LEGACY TO

politics and culture of
revolutionary asian pacific america

LIBERATION

edited by Fred Ho
with
Carolyn Antonio
Diane Fujino
Steve Yip
Designed by ManChui Leung

AK PRESS
EDINBURGH · LONDON · SAN FRANCISCO

BIG RED MEDIA

Legacy to Liberation
Politics and Culture of Revolutionary Asian Pacific America
ISBN 1-902593-24-3

Library of Congress Catalog-in-Publication data
A catalog record for this title is available from the Library of Congress

British Library Cataloguing-in-Publication data
A catalog record for this title is available from the British Library

Published by
Big Red Media
www.bigredmedia.com
bigredmedia@hotmail.com

and

AK Press
PO Box 40682
San Francisco CA 94140

AK Press
PO Box 12766
Edinburgh Scotland EH8 9YE

Printed in Canada.

cover design by ManChui Leung
book design by ManChui Leung
front photo credit: © Corky Lee
back illustration credit: Steve Wong

TABLE OF CONTENTS

DEDICATION

To Yuri Kochiyama (the Mary Choy of New York) and to Mary Choy (the Yuri Kochiyama of Hawai'i).

To Jamala Rogers, Pam Martinez, William Gallegos, the Sanchez Family—comrades from the defunct-League of Revolutionary Struggle (Marxist-Leninist) who fought the rank opportunism to the end and who still stay committed and dedicated to the fight for socialist revolution in the U.S.

To the new generation of activist-fighters—Carolyn Antonio, Diane Fujino, ManChui Leung, Wayne and Gloria Lum, Kye Leung, Xenon and Jerome Yuan.

To Cindy Chalker, the backbone of Big Red Media Inc.

Special thanks to: Craig Gilmore and AK Press for jumping on the project without hesitation and with febrile enthusiasm; Frances Goldin, literary agent/comrade for her supportiveness; Andrea Lockett and Scott Marshall, founding cultural activists of Big Red Media Inc. for their professional advice, help and personal friendship; Steve Yip, Carolyn Antonio, Diane Fujino and ManChui Leung for their on-going work; Gianna Celli of the Villa Serbelloni/Rockefeller Study and Conference Center in Bellagio, Italy; the Djerassi Resident Artists Program; and all the writers and contributors who have made this anthology a vibrant revolutionary tool for generations to come.

INTRODUCTION

Fred Ho

T he idea for this anthology started in December, 1997 in a discussion with a young mixed heritage Chinese American activist. Since the demise of much of the Asian Pacific American revolutionary movement, and much of the U.S. Left in general, she and I were conversing on the critical void in publications today that address the Asian American Left, particularly the hey-day of the Asian American Movement from the 1970s to the mid/late-1980s, an important period when a large number of the Asian American activists committed to community organizing, anti-oppression struggles, etc., were radical, revolutionary, pro-socialism, many even being communists (Marxist-Leninists). As Chris Iijima points out in this anthology, the brightest and most committed of that generation of activists from the late-60s to 1970s were revolutionaries.

In speaking to some veteran Leftists as well as younger radicals, we shared criticisms of existing anthologies which have tended to omit the presence of revolutionary Asian Pacific Americans, particularly Marxists. For example, both <u>The State of Asian America</u> by Karin Aguilar-San Juan (South End Press) and <u>Dragon Ladies</u> by Sonia Shah (South End Press), while important in addressing contemporary issues from a progressive perspective, do not include contemporary Marxist or revolutionary viewpoints nor even adequately discuss (and virtually make no mention of) the revolutionary APA Movement. At least a decade of significant radical activism seemed not to exist for these editors. This sheer omission gives the mistaken impression that this period was either inconsequential to the activism of today or simply irrelevant, due to whatever biases held by these respective editors.

Furthermore, many veteran and younger radicals have expressed major disappointment and disapproval with William Wei's <u>The Asian American Movement</u> (Temple University Press), the first book devoted to this subject. Wei's account misrepresents the Movement both in its character and in its impact and significance, positing it as "essentially a middle class reform movement"—denying the mass character and dismissing the significant impact of the organizing by radicals and revolutionary forces. Numerous historiographical flaws abound as well, including failure to recognize the inspiration and impetus of the Black liberation struggle, the anti-imperialist national liberation struggles in the Third World and socialist China, as well as the systematic and historical racism and national oppression experienced by APAs, as primary reasons for the rise of the Movement. A simple reading of the interviews of veteran Movement builders in this anthology will amend many of the errors of Wei's account.

In resolving to correct these blindspots and problems, the idea for this anthology emerged. I began contacting old comrades from my days in I Wor Kuen/League of Revolutionary Struggle. I reached out to radicals and revolutionaries from the early days of the Asian Movement who continue to be radicals and revolutionaries, including people whom I had major disagreements with and even acrimony towards when I was involved in the Movement's hey-day during the 70s to 80s. Many were very eager and welcoming towards this project. I also found a new generation of militants, radicals and revolutionaries who have emerged politically in the late-1980s and 1990s. In putting together <u>Legacy to Liberation: Politics and Culture of Revolutionary Asian Pacific America</u>, I assembled an editorial advisory team, of men and womyn radicals and revolutionaries from both my generation of the 70s and today's 90s, representing a diverse ideological spectrum and political experience, and with whom I felt I could collaborate. Solicitation letters were sent to our networks across the U.S. outlining the anthology's purpose, goals and timetable. The response well exceeded our expectations.

In working on this anthology, I believe that we have set a new, higher standard of principle for the Movement that allows for inclusive political diversity among the Left without sectarianism or exclusion. Many of the authors in this anthology continue to disagree and hold very opposing positions on a range of ideological, political and historical issues. All of the authors are activists engaged in serious political and cultural work as organizers and leaders in their respective areas. This is not an armchair, academic grouping, but a gathering of many of the fiercest militants and fighters in the Asian Pacific American Movement for at least three decades, from Hawai'i to Massachusetts.

In the late 1990s, a number of significant national gatherings have taken place bringing together both veteran and younger APA Leftists. These gatherings have been very important in rekindling a nationwide discussion around asserting a Left leadership to our struggles. At the same time, these gatherings have also had serious weaknesses, including a blindspot towards the revolutionary socialist-orientation of the late-60s and 1970s, as well as an unwillingness to discuss Marxism, revolutionary theory and socialism. Many of the younger activists, while supporting the need to be "anti-capitalist," "oriented towards the working class," for "self-determination," did not put forward, both in theory and more urgently, in practice, real proposals for ideological and political advancement.

I believe, in order for the Movement to advance, it is important to sum-up the lessons and experiences of the revolutionary movements of the late-1960s to mid-1980s, to make this history relevant to the struggles of today, and to validate the necessity and importance of a revolutionary orientation to attaining full equality, justice and liberation for Asian Pacific Americans. The scope of this anthology from its inception has been the radical and revolutionary Asian Pacific American Left, from its genesis in the late-1960s to today, representing the entire U.S. Inspired and catalyzed by the Black Power Movement, the massive opposition to the Vietnam War, the wave of national liberation struggles in the "Third World," and the general upsurge to transform U.S. society, a generation of Asian Pacific American activists arose from the innercity Chinatown, Japantown and Manilatown communities, from the college campuses and rural agricultural fields. This Movement both sought to end the more than century long oppression of Asian Pacific peoples in the U.S. and to win "liberation" by challenging the very construction of power in U.S. society as part of a larger, overall movement for revolutionary change in this country. Many of these brilliant and dedicated activists looked seriously to revolutionary ideologies and experiences from the "Third World," moving from initial nationalism into Marxism.

This Asian Pacific American Movement (then referred to as the Asian Movement) was unique in comparison to other U.S. social movements in that it was overwhelmingly radical and revolutionary. Although no statistical data exists to verify this assertion, nonetheless, for a small minority group (in 1970s, APAs were about 1% of the total U.S. population), virtually every major community, campus, or cultural campaign, organization and issue had the leading presence of Leftists. The narratives in this anthology document the significance of this presence and its far-reaching impact and influence throughout Asian Pacific America. This profound impact and legacy set the stage for more mainstream, civil rights and social service-type political forces to arise. Even the term "Asian American" itself came from one of the initial radical groups, the Asian American Political Alliance that formed at the University of California-Berkeley, in which then-Field Marshall of the Black Panther Party, Japanese American Richard Aoki, was assigned to organize.

In the first century of Asian Pacific American history since the mid-1800s, due to the extreme and particular oppression, exclusion and segregation of Asian Pacific communities from the U.S. mainstream, the presence and influence of trade union or electoral reformist political forces were virtually absent. For the most part, the main establishment forces in these communities were very insular and conservative, representing merchant interests. The Movement emerged after federal immigration restrictions were removed and a growing number of young people, exposed more to American society, were catalyzed by the radicalism of the 1960s throughout U.S. society. The oral histories contained in this anthology illustrate this dynamic development that emerged from the previous social insularity and restrictive conditions of the Chinese and Filipino bachelor societies and the Japanese American internment camps experience. The explosive emergence of revolutionaries in the APA communities marks the monumental changes that have occured in our communities between the first and second century in this country.

This generation of revolutionary-oriented activists became part of the emergent constellation of American New Left organizations. Yet the story and political importance of the non-white American New Left, and the APA Left in particular, has been overlooked in many published accounts of this important period and in general treatments of U.S. social movements. Asian American Leftists in groups such as the Red

Guard Party, I Wor Kuen, Wei Min She, and other smaller collectives, have left an important legacy to both their communities and to American society as a whole. These radicals constructed a new, collectivist identity—avowedly political—called "Asian American" which promoted and instilled both ethnic pride, pan-ethnic solidarity and a political consciousness of a shared history and experience of oppression. These radical and revolutionary activists were in the leadership of creating Asian American studies on college campuses, organized Asian Pacific student unions and coalitions. They led community battles to resist gentrification and urban redevelopment that threatened to displace and destroy Chinese, Japanese and Filipino ethnic neighborhoods, fought for low-income housing and tenants rights. They linked the issues of racism to anti-imperialism by linking the APA struggle to opposing the U.S. war in Vietnam and Southeast Asia, built solidarity with the struggles against U.S. military bases in the Philippines, in Okinawa, in Hawaii, and were a major grassroots organizing force in the campaign to normalize diplomatic relations between the U.S. government and the Peoples Republic of China. These activists were in the vanguard of fighting racism and the systematic oppression of Asian Pacific peoples in the U.S.—from capitalist media stereotyping, the exploitation of immigrant workers (including farm workers), police brutality and racist violence, to including all forms of inequality and injustice. Many of these activists were womyn and they challenged the sexism within their own communities and organizations as well as the racism and classism in the mainstream feminist movement.

I believe the significance of the APA Movement needs to be fully recognized, documented and analyzed. Beyond historical documentation, I want to provide lessons and summations to be used by radical activists today. Hence, this anthology seeks to analyze from a radical and revolutionary perspective the accomplishments and failures, the strengths and weaknesses, the what-to-keep and what-to-discard of the revolutionary and socialist organizations that emerged from the APA communities of the 1960s and 70s. As much as possible, I have tried to present such summations and analyses from the "first voice"—i.e., from the perspective of those who were actual, leading participants and who still retain a radical perspective today. Finally, this anthology project has fostered new and expanded dialogue between Leftists of diverse viewpoints and positions, from across the U.S. and inter-generationally. This anthology has also given a platform to militant, radical artistic and literary expressions and viewpoints generally ignored by the preponderance of mainstream/assimilationist-oriented cultural publications and literary collections.

Section One: Theory/Practice—Summations of Organizations/ Movements/ Struggles focuses on analyses of strategies for movement-building. It connects ideology (e.g., nationalism, Marxism, Maoism, Trotskyism) with practice. Many of the authors have opposing views, such as between Ninotchka Rosca and Helen Toribio about the KDP and the relationship between the struggle in the Philippines and the struggles of Filipinos in the U.S. Ms. Rosca doesn't uphold the Filipino American struggle as necessarily a vital and revolutionary one, with which Ms. Toribio differs. Ms. Toribio also outlines the former KDP's disagreements with Mao Zedong

Thought which I, Steve Yip and others fully embrace. As editor, I encouraged a full presentation of political views and positions without slander or attack. Some viewpoints are less positive about the Left's legacy than others. I made no effort to "steer" anyone's opinions or views, only that they be clear, forceful and concrete as possible, and that they struggle to come up with a summation and address what each person viewed as the legacy of their organization, both contributions and failures.

Section Two: Personal/Political—Struggles and Lessons focuses on "the personal is political," on how we can learn to handle the relationship between personal/individual issues with the organizational and political requirements of building a revolutionary movement. These essays ask: How did we become revolutionaries? Why did we adopt Marxism, socialism, or whatever philosophical or ideological framework? What were the difficulties, contradictions and errors? Through personal essays, this section critically examines the errors, weaknesses, blindspots and mistakes committed, and proposes methods of handling contradictions such as egomania, sexism/male chauvinism, heterosexism, relationships and personal problems, sexual harassment, harsh forms of struggle/polemics, etc.

Section Three: Legacy to Liberation: Interviews of Movement Builders contains profiles and interviews of elder, veteran militants and revolutionaries, all of whom continue to offer an understanding of how the Movement developed and what must be done.

Section Four: The Arts: Struggle for Identity and Revolution offers poetry that expresses a militant, radical and revolutionary APA consciousness and identity as well as an essay by Korean American dancer/choreographer Peggy Choy on the politics and history of Asian dance in America. I hope this section helps to supplement the paucity of radical APA creative anthologies. Very few essays exist that struggle with APA cultural theory and cultural production and Ms. Choy's essay is a significant and important contribution.

The appendix includes rare Movement documents and internal position papers that reflect important theoretical contributions of APA revolutionary organizing to the American New Left.

Today the number and diversity of Asian Pacific populations in the U.S. has exploded, as new immigration waves of south Asians, southeast Asians, Koreans, and Guamanians, Samoans, Hawaiians and other Pacific Islanders have entered the mainland U.S. and established new communities. Asian American studies and multicultural education is a burgeoning field. A new generation of young APA activists has emerged. Many are gay, lesbian, and mixed heritage backgrounds. They bring new perspectives and challenges to social change organizing strategies. This anthology is only the first step in a process of documentation, analysis and summation. As a first step, there are many shortcomings. This includes not being able to obtain essays from people who were involved in the Workers Viewpoint Organization/Communist Workers Party, a Marxist-Leninist formation that had significant numbers of Asian Pacific cadre and who were involved in major struggles in the 1970s. Many former members whom I approached did not want to revisit that period in their lives, much less attempt a political summation of their experiences.

I regret not having enough visual artwork, photography, cultural theory essays and other forms of literary and artistic expression. As a cultural worker and professional artist, this has been a special interest area for me, which I hope to rectify in future publications which I edit and write.

I additionally would have liked to have found more essays from the "newer" APA immigrant nationalities such as southeast and south Asians, Koreans, etc. Native Hawaiians are not included per se because many assert that their struggle is not part of the APA movement, but a movement for national sovereignty, the right to self-determination including independence FROM U.S. society. However, Peggy Choy, who was raised in Hawai'i and comes from a family of political and cultural activists there, has an important essay on the relationship between the APA Movement in Hawai'i and the indigenous Hawaiian anti-colonial struggle. The poetry of Japanese American poet Richard Hamasaki, who has lived in Hawai'i for more than two decades and dedicated his cultural activism towards promoting Hawaiian language literature and culture, offers a consciousness and sensibility of identifying with and being inspired by native Hawaiian culture, history and struggle. Clearly, the APA Movement has stood in solidarity with the native Hawaiian struggle for cultural dignity, land and liberation and must continue to do so.

Lastly, I have made every effort to be "anti-sectarian" and inclusive of ideological and political viewpoints unlike or contrary to my own. In these pages are revolutionary nationalists, Trotskyists, Maoists, and other political self-identifiers. I have not tried to alter or modify any of the views of the writers, but have insisted on concreteness, clarity and committed boldness. In this way, I believe that we have taken an important step to rebuild the Left, to foster a broad political engagement of the revolutionary and radical Left, and perhaps have set an example for other movements. Obviously the viewpoints expressed in these articles are solely representative of the authors, and in the cases where the authors have stated their organizational affiliation, the collective views of their groups.

I sincerely hope this book will be vibrant and educational reading for both APAs and a general readership interested in social change. While many other books and publications, both academic and activist, address a myriad of social issues and struggles affecting and involving APAs, this anthology is the first to establish an on-going revolutionary legacy. And this legacy has and will continue to have a profound effect on our liberation struggle for full equality through a revolutionary challenge to the system of U.S. monopoly capitalism.

Fred Ho, October 1999

This anthology began at Villa Serbelloni in Bellagio, Italy in June, 1998 and the majority of it was completed at the Djerassi Resident Artists Program, Woodside, California, U.S.A. in July, 1999.

SECTION ONE

THEORY/PRACTICE
SUMMATIONS OF ORGANIZATIONS, MOVEMENTS & STRUGGLES

"Without Revolutionary Theory,
There can be no Revolutionary Practice."

V.I. LENIN

THE BATTLE FOR
THE INTERNATIONAL HOTEL

San Francisco Police
Department Tac Squad
surveying the peoples'
blockade in front of
Everybody's Bookstore.
Trucks unload
demonstrators.

An I-Hotel tenant
speaks to the
crowd at
Portsmouth Square
as part of the
mobilization
process.

The Workers Committee
to Fight for the
International Hotel held
mini-rallies and marches
through the Chinese
community to build
community support before
the assault.

FISTS FOR REVOLUTION

The Revolutionary History of
I Wor Kuen/League of Revolutionary Struggle

Fred Ho

The history of I Wor Kuen, a revolutionary organization that emerged from the New Left among the Asian nationalities in the U.S., begins in 1969 and ends in September, 1978 when it merged with The August 29th Movement, another revolutionary organization with roots in the Chicano liberation struggle. This merger produced a new organization: The League of Revolutionary Struggle (Marxist-Leninist) which lasted until July, 1989.

I became a revolutionary at the age of 16. I became a revolutionary seeking to understand why, even after trying so hard to assimilate and to be accepted, that I still faced racism. I also grew up in a home experiencing constant patriarchal domestic violence which politicized me and which was to later shape my political vision very profoundly, but not until the early 1990s. I now characterize myself as a revolutionary matriarchal socialist, but during my early formative years, I self-identified as a "revolutionary yellow nationalist."

I had a racial analysis that, while anti-imperialist and anti-capitalist, viewed white people, white culture and white-dominated society as the source of the oppression for myself and Third World peoples. Capitalism was wrong because it was a system from Europe and controlled mostly by, at that time, the White peoples of the world. My revolutionary ideas and positions were heavily influenced by Malcolm X and revolutionary leaders, writers and movements in the Third World. We called ourselves Third World people in the U.S. as we identified with the national liberation struggles waged in Africa, Asia, so-called Latin America and the Caribbean and Pacific Islands. (The term "Third World" was coined in the mid-1950s at the Non-Aligned Conference in Bandung, Indonesia of newly independent countries and national independence and liberation movements that sought a "third" path independent of either the First World, western capitalist bloc, and the Second World, or pro-Soviet, so-called "Iron Curtain" bloc.)

In 1975, I joined the Nation of Islam, one of the few non-Blacks to do so, and became Fred 3X. I attended Fruit of Islam drills at 7am on Saturdays at Temple 44 on Intervale Avenue in Roxbury, Boston, sold the "Muhammad Speaks" newspaper on the streets of Boston Chinatown and to Asian American and other activists, fast-

Revised from a speech presented at "Asian Pacific Americans and Revolutionary Socialism," August, 1998 at Hunter College, New York City.

3

ed during Ramadan, prayed to Allah and stopped eating pork which continued for 10 years long after I left the Nation (one of the hardest things for me to do was to give up *cha siu bao*—Chinese pork buns!).

However between the ages of 16-18 I and the Third World Movements in the U.S. were going thru tremendous ideological transition. As a young revolutionary, I energetically participated in the watershed struggle between nationalism and Marxism. It was at this time that I met cadres from I Wor Kuen active in Boston's Chinatown. After fierce ideological debate and political struggle, I was won to Marxism through a combination of different Marxists, including I Wor Kuen, but also cadre from a group called the Proletarian Unity League (which was later to merge with the Revolutionary Workers Headquarters, a split-off from the Revolutionary Community Party to become the Freedom Road Socialist Organization). The I Wor Kuen cadre would later remark that the strength of my newly adopted Marxist ideology was directly proportional to how hard I resisted giving up nationalism. The whole U.S. movement was moving fast to the Left. Virtually an entire generation that sought answers to solving the contradictions of oppression, injustice, exploitation, imperialism, and repression came to Marxism-Leninism as the guiding ideology for making revolution.

While the Black Panther Party had helped to introduce the concept of socialism (popularized in its famous slogan "All Power to the People"), the Black Liberation Movement was still predominantly nationalist until the mid-1970s. A critical forum for the struggle between the ideologies of nationalism and Marxism took place in the African Liberation Support Committee, a nationwide united front of virtually all Black revolutionaries working to build support for the African liberation struggles in South Africa/Azania, Namibia, Angola, Mozambique, and Guinea-Bisseau and the Cape Verde Islands. These liberation movements were largely led by Marxists and socialists, including Sekou Toure, Winnie and Nelson Mandela, Robert Mangaliso Sobukwe, Eduardo Mondlane, Samora Machel, Jonas Savimbi, Robert Mugabe and one of the most brilliant yet not-very-acknowledged leaders/theorists, Amilcar Cabral. (I urge everyone to check out Cabral, particularly his ideas regarding national liberation, culture, identity and socialism). The prestige and practice of these African revolutionaries forced the nationalists in the African American movements to examine the theory and ideology leading those struggles on the mother continent: while waging armed struggles against the white European occupiers, yet the African revolutions were not anti-White, but anti-imperialist, anti-capitalist and often pro-socialist. A magnificent generation of new, young, brilliant, dedicated African American Marxist-Leninist revolutionaries emerged. Unfortunately, for many, their adoption of Marxism contained the serious error of pitting Marxism against the importance of national liberation in the U.S. To their s/heroic credit, many became factory and low-wage workers, organizing directly at the point of production. Yet they gave up building Black-in-form organizations, abandoned cultural work and the arts to the narrow cultural nationalists, believing that the national-in-form organizing, i.e., organizing Black people as Black people was "narrow" and "limited," a wholesale rejection of their own nationalist past. The view of working-class organizing was simply about industrial organizing. The Dodge Revolutionary Union Movement (DRUM), the League of Black Revolutionary Workers, the Black Workers Congress, the Revolutionary Workers League were all significant revolutionary Black working class organizations yet they increasingly "liquidated the national question."

The National Question is perhaps one of the dividing lines in the entire history of the U.S. socialist, Left and revolutionary movements. Simply The National Question is the question of how to win liberation for oppressed nations and oppressed nationalities or minorities. I had become a Marxist by summer 1976 and was investigating the political lines of a number of groups. But after much serious examination of an array of M-L groups, I joined I Wor Kuen in late 1977 largely because of my agreement with them on this vital question.

Let me give a short history of I Wor Kuen. IWK, a Cantonese name that means "Society of the Harmonious Righteous Fist," was taken from the Boxer Rebellion in China at the turn of the century. The Boxers combined mysticism and martial arts, organized as secret societies to oppose western imperialism in China. IWK, as a revolutionary Chinese and Asian American group, identified with the anti-imperialist militancy of the Boxers. IWK first formed as a revolutionary collective in New York City in November, 1969. A few months earlier, in March 1969 in San Francisco, another revolutionary group, The Red Guard Party had formed. Let me run down some of the key highlights of these two groups.

New York I Wor Kuen was made up of radical students, workers and working class youth. It included both immigrants and American-born. The Red Guard Party consisted mostly of Asian American street youth. The Red Guards came out of a youth group called Leway (from the name "Legitimate Ways")—formed in 1967. Leway wanted to unite and politicize street youth and gangs who were constantly fighting the police, racist tourists, and fighting between themselves along the divisions of American-born and immigrant rival youth gangs. Many of these youth had resorted to petty crimes both as a way to get money and as a result of the lack of any youth programs at the time. However, a more politically conscious segment got some money together through a raffle to open up a pool hall on Jackson Street in SF Chinatown and organized themselves as Leway. Leway filled a vacuum in those days when social service and community youth programs didn't exist. Hundreds of Asian American youth would hang out in Leway. Soon after it opened its pool hall, Leway would hold sessions reading Mao Zedong's Red Book, show films about the struggles of Third World people. Leway faced constant police harassment. As often as four times a night, as many as a dozen cops in full riot gear would storm into the poolhall to harass and arrest the youth. This lesson in state violence and power led the most political members of Leway to form themselves into the Red Guard Party in the spring of 1969. As the name stated, they identified with the revolutionary youth of socialist China. The Red Guards also included revolutionary-minded students involved in the Third World Strike at San Francisco City College [for more on the

Red Guard Party, c.f. Alex Hing interview—editor].

Both of these revolutionary Asian organizations on opposite coasts established a revolutionary legacy in the Asian American Movement. Let me highlight this legacy:

Both IWK and the Red Guard Party had organized Serve the People programs based on the Black Panther Party Survival Programs. These programs were more than simply services to meet the dire needs of the community, but revolutionary programs. The slogan was Serve the People and Promote Revolution, yet we find in the late 1990s conferences with the title Serve the People but what's dropped off is the other half: Promote Revolution. What were these programs and how did they "promote revolution"?

In March 1970 IWK launched an extensive door-to-door TB testing campaign in Chinatown. At that time, New York Chinatown had no hospital facilities or clinics or staff who spoke Chinese. IWK led the fight for the newly built Gouveneur Hospital and forced the city to provide a TB x-ray and testing center, which would later become the New York Chinatown Health Clinic. IWK initiated the first draft counseling service for Asian youth and organized them to resist the draft. IWK organized childcare school programs, organized Chinese working-class mothers to form bilingual language programs through the reading of revolutionary materials. These women soon came to be the foundation of IWK's base of support, along with the elderly, many of them part of the bachelor society during the long years of Chinese/Asian exclusion. Elderly Chinese immigrant working class radicals flocked to IWK, many of them militant organizers from the 1930s, 40s and 50s, including leaders of the Chinese Workers Mutual Aid Association in San Francisco.

IWK believed in serving the people by addressing their basic needs which the government failed to do, while constantly promoting revolutionary education, pointing out how capitalism benefited a certain class and exploited and oppressed the masses, how the solution wasn't going to be more funding of social programs but revolutionary seizure of state power by the working class and oppressed nationalities. IWK also educated people politically by organizing them to fight the state, to demand from the system basic rights and services. The result was the rise of the many non-profit service agencies that started in response to the mass struggles and to curtail the growing support for revolutionaries. The ruling class was forced to pour millions of dollars into anti-poverty programs. The Red Guard Party also started Free Breakfast for children and Free Lunch for the elderly programs. All these programs preceded and made possible the youth, senior citizen and immigrant services that exist today. During that time, as revolutionary organizations, IWK and the Red Guard Party never asked for nor took funding from any government agency.

In 1970 IWK and the Red Guard Party began holding discussions. A sharp two-line struggle emerged between day-to-day grassroots organizing for revolution versus a terrorist or ultra-militarist position that advocated armed urban guerilla actions to "incite" the people to revolution. Certain leaders in the RGP saw the group as a revolutionary army and viewed mass work only as a means to support the army. They downplayed the importance of participating in and leading mass grass-roots struggles and did not view revolution as a mass process. These advocates of para-militarism were also proponents of male chauvinist sexual practices: calling for anti-monogamy and collective sexual relations, they viewed the role of womyn as staying at home raising children and supporting the male fighter. After much internal struggle, these positions were defeated. Out of this struggle came an understanding of the role of shared childcare responsibilities between men and womyn. In June-July, 1971 this process of struggle laid the basis for the national merger between these two groups and a central committee was formed with a womyn majority. IWK and later the LRS would establish a distinguished tradition of providing collective childcare for 6 nights out of a week so that its working class womyn cadres could fully participate in political activism.

In July, 1971, the Red Guard Party and I Wor Kuen merged to form a nationwide revolutionary organization, keeping the name of I Wor Kuen. It put forward a 12 point program, inspired by the BPP and Young Lords Party programs but with its own unique and distinctive vision for Asian American liberation including point #4: "We want an end to male chauvinism and sexual exploitation"; point #11: "We want an end to the geographic boundaries of America," i.e., a call for open borders and an end to immigration and emigration harassment; and point #12: "We want a socialist society."

While IWK did call for socialism it still was a revolutionary nationalist organization. In December 1971 at its first national leadership meeting for the new organization, IWK took up the study of Marxism-Leninism. As a young revolutionary group it suffered from the same political void that today's young militant activists of the late-1990s face without any leading, genuine communist party. The old Communist Party USA had given up revolution in the 1940s. Much of the New Communist Left Movement rejected the Soviet Union as a model or leading example because by the 1950s it had invaded Czechoslovakia, Hungary and Poland, (what we called "social-imperialism"—socialism in words, imperialism in deeds), given up armed struggle and opted for "the peaceful transition to socialism," condemned revolutionary nationalism even calling Malcolm X a "police agent." We condemned the CPUSA for adhering to the Soviet Union's jettison of revolutionary principles as "revisionism"—i.e., revising Marxism-Leninism to strip and gut it of its revolutionary essence and practice.

This new movement of young Third World revolutionaries in the U.S. also rejected Trotskyism. The Trotskyists proved to be especially white chauvinist and racist: they subscribed to world-revolution led by a "pure" international working class party and negated the possibility of socialism in individual countries and viewed the Vietnamese national liberation struggle as "bourgeois nationalist" and not really revolutionary. Both the revisionists and the Trotskyists were terrible in liquidating the national question. They rejected the concept that there are oppressed nations within the U.S. borders much less refused to accept that these struggles and movements, on their own, independent from White workers, could be revolutionary.

Therefore they denounced and attacked the groups struggling for the liberation of the New African or Black-Belt Nation in the south, the Chicano Nation, the Indigenous Nations, the Hawaiian Nation, the Aleutian nation in Alaska, etc. The revisionists and Trotskyists, because they don't accept the concept of oppressed nations, oppressed nationalities and national oppression, see only racism and not the occupation of land and territory and the demand for the right of self-determination, i.e., liberation of a territory/homeland and an entire people, as a revolutionary struggle. Therefore they see the solution as integrationism. They see uniting Asians in a common struggle for liberation as narrow, divisive and non-revolutionary.

IWK during the early to mid-1970s was part of the explosion of young revolutionary groups that viewed revolution as the only solution to the contradictions of the U.S. society and the liberation of oppressed nations and nationalities. While organizing service programs and fighting for reforms and improvements in the daily lives of people, IWK and other revolutionaries never believed that justice and equality could be achieved in class society in general and capitalism in particular. In organizing and demanding these services, it constantly did political education to show the need for a new system that put the needs of people and the planet over profit and private ownership.

IWK established its historical boldness in Asian American Movement history by its open support for socialist China by organizing film showings and events supporting the PRC, working in broad coalitions for the PRC to take its rightful seat in the United Nations and to force the U.S. government to officially recognize the PRC. We often had open street battles with the Kuomintang who physically attacked us and our supporters, at events, when selling our newspaper on the street. The KMT also vandalized our storefront office.

IWK understood that a people's liberation struggle was a multi-class united front. The core of IWK's organizing was based among the working class and immigrant Asian Pacific nationalities. IWK organized directly at the workplace among garment, restaurant and postal workers—industries with large numbers of APA workers. Rather than organizing as staff organizers from the outside, as revolutionary socialists we saw our role and responsibility as going directly into and providing leadership from within the site of production. At the same time we organized in the community, fighting for low income housing and opposing redevelopment and gentrification. IWK organized tenants block-by-block. We also recognized the need to support small Asian community businesses from government harassment. We saw that even the community capitalists faced forms of national oppression. We resisted government attempts to shut down small Chinese grocery stores selling Chinese produce and roasted and preserved meats. The government had branded these businesses as "violating health codes." We worked with the small business owners and got the government health ordinances changed.

We rallied support in Chinatown among immigrants who some Left forces regarded as "backwards" and "anti-communist" and "racist" to support Puerto Rican independence, Black and Chicano struggles against police repression, and organized demonstrations through the streets of Asian American communities against U.S. aggression in southeast Asia.

In 1972 IWK expanded its work to build nationality-in-form organizations in APA communities. We worked with veteran immigrant leftists, working class mothers, college students, artists and professionals to form Chinese Progressive Associations in San Francisco, Los Angeles, New York and Boston. These were grassroots activist "mass organizations": they had no paid staff, did not receive funding but raised money from self-reliant membership activities, held open and frequent general membership meetings and democratically elected its leadership. Nowadays, this model of activist mass organization has been replaced by the non-profit agency with paid staff, appointed paid leadership, reliance upon external funding and which is not accountable to any democratic membership process. Beyond these bureaucratic characteristics, today's non-profits virtually do not allow any political space for open revolutionary presence or discussion. Rather than having professional revolutionaries working in them, they have paid professionals autocratically running them.

IWK upheld the importance of nationality-in-form organizing as part of its strategy for winning the liberation of oppressed nationalities and building the overall revolutionary struggle in U.S. society. Unlike other socialist groups of the New Left when they became Marxist and dissolved their nationality-based organizing work for multinational workplace organizing, IWK continued to build progressive mass Asian Pacific organizations in all areas, including Asian Student Unions and their networks like the Asian Pacific Student Union (APSU) on the west coast and the East Coast Asian Students Union (ECASU) on the east coast (which I personally was in the leadership of starting).

We were active in and often were founders of Asian arts and cultural organizations including in NYC Asian Cinevision, Bridge Magazine, Basement Workshop, the Asian/Pacific Heritage Festival; in Boston, the AA Resource Workshop (I was one of the founders), the Dragon Boat Festival; in Los Angeles: Visual Communications, Gidra newspaper; in San Francisco/Bay Area: the various taiko dojos, Japantown Art and Media, Kearney Street Workshop, Ohana Cultural Center, AsianImprov Records, and many others.

We believed in the vital necessity of building national consciousness, pride and identity. In the words of Amilcar Cabral, "National liberation begins as an act of culture." Oppressed people don't begin to fight their oppression until they resist the identity and historical image their oppressor makes of them. APAs face national oppression—oppression for who they are as a people, a systematic oppression that includes annexation or conquest of land and territory, all forms of inequality (environmental racism, greater rates of tuberculosis and health problems, lower pay), stereotyping, suppression of language, denigration of culture and physical features, racism, ethnic violence, etc. Lenin pointed out that imperialism—globally expanding monopoly capitalist domination—makes entire nations into classes, subjugates and inferiorizes an entire people. Unlike colonialism which rules primarily by direct external force, imperialism operates primarily through assimilation: making the oppressed imitate and absorb into the culture and values of the oppressor.

In 1972 IWK expanded into organizing other Asian Pacific nationalities including Japanese Americans and Filipinos. We were in the leadership of the Little Tokyo Peoples Rights Organization, the Committee Against Nihonmachi Eviction, and later in the 1980s, the National Coalition for Redress and Reparations.

However with all this tremendous and extensive mass organizing going on, the 1970s posed new challenges to IWK. First, the rise of state repression and the outright campaign to terrorize, destroy, incarcerate and murder revolutionaries and revolutionary forces. Second, the rise in the strength of the reformists fueled by the expanded democratic space and gains, including massive injections of funding, as a result of the struggles waged by the revolutionary forces. The rise of the anti-poverty programs, non-profits (which interestingly never declare themselves to be anti-profit!) and professional administrators on leash to government and foundation funders. Many of these professionals pushed reformism. Revolutionaries uphold the importance of reforms, indeed they have been at the forefront of leading the struggles for concessions. Reformism pushes reliance upon the system, narrow legalistic changes, cosmetic integration and tokenism. But most dangerously, reformism EXCLUDES revolutionaries and communists. A reformist will work harder to isolate and remove a revolutionary or squash revolutionary views and ideas than they will to fight the state or capitalists.

To take on these challenges, IWK in its years of revolutionary study and organizing adopted Marxism-Leninism-Mao Zedong Thought as its guiding ideology in 1974. Without revolutionary theory, a movement is blind and groping, with no strategic vision or framework. We need to study and integrate the collective, shared and combined lessons and experiences from revolutionary struggle from around the world with our experiences in the U.S. We called M-L "scientific socialism" because as "science," it could be proven. We looked to the revolutions that had been and were being made, all in poorer, economically backward and dependent countries like Russia, colonies like Cuba and semi-colonies like China.

Throughout the 1970s there were many complicated twists and turns in the U.S. M-L party-building movement. Some groups declared themselves to be The Party. However in September 1978, a significant merger took place between IWK and another M-L organization with deep roots in the Chicano liberation movement, the August 29th Movement (ATM). Both organizations dissolved and re-formed as the new League of Revolutionary Struggle (M-L). Within the next two the LRS would merge and unite with several other groups with long histories in varying nationality movements including the Revolutionary Communist League, formerly the Congress of Afrikan Peoples with its prominent revolutionary writer-intellectual leader Amiri Baraka. Other groups that joined the LRS were the Eastwind Collective, a revolutionary Asian American group based in Los Angeles, individuals from the Japantown Collective of San Francisco, the Seize the Time Collective, a Black and Chicano group in San Jose and East Palo Alto, the New York Collective from the Puerto Rican and Dominican movements.

The LRS has certain important features that distinguished it from the rest of the U.S. Left. First, its significant roots in the Asian, Chicano and Black liberation struggles. Its membership was never more than 20% white. Because of its unique positions on the national question, it never liquidated or dropped its nationality-focused organizing. The LRS continued the legacy of IWK's work in the APA struggles. Therefore it is incorrectly posited by superficial historians of the Asian American Movement that the revolutionary part of it didn't continue into the 1980s. The LRS had more APA members and far greater and extensive work in the 1980s than IWK ever had in the 1970s. The LRS, for example, published an APA magazine called *East Wind* that had national circulation from 1981 to 1987. It also had an all-Chinese language magazine, *GETTING TOGETHER*, named after the former IWK newspaper which began in 1970 at first as a simple stapled mimeographed periodical. The LRS' newspaper, *UNITY*, was the only modern tri-lingual American Left newspaper, in English with full translations in Spanish and Chinese. A few other Left newspapers do a token few pages of Spanish, but *UNITY* always had equal pages of all languages which reflected its commitment to the equality of languages.

Second, the LRS leadership and rank and file held a majority of womyn. Third World womyn. For Asian Pacific Americans, this fact refuted the stereotype of Asian womyn as deferential and subservient. It also refuted certain feminist criticisms of the Third World Left as being male-dominated and hyper-macho, or for ignoring gender equality.

Third, unlike the RCP and others that declared themselves to be The Party, the LRS never did. We believed that all the self-declared parties had objectively lowered the requirements for a true party. Though we embraced Mao Zedong Thought, we never called ourselves "Maoists." Chinese communists in China never called themselves Maoists. Marxism was the theory of scientific socialism (or dialectical and historical materialism) developed in the epoch of rising capitalism. Leninism was the development of Marxism in the epoch of imperialism (or capitalism at its highest stage of global hegemony). "Mao Zedong Thought" was the creative application of Marxism-Leninism to the Chinese Revolution with major new developments and applications (such as the National Democratic Revolution, the United Front, the primacy of practice, etc.), but it did not signal nor reflect an advance of M-L in any new historical epoch. Furthermore, the LRS did not support the Gang of Four. The pro-Gang of Four forces asserted that they were "Maoists" while the Hua Guofeng/anti-Gang of Four forces had betrayed "Maoism."

Fourth, the LRS never subscribed to any socialist models. We certainly rejected the Soviet Union as having sold-out socialism. While we had immense admiration and took much inspiration from China, we didn't follow it blindly and actually had certain differences and disagreements with the CCP, including around nuclear energy, the prohibition of trade unions and other positions.

Fifth, by the mid-1980s we had become the largest M-L organization in the U.S. and were a major force in both presidential bids by Jesse Jackson and the successful election of David Dinkins as mayor in NYC. In the APA communities, we were a Who's Who of leaders in labor, community, student, and cultural areas. We had districts in a number of major U.S. cities and were especially huge in California. What's important to understand is the correspondence between the collapse of the once-huge Left in 1989 which allowed for the huge surge by the Right in the state of California. A strong Left is always the counter to the Right. But once the Left is gone, the Right can steamroller its way as it has done in California with the brazen attacks ranging from the campaign against "political correctness," to opposing affirmative action and immigrant rights.

Our sizeable growth and entrance into the mainstream of U.S. political life also accelerated the downfall and demise of the LRS. This is why EVERYONE SERIOUS ABOUT REVOLUTIONARY CHANGE NEEDS TO STUDY AND INTERNALIZE DIALECTICAL MATERIALISM: to understand how things turn into their opposite.

It is my opinion that our ideological deterioration took a precipitous turn when we made the decision to go all-out for Jesse Jackson in national electoral politics. We made the error of Everything Thru the United Front, abandoned our independent revolutionary socialist perspective and principles. Many of our leading activists now hid their socialist identity and politics in order to be accepted by the Democratic Party. We ran much of Jesse's campaign from the local to national level. To get to Jesse, you had to go through us. We were seduced by the power as gatekeepers. Revolutionary theory and study went by the wayside in the justification that organizing and campaign-building took precedence. Unlike other Leftists, we weren't disoriented by the fall of the Soviet Union because we never looked to it. Even Tiananmen shouldn't have thrown us, as we had reservations about Deng Xiaoping.

We can't use international events as excuses. We liquidated, i.e., gave up, Marxism, socialism and revolution, because of our own deterioration, seduced by and subsumed into electoral politics and mainstream acceptance, and the careerism of a handful of charismatic leaders who decided to bail out for corporate and academic careers who had to justify themselves by getting most of the organization to turn against its own history. How could this happen to so many people with decades of history as revolutionaries? Why didn't it happen to some?

While individual case-by-case explanations need to be made, a few general lessons can be drawn.

First, ideological deterioration was key. This is not inherently due to getting older, or growing conservative times or difficult conditions. When we stop studying, struggling to develop and advance revolutionary theory and fall into complacent rationalizations like we're too busy doing mass organizing to bother with study or theoretical questions, then we opt for easy way-outism (the political meaning of "opportunism"—when the Movement becomes Everything and the Final Aim Nothing).

Second, the squashing of democratic struggle and real debate over ideology. Bureaucratic maneuvering, appeals to personal loyalty, ostracism, are used in replacement of open, direct struggle. In a revolutionary organization, everyone has the right to criticize and challenge and debate views and ideas openly and freely. It is this process of struggle in which we Marxists believe that correct ideas, i.e., the truth, emerges. Without this process, we'll go with the flow and take the path of least resistance, rubber stamp leadership, allow petty maneuvering to win.

Third, all of the aforementioned two points feeds into a really horrible thing called "cult of personality"—unquestioning loyalty based on friendship, marriage, mutual self-interest instead of ideological struggle and unity. This in turn produces what I call the "lemming syndrome"—following charismatic/revered leaders off the cliff. If leaders get tired, burned out, bitter, selfish, they should be shown the Exit door. Certain anarchist views promote "leaderless" collective decision-making. While this can work for specific meetings or smaller gatherings, it is difficult with a nationwide group, part-clandestine in which not everyone is known to everyone else. Even anarchists go through splits, cult of personality and lemming syndrome. Leaders must be subject to accountability and removal by democratic struggle.

What is to be done?

We need a resurgence of revolutionary theory and Marxist ideology. Today's activist really needs to study the history of struggle and revolutionary experiences both of their particular movement but also international revolutionary experiences. We need to promote revolutionary consciousness and understand that ideology is KEY to having a framework to advancing strategy and vision and to answer the complex questions.

We need to build independent militant, not non-profit, organizations and resources. A revolutionary and radical media needs to be built and sustained without state or corporate funding. We've done it before. In fact, technology has allowed us to publish, record, video and communicate even easier. What we lack is the political prioritization and organization concentrated in building these resources.

Cultural work and the arts. We need to be constantly creative in all the many visual, spoken word, musical and theatrical expressions and forms to promote revolutionary consciousness.

Finally, what we've begun tonight: an intergenerational and cross-Left dialogue. To share history, lessons, to debate ideas, to lay out differences, to have debate and struggle in a civil, respectful and dignified way with different generations and across the ideological spectrum.

Flo Oy Wong
"Lucky Daughter" 1996
Suitcase, pages 3 and 4
mixed media - suitcase, photos, sequins 20 3/8" x 30 1/2"

SERVE THE PEOPLE — YESTERDAY AND TODAY
The Legacy of Wei Min She

Steve Yip

This essay is an attempt by a founding member of Wei Min She (WMS) to share the experiences of this Asian American anti-imperialist organization. Mandarin Chinese for "organization for the people," WMS grew out of the Asian American Movement of the late 1960s and early 1970s, and existed in the San Francisco Bay Area from 1971-1975.

I think key aspects of WMS' history are very relevant to the present and future struggle for liberation. I feel a particular sense of responsibility and urgency as I listen to, and learn from, the new generation of radical and revolutionary-minded Asian American youth who are hitting the political scene and grappling with questions of political and ideological direction. Important elements provoking renewed restlessness among young Asian Pacific Americans are the current wave of attacks on immigrants, bilingual education, affirmation action, and the rise in anti-Asian violence.

Though WMS existed in very different times, some of the questions we confronted through collective and sometimes heated debates hold many lessons for today: what's the real source of the oppression of Asian peoples, of white supremacy and racism generally? Is it white people and their cultural institutions per se, or was it an economic and political system called imperialism? Was it possible or adequate to create alternative institutions and lifestyles or do we need a revolution? What kind of revolution, and what strategy and organization do we need if we were serious about revolution? Is there a working class or proletariat in the U.S. that is part of an international class with a revolutionary mission?

These were the kinds of questions grappled with by members of WMS in leadership, in workteam meetings, and in exchanges with other Asian and non-Asian organizations. For us, the fight for social equality and justice had moved beyond the question of getting more Asian physicians, lawyers, architects, social work professionals or "savvy" businessmen/women. Some of us had already resolved that those were the demands of a more narrowly focused and aspiring "petit-bourgeois" strata working for their own class interests. But this did not mean we fully understood all the class differentiation among Asians, or within communities like Chinatown. And for those of us gravitating towards greater, more fundamental change, how would we go about this?

Two central, and inter-related, questions and positions concentrated the fluid but steady motion of political struggle: reform or revolution? Nationalism or inter-

15

nationalism? Major points in WMS's development centered around these two conflicting directions as we worked to build radical political movements and organizations in the Chinese, Japanese and Filipino communities in which we were based. Members of WMS would learn serious lessons about fighting national oppression and its relationship to the broader struggle for revolution. I want to focus not just on the history, but on the leap that a section of WMS made from revolutionary nationalism to revolutionary INTERnationalism. Because of this leap, I think the existence of WMS has left an important and lasting contribution to the legacy of liberation.

Three key factors enabled a section of WMS to make that leap: First and foremost, the practical and theoretical lessons forged in the Cultural Revolution in socialist China, and Mao's leadership of that struggle. Two, our close and comradely working relationship with the Revolutionary Union (forerunner of the Revolutionary Communist Party), with whom we conducted joint practice and engaged in vigorous political and theoretical exchange. Three, our determination to go to, link up with, and learn from the working class. For me, the leap from revolutionary nationalism to proletarian internationalism was a turning point that has enabled me to continue serving the people as a revolutionary down through today, as a supporter of the Revolutionary Communist Party (RCP).

Backdrops...

WMS came out of the political ferment of the 60s—part of the Asian Movement which was a stream in the torrent of political upheaval gripping U.S. society and the world. In those heavy days, hundreds of thousands considered the need for fundamental change in the U.S. The fight for civil rights gave way to the Black liberation movement as Black people's struggle boldly challenged Amerikkka's institutionalized racism and white supremacy. This was best articulated by Malcolm X and then by the Black Panther Party. The struggle of Black people played a vanguard role electrifying all of U.S. society—particularly other oppressed nationalities such as Chicanos, Native Americans, and Asian Americans, as well as the powerful multiracial youth and student rebellions against the status quo. In fact, Mao Zedong pointed out:

> *The Afro-American struggle is not only a struggle waged by the exploited and oppressed black people for freedom and emancipation, it is also a new clarion call to all the exploited and oppressed people in the United States to fight against the barbarous rule of the monopoly capitalist class.*[1]

The war in Indochina escalated and escalated, but more significantly, the U.S. was getting its ass kicked in Vietnam, and facing increasingly determined and militant resistance to the war at home. U.S. armed forces were bogged down and demoralized in Vietnam. Outright revolts by American servicemen against the war, against racism and discrimination, and against the entire establishment found its way into the barracks and military installations throughout the U.S. and Europe. Confidence in the powers-that-be was in a downward slide. The stability or governability of U.S. society was a real question for the rulers of this country, especially as growing sections of the middle classes turned against the war. These and many other factors contributed to significant infighting within the confines of the U.S. ruling circles itself.

There was a tide of national liberation sweeping Africa, Asia and Latin America. A key factor on the world stage promoting and supporting revolution throughout the world was Maoist China. It propelled Marxism-Leninism into the national liberation struggles and into imperialist citadels, including the U.S. China too was in the throes of a revolution—the Cultural Revolution—which dared our generation to dream and work for a radically different world (see "Mao More Than Ever" for a more in depth discussion of this). Waves of Asian American youth were radicalized by the combined effects of this social turmoil, especially by the war in Indochina, the Black liberation movement, and the Cultural Revolution.

Although I didn't fully understand what was going on in China as class struggle until some years later, there was something exciting about what was going on in the Cultural Revolution that captured my imagination. I did have some basic sense that it was total revolution—that Mao and the Chinese people were blazing a trail that revolution isn't just about economics and institutions but also about social values and world outlook. I was certainly drawn to the whole thrust of "serve the people"— putting the collective interest of society above self-centered agendas.

...and beginnings

In the fall of 1969, I was a freshman entering the University of California at Berkeley (UCB). I had grown up in the Black community of Oakland, California and was influenced by the rise of the Black Panther Party there. Several of us Asian students had invited the Third World Liberation Front to our high school to speak about the Third World strike at UCB. So when I entered UC, specifically to hook up with "the movement," I immediately joined the Asian American Political Alliance (AAPA). AAPA had helped lead the third world strikes that established ethnic studies at UCB and San Francisco State. We were feeling empowered by these victories on campus that had resulted in the first university ethnic studies programs in the U.S., and we now hungered for greater social change. The newly founded Asian Studies introduced us to many revolutionary writers of the day, especially the works of Mao. We read and discussed Mao's Red Book[2], and Mao's essays such as "On Contradiction," "On Practice,", "Where Do Correct Ideas Come From?" As radical intellectuals, many of us were particularly struck by Mao's comment that

> *...If you want knowledge, you must take part in the practice of changing society. If you want to know the taste of a pear, you must change the pear by eating it yourself....If you want to know the theory and methods of revolution, you must take part in revolution.*[3]

The debate among us students increasingly grew about heeding Mao's call to the youth in China to go among the laboring peoples, to go "serve the people," and learn the theories and methods of changing the world. We resolved to take our radical politics beyond the elitist frontiers of the ivory tower, and to go among those we were being groomed to forsake—our communities packed with the poor, the workers and the oppressed. This weighty decision to reject privilege and join with the masses of people in struggle was a significant rite of passage.

I know a similar crossroads confronts many of the new generation of youth and student activists today. Even though there was a whole mass movement among our generation to do this, it still took a great deal of soul searching and political courage. Many of us were second-generation Chinese Americans, foreign students from Hong Kong and Taiwan, and third-generation Japanese Americans, who were the first in our families to go to college. This carried tremendous social pressures to "make it." Those of us who left the campus for the 'hood still had to weigh abandoning the lure of individual, self-serving careers in favor of serving the people with political activism. Relative to the times then, we were still a minority who boldly embarked on the challenge to go "integrate with the masses" in the Chinatown/Manilatown community of San Francisco. What followed was a period of intense struggle and learning.

In December 1969, I was among the dozen or so people, former AAPA members and others, who opened the doors of the Asian Community Center (ACC) in one of the many basements of the International Hotel. A little more than a month later, we each pitched in $50 to stock and open Everybody's Bookstore in one of the I-Hotel's walk-in-closet-sized storefronts. However primitive our understanding, establishing a community center together with a bookstore reflected our sense of the need for revolutionary theory as well as practice, and of theory dynamically linked to social practice—as a guide to action, to solve the many new and complex questions of the political movement.[4]

Excited by the revolutionary optimism of China's Cultural Revolution, we envisioned ACC and Everybody's Bookstore to be major outlets and platforms to disseminate bilingual news and information about the People's Republic of China, and about other struggles internationally and domestically. During the Cultural Revolution, China put a lot of emphasis on popularizing Marxist-Leninist works, as well as the many concrete achievements of socialism in China. All literature from China were priced cheaply as part of socialist China's policy to assist revolutionary forces internationally, whether it was Mao's little Red Book and collected works, pamphlets by Marx, Engels, Lenin, Stalin, or periodicals from China. Along with ACC's film program, Everybody's Bookstore made progressive and revolutionary literature, art, and theory readily accessible to youth, workers, and activists in Chinatown and beyond.

The response of the community to our film program far exceeded our expectations. It helped us to learn about, and to influence, the aspirations of the community for radical and revolutionary politics. We soon found that films about China, Vietnam or the Black Panthers not only served to popularize struggles from around the world, but also tapped the enthusiasm of the immigrant community to learn about and support these struggles. This was a community that had been suppressed and dominated for decades by reactionary forces such as the Chinese Six Companies, and by the anti-communist government "witch hunts" of the 1950s. We were pleasantly surprised that the most diverse and large audiences, which included many elderly or retired Chinese and Filipino workers, would always attend film showings from or about the Cultural Revolution in China. ACC and Everybody's Bookstore laid the political groundwork for Wei Min She.

From Community Activists to Anti-Imperialists

After a year of organizing various political activities and social programs out of ACC such as the free food program, a group of us decided to form WMS and define our political unity/mission as anti-imperialism. WMS' basis of unity included membership of those who were already revolutionaries, but also those who had not completely rejected the possibility of reforming the system. Being anti-imperialist expressed the stage of development where many of us had come to conclude that the source of our oppression was the imperialist system, but many also had not yet decided that revolution was the solution. Anti-imperialism reflected our political motion as well as the crucial political and ideological influences on us.

As Asian youth searching for the solution to end racism and national oppression, Mao's statements in support of the Afro-American struggle had a big impact on our growing consciousness:

> *Racial discrimination in the United States is a product of the colonialist and imperialist system.... The black masses and the masses of white working people in the United States share common interests and have a common objective to struggle for.... The struggle of the black people in the United States is bound to merge with the American workers' movement, and this will eventually end the criminal rule of the U.S. monopoly capitalist class.*[5]

Mao's statement pointed to the links between national oppression and class exploitation in the U.S.—Black people suffered twice, oppression as a people and in the great majority, as exploited proletarians who are part of the single working class made up of all races and nationalities. But this statement also pointed to a larger strategic link—the revolutionary alliance between the struggle of Black people against their oppression, and that of the multinational working class to end the rule of U.S. imperialism. We sought out the implications of his analysis for the struggle of Asian Americans.

Many of us had started our political lives as revolutionary nationalists who ventured to face issues of what it would take to eliminate all exploitation and oppression. We already understood the fact that the U.S. was a thoroughly racist society. But these kinds of statements by Mao pointed to how racism and white supremacy were built into the very foundation, and were major props, of U.S. imperialist rule. While there were certainly privileges for people of European descent under this system, Mao was saying that the oppressed, and working people/class of all races, share a common fate and a common interest in getting rid of this system. WMS conducted internal study of this and other questions of the day, and constantly struggled to apply what we were learning to our practice. We studied and debated the relationship of getting rid of racism and national oppression, and getting rid of capitalism/imperialism.

Besides works by Mao, Lenin, Marx, and Stalin on this issue, we also discussed and debated major documents by the Revolutionary Union (RU) such as "National Liberation and Proletarian Revolution in the U.S." As mentioned earlier, a key factor influencing us from the beginning was that some members of WMS were also members of, or politically relating to, the RU. Some of us had been reading the RU's theoretical journals called "The Red Papers." In fact I had received early copies of the Red Papers while still in high school, grappling over the importance of revolutionary theory and the road to revolution in the U.S.

The RU was a multinational communist organization founded in 1968 and grew out of the radical upsurges of the time: the antiwar movement, the support for Vietnam and other third world liberation struggles, the Black liberation and Chicano movements, the revolutionary youth movement, and the impact of Cultural Revolution in China. The RU had close relations with the Black Panther Party. It was part of the new communist movement that rejected the old revisionism of Communist Party USA and its Soviet model of socialism. It was applying Marxism-Leninism to the conditions of the U.S.—engaging in political practice while popularizing and struggling for Marxist-Leninist ideology—with the aim of developing theory that could lead to mass armed revolution in the U.S. It put forth the goal of fulfilling the political necessity of forging a new, antirevisionist, that is to say revolutionary communist, vanguard in the U.S., and its Red Papers (1968-1975) contributed to this party-building process.

The relationship with the RU impacted WMS' overall political and ideological direction—on how we would enter into and sum up key nodal points in our development. I think two of these nodal points hold particular lessons for today's activists: One was the Lee Mah workers struggle in S.F.'s Chinatown/North Beach area; and the other was the struggle for the International Hotel.

The I-Hotel: A Stronghold of Resistance

The I-Hotel struggle was a test and learning experience for many Asian radical forces, including WMS. For eight years, the constant issues all of us confronted in stopping City Hall's new eviction attempts, or negotiating with new landlords, were: who are our friends, who are our enemies, and who do we rely on. Did organizing the resistance demand going to the broadest masses to motivate determined and fierce resistance? Or, as some proposed, should we merely be working out a good arrangement with City Hall?

When we opened the doors to the Asian Community Center and Everybody's Bookstore, the block-long I-Hotel complex on San Francisco's Kearny Street was a seething hotbed of Asian youth radicalism. Besides the Asian Community Center and Everybody's Bookstore, it was also home to a multitude of political and cultural rebels: the Chinatown Draft Help/Asian Legal Services; the Red Guards/I Wor Kuen/Chinese Progressive Association; the Kearny Street (artists) Workshop; and the I-Hotel Tenants Association. The battle against the eviction/demolition of the I-Hotel went through many tense twists and turns that lasted from 1969-1977. For us, it focused two critical issues:

On the one hand, it was a protracted struggle for decent low-cost housing for Chinese and Filipino workers, many retired. The I-Hotel sat on the last remaining block of a once thriving Filipino community (Manilatown) that had been sacrificed to the economic interests of real estate developers of "Wall Street West." Particularly outrageous were the cruel economics of racial discrimination and class exploitation—oppressed peoples who had been used to enrich capital were being tossed into the streets like garbage to further the needs of capital. Filipinos and other Asian youth/student organizations mobilized. The I-Hotel became a hallmark and land-mark of Asian community resistance joined by tens of thousands of people from all nationalities and walks of life in the Bay Area. The struggle won very broad support nationally and even internationally.

On the other hand, it was a fight to defend and extend a physical and political space where the overall atmosphere was one of promoting and defending the people's right to fight the power. Many of these activist groups openly promoted aspects of revolution, Marxism, Maoist China and socialism. It was a meeting place and train-ing ground for immigrant and native-born rebels of different ages, nationalities and socio-economic backgrounds, from Iranian students opposing the U.S. puppet, the fascist Shah of Iran;[6] to Asian sisters protesting the sexist Miss Chinatown pageants.

There was a tremendous feeling of a community and a culture of rebellion. Despite the (sharp) differences among the radicals, there was a united front of resis-tance against the real enemy—the power structure and their police. There was a high spirit of community where sexual harassment or other attacks on women were criti-cized and held in check. It was the spirit of people striving to work together to find collective solutions, in the interest of serving the people's struggle by relying on our-selves and not by relying on the enemy to solve our problems for us.

For years, the I-Hotel acted as a beacon and magnet for many to fight the power. The authorities looked on this block of Kearny Street and the I-Hotel as a big red thorn in their side. The political strength/support that had been built through fierce and determined resistance had put them on the defensive for eight whole years. They did not have the political freedom to attack at will but had to carefully wage their own campaign of public opinion before they were able to forcefully evict. And the reactionary forces allied with City Hall and the police, such as the anti-communist Chinese Six Companies, were also held at bay during that time, even as they made many death threats or hired Chinatown youth gangs to attack the radicals.

To paraphrase Mao, our attitude had become "to be attacked by the enemy is a good thing as long as we work to make it a rock they drop on their own feet." That is, we both expected their attacks and responded by even broader mobilization of the

21

people to expose the attacks and fight back. Those years of backing down one eviction attempt after another represented a real concession won through mass resistance.

The military-like assault to evict the I-Hotel on the night of August 4, 1977, was yet another jolting lesson about the absolutely unyielding and heartless nature of this sick system. To this very day, that site is a large hole in the ground after the eviction and demolition—a painful eyesore and reminder that the profit system cannot and will not meet the basic needs of the people like decent low-cost housing. The lords of capital dictated that many of the former I-Hotel elderly tenants die in destitution and loneliness, stripped of the support apparatus and community the I-Hotel had provided. It also shows how threatened the authorities are by a caring and sharing alternative space, even just one city block, when it exists as part of a movement challenging the dog-eat-dog system and its values.

The I-Hotel struggle is a testimony to the fact that the have-nots in society can fight back against the system's efforts to beat down and crush us, and win broad support in such struggles. But the I-Hotel struggle holds another key lesson for today. Since then, I've come to understand that building these kinds of vibrant strongholds of collective resistance—full of cultural and political life—is indispensable to the building of a revolutionary movement.

Fighting Class Exploitation and National Oppression

As part of the mass opposition in the late 60s and early 70s, there was an upsurge among sections of the working class in the U.S. By the early 70s, there were similar stirrings of "labor unrest" among restaurant, garment and other workers in S.F. Chinatown. By this time, WMS' labor committee was conducting joint political organizing with RU members inside various work places, including a number of garment factories. We were also jointly involved in support activities of a number of workers strikes inside and outside of Chinatown, as well as in struggles such as against police brutality in San Francisco. The RU had initiated reclaiming May Day (International Workers Day), and International Women's Day, as revolutionary holidays/celebrations, which WMS also participated in. And the RU was holding discussions and joint work with a number of groups and organizations, among them WMS, about the possibility and necessity for revolution in the U.S., and the need for a vanguard party based on the ideology of the proletariat—Marxism-Leninism-Maoism.

WMS had been working to make a class analysis of the community, investigating the class structures among Chinese people, and the economic, social and political ramifications of this stratification. We were trying to figure out who was the working class, the middle classes, the capitalists—as part of figuring out who were our friends and who were our enemies in building political struggles in the community. One product of our research, maybe simple in retrospect but a real revelation to us then, was coming to the conclusion that there was no such thing as a separate Chinese working class in Amerikkka. In studying the history of the role played by Chinese immigrant workers in the labor history of the U.S., WMS issued our findings in a book titled <u>Chinese Working People in America</u>[7]. During the work on that book, we found that Chinese workers were members of a larger entity—a working class made up of workers of all nationalities in the U.S. (multinational class). We also gained a deeper view of how all the socio-economic stratas of Chinese (and other Asians) in the U.S. suffered various degrees of racial discrimination and oppression as a people.

The Lee Mah struggle broke out in 1974 in this small electronics sweatshop where Chinese workers were paid the typically sub-minimum wage, abused as immigrants and many as women. The workers' attempt to organize brought a lock-out by the company, and WMS organizers began to join the workers in their struggle for their jobs and for justice. While organizing daily picket lines and weekly mass mobilizations of support in conjunction with the workers, many perplexing questions confronted us. We had already learned from other experiences that it was more complex than just a problem of Chinese bosses exploiting Chinese workers.

Some in the Asian Movement argued against being involved in Lee Mah because most Chinese workers were in garment and restaurant and this was a tiny electronics plant—hard to organize and win support based on trade/industry lines. Others argued that support for the workers could and should be built but by narrowly and solely focusing on their economic demands—the improvement of wages and conditions through unionizing. In trying to figure out what to do, WMS organizers grappled with Lenin's classic work <u>What Is To Be Done?</u> and tried to understand whether and how it applied. For workers to become fully trained as class conscious revolutionaries, Lenin had argued that:

> *Working class consciousness cannot be genuine political consciousness unless the workers are trained to respond to all cases, without exception, of tyranny, oppression, violence and abuse, no matter what class is affected. Moreover to respond from a social democratic [revolutionary socialist or communist—ed.], and not from any other viewpoint.*[8]

Comrades from the RU pointed out that the struggle at Lee Mah was both a fight against (super) exploitation of these workers AND was delivering a blow against oppression on behalf of the Chinese community overall. Lenin's point above supported, and had inspired, the slogan promoted by the RU: "Workers unite to lead the fight against all oppression!" This pointed to a political direction of uniting workers of all nationalities to lead the struggle against class exploitation and ALL forms of oppression—to build the revolutionary movement on this basis and NOT conducting the struggle in narrow trade union terms.

WMS, together with the RU, tried to apply this understanding in rallying workers and others to take up the Lee Mah struggle. We began mobilizing broadly in the Chinese community with car caravans and cultural events, unleashing the anger many felt about the discrimination faced by the whole community. We also mobilized rank-and-file workers of all nationalities to join and support the Lee Mah workers. White strikers from other Bay Area electronics factories, Black, Latino and white workers from the post office, city bus drivers, Chinese garment and restaurant workers—would join the picket lines and support activities. We also drew support from Asian students and activists from all over the Bay Area—from S.F.'s Japantown to UC Berkeley's Asian Studies.

It was a small but notable step in our learning the concrete basis and potential for multinational and working class unity—fighting against exploitation, as well as national (and women's) oppression. A whole new horizon was introduced to the Lee Mah workers as well. Some Lee Mah workers would step outside of Chinatown to join White, Black and Latino workers attending political activities such as protests against police murders of Black people in S.F., May Day rallies, and interacting with revolutionaries and Maoist/communist politics.

What would we sum up off Lee Mah, where the workers did not win their immediate economic demands despite a long, hard fight? The struggles around wages, working conditions and unionization going on back then and that are being fought today in sweatshops and low-paid industries are important fronts of the class struggle. The masses cannot just let themselves be ground down into abject submission; and these battles give workers a sense of the power in their unity and determination. But the class-conscious proletariat has to break beyond the bounds of the economic struggle and lead in developing an all-around revolutionary movement that stands for emancipation. To paraphrase Marx's famous statement, "the workers need to inscribe upon their banner—the abolition of the system of wage slavery."

Proletarian Revolution and Ending National Oppression [9]

By 74, most of us in WMS had come to the conclusion that imperialism/capitalism was the problem which required revolution to resolve.[10] We were revolutionaries who had long rejected cultural or narrow nationalism. But we still have to make a leap beyond seeing revolution mainly as a way to solve the oppression faced by Asians (revolutionary nationalism). As we grasped the need for revolution more deeply, we studied Marxism-Leninism and engaged with the line of the RU more seriously.

In 1974-75, the RU was mounting a battle to build a new vanguard party in the U.S. A major debate broke out over the relationship between national liberation and proletarian revolution in this country. Two issues in particular played a big part in further defining WMS' political and ideological development: the difference between revolutionary nationalism and internationalism; and how to wage the most powerful fight against national oppression as part of building a revolutionary movement that can ultimately overthrow the system.

It's important to remember that these debates were taking place in a certain historical context. The national liberation struggles in Asia, Africa and Latin America had been striking righteous blows against U.S. imperialism. In the U.S. itself, the Black liberation struggle had, as I mentioned, played a certain vanguard role in the overall struggle and had in fact pushed the question of revolution to the fore.

In the early 70s, many of the most revolutionary-minded in the Black, Latino, and Asian American movements were turning to Marxism-Leninism—the influence and example of revolutionary China being a compelling factor. Like myself at the time, many of the new revolutionaries gravitating towards Marxism-Leninism also carried the influence of nationalism. Part of the reason for this ongoing influence of nationalism was the low-level of conscious working class leadership in U.S. society.

In these circumstances there was a strong trend in the new communist movement to equate or try to combine revolutionary nationalism and internationalism. There were theories that Marxist-Leninists of the oppressed nationalities should be both nationalists (looking out for your nationality first) and internationalists (concerned about all the oppressed and exploited first); that the masses of the oppressed nationalities could not be won or didn't have to be won to communist ideology; that Black workers—not the multinational proletariat—must be the leading force in the revolutionary movement; that communists who were Black or other oppressed nationalities would be "the vanguard within the vanguard party."

We didn't agree with all these ideas, but we were definitely influenced by them...and we had a lot of sorting out and ideological shaking up to do. What made it especially challenging for me was that I had responsibility for helping to lead many of these discussions in WMS around these issues! In terms of what we were debating, I want to say a few things about nationalism because it was a big question then and is a big question today.

The nationalism of the oppressed nations (and Black people are an oppressed nation in the U.S.) and oppressed nationalities has historically played a major and often positive role in the peoples' struggles. This has everything to do with people rising up against discrimination. It has to do with Blacks, Latinos, Asians, and others reclaiming their histories and asserting peoples' identities against the racism and white supremacy rampant in Amerikkka—in the 60s and today. But what we came to appreciate more deeply through study and debate was that nationalist ideology, even revolutionary nationalism that wants to stand up to the system and wages armed struggle, doesn't point the way forward to complete liberation.

Why? Because nationalism doesn't challenge the fundamental economic and social relations of capitalist and class society, and therefore it can't fully represent the interests of the exploited and most oppressed. Because the nationalist program of everyone looking out for "their" nationality first doesn't provide the basis to build the broadest and most powerful unity of the exploited and oppressed of different nationalities. When you get right down to it, you can't really promote genuine equality between nations on the basis of an outlook and program of "my nationality first."

Nationalism doesn't give you the ability to make the kind of class analysis that we were trying to do of Chinatown and U.S. society. It doesn't enable you to identify different class interests, who should lead in the struggle, and how the working class has to relate to other classes.

Revolutionary nationalism often identifies with other struggles internationally, but it cannot give a full picture of the struggle of the exploited and oppressed as a worldwide battle to move humanity to a whole new stage of history. And nationalism cannot provide truly liberating solutions to some of the most pressing and profound problems in our communities, in the larger society, and in the world...like how to end the oppression of women!

In short, the nationalist ideology is not a guide to ALL-THE-WAY liberation, to overturning and transforming all economic systems based on exploitation and class division, all institutions that perpetuate oppression, and all ideas that reflect and reinforce these things. Nationalism is limited by the class viewpoint of those within the oppressed nations who cannot see beyond "control over the affairs of the nation." At an even deeper level, it's limited by the very horizon of nation and nationhood. You see, communist ideology doesn't have allegiance to any particular nation but to the cause of total emancipation. Communism is internationalism—the ideology of the international proletariat in its world-historic mission to liberate itself and all humanity. The communist revolution not only aims to abolish the division of society into different classes and to overcome the inequalities and oppressive relations between different nations and peoples; it also aims ultimately to move beyond the division of the earth's people into separate nations and to replace it with a genuine community of world humanity.

Only a communist revolution led by the proletariat, and based on the goals and methods of completely eliminating capitalism and class society, can end national oppression and uproot all forms of inequality and social antagonism. Which is why communists are the staunchest fighters against national oppression.[11]

But what does this mean in terms of building the revolutionary movement in the U.S.? The RU back then was seeking to apply and deepen the understanding that the alliance between the revolutionary movement of the multinational proletariat and the movements of the oppressed nationalities is crucial to making revolution in the U.S. And the RCP today has continued developing this approach and the policies for fighting racism on every front and forging this alliance.

Among other things, it means with regard to the struggle against national oppression, the revolutionary vanguard works to unite the greatest number of the oppressed nationalities to strengthen the fight against racism. An early glimpse of this potential, albeit in a primitive form, was how we tried to mobilize all the people in Chinatown and various Asian communities to fight the oppression of the immigrant Chinese workers at Lee Mah. And the people of the oppressed nationalities (popularly termed people of color) do not need to be limited to just fighting their own oppression; people can in fact go from being fighters on one front to becoming fighters for all, as many of us in WMS began to do.

It also means that the proletariat needs to build the fight against white supremacy and racism, and be on the front ranks of this fight throughout society—whether it's the fight against police brutality, opposing "English-only" campaigns, or taking on racist theories of genetic inferiority. At the same time, the vanguard has to carry out work among the middle classes and other sections of society to mobilize them in this fight, and to win them to stand with and follow the lead of those on the bottom of society.

The program of fighting racism on every front and in every sphere of society was something that connected to my own experiences in the struggle and yearning for revolution. Through those tumultuous years in WMS, my own outlook began to change from seeing myself mainly as an Asian revolutionary, putting my people first, and looking at the world and political struggle from that vantage point, to more and more seeing myself as an internationalist—putting the interests of the world revolution first and foremost, proceeding from the standpoint of the international proletariat.

For me and others in WMS, making this transformation to seeing liberation as an international thing was quite challenging AND truly liberating! It meant understanding the source of our oppression as Asians, and the source of all oppression was rooted in capitalist exploitation. It meant confronting the kind of struggle it would take to really get rid of imperialism, and what kind of society and world needed to be brought into being.

Carry Forward the Legacy of Serving the People

I noted with much interest the 1998 "Serve the People" conference in Los Angeles on the new Asian American community activism, and its workshops on "resisting imperialism", "organizing Asian workers", and "The New Asian and Pacific Islander Working-Class." These themes are reminiscent of my WMS experience, and reflect both aspects of the 60s legacy: the imprint left by the upsurges of that period, but also the unfinished task in front of the new generation today—the actual overthrow of the imperialist system.

WMS was part of the revolutionary movement in the '60s that shook U.S. imperialism. It was a time when the need for revolution was a serious consideration for millions. The struggle then had exposed the fundamental injustices of the system, and brought very broad forces together to struggle in unity against it. It identified with people fighting imperialism around the world and fostered international solidarity in the struggle. However, we can't and don't want to go back to the 60s, because as powerful as it was, the 60s didn't go far enough.

Much has changed since those years. Most significantly is the restoration of capitalism in the once revolutionary China of Mao Zedong in 1976. The revisionist (phony socialist) Soviet bloc collapsed in 1989-91, and today the U.S. presides as the chief imperialist over a vast empire. Despite the much touted technological wonders and globalization, imperialism today is imposing ever more brutal and repressive conditions on people around the world. In the U.S., we've seen a vicious war on the poor, on women's right to abortion, on affirmative action, and the criminalization and mass incarceration of the youth, especially Black and Latino youth.

But as Mao said "oppression breeds resistance." There has been a significant, even if initial, rise of new political youth activism these past few years. I have engaged in several intergenerational dialogues with radical Asian Pacific American youth active in the crucial battles of today: stopping the execution of Mumia Abu-Jamal, against police/INS brutality, for women and immigrant rights. In this beginning fer-

27

ment, the current generation of warriors are gaining new experiences, posing new questions, and searching for new explanations and ideologies. I feel ever more compelled to contribute what WMS learned about the importance of revolutionary theory/ideology guiding our activism that can truly liberate all of humanity. Veterans like myself are learning from the diverse experiences and insights of the new generation, and we need to be struggling and learning together about the many new contours and elements of moving forward to revolution.

Though WMS dissolved, many of us have struggled to continue serving the people to the fullest sense—serving the exploited and oppressed of the world by working for world revolution right here inside the belly of the beast. The challenge for veteran activists like myself who never gave up the vision of a radically different and better world—and for the new generation of activists who are beginning the search for the "theory and methods" to do so—is to carry forward the best of the 60s upsurge and to go further and develop the means to actually get rid of imperialism.

My experience through Wei Min She—the organization to serve the people—left me with a firm understanding that imperialism is a global system of exploitation and plunder that must be overthrown through revolution. I came to see that not just any revolution, but only a proletarian revolution—led by the have-nots in society and that aims to eliminate all forms of exploitation and oppression, one that changes society from bottom to top—can end the oppression of Asians and other people of color.

One thing we have today that we didn't have in the 1960s is a revolutionary vanguard. The RCP is very much a product of all the experiences and lessons of the 60s and early 70s—from the Cultural Revolution in China, to the Black Panthers, to the struggles like the I-Hotel. I encourage people to check out and dialogue with the party. The party is armed with a deep grasp of Marxism-Leninism-Maoism, with a developed program and plan for how to organize in the conditions of the U.S. to move towards revolution, and with a liberating vision of a new society.

Today I am a revolutionary communist—my perspective in all the political organizing I'm involved with. I advocate and work for the day when the proletariat and all oppressed peoples, through building a revolutionary movement based on the united front against imperialism, will wage a people's war in the belly of the beast.

The revolution is, in important ways, being made right now in the work of the RCP: the public opinion it is creating for revolution; the battles it is leading now against the system; the way it is moving to make all this strengthen the forces of the people for the BIG battle to be fought on a whole other level whenever and as soon as the conditions for that ripen.

Together the new generation and veteran activists like myself can rally the people against this system to rise up in resistance. We can help develop that resistance into a powerful movement whose aim is not to patch up this sick system or to get our share in it, but to overthrow it through revolution and replace it with a new and better world. We can do this together with our sisters and brothers all over the world who are struggling against the same imperialist enemy.

Through WMS, many of us took the Maoist adages of "going to the masses" and "serving the people" to heart, and in the process, found revolutionary Marxism-Leninism-Maoism on the "road to the proletariat." This is the legacy left by Wei Min She. It is a legacy that I am confident a new generation of Asian activists can learn from and build on.

ENDNOTES

1. "Statement by Comrade Mao Tse-tung, Chairman of the Central Committee of the Communist Party of China, in support of the Afro-American Struggle Against Violent Repression," Foreign Language Press, Peking: 1968.

2. Formally known as <u>Quotations from Chairman Mao Tse-tung</u>, the <u>A Little Red Book</u> was first compiled in the early days of the Great Proletarian Cultural Revolution and disseminated as an important tool for making Marxist-Leninist theory accessible to the broad masses in China and internationally. It trained a whole generation of revolutionaries in the 1960s and outsold the Bible.

3. Mao Tse-tung, "On Practice" <u>Selected Readings from the Works of Mao Tse-tung</u>, Foreign Language Press, Peking 1971.

4. ACC's political platform, as outlined in the bilingual <u>Asian Community Center Newsletter</u>, emphasized moving the community collectively for political action as a means to solve community problems. It stated:

What we see

We see the breakdown of our community and families

We see our people suffering from malnutrition, tuberculosis, and high suicide rates.

We see destruction of our cultural pride.

We see our elderly forgotten and alone.

We see our youth subjected to racism in the classroom and in the streets.

We see our mothers and fathers forced into meaningless jobs to make a living.

We see American society preventing us from fulfilling our needs.

What we want

We want adequate housing, medical care, employment, and education.

What we believe

To solve our community problems, all Asian people must work together.

Our people must be educated to move collectively for direct action.

We will employ any effective means that our people see see as necessary.

5. "Statement by Comrade Mao Tse-tung, Chairman of the Central Committee of the Communist Party of China, in support of the Afro-American Struggle Against Violent Repression," Foreign Language Press, Peking: 1968.

6. WMS developed campus work together with the RU that centered on building a multinational revolutionary student organization on several S.F. Bay Area campuses. In the course of this campus work, we found common cause with revolutionary-minded foreign students who taught us some lessons about the international struggle and internationalism. Most exemplary were our Iranian student comrades who contributed to various battles—from their militant anti-Shah protests to joining in ACC events, and mobilizations at the Lee Mah factory. Many of these Iranian comrades, who returned to Iran to join the revolutionary overthrow of the Shah of Iran, became martyrs to the cause at the hands of the fundamentalist Islamic Republic there.

7. Wei Min She Labor Committee, United Front Press: San Francisco, 1974.

8. V.I. Lenin <u>What Is To Be Done? Burning Questions of Our Movement</u>, Foreign Language Press, Peking: 1975, page 86.

9. In this essay, I use the terms "working class" and "proletariat" interchangeably. The proletariat is the

propertyless exploited class in capitalist society. Its labor is the basis of capitalist production and its poverty is the basis of capitalist wealth. The proletariat includes not only the employed and underemployed but also the A reserve army of the unemployed. The millions of young women who labor in South Asia=s textile and electronic industries, French transport workers on strike, Mexicans who risk death crossing the border into the U.S. to find work, unemployed youth crowding the corners of the South Bronx and South Central L.A.— they are all part of the international proletariat. The proletariat has both the interest and the potential power to make a revolution that will finally abolish all forms of exploitation and oppression.

10. WMS was a pan-Asian organization; additionally, it recruited the J-Town Workteam, a small collective of Sansei activists.

11. For a comprehensive Marxist-Leninist-Maoist analysis of the Black national question in the U.S., including the application of the principle of self-determination, see Cold Truth, Liberating Truth: How This System Has Always Oppressed Black People, And How All Oppression Can Finally Be Ended (Chicago, RCP Publications, 1989). For a response to nationalist arguments raised against communist ideology, see Bob Avakian, "Communism is Not a 'European Ideology': It is the Ideology of the International Proletariat," Revolutionary Worker, February 17, 1991.

DARE TO STRUGGLE

The KDP and Filipino American Politics

Helen C. Toribio

Like most other Left organizations in minority communities, the KDP was born out of the radical movements of the late 1960s and early 1970s. Although there were numerous Leftist and progressive organizations in the Filipino American community by the early 1970s, predominantly student led, the KDP's birth in 1973 signaled the formation of the most organized leftist institution in the history of the Filipino American community.

The KDP was the product of one generation from both ends of the Pacific Ocean, immigrant and American-raised Filipinos. They traced their common revolutionary roots to the Katipunan in the Philippines that was founded in 1892 and led by the working-class hero, Andres Bonifacio.[1] The Katipunan ng mga Demokratikong Pilipino, (translated as the Union of Democratic Filipinos, or KDP) borrowed part of its name from the original revolutionary organization to symbolize a commitment to continue the unfinished revolution that the original Katipunan was not able to fulfill, and to express solidarity with the revolutionary movement in the Philippines.

On the U.S. west coast, American-raised Filipino student ("Fil-Am") activists were immersed in a variety of struggles in coalition with other ethnic groups: Vietnam War protests, demands for ethnic studies, low income housing struggles. In the KDP, their lifetime experience as minorities in the U.S. would highlight the centrality of racism in U.S.-Philippine relations historically and on the Filipino American political agenda. Meanwhile, in the Philippines, a massive nationalist movement challenged the U.S.-backed regime of President Ferdinand Marcos, leading to an open confrontation in 1970 that became known as the First Quarter Storm. Immigrant activists from the Philippines would bring with them a national experience from a movement with an established Left vanguard guided by a strategy for a Philippine revolution. Together, both immigrant and American raised Filipinos would challenge the "old guard" in the community, demonstrating progressive and radical sensibilities which sharply contrasted with the conservative orientation that dominated Filipino American politics.

The plethora of Filipino American student and community based conferences throughout the early 1970s gave rise to calls for a national activist organization. Likewise, the network of Filipino organizations which were established by immigrant activists in major U.S. cities to support the national democratic movement in the Philippines sought to establish a national formation to coordinate their efforts. The Kalayaan Collective of San Francisco, which produced a nationally distributed radical newspaper, initiated the call to organize a national formation. Efforts were underway in the fall of 1972 for a national conference when Marcos declared martial law in the Philippines. Plans for the national conference were delayed as activists immediately responded to martial law, forming the National Committee for the Restoration of Civil Liberties in the Philippines (NCRCLP), a coalition of opposition forces from both the left and right in the Filipino American community.

The national founding of the KDP took place in July 1973 which brought together a variety of political orientations: nationalist, anti-imperialist, socialist, communist, and some still struggling to define their own. The result of intense political debates and discussions was a program that defined the KDP's dual identity: an anti-imperialist program supporting the national democratic movement in the Philippines, and a socialist program, albeit less defined, supporting a socialist revolution in the U.S. For the next thirteen years, the KDP would organize a massive amount of activity from demonstrations to theater productions, produce numerous publications, and conduct its own systematic political education of its rank and file. Leading the organization would be an elected (and selected) group of revolutionaries forming the National Council (NC) who in turn selected the National Executive Board (NEB). The NEB led the day by day operation of the organization which was theoretically democratic-centralist but substantially centralist in nature; activists were expected to "tow the line" on political questions and campaigns as set out by the NEB. The top-down approach, nonetheless, made the KDP function efficiently. Political discussions, organizing meetings, and theoretical studies were always meaningful interactions, even if at times heated, instilling a sense of accomplishment and progress for activists. And the NEB, for the most part, was effective in providing the necessary leadership. The internal reports called the Ang Aktibista prepared by the NEB reflected a systematic and thorough assessment of political conditions in the Philippines and the U.S., and the KDP's role as the political vanguard in the Filipino American community.

Vanguard

From the onset, the KDP set itself as the most "advanced" political force in the Filipino American community. The self-proclaimed role of vanguard was no pretense. The KDP assessed the community's existing leadership to be conservative and out of touch with the times, an assessment supported by numerous experiences by members even prior to joining the KDP. Filipino activism in the struggles for low income housing, ethnic studies, immigrant rights, affirmative action, etc., were largely ignored by the mainstream Filipino community organizations and their leadership. Some activists had grown up with these organizations, attending meetings with their parents and made to dance to traditional Philippine folk music at community functions. Returning to these organizations as activists became an endurance test through endless debates over Robert's rules and statements preceded by a litany of titles and life accomplishments—president, vice-president, doctor, colonel, graduate summa cum laude—before any substantive comment or question was made. The content of these meetings—treasurer reports, beauty pageants, officer installment dinners—tried the patience of activists eager to bring issues of civil rights in the US and human rights in the Philippines into the community's agenda.

Conversely, given the community's relative invisibility in the decades since World War II, raising the community's political consciousness was essential to establishing its presence. Until the 1970s, the Filipino American community had been overshadowed historically by other Asian American communities, and largely ignored in the national political landscape. Through a variety of national campaigns, among them the campaign for justice for Narciso and Perez, the KDP's organizing efforts resonated among Filipinos who sought venues for empowerment and drew attention to the community's concerns from the outside, e.g. the media, government, and other progressive organizations.

From the KDP's perspective only a vanguard organization had the capacity to effect the community's political agenda. In the heyday of inspired "serve the people" activism, the role of vanguard projected activists into organizing the community around a wide field of issues both local and national. All KDP chapters, for example, held common activities (e.g. demonstrations) each September on the anniversary of martial law in the Philippines. In addition, each chapter addressed local issues specific to the area, e.g. foreign-trained nurses in New York and labor organizing in Seattle.

As the vanguard organization, the KDP's goal was to (re)instill progressive politics in the Filipino American community. Progressive politics was not new in the history of the community. To the KDP, however, it had been forty years since progressive Filipinos, some of whom were communists, were active in community politics. Back then, in the 1920s and 1930s, labor organizing was prominent, and Filipino labor activists, including Carlos Bulosan, not only fought for labor rights, but were active in fighting deportations and defending immigrant rights. The KDP found itself struggling with similar issues and sought insight from veterans of the struggles of the 1930s. Oral histories of Filipino former members of the CPUSA, while inspiring, revealed little by way of specific strategies that might have been useful for the KDP in its work in the Filipino American community.[2]

But like the Filipino labor activists of the 1930s, the KDP faced a number of right-wing forces in the community. Prominent among them were the Philippine consulates in major cities around the country. The consulates, like their predecessors[3], maintained close ties with the community to ensure support for the existing Philippine regime and US support for it. By the 1970s, the consulates not only served to promote conservatism in the Filipino American community; they were also sources of intimidation to suppress open opposition to then President Ferdinand Marcos. Thus, wherever the KDP organized or participated in community activities—demonstrations, community conferences, cultural celebrations, etc.—consulate representatives were present taking pictures, making notes of KDP activists, voicing anti-communist rhetoric. The extent of the consulates' intelligence work on the KDP became publicly known in the early 1980s when information was obtained through the Freedom of Information Act (FOIA) on leading members of the KDP. The information was necessitated in the aftermath of the 1981 murders of Gene Viernes and Silme Domingo, KDP members and labor leaders in Seattle. The successful civil trial indicted the Marcos' in the deaths of the two Filipino Americans.

Organized community empowerment efforts in the mainland Filipino American community was almost nil before the 1970s. Filipino presence in American politics was relatively limited to Hawaii where Filipinos held electoral and appointed positions, and were placed in leadership positions in Hawaii's leading union, the ILWU Local 142. Progressive politics elsewhere in the U.S. were even less present in Filipino community empowerment efforts. What progressive activities existed before the 1970s were mainly known by a minority number of Filipinos involved in or sympathetic to the issues directly affecting Filipinos, such as the 1965 Delano grape strike, the 1968-69 student strikes at San Francisco State University and University of California at Berkeley, and the early protests against eviction at the International Hotel in San Francisco. Although these struggles did draw sizable participation from Filipinos, particularly among the young and the elderly, they did not generate Filipino community-wide attention that these struggles deserved. Still, these struggles provided invaluable experience in progressive community empowerment. Perhaps because of the absence of community-wide support, Filipino participation in these sixties-era civil rights struggles are often overlooked, leading to erroneous assumptions that Filipinos were not part of the civil rights movement or were latecomers. In fact, Filipino activism in civil rights existed since the early mass migrations of Filipinos into the U.S.. For decades before the 1960s Filipinos were active in issues both domestic and Philippine related, e.g. labor rights, citizenship, and resistance to deportations, as well as support for Philippine independence and liberation from American colonialism.

The KDP's presence by 1973 systematized Filipino participation in progressive politics. Because of its dual program, the strategy for community empowerment was two-fold: to intervene in U.S. anti-racist struggles, and organize support for the Philippine national democratic revolution including militant opposition to the Marcos regime. In both cases, the U.S. was seen as the primary instigator of the racist and imperialist policies that maintained Filipino racial and national oppression in the U.S. and in the Philippines. Given this two-pronged approach to community empowerment, the KDP organized on many fronts. It initiated community task forces, for example, on education and on immigrant rights. It organized community intervention on the rights of foreign-trained nurses and of 4-H trainees from the Philippines. It participated in coalitions to protect affirmative action and brought in Filipino support for Jesse Jackson's Rainbow Coalition in the early 1980s. For its Philippine national democratic program, the KDP organized the Anti-Martial Law Coalition (AMLC)[4]; initiated the International Association of Filipino Patriots

(IAFP) which focused its attention on the Philippine revolution; and helped to form the Friends of the Filipino People (FFP) to organize support among progressive non-Filipinos in the U.S. for changing the conditions in the Philippines.

Organizing in the Filipino American Community

The KDP's initial priority upon its formation was organizing the diverse opposition to the martial law regime of President Marcos. The KDP recognized that there were various groupings each with its own political orientation, and sought to develop a "united front" against the Marcos dictatorship. One group, for example, was the "traditional" political opposition such as the exiled politicians disenfranchised by Marcos but who would otherwise be in power had Marcos not monopolized the state apparatus in the Philippines. Another was the Filipino left in the U.S. comprising not only of the KDP but included the NCRCLP and independents who were disenchanted with the traditional politicians but not aligned with any organized opposition. Then, there was the non-Filipino opposition, predominantly White anti-imperialists with expertise on the long history of U.S.-Philippine relations.

Between 1973 and 1975 the KDP was instrumental in institutionalizing the anti-martial law opposition. In October 1973, it helped establish the Friends of the Filipino People (FFP) at a conference in Philadelphia. Directed mainly at a non-Filipino audience, the FFP led efforts in lobbying Congress against support for Marcos. In 1974, the first national anti-martial law conference was held in Chicago which established the National Coordinating Committee of the Anti-Martial Law Movement, later re-named the Anti-Martial Law Coalition (AMLC) in 1975. The KDP's role in the AMLC was to "centralize all information from the resistance movement in the Philippines and organize a historical archive for the anti-martial law movement in the U.S."

The KDP's tasks, however, were not limited to centralizing information on martial law. At the local level the KDP organized local chapters of the AMLC; each AMLC chapter was called the Anti-Martial Law Alliance (AMLA), except Hawaii which named its local AMLC chapter the Committee for Human Rights in the Philippines (CHRP). Given the ongoing developments in the Philippines and continuous U.S. support for Marcos, there was no lack of anti-martial activities every year, even during the late-70s which the KDP assessed to be years of ebb in political movements and anti-martial law activism. With the KDP as its backbone, the AMLC maintained vigilance and closely monitored events in the Philippines and on Philippine related legislation pending in Washington D.C. Yearly demonstrations at local Philippine consulates were held every September 22nd on the anniversary of martial law characterized by rallies, marches, picketing, effigy burnings, and sit-ins within consulate offices. Other anti-martial law events included car caravans around local neighborhoods and community forums.

The AMLC's newsletter, the *Taliba* (balita, meaning news in Tagalog, phonetically spelled backward), was the most widely distributed anti-martial law source of information in the U.S. Besides its distribution at demonstrations, thousands more were given away wherever Filipinos were concentrated: workplaces such as hospitals with large numbers of Filipino nurses, Catholic churches, farmers markets, street corners, and residential neighborhoods. Most Filipinos were responsive by taking the *Taliba*, some making critical comments about conditions in the Philippines, others claiming U.S. Filipinos should have nothing to do with the Philippines, and a few eventually supporting or joining local AMLAs.

Among U.S. Filipinos supporting Marcos, the most vocal were in Hawaii where the majority of Filipino immigrants were from the Ilokos region of the Philippines where Marcos came from. In spite of being outnumbered by Marcos supporters, however, the Hawaii AMLC chapter—the CHRP—had its own presence. Its organizing capacity was tested in 1980 when Marcos visited Hawaii, his first entry into the U.S. since he declared martial law. The CHRP confronted Marcos at the Honolulu International Airport, unfurling banners of denunciation a few feet from the podium just as he began his speech to a welcoming crowd. Marcos continued with his speech, heckled along the way with protests about his human rights violations.

While the AMLC symbolized the anti-imperialist side of the KDP's program, it had no counterpart in the socialist side. On this aspect of its political program, the KDP organized a multiplicity of focused community advocacy groups and actively participated in existing community efforts and institutions such as the yearly Far West Conventions in the west coast and local Filipino community councils. Among the numerous advocacy groups the KDP organized, for example, were: the Filipino Education Task Force (1975) to address racist portrayals of Filipinos in school textbooks; the National Alliance for Fair Licensure for Foreign Nurse Graduates (1977) to address the exploitation of Philippine trained nurses in U.S. hospitals; and the National Filipino Immigrant Rights Organization (1979) to defend immigrant Filipinos from deportations and protest anti-immigrant legislation.

The KDP did not always initiate organizing around community issues. On numerous occasions, the KDP became involved in struggles brought to community attention by those directly affected, such as manongs faced with pending housing evictions, 4-H trainees from the Philippines subjected to treatment as cheap farm labor, and Filipina nurses confronted with numerous adversarial situations from labor exploitation to licensure denials to unemployment and deportation. But, as with the AMLC, the KDP provided the activist core that sustained community organizing, facilitated nationally coordinated activities, and provided a progressive perspective in the reporting of community struggles through the KDP's national newspaper, the *Ang Katipunan*. No other Filipino American organization had that comprehensive a capacity to intervene on issues confronting the community.

The KDP's first attempts in organizing national campaigns around its socialist program involved the defense of immigrant medical workers, particularly nurses. In 1975, the KDP helped to establish the Emergency Defense Committee for Foreign Medical Graduates (EDC-FMG) in response to the imminent threat of mass deportations. Local committees were set up in cities like New York, Chicago and San

Francisco to organize resistance to pending deportations and help obtain legal status for those considered "illegal aliens." While spearheading efforts against deportations, the KDP was also increasingly drawn to an even more insidious issue affecting two immigrant nurses in Ann Arbor, Michigan.

The same year the EDC-FMG was established, Leonora Perez and Filipina "PI" Narciso were arrested for allegations of multiple murders at the Veteran Administration (VA) Hospital in Ann Arbor, Michigan. The nurses were accused of poisoning patients at the hospital. A two year investigation into the allegations resulted in an indictment based entirely on circumstantial evidence as admitted by the prosecution. A one year trial ensued in spite of misconduct on the part of the prosecution which included withholding evidence, and contradictory statements by prosecution witnesses including some made under questionable hypnosis. Narciso and Perez were initially found guilty but were later acquitted upon appeal.

Throughout the investigations and pre-trial hearings, the two nurses were under constant pressure to confess by the hospital administration and the FBI. They were subjected to blatant racism, described by a prosecution witness as "a couple of slant-eyed bitches" who were part of a "nation-wide conspiracy of 1800 Filipino nurses out to murder Americans."[5]

Initial support for the nurses was localized, coming from fellow hospital workers, other Filipino nurses, and the Filipino community in the midwest. In October 1976, the KDP Chicago Chapter helped establish the Chicago Support Group to coordinate the national support activities which included fundraising for the defense, community forums, and updates from the trial reported in detail in the Ang Katipunan. Organizing went into high gear when the verdict of guilty was announced: a national petition was begun to demand a re-trial; a media blitz of public service announcements, press releases, and press conferences were held; mass leafletting of informational brochures were distributed; rallies and marches were held outside federal government buildings. In addition, the KDP's cultural group, Sining Bayan, produced a satirical play called "The Frameup of Narciso and Perez," which was performed before Filipino and non-Filipino audiences to educate and garner support for the nurses.

A new trial was granted in February 1978 which never happened as the U.S. Attorney General dropped the charges. The KDP's response to the end of the Narciso-Perez case was not as euphoric as most who supported the nurses. In its last statement in the Ang Katipunan about the case, the KDP expressed disappointment that some attributed the victory to the "system of justice" in the United States instead of the mass movement that pressured the federal prosecution to drop the case. The KDP noted that the Narciso-Perez trial illustrated the racist and inherently oppressive nature of U.S. capitalism, and that the only alternative that could guarantee the rights of minorities like Filipino Americans was socialism. Unfortunately, a unified socialist program did not exist in the U.S. Left. Without it, even self-proclaimed vanguard organizations like the KDP were hard-pressed to elucidate just how a socialist system would work better than the one that granted Narciso and Perez justice in the end.

Contradictions

The variety of organizing activities represented the KDP's dual program, and at the same time reflected a contradiction inherent within the program. Having a dual program meant objectively participating in two separate revolutions, the Philippines and the U.S.. Could a "revolutionary mass organization" like the KDP realistically consider itself as part of two revolutions? Shouldn't one revolution take precedence over the other? And since the Philippine revolution was more advanced, (i.e. having a vanguard party in the Communist Party Philippines and a strategy) compared to the U.S, (having no singular vanguard and no unified strategy), then shouldn't the Philippine work have primacy in the KDP?

In effect, the Philippine work did dominate the KDP's organizing during the immediate aftermath of the declaration of martial law in the early 1970s and throughout the early to mid-1980s with a series of developments, e.g. Marcos' visits to the U.S., the Aquino assassination, and the 1986 Philippine elections that generated the "people's revolution." The priority given to the Philippine support work, however, did not necessarily diminish the KDP's intervention in domestic issues such as immigrant rights. Activists typically took on multiple tasks in both areas and integrated them in numerous conferences and cultural events such as the Far West Conventions and Philippine National Day celebrations.

The integration of both aspects of the KDP's dual program was not always a smooth process, however. Early in the KDP's history the debate over primacy of the Philippine work erupted into an open split with the Chicago chapter in 1975. After intense discussions over differences the chapter was reintegrated—with the dual program intact. The debate in Chicago highlighted not only the question of the primacy of Philippine work, but the question of Filipino nationalism as well. If the Philippine work had priority, then how should the KDP view the fast-growing Filipino community in the U.S.? Given the increasing influx of immigrants from the Philippines, should the KDP view the community as an "overseas" constituent of the Philippines? Or, did an immigrant population settling into American communities and integrating into the workforce mean it was principally a U.S. constituency? The KDP rejected the "overseas" characterization of the Filipino American community as an indication of narrow nationalism, and instead acknowledged the "dual identity" of the community: Filipinos in the U.S. were viewed as integrally tied culturally, economically, and politically to the Philippines through language, remittances to families, and community debates on homeland politics, while they also struggled with their marginalized status as non-whites who were predominantly foreign-born. The KDP's experience in Chicago demonstrated the dual-identity analysis and affirmed the organization's dual program as the chapter became the center for the KDP's defense work for Narciso and Perez, while, like other chapters, it also maintained the Philippine support work with as much priority as Narciso and Perez.

The integrated approach to both aspects of the KDP's program reflected the policy of internationalism that was instituted into the organization early on. As practiced by the KDP, internationalism underscored the role of a revolutionary and his/her political unity with the organization regardless of national origins. In effect it meant, for example, that membership in the KDP was not exclusively Filipino, that a Filipino national in the U.S. could lead in domestic anti-racist struggles, and likewise, a Fil-Am could lead in the Philippine support work. Internationalism was best exemplified by one of the original founders of the KDP, the late Cynthia Maglaya[6]. Forced to leave the Philippines in the aftermath of the First Quarter Storm, Maglaya provided an organic link between the Philippine revolution and the KDP at the leadership level. As a student leader in the CPP-led Kabataan Makabayan (Nationalist Youth), Maglaya brought to the KDP the sensibility of an internationalist revolutionary tempered by direct experience in a revolution led by a vanguard party. Thus, upon her arrival in the U.S. she became immediately engrossed in both domestic issues such as the fight to save the International Hotel as well as in organizing support for the Philippine revolution. She knew the value of cultural work as integral to organizing, which in the KDP translated into placing a premium value on "propaganda" such as the Ang Katipunan newspaper and the Sining Bayan Cultural Group.

By the late 1970s, the KDP's policy of internationalism[7] was both practiced and subverted, at least in the San Francisco Bay Area. On one hand, for example, the KDP took responsibility for the political and theoretical training of its activists especially those who could eventually leave the KDP for the Philippines or for responsibilities beyond the Filipino American community. It also continued to develop fraternal relations with other activists of color and left organizations with similar political views.

On the other hand, internationalism took a back seat to Filipino-centered nationalism (i.e. narrow nationalism) when the KDP minimized its role in the multi-racial, multi-ethnic struggle to save the International Hotel, particularly as the evictions became imminent by 1977, and chose to prioritize campaigns centered by the KDP. A consequence from this episode was an internal struggle which resulted in bitterness on many sides. The organization was engrossed in numerous campaigns, each demanding the allocation of activists. The three-person KDP team assigned to the I-Hotel was criticized for refusing additional responsibilities separate from the I-Hotel and became estranged from the local leadership which, in turn, virtually ignored the I-Hotel at the height of the struggle in favor of the Philippine support work and other Filipino domestic issues. Only the Ang Katipunan paid detailed attention to the I-Hotel, providing extensive coverage during the last few weeks of the struggle before the eviction finally took place. Nonetheless, even though the KDP I-Hotel team was marginalized by the local leadership, they were also flanked in the I-Hotel work by other, more KDP-friendly groups such as the Third World Women's Alliance and the Northern California Alliance, though the three organizations may not have necessarily organized themselves as a left caucus with similar political perspectives on the I-Hotel.[8] This distinguished the I-Hotel work from most other KDP initiatives. Although the KDP regularly sought support from fraternal organizations on the left, it did not achieve the same level of work relations with fraternal groups as the KDP had in the I-Hotel.

Thus, in a way, the I-Hotel struggle was an anomalous experience for the KDP relative to other campaigns it centered. Not being the only left center in the I-Hotel denied the KDP a sense of "ownership" as there were numerous groups who could claim a vanguard relationship to the struggle. Unlike other campaigns, the I-Hotel had a different history: its beginnings pre-dated the KDP; many other left and progressive individuals and organizations from all racial and ethnic groups were involved from the onset; although Filipino manongs were at the center, the character of the I-Hotel struggle was never Filipino-only; and the ten-year span to save the hotel paralleled the evolution of various left formations which, in the late 1960's emphasized "serve the people" activism, but by the late 1970s had become focused on "party-building" with each formation contending to become the vanguard for the U.S. revolution. In these respects, the I-Hotel was unique; no other area of the KDP's work had a similar history or character.

If the I-Hotel provided a catalyst for the internal discord that ensued in the local chapter of the KDP, the I-Hotel struggle was as much if not more indicative of the fragmented and contentious state of the U.S. left as it was evident of the KDP's development by the late 1970s. Given the broad character of the I-Hotel struggle, the KDP had to contend with other left groups for the "correct revolutionary line," e.g. how to appropriately characterize and to lead the struggle.[9] The KDP would face similar challenges in other areas, especially the Philippine support work. In the I-Hotel, the polemical relationships among the various left groups amplified the already bitter struggle against eviction. The internal enmity that developed between the KDP I-Hotel team and the local leadership mirrored, on a smaller scale, that of the Left in general. Relations among activists became antagonistic like the relations between left organizations. Activists struggled over the question of what was a politically correct assessment of the time to warrant how activists were allocated and what tasks had priority.

As a campaign of resistance, the I-Hotel effectively ended when the evictions took place.[10] At the end of a campaign, the KDP routinely conducted a summation, assessing the strength and weaknesses of the KDP's involvement, and extracting lessons learned. But no such summation by the KDP occurred for the I-Hotel.[11]

The falling-out that resulted in the alienation of the I-Hotel team developed in the context of intensified political organizing by the late 1970s, while at the same time membership in the KDP had declined.[12] The intensification of the KDP's organizing coincided ironically with a period of political ebb when social movements were in retreat. The U.S. civil rights movement no longer had the momentum it had ten years earlier, and martial law in the Philippines had become entrenched, secure in its support from the U.S. Regardless of the ebb, the KDP became immersed in many activities which tested its organizational capacity and its leadership capabilities especially at the local level. In the San Francisco Bay Area, just as the I-Hotel struggle was heightening, the KDP also became involved in other important campaigns. The KDP organized the national defense of Narciso and Perez in 1976. When two Catholic Priests were deported by Marcos, the KDP worked on a national speaking tour for them organized by the AMLC in 1977. Mass protests were organized to oppose Marco's "snap elections" in 1978.

Aggravating the already intense level of political work were other responsibilities deemed just as important. During this same period each chapter was charged with developing its own local strategy, which included, for example, positioning the KDP at the center of the Filipino community, i.e. being the vanguard in the most concrete sense. For local chapters, such positioning meant establishing the KDP's leadership in local Filipino community organizations such as Filipino community councils. The weight of responsibility to be a vanguard had become especially intense so that each activist was expected to bear responsibility for multiple tasks in almost every campaign being organized concurrently. Thus, activists whose primary area may have been Philippine support also had duties in domestic campaigns and vice-versa (as expected in the I-Hotel work).

As local chapters struggled to place themselves at the center of their respective communities, the national leadership was also becoming inundated with additional responsibilities. Besides overseeing the day to day operations of the KDP, leading members in the NEB were also addressing the question of a vanguard for the U.S. revolution overall, a question which situated them in a network of Leftists which became the precursor for the eventual formation of the Line of March (LOM).

Embracing and Rejecting Mao Zedong Thought

Aggravating the challenge to explain socialism to a community like Filipino Americans, many of whom grew up in the Philippines under the colonial tutelage of the United States, was the state of the U.S. left itself. Throughout the KDP's existence the U.S. Left was mired in polemics around the question of the correct road to socialism, characterized by many organizational splits and mergers which often reflected the splits in the international communist movement, e.g. China versus the Soviet Union.

Aware of the importance of a "correct political line" that expressed a coherent strategy for revolution, the KDP became one of the antecedent groups that eventually organized into the Line of March (LOM) in 1980.[13] Other organizations included the Third World Women's Alliance (TWWA), the Northern California Alliance (NCA), and the Guardian Clubs (which was formerly associated with the Guardian newspaper). Prior to creating LOM, these groups worked as a network to address the question of "rectifying the general line" of the U.S. movement, i.e., a strategy for socialism. The development of this rectification network in the late 1970s symbolized a break from the influence of Mao Zedong Thought in one segment of the U.S. Left.

The influence of Mao Zedong Thought was especially evident in the Asian American Left in the early 1970s, as it was among radical groups of color, and the KDP was no exception. As a school of revolutionary theory which served to successfully seize state power, Maoism was the model that Third World liberation movements could emulate. In the U.S., Maoism resonated with the 1960s-70s generation

41

of Left radicals because it elucidated the relationship between class oppression at home and imperialist wars abroad, both of which were perpetuated by one and the same enemy, the United States. Compared to the more conservative stance (e.g. peaceful transition to socialism) of older left formations like the CPUSA, Maoism advocated a more militant approach to revolution including the use of armed resistance. And in the heyday of Left radical activism militancy was viewed as a necessity and revolution then appeared imminent. In spite of Maoism's influence, however, the U.S. Left remained largely fragmented. In the early 1970s, the KDP did not yet fully have reason to question Maoism. The progress in the Philippine revolution led by the Communist Party of the Philippines (CPP) was an indication of the successful application of Mao Zedong Thought. The CPP, for example, utilized Mao's strategy of "surrounding the cities from the countryside" which generated gains for the guerrilla warfare led by the CPP's New People's Army.

Maoism also provided the inspiration for the "rectification and re-establishment" of the CPP: to rectify the conservative approach of the old PKP (Partido Komunista ng Pilipinas, the CPUSA's counterpart in the Philippines), and re-establish a new party based on Mao Zedong Thought. Up until the mid-1970s, the CPP was the KDP's principle source of political analysis on the developments in the Philippines. However, international developments emerged which brought Maoism into question not just for the KDP, but others in the U.S. left as well.

In 1975, the liberation struggle in Angola found the United States and China allied against the revolutionary movement led by the MPLA. The MPLA sought and received material assistance, including armed forces, from Cuba and the Soviet Union in light of U.S. support for other Angolan groups contending for power, (i.e. the FNLA and UNITA). China's position in siding with the U.S. underscored the animosity between China and the Soviet Union which had already been developing for decades. The KDP, whose anti-imperialist program always identified the U.S. as the main imperialist enemy of national liberation movements around the world, was among the U.S. left groups that then began to steer away from Maoism.

The CPP, however, remained avowedly Maoist despite the situation in Angola and China's friendly relations with the Marcos dictatorship. By 1979, the KDP was further alienated from the CPP's siding with China on another international development. When Vietnam invaded Kampuchea in late 1978 the leadership of the KDP sided with Vietnam's intervention against the China-supported Pol Pot regime. The CPP continued to side with China on the Vietnam-Kampuchea crisis, a position strongly supported by some in the KDP. Meanwhile, by this time the KDP had also become one of the key partisans seeking a "rectification" of the strategy for a U.S. revolution along with the NCA, TWWA, and the Guardian Clubs. Ironically, the lessons learned by the KDP of the CPP's rectification-and-re-establishment process would serve to draw the KDP away from the influence of Maoism and the CPP. By taking part in the U.S. rectification movement the KDP came into dialogue with those who were beginning to re-examine their position towards the Soviet Union and their relationship with the CPUSA.

The CPUSA had been deemed by the New Left, (out of which numerous Maoist groups emerged in the 1960s and 70s), as essentially a dinosaur: lagging behind the mass movements of the 1960s and remaining uncritical of its stance towards the Soviet Union. Although the old party established an Asian-Pacific Islander commission in 1972 (and appointed a Filipino American as co-chair of the commission), the CPUSA had very little to offer—at least from the point of view of Maoists—by way of leadership politically and theoretically on the question of a general strategy for a U.S. revolution. Political conditions under the Reagan administration provided a catalyst for rectificationists to reconsider what the Soviet Union might have to offer now that Maoism had been discredited. Reagan's policies of social austerity which drastically reduced public programs for minority communities was concomitant with increased militarism evidenced by the development of the so-called "Star Wars" defense system. With the establishment of the LOM in 1980, a process was begun to study the history of the Communist Party of the Soviet Union (CPSU) in how it addressed the growing militarism in Europe during the 1930s which gave rise to fascism. Similarities were drawn between the U.S. in the 1980s and Europe of the 1930s: both faced a growing rightist movement propelled by racism and fueled by a depressed economy. This political assessment led to LOM's assertion for the development of a United Front Against War and Racism (UFAWR).

Though the LOM stopped short of calling the UFAWR a general line for a U.S. revolutionary strategy, the UFAWR nonetheless was a manifestation of the rectification process that was of paramount importance to the LOM. The development of the UFAWR line contextualized how each of the LOM's antecedent groups would then relate to the revolutionary process in the U.S.. For the KDP, it meant re-assessing its political identity that was defined as dual in character: anti-imperialist and socialist. By 1983 the KDP dropped its dual identity and declared itself simply socialist.

In the Philippines, meanwhile, the political and economic crisis of the Marcos dictatorship was precipitated by the 1983 murder of Ninoy Aquino. The massive outpouring generated a popular movement for democracy culminated in the "people's revolution" which ousted Marcos in 1986. The political schism between the KDP and the CPP which had evolved since the mid-1970s deepened even further by the mid-1980s. The apparent absence of the CPP's National Democratic Front in the midst of the people's revolution was viewed by the KDP as the consummate error of the CPP's adherence to Maoism.

By 1986 the KDP was being pulled into two different revolutionary directions: the rectification movement in the U.S. led by LOM, and the crisis in the Philippine Left in the aftermath of the people's revolution. Both were intensifying at the same time. Given these political developments, the KDP did not have the political and organizational capacity it once had to adequately address both situations. Many of its activists were already transferred out of the KDP and taking leadership roles in movements where more LOM activists were needed such as labor and the support work for revolutionary movements in Central America. Rather than maintaining the structure that had served the KDP since its inception, a more radical re-structuring was proposed and implemented. KDP activists who could focus primarily on the Philippines were re-grouped into a Philippine committee (which was independent of LOM); others who continued to work in the Filipino American community on domestic issues like immigrant rights were incorporated into the LOM's Anti-Racist Commission. In effect, the KDP as an organization was dissolved by 1987. However, former KDP members maintained an informal network as activists continued their involvement in both Philippine and Filipino American matters even until today.

Legacies

Although revolution was not realized as many had envisioned in 1970s, the commitment to social change remained. Many former KDP members have continued their activism which was nurtured in the days when they, like others on the Left, thought that revolution was just around the corner. Revolutionary change may take a while longer. Meanwhile, ex-KDP activists are channeling their energies in numerous contemporary struggles: labor, immigrant rights, civil rights, education, health, gay and lesbian rights, to name a few. Some are positioned in the management of social service programs such as those against domestic violence, others are organizers and union leaders; a few are tenured in colleges, fewer became appointed or elected government officials. Most are not as active in the Filipino American community as they were while in the KDP but nonetheless continue to address the issues that affect Filipino Americans as much as other communities of color through their jobs, their volunteer work, or both.

Empowerment remains central to the Filipino American political agenda. The question of how, though, is perhaps more complex now than the limited reform-or-revolution alternatives the KDP struggled with alongside many other revolutionary groups at the time. In the absence of a viable progressive or revolutionary party in the U.S., some former members can be found participating in electoral politics, mostly with the Democratic Party, as the means to empower the Filipino community within mainstream America. For others, however, the Democratic Party remains too reformist, if not altogether conservative, for their participation. Likewise, the few activists who returned to the Philippines have also participated in the electoral arena but not necessarily in the same political formations. While critical of the ruling elite, the CPP, and the fragmented state of the Philippine Left, they have remained active in the debates over how revolutionary changes should occur. Meanwhile, conditions in the Philippines continue to be monitored by ex-KDP members in the U.S. although very little discussion now take place about homeland politics.

Some former members have lamented over the question of a thorough-going summation and assessment of the KDP's history. Although the KDP existed for a relatively short period of thirteen years, those years were characterized by a density of innumerable activities that spanned two countries, two revolutions, and a few hundred activists who entered and exited the KDP at different stages of its development.

It would thus be unlikely that a singular summation and assessment agreed to by all former members would ever be developed. Each of the KDP's many organizing projects could be a subject of detailed study, not just by former members but by anyone with progressive or revolutionary interests. Some ex-members have begun to share their experience with younger activists, and have written personal stories.[14]

A few may reflect on their KDP experience with antipathy. Most, however, will acknowledge that the bitterness was as much a part of the experience as the gratification felt by all in knowing that s/he contributed in the struggle to build a better world. As more and more publications become available about the KDP, it will be up to interested individuals to develop their own composite summation and assessment of the KDP and its legacy.

Postscript

The Line of March was disbanded in 1989 and re-grouped into the short-lived Frontline Political Organization which published *Crossroads* for a few years. LOM's history will be part of an upcoming book being written by Max Elbaum on the history of the New Communist Movement of the 1960s and 70s.

ENDNOTES

1. The full name of the original Katipunan was the Kataastaasan Kagalang-galang ng Katipunan ng mg Anak ng Bayan, and popularly referred to as the KKK. In translation the name stood for the Supreme and Most Reverent Society of the Sons of the Motherland.

2. Taped oral histories were taken in San Francisco of Manongs Mario Hermoso and Pablo Valdez, former members of the CPUSA.

3. During the U.S. colonial period in the Philippines, labor commissioners like Cayetano Ligot were sent by the colonial government to the United States to help suppress union activity by Filipino immigrant laborers. When Philippine consular offices were established in the U.S. by the 1950s, one of their tasks was to help establish Filipino community councils through which the Philippine government kept ties with the Filipino American community.

4. Later became the Campaign to Advance the Movement for Democracy and Independence (CAMDI).

5. All information on the Narciso-Perez campaign are drawn from the Ang Katipunan, years 1977-78.

6. Cynthia Maglaya passed away in 1983 after a long illness.

7. The term "internationalism" is used here to mean: (1) the sense of solidarity that activists demonstrated by working with and supporting domestic struggles beyond their own ethnic, racial, or national group; and (2) supporting struggles outside the United States, e.g., third world liberation movements.

8. A more collaborative relationship among the three organizations would not occur until after the fall of the I-Hotel when the Line of March was formed and activists from the three organizations began to work together in various LOM commissions such as the Anti-Racist Commission.

9. See Estella Habal's article "How I Became a Revolutionary."

10. The efforts to build low income housing on the I-Hotel site, however, have continued since the evictions.

11. It remains unclear if others on the left developed their own summations. Nonetheless, the I-Hotel remains a historical subject for leftists and researchers alike to revisit and analyze for its significance to the Asian American Movement and to the history of the Left in general.

12. Some estimated the KDP had a membership of about 400 by around 1975 but had declined by the late 1970s for various reasons. Some activists were expelled, others resigned to drop out of activism all together, or joined other activist groups.

13. Elbaum, Max, "Maoism in the United States" (1998), Encyclopedia of the American Left.

14. An upcoming anthology of personal stories has been compiled by former KDP members and will be published in the near future.

Waiāhole-Waikāne demonstration at Iolani Palace
Photo credit: Marion Kelly
see "Return the Islands Back to the People: A Legacy of Struggle and Resistance
in Ka Pāeʻaina"

PERSPECTIVE OF A REVOLUTIONARY FEMINIST

Emily Woo Yamasaki

I am very glad to be on this panel tonight on Asian Pacific Americans and Revolutionary Socialism with other activists whose work and histories I respect. My organizations and I have a history of working with many of you. I want to thank Fred Ho, Steve Yip and Wayne Lum for calling this very important meeting. I hope this will be one of many.

Following the theme of tonight's panel, I will be speaking as a member of both Radical Women (RW), a feminist organization, and its sister organization, the Freedom Socialist Party (FSP), and on how I became a revolutionary.

I am a native of San Francisco. I am Asian American of Chinese, Japanese and Korean descent. This explains the Yamasaki and Woo parts of my name, which people often wonder about. As a woman of color and a lesbian, I have gathered strength from the histories of all three cultural aspects of my background . I have received a lot of personal and political inspiration from my mother, Merle Woo. Many of you may know her through her anti-discrimination cases starting in 1981. Merle fought the University of California, Berkeley administration in two multi-discrimination cases. She won them both in the California State Courts on the basis of race, sex, sexuality and political ideology discrimination.

These cases inspired me, as well as other Asian Pacific Americans, feminists, lesbians and gays, students, unionists and many other activists around the country. For some time prior to her firing, Merle had been a public figure in the feminist, especially feminist of color, community. As a writer, she had been featured in various Asian American and Lesbian anthologies. She was a member of Unbound Feet, a collective of Chinese American women writers, and is a leader in RW and FSP. The central issue of Merle's cases was class. Merle was fired by other Asian Americans in the Asian American Studies Department at University of California, Berkeley. These tenured faculty found my mother's radical politics threatening to their personal career goals.

I moved to New York City in 1981. At that time, identity politics were pervasive. These politics were based in ranking identities. For example, as a young Asian American lesbian, I was supposed to be an Asian American or woman of color first. Other parts of me like being a lesbian or a student came second or third. However, I

Revised from a speech presented at "Asian Pacific Americans and Revolutionary Socialism," August, 1998 at Hunter College, New York City.

felt that all aspects of my oppression needed to be addressed at the same time.

I joined RW because its socialist feminist program spoke to me as an Asian American lesbian, as a worker, and as an actor. I had come to New York City to study acting.

A key apart of the RW and FSP program is feminism. Here I'll briefly explain the relationship between the RW and FSP. These are two sister organizations whose affiliation is based on a common program of socialist feminism. RW is an autonomous women's organizations with its own leadership and finances. RW's membership is just women. The FSP is a political party whose members are both men and women who are all feminists as well as socialists. The FSP, as a party, runs candidates in elections and considers the electoral arena an important part of socialist work. Currently, The FSP is running Stephen Durham in the 71st Assembly District in Washington Heights. It has been rewarding for me as a campaign volunteer to hear the enthusiastic response of district residents to the issues of the campaign, such as stopping police brutality, hiring the youth, and nationalizing healthcare, among others. Stephen is here tonight and would be glad to speak with you later about his campaign. Here in New York City, this is the FSP's first electoral campaign. We are excited about the response we've gotten.

One of the principle founders of both RW and FSP was Clara Fraser, an ardent, unapologetic feminist and pioneer of socialist feminism in the U.S. Her words have inspired me and many others, especially when it comes to defining the relationship between feminism and socialism. She wrote, "The logic of feminism is to expand inexorably into generalized radicalism. The survival problems of women can be solved only by fundamental change. And feminist demands lead logically and irresistibly towards the clear necessity for socialist revolution."[1]

These concepts have guided me through 17 years of activism in New York. Clara and others founded FSP out of a split from the Socialist Workers Party (SWP) in 1966 over the issues of feminism and an analysis of the Black movement containing the concept of Revolutionary Integration, which I will talk about later. The founders of the FSP disagreed with the SWP's tail-ending of the Black movement. They uncritically supported whoever was popular at the moment from reformist to cultural nationalists like Elijah Muhammad. The SWP today still waffles on the Black question.

RW was founded in 1967 at the University of Washington campus, primarily to provide a space to build women's leadership as an answer to the sexism in the left.[2]

Returning to my previous comments about the limitations of identity politics, I want to tell you about my experiences in an Asian American lesbian organization, Asian Lesbians of the East Coast (ALOEC). In the mid-80s, a debate broke out in this organization over political priorities. I felt there should be room for diverse perspectives, including my own radical, multi-issue approach. The majority believed, however, that members should focus exclusively on their Asian and lesbian identities, and those who didn't weren't really Asian or lesbian. I disagreed with this.

It is true that many of us are exploited because of our identities as women, people of color and queers. In response, some members of our communities follow the narrow logic of identity politics. This logic leads to a quest for a "safe haven" among a given single community, e.g. Asian or lesbian which doesn't really exist. What is missing from this approach is an analysis of class division. The Feminist Majority says putting women in office is the answer. Well, there are certainly women as well as Asian bosses whose interests are fundamentally opposed to ours as workers.

In the early days of Asian identity politics, if you were a feminist or a lesbian you weren't Asian enough. Especially if you were a radical or a member of a multiracial organization, you were not considered a legitimate part of the Asian American Movement. My mother talks about how when she found her identities as an Asian American through the Ethnic Studies struggle in the '60s, as a feminist and a lesbian, and later as a socialist feminist when she joined Radical Women and the Freedom Socialist Party, she had to "come out" in stages. My experience was different—I was fortunate to have been able to come out all at once!

I benefited from the road that was paved by those who struggled before me. And the multi-issue program of the RW and FSP—demonstrated in both words and action —embraced me as a whole person. These organizations were unique; I didn't have to compartmentalize the diverse parts of my identity to be a part of them, and I joined them in the early 80s. At that time multi-issues wasn't really in yet. An example of this was the Third World Women's Committee for International Women's Day. Many women in the committee refused to consider lesbian issues as equal to other issues like race and class. Their position was largely rooted in a cultural nationalist perspective which puts race first above other issues. I fought this exclusivity in the coalition with the backing of my organizations which were unabashedly lesbian/gay/bisexual/trans liberationist from the get-go.

The multi-issue radical politics I support come out of the traditions of Trotskyism. This means that achieving gender and sexuality equality are intrinsically linked to socialism. Trotskyism embraces the idea that because of our long-standing, ongoing struggle against exploitation and for equality, women are central to revolution. Trotsky said, "...In the world labor movement, the woman worker stands closest precisely to...the section of labor which is...the most oppressed...And just because of this, in the years of the colossal revolution this section of the proletariat can and must become the most active, the most revolutionary and the most initiative section of the working class."[3]

Another Trotskyist idea that made sense to me is that the leadership and democratic rights of the most oppressed—including women, people of color and sexual minorities—are key to a revolutionary agenda. Because of our experiences with multiple oppressions, we have the potential to be dynamic leaders.

A third idea that is central to Trotskyism is that socialism cannot be built in one country alone, especially in an underdeveloped country surrounded by the forces of world imperialism. This reality points to the indispensable role of the U.S. revolution. As U.S. revolutionaries, we have particular responsibility to organize for radical change here. This country is the headquarters of world capitalism. If private property were to fall here, it would open the floodgates to freedom for everyone else. Furthermore, the U.S. is the world's most extreme case of race and gender stratification within the working class. If we can overcome these divisions within our working class, that would be a huge step toward building world revolution.

The theory of Permanent Revolution is the cornerstone of Trotskyism. The main idea here is that socialism can only be realized on a global basis and that even after attaining international scope, the revolution must proceed forward on every plane of economic, technological and cultural existence. There are a number of writings on Permanent Revolution from the Freedom Socialist Party and other sources.[4]

Trotskyism also addresses the need for a revolutionary party. This party must be based on democratic centralism: democracy in discussion and decision-making followed by centralism and unity in action. I would be happy to discuss this later in further detail during the discussion.

In a word, other Asian Americans, people of color and I were drawn to the socialist feminist programs of RW and FSP because they linked all our issues together. During the 80s when a whole group of us joined RW and FSP, it wasn't very popular to conjoin feminism and socialism on the Left. In fact, there were times when we were mocked by the macho Left, when we were dismissed as girls and gays. But it is that inextricable link between socialism and feminism that attracted people like me and continues to attract activists today.

RW an FSP have long been a steadfast part of the Asian American movement, from the legal case of Merle Woo to the struggle for multilingual education. Our members have worked in coalitions around Vincent Chin and David Wong. Radical Women has participated in and collaborated with chapters of GABRIELA Network. Weaving culture and politics, RW and FSP was part of the struggle around the Broadway production of "Miss Saigon." I was a spokesperson and journalist on the protest against the film "Year of the Dragon." To me what is notable is not only the particular role that our Asian American members play in the movement but the fact that we do this work with the full support of the organizations; and our non Asian comrades also actively organize for Asian American issues.

I was also drawn to the FSP because of its formulation of Revolutionary Integration (RI)[5], a guiding concept for its work against racism. RI says that racism is a central and permanent feature of U.S. capitalism. It says also that the overriding direction of the Black movement is toward integration but not reformist assimilation into the status quo. RI initially developed in the 1960s as the FSP's position on the Black movement in contrast to the liberal tail-ending of cultural nationalism, which advocates separatism as the alternative to assimilation into the racist capitalist status quo. This only capitulates to forced segregation which has been an essential component of Black oppression and which sparked the struggle for integration and equality.

I think RI is a powerful tool to fight race oppression in the U.S. not only as it relates to African Americans but Asian Americans, Latinos and Chicanos as well. The race liberation struggle is, in essence, anti-capitalist and revolutionary. My mother,

Merle, wrote the following summary statement about RI: "this is what it's going to take: the creation of a multi-racial/ multi-sexuality feminist coalition for radical economic change: revolutionary integration."

Tonight's discussion is very important. these are turbulent times. With the dramatic fall of the Russian economy just this week and the talk of looming recession, we all have the impression that the world is exploding around us—literally. This is a crucial time for the Asian American Left and the Left in general to unite. We need an effective movement to battle all the attacks on immigrants, on bilingual education, affirmative action, labor and welfare benefits. The list is long and growing!

If we don't build a strong Left alternative, the consequences can be severe. We have seen what has happened historically.

Events like tonight's give us an opportunity to explore points of unity and common work. I think it is important for Asian American Leftists to strategize about how we can educate in our communities to expose the bankruptcy of capitalism and provide an alternative to the Democrats. We need to remember the Democrats are just as bad as the Republicans. The Democrats have led us into virtually all of the wars of the 20th century. Just look at the Clinton Administration's threats to bomb Iraq and its politics on Cuba.

I think most of us are here tonight because we believe capitalism isn't working and that we need an alternative. I'm convinced that socialism is the only humane alternative. My three visits to Cuba confirm socialism's possibilities. I don't see Cuba as socialist yet because as I said before, no country can achieve socialism alone. Cuba is not perfect, but it is a model for what can be achieved in a post capitalist society and makes socialism believable.

My last trip to Cuba was to attend the Women's Encuentro in April 1998. There were 3,000 women from 79 countries at this Havana conference. The majority of participants were feminist and anti-capitalist. These women are a strong affirmation of what I have been talking about here tonight: the connection between feminism and socialism. As a member of GABRIELA Network, I also look to it for inspiration as a feminist and anti-imperialist organization.

In conclusion, I want to emphasize how crucial it is for us to organize for revolution here in the U.S., and to remember that world socialism cannot become a reality without us. Building a revolution here is the best demonstration of solidarity with our sisters and brother in Cuba, the Philippines, China and around the world that we could possible make.

Thank you very much.

ENDNOTES

1. Revolution, She Wrote, by Clara Fraser, Red Letter Press

2. An illustrative source on the history of the FSP and RW can be found in the book Socialist Feminism: The First Decade, 1966-76, by Gloria Martin (published by Red Letter Press).

3. The First Five Years of the Communist International, Vol. I, 1921

4. See Permanent Revolution, by Leon Trotsky, Pathfinder Press.

5. See Revolutionary Integration, available from the Freedom Socialist, 5018 Ave. South, Seattle, WA 98118

Eviction Day in Kalama Valley
Photo credit: Marion Kelly
see "Return the Islands Back to the People: A Legacy of
Struggle and Resistance in Ka Pāeʻaina"

NEW DAWN RISING

History and Summation of the Japan Town Collective

Ray Tasaki

I'm a third generation (Sansei) Japanese American. I experienced internment in a concentration camp during World War II at Heart Mountain, Wyoming, when over 120,000 Japanese Americans (two-thirds of whom were American citizens) were interned as "enemy aliens." After the Camps, I lived through the Eisenhower era, a time of sterile dominant white culture, racism and Cold War paranoia. I spent four years in the U.S. Marines, then twelve years on drugs. I was in gangs and spent time in county and state prisons during this time. But in 1969, while I was immersed in the clouds of psychedelic drugs, the winds and words of revolution, of struggle and change, reached me. I listened and got caught up in this movement to change U.S. society. I joined with others to start survival programs: drug rehab, legal aid, prison outreach, youth counseling, programs for the elderly and infirm. Then we tried to form a revolutionary core to lead and direct the struggles going on, but that core never materialized.

During this period, activists from all over the U.S. were traveling and connecting with one another: seeing, learning, making alliances and sharing. In San Francisco I got excited about the struggles led by the Black Panther Party, the Red Guard Party, Los Tres (a Chicano organization) and all the groups that were emerging in the Bay Area. I moved to the Bay Area in 1971 and starting working with people in San Francisco Chinatown, Japantown, in Berkeley and San Jose. It was at this time that I joined the Japan Town Collective. Here is my view of the history of that group and what happened.

During the summer of 1971, as the Red Guard Party in San Francisco was breaking up, some of its members joined with I Wor Kuen. A few of the Japanese American cadre of the Red Guard Party—people like Stan Kadani, Leo, and Neil Gotanda—a legal person who worked in the legal aid program in Chinatown, San Francisco—went to organize in the Japanese community in Japan Town San Francisco (Nihonmachi).

This core of activists started a study group composed of people from campuses and community groups, about a dozen in all. The study group read Mao's writings, such as "On Practice," to discuss what was happening in the world, such as in Vietnam, in Japan and Okinawa, and also the concept of "serve the people."

Some of the core that was to become the Japan Town Collective came from

53

social service agencies, frustrated about the limitations of that kind of work to address the root causes of people's oppression, alienation and internalized racism and psychological self-effacement particular to Japanese Americans from being interned in camps during World War II.

One important agency that many activists worked in was the Japanese Community Youth Council (JCYC). This was a mass organization that organized programs for the youth in the Japan Town community. While some activists were revolutionaries and Marxist-Leninists, most weren't but they did identify with the progressive social change movement. But the more revolutionary-minded activists were searching for a way to connect the struggle to end the oppression of Japanese Americans with the larger question of revolution.

These activists formed a "work-study collective" which developed the name of the Japan Town Collective. The JTC was seen as a preliminary and transitional step to joining a larger revolutionary organization. Some of the first actions by the JTC were participating in anti-War marches, support for struggles in Japan, especially the anti-military base struggle in Okinawa, and working in different coalitions. One of the first organizing and propaganda tools used by the JTC as guerilla theater skits performed in the community to highlight the struggles against those military bases in Okinawa, about how the bases were expanding and how they affected the people living around the bases. One particular struggle was around the Sanrizuka airbase near Tokyo and its expansion, bringing in more war planes, and how this was opposed by revolutionary students and workers in Japan at the time.

Because the JTC initially did not have a base in the community, the focus was placed on having a center, and from there, developing a broad propaganda and outreach about the Vietnam War, the struggles of Third World people. This center was in a building threatened with demolition by redevelopment. It was located next to a community church. The center was in a building that belonged to the church. A couple of people in JTC had ties to the church, so the church let JTC have use of the building.

The center was used as a base to do propaganda and organizing around opposing the U.S. imperialist war in Vietnam, to do film showings, hold forums, and run a revolutionary bookstore. JTC also worked in the Asian Women's Health Team and did high school organizing through the Asian Alliance at Washington High School. Following the example of the Black Panther Party "survival programs," the JTC offered legal services, health care, a prison program, etc. We started a revolutionary newspaper called *New Dawn* which featured articles about Third World liberation struggles and local community issues. All these activities were aimed at promoting revolutionary education and connecting all the struggles internationally with the Japanese American community.

One of the first large forums was about the United Farm Workers struggle against large agribusiness and corporate farming, and the role that Japanese American Nisei farmers played. The Japanese American Nisei farmers were small farmers, but often took the side of agribusiness against the UFW.

They were pretty adamant in their opposition to the UFW because they felt organizing farm workers would hurt them the most since they were small farming businesses. This forum brought out both sides of the struggle and was pretty enlightening to a lot of the people who attended.

We had film showings about the struggle in Japan and in other countries, especially from socialist China. We showed "The Red Detachment of Women."

From these activities, people started to come forward and participate in different activities. One in particular was the anti-War march in downtown San Francisco to protest the renewed bombing in northern Vietnam. This march was a particularly successful organizing event that brought out a lot of "advanced elements" closer to the JTC.

During that time there was an on-going struggle against a lot of buildings threatened with destruction by redevelopment to pave the way to construct buildings for corporations. This anti-redevelopment struggle was the basis for starting a mass organization called CANE (Committee Against Nihonmachi Evictions).

Many of the JTC cadres and "advanced elements" joined with the tenants to fight against the destruction of the Japanese community. As this struggle developed, some of the cadres from the JTC were pulled out of labor organizing to go into the CANE struggle and to give it leadership. At one time, the JTC had close to two dozen cadres involved in CANE.

The labor organizing at that time done by JTC centered in the garment industry. In this area, JTC and IWK were having joint meetings about strategy, direction and the development of a line in terms of organizing the workers, giving direction and focus to the struggle. I wasn't involved in that work and I don't know why it started to unravel. There was no clear sum-up of that particular period, or the errors that developed, but this was one of the points where the JTC shifted its focus to primarily doing its work in the Japanese community. The relationship with IWK began to come apart. At this time, IWK became engrossed in the overall U.S. revolutionary movement and its take on particular struggles in the world, and how IWK's theoretical, organizational and political line clashed with other organizations like the RCP (Revolutionary Communist Party), WVO (Workers Viewpoint Organization) and most of the centrists (a term then-used to characterize groups that tended to be less critical of the then-Soviet Union, and who disagreed with the Peoples' Republic of China's international line—editor).

JTC, for the most part, withdrew from most of these line struggles going on in the rest of the U.S. Marxist-Leninist movement, being waged in various coalitions. The JTC retreated into its mass organizing in Japan Town. By this time, even most of its line on international struggles was rehashed from Pacific News Service, the Guardian newspaper and some of it even from the bourgeois press.

This theoretical weakness and avoidance crippled its ties to many of the "advanced elements." The JTC wasn't able to lead these people in day-to-day mass organizing who were in the study groups that the JTC led. The JTC lost its ability to give overall revolutionary direction, getting bogged down in day-to-day things, in little victories and responding to the concessions given by the redevelopment agency. The redevelopment agency had a lot of room to give concessions. Although at the time, the JTC saw these concessions as little victories, they really turned out to be little sell-outs, token gestures given to the community.

A lot of these results revealed the JTC's theoretical weakness in being able to give overall revolutionary direction to both the struggles internal to the Japanese American community and also to the line struggle around various struggles going on in the rest of the world. Some of these questions centered on China's foreign policy, particularly at that time, around the struggle in Angola. Irwin Silber, a prominent New Left intellectual and writer, and longtime editor of the *Guardian* newspaper, would criticize and eventually condemn China's international line. There was much controversy and debate in the new M-L movement. The JTC had a difficult time being able to study and develop a position on all these debates. Some JTC cadres united with Silber and what I called these "centrist" lines (soft on condemning the Soviet Union as social-imperialist—"socialism in words, imperialism in deeds—and increasingly opposed to China, particularly its international positions).

This weakness came to a head about 1974 when a lot of the "advanced elements" began to work with IWK, which really isolated the JTC. People were leaving the JTC either for other groups, or burned and turned off by the intensity and stridency of the M-L polemics. The JTC had become so isolated that one night, the few remaining people who still comprised the JTC drove up in the middle of the night, took all of their things from the building in which everybody shared offices, and left. From that day on, they weren't a force to reckon with in the Japanese American community. Nobody hardly ever saw them anymore. I believe that the JTC just faded out around late 1974 or sometime in 1975. Through the years, I hear about different people, about what they're doing, their alignment with various other groups like MLOC (Marxist-Leninist Organizing Committee) which joined the Communist Party USA. Those who did this seemed to just disappear from view.

Just before that period of time, I had left the organization in early 1974. I was turned off from the harshness of the internal struggle. People seemed to turn on one another, questioning people's commitment, making heavy demands and having a tone of self-righteousness and self-importance. It is my opinion that since the JTC leadership and group as a whole was unable and/or unwilling to deal with its lack of political and theoretical development that it turned inward and internal struggle became very dysfunctional. People started accusing one another of not being committed or sacrificing enough. Things got crazy and harsh. However, the JTC did leave a bold legacy in the San Francisco Japanese American community, from its opposition to the U.S.-Japan Treaty that allowed American military bases in Okinawa, to fighting redevelopment of the historic Nihonmachi community, to staging guerilla theater in the J-Town mall to educate the masses in the community. Despite its problems and implosion, in its short-lived history, it represented a revolutionary, organized expression among young Japanese American radicals to fight for the community as part of identifying with a larger, global anti-imperialist and revolutionary movement.

After two years in the Japan Town Collective, I left to join I Wor Kuen, which became the League of Revolutionary Struggle. In 1986 I eventually left the LRS due to a combination of reasons. My commitment was fading. I was dealing with the difficulties of raising kids, and I couldn't keep up with the demands of being in a cadre organization. I also no longer believed that a communist organization in the U.S. at that time was viable, but I think I mostly suffered from a loss of my idealism. Today, I still believe in many of the principles from that time, the need for a revolutionary core to give guidance and leadership to the mass organizations and struggles even though I personally may not be in a position or capable of participating. But I believe its important to uphold the legacy of this period and to understand the lessons, the difficulties and problems.

Waiāhole-Waikāne protest at Developer's Office
Photo credit: Marion Kelly
see "Return the Islands Back to the People: A Legacy of Struggle and Resistance
in Ka Pāeʻaina"

LOSING ITS SOUL?

Reflections on Gay and Asian Activism

Daniel C. Tsang

In 1975, my essay on "Gay Awareness" won the distinction of being the first coming out essay to be published in an Asian American publication. It appeared in the February 1975 issue of *Bridge: Asian American Perspective*.[1] I don't know if the editors had qualms about publishing it or not, but my essay was clearly identified in large type (larger than the title) as "Reader's Turn." I guess no one wanted to take the responsibility for publishing it as a regular feature.

Looking back on it, I can see my words reflecting the anger, yet idealism of the period. I had started the essay with an extended extract from a reader's letter that had appeared a couple of years or so earlier in the same magazine:

"I am Asian, a male and gay. For the past year since I've gotten involved with the Asian Movement, or at least tried, I've been scorned, ridiculed, and rejected by many so-called sincere Asian Movement people, especially the males... the males somehow feel that I'm undermining their male egos. I strongly believe in honesty. I won't pretend that I'm not gay. I'm proud to be Asian. And the two are not mutually exclusive."

The letter was from a brave man, Hung Nung. As I wrote in that 1975 essay, his plea was still being ignored, several years after he penned that letter. And today's more diverse Asian American communities are arguably more tolerant and perhaps understanding of gay people, yet many of our sisters and brothers still agonize over whether or not to come out to family or to members of the community.

In 1975, I spelled America with several k's in the word. I was an angry activist, out to liberate the world. I was then in my 20s, full of youthful confidence and exuberance. I argued in the essay that "oppressors are usually, if not always, quite ignorant that they are oppressing someone." While there is a hierarchy of oppression, I wrote, "the oppressed can in turn become the oppressor." I also suggested that for too long, "gays have refused, or strategically delayed, confronting Asian American straights about their homophobia." I called this a "conspiracy of silence" and an "acquiescence in our own oppression." I attributed this to the "mistaken notion that by not rocking the boat we would gain the respect of the dominant culture."

I also noted that "true liberation from oppression will only come from a radical and revolutionary restructuring of the means of exchange in society, and made a valiant call for my comrades to come out:

> *"In opting for gay liberation, we strike a blow for gay liberation, we strike a blow against sexism, machismo, and political repression. Coming out both as Asian and as gay enables us to relate better and more honestly with our yellow brothers and sisters. It liberates us from one of the major obstacles in the Asian American struggle: the alienation of Asians from other Asians. No longer will Asians who meet on the street avert their eyes; we shall embrace each other with joy. Let us get rid of pretense, and live honestly. Gay sisters and brothers, unite in the struggle!"*

Extracting and re-reading those words here almost 25 years later, I see the idealism and hope that filled my young head. But if those dreams are today unrealized, whose fault is it? Should we blame society, "progress," "technology" or ourselves?

A comparison of the first March on Washington for gay liberation, with more recent developments shows how far we have come, and how far we have yet to go.

I met other gay Asian American activists (e.g., Don Kao, then a University of Wisconsin, Madison, student, who came out there) at a Midwest Asian American Student Conference in Madison soon after my essay was published. By 1979, a growing Asian gay network had developed, and about a dozen of us ended up marching in the October, 1979 March on Washington. That event took place a day after the National Third World Lesbian and Gay Conference at Howard University had ended.

The conference and the subsequent march were highlights for all who attended. Poet Audre Lorde, decked in colorful African garb, addressed the gathering at the conference, asking in her inspirational talk on the conference theme, "When Will the Ignorance End?" This conference, she declared, was an "affirmation of the power of vision."[2] At the conference, we also formed a "Lesbian and Gay Asian Collective," to network among ourselves.[3] And one of us, Tana Loy, a Chinese American lesbian, gave a stirring address, "Who's the Barbarian?" She declared to a round of applause, "You know, we're not that quiet and reserved Asian," but conceded that we have been silenced from each other by racism, sexism, and fear of leaving the closet. Many Asians could not come out at the time because of fear of deportation, she noted.[4] Before the big march, we jointly created a banner and took turns painting the words, in big type, "We're Asians, Gay & Proud." And we decided to march as a group through the Black and Chinese neighborhoods of Washington, D.C., in the first-ever march through those communities by open gays and lesbians. We did that on our way to the Washington Monument, without any hassles. I think the shoppers and dim sum lunch-goers were more surprised than anything else. They just looked at us, speechless. And we kept chanting, "We're Asians, Gay and Proud!"

At the monument, a Vermont poet, Margaret Noshiko Cornell, representing our new "collective," addressed the crowd of thousands at the Washington Monument. Her incredible talk was called, "Living in Asian America," where she challenged the crowd to give up their "white-skin" privilege and "actively support" Asian American lesbians and gay males. "We have a right to our sexuality, to our love and to our racial identities," she declared. And she called for solidarity with our "Third World sisters and brothers, gay and straight," saying we share a common oppression.[5]

As Richard Fung would later describe the events in the Toronto gay liberation magazine, *The Body Politic*, "The homophobia of our 'ethnic' communities and the subtle racism of the gay community combine to isolate us and produce a kind of cultural schizophrenia. But in Washington for the first time I was both gay and non-white and in the majority. The experience was energizing." Richard also wrote:

> *"An Asian caucus was formed by lesbians and gay men with Japanese, Indonesian, Indian, Chinese, Malaysian, and Philippino backgrounds from North America, Asia and the Caribbean. Although our different routes had led us to different experiences in North American gay social life, we were able to find a common bond in the context of the Third World Movement and solidarity with our Black, Latino and Native brothers and sisters. And if for many of us, it was the first time we had spoken with other Asian gays, we immediately recognized each other's stories."* And he asked, *"When will the ignorance end? When there are so many Latin, Native, Asian and Black gay men and lesbians organized and out, that no amount of whitewashing or straightlacing can keep us hidden. Washington was just the beginning."*[6]

Indeed it was, and in the next decade, many of us continued to meet at Don Kao's "farm" in the Catskills in upstate New York, where the people of color lesbian and gay activists from the Lavender Left convened, for comradeship as well as seemingly endless political discussions.

Yet looking back, I sense a totally different movement, either gay or Asian. The goal seems now to be getting a piece of the national pie, not challenging the body politic or restructuring it. Much of the solidarity we felt then can still be found around people of color organizing around AIDS and other community issues, but I sense that the Reagan years (and thereafter), the end of the Cold War, and the advent of the Internet have totally changed much of Asian America so that being an active participant in this transnational capital-based world economy has co-opted many of us. Our institutions of higher education, more often than not, churn out not critical thinkers or community activists but cogs in the machinery of global capitalism. Our hard-fought Asian American and ethnic studies programs have, by and large, severed their community ties to serve academic survival interests. And within the gay movement, the goal is no longer overthrowing a heterosexist state but joining it, seeking approval from the powers that be for gay marriages, for example, or the ability to enter the institutions of repression locally and abroad (the police and military forces). Gay marches on Washington have become predictable and uninspiring, serving mainstream political agendas.

One illustration may suffice. At the North American Asian Pacific Islander Gay Conference in August 1993, sponsored by the Gay Asian/Pacific Support Network (GAPSN) and held at the Lesbian and Gay Community Services Center in Los

Angeles, I was unceremoniously kicked off a panel on hate crimes (to talk about the vicious beating of Vietnamese immigrant Loc Minh Truong in Laguna Beach by gay-bashing kids) because another Asian panelist, Martin Hiraga, then the director of the Anti-Violence Project at the National Gay and Lesbian Task Force, and, ironically, also the head of its Privacy Project, thought it would be bad for his work with the FBI to be seen on the same panel as I was.[7] It turns out, as NGLTF liaison on hate crimes with the FBI (he was co-chair of an ad hoc committee on the issue; the other co-chair was from the Anti-Defamation League, a group then widely accused of conducting surveillance on activist groups), Hiraga routinely met with the FBI, and as he told me after the truncated session, gave them information on what was going on in the community. He had asked for my removal from the panel as a matter of "national security," he proffered, rather grandiosely. This self-admitted FBI informant thought he had to be careful with whom he associated with, since he seemed confident the FBI had me under investigation. As Kathryn Imahara, a staff attorney with the Asian Pacific American Legal Center in Los Angeles, who had replaced me on the panel, later recounted to a gay paper, Hiraga told her that "because of his involvement with the government, and Dan's investigation, that Martin couldn't put his own ability to work with the FBI in jeopardy." When I contacted onetime NGLTF executive director Urvashi Vaid about this, she told me that the task force worked with the FBI to fight hate crimes, not to smear or report on gay activists. Chip Berlet, who monitors Rightwing groups for Political Research Associates in Cambridge, Mass., noted that while it may be appropriate for an NGLTF staffer to work with the FBI on hate crimes, "for the same person to wear the hat of the Privacy Project is a built-in conflict of interest." Berlet added, "It's hopelessly inappropriate for anyone to be spreading these rumors to ingratiate themselves with the cop community at the expense of political activists... It's inappropriate for a major figure in a national organization to be going around slandering people." When Hiraga was interviewed by the gay paper, he only had kind words about me: "Daniel has been an invaluable worker in the movement for ages, since before I even knew there was a lesbian and gay movement he was working in it," he said, but declined comment on the informant charge. The informant later left his job at the NGLTF. GAPSN organizers later apologized to me. And from Privacy Act releases per my request, I found I was not the subject of any formal FBI investigation.[8]

This issue of how to deal with hate is one that is symptomatic of the lack of critical thinking among today's activists. In the quest to punish the perpetrators of hate, I'm afraid our leaders have been too ready to give increasingly more repressive powers to the state to counter "hate crimes." As a community activist (see my other essay in this volume), I get invited to local meetings of a "hate crime" network—composed of people from a whole range of community groups working to fight these horrendous crimes. At one such meeting, at the Orange County, Calif., Human Relations Commission offices in Santa Ana, Calif., I was shocked to see introduced, a half dozen or so FBI agents, all dressed casually (no longer the Brooks Brothers suits of the J. Edgar Hoover era). Turns out, the FBI office in Santa Ana had recently gotten specific approval to treat hate crimes as acts of domestic terrorism. Hence the large turnout of G-men at the meeting.

The recurring image from the past I will always treasure was our identification with other people of color in North America. Yet that sense of solidarity and coalition building across races is largely absent from gay Asian America, except in people of color AIDS work perhaps.   Further, instead of critiquing and challenging the state, our "leaders" have become accommodationists with the establishment. While gay and lesbian Asian groups have proliferated in the U.S., each year holding larger and larger "installation ceremonies," it is politicians and celebrities who are courted and feted at these events. Are we satisfied celebrating now that we seem to have a place at the table, an entree into the halls of power? It is not just in electoral politics that gay street activism has been siderailed.   A long-time GAPSN leader has even criticized West Hollywood's sometimes bacchanal gay pride march (an Asian brother had apparently behaved "obscenely") as too embarrassing for the Asian community. Flaunting our sexuality must be stopped in the future, or we would lose the respect of (straight) society, he argued. This quest for respectability was something, of course, I had criticized back in 1975 as a "mistaken notion" (see above). The joy and fun of a liberating era has been snuffed out by straight-acting, conformist gay Asian activists, who apparently would do anything to be "respectable." Urvashi Vaid subtitled Virtual Equality, her 1995 book, "The Mainstreaming of Gay and Lesbian Liberation." Have we been mainstreamed out of existence? In trying to remake Asian America at the beginning of another millennium, have we lost our soul? What happened? Is being left and gay and Asian passe now? I long for a resurgence.

ENDNOTES

1. Daniel Tsang Chun-tuen, "Gay Awareness," *Bridge,* 3/4 (February, 1975), pp. 44-45. *Bridge* was published bimonthly by Basement Workshop, an important nonprofit cultural group in New York City's Chinatown. It was the first Asian American magazine to circulate nationally. Proud of my background, I had spelled my full name, with my Chinese name in the correct order.

2. Audre Lorde, "When Will the Ignorance End?", *Gay Insurgent* #6 (Summer, 1980), pp. 12-14. *Gay Insurgent: A Gay Left Journal*, a publication I edited, featured a photograph of the march on its cover.

3. "Lesbian and Gay Asian Collective Formed," *Gay Insurgent* #6 (Summer, 1980), p. 14.

4. Tana Loy, "Who's the Barbarian?," *Gay Insurgent* #6 (Summer, 1980), p. 15.

5. Margaret Noshiko Cornell, "Living in Asian America," *Gay Insurgent* #6 (Summer, 1980), p. 16.

6. Richard Fung, "We're Asian, Gay & Proud!", *The Body Politic* #58 (November, 1979), p. 17. Reprinted in *Gay Insurgent* #6 (Summer, 1980), p. 21.

7. This paragraph is based on my own recollections and on reporting by Bill Andriette, "Blacklist Redux: Is the NGLTF Doing the FBI's Dirty Work?", *The Guide* (Boston), December, 1993, pp. 9-10. Hiraga somehow believed that the FBI would be interested in me because of an anthology I edited on the gay age of consent, *The Age Taboo: Gay Male Sexuality, Power and Consent* (Boston: Alyson Publications; London: Gay Men's Press, 1981). Contributors included Kate Millett, Sylvere Lotringer, Gayle Rubin and Pat Califia.

8. The CIA did spy on me, as I discovered in my ACLU lawsuit, *Tsang* v. *CIA*. CIA stations around the world were asked to dig up information on me and on *Gay Insurgent*. We settled out of court for some $46,000 after the CIA promised never to spy on me again, although it would not make the same promise not to spy on other Americans. Spying on the 1st-Amendment-protected activities of American citizens and per-

manent residents was thought to have been barred by a provision of the Privacy Act, passed after the exposes of domestic spying in the 60's. But my case revealed that the CIA, arrogantly, did not believe it was bound by that legal provision, because it was permitted by the National Security Act to conduct counterintelligence activities. After my legal team complained, the CIA also had to remove from its Web-site a statement that it did not spy on Americans. See (my lawyer) Kate Martin, "Domestic CIA Snooping," *Washington Post*, February 20, 1997, p. A22; original letter posted at: http://sun3.lib.uci.edu/~dtsang/cnss.pdf; my op ed piece, "A CIA Target at Home in America," *Los Angeles Times*, January 18, 1998, p.M1-2, posted at: http://sun3.lib.uci.edu/~dtsang/ciatarget.htm; Kimberly Kindy, "Prying Eyes were Watching UCI's Library Activist," *Orange County Register*, January 25, 1998, pp. 1, posted at: http://www.geocities.com/WestHolly-wood/1443/cia_gayspying.html; and Daniel C. Tsang, "Eyes Only: The Central Intelligence Agency versus Daniel C. Tsang," *CovertAction Quarterly*, No. 65 (Fall 1998), pp. 60-63.

YELLOW PERIL TO YELLOW POWER

Asian Activism in the Rocky Mountain Region

Marge Taniwaki

From the mid-1800s, the few Asians living in the Rocky Mountain region engaged mostly in farming and other labor intensive work, but all was not peaceful. In 1880, the Chinese neighborhood in Denver, the capital of Colorado, was razed. Small businesses were burned to the ground, its inhabitants beaten and forced out by racists. One Chinese man was lynched from a lamp post. Five years later, 28 Chinese were massacred in Rock Springs, Wyoming where Chinese workers had been imported for coal mining. We will never know how many others lost their possessions, their jobs, their homes, their lives in other unreported incidents.

Colorado was far enough inland for its Japanese-descended residents to escape imprisonment in the World War II US concentration camps, though one such camp was built in the extreme southeastern corner of the state. The "Granada Relocation Center", as it is known in history books, held more than 8,000 captives who had been shipped primarily from northern California. The inmates of the camp had their own name for it: "Amache", the name of a Cheyenne woman who was the wife of a local cattle baron, John Prowers.

The camp was located in Prowers County near the small, quiet town of Granada, not far from the killing grounds of the Sand Creek Massacre. The local Postmaster needed a postal distinction to differentiate between the town and the prison camp and it was he who chose the name of Amache. It is not known if the Postmaster appreciated the irony of naming a concentration camp after a woman whose people had been forcibly removed from their homes less then a century earlier.

Bordering Colorado on the north, Wyoming also had a concentration camp, Heart Mountain, situated in the northwest corner of the state near the town of Powell. Because of the heroic efforts of Heart Mountain's Fair Play Committee, this camp was the site of the most organized resistance to the U.S. military draft, although there were dissenters in all ten of the major camps.

The only journalist to publish press releases and other documents sent out by Heart Mountain's Fair Play Committee, James Omura was the wartime English editor at the Denver Japanese community newspaper, *The Rocky Shimpo*. Because he editorially supported the Fair Play Committee's demand for full restoration of their Constitutional rights, Jimmie was charged with conspiracy to aid and abet violation of the Selective Services law. Although acquitted, Omura was ostracized by Japanese

American *quislings* and those whom they could influence within and without the community. He was forced out of journalism and had to rely on landscaping, thus becoming one more post-World War II Japanese gardener.

This and other APA stereotypes were challenged a generation later as Asians and Pacific Islanders organized locally and nationally, inspired by the American Indian and Black Power Movements of the 1960s. While still sparsely populated by APA's, the Rocky Mountain region possessed a few areas with communities large enough to support fledgling activist work. Denver had been the natural destination for Japanese released from Amache concentration camp in late 1945. Though many had aspirations to move back to the west coast after accumulating a stake, like sojourners before them, they found it difficult to accomplish.

The Asian American Educational Opportunities Program located at the University of Colorado at Boulder was the developmental cocoon for a number of activists including those who made up the core of the Asian American Community Action Research Program (AA CARP), the first progressive Asian group to emerge in the Denver area in the late 60s. AA CARP was comprised mainly of students, but also included adult and elderly community members. The group included Chinese, Japanese, Korean, Biracial, and Asians raised in Chicano and African American working class neighborhoods. CARP was a haven, a place to test political theories, study Marxist-Leninist ideology, and a support network for a widely diverse community who sought to make social change and contribute to the Asian community. There were other, more conservative Asian vehicles through which one could participate, but none that appealed to the members of CARP.

CARP studied revolutionary history and attempted Maoist-style criticism/self-criticism. Each member would read aloud a section of the subject matter, define phrases, and ask questions. The word "bourgeoisie" was particularly difficult for immigrants to pronounce, but everyone understood the concept. The study sessions were conducted with the guidance of Asian as well as Chicano activists who participated with the Crusade for Justice, the Denver-based nationalist organization founded by Rudolfo "Corky" Gonzales.

One of the problems which emerged in the study group was its collective inability to provide the kind of nurturing support which is necessary to provide closure of a criticism session. Unfortunately, the criticism/self-criticism process often traumatized the recipient without providing a mechanism for rebuilding and reintegration into the group. Though certainly not unique to Denver, CARP was lacking in the personal and organizational resources to overcome this problem and study group participation declined.

Although CARP knew of I Wor Kuen, The League of Revolutionary Struggle, and other worker-based groups, it remained independent and concentrated on local issues and solutions. Members of the cadre went out into the community to assess needs and then structured programs that would be of service and address those concerns.

One of CARP's activities was a Hot Lunch Program for the elderly, mostly Issei, first generation Japanese in the United States. Many of the Issei lived in Tamai Towers, a rent-subsidized high-rise situated at Sakura Square in the last remaining block of *J-Town* in Denver. Other Asian elderly lived in small apartments, often subsisting on canned food heated over hot plates. It was mainly these individuals CARP targeted in order to break their isolation and to provide them with a nourishing meal. CARP planned menus, shopped for large amounts of groceries, arranged publicity, set up home deliveries, and tended to the many other details of feeding over one hundred people in the Buddhist Temple at 20th and Lawrence Street, close to the largest Black and Chicano/Mexicano neighborhood in Denver. Food preparation began the night before in the temple's kitchen. The work resumed early in the morning each day lunch would be served. The cooking of *gohan, misoshiru, sunomono,* and *okazu* was overseen by a *Kibei* who also helped with communication and translation. Because the elderly would never accept charity, a nominal fee of fifty cents per meal was charged while other visitors paid $2.00. Meal tickets were made from colored construction paper and collected at the door. *Sansei* escorted guests to their seats and served tea throughout the meal while inquiring about health and other issues of concern to the Issei.

One of the elderly who came to eat regularly said she always looked forward to the meal because the rice tasted so good, much better than when she cooked for herself. When rice is prepared in large quantities, she explained, it affected the texture and taste enough to be very noticeable to someone who valued the difference.

CARP also ran a Food Distribution Program out of the Nihonjin-kai, the Japanese Association Hall. For a dollar per summer, each person would receive a grocery bag full of fresh vegetables once a week. After making arrangements, members of CARP would go into the fields of Japanese farmers and glean vegetables which were perfectly edible but too large or small for sale to grocery stores. Avoiding the farmer's dog added excitement to the process! Vegetables were delivered to those unable to make their way to the distribution site, thus providing them with at least a brief visit. For those elders who did come, there was time to talk which helped break the isolation which many in the community continued to suffer.

The Children's Cultural Workshop run by CARP provided summer classes for youth from kindergarten through sixth grade. Among the activities were field trips to workplaces which produced traditional Japanese food such as *tofu* and bean sprouts. The children learned from what part of Japan their ancestors came. Another favorite class activity was simply talking about their names, how people made fun of them, and ways in which to handle the teasing.

One of CARP's members taught a class in silk screening. An amusing misunderstanding with CARP's benefactors arose because of the large amount of water used in the silk-screening process. The water bill at the Japanese Association hall increased so much that the Nihonjin-kai representative asked if CARP members were bathing there!

A newspaper published by CARP carried articles on local activities as well as national issues. It provided publicity for the groups programs while helping to hone writing skills.

CARP's attention to intergenerational socialization was a marked contrast to the "generation gap" which existed in Euro-American society at the time. This was amply pointed out at a Halloween party when an elderly Kibei costumed herself as a "Sansei", wearing a colorful poncho, blue jeans, sandals and carrying her daughter's guitar with her long gray hair combed straight down from its traditional bun.

In the early 1970s, Federal funds for organizing became available and caused a split among CARP's members. The National Institute of Mental Health (operated by the then-Department of Health, Education and Welfare) provided the means for Asian and Pacific Islanders to organize and maintain relationships across the mainland United States and Hawai'i. Some members of CARP felt that receipt of Federal dollars would mean strict adherence to guidelines by which the government could manipulate the community. Others in the group looked upon Federal funding as an opportunity to connect with activists across the country and to begin building the structural framework around which social change in society might occur.

Those activists who saw some benefit in utilizing Federal funds went on to participate in groups such as the Pacific/Asian Coalition, a grassroots organization made up of regional representatives from across the country. Another group was the Asian American Mental Health Research Center where Asians conducted research on Asians as opposed to the previous models in which research was done almost solely by members of the dominant society. These networks were the basis for much of the community activism of the time and continue to exist informally today.

Those members of CARP who chose not to participate in federally funded programs undertook other courses of action including the establishment of Denver Taiko, a traditional Japanese drumming group. Denver *Taiko* began with homemade drums rescued from a junk dealer by one of CARP's members after the drum maker, the caretaker of the Nihonjin Kai, had all of his possessions hauled away in preparation for a move to California. Over the years, Denver Taiko has added *shakuhachi, koto, shamisen* and traditional dance. A youth group of drummers is now the training ground for future members.

Though today's atmosphere of cloying interest in so-called "ethnic", that is, non-European cultural activities has made drum groups, dance troupes, and storytellers seem almost commonplace, a generation ago any expression of cultural pride by non-whites was a profoundly radical statement.

In the early 1970s, Denver was divided into quadrants, each served by a community mental health center. The northeastern ghetto center was named for Malcolm X. When finances became a problem because of funders' negative perception of the name, the board reluctantly changed it to Park East Community Mental Health Center. Several of the staff were Asians who dealt with client mental health issues with an overlay of cultural and language differences. A move was made by these Asian staffers to establish an agency which could deal with the growing problems of mostly Southeast Asians who were settling throughout the metropolitan area and were too scattered to receive adequate services under the quadrant system. From early tentative steps, that effort developed into the Asian Pacific Development Center (APDC) which serves not only Colorado, but other western states. While APDC has been severely criticized for receiving funding from right-wing organizations, it provides mental health services which would otherwise be much more difficult to obtain or altogether unavailable.

In 1976, AA CARP "alumni" organized the first Pilgrimage to the Granada Relocation Center located near Lamer in southeastern Colorado. Two busloads of Issei, *Nisei* and *Sansei* traveled in time and distance to remember a part of their history molded by World War II and US injustices. Almost every year since, members of the community have conducted pilgrimages to Amache, modeled on those organized by Sue Kunitomi Embry and the Manzanar Committee of Los Angeles. The pilgrimages include tending the cemetery grounds and conducting a memorial ceremony for those who died in the war and from the harsh conditions which existed in camp. A guided walk through Amache over the hot sand, past the foundations of barracks and guard towers and a shared meal end the day. Fifty years after the last inmates left Amache, the Denver Central Optimists Club secured state historical status for the concentration camp. The Optimists' mostly Nisei members continue to honor their pledge to care for the cemetery and camp site as long as they are physically able.

Throughout the Rocky Mountain region, Asian women have long been a strength in their communities. Some began to hold leadership positions in long established service and social organizations in the 1970s, offices previously always occupied by men. This brought Asian women out from the realm of coffee-serving auxiliaries and into the decision-making process, although real change remains torturously slow. Consciousness raising and support groups formed. Some still meet today, although the emphasis now includes dealing with community issues and information-sharing. The grassroots-directed Colorado Network of Asian/Pacific Women was formed in the early 1980s by some of those same women and was a chapter of a larger national attempt to organize Asian/Pacific women. Unfortunately, it has now evolved into a mainstream group of professional women whose conferences include fashion shows and workshops on how to minimize one's foreign accent. A dangerous outgrowth of this trend is the formation of so-called "Women's Leadership Initiatives" funded by corporate and right-wing entities such as Philip Morris and Coors. Ostensibly formed to train women of color for leadership roles, the agenda is one that rewards abject assimilation into the dominant society and the abandonment of one's ethnic culture.

Since the 1970s, there have been several attempts to form a coalition of the many and disparate Asian and Pacific Islander groups in Colorado. The Colorado Asian Pacific Association was a short-lived umbrella group which attempted to address issues relevant to its burgeoning communities. Unfortunately, the coalition dissolved after struggling with organizational issues and unfamiliarity with each others' concerns. A similar effort called the Asian Roundtable formed in the mid-nineties with a broader base, a stronger support system, and more impetus than earlier attempts. This may be the result of fresh input, new energy, and greater needs brought to the area by the recent influx of new immigrants, especially Southeast Asians and Pacific Islanders. The Asian Roundtable's aim is to address concerns of the more than three hundred Asian groups it has identified within Colorado.

Coalition work with other People of Color has been slow to build with relatively little participation by Asians in Colorado except for a few student organizations and a small network of community activists called Making Waves: Asians In Action. Most Asians still feel that reaching out between Chinese, Japanese, Koreans, Pilipinos and Vietnamese is a major step and few attempts have been made to coalesce with African Americans or Indigenous Peoples, including both tribal members and Chicanos.

An early example of mutual cooperation across ethnic lines was the effort to head off violence between Chicanos and Vietnamese living in the Lincoln Park Housing Project on the west side of Denver. With the liberation of Saigon in April of 1975, large numbers of Southeast Asian refugees settled in various parts of the United States. Many of those who resettled in Denver were placed in an enclave of the recently remodeled Lincoln Park Housing Project whose former tenants, primarily Chicanos, were moved out in order to facilitate repairs. Rumors abounded. There were claims that squirrels were being shot in parks and that pet dogs were disappearing from the Projects and becoming food for the newcomers. There was also great resentment on the part of Chicanos regarding subsidies provided to Southeast Asians for resettlement and education purposes.

Three undergraduate students at the University of Colorado at Denver worked together to contact community members, city officials and law enforcement authorities in an attempt to keep tensions from escalating to the point of physical violence. One of the students was Asian and the other two were Chicanas. Unfortunately, no one listened to the trio and the predicted violence occurred. Homes were robbed, shots were fired into apartments, and cars were vandalized. Inflammatory news coverage only exacerbated the issues. Most of the Southeast Asians moved out of the projects as soon as it was economically possible without actually resolving any of the underlying tensions and concerns with their Chicano neighbors.

In 1988, Denver and Boulder-based Asians created Making Waves: Asians In Action, an overtly political network of activists whose purpose is to bring a more radical point of view to the public. Over the years, participants have included those of Korean, Chinese, Cambodian, Japanese, Malaysian[,] and Biracial ethnicity. Cooperative and coalitional work with other activists of color has included major organizing efforts opposing the celebration of Columbus Day in 1992. Making Waves participated in successfully stopping Denver's previously annual Columbus day parade. Members helped assemble exhibits; served with grassroots medical teams volunteered to cover the parade; were legal observers; and spoke at rallies. Ongoing activities of Making Waves include political theater performances; speaking engagements; sharing of resources and skills with other activists; radio production and commentary; and sponsoring political presentations.

One of the first political presentations sponsored by Making Waves was a community forum featuring James Omura, who was so maligned for his wartime stand on constitutional rights that he withdrew from the Japanese scene until brought to national attention by the Chinese American playwright, Frank Chin. Members of Making Waves maintained a close relationship with Jimmie, attempting to help him with the writing of his memoirs which could bring to light direct collaboration with the United States government by those very people who were his detractors, primarily the Japanese American Citizens League. Jimmie died on June 20, 1994 with his work still in progress.

It is of interest that many influential, official, and governmental agencies and their supporters seemed to be centralized in the Rocky Mountain region, including the Japanese Language School which was headquartered in Boulder. Many of those schooled there went on to join the Military Intelligence Service whose members interrogated captured Japanese soldiers. Continued manipulation of APA's regionally and nationally seems clear, up to and including the myth surrounding Colorado's wartime governor, Ralph Carr, who is touted as a great civil libertarian who invited the Japanese to come to the state.

A careful reading of his radio speech broadcast in March, 1942, shows him calling us "undesirables". A further examination of Carr's personal correspondence on file at the Colorado State Historical society reveal his feelings when he writes to a colleague on the west coast that California should not have to bear the entire brunt of the war and that Colorado will do its part for the war effort by accepting Japanese to come to this state if need be. This is hardly the invitation widely attributed to him. Recent research turned up an uncataloged 1942 article from the *Rocky Mountain News* which quotes Carr as asking for the federal government to intercede and take care of the problem created by Japanese coming to Colorado during *"free evacuation"*, causing his constituents concern over potential competition for jobs.

Governor Carr's supposed willingness to accept persons of Japanese descent into Colorado takes on a less benevolent meaning when one considers the post-war forces that shaped Denver's JA community. There were generally two contrasting elements: those previously interned Kibei considered a loyalty risk for their Japanese education as well as others perceived as security threats and those polar opposites who were among the strongest supporters of compliance with relocation and the fiercest critics of camp resistors who opposed the military draft on constitutional grounds. An almost classic example of US supported strong-man rule occurred here domestically with the elevation of one individual to the status of community spokesman. It is a tactic carried out repeatedly by the United States in other countries, imbuing one person with dictatorial power to keep the populace in line using the ruse of a "democratic" election. Here, anyone who diverged from the loyal American line was and continues to be subject to condemnation in the greater APA community

At least four generations of Japanese in Amerika struggle with the real and savage effects of the internment. The sham reparations which came with the passage of the Civil Rights Act of 1988 was created to buy off an entire community with an apology and the inferred pledge that it was an aberration and could never happen again. But it is happening, right now, and those in power have not even bothered to change the rhetoric. They use the same euphemism of relocation as they remove the Dineh, traditional Navajo, from their sacred lands in northern Arizona so that Peabody Coal Company can strip-mine with impunity, carrying out the coal in huge slurry pipelines which deplete the water table and cause natural springs to go dry. Some of those traditional Navajo men worked as prison guards at Leupp, Arizona, site of one of the citizen isolation camps created to jail "dissident Japanese" during World War II. A number of Japanese American redress and reparations activists have established ties to the Dineh relocation resisters in an ongoing regional process of community activism and advocacy.

In 1997, a Sansei born in the concentration camp at Poston, Arizona, committed suicide after killing several people in a local shopping mall parking lot. Other than spending his formative years in prison, he conducted his life as any dutiful Asian son would have, earning a degree in higher education and serving his country in Vietnam. When he returned from that tour of duty, he cut off all contact with his family and, for years, his relatives were unaware of his location. He used his "reparations" money to buy land near his birthplace where he lived reclusively with only his dog for companionship. Though we will never know precisely what drew him back to his birthplace and drove him to kill before taking his own life, the time he spent in camp was the earliest and most enduring experience of his formative years. Despite the pervasive self-deception of assimilation in to US society, Japanese Americans undoubtedly still suffer tremendous psychological trauma from being imprisoned for no other reason than their ethnicity.

We now know of the tactics used by Euro-America to destroy the Black Panther Party, the American Indian Movement, and other similar struggles. Now the dominant society is using Asians as a managerial buffer between their elite and other People of Color. We have been cast into the role of the New Overseers because we are perceived as easily manipulated and satisfy all of the affirmative action guidelines, just as the Japanese American Citizens League (JACL) was cast into the role of managers of our own peoples repression. If we allow this manipulation and positioning of ourselves to benefit the dominant society, they win again.

Entering into this time of supposedly politically correct multiculturalism, APA's are challenged to more intensely explore and develop a new and deeper understanding and appreciation of ethnicity, culture, and nationalism. This becomes particularly important so that we can engage with other communities, especially communities of Color, on equal footing. Otherwise we may well be relegated to merely providing a predictable annual festival of diversion for the Eurocentric empire which continues to exploit, repress, divide, and dominate all of us. How ironic if the small advances we made in the last generation of struggle against the whitebread monster result in us simply providing costumes and a soundtrack as picturesque entertainment while we are divided and conquered.

72

GLOSSARY

APA: Asian Pacific American

free evacuation: the brief time when JA's could move inland and not be imprisoned

gohan: cooked rice

J-Town: Japanese Town

Kibei: born in US of Japanese descent, raised in Japan

koto: harp-like musical instrument

misoshiru: staple fermented soybean-based soup

Nisei: second generation Japanese born in US

okazu: stew

quislings: collaborators, from Norwegian politician and Nazi collaborator Vidkun Quisling

Sansei: third generation Japanese born in US

shakuhachi: bamboo flute

shamisen: banjo-like musical instrument

sunomono: seasoned vegetables

taiko: drum

tofu: bean curd

Wayne Lum and Yuri Kochiyama in front of the Asians for Jericho banner
Jericho 98 March and Rally in Washington, D.C, 1998
Photo credit: unknown

SUPPORTING U.S. POLITICAL PRISONERS
Incarceration Under U.S. Capitalism

Wayne Lum

People who come out of prison can build up the country
Misfortune is a test of people's fidelity.
Those who protest at injustice are people of true merit.
When the prison doors are opened, the real dragon will fly out.

Ho Chi Minh

As we begin the new millennium, some of the ongoing struggles confronting us in the Asian American community such as racism, affirmative action, multicultural curriculum, immigrant rights, and sweatshop exploitation remain as principal issues. The abusive climate of Right-wing domination resulting in the escalation of police brutalities added another dimension to the Asian American activist agenda. This, along with the mercurial rise of the prison industrial complex completes the vicious order of social control and political repression under U.S. capitalism.

Like anywhere else in the world, political repression produces political prisoners. The U.S. is no exception despite its consistent hypocritical denial of their existence.

U.S. political prisoners are those activists who were imprisoned because of their political activities and/or affiliations. In 1990, many imprisoned activists in the U.S. were identified as political prisoners by an international tribunal held at Hunter College, NYC, after an extensive investigation into each of their backgrounds. There is also a distinct group of political prisoners who consider themselves to be Prisoners Of War (POWs). These individuals, according to their convictions, are in a state of war as members of oppressed nations. Thusly, they refuse to recognize the sovereignty of the U.S. court system.

America has a history of political prisoners. In the 20th century, this government has imprisoned anarchists, communists, war resisters, and labor organizers, but it has also barbarically committed political executions. Two that come to mind are Sacco and Vanzetti and Ethel and Julius Rosenburg. This is not to discount the numerous "hits" made by the FBI and police on members of the Black Panther Party (such as Fred Hampton) and other organizations.

In denying the existence of political prisoners, this government asserts that these imprisoned activists are common criminals. In this very same act, it denies the existence of any movements for fundamental justice in this society. By criminalizing these individuals, the state is criminalizing the particular movements they represent.

I support U.S. political prisoners and POWs because I identify with their struggles. To me, this is a crucial element in organizing to free these prisoners.

According to Rev. Mike Yasutake, in the book Can't Jail The Spirit: "They represent movements of oppressed people in the U.S., mostly people of color, such as American Indian Movement advocates, militant African Americans (former Black Panther Party and Black Liberation Army participants), and Puerto Rican independentists, as well as white anti-imperialists proclaiming solidarity with minority peoples for self-determination." In supporting their respective movements, I separate any support for the right-wing political prisoners who advocate white supremacy.

My work in support of U.S. political prisoners and POWs has its roots in the David Wong Support Committee—a committee devoted to the freedom of a Chinese immigrant. Through this committee I entered the inspiring realm of Yuri Kochiyama, considered by many activists to be the cornerstone of activism for U.S. political prisoners. It is fitting that I spend some time to recognize her monumental contributions in this arena, especially since all of my prisoner support work revolve around her.

Yuri, as a comrade and loving friend, helped navigate me through the 90s in this most challenging work for these freedom fighters. Her endless and tireless efforts in this fight are extraordinary. Yuri's involvements with the Black, Latino, Asian, and all other communities exemplified the unity of struggle. Her determination, focus and love for these political prisoners permeated our meetings as she consistently called for support for these individuals that she characterizes as the "heartbeat" of the movement.

The three support committees in NYC—David Wong Support Committee (DWSC), Yu Kikumura Support Committee (YKSC), and Asians For Mumia/Jericho—were the only Asian based organizations doing specific support work for prisoners. These three committees would not have existed without Yuri as the driving force behind them. They are part of Yuri's legacy of grassroots activism.

I joined the DWSC because the case of David Wong highlighted the issues of race and class as they relate to the Asian community. David is not a political prisoner because he was not incarcerated for political affiliations or activities. There is an argument that all prisoners are political prisoners simply because their incarceration arises out of the oppressive conditions of a racist, capitalist system. However, this only makes them victims of this system. Nevertheless these prisoners like David Wong need to be supported as well since the incarceration of all of these individuals, political and nonpolitical, points to the role of U.S. prisons as a tool of political repression and social control under U.S. capitalism.

My approach in assessing incarceration in this society is seen through the prism of a class/race analysis. My support for U.S. political prisoners and the anti-prison movement is rooted in the fundamental struggle against capitalism.

Capitalism produces a class society—a society of economic inequality. The exploitation of labor—that is to say, when the workers are not paid the full value of what they produce—is part and parcel of this system. The appropriation of surplus value or profit by the few is an act commonly fostered as a right of the owners. On the contrary, I contend that this so-called 'right' is outright theft. Yet, none of these thieves are incarcerated for their acts of appropriation.

From a historical context, theft and violence has been the dominant theme of U. S. capitalism. At the outset, this land was taken by force from the native population through genocide. The enslavement of Africans as a source of free labor was a springboard to the development of capitalism. The exploitation of Asians and other immigrants as cheap labor allowed the profiteers to further expand their empire. Today, this system has reached a global scale where the productive capabilities can be organized to solve the miseries of most of the world. Instead, this imperialist stage intensifies the miseries and disparities of less-developed countries by sapping their labor source and natural resources.

Imprisonment is a political act under capitalism because it is the ruling class that defines crime. Crime is an inevitable product of this system. When individuals seek to redress their exploited conditions through appropriation, it is considered a crime. The elite few who profit the most through their form of appropriation go unpunished. The majority of the prison population is from the working class. Close to half of this population are from oppressed nationalities (especially Black and Latino). Detention centers have become warehouses for many immigrants. According to an article in *The Village Voice* (Mar. 30, 1999), immigrants have become America's fastest growing prison population. It stated that "such prisons stand at the crossroads of anti-immigrant anxiety and the roaring economy of incarceration, raking in profits and , at the same time, barring the supposed threat of teeming masses coming to snatch those profits away." The U.S. prison system has become a central institution of society.

The case of David Wong involves a Chinese immigrant incarcerated in New York State for armed robbery. He was given an unusual maximum sentence of 8.3 to 25 years for his first time offense. While in prison, David was framed for a murder. He was poor and did not speak English fluently. There was no physical evidence nor motivation linking him to the murder. His court appointed lawyer was incompetent and disinterested. He only visited David twice during the pretrial phase - both times without an interpreter. When he did receive an interpreter, she could not speak his dialect. Racist stereotyping was introduced by the prosecution as evidence. The court disallowed affidavits by fellow prisoners supporting David's innocence. Typical of many people of color, David Wong was tried and convicted by an all-white jury of his peers. His status as a poor Asian immigrant made him a vulnerable prey for this frame-up.

Through the years, David has become politicized in his outlook on this legal system and its relationship to capitalism. He had expressed his contempt for capitalism and the racism that reeks throughout this system. Through his years in prison, his illusion of being freed by the same legal system that had framed him dissipated with each step of legal denial for his case. At one point during one of our telephone conversations, David emphatically states: "This system is one big conspiracy. There is no such thing as the three branches of government. It is just one system based on race and class biases."

David Wong's case speaks directly to the Asian community. I support David because his battle links the plight of immigrants to the fundamental struggles against racism and class under U.S. capitalism. I feel we need to support prisoners like David because they are the modern day slaves. The 13th amendment did not eradicate slavery, but changed it into another form. It states: "Neither slavery nor involuntary servitude, except as a punishment whereby the party shall have been duly convicted, shall exist in the United States."

In the case of Yu Kikumura, the battle being waged takes on a global scale. As an anti-imperialist, Kikumura, was accused by the FBI of being a member of the Japanese Red Army and of having connections to Libya. These were Reagan-Bush years when U.S. imperialism included the invasion of Grenada and the bombing of Libya. Simultaneously, the specter of terrorism upon U.S. soil was evoked to create a climate of mass hysteria and support for tighter governmental control. After Kikumura was apprehended, he was immediately tried and convicted by the media, which demonized him as a terrorist.

This railroading was possible because of the criminalization and demonization of political activists. At a time when threats of foreign terrorism upon U.S. soil were being manufactured, a terrorist had to be presented. The complicity of the corporate media exemplifies its role in protecting the class interests of the ruling class.

In contrast, an article published in *The New York Times* on Dec. 6, 1998, reported the conviction of a member of a white supremacist group who had stockpiled weapons in preparation for a race war. He was also found with a handwritten "hit list". This former prison guard was sentenced to five years and ten months. Apparently, this white supremacist did not represent enough of a threat to the ruling class to warrant a thirty year sentence.

I support Kikumura because it is necessary to stand with those who stand with the oppressed struggling against imperialism. The state has been very consistent in its rule by force especially against those who fundamentally oppose the existing order.

Yu Kikumura's case fits the typical formula applied by the government in its mission to corral those who seek justice through fundamental changes in society. He was given an unusually long sentence for a non-violent crime and criminalized as a terrorist. Despite a recent development in which a FBI Laboratory supervisor blew the whistle on a fellow agent who had given perjured testimony in this case, Kikumura still languishes behind the walls of a maximum security control unit in Florence, Colorado.

Of the two hundred plus political prisoners in this country, one stands alone on death row. In the case of Mumia Abu-Jamal, the state is determined to execute this Black, revolutionary journalist. Convicted of killing a cop in a trial that included intimidation and coaxing of witnesses, and a cop-friendly judge (a former member of the Fraternal Order of Police) who had handed down more than twice as many death sentences as any judge in the country, Mumia remains uncompromised in his political convictions.

According to FBI files, Mumia's political activities were under surveillance since he was member of the Black Panther Party in Philadelphia as a teen. As a Black, revolutionary journalist in this city, he presented exposes of police brutality, racism, and other social injustices. This earned him the name "voice of the voiceless." At his sentencing, the prosecution introduced a quote from Mao that Mumia had used— "Political power grows out of the barrel of a gun". Mumia was sentenced to the electric chair based on his political views.

Mumia's case stand alone not only because of his death row status, but because of the large number of supporters that form an intense united front, here and abroad, which it has attracted. Both David Wong and Yu Kikumura have written solidarity statements in support of Mumia. They have linked their battles with Mumia's.

Asians For Mumia (with Jericho added to its name in 1998) was formed in 1995 specifically for the purpose of creating support in the Asian community for Mumia Abu-Jamal. This committee extended that mission to apply to all U.S. political prisoners and POWs with the emergence of the Jericho '98 campaign. Jericho '98 in Washington DC, was the first national mobilization to call for the recognition of U.S. political prisoners and POWs and to demand amnesty for them. It is a contradiction to support Mumia and not other political prisoners because they are the same struggle—defending those activists who were imprisoned for their stand against an oppressive system. Many supporters of Mumia have said that the movement to free Mumia is not about him but about us.

In recent years, there were three events that indicate the buildup of national Asian support for U.S. political prisoners: Jericho 98 in Washington D.C., Millions For Mumia in Philadelphia and San Francisco on April 24, 1999, and the Critical Resistance Conference at Berkeley on Sept. 26, 1998. The Jericho 98 and the Millions For Mumia showed sizeable Asian support, but at the Asian roundtable in Critical Resistance, the classroom of supporters was standing room only and overflowed into the hallway. Asians from different parts of the country linking their particular issues came together to discuss the anti-prison movement. It was encouraging to see the outpouring of Asians recognizing the significance of organizing against the prison system and supporting U.S. political prisoners.

At the Association of Asian American Studies (AAAS) Conference on April 1-3, 1999, at Philadelphia, a resolution was presented by the Asians For Mumia/Jericho in which the AAAS voted in support of stopping the execution of Mumia and for gaining a new trial. However, the third point of the resolution—amnesty for all U.S. political prisoners and POWs did not pass, which is why I emphasize the point that in supporting these prisoners, we need to support their movements. It is the same struggle.

In addition to evoking the name of Yuri Kochiyama earlier, other prominent Asian Americans doing specific work for U.S. political prisoners include Rev. Mike

Yasutake and Nozumi Ikuta of the Interfaith Prisoners of Conscience Project in Illinois, and Prof. Diane Fujino in California.

In summary, I support political prisoners because our struggles are integrally linked with theirs. Our particular struggles against racism, sweatshop exploitation, and police brutality all arise from the fundamental contradiction of imperialism. I stand with those who link their movements to the overall struggle against imperialism.

With the recent surge of interest in the Asian American Movement of the 60s, we should examine more closely the radical roots of that movement. The 60s gave us a historical example of Asian Americans supporting the revolutionary forces in the national liberation struggle in Vietnam. We linked our particular oppression at home to the international struggle against U.S. imperialism.

The campaign to free all U.S. political prisoners means waging battle against political repression. As Asian Americans we have much to gain in supporting these imprisoned activists and their struggles. Living under the same racist, class system, political repression by the state unites all of us in a common struggle. Furthermore, in waging battle for political prisoners, we cannot forget the politicized prisoners such as David Wong. They are the victims of the political incarceration of the poor and people of color. The National Minority Advisory Council on Criminal Justice in 1980 had proclaimed that "America stands as a distinctive example of ethnic, religious, and linguistic pluralism, but it is also a classic example of heavy-handed use of state and private power to control minorities and suppress their continuing opposition to the hegemony of white racist ideology."

The movement to free U.S. political prisoners and POWs should go hand in hand with the anti-prison movement. It is a modern day anti-slavery movement. Asian Americans, as an oppressed nationality in this system, fighting for a more just and humane society through our particular struggles, must add this movement to our political agenda.

DEDICATION

This article is dedicated to all of the U.S. political prisoners and prisoners of war who have put themselves on the line in the forefront of the struggle for fundamental change in a racist, capitalist America.

In 1999, we celebrated the release of the Puerto Rican political prisoners (despite the shackles of the conditional "amnesty"), the expatriation of Silvia Baraldini to Italy, and the release of Laura Whitehorn after 15 years in prison.

I want to point out a great loss this year with the passing of Susan Burnett—a strong, committed fighter for political prisoners, especially Mumia Abu-Jamal, and the soulmate of Brother Ali Bey Hassan, ex-Panther 21 political prisoner.

I would also like to thank Brother Steve Yip, longtime Asian American activist and revolutionary for his constant guidance, politically and personally.

Last, but not least, this article is also dedicated to my dearest friend and mentor, who nurtured me with such patience, tolerated my many mistakes, and led me by the hand through the door of various liberation struggles—Yuri Kochiyama.

LIVING IN TWO-TIME ZONES

Ninotchka Rosca

Advocating for socialism in the Filipino American community has its roots in a hundred-year-old event half-way across the globe, in 1898, when the United States invaded the Philippines while Filipinos were in the middle of a revolutionary war against Spain.

The invasion was one of a three-pronged attack by the U.S. against Spain, in a war subsequently memorialized in textbooks as the Spanish-American War. It was a war fought in neither U.S. nor Spanish territory but rather in the colonial grounds of Cuba, Puerto Rico and the Philippines. All the killing and destruction of property occurred in these countries; none in the two countries supposedly at war.

Despite a declaration of national independence by a Filipino constitutional assembly, the United States decided to keep the Philippines "to educate and Christianize" Filipinos under the so-called "Declaration of Benevolent Assimilation" of U.S. President McKinley. That the Philippines had a university when buffaloes still roamed the U.S., that 90% of Filipinos were Roman Catholics, made little difference. The country was too far and too unknown to the American public to put the lie to this first instance of U.S. black propaganda against a nation of color.

Because Spain ceded the Philippines to the U.S. in exchange for 20 million silver pesos (or two silver pesos per Filipino), there was little outcry against this virtual enslavement of an entire country. Filipinos were thus on their own in confronting the armed power of the U.S. which was technologically superior. The resulting Philippine-American War, labeled—if mentioned at all—in American textbooks as the Philippine Insurgency, killed 1/8 of the population of Luzon. The total related deaths, from famine created by re-concentration (later known as hamletting), disease, search-and-destroy operations, and actual war casualties, have been estimated to run as high as two million.

Today, that would be a holocaust and genocide, and American generals would be tried for war crimes.

The valiant attempt by an outgunned people to drive invaders from their territory surprised a Russian gentleman by the name of Vladimir Ilyitch Ulyanov Lenin. He would recognize it as the first anti-colonial war and war of national liberation in Asia.

We deem this preamble important as it explains the essence of the relationship between the U.S. and the Philippines for the next hundred years; and explains why the adversarial language of the Philippines has been and is Marxist. The liberal democracies of the world had little to say about Filipino desire for an independent nation. This silence would continue to the unspeakable time of the dictator Ferdinand E. Marcos and further, to this day when the archipelago has been turned into a whoredom in the name of economic globalization.

These facts are the wellspring from which revolutionary waters continue to flow, both in the archipelago and in the Filipino American community. This is a singularity: this direct connection between events in the U.S. and events ten thousand miles away. It confers an internationalism to the progressive movement in the Fil Am community, characterizing it as more than a domestic movement for social transformation, more than a simple case of an ethnic group struggling for equality, more than a matter of identity politics. It locates the Fil Am progressive movement squarely within a movement for national liberation on the other side of the globe.

This uniqueness is both strength and weakness. The history of the Fil Am Left shows a constant tension between the need to protect gains made in the larger American society and the need to act in concert with a liberation war in the Philippines. Historically, the Fil Am Left has time and again decided in favor of the former, to its own detriment.

The problem stems partly from a) a lack of critical examination of how the imperial doctrine permeates American society, including its progressive movements; and b) an inadequate understanding of marginalization under capitalism and the inseparable nature of U.S. racism and sexism from imperialist control and disenfranchisement of peoples overseas.

The very presence of Filipinos in the United States originated from such a marginalization. In 1901, with the American war for the conquest of the Philippines still raging, the Hawaii Sugar Planters Association (a misnomer as the members were landowners not tillers of land) was already suggesting to Washington DC that Filipinos be recruited for stoop labor in land wrested from Hawaiians. A natural resource from one colonized people; human resources from another.

By 1906, fifteen Filipinos would arrive; by 1907, 150 more; by 1910, 3,000. As a corollary, very few women were recruited, only some 200 in 1910. These first years would set both policy and pattern for the transport of labor to the U.S., manifesting concretely the inextricability of economic marginalization with racism and sexism.

First, pattern and policy locked Filipinos in a specific kind of work in American society: not only dreary, dingy and menial, but more importantly, without power. What power there was among supervisors and foremen was granted by white Authority. Thus, to this day, Filipino Americans exercise leadership only over their ethnic communities, and only a leadership that does not threaten the white power structure. Fil Am leaders, in general, do not innovate; they implement.

Second, measures were undertaken to preempt historic continuity by coopting genetic continuity. The disproportionate ratio between men and women, coupled with laws against so-called miscegenation, ensured that no distinct community could be established. That way, history, tradition and languages could not be passed on to another generation, thus cancelling what should have been a day of reckoning.

By the 1920s, there would be roughly one woman per 40 men, with the ratio as high as a hundred to one in certain states. In Hawaii, the largest number of women recruited was in1920-1924—around 4,000, even as some 23,000 men were brought in.

The impact of this political control of Filipino men's reproductive rights—similar to women's loss of control of their reproductive rights—was not and has not been studied. That the "boys from the boondocks (*bundok*, a Tagalog word meaning mountain)" were relegated to an "inferior" status not only economically or racially but also gender-wise is attested to by stories of rape and sexual abuse visited upon them. Also by the coup de grace administered by white men who beat up Filipinos up and down the West Coast: crushing the testicles.

The absence of a viable community—which depends largely on the existence of families—deprived the few children there were of knowledge about their origins. History, culture and language were taken from the larger American society, creating a consciousness that was fractured. because it could never fully explain why the person remained different, despite all efforts to assimilate.

Much has been made of the role of unions in Fil Am history. The truth however is that American-based unions were quite late in influencing Filipino migrant workers. Manila, during the decades of recruitment, was already heavily unionized. The first true labor union—a printers' union—was established in the Philippines by Isabelo de los Reyes in 1902. It was re-organized as the core of a labor federation, the Union Obrera Democratica, in the same year and gathered together some 150 unions with 10,000 members. By 1913, there was already a Congress of Filipino Workers celebrating the first official Labor Day in the Philippines—May First.

This "class-for-itself" consciousness was carried by Filipinos to the U.S.. In 1919, Pablo Manlapit, a plantation worker in Hawaii, organized the Filipino Labor Union and in 1920, he joined Japanese labor leaders in the first multi-racial workers' strike which lasted three months. By 1924, the workers' struggle was being met with guns by the police. In September, sixteen Filipino workers and four policemen were killed in Kauai during an unequal gun battle. Manlapit, along with some sixty others, was convicted of conspiracy and sentenced to two years in prison.

Filipino labor leaders and union organizers were routinely charged with conspiracy and then either imprisoned or deported. Union organizers and members were also "diagnosed" as afflicted with Hansen's disease and sent into the isolated leprosy settlement of Kalaupapa, where along with Hawaiians, they were subjected to medical experiments.

It was only after World War II when the International Longshoremen and Warehousemen's Union (ILWU) moved into the plantations. It is a testimony to the impact of Filipinos on U.S. unionization and the impact of unions on Filipino American history that again and again, we are brought to this point in time when two movements for empowerment and social justice came together.

The Left and the Lefts

There is constant pressure to separate the history of struggle of Filipinos and Filipino Americans. It fails just as constantly because there has never been such a separation.

The consciousness of struggle among Filipinos in the U.S. was not one created or molded in the United States. Filipinos came with an intense awareness of oppression and struggle, and from a nearly half-millennium of struggle against colonialism. The war for national liberation—for the creation of a true country and a cohesive people—was a monstrous one. It began with the clash between Ferdinand Magellan and Rajah Lapu-lapu in 1521, continued through the first armed resistance against Miguel Lopez de Legaspi organized by the babaylan, the local priestesses, through the one uprising per year of the 500 years of Spanish colonialism, to the Philippine-American War, the peasant uprisings against U.S. colonialism and so on, to this day when Filipinos continue trying to resolved the acute contradictions of their society. A monstrous war, an incomparably heroic struggle.

In 1906, the printers union in Manila, which established by de los Reyes, adapted the slogan "the emancipation of workers shall be realized by workers themselves." These militant self-reliance and "class-for-itself" motivation as were brought from the Philippines by Filipinos recruited to work in the Hawaii and West Coast plantations and would define the adversarial language as far as these first Filipino Americans were concerned. It pushed them towards organizing themselves, towards joining the trade union movement and later, towards the Communist Party of the USA (CPUSA).

The writer Carlos Bulosan, who was also a union organizer, is much venerated by the Filipino American community. However, that he was a communist, a member of both the CPUSA and the PKP is adroitly hidden. One reason is that the CPUSA never acknowledged this man who was one of the few authentic ethnic heroes within its ranks. At the time, Bulosan could hold membership in the two parties because the relationship between the CPUSA and the PKP echoed the relationship between the U.S. and the Philippines.

The PKP was deemed under the supervision of the CPUSA, never mind that very few of the latter's leadership was knowledgeable about the Philippines and never mind that the PKP was in an armed conflict in a revolutionary situation. Despite these "special relations," the CPUSA was unable to mobilize adequate support for the Philippine revolution in the 1950s.

This bit of history was what compelled a re-established Community Party of the Philippines in the early 1970s to consider the problem of a solidarity and support movement in the U.S., in anticipation of a fascist crackdown in the Philippines. It charged activists and cadres departing for the U.S. with the task of establishing such a movement for the Philippine revolution; it also charged some Filipino Americans who had gone to the Philippines to study and learn with the same responsibility. This meant that these men and women were under the discipline of the CPP, owed it allegiance and reported to it. In return, the CPP lent its prestige, experience and resources organizing work in the Filipino American community.

Out of this partnership came the *Katipunan ng Demokratikong Pilipino*, or KDP, which became the leading organization in the solidarity movement against the Marcos dictatorship for nearly a decade. However, its leadership fell under the influence of the Line of March group, led by Irwin Silber who later recanted his Marxist writings and utterances. KDP members who were gauged to be firmly loyal to the Philippine movement were subjected to intense criticism and if unrepentant, thrown out of the organization. Nevertheless, the CPP maintained its links with the body overseeing KDP's work until members of the latter launched an attack on the Philippine revolution, questioning the CPP's political line, strategy and tactic. There was a parting of the ways.

The KDP rapidly disappeared, underscoring the truth that an organization established and mandated for specific purposes rarely survives too radical a change in objectives. Its disappearance also underscored the rather strange historic fact that without links with the Philippine movement, assimilation of Filipino Americans into U.S. reactionary and/or reformist politics was more likely than not.

These lessons appeared to have been lost on a new political center, the Association of Philippine Concerns (APC) which similarly disintegrated, following a falling-out with the Philippine Left. As with the KDP, the APC could not resolve the issue of what it, as part of American society, wanted from the U.S. and what was needed for the Philippine revolutionary movement.

One tricky question was how the work in the U.S. could be represented and presented in the deliberations of the revolutionary movement in the Philippines. The political distance between the revolutionary practice of one from the other was too vast to even consider them on equal footing. This "secondary citizen" status of overseas Filipino revolutionaries became unacceptable to some of the APC leadership and members of the U.S. Committee. They began to adopt programs which would make the organization and its work more acceptable to the U.S. liberals.

There were wild swings in APC's alliances. It found itself with a peace and nonviolence coalition during the Gulf War. An organization mimicking an underground revolutionary organization in the Philippines was established, but with a program so diffused it declared itself to be "pluralistic." This group barely made it through a year of existence, wracked by internal debates and bickering, and disappeared shortly after its founding. Without a common belief and a common discipline, its members were swept into various issue fads in the U.S., from peace to environmentalism. This was a world view forged from life in the U.S., rather than from the millennium-old revolutionary heritage of the Filipino people.

In the 1980s, history came full cycle when hospitals and Catholic schools began importing RNs and teachers from the Philippines. As these professions were predominantly female, the man-woman ratio within the Filipino American community became instantly lopsided. By the end of that decade, the community was 60% female; in some states, it went up to 70%.

The new demographics was reflected perversely within Left organizations: 70% female membership and 99% male leadership. The faces which confronted the larger society on behalf of these organizations remained male. And certainly, there was little work on women's issues.

In 1989, some 50 women working with various Left groups met in Chicago on Labor Day to found the GABRIELA Network, a Philippine-U.S. solidarity organization. This was in response to the request for assistance by the then-Secretary-General Nelia Sancho. GABNet's founding was an act of both defiance and affirmation. Defiance because the general feeling among various progressive organizations was that establishing a women's organization would divide the already thin forces of the Left. Affirmation because the women were determined to include women's rights and women's issues in the political debate on both sides of the Pacific. Even then, there was this hunch that the Philippines was heading towards an abominable time, as far as Filipinas were concerned. But to clarify its mandate, GABNet decided to work on issues directly linked at the same time to both the U.S. and the Philippines—i.e., bicoastal issues, issues traversing the Pacific Ocean.

GABNet decided to concentrate on a single issue for a long-term campaign—an issue which would serve as the clarifying metaphor for imperialism. At the same time, because it was a sister organization of GABRIELA Philippines, it had to consider the priority issues of that entity.

At the time, GABPhil was immersed in a campaign against U.S. bases in the Philippines. But how to give the problem both depth and a sense of urgency? GABNet posited one theoretical consideration: that U.S. bases in the Philippines acquired a class character similar to that of landlords, in terms of control of the land, control of its produce and the demand for droit de seigneur, the right of the lord to the women of his vassals. The sense of urgency came when GABNet anchored its arguments not on speculations about nuclear war, interventions or such, but rather on the reality of the impact of the bases on the adjacent communities: loss of land, poverty, prostitution, abandoned children, drugs, criminality. These graphically symbolized the impact of imperialism on a nation.

This was followed by the still-running campaign against the traffic in women, including the mail-order bride industry. Roughly a year ago, GABNet began organizing domestic workers under Pinays in America Working in Domestic Settings (PAWID).

From this much-abbreviated history, the following can be deduced:

1. The Left in the Fil Am community has drawn vitality from the revolutionary movement in the Philippines, rather than from the traditions of social transformation movements in the U.S.. There are benefits and there are costs in this kind of arrangement. Among the benefits, being backed by a revolutionary movement actually engaged in armed struggle is a great morale booster. Among the costs, there is a tendency to apply in a mechanical way what is successful in the Philippines to the U.S. arena.

2. Severance of that link inevitably creates an acute dislocation. Often, the vanished core idea or objective and center of discipline are not replaced quickly enough nor adequately enough.

3. The Left on both sides of the Pacific continues to wrestle with the problem of creating a seamless conjoining of (1) a two-fold domestic struggle—against racism and class oppression—and (2) the struggle for national liberation in the neo-colony called the Philippines. Part of that problem could be that the Philippine Left changes its view of Filipino Americans periodically. At one time, they were seen as separate and distinct, citizens of another country and another world; at other times, they were considered a part of the Filipino nation. The latter view, it seems to us, presents severe contradictions.

4. A way has to be found to integrate the struggle against racism and sexism with the struggle for workers' emancipation, to use the words of the Union de Impresores, and with the struggle against imperialism.

5. A Left culture is acutely needed to ensure historical continuity. Bulosan's <u>America is in the Heart</u> was the literary expression and social documentation of the Depression—and it remains the only powerful account of the Filipino's attempt to carve space for himself in the U.S.. The Fil Am Left of the 1960s did not produce any enduring product of its time of activism, whether literature, music, painting or whatever. Neither did the Left of the 1980s. And while there are a great number of cultural products emanating from the Fil Am community, too many speak of generational conflict, generational reconciliation, generational differences. Hardly a one speaks in larger and more epic terms—i.e., evaluating and judging American society from the eyes of one of its ethnic members. The current Left, on the other hand, concentrates on propaganda. More's the pity as this is a monstrous war which will continue to the next millennium.

San Francisco demonstration to support cannery workers
Photo credit: Kent Wong

BUILDING AN ASIAN PACIFIC
LABOR MOVEMENT

Kent Wong

W hile Asian Pacific Americans have been part of the American work force for 150 years, with few exceptions their inclusion in the American labor movement is a relatively recent phenomenon. In years past, American unions were at the forefront of racist anti-Asian campaigns, advocating exclusionary immigration laws and preventing Asian workers from joining unions. The formation of the Asian Pacific American Labor Alliance (APALA) in 1992 was a milestone in providing a voice for Asian American workers within the labor movement, and coalescing Asian American union activists throughout the country. The establishment of APALA has its roots in the Asian American Movement of the 1960s and 1970s.

Revolutionary movements of the 1960's and 1970's domestically and internationally nurtured the Asian American Movement. The Black Liberation and Chicano Liberation movements provided tremendous inspiration to emerging Asian American activists. Asian American activists were drawn together by a common sense of identity as a growing and visible ethnic group, and drew encouragement from the broader social and political forces of the day. Of central importance was a shared commitment to serve the Asian community and work for social change.

Asian American activists were involved in the civil rights movement and the movement against the Vietnam War. Many began to see the anti-war movement as part of a broader struggle against imperialism. Asian Americans led and joined Marxist study groups throughout the country. Asian American activists gained inspiration from the Vietnamese struggle for liberation, and from the Chinese revolution and the teachings of Mao Zedong.

With the development of the new American Left, Asian American activists played prominent roles in a number of emerging Marxist-Leninist organizations in the 1970s. The study of Marxism encouraged many Asian American activists to focus their resources on the working class. Many Asian American activists left college to work as grassroots organizers in the Asian American community, or to seek jobs in factories to build a worker's movement.

Asian American activists established worker cooperatives, set up rank and file committees, mobilized community support, and led worker struggles. In the early 1970s, Asian Americans mobilized national support for the Lee Mah and Jung Sai strikes involving San Francisco Chinatown garment workers. In 1974, Asian

89

American cannery workers organized and brought legal action to protest the blatant racist policies of the Wards Cove Packing Co. in Alaska. In 1981, Gene Viernes and Silme Domingo, two Pilipino labor activists from the International Longshore and Warehouse Union were murdered in Seattle because of their activism and opposition to the Marcos dictatorship. A national campaign demanding justice ultimately uncovered the role of the Marcos dictatorship in their murders. In 1982, 20,000 garment workers marched in New York Chinatown to demand a union contract in one of the largest demonstrations of Asian workers in the history of this country.

Among Asian American activists who persevered in the labor movement, some obtained jobs as union organizers and staff, or were elected to positions of union leadership. But the movement that nurtured and encouraged Asian American activists to enter the working class soon dissipated.

The new wave of Marxist-Leninist organizations tried to link radical theory and practice and tried to advance a bold revolutionary agenda, but none of these organizations grew beyond a small group of dedicated cadre. Their analysis was frequently based on an attempt to apply lessons from Third World liberation struggles to radical social change in the United States. Frequent sectarian in fighting among themselves also characterized these Marxist-Leninist organizations.

By the 1980s, the political climate nationally had changed dramatically. The 1980s were a decade of right wing political leadership represented by President Ronald Reagan, a steady decline in labor union strength and influence, and the dissipation of large-scale social movements. With the fall of the Berlin Wall and the end of the Soviet Union, communist and socialist groups in the U.S., as well as those internationally, faced tremendous internal conflict and many imploded.

The rapid growth and expansion of the Asian American community in the 1970s and 1980s also posed new challenges for Asian American activists. For many Asian American activists, the community they thought they knew was rapidly changing before their eyes. In recent decades, the Asian Pacific American population has continued to expand exponentially. The composition of the Asian Pacific community has also changed dramatically, a community no longer demographically dominated by Chinese and Japanese, but increasing with growing numbers of Pilipinos, Koreans, Vietnamese and other Southeast Asians, South Asians, and Pacific Islanders.

Among Asian American activists who persevered within the labor movement, many maintained a commitment to strengthen linkages between the Asian American community and labor unions. While their activism was consciously grounded in the working class, many still had strong roots with the Asian community.

Although most Asian American activists over the years abandoned idealistic pursuits of building a vanguard party or preparing for working class revolution, many continued to actively support working class struggle and oppose corporate exploitation. Unions were still seen as important democratic worker institutions that could play a leading role in a broader social justice movement. Asian American activists also continued to advance the particular concerns of Asian Pacific workers in opposing both class and racial oppression.

In the 1980s, Asian activists began to set up Asian labor committees in key cities throughout the country. The Asian American Federation of Union Members was established in San Francisco, the Asian Labor Committee was launched in New York, and the Alliance of Asian Pacific Labor developed in Los Angeles. These committees brought together Asian labor activists to work on joint activities, including conferences, labor festivals, and support for organizing Asian American workers.

In 1990, when I was working as a staff attorney for the Service Employees International Union in Los Angeles, I traveled to Washington D.C. to meet with then AFL-CIO President Lane Kirkland to propose the establishment of a national organization of Asian American trade unionists. Those of us who had worked to build local Asian labor committees realized that we would need to establish a national organization to have a greater impact on the labor movement and the Asian American community. We were also interested in developing a broad-based movement for social change that could help to encourage and support others within the Asian community to become involved in worker struggles.

Precedent already existed for such an organization. The A. Philip Randolph Institute for African American trade unionists, the Labor Council for Latin American Advancement for Latino trade unionists, and the Coalition of Labor Union Women for women trade unionists had been in existence for many years.

While President Kirkland seemed supportive, he cautioned that such an initiative might take a long time to be realized. To my pleasant surprise, at the next Executive Council meeting of the AFL-CIO, Lane Kirkland appointed a committee of seven union presidents to oversee the process of setting up a national Asian labor committee. Jay Mazur of the International Ladies Garment Workers Union chaired the committee. For years, older White men had dominated the leadership of the AFL-CIO almost exclusively. So the establishment of an all white committee to oversee the launching of an Asian American labor organization, while it was puzzling to Asian American union activists, seemed perfectly reasonable to the AFL-CIO.

From 1991 to 1992, there were a series of national meetings of Asian American trade unionists, primarily from the three cities with existing Asian labor committees, but also including other regions and key unions with a sizable Asian membership. The early meetings were contentious gatherings. Most of the disputes focused on procedure rather than substance, but the underlying current was grounded in the long history of conflict between the various individuals with previous affiliations from Asian American and Left organizations from years past. Of central concern was the representation of the leadership body of the new organization. Special efforts were made to ensure diversity among the leadership, and to explicitly include Asian ethnicities, geographic regions, gender, and union representation.

The Founding Convention of the Asian Pacific American Labor Alliance in 1992 surpassed everyone's expectations, including the organizers. Whereas we had expected two or three hundred participants, fully 500 Asian American labor activists came to the founding convention. I was elected President, and the other three officers were Pat Lee from the Service Employees International Union, May Chen from the International Ladies Garment Workers Union, and Norman Ahakuelo from the International Brotherhood of Electrical Workers. Matt Finucane from the American Flight Attendant's Union was hired as APALA's first Executive Director. What also surpassed everyone's expectations, was our ability to actually move an agenda. We doubt that the leadership of the AFL-CIO ever intended for APALA to emerge as a social change organization, especially one that was deeply committed to transform the American labor movement.

The AFL-CIO was notorious for maintaining a rigid structure that perpetuated institutional discrimination based on race and gender. People of color and women were marginalized within the AFL-CIO and within the affiliated unions. Groups such as the A. Philip Randolph Institute and the Labor Council for Latin American Advancement were never brought into the formal leadership structure of the AFL-CIO. They were designed to allow people of color to meet, but they were never intended to advance an independent, activist agenda.

APRI received most of their funding to ensure greater African American voter turn out to support Democratic candidates. LCLAA for years was one of the few Latino organizations to support "employer sanctions" against undocumented immigrants, and to support AFL-CIO's cold-war policies in Cuba and Central America. One significant difference that set aside APALA from other organizations within the AFL-CIO was that the APALA leadership included many activists who had been trained in the radical movements of the 60s and 70s.

At the APALA Founding Convention, we chose to focus on two major objectives: to organize the unorganized, and to advance a civil rights agenda for Asian American workers. On the organizing front, the first challenge was to recruit a new generation of Asian American union organizers. The dearth of Asian Pacific union organizers meant that the large and growing Asian Pacific work force was being almost completely overlooked by the labor movement. With few exceptions, unions did not have the interest or capacity to organize Asian Pacific workers. They lacked language skills to communicate with Asian immigrant workers, and they lacked the cultural skills and familiarity with the Asian community to cultivate allies or to develop effective organizing campaigns.

APALA partnered with the AFL-CIO Organizing Institute to establish a new program specifically to reach out and train new Asian American organizers, which has yielded impressive results. In 1992 there were less than a dozen Asian American union organizers nationally. In 1999, there are more than 100 Asian American union organizers. Many of these organizers are young activists with tremendous enthusiasm and energy, and with a strong commitment to social justice.

In 1997, APALA was able to secure funding for a national organizing director. Kathleen Yasuda from the American Federation of State, County and Municipal Employee in Southern California was hired to develop an Asian American worker organizing program. APALA also began to target key organizing campaigns nationally involving Asian American workers, and to provide critical support to campaigns. Through the collective resources of APALA, we now have multi-lingual capacity in many different Asian languages to assist translating materials and in organizing immigrant workers.

On the civil rights front, APALA has emerged as an important bridge between the Asian American community and the labor movement. We have aggressively advocated for affirmative action, immigrant rights, and economic justice. As one of a handful of Asian American national organizations with headquarters in Washington, D.C., we have served as an important political voice for social change. We have coordinated work closely with the Organization of Chinese Americans, the Japanese American Citizens League, and the National Asian Pacific American Legal Consortium around a common agenda for civil rights.

The New American Labor Movement

The development of the Asian Pacific American Labor Alliance has not occurred in a vacuum. There have been major changes that have been taking place throughout the American labor movement that have facilitated the work of APALA.

The AFL-CIO had historically never defined its role as a center for union organizing or as part of a broader movement for social justice. Their role domestically was centered on a political agenda that narrowly aligned labor with the Democratic Party, and internationally they served as a staunch defender and promoter of the Cold War, openly supporting the U.S. War in Vietnam and opposing many Third World liberation movements.

A significant transformation occurred with the 1995 AFL-CIO National Convention. For the first time since the formation of the AFL-CIO, there was a contested election between Tom Donahue, who had served loyally under President Lane Kirkland and the old regime, and John Sweeney, President of the Service Employees International Union. John Sweeney was successful in consolidating some of the major unions to support his insurgent campaign, including the American Federation of State, County and Municipal Employees, the Teamsters, the United Auto Workers, the United Steel Workers, and the International Association of Machinists.

Immediately before the 1995 Convention, the Asian Pacific American Labor Alliance had helped to organize the first national conference of people of color and women within the labor movement. The "Full Participation Conference" brought together APALA, the Coalition of Black Trade Unionists, the Coalition of Labor Union Women, the A. Philip Randolph Institute, and the Labor Council for Latin American Advancement together to discuss a common agenda for action. We resolved to work together to eliminate racial and gender barriers that kept people of color and women out of the leadership of the American labor movement.

The Full Participation Conference had a major impact on the 1995 Convention. Both Tom Donahue and John Sweeney spoke at the Full Participation Conference; both pledged to do more to increase the participation of people of color and women in leadership. The debate that began at the Full Participation Conference carried over to the 1995 AFL-CIO Convention floor. For the first time, an African American delegate on the AFL-CIO Convention floor criticized the leadership of the AFL-CIO for being "too male, too pale, and too stale."

The outcome of the debate resulted in the expansion of the Executive Council of the AFL-CIO, and for the first time in history, a sizable number of people of color and women were elevated as part of the leadership slate. A special seat of Executive Vice President was created, and Linda Chavez Thompson was elected, the first woman and first person of color ever to hold a top leadership post in the AFL-CIO. In addition, Sumi Haru from the Screen Actors Guild was elected as the first Asian American ever to serve on the AFL-CIO Executive Council. This change was a symbolic step forward, and represented the growing role of people of color and women within the labor movement.

The change in leadership within the AFL-CIO, however, was more than symbolic.

The new leadership has taken dramatic steps to change the direction of the American labor movement. This includes allocating greater resources to organizing, restructuring the labor movement to strengthen its effectiveness, improving the public image and profile of unions, and strengthening alliances with its natural allies, such as communities of color, women, gays and lesbians, religious leaders, and progressive academics.

APALA has benefited from the change in direction within the AFL-CIO. In the first few years of this change, more Asian American activists have obtained key leadership roles within the labor movement. These emerging leaders include Pat Lee within the AFL-CIO, Leonard Hoshijo of the International Longshore and Warehouse Union, Richard Leong of the Service Employees International Union, May Chen of the Union of Needletrades, Industrial and Textile Employees, and Day Higuchi of the American Federation of Teachers. APALA's first Executive Director, Matt Finucane, has moved on to obtain a leadership position within the AFL-CIO Civil Rights Department.

While these developments are encouraging, the process of change within an institution as large and bureaucratic as the American labor movement is a daunting task. The AFL-CIO itself has clearly made substantive and significant change. The reality, however, is that the AFL-CIO is an umbrella coalition of individual labor unions. The AFL-CIO itself only controls a small portion of the labor movement's resources. Most of the money, power and influence is still maintained within the national, regional and local structures of labor unions themselves. Unfortunately, most American unions are still clinging stubbornly to the status quo. "Business unionism" is the dominant trend, where unions define their role as servicing members and handling the day to day business of negotiating contracts and filing grievances and arbitrations. Only a few unions have embraced an "organizing culture," where unions commit time, resources, and energy to organizing unorganized workers, change existing power relationships, and transform the labor movement.

For APALA to become effective, therefore, we must strategically link with other progressive forces for change within the labor movement and advance a common agenda. This includes aligning with those unions that embrace an organizing culture, supporting strategic union campaigns to build worker power, and strengthening the convergence of unions and community to advance a social justice agenda. We must leverage the support and power from the Asian community to advance a progressive, anti-racist agenda within the labor movement, and we must leverage the support and power from the labor movement to advance a more progressive, class conscious agenda within the Asian community.

The Next Generation

There is a dichotomy facing most within the APALA leadership team. On the one hand, we are considered the younger generation from the perspective of the older, existing leadership of American unions. On the other hand, we are considered old veterans from the perspective of the new union activists we are aggressively recruiting into the labor movement. For APALA to be an effective voice for social change, it is critical to both strengthen our position within the labor movement, and at the same time to empower the younger activists that are entering the labor movement. This is clearly much easier said than done.

The new generation of Asian American union organizers represents the hope and future of the Asian American labor movement. Unless unions can aggressively reach out and recruit young people, their capacity to sustain work for the long haul is in serious jeopardy. APALA made a strategic decision to recruit and train young people into the labor movement. However, this has not been an easy process.

Young people are attracted to APALA because of APALA's activist orientation, because unions provide an opportunity to pursue careers involving social justice. APALA recruits them with the perspective of what the labor movement must aspire to be—not what currently exists. Many young organizers are filled with idealism, committed to challenge racism, sexism, and injustice. Yet they are sometimes placed in labor organizations that perpetuate the racism, sexism and injustice that exists in society at large.

Organizing has historically been devalued within the labor movement. The work of an organizer has been characterized as "grunt work." Organizers have been evaluated on the basis of how many membership cards they can collect. Organizers are routinely paid less than "business agents" or "business representatives." This is based on the perspective that servicing the members, enforcing the contract, and handling grievances and arbitrations are more important responsibilities than organizing.

There is a current debate on the nature and character of union organizing. Is it mainly a challenge of mobilizing, getting numbers, and winning the campaign? Or is it a challenge of one to one education, developing leadership and building worker organization? Unions are frequently on the defensive, and involved in fierce campaigns with limited resources. Labor education, leadership development, and work place democracy are often perceived as luxuries that unions don't have the time or resources to address.

APALA has been grappling with the challenge of both recruiting and retaining young organizers. While we try to be as honest and straightforward as possible in explaining the current state of the American labor movement, we also try to project a vision of the potential for the future. Young organizers are recruited based on their commitment, passion for change, and for their ability to agitate others and move a social change agenda. Yet it is sometimes these very same attributes that result in conflict within the unions where they work.

In summer 1998, more than 50 Asian union organizers from throughout the country gathered in San Jose, California, for a retreat to discuss the challenges confronting the new generation of Asian union organizers. The sober reality is that in spite of the tremendous inroads Asian American union organizers have made, there has been significant attrition among those who have grown disillusioned with the labor movement.

Many young Asian American activists who were recruited had expressed interest in organizing Asian Pacific workers. Unfortunately, there is very little union organizing specifically targeting Asian workers. The drives that do have Asian workers are usually multi-racial settings where Asian workers are but one portion of the work force. The most blatant examples of sweatshop exploitation and abuse in Asian communities are not even on the radar screen for union organizing. Unions don't have a history of organizing in the Asian community, few have bilingual organizers, and few are familiar with the political and social terrain.

Many young Asian American activists were also recruited with the expectation of joining a movement for social and economic justice. Unfortunately, many of them have been placed in unions or on campaigns where there is lack of democracy and use top-down leadership styles. In the worst cases, organizers have experienced blatant examples of racism and sexism within the union itself.

These challenges led Asian American organizers to convene a national retreat, and to openly and honestly discuss ways to address these obstacles within the labor movement. Organizers discussed the need to strengthen a support network for one another, and also to advocate for specific standards for organizers that provide for their development and well being. Many of us emerged from the retreat hopeful that the organizers will persevere with the labor movement in spite of the difficulties. We are also confident that those who have the drive and patience to persevere will ultimately assume key leadership positions within the new labor movement in years to come.

The Road Forward

APALA has played an important role in advancing an agenda to organize Asian American workers, but we are still in our early stages of development. There are other significant efforts at organizing Asian workers, specifically those who have chosen to pursue an agenda outside the American labor movement. Asian worker centers have grown out of a strong desire to organize Asian American workers, and to fight worker exploitation and abuse within Asian communities. They have also implicitly and at times explicitly challenged the lack of support from established unions to organize Asian workers.

Several independent worker centers have been established in various parts of the country, including the Chinese Staff Workers Association in New York, the Asian Immigrant Women's Association in Oakland, and the Korean Immigrant Workers Advocates in Los Angeles. All have been established with little or no support from labor unions, and have relied on foundations and community-based fund-raising initiatives.

All three organizations have established a reputation of organizing and launching campaigns to support Asian American workers. AIWA and KIWA have maintained good relationships with labor unions in their respective areas, while CSWA has had a more acrimonious relationship with New York based unions. CSWA has been highly critical of unions in New York with regard to organizing and representing Asian workers, and have established independent unions in New York Chinatown. Asian American unionists have been critical of CSWA for advancing policies of "dual unionism," setting up structures in opposition to existing unions. CSWA has also been criticized for attacking the very unions and Asian American union activists who are trying to strengthen Asian worker organizing.

AIWA and KIWA have been active for many years in supporting worker struggles in California. AIWA played a leading role in building a nationwide campaign against garment manufacturer Jessica McClintock, and in bringing national attention to the problems of sweatshops. KIWA has concentrated work on the sweatshop conditions in Los Angeles Koreatown restaurants, and has won back wages and benefits for restaurant workers as a result of hard won campaigns. As community-based advocacy organizations, they have attracted considerable student support, and have served as a progressive voice within the Asian Pacific community in highlighting worker issues. KIWA has also been active in supporting existing union campaigns by the Service Employees International Union and the Hotel Employees and Restaurant Employees Union.

Asian worker centers have emerged as important community based organizations for worker justice. Unfortunately, however, their efforts have not led to unionization of Asian American workers. At the same time, labor unions have been unable and unwilling to commit resources to target organizing in the Asian American community. Without a coordinated effort that will bring together union resources and Asian community resources to organize, the prospects for unionization within the Asian community are still remote. Yet unionization ultimately is the very best way to build worker democracy, provide workers with a collective voice, and strengthen worker power.

APALA is currently launching a national campaign for worker justice, to highlight the exploitation and abuse facing Asian workers, to confront barriers preventing Asian workers from unionization, and to provide needed support to Asian workers who are involved in union organizing campaigns. We hope to work with community based worker centers in this undertaking, civil rights groups, religious networks, and community based organizations, and perhaps collectively we can map out a common strategy that will successfully organize Asian workers into unions.

As we approach the new millennium, the Asian American community today is not the Asian American community that existed in decades past. Our community is complex, multi-ethnic, geographically dispersed, and comprised of many recent immigrants as well as those who have been in this country several generations. We have many small business people, professionals and technicians, and proportionally a larger number of highly educated individuals within the Asian community. Fundamentally, however, the majority of Asian Americans are workers. We need to strengthen a collective understanding and analysis of the power structure within our community, and its relationship to the broader community at large. We need to strengthen a class analysis of allies and obstacles, and advance a movement for social and economic justice.

If we can learn from our experiences within the Asian American movement, I hope that we can build on what we accomplished collectively, while acknowledging and learning from our mistakes. The Asian American movement inspired a generation of activists who dared to challenge the status quo, and who embraced a vision of radical change and social justice. We collectively pushed ourselves to accomplish many things, to lead marches, to organize our communities, to run campaigns, to serve the people. We were motivated by a commitment to build a better future.

At the same time, our movement was marked by sectarian in fighting, by an idealism that was frequently not grounded in reality, and by a serious underestimation of the strength of our opposition. We were also influenced by the broader social and political forces around us, including the ebb of mass social change movements in the United States, the crisis of international socialism, and the pervasive policies of neoliberalism promoted by the U.S. government and corporate interests.

Today, there are opportunities within the American labor movement that have not existed in our lifetime. There is a window of opportunity to transform the labor movement as part of a broader movement for social justice, to build labor and community alliances, and to advance an organizing agenda for Asian workers that will improve their lives and the lives of working people throughout the country. Hopefully, we can draw from our experience within the Asian American movement of years past, and build a more inclusive and more powerful movement that will represent the interests of workers of all colors.

RETURN THE ISLANDS BACK TO THE PEOPLE

A Legacy of Struggle and Resistance in *Ka Pae'āina**

Peggy Myo-Young Choy

Kaulana nā pua a'o Hawai'i
Kupa'a mahope o ka 'āina
Hiki mai ka 'elele o ka loko 'ino
Palapala 'ānunu me ka pakaha.

Famous are the flowers of Hawai'i
Ever loyal to the land
When the evil hearted messenger comes
With his greedy documents of extortion
(from the song, "*Kaulana Nā Pua,*" composed by Ellen Kekoaohiwaikalani
Wright Prendergast in 1893)

*"...the Wasichus [whiteman] came, and they have made little islands for us and
other little islands for the four-leggeds, and always these islands are becoming
smaller, for around them surges the gnawing flood of the Wasichu; and it is dirty
with lies and greed."* Black Elk[1]

Preface

For those of us who survive into the next century, it will be our challenge as Asians living within the belly of the beast not only to be alert to the "gnawing flood," but also to prepare ourselves for the century of the indigenous peoples. The next century is primarily about indigenous peoples' struggles in relation to settlers on their lands and the conditions brought about by the colonizer. Although the U.N. and other organizations have declared indigenous peoples' concerns as priority for the year 2000, and have called for an end to all forms of colonialism by the year 2000, it is the indigenous peoples themselves and their grass-roots supporters who will make it actually happen. As in Micronesia and other Pacific islands, independence has been achieved in some form through the efforts of indigenous peoples themselves. Not only in the Pacific, but in other parts of the world, independence struggles are underway—Autearoa, Tahiti, and Rapanui in Polynesia; East Timor and in other parts of Indonesia, West

---

* *Ka Pae'āina* refers to "The Hawaiian Archipelago."

99

Papua, Kanaki, Bougainville, and even in Kashmir and Tibet.[2] Pacific Island struggles—in particular, the *Kanaka Maoli* struggle in *Ka Pae'āina* —cannot be subsumed under the vague term "Asian-Pacific" (or "Asian/Pacific") without losing a sense of primacy. As Shawnee attorney Glenn Morris says, "We are all indigenous to somewhere."[3] As Asians living in *Ka Pae'āina* and on the American continent, it is true that we cannot underestimate the importance of our home countries in Asia and Southeast Asia in terms of understanding our identities and roots as part of our own resistance process. But we must equally envision our own liberation in the context of the liberation of *Ka Pae'āina* lands. We need to educate ourselves and to listen to those who know[4] about the specific place where we find ourselves living now. We need to be aware of the specific short- and long-term effects of the surges around the islands on which we live.

The need to re-visit the recent and vital history of peoples' struggles on *Ka Pae'āina* land is part of this necessary process of decolonization. My perception of this process as central, is inspired Ngugi wa Thiong'o's thinking in his seminal book, Decolonising the Mind. Included is the notion that in a colonial context, control of a people's culture[5] "is to control tools of self-definition in relationship to others."[6] I expand the decolonization process to the body as well, because our sense of being rooted in the moment, in our identity, has much to do with how we collectively envision, re-vision, and imagine our bodies on a daily basis. To speak of people's history as it ultimately relates to the struggle for the *Kanaka Maoli* (Native Hawaiians),[7] independence is necessarily part of my own process of decolonization as someone who is Korean and whose childhood was spent on *Kanaka Maoli* soil.

During the summers of 1998 and 1999, I interviewed a number of activists—*Kanaka Maoli*, Okinawan, Japanese, Korean, Chinese, Filipino, Caucasian or mixture thereof. They were activists who organized during the period of the late 1960s through the 70s, some of whom are currently active. For many of those interviewed, their motivations in participating in struggle were inspired by a desire for justice, and for a way of life not driven by "lies and greed." What I present here is inspired by their spirit, their commitment and their clarity of perceptions and actions. Although I also include a perspective on what happened much earlier than the 1960s and 1970s (because the state context was defined from the time of contact between the *Kanaka Maoli* and those who invaded), the interviewed activists' stories of what happened and what they thought and felt has fueled and inspired my writing.[8] If there are any inaccuracies because of inevitable bias, I apologize. What I come away with is a sense that the history of struggle in *Ka Pae'āina* is of central importance for all who live in colonial America, and provides a legacy of inspiration even for those on the continent who do not live on islands.

Historical Precedents of Struggle and Resistance

Before devastating contact with the *haole*,[9] people's role as caretakers of the land was of primary importance, and integral to *Kanaka Maoli* culture. *Kumu hula* (teacher/master of *hula* or the dance of *Ka Pae'āina*) John Ka'imikaua of Moloka'i says:

> *"Our people have lived on these islands for 2,000 years. And for the first 1,000 years that our people have lived upon these lands there was no aliʻi [royalty] system."*
>
> *"Before the time of the aliʻi, there was only the makaʻāinana.[commoners] And the makaʻāinana lived upon the land, the makaʻāinana worked upon the land. They were born, they planted, and they died upon the land. It is important for us to reflect the original attitudes of our people from even before the time of the aliʻi."*[10]

Respect for the land is communicated through chants and the *hula*. As a cultural representation of collective consciousness in relation to the land, the *hula* often expresses the struggle between people and nature, and describes the beloved landscape and the "rhythm of daily and seasonal life."[11] A chant, *"Noho Ana I Hilo"* (Living in Hilo), together with the hula convey respect for and love of the land. The chant is by the late *kumu hula* Aunty Edith Kanakaʻole:

Noho ana i Hilo, ka ʻāna kawaū ō Kulukulua,
ʻO Hilo, ʻāna hoʻolūlū lehua, nā lehua makanoe ō uka.
Hao mai ka ua kilihune ō ka nahele
Pū ʻia me ke ʻala ō ka maile o Panaʻewa e.
Kūnou mai nā wai moʻo ō Wailuku, he lua luku e nā kānaka.
I Kaipalaoa e ʻuwā ana i Haili ka leo mūkīkī ō nā manu.
Hoʻolono ai Waiōlama me Kawailepo.
I hoʻokahi me Wailoa a pae i ke kula ō Hanakahi.
Akahi ka manaʻo ake aloha i noho ʻalo ai i Mokuola.
I ola e nā kini e.

Living in Hilo, the damp land of Kulukulua,
Hilo, land of lehua showers, the lehua makanoe of the uplands.
Forcefully strikes the wind-blown rain of the forests
Together with the scent of the maile of Panaʻewa.
The moʻo waters of Wailuku beckon, watery grave of slaughtered men.
At Kaipalaoa all the way to Haili the chirping, sipping sounds of the birds.
Waiōlama and Kawailepo streams comply,
Merge with Wailoa and wash the open lands of Hanakahi.
At last, thoughts of shared love dwell at Mokuola.
May the people be granted long life.[12]

Perhaps because of this historical precedent, this ancient view of the primacy of the land and its care, the peoples' struggles and resistance in Hawaiʻi have related foremost to the land in the past, and relate to peoples' limited access to land today. On the other hand, as a result of *haole* contact—Captain Cook, whalers, traders, missionaries, sugar plantation owners, the military and tourists—*Ka Paeʻāina* has been

101

at the mercy of external forces.

Since 1820, with the first influx of American missionary-colonizers, the people and the land were viewed as resources to be exploited for profit, a view that ran counter to the indigenous view of the land. According to McElrath, the missionary vision was linked to both religion and business:

> *When the missionaries arrived in 1820 under the auspices of the American Board of Commissioners for Foreign Missions, their primary interest, as it was in missions to other parts of the world, was to convert the indigenous people to Christianity. However, the needs of the missionaries to build the infrastructure to promote their religious activities, to grow food, and to get the printed word to converts thrust them into close relationships with the monarchy, thus easing the path to conducting their mission and to furthering their business interests.* (McElrath 1999: 75)

The missionaries were told by the Boston headquarters that they faced a choice between two options—either they would have to become self-sufficient, or they would have to return to Boston and be re-assigned because funds were drying up.[13]

As colonialist-capitalists, the missionaries sought to take control over and exploit the land and its resources for profit through connections with royalty. As early as 1847, missionaries who were part of the Hawaiian Government hierarchy were negotiating with the king. Gerrit P. Judd (as minister of the interior) and Robert Wyllie (as minister of foreign affairs) met with King Kamehameha III and discussed the economic need for land and labor.[14] As Christians, in the name of a foreign Calvinist god, they attempted to disfigure and destroy *Kanaka Maoli* culture, and convert the "destitute, degraded, barbaric, chattering, naked savages." (Blaisdell 1996) Hawaiian traditions were considered works of the devil. The *hula*, for example, was called "savage" and "heathen." (Kamahele 1992: 41-42)

With the acts of the *Māhele* of 1848, and the *Kuleana* Act of 1850, lands throughout the islands were divided among King Kamehameha III himself, chiefs, and the Hawaiian government. The King's lands (crown lands), and the Hawaiian Government lands came to about 60.3 percent (2,477,000 acres), while the lands given to the chiefs made up 38.8 percent (1,600,000 acres). *Maka'āinana* (cultivators of the land) held only 0.9 percent (28,600 acres) of the land, leaving about 71 percent of adult males and their families landless. (Kelly 1999) *Haole* were able to buy land before lands were awarded to the *maka'āinana*. Land became both privately owned property and a commodity for sale—pillars of capitalism. The notion of land held communally was annihilated. Loss of sovereignty was inextricably connected with the loss of land. (McElrath 1999:76) The *Kānaka Maoli* were "locked down," as prisoners in their own land. For example, if they were found wandering about and could not deliver a good reason, they were jailed, or were forced to work on sugar plantation fields for a year. If *Kānaka Maoli* did not pay their land taxes, the government would take their land away. A law was upheld that any land, the produce of which you took to market, could not be awarded to you. The original *kuleana* award could not include land on which one could grow a crop for sale, and could only include the lands on which one grew crops to feed one's family and one-self.[15]

The "deals" the colonizers cut not only with the king but also the chiefs, paved the way for the development of the sugar industry and later the pineapple industry. Asian labor was imported and exploited to provide the engine for this development; 200 Chinese workers arrived on the S. S. Thetis in 1852. Their five-year contracts earned them $3.00 per month. Other laborers followed from Japan, Portugal, other Pacific islands, Germany, Korea, the Philippines, Russia, Spain, Norway and Puerto Rico. (McElrath 1999:77)

In 1893, the U.S. invaded the islands, in support of the local *haole* camp against Queen Lili'uokalani. In 1895, two years later, a Royalist-led revolt of 200 civilians was crushed by a 1000-strong Republic of Hawai'i (ROH) militia, resulting in deaths of an ROH guard and two royalists, as well as the incarceration of 191 royalists. The queen was imprisoned in Iolani Palace, and forced to sign an abdication statement (Blaisdell 1996).

> *Mahope mākou o Lili'u-lani*
> *A loa'a 'e ka pono a ka 'āina:*
> *Ha'ina 'ia mai ana ka puana*
> *Ka po'e i aloha i ka 'āina.*

> *We back Lili'uokalani*
> *Who holds the rights to the land*
> *Tell the story*
> *Of the people who love the land*
> (From "*Kaulana Nā Pua,*" 1893)

An annexation treaty was introduced to the U.S. Senate by President McKinley in June 1897, declaring the self-proclaimed *haole* oligarchy, "the Republic of Hawaii." (1989-1999 Komike 1998: 4) With their right to govern their own home-land denied, three organizations of *Kanaka Maoli*[16] collectively resisted by organizing rallies and circulating petitions. On September 7th and October 8th, in the year 1897, thousands of *Kanaka Maoli* rallied at Palace Square, and 21,269 *Kanaka Maoli* signed the *Hui Aloha 'Aina's* petition against annexation called, "*Palapala Hoopii Kue Hoohui Aina a Ka Lahui*" (Petition of the Nation Protesting Annexation). The petition was taken to Washington and presented to then President McKinley and the U.S. Congress. (1989-1999 Komike 1998: 4)

For annexation to work, inter-ethnic distrust was encouraged as a strategy of control. Aoudé describes the formation of the division between the *Kānaka Maoli* and other ethnic groups:

> *The development of the plantation system was an integral part of the transfor-*
> *mation of the Native Hawaiian pre-contact system to full-fledged capitalism. By*

the time Hawai'i was annexed to the United States in 1898, the plantation society had developed into a caste-like system with the haole oligarchy in power and ethnic minorities on the plantations, mainly Chinese and Japanese, at the bottom. The haole oligarchy was able to drive a wedge between the Native Hawaiians and the other nationalities....

...[In 1901,] Native Hawaiians comprised about two-thirds of the voters in the Territory. ...To check this potential threat, planter Henry Baldwin met Prince Kuhio Kalaniana'ole ...to convince him to run as a delegate to Congress against Robert Wilcox, the candidate of the anti-haole Home Rule Party. Baldwin argued that Native Hawaiians and haoles needed to join forces against "the rising Oriental tide." ...Kuhio agreed. The deal was made in order to have the Native Hawaiians serve the interests of the haole oligarchy. (Aoudé 1998: 268)

Plantation housing was segregated by ethnicity. Solidarity between groups was discouraged. In fact, Korean labor was imported as scabs to break the Japanese strikes protesting work and living conditions. For the most part, strikes were by single ethnic groups. For example, in 1909, 7,000 Japanese workers went on strike in protest of their pay of 69 cents a day and their poor working conditions. Actions of state control followed:

Merchant Street attorneys broke into the offices of a Japanese newspaper to dynamite the safe and collect evidence that put the strike leaders in prison for "interfering with plantation operations." One hundred Japanese were arrested. After three months of goon-squad harassment and court injunctions, the workers, many now sick and destitute, trudged back to work. (Kent 1983: 86)

However, inter-ethnic solidarity was behind the lengthy and massive strike of 1920 wherein Japanese and Filipino plantation workers joined forces. The reactionary response of the state and the Big Five[17] indicated a threatened elite:

...the Big Five whipped up a racist, red-baiting press campaign against the strikers: "IS CONTROL OF THE INDUSTRIALIZATION OF HAWAII TO REMAIN IN THE HANDS OF THE ANGLO-SAXONS OR IS IT TO PASS INTO THOSE OF THE ALIEN JAPANESE?" Thousands of workers and their families were evicted from their corrugated houses on plantation property... Makeshift camps were strung out along dirt roads from Pearl City to West Honolulu, and in the city itself, camps, parks and temples. As people died...they said, "Don't give up the fight. Fight for the righteous cause." After six months the strike was smashed...(Kent 1983: 86)

Ka Pae'āina's "enslavement" to the U.S. economy was underway prior to annexation. Between the years of 1887 and 1891, with 91.20 percent of Hawai'i's foreign trade to the U.S., Hawai'i was already its economic satellite. (Kent 1983: 58)

After the territory made its transition to statehood in 1959, the islands' sugar economy transformed into a tourist-run economy, made possible by global capitalist and technological changes, and the rise of the Democratic Party which had begun in 1954. (Aoudé 1998: 269) Aoudé describes these conditions which created a period of economic boom (1959-1990) at the expense of the poorer multi-ethnic peoples, particularly the *Kanaka Maoli* and the Filipino populations:

> *Corporate investment, jet airplane travel, and the political apparatus were essential ingredients for transforming the Islands into a major tourist attraction, with such supportive economic activities as construction, finance, and real estate development. In the boom years, GSP real growth averaged 5 percent annually.* (Aoudé 1998: 269)

The Pacific Rim and Military Hegemony

Along with the development of the U.S. capitalist economy with *Ka Pae'āina* as a dependent satellite, in the global context, the islands were also a crucial strategic link in the U.S. imperialist "Pacific Strategy" of empire building. Prior to annexation, *Ka Pae'āina* was not only a site which America could mine for its natural resources and labor, but it also was a strategic site in the Pacific basin serving the purpose of U.S. "national security." Because the plantation elite had secured the islands as a U.S. military base and territory in the Pacific basin, the U.S. gave them free reign to gain access to both political and economic power in the islands. (Kent 1983: 67-69)

The first *haole* military invasion is marked by Captain Cook's entry into *Ka Pae'āina* waters in 1778. In 1814, the first U.S. warship arrives in Honolulu, and by 1826, U.S. warships begin cruises to *Ka Pae'āina* on a regular basis. In 1887, the Navy is given a seven-year lease to Pearl Harbor. The 1893 overthrow of Queen Lili'uokalani is supported by the U.S. marines and sailors. (Ferguson et. al. 1994: 184) *The Honolulu Advertiser* headlined its article on the 1898 annexation with "HAWAII BECOMES THE FIRST OUTPOST OF A GREATER AMERICA." (Kent 1983: 68) In fact, annexation occurred largely because Pearl Harbor was a crucial base for the U.S. military in its conflict with Spain during the Spanish-American War (which lasted from April to December 1898). As a result, the U.S. was able to gain hegemony over the Philippines and Guam in the Pacific, and Puerto Rico and Cuba in the Caribbean. (1898-1998 Komike: 6)

O'ahu's Pearl Harbor became the heart of the illegal U.S. military occupation of the islands, with a military camp, three barracks, four forts, and two airfields erected at other locations on the island. O'ahu was the island for "R and R" for the U.S. soldiers fighting in Vietnam. Kaho'olawe was taken over as U.S. military land in the 1940's, and for nearly 50 years until 1990, was a target for bombing exercises, destroying its ecology, indigenous sacred burials and other sites. Military exercises have also been held at Makua since 1943, and continue today both at Makua and Pohakuloa. (Ferguson et. al. 1994: 184, 187; 1989-1998 Komike: 6) Highways, including H3, were built for military expediency when necessary. The U.S. escalated its military presence and arms stockpiling on *Ka Pae'āina* lands and in its waters, a process continuing today. Ferguson, Turnbull and Ali report little known statistics.

105

Stored on Oʻahu are an estimated 3,000 nuclear weapons. Over 150,000 military personnel and dependents live in Hawaiʻi. Since annexation, over 200 executive orders have declared land for military purposes, with 140,000 acres of ceded lands used by the military. (Ferguson et al. 1994: 188) Nuclear submarines home-port in Pearl Harbor and off-load their "spent" nuclear rods. The U.S. plans to home-port three nuclear-propelled airplane carriers (two have been already completed) in Pearl Harbor.[18] *Ka Paeʻāina* continues to be of strategic importance for the myth of "national security," as the U.S. eyes North Korea, and the potential threat of China, and perhaps Japan. Military, political and economic might, and the subjugation of the indigenous are the four, mutually-supportive legs of the "beast." Just as the missionaries turned businessmen in order to make permanent their settlement in *Ka Paeʻāina*, the U.S. makes military production a big business venture as well. So in the 1960s and 70s, the U.S. "military industrial complex"[19] was the term that activists used to refer to this interdependency of power, arms and capital.

Contemporary Struggle and Resistance

"*We're* not trespassing. *They're* trespassing."
Michael Grace, 1993 Tribunal Witness[20] (Hasager et. al. 1994: 1)

In the 1960s through the 1970s—during the so-called economic "boom" period—there was a confrontation between different ways of life, and different ideologies. The state—continuing its drive for profit at all costs—operated deceptively, without an ear to the people, and made deals and plans with big business, developers, and landowners behind closed doors. There was a rush to develop *Ka Paeʻāina*. Plans were made to convert land into parks, upper-class housing, and tourist resorts. These lands were often already inhabited by farmers and the poor. The "gold rush" actions on the part of the state to develop the land, as well as the military's actions to desecrate the land, were met with resistance from groups which represented a unique confluence of ideology, political actions, collective consciousness, and a growing understanding of indigenous ways of life. Influenced by the *Kanaka Maoli aloha ʻāina* (love of the land), and by the less evident yet simultaneously occurring indigenous process of recapturing and redefining a sovereign identity, actions occurred which marked this period as a crucial time in which people were not afraid to stand up against the state. Actions were carried out by "local"[21] people who believed in resistance and struggle along lines of class, ethnicity and or/national identity. During the late 1960s through the 1970s, a strong focus for peoples' struggles centered on the land and people's lack of access to it. Fueling community actions and movements was a growing consciousness on three general fronts—Third World awareness, self-education, and networking.

Third World Awareness

There was the growing awareness beginning with the peace movement (beginning in the 1960s)[22], that the war in Southeast Asia—the Vietnam War and the bombing of Cambodia in 1970—was a rich man's war,[23] and was immoral and racist. An international perspective was present in progressive organizations beginning with the Communist Party which began in the 1930s and 40s and ended with the McCarthy era in 1953. Other groups which developed in the 1970s—including the Revolutionary Communist Party, Communist Party Marxist-Leninist, Workers Viewpoint (later Communist Workers Party), Line of March, and *Katipunan ng mga Demokratikong Pilipino* (KDP)—shared an awareness of struggles in other parts of the world including the Vietnam War, but also struggles closer at hand on the U.S. continent. While in most cases, these groups began with initial contact with members of U.S. continent-based organizations, the situation was fluid in that membership in these groups did not make or break the particular struggles in *Ka Pae'āina*. At times, membership followed initial involvement in certain struggles. The ideology of these groups supported consciousness which was already forming prior to and during the active years of particular organizations.

Self-Education

The focus of self-education was deepening one's understanding of one's own ethnic roots, and of larger communities—a "local" community and a "Third World" community. The notion of politically and culturally empowering oneself and one's community came from the Black Power Movement which began in the 1960s on the continent. Hawaiians deepened their own awareness of their own history through knowledgeable elders (*kapuna*) in the community, through reading works of *Kanaka Maoli* historians Kepolino and Kamakau[24], they studied *Kanaka Maoli* language to begin to reclaim their culture[25]. There were some Hawaiians who were turning westward towards other parts of the Pacific to educate themselves. For example, direct contact was made with other Pacific island peoples, like the Maori, the Kanaks, and the aborigines of West Papua.[26] Political literature from New Zealand was available, as well as other legal documents, including the "Treaty of Waitangi."[27] There was an excitement about and respect for indigenous as well as Asian and Southeast Asian performance—Okinawan, Chinese, Korean, Filipino, Japanese, and Javanese. Courses on all of these dance and music traditions were taught through the University of Hawai'i Music Department. Ties with community groups were made. A blossoming of *hula halau* (literally "houses of hula") occurred. Innovative and dynamic *hula* were created, by visionary *kumu hula* such as Johnny Lum Ho and Aunty Edith Kanaka'ole on the Big Island. Alongside chanting and *hula* one could hear a fresh, contemporary sound in Hawaiian-style popular music through groups such as Sunday Manoa, Hui O'hana, Kalapana, and Olomana, and through the solo voices of George Helm,[28] and Liko Martin who composed "Waimanalo Blues." The Ethnic Studies Program on the University of Hawai'i at Manoa campus brought heretofore unknown history, research[29] and radical theory through lecturers, professors and community speakers. Curriculum included conducting research, taking geo-political tours to sites of community struggle, supporting community actions at rallies, demonstrations, and occupations. Off-campus study groups emerged which served as catalysts for ideological exploration—mostly drawing upon Marx, Lenin, Mao, as well as local research, ethnic and political history. Alliances were formed between communities, students and other activists, and with activists from outside of *Ka Pae'āina*. The radical critique of capitalism was contextualized in terms of the local situation. Whereas, Marxist-Leninist analysis focused on Europe and its historical "progressive" march towards modernization,[30] study groups discovered local differences in the application of the analysis. Perspectives took into account the importance of the land, the multi-ethnic make-up of *Ka Pae'āina*'s population, and the "spiritualism" present in the life style of the *Kānaka Maoli*. Several women's groups formed. For example, the Women's Union (originally called Hawaii Women's Group) formed in 1971, because "As women we feel a need to come together to understand our oppression and to organize ourselves to work for our liberation. ...[We] must also support our sisters whose political consciousness has not yet reached the level where they recognize their oppressed condition."[31] Sub-committees included the Childcare Committee, and the Prison Committee which investigated the conditions in women's prisons, and detention homes for adolescent girls. Position papers were shared including, "Young Lords Party: Position Paper on Women," and excerpts from "Colonized Women: The Chicana" by Enriqueta Longauex y Vasquez in Sisterhood is Powerful, and "What is the Revolutionary Potential of Women's Liberation?"[32] One cannot underestimate, as well, the important educational contribution of the activist presses which disseminated alternative points-of-view, including the *Hawaii Free People's Press*, and the presses run by John Kelly,[33] and "Van."[34] Groups active in different struggles also published their own papers, such as *Kokua Hawai'i's Huli*,[35] and Third Arm's *Working Together*.

Activist Networks

Activists created networks by traveling abroad to places that included New York, Puerto Rico, Cuba, and other parts of the Pacific. There were also visits to *Ka Pae'āina* on the part of activists from the U.S. continent and from other parts of the world. Peoples' struggles took place in different locations on O'ahu—for example, in Kalama Valley, Waiāhole-Waikāne valleys, Chinatown in downtown O'ahu, Ota Camp, Hale Mohalu, "Stop H-3 for People, Land and Sea," He'eia Kea, Mākua Valley, and Sand Island. There were also actions on other islands—including at Niumalu Nāwiliwili on Kaua'i (to stop the resort); on the island of Kaho'olawe (to stop the U.S. military bombing exercises).[36] These struggles involved organizers who were of the community who came together with supportive "outside" activists, including students, who were not residents of the community engaging in struggle. Groups involved in one struggle often supported other struggles as well. While each one of these struggles is a significant chapter in the peoples' history of *Ka Pae'āna*, I will focus on three cases in particular—the Kalama Valley, Chinatown and Waiāhole-Waikāne struggles. Kalama Valley was the "watershed" struggle which was not in itself a victory but was crucial to what followed—*Kanaka Maoli* empowerment and the movement for sovereignty. Those involved in the two other struggles—

Chinatown, an urban context, and Waiāhole-Waikāne, a rural context—could each claim victory on some level.

"*Huli!*":
Kalama Valley and the Roots of the Contemporary Independence Movement

"People talked about Wilcox[37] and Liliʻuokalani, but it was far away. Kalama Valley for us was the beginning of change…it was the basis for the independence movement, the beginning of awakening." Kihei Soli Niheu[38]

"Kalama Valley was the beginning of Hawaiian consciousness." P.T.[39]

"Kalama Valley was real important. I really felt it was a way for me to express my feelings for Hawaiʻi." Ray Catania[40]

The Kalama Valley struggle brought together a particular land struggle with the anti-war movement, and brought to fore issues including "local" activism versus *haole* support, Hawaiian sovereignty and identity, and land linked with class struggles. John Witeck summarizes:

With Kalama Valley, you really had a landmark struggle. You had the antiwar movement, SDS, The Resistance,[41] Youth Action, all now looking at this small valley across from Sandy Beach, on ʻEhukai Road. Bishop Estate—a huge landowner, allegedly acting for Native Hawaiians, but actually an instrument of colonization—was letting Kaiser, a major company, have that land to develop into affluent housing. Because Kaiser got major defense department contracts, the antiwar movement saw that taking Kaiser on in Kalama Valley, where they were destroying the lifestyle of yet another people, was a very important way of connecting issues. In fact, the People's Coalition for Justice and Peace did a week-long march around the island in the summer of 1971 that linked the issues of Vietnam, Kalama Valley, and the atomic bombing of Hiroshima and Nagasaki. Over one hundred people participated. The march linked issues that many people cared about in one package—all aspects of a system that didn't care about people, that put profit, militarism, and capital expansion above the lives of people.

So we united with the pig farmers and the Hawaiian families, and we decided that there should be a stop to it. With Kalama Valley, talk of Hawaiian sovereignty and independence was first put into action with the idea that people should refuse to move, should occupy land, and develop new alternatives for the use of that land. (Witeck 1996: 345)

Young activists from Concerned Locals for Peace began the first Kalama Valley sit-ins with 20 to 25 people. The first arrests included between 10 and 12 people.[42] The residents themselves took a stand. George Santos—a Portuguese pig farmer and resident of ʻEhukai Road—stood out as a fighter. He grew up on the tough side of town, on Bethel Street in Honolulu. During the struggle in the valley, along with Santos, there were other families still there—the Richards, Moose Lui's family, Ah Ching Poe, and Manny Botello. But George took a strong stand, and was the last of the farmers to leave Kalama Valley. He galvanized other residents who were also being disenfranchised. He saw things clearly.[43] G.K., who was one of the core activists who occupied the valley, reminisces about George: "The one thing I always loved about him—his irreverence. In his hard hat, he was so wise. His most favorite statement was, 'Dere jus' a bunch of clowns.'" Young activists' occupation of the valley involved setting up camp. One activist, who was still attending a girls' high school at the time, remembers: "I used to help George with his slop runs. We were occupying the valley. We built tents, latrines. ...We would have long meetings at George's house." There were around 17 organizers from outside the valley who were very involved.[44]

Out of the struggle emerged an organizational structure, a group called *Kokua Kalama* (Help Kalama). The organization became a magnet for the radical Hawaiians who began to question authority. Others who were part of the organization included activists of different ethnicities, including Filipino, Korean, Japanese, *haole*, or a mixture thereof. Women of different ethnicities (including Hawaiian, Korean, Japanese women) took on key leadership roles alongside the men. Along with actions supporting the remaining farmers and residents through occupation of the valley, key questions were raised which related to class, identity and the duty of the state to its people. Who is Kalama Valley for? What is the fiduciary duty of the Bishop Estate trustees to their people?[45] For the first time, activists raised the questions of who has legitimacy to lead, versus who should take a supportive role? Hawaiians—including activists who were among the first to be arrested—had come to the forefront of the struggle, and there was the awareness that Hawaiians and "local" youth and community members—those born and raised in Hawai'i—were taking a stand on a local issue. Locals were acknowledged as having a crucial role to play in Kalama Valley.[46] One activist reflected, "...The important thing was local kids coming to the forefront to lead their own struggle."[47]

Kokua Kalama changed its name to "Kokua Hawai'i" to go along with the radicalized perspective that peoples' struggles went beyond just Kalama Valley. This change was linked to the influence of the Black Panthers and the Young Lords. Like the Panthers, and aside from most of its members sporting "beige berets," the organization developed a 10-point program which had the following foci: begin with land and housing struggles, stop all evictions, people have a right to the land, anti-military and anti-big land owner stance, no welfare cuts. Joining forces with S.O.S.,[48] the organization succeeded in mobilizing around 2,000 people for a rally at the State Capitol, which included advocacy of independence from the U.S. for Hawai'i. They also supported struggles in other communities.[49] The group put on two historic benefit concerts, called *"Huli Kakou,"* to raise money for evicted families and bail money for jailed activists. The concerts drew crowds to the Waikiki Shell to see unique programs which combined music, hula, as well as guerilla theater.

"Plantation Days," for example, showed the influence of Chinese socialist society on the immigrants who came to work in the sugarcane fields from the Philippines, Japan, and so forth. George Helm with his musical partner Homer Hu, was one of the first to come forward to commit to being on the roster of performers.[50] The greats of Hawaiian performance sang, including Alfred Lopaka, Palani Vaughn and Genoa Keawe. Popular groups performed, including Hui O'hana and Olomana. Lono, the *Kanaka Maoli kahuna lapa'au* (spiritual leader), gave the opening chant.

On the day that Bishop Estate sent in a bulldozer, three people (including Witeck) were arrested while occupying one resident's house to hold-up the demolition. (Witeck 1996: 345). Witeck observes:

The Bishop Estate spokesman ordered the Bulldozer to knock the house down on us. I was with a woman who was six months pregnant. The Hawaiian bulldozer operator—a huge guy named Tiny—roared the bulldozer within a foot of the house, stopped it, got out, threw the keys in the grass, and said, "I ain't going to do it!" It was dramatic. Within a week, other people were arrested. The occupation lasted for over a year. (Witeck 1996: 346)

During the final days of the occupation, and before the final arrests occurred, the controversy arose of who would stay (to be arrested) and who should leave the valley. It was agreed that the *haole* activists should leave.[51] Witeck reflects on this decision:

The Kalama Valley activists wanted to have a tactical separation, to show that this is not outside agitators, or hippie culture, or drugs, or anything else. This was a stand of local people for their local culture and for their identity. So they made that stand. For myself, as a haole with Civil Rights movement experience, it was sort of a repeat of that understanding in the mid-60s that whites may have a different role to play than Black activists, that we needed to work with our own communities. (Witeck 1996: 346)

There were those like G.P. who consented to leave. "When it was clear that his role was going to be secondary, he began to do a lot of G.I. organizing...[which] took him to the Philippines."[52]

The state muscled its way in and ended the occupation. Police moved in 300-strong, with helicopters, and snipers (Witeck 1996: 346). Mary Choy recalled the day of eviction:

On Mother's Day, May 21, 1971, the showdown between George and other Hawaiian tenants on the land and the Bishop Estate began. The State of Hawai'i's special force was there in full battle dress and assault weapons. Ironically, many of the force were men of Hawaiian ancestry. Following a discussion of who would stay and be arrested or leave, thirty-six of us decided to stay. The young people then climbed to the rooftop of George's house, to be brought down one-by-one by the police, fingerprinted on the spot, driven away in police cars to the old police station on Young Street. George was the first to be dragged out of his house. His pigs, including piglets, were removed, many to die later from inhumane treatment. (Choy 1996: 182)

Another activist remembers, "The arrests were in May 1971. I was on the roof. I was holding a banner, "Yankee Go Home" with K. and H. Sam Lono came in the day of the arrests. ...He gave a blessing ...in a *kikepa* [*Kanaka Maoli* garment cloth tied over one shoulder]. The HPD [Honolulu Police Department] were standing around. He spoke harsh words with the bowl, and the HPD stepped back (many of them were Hawaiian). ...We sang *"Moloka'i Nui Ahina,"* "We Shall Overcome," and *"Ehuli Mako."* ...[we] pulled the ladder up when we saw the police come in. People were standing around on the ground—M.C., R.I., Danny (one of Moose Lui's friends) were milling around. George was also on the ground. They were the first to be arrested.[53]

Although the struggle died with the arrests of activists, and the eviction of pig farmer, George Santos[54], along with other remaining residents, the important lessons had taken root.[55] Some took the idea of local struggle for the poor farmers and residents of Kalama Valley, and went onto the idea of local independence, the idea that Hawai'i was a nation.[56]

Chinatown: From Ideology to Practice

"...The true revolutionary is moved by strong feelings of love. It is impossible to conceive of an authentic revolutionary who lacks this quality. ...For them there is no life outside the revolution. If they are to sidestep dogmatic extremes, sterile scholasticism, and isolation from the people, they must possess a full measure of humanity and a sense of justice and truth. Theirs is a daily struggle to transform their love of living humanity into concrete deeds, into acts that will serve as a mobilizing force and an example."
Che Guevara, from "Socialism and Man in Cuba" [57]

"Basic needs, no mo' kukui weeds!" (Third Arm slogan)[58]

Alongside the community actions in Kalama Valley and at other locations in the islands, a process of education, research and ideological study occurred which created a framework for action. This process occurred through vehicles such as the Ethnic Studies Program which began in 1969 (itself an historic struggle)[59], and through study groups such as the underground "Pacific Rim Collective" (or the "Kaimuki house") which began in 1970.[60] The Kaimuki house's vision of "collective consciousness" was largely provided by H.T., who had returned in the same year from study on the "mainland,"[61] having had some experience with the Civil Rights movement. The group studied a range of radical thought, including Fanon, Marx, Lenin, Mao, Che Guevara, as well as the Panthers, Hawaiian history, and ethnic studies.[62] Some others who joined the collective were returning or coming from "mainland" colleges and universities. They had begun to be radicalized through their own self-education, their own perceptions of global events (particularly the Vietnam War[63]), and through their own experiences on different "mainland" campuses and working in different communities. D.C. was in Madison at the time of the "Dow Chemical riots" at University of Wisconsin-Madison. In California, D.C. and D.L. met activists from Hawai'i who influenced their later joining the Kaimuki house. D.L. had gone to the Third World Liberation College at San Francisco State, met Hawai'i activist K.H. at Berkeley. He later went to Cuba as part of the Venceremos Brigade in 1970. D.W. also met Hawai'i activists while he was going to school at Rochester. G. was at Columbia during the anti-war SDS riots in the late 1960s. He became involved in the "Chickens Come Home to Roost," an anti-eviction coalition involving African Americans, Latino and Japanese residents. Prior to joining "the house," they had already been inspired by books, such as The Autobiography of Malcolm X, and Fanon's The Wretched of the Earth. They had been exposed to Black activists like Eldridge Cleaver. They also had experienced struggles on active campuses, and had met activists from Hawai'i who were either teaching or on speaking tours. One activist who was loosely affiliated with "the house" remembers the impact of, as well as the limitations of the "movement" and the study sessions:

> *"I was attracted to the movement. I was "ku'u ǎina" (country girl). I would watch them [the Asian activists] ...more socially skilled than I was. ...[What we got from reading Marx, Lenin and Mao was]...how to make something out of nothing. Disenfranchised groups were using a methodology to fight the rich and powerful. ...I realized without true economic and political analysis the [power structure] would continue to skim off leadership so poor people would stay in their place. So I was very attracted to study. I learned the limitations of grass roots struggle without analysis. ...But I [also] learned the potential of masses. I wanted collectivity, and knew I couldn't do it by myself. All that study and no action. I need action. When the call came from Kokua Hawaii, I walked into the valley by myself. I was drawn to this ...very real struggle." G.K.[64]*

Nevertheless, as G.K. acknowledges, "the house" offered analysis. D.C. remembers that they began to focus on Hawai'i—its colonial history, its relationship to the U.S. and to the "military industrial complex," and the tourist industry. Yet, there was also a broad, Third World consciousness which was anti-colonialist, anti-imperialist, and anti-Vietnam War.[65] For the activists, the ideas of Marx, Lenin and Mao pointed to the need to "serve the people, serve the workers, and to meet the people's needs."[66]

Working Together

"We took Marxist-Leninism into Chinatown."[67]

In April, 1971, Third Arm[68] was set up in Chinatown in downtown Honolulu by a group of about ten to fifteen activists, some of whom had been part of the Kaimuki house, and students. They first rented an abandoned storefront at 21 North

Pauahi Street which they renovated, then expanded by moving in next door which was also an abandoned storefront. It first began as a place for draft counseling, but most of the residents were old men, including retired plantation workers, who were not of draft age. Upon hearing that urban renewal plans for Chinatown had been approved, they realized they had stumbled upon a more relevant struggle. Their focus changed from draft counseling to anti-eviction community organizing. Through petitioning, the activists became the representatives for the community on the Chinatown Citizens Committee. They devised a strategy in which members were assigned to take responsibility for certain blocks within a larger 36-acre block area (including the boundary streets of Beretania, River, Nuuanu, and Nimitz Highway). They divided the block into four sub-blocks with yet smaller blocks within for strategic organizing purposes. [69]

A conference was held in the dance hall above the Tin Tin Restaurant on Maunakea Street.[70] A 12-point program was developed. (See Appendix I.) Different programs were started to "meet basic needs" of the community—a youth program, employment opportunities opened up for residents through the organizing of a "co-op"[71] and the newspaper, *Working Together*, was published by Third Arm and sold at 15 cents an issue. Weekly movies were also shown, such as films from China, such as, "The White Haired Girl" and "Red Detachment of Women." They were shown at Third Arm, and were also taken into the back alley courtyards of the remaining residents' housing. The free health clinic began because someone collapsed out in front of Third Arm.[72] The clinic sponsored a para-medic training program, distributed health information in Chinese and Ilocano.[73] Cezar Chavez came to visit, supporting Third Arm's efforts at community organizing.[74]

A small cadre began living in a small unit in Chinatown in order to further "integrate" into the community. When it came to the landlord wanting to evict the group, H.T. (who had become an attorney) stepped in. The Third Arm evolved into PACE (People Against Chinatown Eviction) because the activists believed that the residents themselves should be the base.[75]

Political analysis was distilled into pragmatism emphasizing collectivity and class-based justice in the community context. "There was a relationship between study and life....We cared for people, we had a stake in what could happen...People should have control over decisions affecting them, over their own lives. Collective interests should be taken care of."[76] Local research and ideology were synthesized into a preliminary assessment report of the Chinatown community. (See Appendix II.)

Interviewed activists felt that the community-building process was difficult and marginally successful. In retrospect D.W. reflected, "Who benefited more? The students [activists] or the residents?"[77] However, whereas before, residents were isolated and did not know what was going on around them, the activists succeeded in educating the community in several ways. They informed the residents about plans for a large high-rise and other developments that were not in their interest. They helped residents to understand their benefit rights and how to get them from the system.

They rallied residents like Charley Minor (who was already somewhat of a leader[78]), and Charley Hazard to testify at public hearings. They organized a large anti-eviction coalition demonstration in the mid 70s, which moved from Chinatown to the Housing and Community Development Office. The office was taken over; a few arrests followed. Other later marches were organized by PACE. They managed to slow down urban renewal projects significantly; some low-rise units were built, and residents were given priority to come back to their neighborhood.[79] Commercial developments such as Kukui Plaza followed. It was apparent that "the seeds of capitalism were already in Chinatown."[80]

Waiāhole-Waikāne: "People United Will Never Be Defeated!"

"I learned that our government is corrupt. I also learned that there is a difference in classes of people. There is a class struggle." Hannah Salas, resident of Waiāhole Valley[81]

The land in Waiāhole and Waikāne valleys on the windward side of O'ahu was controlled by Mrs. Loy McCandless Marks, the granddaughter of Lincoln Loy McCandless. McCandless had been part of the *haole* oligarchy, a "rebel" democrat who had acquired land in the valleys. The community itself was made up of about 100 families,[82] and was multi-racial. Almost all of the residents (about seven-eighths) lived in the valley of Waiāhole during the period of 1973 to 1974 when the struggle took place.[83] Hawaiians lived with Okinawan farmers, along with Guamanians, Filipinos and Chinese (or mixture thereof), and most were tenants and working class people. Key community members were residents for the most part. For example, Pat Royos was born and raised in Waikāne, moving to Waiāhole in 1966. Her father was a full-time farmer and raised chickens, dogs, pigs, and grew string beans, Chinese peas, and bananas,[84] as well as raising 10 children. Hannah Salas was born and raised in the valley. Guy Nakamoto, who was Japanese, was president of the Association at one time and was committed to the struggle. Together with a few other residents, he took a slide show about the struggle to different groups around the island.[85] However, some landowners and some farmers did not live in the valley and commuted on a daily basis. Okinawan farmers had also lived and worked in the valley for a long time. Considered one of the "iron people" in the struggle,[86] Sei Serikaku, one of the Okinawan farmers, lived in Kahalu'u, had attended school with valley children, and later commuted to the valley to farm. He rented land from Mrs. Marks, and had grown vegetables there since 1948. His parents were from a farming village in Okinawa, and were the first Okinawan farmers in the valley.[87]

Kihei Soli Niheu talks about the multi-ethnic mix of those who were prominent in the struggle:

In the Waiāhole-Waikāne struggle, we worked with Bobby Fernandez, Bernie Lam Ho, Hannah Salas and her husband and their Guamanian contingency. Many Chamorro farmers and residents were involved. They were strong; it was beautiful. And, of course, Ike Manalo and some of the Filipino contingency were key persons. (Niheu: 50)

During the summer of 1973[88], community people came together because they were alarmed at "seeing surveyors coming up and down their roads and out of their fields, and there was an agricultural economist going around talking to people asking them their attitudes about development."[89] Resident Pat Royos[90] describes the first meetings that occurred, and her growing awareness of the development plans:

My girlfriend, Pally Kawelo, and I were working with Bob Nakata[91] who got us involved in a survey, asking farmers questions. I found out they [developer Joe Pao and the state] were planning to develop ...through my cousin, [who was going to be contractor] Moon Palanka...[I said,] ...couldn't be because the survey was about the agricultural part...Bob [Nakata] ...met with Bobby Fernandez, and felt we should have a meeting with tenants, farmers and landowners to talk about what's going on. I was shocked. We knew about Ota Camp, and knew about Kalama Valley. Couldn't be us! Bob Nakata himself didn't know. My cousin said, "Aunty Pat, I think you guys wasting your guy's time. The first meeting ...[I met] with Bobby Fernandez, Bob Nakata...Bobby Fernandez felt we should start meeting with a committee and let them have input. Bobby Fernandez got a hold of landowners, made the most phone calls. It was at the Waiāhole School cafeteria ...jam-packed. Bobby Fernandez conducted the meeting. Everyone was shocked. There was a lot of concern. A lot of people was offended. Then Bobby Fernandez (who was the first president of the Association, a small landowner whose family has been here a long time), felt we should have a steering committee. Bob Nakata was involved. See, Bob Nakata's uncle wanted landowners involved...I was angry, hurt, and concerned. Since we organized, I'm just going to follow through."[92]

Prior to the first meeting, the valleys had also drawn the attention of "outside" student and community activists. The balance of the "outside activists" and the community organizers was delicate. Nakata felt that it was crucial that not too many "outsiders" were brought in so the community would not pull away.[93] Yet, the core outside activists played a role in helping to facilitate the changing consciousness and crystallize action.[94] One activist saw their role as that of raising political questions in the context of what was happening in the valley. What is the nature of power? How do we fight—with what strategy and tactics? Class analysis was introduced on the assumption that "we can't trust politicians, can't rely on them. We need to build people power, and to rely on people to force decision makers to do something."[95] Analysis was inspired by Marx, Lenin and Mao, but there was also a strong Saul Alinsky perspective.[96]

In the course of conducting land research, P.T.—a key activist in the struggle—discovered the applications for re-zoning development in the valleys. Community organizer, R.K. got P.T. in touch with resident Bobby Fernandez and Bob Nakata, who was conducting his own investigation of the development plans. Nakata had heard from a planner, "Watch out for Waiāhole-Waikāne."[97]:

> *We had gone through a planning process; I was going around to different parts of the community asking, "Okay, how do you want to see our community develop?" We were trying to be proactive—and developers were not cooperating...*
>
> *The first place we went to was the Land Use Commission where we found a letter from Mrs. Loy McCandless Marks, the owner of the property, and she had plans for 7,000 condo units in those two valleys, which at that time probably had 120 families...Then we talked to Life of the Land, which was one of the active environmental groups at the time. We talked to Legal Aid, which at that time, played a much higher role than it does now in terms of community struggles*
>
> *We later found out how much power we were up against—there were City officials and legislators, there were judges, there were labor leaders, all involved with the developers. The name of this development company was Windward Partners. We found out really quickly what we were up against.* (Nakata: 61-62)

Compared with other struggles, the activists made direct contact with community people, and became involved early on before developers could scare people into leaving their homes.[98]

"If You Invest, We Protest!"

One of the earlier actions was the community demonstration downtown in front of Honolulu Federal Savings and Loan, the company financing Joe Pau. The message was, "Our own money is evicting us." The aftermath had Honolulu Federal "traumatized" and some churches began withdrawing their money. Sei Serikaku felt the action was worth it:

> *Honolulu Savings and Loan provided the finances for Joe Pao, the developer. We went to ask to not finance them. We had it all planned. We had a demonstration at Iolani Palace. If they refused, we were going to ...picket. Masuo Murawaki collected passbooks [of those who held accounts at the bank]. We presented them in a dramatic fashion. Our money was helping us to be kicked out...Later we went to the Kaneohe branch. At first froze the money, then we could take it out...Churches were withdrawing money. We used to meet every night. It was rough. I had to support my family. It was worth it.*[99]

Sympathetic journalists including Gerald Kato and Kay Lynch ran editorials on "communities in struggle."

The initial steering committee which formed was made up of largely petit-bourgeois forces who had first come to the forefront—there were some landowners, those that leased land for business reasons, independent business people, as well as small farmers who made up the bulk of the committee. The membership hardly included any working class tenants. The activists felt they were not going to win the battle for the people. P.T. met with the working class tenants by going door-to-door, and urged them to join the steering committee. When the working class tenants and, in particular, the women became members, the committee dynamic changed overnight. They were willing to fight.[100] P.T. observed:

The women were central to the struggle. Pat Royos, Hannah Salas, and Mrs. Cortuna were some of the most resolute fighters. There were other strong older women involved, including Mrs. Manatad and Mrs. Batalona. When the women joined the steering committee, the original members stepped aside and the committee became radicalized. When the judge [Arthur Fong] gave the eviction notice, they yelled, 'Hell no, we won't go!'[101]

Hannah Salas recalls the collective spirit required:

The attorney [M.H.] told us we're going to get it. He planned to give a signal when the judge was going to say, "You have to remove yourself." We would yell, "Hell no, we won't go!" We practiced for more than one month. We all had to do it all at once.

The women planned and carried out high-profile actions.[102] During demonstrations, a core of women residents organized themselves and were known as "The Up In Arms Committee"—including Pat, Hannah, Mapuana, Manotad, Aunty Nene, Rusty and Phyllis. They felt that they needed to learn how to use arms, and had target practice. The women strategized about what they could do to put themselves on the offensive in the case that the police threw gas, and so forth.[103]

Other actions continued to capture the press. Rallies were held. One rally and concert was held in the valley in the yard of the Camp family. George Helm, The Makaha Sons of Niʻihau, and Olomana were heard by hundreds of people.[104] Prior to the issuance of the eviction notice, the residents enacted a mock resistance exercise. Some residents dressed up like police. The women decided that they would surround the houses and link arms like human chains. They made up the front line. The "fake police" tried to break through the front line. Via the media, the demonstration served as a warning to the authorities. The message was: We hope that your inaction will not bring this about; we're serious about not moving.

Dramatic actions were not devoid of analysis by the active community members. For example, Hannah Salas spoke at a demonstration for the first time, expressing her critique of the "system":

"System" was the term that got me. That was what I learned through the process, and I found it to be true. I was asked to be a speaker at a demonstration. I looked at it as a monster, I used the octopus. The government rules it and [it] has its legs into everything, and we're all fishes. It injects ink, the ink is "divide and conquer."[105]

Sei Serikaku, who had been inspired by the Narita farmers in Japan, reflected on the nature of the state and people's response to state control:

"The politicians learned that Waiāhole people will not tolerate any b.s... We can be very proud of what we accomplished here because this is one of the few land battles in Hawai'i won by residents who want to keep [the] country [as rural] country... We were all very, very afraid about losing the land, ...It was the first time any of us had faced such a situation. We didn't know what to do, how to stop it, how to fight the big boys. If I had to leave the farm I would be working for some company in a menial job. Farming's all I know. ....They [activists] were the ones who taught us how to protest, do civil disobedience and organize against the big boys. They taught us the militancy we needed to get the courage to fight back. I used to think activists and protesters were really crazy. Guess you're never too old to learn...Before human beings leave this earth we want to do something significant. This is my legacy."[106]

"...I knew about our history...We've worked there a long time. It was a do or die thing for us...the Big Five controlled everything...there were inter-locking directorates of [people] sitting on each other's boards...What really angered me was how people prostituted themselves and our own people.[107]

There was not always consensus within the community, and there were conflicting perspectives as to which strategies were best. There were some who still wanted to talk with Joe Pao and Mrs. Marks.[108]

"Being Nice Wasn't Working"[109]

Negotiations stopped. When the eviction notices were sent out and the eviction date set, the word went out, "Occupy!" When the eviction writs were served, about 150 residents came en masse for a demonstration at the *poi* factory at the corner of Waiāhole Valley Road and Kamehameha Highway, with the media as witness:

We gathered the writs of eviction...Mrs. Cortuna ripped the writ and burned it. Then the occupation of the valley [happened]...There were a lot of people...People were waiting...At 11 p.m. at night, the siren went off. We decided to block the houses. A lot of us were scared. We held hands.[110]

Other residents also destroyed their writs. There were 500 supporters ready to stay. The occupation began.[111] There was already a broad base of support—from people working for organizations such as the Waianae Rap Center, Kuhio Park Terrace activists, American Friends Service Committee, even church groups like the Methodists, activists from neighbor islands, and supporters from other struggles going on simultaneously (e.g. Ota Camp, Chinatown).[112] Kathy Hoshijo[113] cooked, and there were people from the University of Hawai'i campus. M.H. was a local *haole* lawyer and member of the steering committee, who fully supported the struggle to such an extent that he lost his job at his law firm. Two strict rules were exercised—no guns, and no alcohol or drugs. Drills in case of an air-raid or police invasion were practiced. C.B. operator volunteers, organized by Bobby Fernandez,[114] were used to see if the sheriffs were coming. A road-block on both sides of the high-way entrance to the valleys was set up by the community and supporters. Supporters in Kahaluʻu blocked the road at one end, while others blocked Kamehameha Highway near Waikāne. Traffic was backed up all along Kam Highway. A police officer, captured in between the two roadblocks, drove back and forth trying to get out. Ariyoshi, who was governor at the time, wrote in his memoirs that he did not want to set foot in the valley for fear of "personal harm:"

> *The people responsible for my security insisted that I not go. I said I thought it was important, but they said I would be endangering not only myself but others who went with me. A large element of the people in the demonstration were pri-marily—and sincerely—concerned about Waiahole. Another element was anti-democratic and antagonistic to the interests of America.*[115]

In his place, the governor sent a group of mediators, mostly of Hawaiian ances-try. The residents felt that "they were hard-headed, not mediators."[116] One hour after the roadblocks went up, the residents were given the assurance that the state would not intervene that night. The next morning, Ariyoshi announced the state's intent to purchase the valleys. But it was not until twenty years that the residents finally were given 75-year leases.[117]

In assessing the strengths of the struggle and what was learned, Hannah Salas and P.T gave their analysis of what worked. Hannah Salas reflected that, "The key is that the leadership has credibility. They have to struggle with everyone else, too."[118]

P.T. offered his opinion:

> *The activists had to be in early. The most resolute fighters need to come to the forefront, and have to come as soon as possible, joining with other resolute fight-ers. The struggle was broadly built—including the middle class and students. The people have to win over public sympathy proving that they can be effective and doing their utmost repeatedly through the system (e.g. meetings with the mayor and land use commission, etc.)...The question of lifestyle reached a broad-er base—[touching issues such as] the Hawaiian land struggle, the family, ten-ants versus owners, with local people at the center...You've got to make your own analysis. "If you make your own bed, you got to sleep in 'um"*[119]

Hoʻo Kuʻo Koa (Independence)

> *It takes a lot of courage to survive in this world. The struggle never ends. It's just part of a book. But there's another chapter.* Hannah Salas[120]

> *We must not therefore be content with delving into the past of a people in order to find coherent elements which will counteract colonialism's attempts to falsify and harm. We must work and fight with the same rhythm as the people to con-struct the future and to prepare the ground where vigorous shoots are already springing up...A national culture is the whole body of efforts made by a people in the sphere of thought to describe, justify and praise the action through which that*

people has created itself and keeps itself in existence. Frantz Fanon[121]

After the 1970s, for the most part, many of the activists (particulary those who had been students at the time) became focused on their career paths. In particular, the Asians (who were among the "outside activists") appear to have had more opportunities to be employed by "the system," albeit many tried to apply the progressive perspectives they had absorbed earlier, and to work in the area of labor unions, law and social work. There were fewer Filipinos who had been involved in peoples' movements in comparison with those Asians of Chinese, Japanese and Korean heritage.[122] Of those interviewed, the *Kanaka Maoli,* and particularly the grassroots activists in Waiāhole-Waikāne, still felt committed to working collectively to transform and re-claim *Ka Pae'āina's* future. This includes the residents of Waiāhole-Waikāne, even though their opportunities for economic, social and political advancement have not been forthcoming. Hannah Salas reflected:

> *"Our kids gotta take over. If they don't, all we fought for is down the tubes. We got to get them involved. Our own families are moving out to where they can afford to live—Las Vegas, Oregon. People of Waiāhole-Waikāne need to be educated to continue this fight...Now the giant is sleeping. We have a long-term lease. It's the enemy's way of shutting up the parents. Down the road, we'll catch them again. That's why we need to educate our children and not only our children. "[123]*

Other residents continue to fight for their rights using skills they learned during the earlier struggle. Pat Royos is now involved in an organization she helped to found, called *Na Tutu,* which is a group of grandparents fighting for the rights of their grandchildren, or other children taken away by the Child Protective Service. She also sees a continuing legacy is necessary:

> *Now we're fighting for the rights of our grandchildren. Going up against the system, we're still using it. Whatever we've learned, we use in whatever we take on. We're carrying it on...We're not afraid to buck the system. We're not afraid of the governor or whoever.[124]*

Both Hannah Salas and Pat Royos want to see the establishment of a community center, which would include a research library housing a record of their struggle as a legacy for the children of the valleys. Others from the valleys, like Sei Serikaku and the Rapoon brothers, are involved with the controversy over water rights. The Rapoons are "reclaiming" valley lands and are opening it up for *taro* cultivation to return to indigenous land use. [125]

However, there areothers, such as Dean Alegado, Professor of Ethnic Studies at the University of Hawai'i at Mānoa, who acknowledge the need for continued engagement:

> *"At our age at that time, we couldn't make all these big changes overnight. One year or two year plans at the most. That's why Marion, Ah Quon, Mary and*

> *Duke Choy [the older generation activists], who have seen it all and yet are still engaged. We have to continue to be engaged...We should have been persistent. We needed a more long-term view of the struggle...A lot of us knew we would be here, a part of the scene. If you're going to be part of the scene, there should've been more continuity from earlier generations. If you're going to be here and committed to this kind of philosophy, stick it out. But we don't have that old division of labor, the "coherent forward march towards progress."* [126]

The future freedom of *Kanaka Maoli* and non-*Kanaka Maoli* alike is linked with continued struggle to liberate the land. The success of the peoples' movements which occurred in the 1970s were contingent upon the meeting of critical consciousness and grass-roots organizing grounded in the specific communities which were threatened. The seeds of *Kanaka Maoli* independence were sown during this period beginning with the Kalama Valley struggle. Since then, the sovereignty movement has come to the fore.

Asians generally have not been engaged in support of the *Kanaka Maoli* movement, and have appeared apathetic when it comes to the sovereignty debate—albeit complex and problematic as it is. The *Kanaka Maoli* movement has its own history and its own leadership. Since the early 1970s, less publicized organizations emerged predating Kalama Valley which were nonetheless significant. Between 1970 and 1971, Louisa Rice began the Aloha Movement to seek *Kanaka Maoli* reparations. In the late 1970s, *Hoala Kanawai* (Awaken *Kanaka Maoli* Law) was founded by Josiah "Black" Ho'ohuli and Mitsuyo Uyehara. Based on legal research, they began to use the notion of "ceded" lands. "Ceded" is an adjective to describe "lands that were clearly stolen, *Kanaka Maoli* lands passed from a lesser (the Republic of Hawai'i) to a greater thief (the U.S.)." [127] The intent of *Hoala Kanawai* was to manage the ceded lands and the Hawaiian Home lands. Their attempt to establish such an arrangement was aborted by the state's setting up of the Office of Hawaiian Affairs (OHA) in 1979. Another key organization, *Ka Lāhui*, was founded in 1987 again by Josiah "Black" Ho'ohuli, Mitsuyo Uyehara and Mililani Trask. At the time, the group saw OHA as a tool of the state, and they sought recognition by establishing a separate government. [128] Seen as a "sovereignty initiative," the organization sought federal recognition. [129] It has elected representatives from all islands and the continental U.S. According to *The Native Voice: Ka Leo o Ka Lāhui Hawai'i*, they "follow a democratic process and propose a nation-within-a-nation model of self-governance." [130]

Me Ka Ho'omau (Continue the Struggle)

The freedom of the peoples living in *Ka Pae'āina* is contingent upon three critical components—the liberation of *Ka Pae'āina* lands, de-colonization of peoples' minds and bodies, and independence of the *Ka Pae'āina* nation. There are vital questions that need to be asked, not in conclusion but as continuance of the struggle, and as an opening interchange between *Kānaka Maoli* and those who are settlers. The more inclusive and open this discussion and debate can be, the greater the hope for independence. Here are what I consider to be some of the key questions.

The notion of "sovereignty" has been co-opted by the state. Increasingly evident is government support of a few organizations while ignoring others, a tactic to split and co-opt the *Kanaka Maoli* community. The state-endorsed group, *Ha Hawai'i*, began as an advisory committee, but quickly became a non-governmental organization to gain access to funds for "educational purposes." The group called for a *Kanaka Maoli* vote to legitimize their process of defining a sovereignty process, which could pave the way for their eventually becoming the "governing nation." However, the group's authority is highly suspect given the meager support they won in a series of votes they initiated. The group nevertheless has elected delegates and plans to form a constitution for an independent *Kanaka Maoli* government with funding support from outside the state. OHA, a department of the state, directly sought funds from the state in its attempt to capture the leadership position of the *Kanaka Maoli* nation as well. Keanu Sai's group maintains that the *Kanaka Maoli* kingdom was never abolished and that the land was stolen by the U.S.government. The group with the largest following among the *Kanaka Maoli* is *Ka Lāhui*. This group is ignored by the state. Senator Daniel Inouye, a powerful voice in state and federal politics, is not concerned about true sovereignty even though he claims to be in his public statements. Rather, he is focused upon his desire to have the *Kanaka Maoli* to be recognized as Native Americans, and as tribes, so that they can receive federal monies. This would mean that *Kānaka Maoli* would be wards of both state and federal governments with no sovereign or independence status whatsoever.[131]

Will sovereignty succeed on the strength of the long-term vision of *Kanaka Maoli* leaders—a vision extending into the future beyond the state-controlled notion of "sovereignty"? How much is "sovereignty" dependent upon the "sympathy and support of the rest of the community?"[132]

Revitalization of the indigenous concept of *ahupua'a* has long been a goal for some *Kānaka Maoli*. *Pua'a* means "pig." *Ahu* is "a platform on which an offering is given." *Ahu pua'a* refers to a land section. In pre-colonial times, the chief of this section gave an offering at the border of the land section to the *ali'inui* ("ruling chief") as an appreciation for allegiance. Every year at *Makahiki* time the *ali'inui* came to collect the offerings from the people, and each *ahupua'a* chief to whom he had assigned the use of the land in his district.[133] More loosely, *ahupua'a* can also mean, "those who are living in the *ahu pua'a*, implying that all people work together, participate and share in the provision of the basic necessities of life—food and shelter." Even if we ourselves are not *Kanaka Maoli*, whether or not we live on *Ka Pae'āina* soil or on the continent, how useful is it for each one of us to attempt to understand this in the context of wherever we are living? One of the goals of the *Kānaka Maoli* movement is to restore, revitalize the *ahupua'a*. As Kekuni Blaisdell says, "Even if you live in a condo, you can and should grow *taro* in a pot."[134] In order to live in true harmony with the land, and for the land to truly benefit everyone, a classless society is needed (as in the times before the *ali'i*). Can sovereignty have a class con-

123

sciousness?[135]

Capitalism has proven itself to be an enemy of the *Kānaka Maoli*. From the time of the missionaries, indigenous strategies of livelihood were re-defined as primitive and evil. What was set down in its place were the basic tenets of capitalism as envisioned through a colonial Christian gaze. What was seen as "modern" and "right" were notions such as individualism, the holding of private land and wealth, the taking of more profit than you give.[136] Can *Kānaka Maoli* arrive at self-determination under capitalism?[137] What is the process of decolonizing the mind/body which needs to occur if sovereignty is to come from the people and not be forced upon the people from above, by the colonial establishment—propped up and controlled by the U.S. government? How will cultural and spiritual education—including the *hula* and other kinds of performance—be part of this process so that this is not simply an economic-political process?[138] How will participation-by-all be part of this process?

The U.S. will insist upon holding onto *Ka Paeʻāina* as an economic and military base in the mid-Pacific. In time, the U.S. may be pushed out of East Asia and may need to pull back to Guam and *Ka Paeʻāina*.[139] In order for independence to occur, the U.S. must withdraw and the land must be returned to the *Kānaka Maoli*. How? Which lands? What of the prime lands occupied by the military? What of the lands and waters that house the nuclear arsenal, submarines, and carriers?[140]

Through colonialism and imperialism, the U.S. expanded its borders by invading and colonizing Hawaiʻi to increase its territorial might. To this day, its military occupies the islands even though it is designated a "state of the union."[141] It has only been 40 years since the United States incorporated *Ka Paeʻāina* as a state. Can we begin to conceive of the U.S. as differently configured? Can we begin to understand that land is not permanently a political possession of any power, and that rights to lands can shift as can boundaries.

The U.S. political boundaries have shifted over time. We may live on islands or live on the continent where the "*Wasichus*" have created islands called "reservations" for the indigenous peoples, and other kinds of prisons for the poor and those of color. Although the Asians once came here under forced labor conditions, many have now become part of the settler colonial society. Asians can and have supported the *Kānaka Maoli* movement for independence. It is my belief that the return of the land to the people is inextricably part of the Asian struggle in America for equality. True justice cannot occur without the return of the land to the *Kānaka Maoli*. As Asians, whose side are we on? On the side of the *Ka Paeʻāina* nation or that of U.S. imperialism? Are we part of settler colonialism or do we stand with those who fight it? What is our own commitment to the long-term vision of independence? Hilda Hulkward-Harawira, the Maori anti-nuclear sovereignty activist, looks to this future and reminds us that, "Independence is irreversable and irresistable."[142]

Mele o Kahoʻolawe by Harry Kunihi Mitchell
Aloha kuʻu moku
O Kahoʻolawe
Mai kinohi kou inoa

O Kanaloa

Kohemālamalama

Lau kanaka ʻole

Hiki mai nā pua

E Hoʻomalu mai

Alu like kākou
Lahui Hawaiʻi
Mai ka la hiki mai
I ka kā kau aʻe
Kū paʻa a hahai
Hōʻikaika na kanaka
Kau liʻi mākou
Nui ke aloha no ka ʻaina

Hanohano nā pua
O Hawaiʻi nei
No ke kaua kauholo

Me ka aupuni
Paʻa pū ka manaʻo
No ka pono o ka ʻaina

Imua nā pua
Lanakila Kahoʻolawe

Song of Kahoʻolawe

Love for my island, Kahoʻolawe
From the beginning your name was
Kanaloa
You are the southern beacon, barren,
without population
Until the rescue by nine young men to grant
you peace.
Let us band together people of Hawaiʻi

From sun up to sun down
Stand together and follow, be strong
young people
We are but few but our love for the
land is unlimited.
Honored are the young people
of Hawai'i nei
For their civil protest against the government
Together in one thought for the good
of the land
Go forward young people, bring salvation
to *Kaho'olawe*[143]

Acknowledgements

In gratitude, I acknowledge the people I interviewed—for their time, inspiration and insights. A special *mahalo* to Marion Kelly and Kekuni Blaisdell for their generous gifts of information, encouragement, translation help and editing. Thanks to Deborah Weiner for her editorial assistance, and to J. and Patrice Choy for their perceptions. Lastly, I wish to thank my parents, Mary Whang Choy and Duke Cho Choy. Without their guidance and actions reflecting their commitment to the communities working for deep change, even the writing of this would not have been possible. *Kamsahamnida.*

APPENDIX

Appendix I. <u>Chinatown 12-Point Program</u>

In order for people to have self-respect they must have direct control over their daily lives. This means in our work place, we and our fellow workers should make decisions concerning our work rather than one person (usually the boss). The same is true for a community; we and our fellow neighbors should make decisions about our community rather than one agency (usually da city). Only in this way—community control—can our needs be met.

Because Chinatown is our home, we support the following 12-point program for Chinatown in order to provide for the basic needs of our community:

We, the people of Chinatown, must determine for ourselves what happens to Chinatown and how we want to change it.

Chinatown must remain a community which serves its people and not the wishes of tourists, the rich, big business, or any other outside interest.

The people of Chinatown must carefully discuss any changes planned for Chinatown. Any agency doing planning and improvements for Chinatown must sign a contract with people of Chinatown, as represented by an active community-controlled organization.

We want our cultures preserved. We want education and recreation that reflect our peoples' true history and the facilities to hold these activities in.

All planning and actual improvement of Chinatown should employ local resources.

There should be increased health facilities and social services in the com- munity. These should be staffed by community people.

If improvements are made in our community, they should be done with rehabilitation as an on-going process, not through total clearance and destruction.

Small land ownerships, shops, buildings, etc., should be maintained.

Small commercial shops should remain at current styles and rent levels; the open air markets should also be maintained.

We must have decent, low-cost housing.

We must have employment for people of all ages in Chinatown.

We support similar programs of community control for all local communities in Hawaii.

"BASIC NEEDS, NO MO' KUKUI WEEDS"

Appendix II. Excerpt from Report on the "Chinatown Community," July 1971 (pages 7-8)

...The problem is to find a common denominator within the community. What is a universal contradiction that all or most of the interest groups face having to exist or work or hang out in Chinatown? What problem or contradiction will rally the most support in the community? If such a contradiction is found and usually through investigation a contradiction of this nature will emerge, organizing of the various elements within the community must begin to happen. But it doesn't happen without any effort, energy or struggle being expended. What then may be one possible rallying point for the community as a whole? Because the Chinatown people are mainly elderly, retired, single men of working class backgrounds a general feeling in the area is one [of] uselessness and non-productivity. These are the people which society has deemed worthless and has relegated to waste away on a shelf marked "out of commission." But these people for the most part are still capable of being productive and useful contrary to the arbitrary role that society has forced upon them. Because they have been forced to "retire" they have lost what little economic power they once had when they were employed. Restoring economic power and eventually political power into their hands is what must take shape if self-determination of these people's lives is to have any meaning. This may be done through work projects where the people make items which they can then sell. A community cooperative could be developed. A union type set up could also be worked out as far as employing carpenters, electricians, painters, etc., to work on the structures that presently exist in the area. Through the set up of education classes political education and thus ultimately self-determination and control over one's community can begin to take shape. Through education people can gain an awareness of their past histories, their roots, and identities, the part they actively took in shaping Hawai'i, and the part they must to continue to play if Hawai'i is to regain her independence and if the local people are to take back the universal right to say how they live their lives...

So far we have been working most closely with the residents. In the view of Third Arm as of this point, it is the residents who stand to lose or get fucked the most. For them it is a natural happenstance in their lives. Their loss is not only being forcibly moved from homes which some of them have inhabited for several decades but also more of the emotional traumas of being relocated and shoved about, never having the power and support or collective effort behind them to determine for themselves what happens to their lives.

SOURCES CITED

Aoudé, Ibrahim G. The Ethnic Studies Story: Politics and Social Movements in Hawai'i, in Social Process in Hawai'i (1999), vol. 39, Honolulu, Dept. of Sociology, University of Hawai'i at Mānoa.

Ariyoshi, George R. With Obligation to All (1997). Honolulu, Ariyoshi Foundation.

Black Elk Black Elk Speaks: Being the Life Story of a Holy Man of the Oglala Sioux (1988), as told through John G. Neihardt, Lincoln, University of Nebraska Press.

Blaisdell, Kekuni "Ka Manawa (Chronology) for Sovereign Sunday, January 14, 1996," July 11, 1997 (draft).

Choy, Mary "Mary Choy," in Autobiography of Protest in Hawai'i (1996) by Robert H. Mast and Anne B. Mast, Honolulu, University of Hawai'i Press.

Fanon, Frantz The Wretched of the Earth (1966), New York, Grove Press, Inc.

Ferguson, Kathy, Phyllis Turnbull and Mehmed Ali "Rethinking the Military in Hawai'i," in Hawai'i Return to Nationhood (1994), eds. Ulla Hasager and Jonathan Friedman, International Work Group for Indigenous Affairs, Doc. No. 75, Copenhagen, pp. 183-193.

Guevara, Che Reminiscences of the Cuban Revolutionary War (1998), transl. Victoria Ortiz, New York, Monthly Review Press.

Kanaka'ole, Edith "Ha'aku'i Pele i Hawai'i!" (1978), LP, with Pualani Kanaka'ole and Nalani Kanaka'ole, Hula Records, Inc.

Kamahele, Momi "Hula as Resistance," in Forward Motion: Asian Americans and Pacific Islanders: Changing Realities, Revolutionary Perspectives, Volume II, No. 3, July 1992, eds. Fred Wei-han Ho, Meizhu Lui, Ellen Somekawa, Dao Tran, Jamaica Plain, MA, Red Sun Press.

Kelly, Marion Statistics and charts on Hawai'i land history were developed and compiled by Marion Kelly as part of her research and were provided by the author on 8/27/99.

Kent, Noel J. Hawai'i, Islands Under the Influence (1983), New York, Monthly ReviewPress.

1898-1998 Komike "Self-Determination: Newsletter of the Kanaka Maoli Tribunal Komike," March 1998, Kanaka Maoli Tribunal Komike, Honolulu.

McElrath, Ah Quon"Race Relations and the Political Economy in Hawai'i," in The Ethnic Studies Story: Politics and Social Movements in Hawai'i, Social Process in Hawai'i, Vol. 39, 1999, ed. Ibrahim G. Aoudé, pp. 74-84.

Miyazuki, Hirokazu "Sansei Radicals: Identity and Strategy of Japanese American Student Activists in Hawaii," in New Visions in Asian American Studies: Diversity, Community, Power (1994), eds. Franklin Ng, Judy Yung, Stephen S. Fugita, Elaine K. Kim, Pullman, Washington State University Press, pp. 173-187.

Nakata, Bob "The Struggles of the Waiāhole-Waikāne Community Association," in The Ethnic Studies Story: Politics and Social Movements in Hawai'i, ed. Ibrahim G. Aoudé, Social Process in Hawai'i (1999), Volume 39, pp. 60-73

Niheu, Soli Kihei "Huli: Community Struggles and Ethnic Studies," in The Ethnic Studies Story: Politics and Social Movements in Hawai'i (1999), ed. Ibrahim G. Aoudé, Social Process in Hawai'i, Volume 39, pp. 43-59.

Waiwai'ole, Healani "New Leadership in Ka Lāhui Hawai'i," in The Native Voice: Ka Leo o Ka Lāhui Hawai'i, Spring 1999, Honolulu, Ka Lāhui Hawai'i, p. 1.

Wa Thiong'o, Ngugi Decolonising the Mind: The Politics of Language in African Literature (1986), London, James Currey.

Witeck, John "John Witeck," in Autobiography of Protest in Hawai'i (1996), by Robert H. Mast and Anne B. Mast, Honolulu, University of Hawai'i Press, pp. 337-352.

Working Together, January 1973. Honolulu, Third Arm in Chinatown

ENDNOTES

1. From <u>Black Elk Speaks: Being the Life Story of a Holy Man of the Oglala Sioux</u> (1979), as told through John G. Neihardt, Lincoln, University of Nebraska Press, pg. 9.

2. Islands in Micronesia which have some form of independence include the Northern Marianas (pact of free association), the Federated States of Micronesia (free association), the Marshalls (free association), Belau (independent but agreed to U.S. demand of taking out of their constitution a clause which bans nuclear materials from the island). Western Samoa and the Cook Islands have forms of independence from New Zealand. Other island struggles include Western Papua (turned over to Indonesia by the U.N.), East Timor (struggling with Indonesia), Kanaki (New Caledonia, struggling for independence from France), Tahiti (a "province" of France struggling for independence), Bougainville (western part of the Solomon Islands, struggling with New Guinea for independence), the Maori are struggling to get lands back and to be recognized through the Waitangi Tribunal, the Chamoru Nation (or Guam, the U.S. treats this nation like a territory), and Okinawa (protesting U.S. military presence, still a colony of Japan).

3. Glenn Morris shared this in a personal conversation with Patrice Choy. Glenn Morris is also Director of the Fourth World Center for the Study of Indgenous Law and Politics, University of Colorado at Denver, Director of AIM, Denver Chapter. He served on the advocate prosecutor team for the "Ka Ho'okolokoloui Kanaka Maoli" (1993 The Peoples' International Tribunal Hawai'i MANA'O).

4. "Those who know" refers to the *Kanaka Maoli* who know about the land, water, wind, and about how things grow on the land, who know about the cultural, spiritual and scientific way of the *Kanaka Maoli*, and are committed to the long-term process of decolonization and self-determination. There are also those who support with their knowledge of the land, law, politics and culture who are not *Kanaka Maoli*.

5. Included in the idea of culture are processes of language, performance, perceptions of collective history and knowledge, which are negotiated by political and economic processes.

6 Wa Thiong'o, p. 16.

7. "*Kanaka Maoli*" has been used recently. However, because during the 1960s and the '70s, the term "Hawaiian" was more generally used, I use the terms interchangeably, just as I will use the term Hawai'i and *Ka Pae'āna* interchangeably.

8. I spoke with 26 people who were or are active in peoples' struggles during the summers of 1998 and 1999.

9. "*Haole*" means "foreigner," "white person." The first recorded contact with the haole was on January 18, 1778 when James Cook of the British Admiralty brought to the islands firearms, fatal diseases, alcohol, tobacco and Western ideas. This time marks the beginning of the process of depopulation and collapse of *Kanaka Maoli* society. (Blaisdell 1997) The rapid decimation of the population is well-documented. According to Ah Quon McElrath: "Many historians have accepted 300,000 as the number of Hawaiians in 1778, said to have decreased to half by the time of the missionaries' arrival in 1820; further, that by 1860, the Hawaiian population was said to have dropped to sixty-seven thousand, or about 22 percent of the 1778 number." (McElrath 1999: 75) David Stannard estimates that at the time of contact, the population was about 800,000. (Kamahele 1992: 46) In 13 years, between the years of 1823 and 1836, the population is said to have declined by 23.5%. (Kelly 1999)

10. John Ka'imikaua spoke these words on Moloka'i, on August 16, 1993, as part of his testimony for Ka Ho'okolokolonui Kanaka Maoli (The Peoples' International Tribunal Hawai'i MANA'O). This quote is from the publication, "Ka Ho'okolokolonui Kanaka Maoli—1993 The Peoples' International Tribunal Hawai'i MANA'O," (1994) prepared by Ulla Hasager, Iokepa Campton, Mona Bernardino, Haunani Bernardino, Hiko Hanapi, Kekuni Blaisdell, Teresa Black, and edited by Nalani Minton. Published by Honolulu Publishing Co. and Rudolf Helder.

11. Momi Kamahele, "*Hula* as Resistance," in <u>Forward Motion: Asian Americans and Pacific Islanders: Changing Realities, Revolutionary Perspectives</u>, Volume II, No. 3, July 1992, eds. Fred Wei-han Ho, Meizhu Lui, Ellen Somekawa and Dao Tran, p. 40.

12. The late Aunty Edith Kanaka'ole of the Island of Hawai'i, *kumu* (master/teacher) *hula* of Halau O Kekuhi, was known for her dynamic ancient Hawaiian hula style, *'aiha'a*. This chant is from the liner notes of the LP record album, "*Ha'aku'i Pele i Hawai'i!*" (1978), by Edith Kahaka'ole, with Pualani Kanaka'ole and Nalani Kanaka'ole.

13. Marion Kelly, personal communication, 9/17/99.

14. McElrath quotes a communication from Judd and Wyllie from Ed Beechert's <u>Working in Hawaii: A Labor History</u>: "I most respectfully urge your Majesty the policy of granting lands in the most liberal manner to all of your subjects—of extending cultivation or grazing over your whole islands—of encouraging foreign labor whenever native

labor is found insufficient for the quantity of land to be cultivated, and receiving kindly and liberally those foreigners of good character who may come..." (McElrath 1999: 76-77)

15. Personal communication with Marion Kelly, 10/11/99.

16. The organizations were Hui Aloha 'Aina o Na Kane [for men], Hui Aloha 'Aina o Na Wahine [for women], and Hui Kalai'aina. (1898-1998 Komike 1998: 3)

17. The Big Five companies—Castle and Cooke, C. Brewer, American Factors, Theo H. Davies, Alexander and Baldwin—became the most powerful firms in the islands, a pattern well-established by 1910. Having inherited political and economic power from their early missionary and merchant forebearers, these companies fueled a haole-controlled empire in the islands through monopoly of plantations, banks, insurance and trust companies, shipping lines, railroads, retail and wholesale outlets. (Kent 1983: 70)

18. Marion Kelly, interview 9/17/99, Honolulu.

19. Prior to leaving office, president Dwight D. Eisenhower warned the nation about the power of the "military industrial complex." Later, activists took up use of the same phrase from their own perspectives.

20. Hasager et. al., p. 1.

21. The term "local" refers to people of different ethnicities (of color) who live on *Ka Pae'āina* soil. This term was used beginning in the 1970s to collectively define people who were born and raised in the islands but were not necessarily *Ka Pae'āina*. It was used to distinguish people from the *haole* and those who were not born or raised in the islands.

22. The peace movement in Hawai'i was largely *haole*-led.

23. Telephone interview with Ray Catania, 8/5/99, Honolulu.

24. Telephone interview, Kihei Soli Niheu, 8/4/99, Honolulu.

25. Marion Kelly felt that Save Our Surf (S.O.S.) began to challenge the state on dominant issues such as tourism. They protested a plan to add sand to Waikiki Beach for more beach, which would destroy the surf sites, like "Baby Queens." Through this struggle the point was made that environment and surfing are part of culture. The young people got to know about the ocean. This set the scenery for the involvement of Hawaiians in the struggle, to "reclaim one's culture." (Interview with Marion Kelly, 7/29/99, Honolulu.)

26. Interview with Kihei Soli Niheu, who was one of the first to seek out this Pacific arena education.

27. Kihei Soli Niheu, 8/4/99.

28. George Helm who became renowned as the activist who mysteriously was lost at sea with Kimo Mitchell in the struggle over Kaho'olawe. Other key people involved in the struggle were Walter Ritte and Richard Sawyer, Emma De Fries, and Aunty Mary Lee. This was the struggle in which the role of the *Kanaka Maoli kupuna* was sought for support. There was a return to acknowledging the value of spirituality, and the sacredness of the land. Basic beliefs were shared, for example, that the Earth Mother is *Papa* and the Sky Father is *Wakeo*; "the entire cosmos is living and everything is sacred, the winds, waters, rocks, rainbows, everything communicates and is conscious." (Kekuni Blaisdell, Interview, 8/2/99, Honolulu.)

29. Marion Kelly was invaluable to the program. In 1969, she taught the course "Economic Change in Hawai'i." She brought to her students a mature and strong political perspective, as well as her landmark research on Hawai'i's land issues.

30. Interview with D.A., 7/29/99, Honolulu.

31. From "Minutes – July 30, 1971," provided by Lucy Witeck.

32. I wish to thank Lucy Witeck, member of the Women's Union, for providing these materials.

33. P.T. brought my attention to this.

34. Telephone interview with Ray Catania, 8/5/99.

35. "*Huli*" means "to overturn," "to make the lowest the highest." (G.K., telephone conversation 9/22/99)

36. Although this article does not do justice to all these important struggles, I urge others to continue to research and write down this legacy. One crucial story still shrouded with unanswered questions is the activism of George Helm and Kimo Mitchell in relation to their premature deaths when they went out to the island to protest its bombing. A tribute to Helm and Mitchell was edited by Rodney Morales, *Ho'iho'i Hou*, and published by Bamboo Ridge in 1984. A telegram was sent by George Helm, Francis Ka'uhane and Charles Warrington to president Jimmy Carter on February 2, 1977, which indicates something of the clarity and forthrightness of the collective vision of Helm and his co-activists:

"DEAR MR. PRESIDENT

UNITED STATES NAVY HAS SUSPENDED BOMBING OF TARGET ISLAND OF KA'HO'OLAWE HERE IN HAWAII BECAUSE OF OUR INVASION. TWO NATIVE HAWAIIANS WALTER RITTE AND RICHARD SAWYER REMAIN ON THIS ISLAND SACRED TO US HAWAIIANS AND WILL CONTINUE TO OCCUPY IT UNTIL BOMBING OF OUR HEIAUS (SHRINES) AND DESTRUCTION OF OUR CULTURE IS PERMANENTLY STOPPED.

AS PRESIDENT YOU HAVE AUTHORITY TO RESCIND EXECUTIVE ORDER 10436 ALLOWING BOMBING. AS NATIVE HAWAIIANS WE INVADED KAHO'OLAWE TO PROTEST THIS DESECRATION WE HAVE VOLUNTARILY RETURNED TO HONOLULU TO TELL THE WORLD OF THE SACRED NATURE OF THE ISLAND AND TO CONVEY THE DETERMINATION OF RITTE AND SAWYER TO REMAIN ON KAHO'OLAWE. OTHER HAWAIIANS ARE NOW PREPARING TO JOIN THEM IN THIS INVASION.

WE NATIVE HAWAIIANS WANT YOU TO HEAR OUR VOICES. CONTINUOUS DISREGARD OF OUR SERIOUS INTENTION HAS FORCED US TO TAKE THIS ACTION. WE ASK TO MEET WITH YOU PERSONALLY TO DISCUSS THIS INCREASINGLY CRITICAL SITUATION, ALONG WITH CONGRESSMAN DANIEL AKAKA THE COUNCIL OF HAWAIIAN ORGANIZATIONS AND THE PROTECT KAHO'OLAWE OHANA. WE AWAIT YOUR RESPONSE AT PHONE NUMBER 808 841-5961. WE CANNOT OVERSTATE THE SERIOUSNESS OF THIS SITUATION. WITH RESPECT, GEORGE HELM, FRANCIS KA'UHANE, CHARLES WARRINGTON

37. On July 30, 1889, Wilcox and 150 royalists take over the palace in an anti-Bayonet Constitution protest. The revolt is quelled, killing seven and wounding 17 *Kanaka Maoli*. (Blaisdell 1996)

38. Kihei Soli Niheu, telephone interview, 8/4/99, Honolulu.

39. Interview with P.T., 7/14/99, Honolulu.

40. Telephone interview with Ray Catania, 8/5/99, Honolulu.

41. See Hirokazu Miyazaki's article, "Sansei Radicals: Identity and Strategy of Japanese American Student Activists in Hawaii."

42. Interview with S.M., 7/15/99, Honolulu.

43. Interview with G.K., 7/16/99, Honolulu.

44. Interview with C.S., 7/17/99, Honolulu.

45. Telephone interview with Kihei Soli Niheu, 8/4/99, Honolulu.

46. Telephone conversation with J., 9/13/99.

47. Interview with P.T., 7/14/99, Honolulu.

48. S.O.S. or Save Our Surf was organized by John Kelly and mobilized youth to take action against state plans which would bring environmental destruction, focusing on surfing spots which were threatened with development.

49. Witeck 1996: 346.

50. Personal communication with Patrice Choy, 9/22/99.

51. Some *haoles* resented the decision, but others agreed because they supported the importance of "locals" showing that they were taking a stand. It was a turning point and difficult moment; some activists had partners (some who were also activists) who were *haole*.

52. Interview with C.S., 7/17/99, Honolulu.

53. Ibid.

54. Interview with G.K., 7/16/99, Honolulu.

55. At the district court level, those arrested were found guilty. At the circuit court level, the charges were dropped.

56. Interview with S.M., 7/15/99, Honolulu.

57. Che Guevara, pg. 8.

58. The city blocks known as the "Kukui" area had been cleared of poor residential housing for some time with just weeds remaining. Third Arm activists pushed for the building of housing for the poor former residents.

59. The Ethnic Studies struggle is crucial to the people's movement history in *Ka Pae'āina*. See The Ethnic Studies Story: Politics and Social Movements in Hawai'i, edited by Ibrahim G. AoudÈ.

60. Hirokazu Miyazaki has written about the role of *sansei* (third generation Japanese) activists in Hawai'i. See his article, "*Sansei* Radicals: Identity and Strategy of Japanese American Student Activists in Hawai'i."

61. Ibid., pg. 180.

62. Interviews with P.T. (7/14/99), S.M. (7/15/99), G.K. (7/16/99), Honolulu.

63. "The Vietnam War was 'our' war. It impacted our lives." (Interview with D.C., G., D.L., 7/20/99, Honolulu)

64. Interview with G.K., 7/16/99, Honolulu.

65. Interview with D.C., 7/20/99, Honolulu.

66. Interview with D.C., G., D.L., 7/20/99, Honolulu.

67. Ibid.

68. The name was taken from a chapter title in the book Fanshen. The "third arm" was the "collective arm." (D.C., interview 7/20/99, Honolulu)

69. Interview with D.C., G., D.L., 7/20/99, Honolulu.

70. Interview with D.W., 7/22/99, Honolulu.

71. D.L. tried to train people in woodworking. Residents also made "dust pans" out of tin cans, and candles. (Interview with D.W., 7/22/99, Honolulu)

72. Ibid. Dr. Duke Choy was instrumental and served as clinic doctor for 12 years.

73. Working Together, January 1973, p. 4.

74. Interview with D.C., G., D.L., 7/20/99, Honolulu.

75. Ibid.

76. Ibid.

77. Interview with D.W., 7/22/99, Honolulu.

78. Ibid.

79. Interview with D.C., G., D.L., 7/20/99, Honolulu.

80. Interview with S.M., 7/15/99, Honolulu. S.M. said that RCP had this view during the Chinatown struggle.

81. Interview with Hannah Salas, 7/25/99, Waiāhole Valley.

82. Interview with Sei Serakaku, 8/1/99, Kahaluʻu.

83. Telephone conversation with P.T., 9/26/99.

84. Interview with Pat Royos, 7/25/99, Waiāhole Valley.

85. Nakata says that P.T. helped to put the slide-show together (Nakata: 63).

86. Ibid.

87. Interview with Sei Serakaku, 8/1/99, Kahaluʻu.

88. Bob Nakata says the meeting was in April of 1974. (Nakata: 62)

89. Bob Nakata describes how he got involved, when he attended his first meeting in the valley. (Nakata: 61)

90. Pat Royos still lives in Waiāhole raising her family. At the time of the struggle, her husband, Jose, was working at Pearl Harbor at the time of the struggle, with Pat staying home to raise her children and taking care of the family. They also raised chickens, dogs and pigs. (Interview with Pat Royos, 7/25/99, Waiāhole Valley)

91. Bob Nakata grew up in the area, attended school in Waiāhole Valley and was familiar with that community. He went to seminary in New York City and returned home in 1972. (Nakata: 60)

92. Interview with Pat Royos, 7/25/99, Waiāhole Valley.

93. Nakata, p.63.

94. Interview with P.T., 7/14/99, Honolulu.

95. Ibid.

96. Telephone communication with P.T., 9/26/99.

97. Nakata, pg. 61.

98. Interview with P.T., 7/14/99, Honolulu.

99. Interview with Sei Serakaku, 8/1/99, Kahaluʻu.

100. Bob Nakata reports that P.T. had helped with the assembling of the slide show. (Nakata: 63)

101. Ibid. There were also women "outside activists" who took the lead, including women of Hawaiian, Korean, and Japanese ethnicity.

102. Interview with P.T., 7/14/99, Honolulu.

103. Interview with Hannah Salas, 7/25/99, Waiāhole Valley.

104. Ibid.

105. Ibid.

106. Serakaku 1998, pp. 5-7.

107. Ibid.
108. Ibid.
109. Interview with Hannah Salas, 7/25/99, Waiāhole Valley.
110. Ibid.
111. While there had already been people occupying the valley, the occupation as recognized by the media began after the writs were rejected by the community.
112. Interview with P.T., 7/14/99, Honolulu.
113. Kathy Hoshijo was known for her cooking on local television featuring "natural" recipes with local ethnic flavor.
114. Interview with Sei Serakaku, 8/1/99, Kahaluʻu.
115. Ariyoshi, p.114.
116. Interview with Hannah Salas, 7/25/99, Waiāhole Valley.
117 Interview with P.T., 7/14/99, Honolulu.
118. Interview with Hannah Salas, ibid.
119. Interview with P.T., ibid.
120. Ibid.
121. Frantz Fanon, The Wretched of the Earth, p.188.
122. Ray Catania, says his current employment as a nurse's aid comes from his desire to "serve the working class."
123. Hannah Salas, ibid.
124. Interview with Pat Royos, ibid.
125. Waiāhole ditch was built at the turn of the century, which served the function of diverting water from the windward to the leeward side for the growing sugar industry. (Kekuni Blaisdell, interview 8/2/99, Honolulu) When sugar plantations closed down on the leeward side of Oʻahu, the water still remained diverted, and the state leased land to independent farmers. Kaneohe Bay became contaminated, polluted, and fishponds had to be abandoned. (Ibid.) Currently, "more than half the water from Waiāhole Stream was diverted there. We need fresh water for our bay." (Interview with Sei Serikaku, 8/1/99, Kahaluʻu) Fresh water is needed to go into Kaneohe Bay, and keeping the water in the stream (and not diverting it) is important for indigenous stream life. *Opu* (indigenous kind fish) go down into the salt water then come back, and cannot do so unless there is enough water. (Interview with Marion Kelly, 7/29/99, Honolulu)
126. Interview with Dean Alegado, 7/29/99, Honolulu.
127. Interview with Kekuni Blaisdell, 8/2/99, Honolulu.
128. Ibid.
129. Ibid.
130. "New Leadership in Ka Lāhui Hawaiʻi," by Healani Waiwaiʻole, in *The Native Voice: Ka Leo o Ka Lāhui Hawaiʻi*, Spring 1999, Honolulu, Ka Lāhui Hawaiʻi, p. 1.
131. Marion Kelly, Personal communication 10/30/99.
132. P.T. is of the opinion that larger community support is necessary. (Interview with P.T., 7/14/99, Honolulu)
133. Marion Kelly, personal communication 10/4/99.
134. Interview with Kekuni Blaisdell, 8/2/99, Honolulu.
135. Thanks to Ray Catania for this insight. (Personal communication, 10/25/99.)
136. I thank Marion Kelly for the refinement of my basic idea here. (Personal communication, 10/4/99)
137. Aoudé is of the opinion that the idea of sovereignty co-existing with capitalism is an impossibility. (Interview with AoudÈ, 7/14/99, Honolulu)
138. I do not wish to imply that this is not already happening. *Kanaka Maoli* are educating themselves, their children and *hula* is integral. I am challenging non-*Kanaka Maoli* to support this process.
139. Interview with Oliver Lee, 7/23/99, Honolulu.
140. In 1973, Ray Catania (then a member of Kokua Hawaiʻi) had called for the return of military lands to the people. This is not a new idea.
141. Personal communication with Marion Kelly, 10/11/99.
142. Personal communication with Kihei Soli Niheu, 10/10/99.
143. The song text appears in *Hoʻihʻi Hou* (pp. 86-87). I have had the help of Kekuni Blaisdell's editing, along with the incorporation of the "official" translation from the State of Hawaiʻi Kahoʻolawe Island Reserve Commission (care of Momi Lovell).

Asians for Mumia/Jericho
Millions for Mumia demonstration, Philadelphia 1999
Photo credit: ManChui Leung

A BRICK IN THE UNITED FRONT

South Asians Against Police Brutality and Racism

Tinku Sengupta

In the summer of 1997, shortly after the brutal police torture of a Haitian immigrant named Abner Louima, a group of friends got together to make a banner and posters for a march against police brutality. Our small group had committed to going and made plans to meet and march together from Brooklyn to Manhattan. A few people from this small group of friends called on other contacts and acquaintances, with the idea that many of us could meet in Brooklyn and march under one banner. Although there was no name for us at the time, that was the seed of what would later become South Asians against Police Brutality and Racism. Even in its early stages, this group was unique. It was a political meeting point of various groups whose relationships have been traditionally fraught with tension. It was a meeting point of both first and second generation immigrants from different South Asian nationalities, of people involved with various and separate community organizations and affiliations, and of people with very different political ideas and backgrounds. There had been other occasions for which this mix of people came together to support each other, most notably the New York Taxi Workers Alliance strike in May of 1997, which brought out a large number of South Asian taxi workers and their supporters. However this march was different. When we formed, in 1997, among South Asian immigrants, dialogue and outreach about police brutality had essentially not yet begun. But by 1999, attention to police brutality had dramatically increased. On the front page of the June, 1999 issue of the South Asian community newspaper, *India in New York*, there is a photo of people carrying a red banner with the words, "South Asians Against Racism and Police Brutality." Inside, there are three full pages dedicated to this issue. All this in a free paper available in South Asian restaurants and shops throughout New York City.

It has been a conscious choice for us, as South Asian first and second generation immigrants, to become active and visible in the struggle against police brutality. There are many reasons for this. One important reason is that it allows us to join in an united front with Blacks and Latinos, to lend more voices to their fight against this epidemic of police crimes. Another reason is that, although it has not been a widely discussed issue in the South Asian community, police brutality and harassment is not uncommon, especially against South Asian youth and immigrant workers.

135

Self-organizing has been a way for us to resist the ways in which populations are manipulated in this country, where workforces are shifted at will and "model minorities" are put up as smokescreens to hide the deep inequities and flaws of this system. Immigrants from South Asia, like all immigrants, have very much served the economic and political needs of this country, allowing it to sustain its empire and still portray itself as the "land of the free and brave." We see our oppression, as South Asians in the U.S., as part of the global economic and political system, which feeds off the oppression and exploitation of most of the world for the benefit of a few. Most of us are here because our countries of origin, as a result of years of colonialism and imperialism, do not have the material resources that are available in the U.S. Some of us, especially those of us who are second generation immigrants, were able to tap into the system and become a solid part of the middle-classes here, but others of us are struggling and finding ourselves under constant threat of poverty, homelessness, and deportation. Although we see ourselves as oppressed minorities in the U.S., we recognize that our relationship to this country's history is different from the more direct colonial relationship between the U.S. and its Native American, Black, Latino, and many Asian/Pacific minorities. For instance, the U.S. has a longer, more directly colonial and military relationship with the Philippines than it has with South Asia, although we do, like so many parts of the Third World, fall under its global capitalist exploitation of resources and labor. The nature of our oppression changes also based on our class and religious backgrounds, gender, immigration status, among other factors. Therefore, we cannot separate our oppression from all other oppressions.

We also see ourselves as a small, emerging part of the Asian Pacific American movement. The migration of South Asians to this country is similar to the migration of many other Asian groups. On the other hand, we recognize that the U.S. has different economic and political interests all over Asia, and that changes the circumstances of our migration. We have united with groups such as Asians for Mumia/Jericho, and many of us have a background of study in Asian Pacific American history. We aim to add another voice and perspective to this vast and diverse history, rather than allowing right-wing and liberal elements of the South Asian community to dominate the recording of our stories.

Before 1965, the United States still had national origin quotas restricting the entry of Asian immigrants. 1965, in the midst of the Cold War and a changing economy, was a time when it was practical and politically expedient to revise discriminatory immigration laws. It was no longer viable to encourage more immigration from Western Europe. Ireland, Britain, and Germany had long since stopped using up their quotas, while other countries had huge backlogs. The United States would have to attract skills and labor from elsewhere. Furthermore, it was a time of widespread questioning of American propaganda, even among the middle-class, forcing a look at the country's "undemocratic" past and racist domestic and foreign policies, as the Vietnam War continued to escalate. America had lost much of its credibility, at home and abroad. So, the immigration policy changed, but the new immigrants had to be able to pay. The 1965 Immigration Reform Act attracted scores of middle-class professionals from India and other parts of South Asia. They became a perfect buffer between black and white, rich and poor. Here were dark people, previously excluded, who were coming in large numbers to finally take part in the American dream. By and large, they were successful, providing skills and labor for the post-industrial, service economy.

In the meantime, the two imperialist blocks of the Cold War, NATO and Warsaw, had carved up the world for their use. As a result of years of colonialism and imperialism, there was tremendous uprising all over the world. In South Asia, there were revolutionary and nationalist movements in Sri Lanka, Bangladesh, India, and in Pakistan to a lesser extent. These movements politicized a large number of people in those countries. Many of them would later come to the United States, bringing their political knowledge and ideas with them. Although the NATO imperialists, led by the United States, were the eventual victor of the Cold War, America's power was not completely secure. There was a new united Germany; Japan was still an important economic force, and the possible realignment of the former Soviet Union could present a threat to the new world order. America had to remain economically and politically strong to maintain its position. To be competitive in the world market, the country needed limitless supplies of surplus labor, pulling down labor costs. To keep up its power over territory and resources globally, it needed a strong military presence in other parts of the world. To do that, the U.S. must have the cooperation and support of its own population, who will fight these wars abroad. In order to juggle all of this, the United States has relied on repressive measures of various sorts. We have seen how effectively anti-immigrant and racist sentiments are spread to mobilize people behind video game-like bombings in Iraq, Afghanistan, and Sudan. We have also seen how police brutality has been used to terrorize and control inner-city youth.

In the early and mid-1980s, immigration from South Asia decreased. The Immigration Reform Act had run its course. But for the last ten to twelve years, the floodgates have again been open to South Asians, and in these years, many more Pakistanis and Bangladeshis have come into the country. There has been a need for a working class population of immigrants to take the place of poor and lower middle-class Blacks and Whites that have moved out of low-wage production jobs. The current massive surplus of labor allows the U.S. to shift people at will and manipulate tensions – Whites against Blacks and Latinos, Blacks and Whites against immigrants, and immigrants against Blacks. Because Latinos and Blacks have united considerably, the Immigration Reform Act of 1998 has hit Hispanic immigrants the hardest. America has closed that front, and opened the South Asian front.

A second generation of South Asians have grown up here, many of them experiencing much of the racism and alienation of American society. A recent wave of immigrants have grown up in the same generation, but have been politicized by the struggles and uprisings of their home countries. These two groups of South Asians are meeting, talking, and exchanging experiences and ideas. And under the current atmosphere of repression, where the brutal nature of this system can reveal itself, they are witnessing the experiences of other groups and uniting with them. These are the underpinnings of how we came together as South Asians against Police Brutality and Racism.

In 1998, the group that started amorphously as we walked across the Brooklyn Bridge in 1997, grew in number. When we first started to create a visible presence at marches and rallies, beginning with the Abner Louima march, many of us were wary of how we would be seen. We were always warmly greeted and supported in our efforts. And when we have done outreach in the South Asian community, many took the time to listen and talk with us. Along the way, we became encouraged and strengthened by people's responses to us. We also began to network with other progressive South Asian groups, such as the South Asian Lesbian and Gay Alliance, South Asian Women's Creative Collective, Taxi Workers' Alliance, and Workers' Awaaz, a group that organizes South Asian domestic workers. We joined them as part of a South Asian Activist Taskforce, which was designed to create an alternative presence around the India Day and Pakistan Day Parades. We held up placards at the Pakistan Day Parade that said, "Stop the bombing of Afghanistan and Sudan." We got involved with the family of a young Indo-Trinidadian man, the victim of a racist attack in his Queens neighborhood. And throughout 1998, we had been building towards getting a visible contingent on South Asians to participate in the October 22nd National Day of Protest to Stop Police Brutality, Repression, and the Criminalization of a Generation. This is perhaps the process that most contributed to our growth. We went out into predominantly South Asian neighborhoods to leaflet, poster, and talk to people about their experiences with police brutality. In so doing, we realized that police brutality is, in fact, a reality for many South Asians. Others voiced opinions about the general state of repression that they feel, particularly under the current regime of Mayor Giuliani. We also organized a forum to address the issue of police brutality within the South Asian community. Here, South Asians heard from Margarita Rosario, one of the founders of Parents against Police Brutality, whose son and nephew were both shot in the back by two cops, former bodyguards of Mayor Giuliani. October 22nd was a huge event for us. We brought a large and vocal crowd, and through the organizing for that event, we became South Asians against Police Brutality and Racism.

Protest is an essential part of our work. We believe in the importance of showing the powers that be that people are watching and willing to take to the streets. We have taken our banner to many protests, including the Million Youth March, Racial Justice Day, the April 24th Millions for Mumia March in Philadelphia, the Ten Mile March against Police Brutality in New Jersey, many marches and rallies in response to the killing of Amadou Diallo, and smaller rallies and marches on behalf of individual families. We have also supported the Stolen Lives Project, an attempt to document cases of people killed by police in the United States since 1990. The latest book has recorded more than 2,000 names, exposing the symptomatic nature of the epidemic.

We are a group of progressive South Asians, but we do come from a number of different political backgrounds. Some of us believe in revolution and support the people's wars in Nepal and Peru. Some of us believe in revolution, but our ideas about the theory and practice of it are still in formation. Some of us believe in reform and work closely with other groups that provide services through non-profit or community groups. Some of us are new to political action, but have the necessary rage to begin. We support many progressive and revolutionary movements, including the struggle to free Mumia Abu-Jamal and other political prisoners, the movements against America's imperialist wars in the Gulf and other parts of the world, and movements on behalf of immigrants, workfare workers, taxi workers, and street vendors. Various members of the group conduct their own political studies, delving into Marxist and revolutionary literature. However, we have not undertaken any formal political study as a group. We exchange ideas and literature informally, but have centered most of our group discussions on strategy, purpose, and policy.

Our mix of national identities, political ideas, class backgrounds, and life experiences, is unique. With all these issues and differences, we have been successful in maintaining unity and moving forward in our work. We are at a point now where we can define ourselves more clearly and develop a more formal structure. We recently finished a draft of our first mission statement, and have begun to have regular meetings, beyond just the nitty-gritty planning meetings. This stage of our development is exciting, because there is more time to consider questions that did not seem so immediate before. What is our role in the South Asian community? There are a number of groups that have begun to challenge the rightist establishment in the South Asian community, and we have supported and been supported by those groups. But as an internal progressive movement, it is at the very beginnings of developing a class analysis and class consciousness. So far, SAPBR's focus has been limited, to create a visible and vocal South Asian presence in the fight against police brutality. In so doing, many class issues within the South Asian community do emerge. How will we integrate an emerging class analysis into our workings as a group? How will we resolve differences within the group? This article is our first attempt to document our brief history. It is a crucial time for us. We are poised to push the limits and redefine the nature of South Asian political action in this country.

Asians for Mumia/Jericho contingent
Millions for Mumia demonstration, Philadelphia 1999
Photo credit: Wayne Lum

RADICAL RESISTANCE IN CONSERVATIVE TIMES
New Asian American Organizations in the 1990s

Diane C. Fujino and Kye Leung

Thirty years after the emergence of the Asian American Movement, new Asian American formations continue to expand the struggle. However, like other U.S.-based social movements, the Asian American Movement today is qualitatively different than in the 1960s and 70s. The political-economic landscape of the 1990s is much more conservative. Economic restructuring, the rise in conservativism, including Asian American neo-conservatives, and FBI and police repression past and present, have left the radical movements in a weakened condition.[1] Within the Asian American Movement, we witnessed the dissolution in the late 1980s and early 1990s of revolutionary formations with substantial Asian membership such as the League of Revolutionary Struggle. Yet radical Asian American organizing continues, primarily among the youth. And it is our contention that early 1998 marked the beginning of a qualitative upsurge in the Movement.

This chapter focuses on five radical Asian organizations that formed in the 1990s.[2] We did not include liberal or progressive groups such as social service agencies, non-profit organizations, nor worker's centers; nor radical formations that primarily focus on homeland anti-imperialist struggles given the focus of this anthology (though we recognize the continuity between local and international activism); nor Asian American activists in multiracial or predominantly White revolutionary groups. We chose to focus on groups rather than individuals because it takes organization to create sustained social change. While the groups examined here represent the majority of radical pan-Asian organizations that have emerged in the 1990s, there are a few new radical formations that were not included; we were unable to contact them or they had already dissolved by the late 1990s. In addition, we are not highlighting new Asian formations in New York City that are already represented in this anthology (articles by Wayne Lum and Tinku Sengupta) and tend to have progressive politics. While preliminary, this paper is the first to examine the contours of radical Asian American organizations formed in the 1990s. We hope it will lead to further explorations into radical Asian America.

Background on New Radical Organizations

This chapter examines five radical Asian American organizations: API FORCE, ASIAN!, ACTION, the Asian Left Forum, and the Asian Revolutionary Circle. The assessment of these groups is based on interviews with members, published documents, internal papers, informal conversations with activists, and our direct participation in some of these groups and in the Asian American Movement.[3]

Members of API FORCE, or Asians and Pacific Islanders for Community Empowerment, came together in Northern California at a September 1994 meeting to discuss "The State of the Asian American Movement." Out of that meeting, and simultaneous with the frustration various Asian American activists experienced over cultural insensitivity in the Proposition 187 campaign, about a dozen activists established an organization to voice progressive concerns of the Asian and Pacific Islander (API) community. API FORCE was founded in January 1995 through the leadership of Eric Mar, George Iechika-McKinney, Dan Nishijima, and Rhonda Ramirez. The mission and purpose of API FORCE, as identified in its membership booklet, is to: "analyze mainstream political thought and develop progressive ideological alternatives; empower Asian and Pacific Islander communities through education, political participation and grassroots organizing; and support and be a resource for other organizations working for Asian and Pacific Islander empowerment and against racism, sexism, homophobia, xenophobia, classism, and oppression in all its forms." API FORCE calls itself a "progressive," mass-based organization, an ideology that is reflected in the language of its mission and purpose and in some of its activities, especially in the electoral arena. In addition to the 1994 anti-immigrant Proposition 187, API FORCE organized around Proposition 209, the anti-affirmative action initiative passed by California voters in 1996; immigrant rights in response to the passage of the 1996 Welfare Reform Bill; and the successful electoral campaign of Tom Ammiano to the San Francisco Board of Supervisors. Among the five groups, API FORCE works the most within establishment channels. But API FORCE's other activities and Principles of Unity, modeled after the Black Panther Party's ten-point platform, reveal a radical politic, especially in its efforts to promote political education on North Korea and to expose the impact of U.S. militarization on Asian women. Also, one of the points of unity reads, "...We want to democratically transform the U.S. economic system of globalized capitalism and replace it with a truly egalitarian society in which all people can attain their full human potential." While API FORCE has veteran activists, the active membership is mainly in their twenties. There is also a diversity of Asian backgrounds and more women than men in the group. Currently, George Iechika-McKinney, Jung Hee Choi, Sun Lee, Rand Quinn, and Sinai Tongol sit on the Leadership Council.

ASIAN!, or Asian Sisters (& Brothers) for Ideas in Action Now!, began in November 1994 in Santa Barbara, California, after students in an Asian feminism class attended a Los Angeles rally protesting Jessica McClintock's failure to pay Chinese garment workers. Diane Fujino, Robyn Rodriguez, and Cheryl Deptowicz established ASIAN! as a radical political group to uplift humanity, with an emphasis on improving conditions facing Asian and Asian American women. As men joined the group, the name changed to include "brothers," but the focus on women's leadership remained. Given the lack of radical activism in Santa Barbara and in line with

ASIAN!'s belief that systemic oppression underlies and connects multiple issues, ASIAN! has organized political forums and campaigns around, among other topics, garment workers; sex industry; political prisoners, particularly focusing on Puerto Rican POWs and letter writing to California political prisoners; and anti-imperialist struggles in the United States, Philippines, Hawaii, North and South Korea, Okinawa, Puerto Rico, and Africa. ASIAN! has introduced political issues to the campus community and its membership by bringing prominent radicals to speak on the UCSB campus, including Yuri Kochiyama, Geronimo ji Jaga, Ramona Africa, and Rafael Cancel Miranda. ASIAN! also organized coalitions to oppose attacks on affirmative action by the University of California regents and by Proposition 209, and since 1995, organized to save the life of Mumia Abu-Jamal, the only political prisoner on death row. Despite a desire to include community members, ASIAN! remains a small, predominantly student group with substantially more women than men and a diverse Asian membership in addition to a few non-Asian members.

ACTION, the Asian Pacific Islander Collective to Initiate Opportunities Now!, formed in 1995 to focus on Asian American youth organizing in Los Angeles, primarily through cultural-political work. Under the leadership of founder Jason Nawa as well as Tracy Kiriyama, Sunny Le, and Ryan Yokota, ACTION became an organizing space for recent college graduates, college students, and high school students. The group functions with a non-hierarchical, collective structure, with an emphasis on developing leadership skills, raising political consciousness, and building a group culture and personal relationships among members. Its radical ideology is reflected in its Principles of Unity, which include community control of institutions; opposition to global capitalism, racism, sexism, and heterosexism; and basic human rights for all people. Through their two Art Attacks, the group used cultural-political work to reach out to youth and publicize community issues. In conjunction with the 1960s and 70s Asian American Movement group, Yellow Brotherhood, ACTION started a tutorial project at Culver City High School, which has served to provide concrete services as well as to link the youth to the previous generation of activists. While initially located in Little Tokyo, ACTION soon became pan-Asian in membership; about half its members are women.

The Asian Left Forum (ALF) represented the first nationwide meeting of veteran and newer Asian American Leftists in the past couple of decades. Held on May 17, 1998, in Los Angeles, following the "Serve the People" conference on Asian American community activism, this all-day, non-sectarian meeting brought together about 100 activists, double the anticipated attendance, to "strategize radical politics in Asian communities in the United States," with a focus on the struggles of working-class immigrant communities. The ALF called for Asian American Leftists, radicals, and revolutionaries to unite, and its principles of unity identified global capitalism, imperialism, racism, patriarchal domination, and heterosexism as the root causes of oppression. Still, the forum itself focused on a progressive-to-radical agenda. Local chapters in the Bay Area, Los Angeles, and New York have, to varying degrees, continued the work, organizing forums on anti-imperialist struggles in Asia, including Okinawa, Korea, the Philippines, East Timor, and Burma; the Kosovo war; the prison industrial complex; and the role of electoral politics in revolutionary organizing. While the ALF is comprised of diverse membership in terms of age, activist experience, political ideology, gender, ethnic background, and geographic location, the active core is predominantly twenty-something. Jung Hee Choi, Alyssa Kang, Sun Lee, Eric Tang, and Ryan Yokota sit on the National Planning Committee. A second national meeting is planned for early 2000.

Asian Revolutionary Circle (ARC) emerged in Boston in Summer 1998, after its founders, Kye Leung, Meizhu Lui, and Kim Mach, met at the Asian Left Forum in Los Angeles. ARC, initially called Asian Roots and Community, began as a group of liberals, progressives, and radicals who came together to explore issues of identity and "to reclaim our stolen history." But within six months, through struggles over ideology, ARC became increasingly radical and the more liberal members left the group. Its name changed to reflect its new revolutionary politics. Its Ten Point Platform reflects this radical ideology, focusing on self-determination, reclamation of Asian American history, and an end to racism, sexism, heterosexism, class exploitation, and imperialism. ARC holds weekly political study groups for its members, organizes talks on Asian American history and racism in local high schools, raises funds to provide an after-school program and free books on Asian American history to students, invites veteran activists to speak at their meetings, and supports the Chinese Progressive Association in organizing residents to oppose gentrification in Boston's Chinatown. Its focus on Chinatown reflects its commitment to the community as well as its predominantly Chinese membership, although ARC strives to be pan-Asian. Its membership, half of whom are women, is predominantly high school and college students.

Political Assessment of New Radical Organizations

What can an examination of these five organizations tell us about the state of new organizing in radical Asian America? Here we are look for themes, commonalities, and differences among the groups to shed light on the nature of radical Asian American organizing in the conservative 1990s.

Continuing the History of Radical Resistance

Radical groups that emerged in the 1990s have the opportunity to learn from experienced Asian American activists. Though many activists of the 1960s and 70s are no longer active today,[4] there remains a substantial number of veteran activists who maintain a radical ideology, some of whom are active in the Movement today. To varying degrees, younger activists have turned to the veterans to learn from their experiences. API FORCE began through the combined efforts of veteran and newer Asian American activists. Even today, when most of its active membership are in their twenties, the veterans continue to provide an important source of guidance and support. The ALF, though initiated and maintained largely by young activists, was unprecedented in its ability to bring together a sizable number of veteran and newer activists. ARC has consciously sought out veteran Asian activists in the Boston area, organizing speaking engagements by former members of the revolutionary organizations, I Wor Kuen and the League of Revolutionary Struggle. Ten ARC members also traveled to New York City where they met with veteran revolutionaries, many of whom they had never heard of before, including Yuri Kochiyama and Fred Ho. ASIAN! has invited numerous Asian and Pacific Islander radicals to Santa Barbara for public forums accompanied by potlucks and/or political education studies: Yuri Kochiyama, Rev. Michael Yasutake, Mitsuye Yamada, David Monkawa, Fred Ho, Haunani-kay Trask, and Pilipino leaders of BAYAN Rafael Baylosis, Rafael "Ka Paeng" Mariano, and Joe Navidad. And in Los Angeles, ACTION has had the opportunity to meet with veteran activists such as former Yellow Brotherhood members Kenwood Jung and Nick Nagatani.

What is clear is that these newer formations are aware of their connection with the past generation of radicals. It is because of the efforts of the previous generation of Asian American activists—for example, via ethnic studies and Movement publications—that the current generation knows some of its radical history. Moreover, the current generation is continuing the effort to uncover the still little known history of revolutionary Asian America. In doing so, the younger activists are seeking the guidance of the experienced activists, drawing inspiration from them, and encouraging the veterans to work with the youth to create change today. As API FORCE states on their website: "We walk into the new millennium in the footsteps of our ancestors—the railroad builders, miners, anti-imperialist exiles, farmworkers and farmers, picture brides, laundrymen, teachers, cannery and garment workers, union and student activists, and revolutionaries. We acknowledge our Asian and Pacific Islander people's historical continuum of struggle and resistance to oppression in the United States and carry on our work in this proud tradition."

Radical Organizing in the Conservative 1990s

It is important to notice that these groups emerged beginning in the mid-1990s. While there has been a continuity of political organizing in the U.S., there are also fluctuations in the strength of the Movement. The mid-1990s, especially in California, represents one of those shifts. Beginning in 1994, the Right-wing implemented and California voters passed a series of conservative initiatives designed to roll back the gains of the Civil Rights Movement: Proposition 187 attacked immigrants rights; Propositions 184 functioned to criminalize and imprison youth, the poor, and people of color; Proposition 209 banned affirmative action; and Proposition 227 banned bilingual education. Because repression breeds resistance, these measures—along with the scheduled state execution of Mumia Abu-Jamal in 1995—generated mass progressive organizing. In this context, API FORCE was established to organize for immigrant rights, affirmative action, and welfare reform. While other factors influenced the creation of ASIAN! more directly (the convergence of its three founders in a UCSB Asian feminism class) and ACTION (the founders' need for organizational space after college), the right-wing initiatives also

145

influenced the formation and early activities of these groups.

Also in response to the increase in right-wing activity throughout the nation, along with stepped up economic restructuring and neoliberal policies globally, it is our contention that the Movement began a qualitative upswing in early 1998, motion that had been building since the mid-1990s. In 1998 alone, there was an exceptional number of nationwide gatherings of activists in the Asian American community (Serve the People conference on Asian American activism at UCLA and the Asian Left Forum in Los Angeles, both in May 1998), in the African American community (Black Radical Congress in Chicago in June 1998), and on issues of political prisoners and prisons (Jericho 98 march and rally for political prisoners in Washington D.C. in March 1998; Critical Resistance conference on the prison industrial complex at Berkeley in September 1998). Moreover, 1998 represented 100 years of U.S. colonialism in Hawaii, Guam, Philippines, Puerto Rican, and elsewhere. Related to this, significant activity in the Puerto Rican movement has taken place in 1998 and 1999. Large marches and rallies in multiple cities were organized to protest a century of U.S. imperialism; students shut down the San Juan airport to protest the privatization of the telephone company; unprecedented numbers have been protesting the U.S. military presence on the Puerto Rican island of Vieques since a U.S. bomb killed a civilian in April 1999; and in September 1999, eleven Puerto Rican political prisoners, incarcerated for close to 20 years, were released from prison. Grounding these events in imperialism is significant. One of the important revolutions in contemporary times is the Zapatista struggle in Chiapas, Mexico. And this revolution was kicked off in response to 500 years of Western conquest of Indigenous Peoples.[5] In 1999, the Zapatista revolution inspired students to shut down, for six months at the time of this writing, the largest, public university in Latin America, the National Autonomous University of Mexico (UNAM), in response to International Monetary Fund impositions to raise tuition fees, and to fight for the democratization of the university. Also during this period, in Asia and the Pacific Islands, workers and students have organized massive protests against International Monetary Fund austerity measures as well as the massacre in East Timor. It was in this context of increased activism that the Asian Left Forum was organized. And this nationwide gathering inspired the formation of ARC in Boston.

Given the socio-political climate, what does it mean to be radical in the 1990s? The revolutionary fervor that characterized the 1960s and 70s, with its militant actions and socialist and/or revolutionary nationalist ideology, has dissipated. And while revolutionaries continue to be active in the 1990s, the overall nature of the social movements has changed. Today, the radical wing of the Asian American Movement is characterized by groups that critique racism and capitalism and seek to transform social institutions, but do not actively work to build a radical working-class movement or to create a socialist state. Still these groups can be identified as radical because their analysis of society and their practice are rooted in systemic oppression, namely, capitalism, imperialism, racism, sexism, and heterosexism. The statement by API FORCE sums up the radical ideology of these new groups: "We...are committed to building a world of peace and justice, where people's needs come before corporate profits. We envision a new society based on multiculturalism, democracy, mutual respect, and economic and social justice for all."[6] Yet contrast this to the Twelve Point Platform of I Wor Kuen (IWK), an early 1970s Asian American group, which explicitly called for socialism, community control of not just institutions but also of land, and preparation "to defend our communities against repression and for revolutionary armed war against the gangsters, businessmen, politicians, and police."

Modeled after the platforms of IWK and the Black Panther Party (BPP), four of the five groups have developed Principles of Unity or platforms that guide their actions. While it is widely known that the BPP influenced many revolutionary groups including IWK, it is little known that one of the three authors of the BPP's platform is a Japanese American revolutionary who was a high-ranking leader in the BPP (see Richard Aoki interview in this anthology). Moreover, given the increased conservativeness of the 1990s, it is not surprising that none of the current groups have as revolutionary an ideology as IWK. Still what is radical about the platforms of these new formations is their opposition to global capitalism, imperialism, racism, sexism, and heterosexism. ASIAN! too explicitly supports this radical ideology in their Guiding Principles. In addition, ACTION, ARC, and API FORCE call for basic human rights for all people, including affordable housing, food, universal health care, a living wage, and a multicultural education, and for environmental justice—the latter being a new demand not identified by IWK or BPP.

In the context of the 1990s, with its conservative mainstream politics and low revolutionary activity, it is not surprising that radical—and not revolutionary—Asian American groups would emerge. After all, it is difficult today to build an Asian-focused revolutionary party. Many of the newer radical activists are not ideologically or organizationally prepared to establish a revolutionary party; many of the veterans who previously were in cadre formations have personal and political differences that continue to preclude their unity; and many young people, new to politics, are not ready to join a revolutionary group. Moreover, given that multiracial or predominantly White revolutionary groups exist today, many of which include a few Asian members, some would argue that no revolutionary Asian organization exists today because there is no need for nation- or race-based organizations. As global capitalism expands and the meaning of national boundaries becomes less relevant, activists will no longer organize around nation- or race-specific formations. We disagree with this argument. By contrast, that these five radical Asian-specific groups have emerged in the 1990s and that their ideology embraces the need for API community control of institutions and resources points to the continuing significance of nation- or race-based organizing. Certainly, most activists today agree that one's analysis must be international in focus. But this does not preclude working towards control of institutions, resources, and land bases by communities or sovereign nations in conjunction with, or as a step towards, international socialism.

While broadly defined as radical, the five groups do self-identify with somewhat different ideologies. Most notable is that API FORCE consciously chose to organize a progressive organization, even though many of its initial members were radicals. Even the Bay Area, one of the most politically conscious areas of the country, lacked a progressive API presence in the 1990s. So API FORCE believed that broad based support was needed before building a revolutionary party. In addition, ARC is the only new Asian-specific organization to use the term "revolutionary" in their name. The other groups have "safe" names that in fact do not reflect their radical politics. Compared to other groups, ARC uses more revolutionary language. For example, ARC calls its statement a "Ten-Point Platform," after the BPP and IWK; by contrast, ACTION, ALF, and API FORCE use the more generalized language of "Principles of Unity." But in most ways, ARC's practice does not appear any more revolutionary than the other groups. It is our contention that underlying these expressed differences, the ideologies—and especially the practice—of these five groups are actually quite similar.

Changing Social Realities

When activists talk about changing social realities, they think of change at two levels. At one level, activists work to challenge oppressive institutions and systems in order to improve the quality of people's lives. At another level, activists themselves get transformed as they participate in the collective struggle for justice. Through the grassroots movement, activists learn organizing and leadership skills, sharpen their political analyses, expand their knowledge base, and significantly, grow in their ability to interact with people in humane ways while striving to build the new social relationships needed in a non-capitalist society. Change at either level is no easy task. But these new groups have attempted to create social change at both levels.

At the societal level, API FORCE works to challenge institutional power through the legal and political systems. After the passage of 1996 Welfare Reform Bill, which affected low-income Asian Americans, API FORCE embarked on a long-term campaign for economic and social justice. As part of this, they organized to re-elect Tom Ammiano, an openly gay, White progressive community activist, to the San Francisco Board of Supervisors. Here API FORCE differs from liberal groups in its criticism of both the Democrats and Republicans, between whom API FORCE sees few differences. As a progressive-to-radical grassroots organization, API FORCE does not view electoral politics as their main political strategy or ultimate goal, but advocates that "electoral politics, as in everything we do, should be used as a tool to build a stronger, more unified left and progressive movement."[7] API FORCE's support for Ammiano was part of an overall strategy to gain economic justice based on Ammiano's strong support of programs providing food, affordable housing, and living wages to the poor. As API FORCE wrote in their 1998 newsletter: "Organizing around issues, rather than individuals, will help give more focus to broader concerns of social justice and change. However, it is not enough to simply push for yes or no votes. Without also bringing left and progressive ideas into electoral organizing, a strong grassroots base will not be sustainable after election day."[8] After getting a politician committed to food, housing, and wages elected as President of the Board of Supervisors, API FORCE moved into Phase II of its economic justice campaign: Getting a food stamp program written into the 2000 budget.

API FORCE members gained much organizing experience through the Ammiano campaign. By reaching out to people on the streets, they learned how to communicate with people—what to say, what language to use, and to whom to speak: "The people who responded most to what we had to say about affordable housing and food stamps were mothers shopping with their children, the elderly and young adults struggling to pay the rent. We gained the most support from these kinds of folks, talking with them about issues that affect all of our lives."[9] They also faced sharp criticism for supporting Ammiano over less progressive Asian American candidates. But this struggle exposed the politics of different groups and API FORCE discovered who their political allies were.

Like API FORCE, ASIAN! also worked through the grassroots electoral process to organize against Proposition 209, the anti-affirmative action initiative passed by California voters in 1996. Although Prop. 209 passed statewide, in areas where active anti-209 campaigns were organized, the initiative was defeated. Here ASIAN! played a leading role in the UCSB coalition and API FORCE's efforts helped to sway the Bay Area Asian American community. It is important to distinguish the work of radical groups like ASIAN! from that of liberal groups that also work on reform campaigns. While many liberal groups see affirmative action as an end in itself or as a means for reducing discrimination, radicals argue that affirmative action was a concession the U.S. government gave to the people at a time when the radical Movement was demanding community control of the workplace and schools. Through their anti-209 work, ASIAN! educated the community about how the 1960 Master Plan in California created a system which tracked poor and minority students into vocational jobs and sharply reduced their access to the university. ASIAN! contrasted the 1990s call for affirmative action to the 1960s call for open admissions for all people of color into the university. Still, unlike a few revolutionary groups who shun reform work as counter-revolutionary, ASIAN! fought to save affirmative action in California and throughout the University of California because they recognized that college and work opportunities would be cut off for people of color, women, and the poor were they to lose even the mild benefits of affirmative action. Thus countering repressive electoral measures is necessary, but not sufficient. Working on reform does not make one reformist; here radical groups differ from liberal formations. Like most radical and revolutionary groups, ASIAN! believes it is imperative to improve concrete conditions of people's lives while providing a radical analysis of social issues and fighting for militant and just—and not simply moderate—demands.

ASIAN! has also helped to politicize the UCSB campus by organizing speaking engagements for radical activists. They have used these events to make connections to larger social issues. For example, when ASIAN! brought Geronimo ji Jaga to campus in February 1998, he had acquired celebrity status—at least among progressives and Leftists. The former Black Panther had recently been released after serving 27 years for a crime he did not commit. Recognizing his popularity and the sparse mainstream interest in political prisoners, ASIAN! capitalized on his presence to discuss the general issue of incarcerated activists and to mobilize for Jericho 98, the nationwide march and rally for political prisoners—issues strongly supported by Geronimo. Moreover, by organizing forums on, among other issues, Asian women in the garment industry, Puerto Rican independence, and U.S. government efforts to dislocate the Dineh (Navajo) from their ancestral lands in Big Mountain, Arizona, ASIAN! has brought awareness—and a radical analysis—to little known issues. As a result, campus organizations look to ASIAN! to provide political leadership, and significantly, the campus as a whole has grown in its political organizing. Focusing on a younger—and possibly less petty bourgeois—constituency, ARC and ACTION have helped to politicize high school students. ARC holds workshops on Asian American history and activism for high school students and is fundraising to establish an after-school program to regularize these studies. And ACTION established a tutorial program for local high school students, including the children of former Yellow Brotherhood activists.

The group the ALF targets is the community of activists. Through its May 1998 forum, the ALF has been successful in advancing nationwide discussions about the Asian American Left; creating increased dialogue among Asian radicals regardless of their involvement in the ALF; bringing together veteran activists, some of whom had not interacted in years; and bringing together newer and more experienced activists. In part due to the ALF—from the networking developed there to the Forum's inspiration to strong criticism of it—noteworthy Asian American political formations and projects have emerged, including two anthology projects on the radical Asian American Movement, the Asian American roundtable at the Critical Resistance conference, ARC, and the Ad Hoc committee in New York City that organized two panels of veteran and younger activists discussing the revolutionary Asian American Movement. But in other ways, the ALF has faced serious problems in building a radical or revolutionary Asian American presence. Perhaps its most significant problem is its lack of vision and purpose. At its May 1998 meeting, the ALF was unable to define its ideology or even to be clear that it was a Left formation. While its Principles of Unity are clearly radical, the group's unwillingness to discuss a working definition of "Left"—which some define as socialist and others as any politic left of liberal—resulted in a lack of ideological clarity. In addition, the ALF suffers from a confusion over its organizational structure. Though the National Planning Council agreed that the ALF would function as a "united front" and not a network or cadre organization, there is confusion among the general Asian American Left, and even among the ALF leadership, as to the function that the ALF should serve. These problems help to explain why the ALF is struggling to organize its first follow-up meeting to the initial forum.

The local chapters of the ALF have been more active than the nationwide body. Even so the locals, which function with great deal of regional autonomy, have done less work than hoped for over the past year and a half. Still their programs have served to raise political consciousness. In the Bay Area, the activists organized political forums on the role of electoral politics in revolutionary organizing, on student movements, and on examining the role of non-profit organizations in creating social change. The Los Angeles ALF has organized five forums: one on the labor movement; two on international solidarity work around anti-imperialist struggles in Okinawa, Korea, the Philippines, Burma, and East Timor; one on the war in Kosovo; and one on prison issues, focusing on the Juvenile Justice Initiative in California. In addition, the Los Angeles ALF worked with the local chapters of the Black Radical Congress and New Raza Left to form a People of Color Coalition Against War. New York City ALF has organized forums on the prison industrial complex and about young Korean, Pilipino, and South Asian activists working in international solidarity movements. The focus of much of ALF's work has not been on educating the public per se, but rather on studying methods of organizing. For example, Los Angeles activists explored ways people can conduct international solidarity work, and Bay Area activists discussed the role of electoral politics and non-profits in radical organizing. As such, the forums serve primarily as internal studies, though they are open to the public.

A look at the diversity of ALF's programming reveals its multi-issue approach, which is also reflected in ASIAN! and, to a lesser extent, in the other groups. These radical groups focus simultaneously on multiple political issues (e.g., worker's rights, anti-imperialist struggles worldwide, the prison industrial complex) because of their ideological belief that these issues are interconnected and rooted in capitalism and imperialism, in addition to racism. Thus, these groups, to varying degrees, find themselves tackling multiple issues simultaneously and striving to expose the underlying systemic causes.

In addition, the five groups oppose sexism in society and within the Movement and work to promote women's leadership. ASIAN! began as a women's group to provide an organizing space for women to develop leadership skills in an environment free of—or less affected by—male dominance. Even though men have joined, women, in theory and practice, have the primary leadership roles; there have been few, if any, problems with sexism within the organization; and they implemented a policy that an Asian woman (alone or in conjunction with another member) must represent the group at public events. API FORCE established a Women's Collective in 1998 when they learned about sexual harassment occurring in a progressive API community organization. In addition to establishing a sexual harassment policy, API FORCE initiated an open letter, endorsed by other API groups, calling progressive activists and organizations to address sexism in the workplace and in the movement for social justice. Though currently inactive, the Women's Collective also published a women's issue of the 'zine, The World is Yours, to create a space for API women to voice their ideas. The ALF also mandated that at least one women will be among the two local representatives to the National Planning Council. The five groups also oppose heterosexism, though their sparse programming on gay and lesbian issues has resulted in few open queers among their membership.

These radical formations also have serious shortcomings. All of the groups suffer from small numbers of highly dedicated activists—no doubt, in part, a reflection of the times. Despite many activists' realization that effective organizing can be accomplished with a few committed organizers—quality is indeed more important than quantity—the small numbers do put a strain on the campaigns and on the activists themselves. In addition, groups like ASIAN! and ACTION suffer from fairly high turn-over rates. ASIAN!'s membership is affected by the nature of campus-based organizing—students often join political groups late in their college career and then graduate—and because, unlike major cities, most students leave the Santa Barbara area after graduating. ACTION has had three distinctive generations of activists in the four years of its existence, largely because after gaining community organizing training in ACTION, they move onto other projects and organizations. As a result, these groups must constantly focus on recruitment—and retention—efforts. Moreover, it is difficult for the groups to advance their politics when there are few stable, advanced members among the constant influx of new, inexperienced members.

Moreover, the overwhelming presence of college students and professionals—and the limited participation by the lower-echelon working class—affects the practice and commitment of members. Though the resources of students and professionals enable them to work for social change, their middle-class status and options allow them an out when the work gets too demanding. The predominant student membership of ARC also helps explain why they believe that "the youth will be in the proletarian vanguard," in contrast to the emphasis placed on the working class by revolutionary socialist groups. Still, many of the activities of these groups reflect their ideological commitment to the immigrant and working-class poor. For example, API FORCE is pushing for a food stamp program, ARC works in Boston's Chinatown, and ACTION, ALF, and ASIAN! have supported working-class labor struggles and issues of prisons and political prisoners.

Finally, the lack of ideological clarity in all these groups presents problems. As Fred Ho noted: "In fighting the system, the question of ideology is key: If you're opposed to sexism, homophobia, worker exploitation, state repression, racism, etc., then what do you replace these with? What is the goal of activism: reform or revolution? What is fundamental to making real, systemic social change: Changing political officials, legislation and media representation, or political and economic power via ownership and control over the means of production?"[10] Within ASIAN!, a conscious decision was made to be opposed to systemic oppression without advocating a replacement system such as socialism because few students are politically ready to join a socialist group. This decision has proven correct for work on their particular college campus where radical organizing is sparse. But as members develop politically, they begin to ask the same questions posed above by Fred Ho. And ASIAN!'s ideology is unable to provide the answers. Likewise, the lack of ideological clarity is a major reason why the ALF has had difficulty moving forward, and also helps to explain the retention problems within ACTION. API FORCE's lack of ideological clarity seems to present less of a problem, possibly because as the least radical of the five groups, API FORCE members struggle less over radical alternatives. Within ARC, a struggle over ideology six months ago resulted in the group embracing a more radical politic and in driving out half of the membership. Though it is too early to assess the impact of this change, ARC members do believe that a smaller group of committed radicals will create more effective social change than a larger group of liberals.

To increase ideological clarity and radicalize its members, ARC and ASIAN! have implemented regular political education studies into its meetings. ARC has weekly study groups in which veteran activists guide the group in grasping Marxism, Leninism, and Mao Zedong Thought. In addition to its public forums, ASIAN! has political study sessions once a month during the academic year and more rigorous studies during the summer. ASIAN! also requires that new members attend a series of study sessions to became familiarized with ASIAN!'s politics. ACTION implements its political education primarily through its leadership training, where readings introduce members to race, class, and gender issues. Eventually, at the end of the training, members are introduced to basic Maoist readings such as "On Practice" and "On Contradiction" that help guide their practice. ALF and API FORCE gain political education through their public forums.

Despite their shortcomings, these groups have been able to raise consciousness among their members and, to varying degrees, among their communities. They have also made some concrete changes to better their communities. And in the process of working to create change, the members have learned organizing skills and gained self-confidence, acquired some ideological training, and have tried to grow as human beings and as political activists. What is commendable is that these activists, mostly in their twenties, have been struggling to effect social change despite the conservativeness of the times and the vacuum of revolutionary leadership.

Organizational Structure

The organizational structure of the five groups resembles that of the mass-based organizations of the 1960s and 70s more than that of Asian American cadre formations of a generation ago. Today's Asian American radical groups are structured to allow flexibility—so members can be involved according to their time availability, commitment, or desire. It seems the groups need to be flexible in order to retain their membership. If they demanded higher discipline—including giving high priority to the group's work, active participation in planning activities, attendance at all or most meetings, and demands for a revolutionary consciousness and practice—many members would leave. Certainly, there are multiracial or predominantly White revolutionary groups that require high levels of discipline, but no such revolutionary Asian American group exists today. Among today's radical groups, there are two main forms for organizing: The smaller groups operate on collective leadership and the larger groups have a more delineated structure.

As small, localized formations, ARC, ACTION, and ASIAN! operate based on collective decision-making, with high levels of democracy. These groups believe that the collective can accomplish more than the individual. Also, the collective process helps members feel a sense of "ownership" for the group—that they are responsible for the successes or failures of the group and that they can contribute to its activities and direction. These groups believe in the need for democracy and for enabling members to voice their opinions. The structure of these groups matches their objectives of building the leadership of youth, of women, and of APIs. They recognize that internalized sexism, internalized racism, and cultural values such as respect for authority can create obstacles to speaking out. With encouragement and practice, many members gain the confidence and skills to formulate political ideas and articulate them. The collective operations of these groups also help to foster closer social relationships among members, as do their weekly meetings.

It is important to recognize that the small size of these groups, usually less than a dozen members, makes it possible to operate based on collective leadership and collective decision-making. ASIAN! knows this from experience. After the defeat of Proposition 209 triggered a desire for action, ASIAN!'s membership more than doubled to close to 30 people. ASIAN! continued to try to operate based on collective leadership because members were reluctant to implement any hierarchical structure. The results were disastrous. Members were generally frustrated with the slowness of decision making and bored with all the talking. It was hard to keep track of who was responsible for various tasks, making accountability difficult to manage. Another frustration was that the larger size made it difficult to develop the personal relationships and closeness that helps build group unity. Though members are still reluctant to move away from collective decision-making, at a retreat to assess its internal functioning, ASIAN! decided that should it get large again, it would need to quickly implement an administrative committee that would be charged with making sure decisions are implemented and holding members accountable. The entire group would still make major decisions. An unfair hierarchy could be avoided by opening the administrative committee to anyone who is willing to do the work. Part of ASIAN!'s reluctance to implement a less collective structure stemmed from their misunderstanding of collective leadership. They thought, as many people do, that collective leadership means everyone must participate equally and have equal influence in the group. But as George Iechika-McKinney noted about API FORCE, "Hierarchy is based on level of involvement. We want to acknowledge that people who do more work should be valued." This statement recognizes that within any volunteer organization, some people are more willing or able to take on responsibility and leadership. And these people will have more influence on the direction and activities of the group; that is, they possess more "legitimate power" based on, among other factors, commitment, hard work, and political experience. What does need to be guarded against is when individuals gain "unearned power"—influence ascribed because of, for example, social status or friendship—or when individuals are shut out of leadership positions because of structural forces such as sexism or the lack of childcare. But sometimes it is difficult to disentangle legitimate power from unearned power. In ASIAN!, the most politically experienced person is also the only professor among its predominantly student membership. And in API FORCE, where highly committed members have become friends, there have been times when organizational work was done through friendships rather than through organizational mechanisms. Here, API FORCE, ASIAN!, and ACTION are aware of internal power dynamics and have changed their structures or otherwise worked to reduce unearned hierarchies.

Along with its collective structure, ACTION and ASIAN!, in particular, are designed to build the organizational and leadership skills of young people. ACTION, working in conjunction with a progressive community organization People's Core, implements a curriculum to teach its members community organizing skills. ASIAN! makes leadership training part of its formal structure. Members are encouraged to take on leadership, and because most are new to activism, this requires pairing a more experienced member with a less experienced one. In reality, a more experienced person may be someone who has organized an event only once or twice before. In addition, ASIAN! also established positions for members to train others on how to facilitate a meeting or public forum, to access funds from the university, or to access the media. In the other groups, leadership training also occurs, but through more informal mechanisms.

The size of API FORCE—about 60 members, including some 20 among the active core—precludes a collective model of organizing. Instead, API FORCE has, by far, the most delineated organizational structure. Overseeing the entire organization is the Leadership Council, comprised of the three divisional leaders and two at-large members. Its Politics Division organizes activities through its committees on economic justice, anti-Asian violence, Korean and international solidarity, and the women's collective. It also has two other divisions: Resource Management and Communications. The committees function with a fair degree of independence and any two members can form a committee. While many members join API FORCE through one of the committees, anyone who agrees with the Mission Statement can be a member regardless of their degrees of involvement. The Leadership Council meets once a month and the committees meet as needed.

As the only national formation, the ALF has a different organizational structure than the localized groups. Each ALF local chapter—Los Angeles, Bay Area, New York—operates with a high degree of regional autonomy. The minimum requirement is that ALF activities abide by the Principles of Unity. The locals meet irregularly, though they tend to meet once every month or so. In addition, the National Planning Committee—comprised of two representatives from each local, at least one of whom must be a woman—was established to develop national meetings. Today, three women and two men (New York has only one representative), all in their twenties, form the National Planning Committee.

An Upsurge in the Movement?: What Is To Be Done

In the 1990s, radical, grassroots Asian American organizations are working to counter oppressive systems and transform social institutions in an effort to build a more egalitarian society. They differ from social service agencies, non-profit organizations, liberal electoral groups, and other formations that are closely tied to the establishment. At the same time, today's formations differ from the revolutionary groupings that existed in the 1960s and 70s and even into the late 1980s. The new organizations are not as revolutionary in their ideology or actions and, as non-cadre formations, demand less discipline from their members. Yet what is remarkable is that there is a core of very committed activists—mostly in their twenties and often women—who are developing their organizing skills, strategies, and theoretical frameworks in a relative vacuum of revolutionary leadership.

These new radical formations operate with greater flexibility compared to the revolutionary Asian American organizations of the 1960s and 70s. They try to find ways for members with varying amounts of time and commitments to be involved. The need for flexibility reflects the conservatism of the times as well as the professionalization of activism. Certainly, the political fervor of the 1960s and 70s helped to popularize activism; similar conditions do not exist today. Plus, increased economic pressures mean that students must work longer hours and take larger course loads to avoid paying high tuition fees for additional semesters. What then drops off is student activism. Concomitantly, Asian American college graduates have greater opportunities to work in professional arenas, at least compared to a generation ago. Consequently, Asian American student activists often seek professional ways to express their political concerns—by working in social service agencies, non-profit community organizations, and in the cultural, educational, and legal arenas. This becomes problematic when this work replaces direct participation in the radical, grassroots movement. This can occur when a lawyer's activism is limited to pro bono work, when a cultural worker produces political poetry but fails to help organize for social change, or when one's social service or union job eats up all one's time so there is no direct engagement in the radical, grassroots movement. No doubt, the weakened state of the radical movements also makes professionalized political work more attractive. Frequently, young activists complain that no revolutionary organization exists that they want to join. Given the demands on people and the limited outlets for radical and revolutionary organizing, the radical organizations examined in this paper find that if their membership requirements are too high, members drop out. By contrast, some members leave these groups because they are looking for more advanced politics. Thus, it becomes necessary to create a variety of spaces, including revolutionary organizations, for Asian American activists.

One positive effect of the flexible approach of these new organizations is seen in their effort to develop the types of social relationships that do not reproduce the oppressive relations displayed under capitalism. Like in the past, political organizing today leads to friendships based on similar values, commitments, and activities. But today's groups are less harsh in their criticisms and less focused on determining the correct political line. This aids in building new social relationships, ones that will form of the basis of a new non-capitalist society. But today's new groups tend to err in the other direction—of not holding each other accountable to high standards and not giving enough constructive criticism—which tends to undermine the effectiveness of political organizing and individual growth.

What is needed is a revolutionary wing of the Asian American Movement. If we are correct that the current period represents the beginning of a qualitative upswing in the movements for social change, then the time is ripe to build the infrastructure to promote that growth. Activists will create those changes and, in turn, a changed environment, with mass popular support and revolutionary leadership, will facilitate advances in the Movement. Community-based progressive forces and radical formations already exist in the Asian American community. But we need to build Asian-focused revolutionary organization(s). As evidenced by the efforts of the ALF, this is an ambitious and difficult task. But it is called "the struggle" for a reason. To create this force, activists will need to intensify their commitment to social justice, reduce their reliance on professionalized activism, and increase their willingness to sacrifice for the future generations. This new revolutionary group might be worked out through the ALF, if it can overcome its problems. Otherwise, activists will need to develop a new formation that has ideological clarity, revolutionary politics, and clear goals and organizational structure. It will likely take the combined efforts of newer and veteran activists, the latter of whom will need to let go of old interpersonal conflicts and even outdated ideological disputes to achieve a principled unity. And it will be important for any new formations to replicate the models of organizing that promote women's leadership, as happened in the League of Revolutionary Struggle and is occurring in many of the new radical groups. But this new formation will also need to incorporate a wider range of the community than the students, professionals, and heterosexuals now dominating the radical Asian American Movement. If Asian revolutionaries can accomplish this, they will push forward not only the Asian American Movement, but also the entire U.S. Left. And the committed youth and women of these new radical organizations are in a prime position to facilitate this motion.

ENDNOTES

1. See Jeremy Blecher & Tim Costello, Global Village or Global Pillage: Economic Reconstruction From the Bottom Up (Boston: South End Press, 1994); Ward Churchill & Jim Vander Wall, Agents of Repression: The FBI's Secret War Against the Black Panther Party and the American Indian Movement (Boston: South End Press, 1988); Michael Omi & Howard Winant, Racial Formation in the United States, From the 1960s to the 1990s (NY: Routledge, 1994); Paul Ong, Edna Bonacich & Lucie Cheng, "The Political Economy of Capitalist Restructuring and the New Asian Immigration," in Ong, Bonacich & Cheng (Eds.), The New Asian Immigration in Los Angeles and Global Restructuring (Philadelphia: Temple University Press, 1994, pp. 3-35).

2. Although there is no single definition, we use the term "radical" to refer to the root cause of a problem—particularly capitalism and its global extension, imperialism, as well as racism, sexism, and heterosexism. Radicals analyze problems and devise strategies for combating systemic oppression. "Revolutionaries" go further than radicals in not only naming the problematic system, but also in advocating a replacement system such as socialism. By contrast, "liberal" groups tend to focus on the immediate problem without connecting it to larger structural forces. From a radical perspective, liberals are problematic because they are

swayed by their own self-interest (see Mao, "Combat Liberalism"). "Progressives" lie in between liberals and radicals. While they see race, gender, and class inequalities, their solutions often do not embody opposition to capitalism per se. Certainly, these categories are nuanced and complex, and an individual may not fit neatly within any one grouping. To give a concrete, yet simplified, illustration: Liberals oppose the low pay and difficult work conditions of garment workers, but only to the extent that paying higher wages does not significantly increase their clothing costs. Progressives oppose race, gender, and class inequalities, but it is radicals who advocate that labor exploitation is inevitable under capitalism, an economic system that requires low wages in order to increase the profits of the few big business owners. And revolutionaries argue that the only way to end labor exploitation is to build a socialist or communist society. Here we are examining one's political ideology and practice, which goes beyond the tactics one may use. We do not identify political orientations based on tactics because people with different politics can use the same tactics (e.g., civil disobedience). Thus, the militancy of a tactic can be decoupled from the analysis of the problem.

3. We are grateful to the following people for providing interviews, information, and materials about their organizations: Betty Chan, Caroline Choi, Sumaya Dinglasan, George Iechika-McKinney, Don Kim, Nadia Kim, Soudary Kittivong, Sun Lee, Meizhu Lui, Daniel Magpali, Mo Nishida, Robyn Rodriguez, Jee Ryu, Eric Tang, and Ryan Yokota. We appreciate insightful feedback on an earlier version of this manuscript from Betty Chan, Fred Ho, George Iechika-McKinney, Nadia Kim, Sun Lee, Mo Nishida, and Ryan Yokota. Thanks also go to the numerous activists with whom we have had informal discussions.

4. The FBI's COINTELPRO succeeded in murdering radical activists, imprisoning them, scaring them out of the Movement, and creating such a disruption in the revolutionary movements, especially in the African community, that many organizations collapsed and activists left the Movement. In addition, internal conflicts, familial and work demands, and limited resources undermined the revolutionary movement. By the mid-1970s, the visible revolutionary Asian American Movement had mainly dissolved. But Asian revolutionaries continued on throughout the 1980s in formations like the League of Revolutionary Struggle, which was two-third people of color, and to the present as independents or members of predominantly White or multiracial organizations.

5. While the Zapatistas struck on January 1, 1994, to protest the North American Free Trade Agreement, the original decision to start the armed phase began in 1992, with the commemoration of 500 years of conquest (Medea Benjamin, "Interview: Subcomandante Marcos," in Elaine Katzenberger (Ed.), First World, Ha Ha Ha! The Zapatista Challenge, San Francisco: City Lights, 1995, pp. 57-70).

6. "An Introduction to API FORCE," API FORCE's website, www.api-force.org.

7. "The Role of Electoral Politics in Progressive Organizing: Issues Not Candidates," The Force, newsletter of API FORCE, 1998, 1.

8. Ibid.

9. "Economic Justice for San Francisco," from API FORCE's website, www.api-force.org.

10. Fred Ho, "The Good, the Bad, and the Ugly-But-Necessary," in the present anthology.

THREE DECADES OF CLASS STRUGGLE ON CAMPUS
A Personal History

Merle Woo

Introduction

Without hesitation I can say that the 27 years I spent teaching as a lecturer in academia was one long class struggle. For those readers who are not campus workers, let me say that all the things that you see at your workplace happen on campus. It's all there: the fierce and ugly competition, the fighting for basic workers' rights, such as job security and health benefits, raises and promotions, and the betrayals of selling workers out and *firing* them for a piece of the managerial pie.

The two conflicting sides of labor have been consistent: on one side are college administrations, deans, and those tenured faculty members who are opportunistic and careerist trying to maintain the status quo of capitalist education and hierarchical power structure; on the other side, the bottom-most rungs of the ladder – progressive and radical lecturers, some tenured faculty, staff, students, and community activists.

I've been involved in a 27-year struggle over students' minds, hearts and bodies. Most students wanted a degree, so that they could get a decent paying job. At the same time they wanted tools to survive as whole human beings: to develop self-confidence and independence of thought. They wanted tools to change their communities. These were the students I would fight for. The students who were oppressed in some way or another —and all of them were! People who had been denied the real history of their people: the resistance, rebellion and heroism in the face of the strongest international ruling class in history.

One of my major goals in teaching has been to help students discover the *truth* that the debased and inferior status of people of color, women, and queers in American society is because the bourgeoisie needs to justify their super-exploitation of us for profits. I wanted them to understand that capitalist educational institutions' real focus is to maintain the majority's conformity to the status quo and collusion with our oppression. I wanted them to grow into empowered individuals who, by working collaboratively and together, could educate themselves to reach their own potential as gifted human beings under this dehumanizing and degrading system.

If we are to learn how to think for ourselves, to be critical of elitist, White, patriarchal, heterosexist education, we need to change the entire way we have been taught in the past. Our activism upsets the apple cart of keeping us mentally subservient and accepting of the status quo.

Implementing the Goals of the Third World Student Strikes 1969-1978

From 1968-1969, students, faculty, community and radical activists led Third World Strikes across U.S. campuses. Despite police brutality and attacks by campus administrators, they were tenacious, united, and they won ethnic studies, affirmative action, the Educational Opportunity Program, and the promise of an autonomous Third World College. They also won student participation in decision-making, the hiring of faculty who were community activists as well as academics, and the implementation of community-related courses.

In the Fall of 1969, I was hired to teach in the Educational Opportunity Program (EOP) in English at San Francisco State. How easy it was then to get hired. Like brand new reading and comp lecturers today, we were dedicated and prepared to put in 60-hour weeks to help our students.

Bertha, my Black colleague, was "walking the halls" of Laney College in Oakland, when someone stopped her and asked her if she wanted to teach in EOP at State. I was the only woman of color getting a Masters in English at State in the Spring of 69, so I was "stopped in the hallway" too, and asked if I wanted to teach.

We were a diverse group of young people: Anita, a Chicana; Bertha, Black; Art, Black; Jeff, Chinese American; Jim, a White working-class guy, and me, a Chinese-Korean American woman. Later came Teresa, who was American Indian.

High school students also were given an invitation to come to college. They were all of color, and had never expected to find themselves on a college campus.

I had not read anything by a Black writer or an Asian American writer in 1969. I had gotten all the way through a graduate program in English literature and had not even heard of Ralph Ellison.

The lecturers were radicalized immediately. Nothing prepared us to teach the students. We were furious that our own education had been so filled with censorship.

Of course, in typical big business fashion, the college administrations had no intention of keeping their agreements. They also knew that we were totally inexperienced in the workings of the bureaucracy of academia. They had no plans to give us the inside story—the real deal. We floundered but persisted.

Ethnic studies and women studies were founded on theories of liberation based on revolutions and national struggles for independence happening in the Third World, especially China, Cuba, and Africa. Within the U.S. the Black Panther program was also influential. "*Self-determination*" and "*relevance*" were key concepts. We were learning our histories of oppression and, more importantly, our resistance. Democracy in education was about students taking the power to direct their education and taking full responsibility for it. In other words, these studies were about changing society. Funding and corporate business go hand-in-hand behind the doors of the boards of trustees. Why would college administrators support students learning how to be radicals, to change society at the root?

We didn't know how to organize then. The university's takebacks began immediately, in the Spring of 1969. It started with one or more lecturers being *terminat-*

ed each year. To this day when I tell people I got *terminated,* liberals (always giving the benefit of the doubt to management) become picky and ask, "Do you mean really *terminated*? Or do you mean *let go*." Come on. There's no difference what anyone calls it if the bosses take our livelihood away! Budgetary reasons, temporary status, dropping our courses: we're gone.

At the end of each and every semester I had to go in to the Dean's office and make sure in person that my courses such as "Third World Literature" or "Lesbianism: An International Perspective", etc., would be on the course schedule for the next semester. My job was never limited to the inspirational joys of exchanging ideas in the classroom. As a lecturer, I had to fight every semester to keep my job and go to meetings to make sure my classes stayed on the curriculum. If I didn't fight, both my ideas and I would be out in the street.

Contrary to accusations, radical teachers don't sacrifice college skills to rhetoric or to *political correctness* (a favorite Rightwing term to invalidate our studies). We taught students how to write and how to think for themselves. When a bunch of EOP students were thrown out of school, Danny Villareal said, "We'll take these skills to hustle better on the street."

Lecturers had it bad. But students had it worse. Our EOP students had to keep a "C" average while they were working 20 hours a week. I saw them stand in line at financial aid and be treated like the dregs of society. The first generation college students—both American-born and immigrant—had the most difficulties.

We couldn't find anything about people of color in print at the college bookstore. So we went out into our respective communities. We took my old reel-to-reel Wollensak and dragged it with us everywhere to tape oral histories of our elders and new poets. N.Scott Momaday's House Made of Dawn and Ralph Ellison's Invisible Man became popular in our curriculum. I taped the oral history of Joe Bill, an Alaskan Native EOP student. Students loved hearing him, because they could identify with his history, and he was right in the classroom with us all.

AIEEEEE: an Anthology of Asian American Writers came out in 1971, by Howard University Press. And although their sexism was exposed in their introduction, the editors coined the term "racist love" to most accurately characterize the way Amerikkka treats Asian Americans. Asian American men and women have been oppressed by both racism and sexism because both have been forced into primarily women's work, such as domestic servants, launderers, cooks, and, in addition for the women, prostitution. Asian men's physiques are stereotyped as androgynous because they are comparably smaller, with "delicate" features, have less body hair than White men, etc. Asian American men need to create solidarity with women against our common enemy. But it has always been easier to scapegoat women as the source of men's problems.

Right after AIEEEEE! in 1972 came Third World Women, a Third World Communications publication in San Francisco. Among the fiery entries were a translation of a poem by Sor Juana de la Cruz, and poems by Kitty Tsui, the first Chinese American lesbian poet I'd ever read! These were exciting, heady times. Asian

Americans and women of color were becoming visible as militant protesters against our invisibility and subjugation.

In 1971, I withdrew from the Ph.D. program in English at UC Berkeley. It was mostly White, mostly elitist and arrogant, mostly irrelevant in comparison to what I was teaching and learning in my other life at State. I was living a deep paradox. At foggy State, I was alive. I'd bring my kids, Emily and Paul, to school with me, and all the lecturers in the "bull pen" played with them. They had a great community during those years. They came to classes, watched movies in the library.

Lecturers spent a lot of time talking politics and education in that room. I remember Anita once saying, "Well it's fine to be a revolutionary and tear things down, but you gotta have something to take its place!" Art, always the philosopher, used to say, "The point of education is not to reveal our knowledge to students, but to reveal theirs to themselves." Bertha taught me about Black women poets and writers, like Paule Marshall and Ann Petry.

Each year we lost one lecturer or two, and each year we'd say to each other, "I'm so pissed. Shall I write a letter of protest or something? But what would happen to my recommendation letter? What would happen to you?" Until finally, I was the only one left. White, academic intellectual lecturers took our places. They had no regard for the students who were in the classroom, who were also becoming whiter. When I left, one new lecturer called the students "EEEOPS," as if they were donkeys.

One thing I know we accomplished and that was to teach our students that standard English was a dialect of English, a skill, and our proficiency at it had nothing to do with our humanity or intelligence. "Broken," "mutilated," "bad" English did not apply to us or to our families and communities. Black English. Cantonese English. Spanglish. We gave English color. But necessity made us understand that we had to be skilled in standard English to communicate with most people.

The Fight to Maintain a Democratic Asian American Studies 1978 to 1982

In the Spring of 1978, I applied for a full-time lecturer position in Asian American Studies (AAS), UC Berkeley. That Spring at State I also put together and taught Third World Women's Literature in the new Women Studies Department. I felt like I was finally becoming myself. That was thrilling to me. I had evolved into being a proud Asian American and now, I was out as a proud feminist.

I actually believed I was being invited to teach in AAS, UC Berkeley because I was a feminist and now a writer (for the more I became myself, the more I felt I could write). I really started writing when I came out as a lesbian and became whole as a Trotskyist feminist and a member of Radical Women and the Freedom Socialist Party, whose program emphasized that because of all the things I am–Asian American, woman, lesbian, low-paid lecturer, single mother—I could be a leader in the movements for radical social change.

I thought I was coming home when I got hired in Asian American Studies!

It took one year to realize that all was not well in AAS. I was teaching the humanities courses. But I also coordinated the Reading and Composition program and so was placed above the other long-time lecturers, who were there before me. By placing me above the other long-time lecturers, the tenure-track faculty used me to punish the lecturers for talking back. The lecturers leveled their animosity at me instead of the tenured faculty.

In my second year, students asked me to write a support letter protesting the ladder-rank faculty's elimination of the community-language courses, Cantonese and Tagalog.

This one letter in support of the students was the only and last straw, that turned the tenure-track faculty against me like they were already against the other lecturers. Suddenly, I was the enemy of the powers that be. But the lecturers weren't going to organize with me. And I had learned from my years at SFSU, that if you don't organize together you lose.

At the same time, in 1980-81, not coincidentally, AAS faculty were coming up for tenure. That's why they started eliminating the community-language courses ("all you learn is how to order from a Chinese menu"), and community-related courses. If they were going to get tenure, they had to play ball with the administration. And, as I said, college administrations will never accept ethnic studies, women studies, queer studies. They were pressuring the tenure-track faculty to shift to the right, to become more academic, more respectable. The question has always been: were we going to remain true to the communities who put us on campus or become extensions of bourgeois academia? The opportunistic and reformist armchair Leftists went for the latter.

So what if in one semester students can only read a Chinese menu? That can be an achievement for a third or fourth generation Chinese American who hasn't been exposed to any Chinese languages at all.

Keep young people down, ignorant, destablized. Make them compete for every good grade they get. Students have no economic power so their survival depends on grades. Not knowledge, or maturity or integrity. Academic life depends on grades and degrees and the false promise of a good job in the future. Turn them into arrogant snobs, ashamed of their immigrant or poverty-stricken, "uneducated" ancestors.

There was pure joy in seeing so many Asian American students change from being subservient to authority to asking questions about every lie they had been fed, and being angry at being kept ignorant of their heroic past. They changed and started collaborating together for certain goals. We used to call the little open courtyard in front of Dwinelle Hall "Asia Gardens."

In one of my Asian American Studies freshman classes, it was the end of the semester of working very hard. Students organized and signed a petition to be freed of taking a final exam. That was a good one on me. What a laugh we had. They didn't have to take a final either.

Asian American Studies was becoming more academic, pushing our history into the dust bin of "That was then; it's so different now." The community-related courses were eliminated. And by 1981, the three long-time lecturers were fired, as well as

a community-activist librarian.   But not before we had a spirited teach-in and boy-
cott of Asian American Studies.   We educated on the history of ethnic studies and
affirmative action on campus.   We wore red armbands saying "Save Asian American
Studies." Balloons drifted over Dwinelle.   Other lecturers from other programs, like
Wendy Rose, the great Native American poet, took her classes to our teach-ins.   She
supported us and connected to us because she was a lecturer not only at UC but in
the community college system.   In addition the UC bookstore refused to carry her
books of poetry *even though* there was a policy that all faculty publications were fea-
tured at the bookstore.   Many of us still aren't equally human under the U.S.
Constitution.   Many of us lecturers aren't real faculty at UC Berkeley.

During this time, I was also involved with Unbound Feet a collective of six
Chinese American performance poets including myself, Nellie Wong, Kitty Tsui,
Canyon Sam, Genny Lim, Nancy Hom.   We were together for almost two years.
Three of us were out lesbians.   We received incredible support.   But, in 1981, we
split over statements Nancy Hom and an AAS woman student made at an Unbound
Feet performance at UC Berkeley, which criticized the AAS faculty for breach of con-
tract made with the six of us and also for the elimination of the Third World student
demands.   Genny, Nancy and Canyon accused Nellie, Kitty and me of *coercing* them
into making the statement.   But in actuality they admitted that the AAS tenured fac-
ulty were influential and sat on grant boards.   This split gave impetus to my firing
soon after.

I was now a writer, writing autobiographical *fiction* about a woman's alcoholism,
her coming-out as a lesbian, a radical.   This was grist for the mill for Ron Takaki,
Ling-chi Wang, Sucheng Chan, and Elaine Kim.   They couldn't get me on my teach-
ing, so it was my *rampant* alcoholism, the lesbianism, my membership in Radical
Women and the Freedom Socialist Party that they spread their dirty little rumors
about. They wanted to ruin my reputation as a professional teacher and principled
activist.   And I gave them even more grist when I spoke at the 1981 San Francisco
Lesbian and Gay Pride Rally and March.

According to one AAS student, Ling-chi said, "I was for gay rights before all
those new converts started coming out of their closets." A tenured faculty member
in another Ethnic Studies Department told me that Ling-chi remarked, "All she cares
about is her radical politics and her poetry readings." They tried slander. They tried
to invalidate my political support of the students.

But you know what?   During discovery in preparation for the trial against
them, we demanded that UC Berkeley hand over documents.   Well, they handed
over 3000 pieces of paper, and a couple of us had to copy it all in one day. There was
a little 3" X 5" scrap of paper that fell to the copy room floor, and it was a short
memo addressed to then Vice Chancellor, Roderic Park.   It said, "Rod, you've got to
do something quick! Merle Woo is *beginning to sound respectable*. Su"

It had become crystal clear to me that there exist internal social differences
between those who defend the interests of the *establishment* in our communities
against the majority who have very little power and resources.

In both Women Studies as in the women's movement, and in Asian American Studies or the Asian American Movement, there is the *establishment*. Just like bureaucrats, they skim the cream from the top and keep the goodies for themselves. They live off our collective oppression. They sit on grant boards. They control the monies and the funding. They're put in control of the direction of departments and movements. Their job is to keep the lid on rebellion. Then to add to the problem radical feminists and cultural nationalists refuse to expose this privileged layer of their own communities. Radical feminism is a political theory that is based on seeing men or patriarchy as the enemy because of the pervasive sexism in society. Cultural nationalism, in a parallel way, sees Whites as the enemy because of the pervasive racism in society. Both are cynical ideologies because they don't believe in solidarity across gender or racial differences respectively. Both ignore the class divide within each group.

The Case Against UC Berkeley 1982-1984

During my time in Asian American Studies, I had become active in the American Federation of Teachers (AFT). The union had come to understand that tenured faculty and lecturers are in competition for teaching jobs (that's divisive capitalism), and so, while before tenured faculty and lecturers were in the same unit, lecturers now finally got representation as lecturers with a particular set of needs and problems.

In my fourth year in Asian American Studies, UC passed a new four-year limitation on *visiting* lecturers. This meant that after teaching for four years, no matter what, visiting lecturers were let go. And so it was this revolving door of a four-year rule that AAS used to fire me. During this period, some *full-time* lecturers were still getting the equivalent of tenure, called *"Security of Employment."* Between 1981-1982, Ron Takaki, demoted me, without telling me from *full-time* lecturer to *visiting* lecturer, so I could never qualify for Security of Employment and could now be fired under the four-year rule.

The first thing Radical Women and the Freedom Socialist Party did was to help form a Merle Woo Defense Committee (MWDC). Then AFT stepped in for me and the lecturers and filed an unfair labor practice with the Public Employment Relations Board against UC, for implementing this anti-lecturer rule. AFT featured me as their prime example on the Berkeley campus. We came to find out that I was the only one Berkeley had used the rule on. The Administrative Law Judge, who happened to have been an ally of Cesar Chavez, declared the four-year rule an unfair labor practice, and UC was ordered to rehire me. That was in 1983. UC refused.

Then we filed complaints in federal and state courts charging violation of my free speech rights and discrimination based on race, sex, sexuality and political ideology. Students, unionists, and community activists supported my case because I represented so many segments of the majority of us. But it wasn't all support, though. One Asian American male ex-student of mine replied when I asked him for help: "Why don't you go get help from those White feminists (read *lesbians*) of yours."

Some Asians, women and gays hated my Trotskyist feminism and its multi-issueism. And here we were fighting for the equality of Asians, women, and gays! Some feminists were racist and some unionists were labor bureaucrats and wouldn't support me.

But there were about 20 staunch members of the MWDC, among them Nancy, Irene, Edgar, Peggy, and Cass who did research, organized support and wrote briefs. Hundreds of well-known activists, academics, writers, even mainstream Democrats endorsed the case.

And we in Radical Women and the Freedom Socialist Party and our radical lawyers wrote the politics in the legal briefs. Socialism on Trial is a book containing James P. Cannon's testimony at one of the most important political trials in U.S. history. He was among 18 leaders of the Socialist Workers Party and the Minneapolis Teamsters Union who were found guilty of "conspiring to advocate the overthrow of the U.S. government." Their defense strategy in the trial was to use the courtroom as a platform for educating the public about socialism.

We were going to do just that — my complaint would be an education about my socialist feminist politics and what I saw as a real democratic education. We also included in the complaint the fact that at Berkeley, Ethnic Studies faculty were paid less than faculty in other departments and that within Ethnic Studies women were paid less than men! And always on every campus, college administrators and deans were making annual salaries in the hundreds of thousands of dollars.

Our many workparties were lively and spirited. We fundraised by organizing forums on *free speech on the job* right on the Berkeley campus. We got support from the Left wing of every movement. And the alternative press was great, among them, *The Boston* and *Seattle Gay Community News, Plexus, Off Our Backs, Hokubei Mainichi* (which always included our entire press releases), and even *East/West* where Ling-chi Wang had an influential position.

In the Spring of 1982, Mary Dunlap, who was my lawyer in the first case, and I met with UC Counsel. We had come to negotiate, because one of the AAS longtime lecturers had come forth and agreed to testify for me. There always exists the potential for people to change! This ex-lecturer was willing to testify that Ling-chi Wang had said, "It is inappropriate for a lesbian to represent Asian American Studies."

I was reinstated to the Graduate School of Education in 1984 and received back pay for the two years that I was fighting the case.

Back to Activism at UC, Retaliation and Another Battle 1984- 1991

Of course Asian American Studies wouldn't take me back. And so for the next two years I taught in the Graduate School of Education, where I trained tutors in bilingual education in the community centers and high schools. Students who were teaching in Peace and Conflict Studies asked me to be their faculty supervisor in "Organizing Across the Color Line" and "Multicultural Lesbian and Gay Studies." I became a member of Lesbians and Gays against Apartheid. Radical

Women/Freedom Socialist Party organized forums on radical and progressive faculty who had lost their jobs by speaking out and who had won reinstatement. AFT asked me to sit in on negotiations regarding maintaining academic freedom for tenured faculty who were protesting UC's millions in investments in South Africa.

In the Spring of 1986, I was fired again — this time under the ruse that I was being paid from a special fund from the office of the Vice Chancellor (Roderic Park). Of course this violated the *equal treatment* rule for employment, i.e., that I was not being treated the same as other lecturers in the UC system. The MWDC, RW and FSP regrouped, and we filed a union grievance. Bill Carder, the AFT lawyer, and Roz Spafford, my union rep, were my advocates. It took three years until 1989 to get to arbitration. But UC tried its delaying tactics even then by saying their UC labor representative was sick and had to postpone arbitration till the next day.

UC had tried to sabotage us because we had organized nearly 50-60 people to attend the hearing. Instead, we started marching around the building, chanting, "Take two aspirin and come to arbitration!" Unionists from the California Faculty Association and lecturers from State crossed the Bay to support me. Leo Kanowitz was the union arbitrator, and although arbitrators are supposed to be neutral, he was a law professor at Hastings (a UC school). We won the arbitration and Kanowitz ruled that I had been treated unfairly and was to be immediately reinstated, but he wrote that my firing was not deliberate and refused to state that it was because of retaliation and continuing discrimination, which we had claimed and given ample evidence to support.

From 1989 to 1991, I tried to get reinstated. I had to interview in the Rhetoric Department ("The Reading and Composition committee has decided that we will no longer teach *ideas* in our reading and composition courses across campus. And that means you, Ms. Woo. We don't want you.") I interviewed with Asian American Studies and they said, "If we have to hire you, we will have to terminate all the other lecturers who've been teaching here because of budgetary limitations. Do you want that?"

UC hired a San Francisco law firm to fight my reinstatement. They tried to drag me in for a psychiatric examination. But we couldn't find a lawyer. Our previous lawyers had been good, but they hated that the Defense Committee insisted on playing an active role in the legal proceedings.

The Defense Committee (which had stayed together just in case) hit the law books and did our own research. We took UC's demand for a psychiatric examination to Alameda County court and won. The judge even said that if UC played any more of these nasty acts of intimidation, she'd personally throw economic sanctions at them.

By 1991, the Defense Committee chose to drop fighting for my reinstatement. I had just had a double mastectomy, and I wasn't about to be in litigation until I died.

Nine years before, in 1982, Radical Women and the Freedom Socialist Party had agreed that the best way to support me was to have a coordinator of the Defense Committee to keep the overview of the legal and public angles of the fight and to help organize supporters. I never would have won without Karen Brodine and Nancy Reiko Kato, the two coordinators of my two cases against UC.

Although never reinstated, I had won backpay for all the years I fought UC and received a "ditto to you, too" check for $75,000. Most importantly I had won three legal victories against them.

In 1983 and then from 1987, I had been a part-time lecturer in Women Studies back at San Francisco State, and this was the location of the final class struggle of my teaching career.

Women Studies Students Carry on a Courageous Tradition 1987 to 1997

Up to about 1988 the Women Studies Department at San Francisco State was comprised mostly of lecturers. Although there was the usual revolving door for all the lecturers, there was still a modicum of democracy. Students and lecturers still had a say and a vote in decision-making processes, not only in Department meetings, but also in curriculum and hiring!

I learned the false unity of cultural nationalism when I was fired from AAS. And I learned about the hypocrisy of the extreme form of radical feminism, lesbian separatism, when I was trying to get hired in Women Studies in 1983 (after my first firing from UC Berkeley). I was interviewed by the hiring committee which was comprised of one faculty member, a lesbian separatist, and two students, one a lesbian of color who happened to have been an EOP student of mine in 1976. The lesbian separatist declared she didn't want to hire me because, as a radical, I wouldn't be trustworthy in a classroom. Well the students outvoted the lesbian separatist and I was hired and worked there for a semester or two, until I got reinstated to UC in 1984.

It wasn't difficult, then, to go back to teaching in Women Studies at SFSU in 1987 (after my second firing).

I'd like to digress a moment and say that class inequality permeates the different "levels" of college campuses. I've taught in community colleges, state universities, and in the UC system. At UC, I taught two classes which equaled a full-time load, had teaching assistants for every class and made $30,000 a year in 1982. At SFSU until I was fired, I made $500 per class per month with five classes being a full-time teaching load for lecturers and four classes being a full-time teaching load for tenured faculty. At Vista, a community college, I made even less than that. And the teaching load is about 1/3 heavier than at the State Universities.

With that in mind, let's return to Women Studies where one lecturer, Chinosole, was up for tenure. At an initial staff meeting with this new situation, Chinosole said that she wanted a permanent situation where she would teach three classes all the time, but get paid for four. This was not standard practice across campus.

Basic arithmetic says that if she got this teaching load on a permanent basis (which she did get as well as did the following two tenure-track faculty hired in Women Studies), we would have less money for hiring lecturers and increasing undergraduate classes. Every course paid for, but not taught, meant one less class or one less lecturer. So we suggested that we discuss it further. The point for us was that it was reasonable to have a three-course teaching load. We knew tenured faculty had to publish, and we supported that. But, of course the university administration was squeezing us to death and making it so that once again we were divided and pitted against each other.

Maybe we could alternate semesters when Chinosole would be paid for four while teaching three, and then we could possibly maintain the numbers of undergraduate courses. Lecturers and students wanted to organize together and demand from the Dean that we get more funding for everyone. Why does it always have to be either/or? Why not *both*? We *supported* stabilizing Women Studies with more permanent tenured faculty —we just didn't want it to be at the expense of lecturers and undergraduate courses. Once we had had about 18-20 undergraduate courses. By 1997, we were offering about 11.

In addition because funding for departments and programs depends on the amount of FTE's (full-time equivalency) or how many students are taking classes, our undergraduate courses leapt from 25 students to over 40, and introductory and basic history courses leapt to 120. This increase had to happen because graduate courses are seminars with 15 students or less, and the undergraduate program had to carry the balance of the load.

There was not going to be any solidarity. In her own self-interest, Chinosole became an instant enemy of the lecturers and soon, with the university's support, started hiring more ladder-rank faculty who were less feminist and radical and more academic. The class struggle had started in earnest. Inderpal Grewal, from UC Berkeley, a strident anti-Marxist and post-modernist, joined the tenure-track faculty.

Once again, every spring there were spirited departmental meetings where students and lecturers protested the cutting back of classes, the laying off of lecturers, and the loss of student democracy. But inevitably lecturers and undergraduate classes were squeezed out.

Up through the 80s, lecturers and students had participated in democratic decision-making in both curriculum and hiring. Campus-wide policy stated that departmental meetings were open to students. By 1997, lecturers and students had absolutely no voice in the running of Women Studies. It became well-known on campus that we who had had the most democracy on campus now had the least democracy of any other department.

It had been campus policy that lecturers had a vote equivalent to the amount of time they were teaching, e.g., if a lecturer taught one class, she got 1/5 of a vote, etc.

The tradition in Women Studies up to 1995 had been that lecturers got one vote based on the principle of democracy. By 1995, we were back to the proportionate vote.

At every campus I have taught, one of the college administration's tactics to put a lid on student activism was to create graduate programs at the expense of undergraduate studies —the theory being that graduate students tend to be much less active on campus than undergraduates. In my experience this has been true. Of course there are always exceptions — for example, UC graduate teaching/research assistants have an economic relationship to the administration. They have been militantly organizing for years and only recently obtained collective bargaining power for their Association of Graduate Student Employees. In a parallel vein, lecturers, as a group, have always been more active and pro-students' rights than tenured faculty. Go to the bottom rung of any ladder and you'll find the most militant rebels. There have been exceptions in this case as well. Many tenured faculty have remained radicals and student advocates no matter what their status and income. One was Mina Caulfield who having received tenure, remained true to the original democratic goals of Women Studies.

So with our little pittance for Women Studies, the Vice President, Marilyn Boxer started implementing a Master's program knowing full well that this would come at the expense of the undergraduate major and lecturers.

Political differences played a major role in who was to survive in Women Studies. It was a no-brainer over who the college administration and the Dean would support.

Chinosole, a cultural nationalist, did not threaten the administration because she wouldn't build alliances; she deeply distrusted that political strategy. Inderpal, a post-modernist, wouldn't be at the forefront of organizing against the administration either. Cynicism plays a strong role in both political ideologies as well as ignoring class differences and playing up to privilege.

Chinosole dropped her membership in and Inderpal never joined the California Faculty Association (CFA) and so broke a proud Women Studies tradition when everyone was in the union.

The lecturers, including Fabienne McPhail, Ruth Mahaney and I, were long-time organizers and activists; we were feminists and radicals, we were out lesbians, and we supported students' rights. We also supported Jewish students when they tried to get the tenured faculty to support courses, in name only, on women in Jewish Studies, but they refused.

Inderpal eventually became chair of Women Studies. Under her regime, she put on a Women Studies Conference and refused to allow Fabienne McPhail, a Black feminist lesbian scholar and activist, whose focus was Violence Against Women of Color and me to present any papers.

We were attacked professionally. But they could never actually come out and say we were bad teachers. The ongoing debate about my graduate class, "Lesbianism: an International Perspective" really showed how political differences affected my job security.

First, Inderpal influenced many of her graduate students that anyone without a Ph.D. should not be teaching graduate courses. Then, she said that I was teaching that there is only one global perspective on lesbianism. Her position was that lesbianism was a western construct and did not exist outside of the United States.

She attacked Marxism because, according to post-modernists, Marxism is a *meta-narrative* or a theory which makes connections in the world based on economics and an analysis of capitalism. Using her post-modern method, she demeaned organizing because there is no one central issue people can gather around. Obviously post-modernism is a cynical and conservative theory which views hegemonic systems of oppression as unrelated and dispersed. Inderpal attacked the integrity of my class and my teaching. Although I have never simplistically used the term *lesbianism* to describe the many, many sexualities possible in human cultures, I did make the connections in societies which were patriarchal and imposed the institutions of the monogamous nuclear patriarchal family and private property. I saw where capitalism and imperialism had become global and enforced its *civilization* on every group of people. By extension, every patriarchal culture based on the family will oppress lesbians, gays, bisexuals, and transgendered individuals, because they challenge sex role stereotyping which enforces male superiority over the female, the woman's free labor in the home, and by extension, her low wages in social production. In addition, queer liberation movements inspired by the 1969 Stonewall Rebellion in New York City had become international.

At the same time, however, we studied sexuality in non-western cultures, especially indigenous cultures in the Americas, Australia and Africa and saw the reality and possibility of the acceptance and respect of diverse sexualities where peoples were organized around collective, matriarchal systems without the curse of private property and inheritance.

Something deeper was going on. Women Studies was evolving into an anti-feminist, anti-lesbian department. It was deplorable that certain classes got struck simply because the powers that be didn't like the ideas taught. One long-time lecturer (and I mean long-time as in decades) was dropped because she taught "Women and Spirituality", a class based on radical feminist theory. I'm no advocate of radical feminism myself, but isn't democracy about diversity and tolerance, allowing students to choose? The lesbian-centered courses were dropped and the lecturers who taught them, including myself.

But not before students and lecturers fought back. We could have been so much stronger if the lecturers had organized in solidarity and with hope. But cynicism, cultural nationalism and radical feminism weakened us. Our temporary status contributed to lecturers giving up and moving on; cultural nationalism prevented a few Black lecturers from any public criticism of Chinosole, and radical feminism prevented some White lecturers from openly coming out and breaking with the Dean, Nancy McDermid, and Assistant Dean, Jane Gurko. They had once been, in better economic times, supporters of the democratic, lesbian-positive and community-oriented Women Studies. But they were now management with high salaries and were tied in to the college administration.

The university's strategy had been to hire careerist women of color who would block a progressive Women Studies from developing. Many liberal White women sympathized with us but kept silent. What would they look like if they were to criticize the women of color tenure/tenure-track faculty? Inderpal depended on White liberalism, because she effectively silenced critics by accusing *them* of being anti-affirmative action.

The California Faculty Association held back. Other faculty of color, including *feminists*, said our battle to survive was just personal in-fighting. And we were losing our jobs. Feminism and Marxism had definitely become *post-*.

The undergraduate students who saw their Women Studies program degenerating continued to organize. Under these embattled conditions, a core of lecturers kept our jobs and maintained some kind of student democracy for seven years, from 1990-1997. This was a great victory in and of itself.

One of the most militant marches was led by the student leaders who in the Spring of 1997 marched and chanted through every floor of the Humanities Building. Fabienne had been fired, and I was next. The number of undergraduate classes had dwindled to the point that there were barely enough classes to maintain a major in Women Studies. Students had even begun to raise funds themselves to keep the undergraduate program intact. They had a list of foundations and donors who were open to helping us survive. Inderpal, however, blocked this by declaring that any money coming into the Department could not be earmarked either for lecturers' salaries or the undergraduate program. So students marched.

Inderpal barricaded herself in her office and called McDermid to stop them. Students pushed picket signs under Inderpal's door and went back into the halls. McDermid ran out of her office and tried to stop the students, but every floor she went to, she was too late and could hear the students chanting distantly who had marched on to other floors.

We continued to barge into departmental meetings, even though we no longer had a voice. I remember one new faculty, A.J., saying to me, "I can't believe it. When *I* was a lecturer, I would never have dreamed of taking my students from class and going to a meeting." I guess that's why she was hired on the tenure track.

Students organized petitions, letters, rallies. They wrote articles and were published in local campus and community newspapers. Student leaders included Vita, Sara, Kelly, Joy, Deborah, Josephine and many, many others. Feminists and long-time lesbian activists in the community, like Del Martin and Phyllis Lyon demanded to meet with Inderpal. But by 1997, some of us were actually glad to leave, including myself, because the educational atmosphere had become suffocatingly stale.

Epilogue

It is now the era of post-affirmative action. Last Spring (1999) on the UC Berkeley campus, Ethnic Studies students went on a hunger strike and took over Barrows Hall, the home of Ethnic Studies, in order to protest takebacks and to make demands including an Ethnic Studies research center on gender and race, the hiring of eight more tenure-track faculty, the funding of a community mural and increased funding. Since then several students have been brought up on charges of resisting arrest, battery and assaulting campus police. This Fall there may be no amnesty and a couple of student leaders who are Black and Puerto Rican may be expelled. Ling-chi Wang and Ron Takaki are still at the helm and taking credit for any positive advances made by the students. When students were told they had won their demands last spring, Ling-chi was seen to be waving from a window like Evita. Now it is said that this faculty may be working to nullify the agreement made with the students.

Why has nothing changed? Obviously because we are still living under this for-profit system. But we have tasted freedom: there is no doubt that every single student who has been involved in activism and taken responsibility to get a decent and democratic education will have been forever changed by exerting individual power in solidarity with others. For once they have been subjects in their own destiny rather than passive, objects acted upon by others.

But once our eyes are opened to the realities of capitalist educational institutions can we ever close them again? Many will try as they move into the corporate individualistic world, but many will not.

Some have come to understand that it's worth devoting our lives to standing up for ourselves and others and to organizing together to create a better world for advanced human relations. They've joined the revolutionary movement to destroy capitalism and, especially, its ugly super-exploitation of the bottom-most of the working class: people of color, women, queers, the disabled, the young and old. This way of life is not difficult at all when we can envision what education could be like under a socialist democracy, where every child has access to quality education, where students are taught to think critically and to speak out. And where each individual can choose something they would love to do and can do it: from each according to her/his ability, to each according to her/his work.

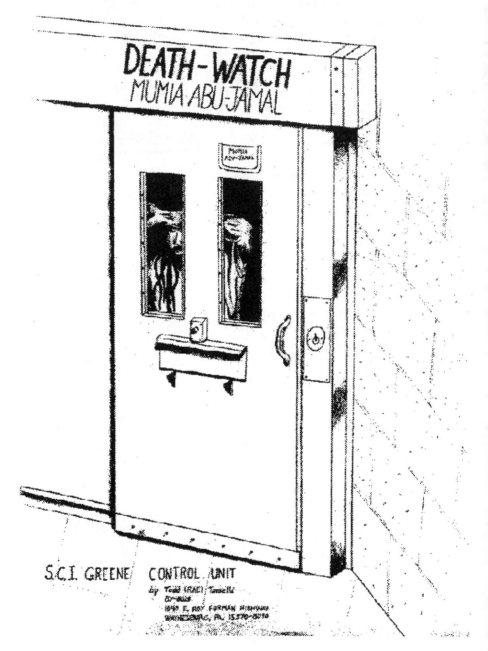

Ilustration credit: © Todd Hyung-Rae Tarselli

SECTION
TWO

PERSONAL/POLITICAL
STRUGGLES
&
LESSONS

"Mask no difficulties, tell no lies, claim no easy victories."

AMILCAR CABRAL

The day of eviction: August 4, 1977 Thousands form a human barricade in front of the I-Hotel to try to physically block the police from entering

Mass mobilization to block possible eviction attempt.

Veteran Chinese labor activists lead rally of the Workers Committee to Fight for the International Hotel in Chinatown

THE GOOD, THE BAD, THE UGLY BUT NECESSARY

Lessons from the Struggle

Fred Ho

As I Wor Kuen/the League of Revolutionary Struggle was liquidating Marxism, socialism and revolution in 1989, and I was thrown out for challenging the underhanded manu-veuring of this process, I went through a watershed period in my life. Up to this point in my life, for 14 years, I had belonged to some form of cadre organization. And the majority of these years—over a decade—were with IWK/LRS.

The organization was my family, my closest friends were other cadres, I had romantic relationships with womyn in the organization, my very direction and understanding of life and the world had been shaped as a rank and file cadre. I never was in leadership, even though by the late 1980s I had achieved some degree of prominence and accomplishment as a cultural worker and professional artist. The organization had evaluated me as someone with high level of commitment, creativi-ty, energy, discipline and ideological clarity but I had severe weaknesses of arrogance and individualism.

Especially by this time, with the wholesale redirection of the organization into electoral politics tailing Jesse Jackson nationally and David Dinkins here locally in NYC, I was increasingly distancing myself from the mainstream of the organization and especially its leadership, one of whom had been my roommate for 6 years. As cadres were being assigned to do work for Jesse and Dinkins, I conveniently made myself unavailable by travelling more often for out of town gigs. Yet I still had faith in the revolution; I never wanted to quit. I had to be thrown out. When the LRS Central Committee announced that it was "reevaluating" Marxism and the validity of socialist revolution, I welcomed the chance to do battle against the sweeping tide of reformism. But the LRS leadership was so despicably underhanded. While attempting to destroy Marxism-Leninism, it used Leninist democratic-centralist organization to do this dirtywork. There was to be no real struggle, only a controlled, railroaded operation to rubberstamp the leadership.

Rather than allow full, open, democratic debate about the validity of Marxism, of socialism and revolution, the opportunist leadership used their centralist authori-ty to push their views, to pull on personal loyalty, to use their prestige and leadership position in the organization to lobby their agenda. The pro-socialist minority oppo-

Revised from a speech presented at "Aziatic Uprising: An Inter-generational Dialogue" November, 1998 at Columbia College, New York City.

177

sition was not allowed to have organizational resources to communicate and coalesce. In the end, the majority not surprisingly got their way, keeping the organization finances and press, leaving the opposition who didn't want to submit to their opportunism with nothing, literally having to start from scratch. Because the "debate" was done without open identities (i.e., the cadres' real names), the minority was at a huge disadvantage as it couldn't even know who shared its positions.

By 1990 I was in a new period of my life, trying to figure out what destroyed the movement and how to proceed as a revolutionary and with my life. I was 32 years old, had bought my loft and dealing with a huge monthly mortgage (though I've always had tremendous financial discipline, even when I was paying $195 a month in rent and yet earning only $250 a month in income). I had no interest in getting married or having children or raising a family. I was beginning to earn a living fulltime as an artist. It seemed like a new activist movement was emerging, however very different than the revolutionary movement in which I came of age. This late 1980s, early 1990s activism was dominated by the politics and organizing of ACT UP! In New York City Asian American activism, the Committee Against Anti-Asian Violence (CAAAV) was emerging, along with the Chinese Staff and Workers Association (CSWA), both of whom were founded by virulent anti-communists, who were former members of the Workers Viewpoint Organization/Communist Workers Party and the Line of March organization who had bitter hatred for these past groups and their experiences within them. Anybody viewed in the old AAFE/CWP (then-Asian Americans for Equal Employment, later-Asian Americans for Equality/Communist Workers Party) vs. IWK/LRS (I Wor Kuen/League of Revolutionary Struggle) days was a pariah.

Younger, early 20-something activists were emerging. The battles in the City University of New York system to save open admissions and to oppose tuition hikes were being led by working class students from Baruch College, the Borough of Manhattan Community College, Hunter...I attempted to connect with these younger budding revolutionaries. Some of them came to me, yet I believe I was primarily making the effort to seek them out. Many of them were too young and had no or little knowledge or experience with the New Communist Movement of the 1970s and early 1980s. By the 1990s what was left of the Left wasn't too appealing. And with all due respect to the Revolutionary Communist Party and to Trotskyists, many of these younger activists associated socialist party-type formations as White-dominated, self-promoting, bullying sectarian cults out to hock their own newspapers and recruit into their ranks.

The politics of ACT UP! were largely anarchistic and heavily influenced by Alinskyism, though many activists in ACT UP! were not self-conscious Alinskyites as were the people in NYPIRG (New York Public Interest Research Group) or ACORN (Association of Community Organizations for Reform Now). The main features of this political tendency were:

(1) anti-ideology (embracing post-modernism's anti-historical/no-grand narratives/no-fundamental philosophy position);

(2) heavily into disruptive actions (civil disobedience, ZAPs, etc.);

(3) anti-leadership and pro-collective decision-making, let's-discuss-everything style of ultra-democratic open townhall-style meetings;

(4) very media saavy;

(5) very militant and yet not revolutionary (Fight the State but not Overthrow the State);

(6) very middleclass, intellectual and professional-friendly proclaiming to have "space" for all identity politics (especially for diverse sexual identities including Gay/Lesbian/Bi-sexual/Transgender).

In the Asian American activist circles, many of these younger activists were from very middleclass backgrounds, graduating from elite schools like Columbia or Brown. They were sincerely looking to organize in immigrant and working class communities but did not understand the need for class-transformation. (An understanding of class was dismissed as that old Marxism stuff.) They took full-time organizer jobs in non-profits and in many ways resembled the generation before them, putting in sleepless hours as activists. They became the Asian American Movement of the 1990s, a movement that still took to the streets but without ideology, revolutionary organization and a goal. Many of these 1990s activists viewed themselves as making social change: they saw many of my former comrades who had abandoned a revolutionary politics and identity as part of the problem and no longer part of the solution.

But these younger activists could offer no solutions and by the election of Bill Clinton, ACT UP! and many similar movements had become quickly co-opted into the Democratic Party, like many of us were by Jesse Jackson a decade earlier. Let's examine the contradictions:

In fighting the system, the question of ideology is key: if you're opposed to sexism, homophobia, worker exploitation, state repression, racism, etc., then what do you replace these with? What is the goal of activism: reform or revolution? What is fundamental to making real, systemic social change: changing political officials, legislation and media representation; or political and economic power via ownership and control over the means of production? The overpromotion of collective decision-making masks the reality that power is held by those who can meet for endless hours, who facilitate (in reality, frame) the agenda—mostly educated middleclass people who have flexible hours, salaries or family trust funds or subsidy, etc. Ultrademocracy without a basis of ideological and political unity is often task-oriented and doesn't further a disciplined political strategy, much less prepare people to do battle with other political forces and the state, which are VERY organized and prepared. Ultimately, revolutionary change requires new political organization: if you oppose the bourgeois imperialist state, then what do you replace it with and how will this be done? Or, as Huey P. Newton pointed out, the fascist ruling class won't become Buddhists overnight.

Because of the lack of serious regard for ideology, often I found myself in debate with these post-modern influenced activists, many from very white-assimilated backgrounds. They objected to "privileging" any type of oppression, thereby blurring and conflating all oppressions in a false equality and inclusivity. That's the fallacy of the "race/gender/class" analysis and equation: it disregards the fundamental root of all oppression: class. That it is possible to envision capitalism to include womyn, diverse nationalities and sexual minorities, but impossible for capitalism to not have classes. This everything-is-everything, least-common-demoninator approach to politics and ideology objectively liquidates the national question, projects a false, reformist feminism and never targets the root of inequality in its celebration of "difference."

Nonetheless, I have been very inspired and learned much from the new generation. Let me point out some examples:

1. The broadening of the concept of "the political is personal" in issues of personal health and personal conduct and ethics;

2. Greater tolerance and acceptance; the less egocentrism and generally less harsh approach towards one another, a greater tolerance and acceptance, though I still encounter some pretty judgmental anarchists who'll criticize everything about your personal practice that doesn't conform to their expectations;

3. The energy and dedication many have shown in a period where there are no revolutionary beacons, when defeats are many and victories are few, when organizing and advocating radicalism is much more difficult.

The weaknesses are, from my point of view, many—though this young generation is not to blame as we who came before have not left much for them to build upon. These include:

1. The lack of study, an even outright pride in being anti-study and anti-theoretical;

2. A weak national consciousness from growing up in the period of integration and consumerism which confuses wearing an X-cap with studying and putting into practice Malcolm X's revolutionary legacy;

3. A lack of revolutionary courage, to give up going to graduate school and to go to organize at the workplace, in factories, sweatshops, industry; or to start up disciplined revolutionary collectives and organizations to be new examples instead of complaining about how dismal the Left is.

But we of the previous generation have our share of problems and weakness including:

Sectarianism: for example, the I-refuse-to-do anything-with-a-Maoist or a Trotskyist or an Anarchist positions;

Tendency to still hold on to dogmatic, bookish formulations, though important questions such as the existence and importance of upholding the Black Nation, the concept of the dictatorship of the proletariat, the vanguard party, etc., are still vital and key questions to debate and figure out;

Our addictions to homophobia, male chauvinism, white chauvinism, economism, to nicotine, alcohol, the nuclear family.

However, our legacy which I hope the younger generation will respect and learn from, includes:

We did indeed develop new revolutionary theory particularly around the national question and white-settler colonialism. We defined an entire generation, challenged U.S. ruling class power and built revolutionary organizations (many of which succumbed primarily to right opportunism and imploded, meaning that they gave up the struggle for revolution and accommodated themselves to reformism, electoral politics, academia and social democracy—socialism in words, Democratic Party politics in deeds).

Every movement, every organization will face critical crossroads. This is inevitable given the inevitability of the many twists and turns of the struggle. I would finally like to share with you what I think are some of the dangers to guard against:

1. While struggle can get intense and even heated, guard against harsh, undignified, negative treatment of dissidents and opposition viewpoints.

2. Be vigilant and oppose behind-the-scenes maneuvering, the manipulation of the stacking-the-deck at meetings, the intrigue and machinations of blocking that pretends to uphold open debate but in reality is factionalizing.

3. If antagonism is constant, then unity isn't real.

4. Try to keep the debate at the level of politics and not gossip, hearsay or attacking individuals. Struggle is not about trying to wound or discredit comrades with opposing positions, but to persuade and convince, not defeat and personally attack.

5. It's definitely NOT healthy when purges and railroads happen.

6. While people can and should be passionate and sharp in their criticisms, the tool of criticism/self-criticism should be used respectfully, in a dignified manner with no personal vituperation.

7. Be watchful of bureaucratism, i.e., people getting props and prestige perks just because they co-sign with leaders, i.e., mediocre philistine administrators who yes the top leadership in the presumption that leaders are always the "clearest" and the "most" of any quality considered a credential to being in leadership.

Democratic-centralism is supposed to be the organizational method of operation for revolutionary organizations fighting the state. The state has a military structure and method of operation that enables it to be decisive, efficient and highly effective against its enemies. Likewise, a revolutionary organization must protect itself from state attack and infiltration and still be politically effective in the mass movements. Revolutionary organizations therefore have "open" (publically known) and "closed" (secret) members and areas of work and operation. Democratic-centralism is the organizational principle: full, open debate of views and positions, voting to settle disagreements and differences, the minority must abide by the majority, lower organizational bodies (such as cells or units) must submit to higher bodies (district/city leadership committees and national bodies). However, what becomes problematic is the relationship between individuals: whether a central committee leader shall have authority over a rank and file cadre, i.e., to give them commands without collective agreement. Obviously, in a military engagement (when the revolutionary organization is in armed struggle with the state) this may be necessitated, but in non-military stages of struggle, then commandism, centralism and concentrated power should be avoided.

No leadership body should ever be presumed to be permanent. Democracy is always undermined and mitigated in the presence of secrecy. Cult of personality will contradict collectivity as the advantages of leaders include control of and greater access to communications, ability to leverage fame, prestige and authority. The top can reach greater numbers of the rank and file than a single rank and file cadre can reach the entire organization, especially if it is nationwide.

While there are never any guarantees against abuses of power and authority, the best deterrent and safeguard is constant political education. Political education should never take a backseat or be allowed to slide because of the mounting mass work. It is both the organization and the individual cadre's responsibility to promote and to develop with each person critical and analytic thinking, creativity, passion and compassion, resourcefulness and expertise (both specialized and general). The ultimate goal of a revolutionary movement is to create new, revolutionary human beings who do not replicate the hierarchal and oppressive behaviors and practices of capitalist society, but who personify and embody liberating relations and conduct.

Each young radical must ask him/herself: Am I a revolutionary? How should a revolutionary movement be built? What should I be studying? What more can I learn from the history of past revolutionary groups and movements? How must I transform myself to transform the world? Hopefully, the veterans can share their experiences and be supportive, yet, as Frantz Fanon pointed out, Each generation must find its own mission and either fulfill or betray it.

MAO MORE THAN EVER!

Dolly Veale

Marxism consists of thousands of truths, but they all boil down to the one sentence, "It is right to rebel."

*Mao Zedong**

A Legacy of Rebellion

There IS indeed a proud "legacy to liberation" to push forward from the 1960s into the new millennium. One expression of this today is a strong anti-imperialist awareness among many young Asian/Pacific Islander activists. We need to raise the level of our struggle so that 30 years hence, we will not be locked in the same elitist institutions, under the same oppressive capitalist system, waging the same battles over and over again, such as the fight for affirmative action or against police brutality. In the spirit of advancing our struggles to the fullest extent—the actual realization of our liberation—I am contributing the following reflections and reminiscences of past experiences and lessons as fuel for future struggles and victories. My perspective is decidedly Maoist—as a founding member of the Revolutionary Communist Party, USA (RCP) since 1975, and a spokesperson for over 15 years.

I was initiated into the Asian movement when I transferred to U.C. Berkeley in early 1970. Asian Studies had been established by the Third World Strike a year earlier, and I enrolled in some of these classes. Students like me were drawn to Berkeley for its rowdy antiestablishment rep. It was new and exciting to attend UCB and find courses that broke with the boring and conventional mold: regurgitation masked as education; indoctrination in white and male supremacist history and cultural values; memorization for a grade and engaging in bizarre forms of abstract reasoning.

In late April 1970, the U.S. invaded Cambodia which provoked a surge in the antiwar movement, including a surge in Asian youth involvement. In the wake of the Third World Strike and establishment of Ethnic Studies, there were a lot of sentiments about the war being a "racist, genocidal war against Asians." For the first

---

This is an expanded version of a presentation I gave at the conference "Crossing Over: Ethnic Studies and Radical Politics Beyond the Schooling Industrial Complex—A Strategy Session and Thirty Year Commemoration of the U.C. Berkeley Third World Strike". The conference took place on April 9-10, 1999 at the University of California at Berkeley. The workshop was titled "Mao TseTung*, the Black Panthers, and the Third World Strike"—a theme which intersects with the theme of the following essay

183

time, I felt compelled to join with thousands of others at UCB in the militant protests against the war. I was inspired by the fierce determination and unity of many of my fellow students, of all races. Students and others, armed only with rocks and bottles, resisted in the face of being clubbed by police batons, sprayed with tear gas and nerve gas from helicopters, mass arrested, shot with rubber and real bullets.

In early May 1970, the national guard shot and killed 4 white students at Kent State, Ohio, followed by the killing of 2 Black students at Jackson State, Mississippi. When I was arrested at the height of these student protests and banned from campus, Richard Aoki was the only professor to tell me "you deserve an A for activist." It was the most deserved "A" I ever got in school, and taught me profound lessons that I would later understand as revolutionary principles: 1) it's right to rebel; 2) the point of knowing the world is to change it; and 3) taking risks in the fight for justice is a badge of honor.

But that arrest also shattered my illusions about the democratic process and the right to dissent in this country. I could see that the "right" of the U.S. government to drop tons of bombs and napalm on women and children was protected by its police and its military. I learned first-hand that immigrants and native-born alike have the "right" and freedom to go along with an unjust status quo, or else. And the murder of students at Kent and Jackson State reinforced my doubts that the war could be stopped through voting[1] or other forms of pacifist protest.

Opposing Imperialist War, Supporting People's War, and Learning About Internationalism

Like many others, I began to identify with and support those waging armed struggle in Southeast Asia for national liberation, like the beautiful Vietnamese women freedom fighters with their AK47 rifles. I was one of 300 women from the U.S.—many were young Asian Americans—who rode buses to Vancouver, Canada to meet women from North and South Vietnam, Laos and Cambodia. We were thrilled to meet face-to-face with those engaged in a people's war for national liberation against U.S. imperialism. One of them, Dinh Thi Huong, relayed her story about spending 6 years in the infamous tiger cages of South Vietnam where she "survived the years of torture and deprivation to join the liberation movement upon her release...to fight against the Americans and [their] puppets."[2]

Though we didn't fully comprehend all that was involved at the time, many of us were greatly attracted to the revolutionary and internationalist stance emanating from then—Maoist China. China gave tremendous support to the wave of national liberation struggles in Asia, Latin America and Africa. They provided material aid to Vietnam and other revolutionary struggles. They boldly promoted Marxism-Leninism. China served as a beacon and a base area for the world revolution. Millions rallied in Tiananmen Square in support of the Vietnamese struggle against the U.S., as well as in support of the rebellions of Black people inside the U.S.

Mao's calls of "Dare to struggle, dare to win!" and "People of the world, unite and defeat the U.S. Aggressors and all their running dogs!" connected with our own aspirations for justice and equality. China's staunch positions and actions propelled many Asian youth in the antiwar movement toward basic internationalist sentiments—that the exploited and oppressed people of the world had a common enemy and a common struggle. Our solidarity statements to the Vietnamese people would reflect this growing consciousness:

> *The vicious imperialism which seeks to commit total genocide against the proud people of Indochina is the same imperialism which oppresses those of us here in North America by creating dehumanizing conditions in our Chinatown, barrios, Black ghettoes and reservations. We struggle together to build a society which fosters cooperation, rather than competition; and justice without exploitation or racism, with love and power to all people....To all of you we give our pledge that we will fulfill our duty, we will build and intensify our struggle to smash imperialism from within.[3]*

Mao and the Black Panthers

To paraphrase Mao, when the oppressed fight back, they look for philosophy to guide their struggle. As soon as I got out of Berkeley City jail after that arrest, totally penniless, I looked for a way to satisfy my hunger and thirst for revolutionary theory to make sense of the world events engulfing me. I ran over to Yenan Books, then a radical bookstore next to People's Park in Berkeley, and volunteered to be on their staff. I sat behind their store counter and read all day.

Now, even though I had made it to UCB, I was no intellectual. I had only learned English 8 years earlier after my family emigrated from Shanghai, China via Hong Kong, and between our diaspora and our poverty, we never had anything more than a few raggedy text books in our home while I was growing up. But now I began to read everything—"Wretched of the Earth," "Pedagogy of the Oppressed," the Black Panther Party (BPP) newspaper, things like that. I even read "The Origin of the Family, Private Property, and the State" by Frederick Engels simply because of its intriguing and provocative title, not yet aware that it was Marxist or communist. From the get, a critical concern for me and many of my comrade-sisters was the unequivocal elimination of not just white supremacy, but male supremacy. These twin unrelenting concerns would eventually lead me to the most thorough-going revolutionary philosophy/ideology, Marxism-Leninism-Maoism.

Given my family history, I didn't read Mao at first. Months later, one of the S.F. Chinatown Red Guards quoted from Mao's little Red Book during a mass meeting at the I-Hotel. It was upsetting, and rather ironic, because my family had left China in 1955 and my mom had told me never to listen to reds, and here I was. But the whole youth upsurge of that time forced me to be open minded. So I read it and found that it actually made sense! Despite an endless stream of lies and slanders about Mao and the Cultural Revolution so pervasive today, my own journey to Mao shows that the truth backed by a revolutionary movement is more powerful than popular prejudices and misconceptions backed by individualistic sob stories.

Struggles against the Vietnam war, for Black liberation, for affirmative action and ethnic studies, were part of our generation rising up and calling into question the unjust and unequal foundation of this society—the economics, the politics, and traditional social relations between men and women, workers and intellectuals, whites and people of color, youth and elders, etc. All this was part of the rebellion that rocked our generation here and internationally in the late 1960s and early 1970s. Rebel students had been shot down in Mexico. Rebel students in France had raised a slogan that captured our attitude "Be realistic: demand the impossible."

Like many others, I began to question and reject the traditional methods and goals of capitalist education. We would laugh about "educated fools from uneducated schools." We began to see our university education as a reflection and a concentration of the me-first, dog-eat-dog society. We disdained the aspirations for self-serving careers or for administrative positions over those on the bottom rungs of society. We saw the battle for equal and relevant education as part of a larger rebellion against society's multi-faceted inequities. We began to discuss and debate alternatives.

It was part of this debate and discussion, more of which needs to happen nowadays, that many of us began to evaluate the Black Panthers and Mao Zedong more seriously. At that time, the BPP represented the vanguard element fighting for the liberation of Black people, a struggle that was pushing forward the whole revolutionary upsurge in this country. They influenced many of us to begin looking for radical solutions to get OUT of the system's madness completely. They helped make the connection between the struggles against U.S. imperialism abroad and the struggles within the U.S., such as between Vietnamese and Black liberation.

During their revolutionary days, the Panthers had told Bob Avakian, today's RCP Chairman, that Mao Zedong was "the baddest muthafucka on the planet earth!" They saw that people in revolutionary China had political power, the kind of power the oppressed needed and wanted here in the U.S. They challenged millions like myself about whether this system could be reformed, or whether armed revolution and socialism were the solutions to root out the problems we saw worldwide, including inside the U.S. There are people in the RCP who had been members or close supporters of the BPP, and in many crucial ways the RCP is standing on the shoulders of the revolutionary legacy of the BPP and carrying it forward.

Mao and the Struggle against Soviet Revisionism

I mentioned that one of the great features of the 1960s and early 1970s was the spirit of debate and the discovery of revolutionary theory. We wanted to know what revolution was all about and how to get there. One big question was the role of the (then) Soviet Union and their U.S. ally, the Communist Party USA (CPUSA). We wondered why their position on everything was downright conservative, even though they called themselves communist.

Through many first hand accounts of travelers to China during the Cultural Revolution, as well as a vast array of literature from China, activists like myself were learning about the many radical achievements in China. We heard about the kind of soul-stirring struggles that were being waged to bring about momentous changes in Chinese society, for example the development of new and liberating roles for women.

But also coming out of China were challenging theories, including a radical critique of the Soviet Union. Mao was calling out the Soviet Union as revisionist, saying that the Soviet Union was not a genuine socialist society. We began to check out this analysis. Many young radicals like me had not been particularly impressed with the Soviet Union—it seemed so un-revolutionary, like a big welfare state that "took care of people." By contrast, we could see that in China, the people were being unleashed to make sweeping transformations in all realms of society. We were learning about the difference between revolution and revisionism.

What is revisionism? It means to revise, a revision of Marxism. Marxism is the science and ideology of revolution—it's about turning the world upside down and eliminating classes and social divisions. Marxism is the theory and method to free humanity through revolutionary struggle. Revisionism however is a non-revolutionary, non-liberating notion of socialism and communism. It pays lip service to Marxism and revolutionary change, but it does not promote overturning all existing social and economic relations. Mao said that Marxism hold thousands of truths but boils down to the truth that it's right to rebel against reactionaries. Put simply, revisionism takes the rebellion out of Marxism.

Now from its very beginning, Marxism has been locked in struggle against political trends and theories that would turn the workers' movement and liberation struggles away from the goal of emancipation. But something new happened in the Soviet Union in the mid-1950s: revisionism had come to power in a socialist society.

After Joseph Stalin died in 1953, a new privileged elite at the top levels of the Communist Party in the Soviet Union took over. Nikita Khrushchev was their point man, and starting in 1956, he launched an attack on the theory and practice of socialist revolution by way of an attack on Stalin. He said that classes and class struggle had died out, and that the Soviet Union no longer needed a dictatorship of the proletariat, that is the dictatorship of the working class, over old and new exploiting classes. He said the proletariat no longer needed a vanguard party, its instrument of achieving and exercising state power. He said that the task of the Soviet Union was not to revolutionize society but basically to increase production, raise living standards, and surpass the technological levels of the West.

He led the Soviet Union to turn its back on world revolution. He said that socialism could peacefully coexist with U.S. and other imperialism. He preached that violent revolution is no longer needed, that fundamental change can come about peacefully. As noted earlier, in the 1960s national liberation struggles in Asia, Africa and Latin America were slamming the U.S. hard, but Khrushchev and the Soviets wanted to cool out these struggles; he talked about how these struggles made the world a more dangerous place. This was the same line that the CPUSA followed and promoted here.

This was Soviet revisionism. Khrushchev set out to do 2 things: 1) to restructure the Soviet economy along capitalist lines. Once again workers were being exploited, but in the name of socialism and communism!; 2) to attempt to ram these "creative ideas" down the throats of communist parties around the world, including those on Mao and the Communist Party of China.

Starting in 1956, Mao led the way in analyzing what happened —what went wrong—in the Soviet Union. In 1963, the Chinese Marxist-Leninists went on the offensive and began publishing several polemics—deep critiques exposing the counter-revolutionary essence of Khrushchev's revisionism. They taught that the proletariat needs to keep its grip on political power in socialist society. They taught that you can't achieve real socialism without violent revolution, and popularized the slogan that "political power comes from the barrel of a gun." As noted earlier, they vigorously upheld and supported the tidal wave of national liberation struggles around the world.

Mao also put forward a beginning analysis of the nature and forces of class struggle in socialist society, and why the revolution has to continue under socialism. This laid the foundation for Mao's all-important theory of the danger of capitalist restoration under socialism.

Mao had drawn a sharp dividing line between revolution and revisionism. The Soviet Union retaliated. It withdrew economic aid and advisors, and made military threats against China. But Mao was fearless! He continued to fight for revolution in China and throughout the world. He then applied the lessons of fighting Soviet revisionists to the struggle inside China against revisionists like Liu Shaoqi and Deng Xiaoping. The need to prevent the same fate in China—capitalist restoration—was the basis of the Cultural Revolution initiated and led by Mao and in which his close comrades, the so-called "gang of four", played a leading role.[4]

Mao's struggle against revisionism in the Soviet Union and China played a pivotal role in rebuilding the revolutionary Marxist-Leninist movement in the 1960s. It gave direction and inspiration to revolutionaries all over the world: from the Philippines, to Peru, to Nepal, to the U.S.[5] Though activists like myself did not have a very developed understanding of what revisionism was about at the time, the battle between real and phony communism profoundly affected how I came to grasp Marxism as the most revolutionary ideology there is.

While it is beyond the scope of this essay to explore in full[6], I want to note here that revisionism continues to be an influence in today's political movements and debates. It shows up in theories claiming to be "Marxist" that say overthrowing the system is neither possible nor necessary in advanced capitalist societies. It purports that the '90s technological advances have rendered revolutionary vanguards, the dictatorship of the proletariat, and planned socialist economies outmoded. It insists that if you want to organize people, you have to stick to immediate bread and butter issues because you can't win people to a revolutionary vision of turning society and the world upside down. At the height of the 1960s revolutionary upsurge, these revisionist theories were discredited among large sections of rebel youth, especially those increasingly inspired by Mao and the Cultural Revolution in China.

Revolution within a Revolution

As the most radical youth all over the world fought the many outrages of capitalism/imperialism in the 1960s, we searched for and found a mirror image in the youth of China's Cultural Revolution. From 1966 to 1976, like the rest of our generation, China's youth were fighting for revolutionary change. The big difference was that they were part of a process of making a revolution within a revolution! This was totally unprecedented. Mao was leading the masses to solve the problem of how to deal with a section of revolutionary leaders that had come to power under socialism and had become a new elite, a new privileged class of exploiters.

The Cultural Revolution was about the masses being mobilized to rise up against top communist party officials who wanted to drag things back to capitalism. It was about the masses of people making deeper and more profound changes throughout society, and more and more becoming masters of society. And for 10 years the Cultural Revolution succeeded in carrying the socialist revolution forward, until 1976 when reactionary forces launched a coup after Mao died. The distinctive thing we saw in the youth and workers in China was this: they were pointing the way forward ideologically and practically about how to advance a revolution until classes, all oppressive divisions of labor, all vestiges of inequality and injustice are eliminated everywhere in the world—that's communism. This vision provided us with a model of a the kind of vibrant society we wanted to strive for and to live in.

The rebel youth called Red Guards were high school and college students—mainly high school. They first sprang up in Beijing as a movement of youth critical of the remnants of old values in China's educational system. The old outlook was to study hard and become a well-off intellectual. In 1966, a young woman instructor at Beijing University had put up a wall poster blasting university and party officials for blocking students and young faculty from carrying out revolutionary criticism and struggle. Conservative forces in the party and the government had tried to put a lid on the growing movement.

Mao responded by issuing his own wall poster saluting the students and calling on the masses to "bombard the headquarters." Mao's message was that it was right to rebel against revisionism, and that it was necessary to confront conservative forces, especially the capitalist roaders at the highest levels of the party and government who were holding society back and keeping the people down.

In the words of one former Red Guard: "[T]he first important impact on the young generation was the call from Mao to participate in political struggles, to understand thoroughly what was really going on in the society. The immediate aspect was issues relating to education [where] the educated youth, the graduating students would not be able to do any hard work, any manual work, any common people's work. They would just know how to read books. They were trained to be a superior person, not a common working class member. So if this kind of education was to produce a great number of students, those students would only expand the 3 differences: the difference between mental and manual labor, between rural and urban, between workers and peasants...[I]f we kept going like this...the color of the country would turn from red to some other color."[7]

This was a challenging view of what education should be: Education that aims to eradicate instead of reinforce inequalities and divisions; education that teaches about the real lives and real struggles of working people whose labor makes the world go round: education that criticizes and discards self seeking competition, blind obedience to convention and authority; education that links theory with practice, such as linking the research lab to the medical clinic.

Many of us admired the vanguard role played by these Red Guards in fighting against inequality, elitism, hierarchy, and the danger of revolutionaries selling out and becoming new exploiters. They were a new kind of intellectual that we began to emulate, revolutionary intellectuals who made knowledge serve the needs of the great majority of people instead of appropriating it as private property. Millions of youth were encouraged to travel all over China—with free train fare, food and lodging—to take revolutionary politics, culture, and even medical care to remote villages as well as to factories. The youth mixed it up with the workers and peasants like never before.

As workers and peasants entered the struggle under the leadership of the revolutionary headquarters in the party, the Cultural Revolution deepened. Workers overthrew capitalist roaders and new institutions of proletarian power were created. The masses developed many new social innovations, called "socialist new things." One example was "barefoot doctors"—young paramedics, many of whom were peasants, who trained for a short period then returned to the countryside, extending basic health care to millions in remote areas of China. Feudal operas gave way to uplifting works of art that put rebel workers, peasants, youth and liberated women on center stage—art created about them but also BY them. Factory life was transformed and the old system of one-man management was replaced with new collective forms—managers participated in productive labor and workers participated in management. A decisive achievement of the Cultural Revolution was that the Party itself got revolutionized, and the link between the Party and the masses was strengthened.

Today we are told that socialist economies don't work[8]. We are told that the Cultural Revolution was an economic disaster. The truth is that Maoist China was developing an economy that was both meeting basic needs and overcoming the inequalities of society. Using a radical and different approach of "grasp revolution, promote production," socialist China showed that great economic developments can be made by relying on the creative energy of the people, and not reliance on faceless bureaucrats making all the decisions. They showed that an economy does not have to be organized around private ownership, profit and greed. The Cultural Revolution stirred deep ideological self-examination of the whole "me-first" mind-set of capitalism. Imagine a society organized around the principle of "Serve the People"!

The "Serve the People" Legacy

Influenced by the Red Guards and the spirit of "serve the people," there developed a mass movement among tens of thousands of us—students and youth—to go to (or back to) the working class and the communities of the oppressed. For me, it meant dropping out of college and returning to the factory, as well as going to S.F. Chinatown/Manilatown to join the revolutionary activists already there. Once there, the hard question posed itself concretely: "What is to be done" to implement our lofty ideal and apply the brilliant examples from socialist China to our communities that would really make a difference?

At the time, there was no revolutionary organization with a developed strategy, plan, program or leadership on how to concretely "smash imperialism from within," much less a vision and plan to rebuild a new society like what we saw in China. Like many others, I checked out working with many of the radical groups on Kearny Street/I-Hotel at the time, and eventually I settled on relating to Wei Min She (WMS). Before joining WMS, I was to learn some lessons about what it would take to "serve the people" for real.

Emulating the radically different health care system in China, I helped launch an alternative health clinic in S.F. Chinatown in 1971. Along with some medical students and community activists, we opened a free health clinic in the basement of one of the Ping Yuen (housing projects). We enthusiastically rounded up old donated medical equipment for a volunteer staff that included a couple of doctors, and held clinics 2 nights a week. But this turned into an all-consuming effort to gather resources and provide medical care that wasn't shoddy (and dangerous) for a desperately poor population. The steering committee had bitter arguments over the direction of the clinic and the actual quality of care we were delivering. Some argued we should get government grants and go "legit," while others argued against becoming poverty program administrators of crumbs from the establishment, or a "new breed" of social workers for capitalism.

After a year of struggling, the clinic was abandoned in the face of hard questions we didn't have answers to. How to get resources for even a minimum level of care (such as paid staff, funds for malpractice insurance, medical supplies and equipment) and not become part of the system we want to fight? What of the systemic socio-economic factors, the poverty and discrimination, that endlessly generated the many diseases people had in Chinatown? While dressing the wounds, how do we get rid of the great wound maker[9]—the profit system? A WMS member in the Revolutionary Union (forerunner of the RCP) had actually cautioned me about these contradictions at the onset of my venture. She noted that my heart was in the right place, but such an attempt at piecemeal reform of capitalist health services was a mine field of frustrations and burn outs. Typical of many young people (even in the '60s), I decided to go try things out for myself.

Summing up the failed clinic attempt a year later, I was relieved that the attitude of my RU/WMS friends was far from "I told you so." Instead, there were insights about how and why China was able to "perform miracles" in their health care system: that the proletariat had state power there and thus could allocate resources on a grand scale to meet the needs of the people; and it was part of mobilizing and empowering the people themselves and their initiative to struggle and transform the world around them. This helped to delineate what was correct from what was incorrect in our conceptions of trying to "serve the people", and whether or not we could truly do so within the framework of capitalism. Personally, the clinic project drove home the point from Mao that "without state power, all is an illusion." And promoting illusions, despite our best intentions, was objectively dangerous, particularly in the field of medical care.

For me, this experience became part of a dynamic but dogged process of measuring social practice in relationship to the goal of a radically different social system. We were learning that you have to fight oppression and fight for the needs of the people, like healthcare for the poor, AS PART OF building a revolutionary movement. We began to learn how the whole foundation of the capitalist system is based on exploitation, and why nothing short of revolution could fundamentally get rid of ALL the misery around us. We struggled to understand how the proletariat is the most anticapitalist class in today's society and the most thoroughly revolutionary class in human history. It stimulated many of us to get deeply into studying the revolutionary ideology of this class—Marxism-Leninism-Maoism—and to apply its outlook and methods (such as criticism/self-criticism) to our political organizing.

Ideological Struggle: Deepening Our Struggle and Commitment

We found that being a revolutionary was an exciting and ceaseless process of learning and changing the world. We discovered that engaging in ideological struggle, far from diverting us, would energize us and lead to new horizons of tackling difficult problems. We could not be afraid of discarding former prejudices.

From my rebel student days, when my concern was on the liberation of Asian peoples, it was always coupled with concern over the liberation of women. I could not imagine being part of a revolution that left the sisters of the world in misery, especially in the "third world" countries where feudal traditions are incredibly brutal, traditions that I had tasted first-hand during childhood. A key inspiration that convinced me of the need for PROLETARIAN/COMMUNIST revolution was the concrete transformations of the Cultural Revolution, especially its effects on liberating women.

The whole process of struggling for Marxist-Leninist-Maoist ideology also meant putting my own life experiences into a larger context and goal: making a leap to being out for nothing less than wiping out and tearing up the roots of oppression not just in one place, one country or region, and not just for one group or nation, but worldwide and for humanity overall. This leap meant becoming a member of the RCP—to become a proletarian internationalist in word and deed—to carry out the historic mission of the working class to liberate ourselves and the whole human race. Becoming an internationalist also meant this life- long commitment: to support revolution and revolutionary struggles against imperialism everywhere in the world, AND to do our share in making the greatest contribution to the world revolution where we live—in the belly of the beast.

Revolution in the Belly of the Beast

For 25 years, I've been part of the RCP's efforts to continuously develop its strategy—building the revolutionary movement and laying the basis to wage and win the armed struggle to overthrow the rule of capitalism when the conditions are ripe.[10] I know that a lot of people who truly hate this system and would like to see radical and fundamental change don't think a revolution is realistic in a country like the U.S. And some activists conclude that the best we can do is to fight to force the system to be less savage. I have several responses to this.

First, U.S. imperialism is not all-powerful. Let's not forget that the Vietnamese people's determined struggle defeated the U.S. with all its military and high tech might. Second, in terms of the situation in the U.S., one of the most important things we learned in the 1960s was that conditions can change very sharply. Over a period of just a few years, perhaps hundreds of thousands of people became revolutionary minded, and many more either participated in various forms of resistance or were sympathetic.

Obviously, there is not that kind of ferment and tumult today. But the authorities do have a great deal of concern about how stability could unravel in the U.S. They definitely take the potential for rebellion and upheaval quite seriously. Look at how the power structure is feverishly enforcing brutal and repressive conditions on those they impose the worst oppression and exploitation—on more police, prisons, surveillance, etc. as well as building up their right-wing militias.

We in the RCP think that revolution in the belly of the beast is not only necessary but possible. Everything we do is to put into effect a strategy we call "the united front against imperialism under the leadership of the proletariat". We are working to unite all who can be united against the system's attacks, and to help people get a sense of their own strengths, and the enemy's weaknesses, as we join with the people to fight back. This unity of people from different nationalities and different backgrounds is how people learn why the system is our common enemy and why it has to be overthrown.

And we work to bring the fierce determination and strength of the have-nots, the proletarians of all nationalities, into this mix—whether in the struggles against the abuse of immigrants or the abuse of women. We especially build what we call the solid core of the united front—which is the revolutionary alliance of proletarians of all nationalities fighting against ALL oppression and exploitation, with the struggles of the oppressed nationalities (i.e. Black people, Latinos, Asians, Native Americans, Puerto Ricans etc.) to end their oppression.

Writing this essay at the end of 1999, the situation in the U.S. is not yet ripe for being able to bring the system down through mass armed revolution. But it is time to step up political work to prepare for such a time, whenever it does come—and that might not be as far off as some people think. Why do I say this? Because this system exists by exploiting and oppressing people, there is bound to be repeated resistance of various sizes and intensity.

It may be helpful to recall the 1992 L.A. rebellion, a rebellion that showed the revolutionary potential of the have-nots in U.S. society. This uprising of Black and Latino proletarians and youth drew in the support of some Asians as well as some white people. It made the local power structure jump back, signified by Police Chief Daryl "Gestapo" Gates losing his job. It called forth rebellions and mass protests all across the country, and drew a lot of support and sympathy from many middle-class people.

Even as the powers-that-be worked overtime to inflame conflicts between Korean store owners and Blacks, there were also protests of Korean people in L.A. following the rebellion where justice for Rodney King was a political demand. More recently, there has been an increasing number of Asian youth in the movement against police brutality across the U.S., as well as in the battle to stop the execution of the only political prisoner on death row, Mumia Abu-Jamal. These further express the basis to build unity as we resist the system's attacks.

There are bound to be major flashpoints in the struggle between the people and the system that hold the potential to erupt into serious crisis. The Asian financial meltdown shows how quickly things could spin out of control for the imperialist system. And what would be the impact on the situation in this country if there was an uprising in Mexico followed by U.S. troops crossing the border to help suppress it?

These kinds of developments, or some combination of them, could create a radically different situation quickly, where the prospects of a revolutionary crises could develop. But a profound lesson from the 1960s legacy is that such crises by themselves will not bring down and defeat the system. Again, that requires revolutionary leadership with deep roots among all sections of the people, that has actually done the preparatory work to be able to seize the openings provided by such crises. This makes stepping up the efforts to build a powerful revolutionary movement, as well as revolutionary organization, an urgent necessity for the new generation. And many young warriors have already stepped to the frontlines of some of the key battles of the '90s.

Conclusion

Twice in the past century, in the Soviet Union and China, those on the bottom of society have tasted the future. Yet twice on that road to the future, the proletariat met defeat—first in the Soviet Union in 1956, and then in China in 1976—where the revisionists seized power and restored capitalism. We live in times when the ruling classes are using these setbacks to hammer away at the message that communism is dead. What should we conclude from this? That revolution and socialism are bound to fail? That the liberating ideology of the proletariat is flawed? Not at all. To begin with, we can't forget what was in fact accomplished when the masses had power. Second, the accumulated experiences so far, especially the lessons of the Cultural Revolution in continuing revolution under socialism, have made the path and understanding of how to bring about and advance such a revolution clearer. And we need to be clear about what we are fighting for and what it will take to get there:

As compared with all previous revolutions in which one class overthrew anoth-

194

er, proletarian revolution seeks to make those two radical ruptures of which Marx and Engels spoke: the radical rupture with traditional property relations and traditional ideas. It seeks not to replace one form of exploitation with another but to do away with all forms of exploitation and indeed ultimately to eliminate all class distinctions. So, for this very reason, we can only expect and must be prepared for the fact that the proletarian revolution will be even more tortuous than previous revolutions; will undergo a longer, more complex process of revolution and counter revolution before it reaches its final goal of communism worldwide.[11]

As we enter the new millennium, capitalism has ever more become a total disaster for people here and around the world. This is a system that exploits billions of people, that robs wealth and plunders resources, that threatens the very ecology of the planet. But there is resistance, there is revolution, and there is Mao's powerful legacy. In Peru, Nepal, and the Philippines, Maoist Communist parties are leading people's wars.

Proletarian revolution is alive, and it is needed more than ever. Only then can we create an economic and social system based on co-operation, meeting the needs of the people, and overcoming ALL forms of inequality. Only then can we build a world where there's no more haves sitting on top of the have- nots, no more racism, no more male supremacy, no more one nation dominating another/others.

We need a deep understanding of the revolutionary process. We need to link our political organizing with a liberating vision of a world without exploitation and oppression, which I believe Marxism-Leninism-Maoism[12] provides. As we engage in struggle together, it's good and necessary to also discuss and debate what it will take to bring about a radically different world. To really carry forward the "legacy to liberation" means critically summing up and applying the lessons of the 1960s and the experience gained since then, so we can go further and finish what the 1960s left undone—making revolution.

Mao has the last word: "The future is bright; the road is tortuous."

ENDNOTES

1. In the 1964 presidential election, Lyndon Johnson was the peace "dove" candidate; his opponent Barry Goldwater was the "hawk" warmonger. Johnson won by a "landslide" and proceeded to escalate the war in Vietnam. In the 1972 presidential election, Richard Nixon was the "hawk" and George McGovern was the "dove". Nixon won but was forced to withdraw U.S. troops from Vietnam. The war was brought to an end mainly because the U.S. was defeated by the heroic struggles of the Indochinese peoples, as well as shaken by the powerful anti-war upsurge here. These are just two dramatic illustrations that the most important decisions in U.S. society are not mainly governed by the electoral process.

2. "Six Years in a Tiger Cage," Asian Women Journal (U.C. Berkeley, Bancroft Library 1971) page 83.

3. Ibid, page 85.

4. The so-called "gang of four" were Mao's widow Chiang Ching, Chang Chun-chiao, Wang Hung-wen, Yao Wen-yuan. They were arrested after Mao died in 1976 and put on trial by the revisionists who rule China today. For more detailed explanation, see Mao Makes Five: Mao Tsetung's Last Great Battle (Chicago, Banner Press, 1978) edited with an introduction by Raymond Lotta, which has documents from the "gang of four"

as well as from their revisionist enemies such as Deng Xiaoping.

5. Today, the Revolutionary Internationalist Movement (RIM) is a grouping of Maoist parties and organizations who are continuing this legacy in a dozen countries around the world. Among those participating in the RIM are the RCP, USA as well as the Communist Party of Peru, and the Communist Party of Nepal (Maoist). For an exclusive look into the Maoist revolution in Nepal, see "Dispatches: Report from the People's War in Nepal" in the *Revolutionary Worker* newspaper, which began with issue #1014, July 18, 1999.

6. For an in-depth and rigorous analysis of revisionism in today's world, see "Phony Communism is Dead, Long Live Real Communism" (Chicago, RCP Publications, 1992) by Bob Avakian.

7. "Running with the Red Guards" an interview with Yi Wang, a former Red Guard in China, *Revolutionary Worker* #386, December 12, 1993.

8. See MAOIST ECONOMICS and the revolutionary road to communism. The Shanghai Textbook (New York, Banner Press, 1994) for a thorough discussion of socialist political economy .

9. Chapter 17 of Quotations from Chairman Mao TseTung (Peking, Foreign Language Press, 1972) is titled "Serving the People". Mao refers to Dr. Norman Bethune, a Canadian communist and physician who went to China and died while treating the Red Army. Mao called on the Chinese people to emulate Bethune's selflessness. Many of us involved in alternative health care were influenced by Mao's call, as well as the life of Dr. Bethune traced in the book The Scalpel, the Sword (Boston, Little, Brown and Company, 1952), especially its last chapter "The enemy—those who make the wounds."

10. In The Asian American Movement (Philadelphia, Temple University Press, 1993), a very conservative account by William Wei, which among many inaccuracies and distortions on AAM history, contains the statement that "Except for the bookstores it operates, the Revolutionary Communist party has all but disappeared...". Even a cursory investigation would have revealed this to be factually incorrect. But for Mr. Wei, it might reveal some idle but wishful thinking?

11. See "The End of a Stage—the Beginning of a New Stage, Two Talks by Bob Avakian," in *Revolution* (Chicago, RCP Publications) issue #60, Fall 1990.

12. Marxism-Leninism-Maoism (Maoism for short) is the science and ideology of proletarian revolution as it has developed to the present day. For a short summary, see the Declaration of the Revolutionary Internationalist Movement and Long Live Marxism-Leninism-Maoism (India, Chithira Printers and Publishers, 1998). For a comprehensive historical overview, see Bob Avakian, Mao's Tsetung's Immortal Contributions (Chicago, RCP Publications, 1979).

Both spelling of Mao's name are used in this essay for the sake of accuracy in referencing other articles or events. All the Maoist materials referenced in this essay can be obtained through Revolution Books at 2425C Channing Way, Berkeley, California, 94704.

HOW I BECAME A REVOLUTIONARY

Estella Habal

How I became a revolutionary initially had to do with the conditions of my life and how dissatisfied I had become with myself and my life, feeling trapped within it and wanting a way out. A series of circumstances within my own life and influential people led me in the direction of revolutionary politics. In other words, being in contact with "the movement" was indispensable for my development as a revolutionary. Without it, I could have easily gone in another direction. The pull of "the revolution" was both seductive and intoxicating.

Moving to San Francisco in June, 1971 was a turning point and a beginning of my commitment to revolutionary politics and a new life. I had literally run away from a five-year marriage that was the product of two teenage pregnancies and a lot of ignorance. I felt the whole world had opened up to me. Feeling both empowered and scared with two baby boys to raise on my own, I knew that life would be hard. My experience as a young mother and college student had already prepared me somewhat for the adventures ahead.

Twelve days before my sixteenth birthday, I gave birth to my first son. I pleaded with my father that I did not want to be married. He told me that I had no choice. Marrying the father of my baby was the only way to save the family name from the disgrace of pregnancy out of wedlock. So, at a tender young age, I married a Filipino boy who was only two years older than me, in what was called in those days a "shotgun wedding." A year later, I gave birth to another baby boy.

Years later my father tried to convince himself that my husband's family probably planned our match because our family was supposedly more prestigious in the community. In fact, there was not much difference between the two families. Although my family was a bit more "assimilated," both were poor, working class families struggling to survive in the "Filipino barrio" of a small town, Seaside, California. Both of our fathers were World War II veterans, both families were large (about 6 children), both mothers and siblings had to work to make ends meet. My sisters and I, as teenagers, worked in the Salinas fields, just like my husband's brothers and sisters. Nonetheless, my marriage was not a "match made in heaven"—and as a young teenage wife and mother of two children, I felt trapped and deeply unhappy.

Graduating from high school was an early test of my perseverance and strength. My ninth, tenth and eleventh grades were spent in a special high school program

197

which allowed young girls like myself to continue school at home by telephone. Many of the other girls were like me, shunned by their schools because they were pregnant or teenage mothers, or physically disabled. Luckily, birth control pills were made available in the mid-1960s and I was able to keep from being forever pregnant and able to enroll in the normal high school with other kids my own age. By the time I reached twelfth grade, I excelled in school, made the honor roll, joined the debating club, and spoke about social issues at the local Lion's Club luncheons. I longed so much to be like the other kids, but I knew I was different, I was already a mother with two children. Not surprisingly, my senior classmates at Carson High School voted me "the most serious."

Part of my feeling trapped had to do with my aspirations to become something other than a farm worker or housewife. After high school, I worked for several years, but felt a yearning to learn more—I wasn't even sure what. I decided to go to college. I remember my husband could not understand why I would be interested in attending college, especially since I was already making a decent living as a clerical worker. After all, I had a white collar, civil service job at Harbor General Hospital in Carson, California. By my husband's standards, I'd already achieved my goals. He viewed graduating from high school more than enough and going to college was an excessive luxury—besides, all hands were needed to work. I knew he could never understand our estrangement and my aspirations, and give me the trust and support I needed.

Fortunately, I had the support of my mother and father. My going to college was seen as a big step for the whole family. I was the first of my generation to attend college. Both of my parents came from poor peasant backgrounds in the Philippines, and none of my siblings had the level of academic achievement or desire to finish college at the time. My mother was willing to baby-sit my boys while I began to attend classes in the fall of 1969.

I was intellectually curious and enjoyed the bustle of activity at Long Beach State College. At the time it seemed that the campus teamed with revolutionary fervor and youthful activities. Students for a Democratic Society (SDS) had a chapter on campus, but Filipino students like myself (there were only a handful of us back then) were more attracted to the other minority student organizations rather than groups that were monopolized by white males. There were also very few black students on campus. I do remember seeing Angela Davis on campus once, she was already famous with her big, wide Afro. Although I didn't believe for a minute the newspaper claims that she tried to smuggle a weapon (inside her hairdo) into San Quentin in the ill-fated attempt to break George Jackson and others of the "San Quentin Six" out of prison—still her appearance frightened me.

My first introduction to Marxist, revolutionary politics was by Chicano students in an organization called United Mexican American Students (UMAS) to be renamed later as MECHA which included the concept of Chicano. The Mexican revolutionary style did not seem to scare me so much. Ironically, I donned the beret and *la bandaleria* with ease (more for show than actual use). Perhaps because of the similar Spanish colonial history, the same Catholic background, a similar working class, immigrant culture, whatever, I felt an affinity for Mexican students (the term Chicano came later). Those students taught me about the popular Mexican historical figures, such as Emiliano Zapata. Through the exposure, I knew more about the father of the Mexican revolution before I even learned about their Filipino contemporaries who had fought against Spain and the United States as well.

After my exposure to revolutionary politics, "campus life" shrank and felt like "small potatoes." Although I don't remember the exact moment, I decided to drop out of school and embark on a new life. The idea of returning to school never entered my mind when I had become a revolutionary. I felt that learning from people in the "movement" was more productive and interesting. If I had to do it all over again, I feel that I would have done the same.

Opportunity knocked when I got the chance to run away. Fleeing an oppressive marital situation, I hooked up with another man, packed up my kids and left Los Angeles in June 1971 for San Francisco and adventure. When I arrived I went immediately to the International Hotel (IH), which was at the time a Mecca for Filipino activist youth throughout the West Coast. Only a year before I had visited the hotel with a group sponsored by SIPA (Search to Involve Pilipino Americans) from Los Angeles, a group which I had helped start. SIPA was a youth group of Filipino Americans that brought Filipino culture back to young Filipino Americans who had been assimilated into American culture and had no knowledge of their history or culture. Through funding, SIPA became one of the stable Filipino community institutions in Los Angeles that not only brings culture but important social services to the community. It still exists today.

At that time, institutions like the media and schools exclusively projected White American culture and history, more specifically, European and American White Anglo Saxon Protestant culture. Most Filipino parents agreed with the status quo because they thought that was the way to get ahead. They felt that racial discrimination would not happen if their children became fully American and forgot their Filipino roots and culture. So, of course, young Filipinos learned to speak in impeccable American accents, ditched anything that resembled Filipino because it was considered inferior to European and white American values and culture. The new generation of Filipino youth was totally assimilated and spoke no Filipino languages or dialects.

It is hard to describe one's feelings when you discover that you do have a history worth studying and a culture to be proud of. The civil rights movement and the ideas of Black Power had influenced many of us who were willing to listen. We owe a debt to Black people in this country who opened the doors for us. Minority peoples became empowered. There was a tremendous pride in our own people's contributions to American society. We began to understand the role of racism and the inferiorization of Third world peoples. Anti-colonial movements around the world stirred us. Although I was not completely aware of all of this at that time in my development, it was part of the background and atmosphere of the time.

For Asian Americans, especially Filipinos, the International Hotel struggle was a movement that galvanized students and youth. What was initially an anti-eviction battle in San Francisco of Filipino elderly beginning in the fall of 1968 became the Asian community struggle for all the youth. Those were defiant times; the Filipino old-timers had already organized themselves in the face of eviction notices in December 1968 and refused to move. Students from all over would descend on the hotel every weekend and volunteer their efforts to renovate the hotel as a concrete expression of support for their struggle. Little did I know that I was later to return to the anti-eviction battle of the IH as a full time organizer years later as a member of the KDP (the Union of Democratic Filipinos—see Helen Toribio's article).

It seemed my fate was sealed, that day I returned to the International Hotel I met Rodel. He was a revolutionary from the Philippines who was both a novelty and a mystery to me since I had known only "assimilated" first and second generation Filipino Americans most of my life. He was the first young immigrant I had met who had only recently arrived from the Philippines. He was an exiled student activist who came to the US in the face of the increasing repression of the Marcos regime (this was maybe a year or so before the declaration of martial law).

Rodel helped me get my first job in San Francisco. He knew of an opening at San Francisco Newsreel, an anti-imperialist film collective. I was intrigued by the possibility of making films. They accepted me because they needed minorities or "Third World people." That job was my first entry into organized Left-wing politics. Through the medium of revolutionary documentaries and films I became aware of many other people's movements, both in the US and throughout the world.

I stayed with the Newsreel collective about two years from 1971-73, during which time my main responsibility was in the area of film distribution. Those years were the height of the Anti Vietnam War Movement, we would get rental orders from all over the country, mostly from radical student groups. The most popular films I remember were about Vietnam and Cuba, the Black Panthers, Young Lords and DRUM (Detroit Revolutionary Union Movement). My task was to process the orders, ship out the films and do routine maintenance on them to ensure they were in good working condition. Another part of the collective concentrated on actual film/documentary production. Unfortunately I never got my turn to be trained in film production. As I look back, part of it was that I was young with no film making experience, but another part I'm sure, was that I was a mother and a woman of color. This issue of "de facto" segregation came to fruition a year later when the "Third World caucus" decided to split from S.F. Newsreel.

The Newsreel collective participated directly in the anti-war movement, and although it considered itself an educational "arm" of the "movement" (and not a political organization as such), Newsreel was widely known and respected in movement circles. I remember representing the Collective in the "Spring Mobilization" (Mobe) of 1972, a nation wide coalition of student and community organizations opposed to the Vietnam War. In the San Francisco Bay Area, it started with a march and ended with a rally at Golden Gate Park. The "Spring Mobe" was the first time I had helped organize anything that big—tens of thousands of people showed up on the day of the march. We leafleted the demonstration and had secured a large auditorium next at Kezar stadium and showed films all afternoon to hundreds of folks who had marched that day.

"Collectives" back then were a "total experience." For example, the members of Newsreel tended to organize themselves into "household collectives" as well. I remember people were careful to call it a collective and not a "hippie" commune. It was a living arrangement based on necessity rather than any principles that people should share everything. In the collective certain things were shared (in theory anyway) – rent money was pooled according to an agreed upon amount, household cooking and chores were shared, and even childcare was carefully planned. One of the purposes of the collective which attracted me was to liberate people, especially women, from household drudgery so that they could participate in more meaningful, productive work. Weekly "house meetings" were organized to engage in "criticism/self-criticism" over household tensions that inevitably would arise out of dissimilar backgrounds and expectations. Another woman and myself were mothers, so all the members of the collective took turns with doing childcare. I gave birth to my daughter while living in the Newsreel Collective, which gave the household four young children, in total, to deal with—quite a task!

However throughout this experience, I felt a need to center my political growth and development closer to Filipinos and the Filipino community. Although I had learned from my experiences at SF Newsreel and was grateful to the people in the collective for helping me with my children, I felt alienated politically, as my tasks within SF Newsreel seemed to become more bureaucratic. Whatever reservations I had were resolved when I met Cynthia and we became very close friends.

I first met Cynthia during a planning meeting for an anti-Vietnam War demonstration protesting the use of biological warfare on the Vietnamese people. I played the Vietnamese woman in a skit displaying the atrocities of the American military against the Vietnamese. After the meeting, Cynthia approached me and asked me to come to a meeting of the Kalayaan newspaper collective. Although she explained the politics of the organization, I didn't fully understand what she said, something about national democracy. All I needed to know was that it was a Filipino revolutionary organization and was happy to find out that there was one. I was ready to join. Revolution meant joining like-minded Filipinos.

Cynthia's appeal was her warm and winning personality, her knowledge of Philippine politics and her indomitable faith in the human race. Back in the Philippines, she had been in the National Council of "Kabataang Makabayan," part of the left and progressive movement in the Philippines that promoted the politics of national liberation, anti-imperialism, and democracy for the poor and true land reform for the peasants. Like a number of other student activists she gave into family pressure and went into exile (at least temporarily) to the United States in the face of mounting government violence and repression.

To me, Cynthia's greatest influence and contribution within the KDP was her ability to bridge the political and cultural differences between recent immigrants and

Filipino Americans. She laid the cornerstone that allowed us to build a truly integrated organization of Filipino immigrants and Filipino Americans. Most of the Filipino Americans came from relatively poor, working class backgrounds, while the majority of the exiled student activists from the Philippines were from more privileged backgrounds. The class "chemistry" between the two groups was often not good, and at times the chasm seemed unbridgeable. Yet the confidence of the KDP that we could work with this contradiction and overcome much of the differences in pursuit of our common goal—in no small part was due to the role Cynthia played in the early, formative years of the organization. For example, Cynthia often suggested promoting persons of working class backgrounds to leading positions if they had potential. This situation sometimes would cause resentment by others of more privileged backgrounds because they felt "de facto" more qualified. Cynthia would smooth the state of affairs by explaining what our political tasks were and how each person complements our strengths. In the area of "mass work," she would explain that working class people had a deeper understanding of the conditions needed to lead the work, while the more privileged had the social ease to move in different social strata. She would talk about collective work that was greater than its parts. Her leadership usually got us moving forward.

Kalayaan's headquarters was in the back of a storefront in the International Hotel. Originally conceived as a propaganda/organizing team in 1971, Kalayaan's main purpose was to distribute, a Filipino newspaper with an anti-U.S. imperialist, anti-racist, and anti-national discrimination perspective nationwide. After a year of propaganda work, Kalayaan decided to become a more "all-sided" and disciplined "underground" collective. I didn't bat an eye at this development. In fact, I thought it exciting that I could participate in a movement that championed the working class and poor in both the United States and in the Philippines. I remember quoting Marx to myself, that I had "nothing to lose but my chains."

I was still with the Newsreel Collective when I began attending the early meetings of the Kalayaan organization. I remember having both the pains of pregnancy and the anticipation of revolutionary activity in the Filipino community. My daughter was due the following fall, and I decided then to name her Kalayaan Guerrero, translated – "freedom fighter." When friends would ask how Kalayaan was, I always answered, "getting bigger everyday." You can imagine their shock when they discovered later that I was not talking about the newspaper!

But how was I going to deal with being a mother in a movement that was primarily composed of young people without children? Again I knew I was different, but that did not deter me. Taking my inspiration from stories about Communist China, I knew that childcare could and should be taken into account in order to encourage women's full participation. After all, even Chairman Mao said the "women hold up half the sky" ... and in those days that was enough to settle any argument! At first I sought childcare in a Chinatown day-care center organized by leftists to care for their children and those of other working people in the community, but this did not work out for me. My persistence paid off though, when my comrades in the Kalayaan (and later the KDP) helped with childcare while I did my political work. I never entertained utopian ideas that the "collective" or even "socialism," could fully take care of children. I knew that I was the primary caregiver and that the burden of responsibility for raising my kids would still remain with me, regardless of the amount of help I received. Deep down I knew that being a mother would pose limitations on my political activity, no matter what. Difficult decisions regarding where to place my time and focus and attention were before me everyday . . . and at times I resented that others did not have to confront the same problem. The tensions created by the demands made by my leadership in the Movement and the needs of my children would remain constant throughout much of my life, a contradiction always to be negotiated and renegotiated again and again and again.

The first major decision that affected my participation because of my family conditions was at the first KDP National Council meeting in 1974. The Kalayaan organization was just one of many local groups which decided to form a national organization of Filipino immigrants and Filipino Americans called the *Katipunan ng mga Demokratikong Pilipino* or the KDP. It had a dual program – support for national democracy in the Philippines and democratic rights for Filipinos in the United States. It was both anti-capitalist and anti-imperialist but explicit support for socialism came about seven years later in 1980. These politics reflected the conditions in the Philippines and in the United States. In the Philippine situation, a national democratic stage was needed before socialism. In the United States, minority peoples were part of the working class and we believed that democratic rights must be extended to minorities first. There was also a recognition that there was not a leading Communist Party in the United States and the task was to rectify and reestablish it. How that was to be done was tabled for the future.

The KDP was patterned after the form of the youth organization in the Philippines, a revolutionary mass organization, not a party cadre organization, as some may think. The process for arriving at decisions was called democratic-centralist, although at the time I never thought it might have been at the root of some errors. Even with our inexperience, we felt a collective leadership was necessary to lead the mass membership. If disagreements appeared, they were usually resolved at the leadership level. Democracy occurred on the chapter level and ultimately at national congresses, which occurred every other year.

At our Founding Congress in July 1973, I was elected to the National Council. I was then nominated to become a member of the new National Executive Board, the day to day national leadership body of the KDP. I thought intently about my revolutionary tasks and how exciting it would be to build a national organization from the ground up. However, after much soul searching, I realized that the tasks would be too encompassing for a mother with three young children—so I declined the offer. The Council reluctantly acknowledged my conditions and chose someone else to fill the position, a young Filipino American woman who had similar working class credentials as myself, but no children. I was then assigned to help build the local KDP chapter in the Bay Area.

Ironically, my political work in the local San Francisco area over the next ten years may have been even more time-consuming than a national level assignment, which had a more methodical and controlled aspect to it. This situation was like burning a candle at both ends. My assignments in the KDP were on many different levels and many different leadership bodies—the San Francisco chapter leadership, the Northern California Regional Executive Board, a special team assigned to lead the work at the International Hotel, and then finally in the National Education Department. My life was filled with a constant flurry of activity, with "mass work" as well as with internal leadership responsibilities. At times I could hardly keep my head above water ... and I'm saddened to say, I was constantly slipping in my responsibilities to my children.

The leadership responsibilities on a chapter level were separated into internal work and mass work. For internal chapter building, the chapter leadership of three people met once and sometimes twice a week to go over the communiqués and political work that the chapter was conducting. This usually involved particularizing KDP national campaigns to the local conditions, and due to our inexperience, often found us meeting way into the midnight hours. Internal duties also included meeting with prospective members for two to four weeks to orient them on the political program of the organization. There were also biweekly chapter meetings to study new documents from the national leadership or educational materials. There were also dues to collect, reports to be written, and on and on.

The chapter level leadership was also expected to participate directly in the mass work or community organizing efforts. The activities and campaigns were so numerous they blur in my memory, as I grow older. As an example, I remember the Narcisso and Perez case in 1975; two nurses in Michigan wrongly accused of murdering their patients for whom we organized local Filipino community support. We distributed flyers at churches, hospitals, and work places where Filipinos were concentrated. We organized "mass meetings" with our contacts to discuss the issue. We circulated petitions, etc. Sometimes our mass activities went beyond the expectations and capabilities of the KDP. For example, for two to three years I helped a Filipina registered nurse, who worked at Blue Shield insurance company, launch a class action suit on behalf of Asian Americans, probably one of the first of its kind. A few years later, a strike ensued at the same company and the KDP was enlisted to do support work for the Blue Shield strikers. We organized a community support team for the strikers. In addition to the "mass work" we also had "propaganda work," which typically meant selling the KDP newspaper, *Ang Katipunan* (AK). We sold AKs at 5:00 am early weekday mornings at work sites where there were lots of Filipino workers such as the Blue Shield company, Saturday mornings at 9:00 at the Farmer's Market, early Sunday mornings in front of key churches or during special community events. Last but not least, we were all "on-call" to do occasional cultural work, mainly singing, at demonstrations. Most of these activities were happening at the same time.

When I worked on the Regional Executive Board, I traveled constantly between San Jose, Sacramento, Oakland and San Francisco to meet with chapter leadership bodies in those cities and to assist in developing their local plans. Many times this meant attending their organizing functions, as well as their internal recruitment meetings. I was engulfed by these activities daily . . . and for years. And while it was exhilarating, it was exhausting and life-consuming as well.

By this time, childcare had become institutionalized within the organization, and I lived in a collective household especially designed by the KDP to help me with my responsibilities to my children. By now, however, my boys were about nine and ten; they had started to get into trouble with the police, mainly mischievous and petty stuff—but for a mother, terrifying nonetheless. I personally could not find the time to help them with their homework. They were beginning to be regular truants at school. Although my comrades often helped, they could not deal with the teachers and the schools. I felt that no one really understood my emotional crisis and the stress of attempting to raise two adolescent boys in the "barrio" Mission district who already had juvenile records before they reached teenage years. I was also a single mother and on welfare with three children to support. I felt increasingly alone and in despair.

To top it all off, the crisis at the International Hotel was mounting—the decade old stalemate between the housing needs of the elderly Filipino and Chinese people and the forces of capital and private property was coming to its inevitable showdown. Our strategy was to forge a broad alliance (which in those days we referred to as a "popular front") to force the city to accept responsibility for providing low income housing in the neighborhood—while simultaneously organizing the tenants and their staunchest supporters to resist eviction to the very end—easier said than done ... but that's another story all together.

The International Hotel (IH) assignment from the fall of 1975 to winter 1977 was probably the most difficult political task I had encountered so far, both in scope and depth. Outstripped by the nerve-racking round-the-clock demands of the struggle, intimidated by big capitalist interests which threatened eviction at least five times, harassed by some other Asian leftist groups as being "centrist reformists"—the work was stressful to the breaking point. In the context of the IH, KDP was considered "centrist reformists" because we were willing to negotiate with city officials to broker deals instead of only relying on the masses. We never called for revolution in any of our literature and the KDP basically considered the IH a struggle for low-income housing, a people's struggle for human rights over property rights. Even though we considered this demand a reform, we also understood the potential for education among the "masses." That is, the struggle for reform was an important process towards politicization about the capitalist system. On the other hand, concrete reforms were about the extension of civil rights to minority peoples.

A major difference with the other Asian leftists on the Kearny Street block was that we did not feel that getting a deal with city government was necessarily a betrayal of the masses. By the time, the KDP entered the struggle as an organization rather than as KDP individuals, the Asian American Left had already been firmly rooted in the IH. A few KDP members had already become leaders within the IH struggle and leaders of the new International Hotel Tenants Association (IHTA), formed to con-

solidate the tenants. Unfortunately, each group was vying for political and organiza-
tional supremacy. Their storefronts on the Kearny Street block gave them legitimacy
in the IH struggle (the organizations rented the storefronts from the I-Hotel). But
it was the Filipino old-timers who had been in the leadership and the KDP members
already had an organic connection. The differences seemed larger then because of the
severe sectarianism between the groups. Although each group believed that private
property rights vs. human rights was at stake, each group had its own emphasis.

The Asian Community Center essentially believed it was primarily a struggle of
the working class while acknowledging minority oppression. The Chinese Progressive
Association (which had much influence from I Wor Kuen, later the League of
Revolutionary Struggle) thought it was primarily an attack on national minority
oppression. The KDP placed emphasis on housing for the working class, poor, and
the destruction of Manilatown.

These apparent political differences also led to the development of support orga-
nizations by each group. The KDP did not form its own support group because it
did not think that a Filipino organization could or should be leading a working class
struggle. Instead, the KDP called in other housing experts and progressives to work
on committees set up by the IHTA. The KDP's "independent analysis" of the strug-
gle was printed in the newspaper, *the Katipunan*. Nor did we not think it was prop-
er to highlight the KDP within the IHTA. Besides, the emphasis on the city's respon-
sibility for low-income housing was a sentiment shared by members of the IHTA.
Education about the need for liberation in the Philippines from anti-imperialist rule
was confined to forums, educationalal programs, and newspapers outside of the IH
struggle.

The other Asian Left groups formed their own support committees and at times
were able to gather tenants to attend their rallies. The Asian Community Center
which was allied with the Revolutionary Communist Party formed the Workers
Committee to Support the IH and Victory Building. The Chinese Progressive
Association group developed the Coalition to Support the I-Hotel. Most supporters
outside of the struggle thought that there was basic unity and did not see the frayed
edges of disunity.

With my personal life in shambles, the final straw for me was the failure to get
support from the KDP itself. The KDP team members of the IH were charged with
being "maverick and elitist veterans," not accountable to the local and regional KDP,
because we felt we had enormous tasks at the IH and should be exempt from addi-
tional tasks. We were essentially browbeaten to accept additional responsibilities in
the local on top of all the IH tasks. Sleep deprivation and personal lives were not
taken into consideration.

The San Francisco leadership body in particular seemed to have no appreciation
of the significance and scope of the IH struggle. This insensitivity may have arisen
because of the rising support work for the Philippines in spite of the reported ebb in
the Philippine political struggle (perhaps a nationalist turn?). This contradiction was
evident during a KDP Regional Conference in which the IH was not even considered

as an area of work to be reported on or analyzed. This contradiction made it difficult to utilize the KDP organization to flank us during the peak of the IH struggle, which was a bit of an embarrassment. (The style of "browbeating" comrades into submission was tolerated for a while until it ran into other political problems and the KDP national leadership stepped in to repair the damage. That type of behavior was later targeted as ultra-left, but for me, by that time the damage had already been done.)

I was extremely demoralized politically and completely drained in my personal life, unable to struggle. Meanwhile, during the last months before the eviction of the tenants at the IH, my life fell apart. Overwhelmed and unable to get help for myself, distrustful of the organization, I considered suicide as an escape. But this was too drastic—and believe it or not, what kept me from it was the gnawing question, who would take care of my kids? Feeling guilty about quitting in the middle of the struggle, I limped along in my political work. I could not concentrate on anything. I closed myself off and went around almost in a trance. (Today I would know to call this clinical depression; back then we termed it "vacillation").

Finally after the eviction of the IH tenants on August 4, 1977, I had to leave the Movement. For the sake of survival I quit everything. People at the IH thought I had abandoned them, and in a way I had. Except for a few close friends, the KDP did not seem to care about my crisis—in fact they refused to accept my resignation. I was even assigned to an electoral campaign in the fall of 1977 to get voters to make a confidence vote for the IH. But I no longer went to KDP meetings, did not answer my phone, and tried slowly to repair my life. I decided that I should work again (I had been on welfare for years). I wanted a more stable life for my kids, a few material goods like good food on the table and a mother more available to them such as helping them with homework. I was criticized for being "bourgeois" because I wanted to get a job. If being on welfare and a mother of three children, and wanting food on the table for them was bourgeois, so be it. I defied the leadership and got a job.

For a year I went on repairing my life this way. But I could not stay completely away from politics. The feeling of isolation and disempowerment proved too much. So, finally, I asked to be transferred to political work which was not so demanding. The National Education Commission needed someone to lead its education work and it was considered a very important task in the KDP. The education program was composed of Marxist-Leninist classics and readings from the revolutionary movement in the Philippines. KDP put a premium on learning the Marxist method of dialectical and historical materialism as well as gaining a common theoretical language in the organization. Unless KDP activists had gone through this type of education and training, they were not considered "all-round" activists. I enthusiastically embraced my new assignment and I was also glad not to have to be in the local chapter any longer. The memories were too raw. I studied and educated myself in the theory of Marxism-Leninism. Although the assignment was difficult for me, it gave the stability and breathing space I needed. This new assignment probably saved me from becoming an embittered reactionary.

But then my physical health took a precipitous turn and I lay sick with an ulcer, suffering probably from a nervous breakdown. My saving grace was close friends and my family, especially my new husband, Hilton, who knew my quiet despair and gave me stability and support. (Oh yes, he also gave me my fourth child and youngest son, Isaac, a few years later.) For a year, I could manage little more than to tend to my health and my personal life. After I became well again, I never returned to the KDP. The KDP, by 1981, had become a part of the trend that was actively involved in the rectification and reestablishment of a new Communist Party in the United States. The education work led by the KDP now became the work of the Line of March. The Marxist-Leninist Education Project (MLEP) was the evolution of that education work in the KDP. I joined the Line of March, a Marxist-Leninist organization, an organization which was part of this party-building process.

My political work in the Line of March, although demanding, did not come close to the level of intense activity in the KDP. I was assigned to various areas of work to shore up political and educational work in the Line of March. For a short while, maybe a year, I was involved in the Women's Commission. My most long-lasting assignment was in the Labor Commission, focusing on solidarity with Central America, which in the 1980s was probably the leading Left campaign. I traveled to El Salvador twice in the early 1980s. From these direct experiences, my commitment to end injustice and desire for socialism became stronger.

Although the description of my experience in the KDP, in particular the last few difficult years, may seem harsh—I would never trade it for anything. As a Filipino American of the 60's generation, the KDP provided the most concentrated political, social and ideological transforming experience. The greatest feeling was a sense of empowerment, optimism and destiny. During that period KDP members worked tirelessly to accomplish concrete tasks which yielded tangible results, while at the same time having a broad vision that encompassed not only our "Filipino struggles," but the whole world!

The KDP changed my perspective and my life. On the one hand, I was always attracted to seeking out my roots as a Filipino because so much of my history was kept secret from other Filipino youth and me. But for me, sentimentally looking to the Filipino past was not enough. My identity had to also be forged in the direction of the future. And the "future" I found was full of promise and optimism—revolution and Marxism. The risks were great and some of the sacrifices were heavy, but I was convinced I was dedicating my present life for a better future ... not just for me, but for human kind. In some ways, my faith in the revolution was somewhat idealistic and utopian, but I still have not stopped dreaming.

My experiences in the Line of March were not as earth shattering but they were transformative nonetheless. Looking back, I realize that building a Party has class, racial, and gender dynamics which are difficult obstacles to overcome. I'm not sure the Line of March had the experienced people beyond the theoretical knowledge to overcome them.

When people hear the bits of my history that I relate here, they may wonder how a teenage mother, then a single mother with three children on welfare, and later a mother of four could have done so much under such extreme circumstances. Certainly my personal background as a child of a poor peasant immigrant family gave me the "work ethic" to try to succeed, but I believe that many of us did extraordinary things because the "revolutionary times" we lived in seemed to call for it. Our generation of youth knew no boundaries or limits. Youth all over the world were turning the tables, demanding to be heard, wanting to change the world with a sense of urgent necessity. The rallying cry by the French students in 1968 captured our youthful optimism and audacity, "Be realistic; Demand the impossible!"

Activist radicals and revolutionaries were on the forefront of everything in those days. If you were a woman like myself, you did it all and then some. We had children, divorced husbands we did not love and who held us back, demanded that our social, personal and even political needs be met. We not only organized quality childcare for our children, but we also fought hard to win issues that we passionately believed in. My individual energy and power were doubled, quadrupled by a social movement and an organization like the KDP. Learning about the dynamics of society in the Line of March and seeing first hand many kinds of peoples from different class backgrounds helped me to put my life in perspective. Without this revolutionary life, I may have ended up dead, literally or spiritually.

Of course, there were intense social and personal costs. I was reminded of the heartaches of being an activist and a mother when I read an article of a woman leader, Rachel Carson, honored during a world conference for her activism on environmentalism. She shared her pain about how her children were estranged from her as she got more involved. My heart still aches when I think of how my children must have suffered during my activist days due to the splintered attention I paid to them. Although my older children survived our life to become compassionate and productive human beings, I still wonder if they could have accomplished more than they did if I paid more attention to their schooling.

Perhaps, the greatest affirmation of my activist life came from my own children. During the tenth anniversary commemoration of the International Hotel eviction in August 1987, my oldest son Anthony commented, "Mom, I finally understand why you fought so hard. You did real good. I'm proud of you. I am glad you did this." His comments helped heal some of the guilt I carried around for years.

The revolutionary movement opened my eyes to the vastness of human potential, collective and individual. In short, the movement gave me invaluable social organizing skills, as well as analytical and academic proficiency which I probably could not have learned anywhere else. It's no small wonder that today I find myself back in school, working hard to finish my Ph.D. and become an educator. I keep dreaming. I keep struggling. I still believe revolution is possible; it just comes in many forms, sometimes subtle, sometimes dramatic. But I no longer think revolution necessarily entails a war with many lives lost or revolutionary violence exacted against the enemy. I do believe that we must constantly struggle for peace, social and economic justice.

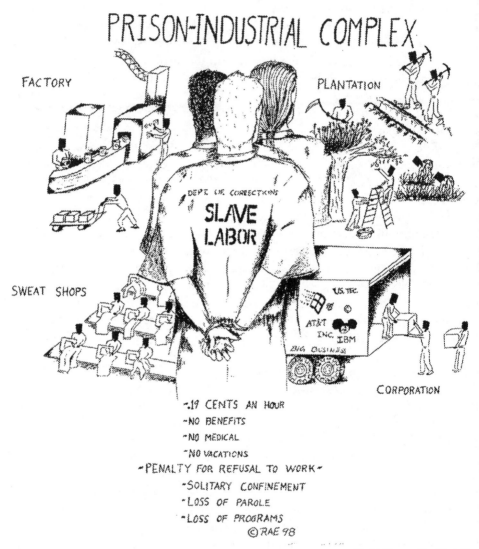

Todd Hyung-Rae Tarselli

PERSONAL LIBERATION/PEOPLES' REVOLUTION

Moritsugu "Mo" Nishida

I've been asked to explain how three possibly conflicting world views are reconciled in my thinking. Namely: 1. Buddhism; 2. Native American Red Road; and 3. Marxism-Leninism-Maoism.

The following are what I understand to be the main points of each that are important to me.

Buddhism

The Buddhism that I feel closest to is from the Mahayana trend (versus Hinayana) and is basically the teachings of Nichiren Daishonin, who taught the primacy of the Lotus Sutra and the chanting of the Mantra, "Namu Myoho Renge Kyo." "Namu" (to become one with/unite with/emulate, etc.); "myoho" (mystic law, the law governing the universe, universal law); "renge" (lotus blossom); shows the simultaneity of the law of cause and effect, the flower and seed are produced at the same time; and "kyo" (Sutra, teachings, etc.).

The basic teachings of all the trends that I unite with are:

A. On his death bed, the historical Shakyamuni Buddha told his disciples to "seek their own enlightenment, since each person was solely responsible for themselves" (paraphrased).

B. In Buddhism, it has been observed that we are continuously involved in ten emotional/mental states during our life time at any given moment. They are: 1) Hell; 2) Hunger; 3) Animality; 4) Anger; 5) Tranquility; 6) Rapture. These are the "lower" six worlds that are brought on by the environment around us. After we achieve a certain level of experience or training we can see/feel: 7) Knowledge; 8) Self-Realization; 9) Bosatsu; 10) Buddhahood. These last four, called "higher states," are self-induced and are not dependent on the environment.

This expansion is: Knowledge (what one gains when we listen to others, read books, learn from others); Self-Realization (what one gets when we observe nature and contemplate on what we saw/felt/experienced; Bosatsu (the self-motivated need/desire to help others); Buddhahood (realization of and unity with laws of the universe).

C. In Mahayana, it is taught that there are people, Bosatsu, who deny their own "last step" to enlightenment and work to "serve the people" in order to help them help

211

themselves towards enlightenment, so that at some future date, all of us on Mother Earth can take the "last step" together and in process deny the importance or "specialness" of enlightenment.

D. Buddhism also does not postulate a "Creator." It would seem to acknowledge "creation" and then focuses on the "law(s) of creation." We believe in a Universal Law; God may be present, but His presence is manifested through the "Law."

E. The Law of the Universe (the law of cause and effect), as I interpret it, is dialectical and historical materialism, the manifestation of "one divides into two."

Native American Red Road: The Lakota White Buffalo Calf Pipe Teachings

As I understand the simpler parts of it, the teachings of this way are based on the concept of harmony through sacrifice, simplicity and helping others. Two fundamental parts are a desire and practice of seeking harmony between all peoples (the four colors of the two-leggeds: Red/Brown, Yellow, Black and White) and harmony between the two-leggeds and our Earth Mother.

We make offerings through self-sacrifice and prayers in ceremonies and rituals, of the sweat lodge, flesh offerings, vision quests ("fasting"), sun dances, etc. We do these voluntarily so that others may live. That is, those who may have no choice in suffering, who may have their suffering lightened by our efforts and sacrifices.

Sacrifice, as I understand it, on this road means nothing material outside of your skin. The Earth Mother and Creator gave all of that to you in the first place, the only thing that is yours that you can sacrifice is from your hide in. That is, to deprive yourself or endure giving up comfort or food, sleep, water, etc.

For me, the subtle rewards of spiritual growth that are a direct benefit of this practice is a benefit in itself. How does it show? Really not clearly, but I have a clearer appreciation of life, all of its manifestations. Simple things are rewarding. I believe I'm learning real patience, my ego needs have diminished to a degree whereby being a worker begins to have a bright perspective that I never dreamed of.

There is nothing wrong with being "poor" or "just a worker." With the spiritual dimension, you're growing and advancing in all different directions. So I don't feel any envy or need to justify my life. Explain, yes, but justify, no!

The Bosatsu implications of the Red Road should be apparent. That Buddhism has been corrupted by the "modern age" is only too obvious. So for me, the Bosatsu ideal motivates my practice to carry out the two principles of the Red Road.

The long term view of spiritual evolution towards an enlightened state of the world, when we've overcome ego, greed, lust, etc., etc. (i.e., the lower six worlds), is the communist epoch in my view. The practical road towards that place and time on the personal liberation side is the Red Road.

The question of absolute pacifism that comes up in both Buddhism and the Pipe Carriers on the Red Road is resolved for me in the Bosatsu Way and the non-Pipe Carriers on the Red Road. Both of these views are directed towards "personal liberation" and are weak on the question of authority and power, Buddhism more so than the Red Road. Is there violence today? Is there oppression and exploitation? If so, then "wherever there's oppression, there is resistance." Do we want to be free? "By any means necessary!"

So for me, the telescopic view of my practice is: To struggle for my eventual enlightenment through the practice of learning to cooperate with my sisters and brothers in struggle and for harmony with our Earth Mother through the healing and nurturing processes within the Democratic Circle.

Marxism-Leninism-Maoism

M-L-M and being engaged in the people's revolution gives me a solid footing in reality—of class, national and gender struggle and class analysis. Without this world view, the other two lead to begging the powers for relief or praying that they'll turn into "nice" people or "good" guys. M-L-M gives me the tools, ideologically/politically/organizationally, to know that we, the working class and oppressed peoples, represent the overwhelming majority of the people on this planet. In order to achieve the highest order of cooperation and benefit, we must work for the interests of this overwhelming majority: us. Which simply means to me, harmony amongst the largest majority of people in the community, nation, country and the world; and harmony between this majority and our Earth Mother. Serve the People!

In my darkest hours, where I felt that people who I trusted, turned their back on and ignored principle, my self-worth and self-esteem took an ass-whipping as I became a worker. The downtown Little Tokyo living conditions were depressing and drugs were the only help for me to dull the pain, but it was killing me. Marxism-Leninism-Mao Zedong Thought kept me dreaming and maintaining some "serve the people" work, but was not enough.

M-L-M has been the cornerstone of my world view for at least 25 years. With Buddhism and the Red Road, the spiritual dimension that was missing in my early years is now present. M-L-M has been the beacon and guiding light for the left side of my brain. Buddhism and the Red Road now give my brain's right side a chance to grow and develop, enabling me to achieve some balance and harmony between these two hemispheres of my brain.

I'm a student of Marx and Engels, the discoverers of the laws of dialectical and historical materialism. I appreciate the attempts by Engels to teach dialectics to us. In particular, his discussion of spirituality, in the later days of his life, are important to me. In effect, he said that he and Marx attacked blind faith and dogmatism promoted by the church. Many people confused this as an attack on spirituality. Engels said that we are not just the product of food, our work, etc., but of some "higher form" of energy. Years later, Einstein would show this mathematically, and the atomic bomb would show this materially, the concrete relationship between mass and energy.

I believe that dialectical materialism is the most comprehensive description of the universe and that historical materialism is the most profound description of the development of human society.

The Paris Commune showed the need for a revolutionary ideology and party,

213

and the Russian Revolution showed the need for a disciplined party. We today are faced with choices, forks in the road, necessary refinements to choose from.

Lenin applied the laws of dialectical materialism to world economic development and exposed imperialism. He applied the same laws to party development, to party-building and discovered democratic-centralism.

If anyone read Lenin's writings during the debates with the Mensheviks, and how Lenin conducted these vigorous struggles over differences, especially during the second congress of the Russion Social Democratic Labor Party, one has to be impressed by his commitment to democracy. Especially the need for the minority to be heard. Lenin calls them all kinds of names to be sure, and argues his case against them in a systematic way, but at no time does Lenin advocate shutting them up. In fact much of his writings are about making sure that their voice can be heard. Chairman Mao expressed this openness and encouragement for debate as well.

The dogmatists, in particular Stalin, show a disrespect for the views of others. Stalin, I believe, will in time be shown for what he really was: a dead end road of backwardness that fucked the world movement up for fifty years. Stalin developed dogmatism to its hilarious and murderous peak: bureaucratic-centralism (all centralism, no democracy) and showed his one-sided ass in his much studied "Bible" of the New Left, A Short Course in the History of the Communist Party of the Soviet Union.

In my own political development, I wasn't all that clear on Stalin until I read "On the Question of Stalin" in the seven letters of the Chinese Communist Party polemicizing with the Russians. After that breakthrough, I became more critical in my analysis of Stalin's teachings and more importantly, of his practice.

Let me now explain how my political thinking and practice has developed.

At first I was a sympathetic by-stander to the civil rights struggle. I was sympathetic to the Afrikan people's struggle from my own experience as a member of a minority nationality—Japanese Asianamerikan: from the oppression my family faced in the camps during World War Two. I began to study our history and to work directly in my own community [for more in-depth, c.f. Nishida interview—editor]. From that, it was an easy step to become an Asianamerikan revolutionary nationalist and a follower of the teachings and example of the Black Panther Party, in particular, their emphasis on the Little Red Book and the teachings of Chairman Mao and his serve the people line. After the Cointelpro [the U.S. government's counter-intelligence program to disrupt and destabilize radical, particularly Black and Native American, groups—editor] murders of up-and-coming young Panther leaders such as Bunchy Carter and John Huggins in Los Angeles, Mark Clark and Fred Hampton in Chicago, and the neutralizing of Huey P. Newton, Bobby Seale and Eldridge Cleaver, etc., after the Panther splits and police killings, many of us came to a crossroad.

The Panther's lumpen-as-leadership line had proven bankrupt as the lumpen leadership could do nothing to defend itself or retaliate. We returned to the working class, yet we did not study Mao to deepen our understanding of his views and practice. I was swayed by the thinking that dismissed Mao as a peasant revolutionary whose ideas only applied to Third World countries and didn't apply to us in the U.S. Our group thought these anti-Mao critics were wrong, but we were still influenced by them.

This group I belonged to [East Wind Collective—editor] then fell for the "study, study, study" line of the "new dogmatists," those who touted the "classics" of Marx, Engels, Lenin and Stalin. In the process, we got hooked on the sly to Stalin's organizational line and more importantly, to his practice in organization: dogmatism and bureaucratic-centralism with all centralism and no democracy, rationalized in the notion that "the center knows all" [i.e., don't challenge or question leadership—editor]. After some years of practice, some of us saw that there was too much ego-tripping with self-proclamations of "the main trend," "the most correct _____," etc., etc., etc. Makes me wanna puke. Got sick of the bullshit and backed off, I went back to basic Mao: serve the people and the mass line.

I also studied Amilcar Cabral, a founder of the Party of Revolution of Guinea-Bissau and the Cape Verde Islands (PAIGC), who showed us in theory and in practice through defeating Portuguese and western imperialism there. He, like Mao, was not considered a Marxist by some European "Marxists." Mao and Cabral are my two teachers of Marxism.

Through such campaigns as the Great Leap Forward and the Great Proletarian Cultural Revolution, to me Mao showed a great faith in the common folk. A deep regard for us as the real leaders and rulers/ruling class of a socialist society, and not the party. I came to understand via Mao that post-revolutionary society must consist of a whole series of cultural revolutions to empower the working class and the peasantry as the working class-to-be.

Cabral showed us a practical understanding of the mass line: that concrete investigation must be the basis of line development and practice. Even further, he showed how the people's culture is the basis for development of revolutionary consciousness and organizational practice. I believe his most important teaching is the emphasis placed on "class suicide." That is, intellectuals who make up the elite of the movement must give up privileges, prestige and self-importance and become one with the overwhelming majority of the people, especially after the seizure of state power. Look out Nelson Mandela!

To me, Mao and Cabral have extended the limits of European interpretation of Marxism. Mao beyond the making of "socialist revolution" into the real "transition stage." And Cabral who refuted the European dogmatists who took Marx's statement that "there is no history without class struggle" literally, and tried to wipe out "early hominid development," including Asian, Afrikan and Indigenous Amerikan tribal peoples' histories. Cabral showed how peoples who had not achieved class stratification controlled their own destiny and made their own history. But when they lost that control to European colonization, they had to struggle against imperialism and colonialism to regain it.

As far as U.S. teachers, I consider myself a student and follower of Malcolm X, especially his teachings on the Black united front, his concept of race pride, self-reliant economic development, and geographic concentration as a basis of political power. Incidentally, I use "Black" in the generic way Malcolm saw things: Non-White.

I decided to "penetrate the class" and become a worker in Little Tokyo. The resulting heartbreak and disappointment of not being accepted at first, of being put down for being a worker, the depression of living in the miserable conditions of Little Tokyo, all led me to a ten year run with drugs and self-pity. The heart was willing but the head was in Cloud 9 and "sho was heavy."

I had lost faith in myself, our people and our working class. To regain that lost faith, I turned to Buddhism. Our sect taught that spiritual growth was a triangle: faith, practice, and study. I slowly worked my way out of the pit I had fallen into. The giant kick in the ass came when my father threatened to disown me and bar me from seeing my mother. I finally came to terms that I was sick. I had not cleaned myself up completely before my mom passed away. I will regret that for the rest of my life.

A friend of mine took me to see Ernie Peters (Longwalker), a real Medicine Man. I asked him for help in my addictions. He advised me to follow the sweat lodge way no matter how long it took. I followed his advice. I'm now drug, alcohol and tobacco free. Now I know why Marx and Engels turned to the American Indians for their inspiration for the communist utopia: "From each according to their ability to each according to their need."

In my journey on this oldest of "red roads," I've found the spiritual center that I longed for. This road teaches me "sacrifice so that others may live." It teaches keeping your life simple and close to mother earth and helping your sisters and brothers. The consistent message of all indigenous peoples is "harmony." Harmony between two-leggeds and between the two-leggeds and our Earth Mother. This original message is the only one that makes sense to me and does not contradict my understanding of Marx, Engels, Lenin, Cabral, Mao or the different Buddhas.

This reconciliation of "the peoples' revolution and personal liberation" has saved my life, my sanity and given me the confidence to look to the future with real optimism, rather than "revolutionary" suicidal tendencies. In fact my life has changed so radically. I'm now happily married and father of a new born son, events which ten years ago would have been unthinkable. Ten years ago, to have married would have only invited heartbreak and I had viewed marriage as a possible weakness when my life was committed to die for our people. I had viewed bringing children into this sick and perverted society as torture. Have things changed? Of course not, but I've changed! I have gained confidence and faith in myself, in others, and in the working class, to face the future. Even if the human experiment on this blue planet is doomed to failure, I know that I can't abandon nor ignore my place in the scheme of things. I'm a peoples' warrior and I don't have any choice but to fight back.

KNOW YOURSELF! KNOW YOUR ENEMY! KNOW THE DIFFERENCE!

SERVE THE PEOPLE?

Challenges in Little Saigon

Daniel C. Tsang

Chairman Mao exhorted, "Serve the People!" But what happens if the community in which you are trying to do work is conservative (with some elements even Rightwing)?

This analysis stems from recent grassroots work with the Alliance Working for Asian Rights and Empowerment (http://go.fast.to/aware), which has been monitoring police abuse in Orange County, California, since 1993. I helped start that group after a group of Southeast Asian teenaged girls were stopped and photographed by Garden Grove, Calif. police for law enforcement gang files. Since then, the group has passed out "Know Your Rights" cards, held community forums to educate various communities about our civil rights, and visited Asian inmates in Orange County Jail.

AWARE works "behind the Orange Curtain," but in fact, the demographics of the county are changing rapidly, with more and more Latinos and Asians moving to the county or being born there. No longer is Orange County lily-White, although portions tend to be whiter than not (such as South County). Outsiders often dismiss the county as conservative and Republican, but even among the voting population, there is change. As I write, for the first time in several decades, Republican registration has fallen below 50%.[1]

These demographic shifts have also affected Little Saigon (Westminster), the symbolic heart of the overseas Vietnamese community. Although figures vary widely, between 100-200 thousand people of Vietnamese heritage live in and around Little Saigon. While outside observers may hear or read about the area only when there is a gang shooting or another anti-communist protest, the prevailing media image of virulent anti-communism masks much of what is going on beneath the gaze of the outside world.

To be sure, there is no denying the long and sordid history of virulent anti-communism in and around Little Saigon.[2] In the 1980s, Vietnamese American editors who "slipped up" and recognized the reality of the existing government of Vietnam would be routinely vilified, their newspaper offices or delivery trucks torched, or themselves even killed. A Caucasian professor at California State Fullerton, Ed Cooperman, was even shot to death. A Vietnamese immigrant student he mentored was subsequently convicted of his killing, but the guy spent just a few years in prison, before ending up working for the Rightwing lawyer and one-time Nixon aide, Alan

M. May, who had defended him. Cooperman headed a scientific exchange group that brought much-needed material to post-war Vietnam. For many years, then, history will record that a vocal group of anti-communist counterrevolutionaries held sway in Little Saigon, intimidating and threatening critics into virtual silence and conformity. Its influence reached its peak in 1999, when thousands of demonstrators kept a video store that had displayed the Vietnamese flag and a portrait of Ho Chi Minh under seige for what turned out to be 53 days.[3] Some protesters even attacked the storeowner, Tran Van Truong, and beat him up. His lawyer, Ron Talmo, was also attacked later that same day.[4] And in my own case, students of mine told me during that time that there were people, apparently former ARVN soldiers, openly discussing "what to do with that UCI writer" at a Little Saigon restaurant, and would bide their time waiting to kill me, after I wrote an op-ed piece for *The Los Angeles Times* suggesting that Vietnamese American youth felt anti-communism to be passe.[5] As of this writing, I'm still alive and kicking.

What I am suggesting is that although the demonstrations in 1999 may at first glance show Little Saigon united in the fight against communism, in fact, as later events indicate (the demonstrators are now squabbling over what happened to the "donations" they were given), it has been difficult to keep the community unified. Part of the reason is that, as in other minority communities, the onus of surviving in this post-modern society weighs heavily on Little Saigon's inhabitants, so that symbolic issues, such as anti-communism, will stir the emotions, but will not bring food to the table. Years of immigrant bashing, affirmative action cutbacks, and gang hysteria under Pete Wilson in California have taken their toll. Even Gray Davis, a Democrat who succeeded Wilson as governor, has veered well to the Right on law-and-order issues, while promoting at times a Republican agenda (with some exceptions). For the person on the street in Little Saigon, survival issues have to matter more than something more remote like fighting communists. (For some, admittedly, the search for commies here is not remote, of course.)

Even the recent shift of tactics by the demonstrators to one of "human rights" advocacy is just the other side of the same coin, since it still sounds very much like commie-bashing, akin to the protests over human rights in the then-Soviet Union. It is also extremely hypocritical, as the 1999 events demonstrated: Tran Van Truong, the video store owner, was not accorded any "human rights," In fact, demonstrators yelled they wanted him dead! So "human rights" is just another slogan, but a campaign some former Vietnamese American "contras" are now ready to embrace, having shed their khaki gear for suits.[6]

One issue important to many Asians has been that of police harassment, specifically, racial profiling. Governor Davis, in fact, as I write, has just vetoed a bill that would have mandated police agencies across the state begin collecting race and ethnicity data on drivers they stop.[7] But there has been a blind spot among many of the proponents of the legislation, who have focused on "driving while black or brown,"[8] while ignoring the pervasive problem of police stopping Asian drivers, especially in parts of Orange County, California.[9] Back in the early 1990s, when this issue did not have the national attention it now garners, Southeast Asians and other Asians in the county were routinely being pulled over, or just stopped in the street, by police gang units.[10] As a result, we helped some teens fight back; the ACLU took their case, and in the eventual $86,000 settlement, the Garden Grove police department was forced to revise the way it questioned "field detainees."[11]

As part of our outreach, we held many community meetings, including in the heart of Little Saigon. One incident illustrates a dilemma I once faced. At that event, I noticed the leader of the community group that had lent us the facilities, and went up to shake his hands. The same pair of hands had just days earlier, ripped apart the flag of Vietnam because it is communist. As someone who supported Ho Chi Minh's ultimate victory in Vietnam (after his death) over the imperialist forces, I, of course, did not agree with what he had done. But he had been the only group willing to lend us—free of charge—a large auditorium where we held our forum. We thought that the others we had approached were scared of knocking the police; and indeed, as we were to start the meeting, we found out that the authorities had called trying to force the group to cancel the meeting.

So I was happy to shake this anti-communist leader's hands. In doing community work, then, especially in a community led by such staunch anti-communists, it is necessary, indeed, to work in coalition even with those for whose politics you have a distaste. And the arrangements could not have been finalized without the active work of Vietnamese American members of our group, who were no friends of communism, but who recognize that someone had to tackle local problems, and that anti-communist rhetoric would not be sufficient for solving societal problems here.

Was I compromising myself and the work of AWARE by shaking this community leader's hands? I think not. Composed of street insurgents, AWARE was not generally liked by the establishment, especially law enforcement; what we came to realize was that social service agencies that were dependent on "soft money" also didn't like us, since they tended to be cozy-cozy with law enforcement. Their "outreach" programs to reach "gang members" often depended on the cooperation of gang units and probation departments. Hence we were grateful that this group was willing to work with us, offering us space within walking distance of many residents. Another time, perhaps I would not have agreed to work with this group. But I'm a pragmatist, and besides, there was no attempt to censor in advance what we would say. In the best of worlds, one would sit down and discuss with the group and come to agreement over a set of "principles of unity." But when we got the space, it seemed a godsend. Still, one must constantly remind oneself of the need to remain true to one's own principles.

Our principles included serving the oppressed. Given our primary focus on race and policing, our constituents, as it were, spanned all classes. Race, ethnicity, and youth appear to be the main reason police target certain individuals.

In fact, as I have argued elsewhere, the "moral panic" over gangs since the end of the Cold War has necessitated the need to construct new enemies:

Yesterday's Communist or Viet Cong is now today's gang member. Yesterday's fellow traveler is today's gang associate. Just as it was hard to identify who was VC in Vietnam, today's police find it hard to identify Asian gang members in the U.S.[12]

Illustrating the close connection between the Vietnam War and the current gang hysteria, a self-described cop ("Nathan Hale") once wrote me:

> *I first began arresting Asians while I was an MP in Saigon. As a stateside cop, I've found Asians (particularly Vietnamese punks) to be even more vicious. Any — and let me emphasize the word ANY—tool that can be brought to bear in the war against these little gangsters should be implemented—their civil rights be damned! I also feel that all card-carrying members of the American Criminal Liberties Union should be hung by their balls in front of Asian Garden Mall.[13]*

With gang injunctions the rave among law enforcement, and the state now viewing any youth gathering as potentially subversive, the ground is ripe for doing movement work among youth so targeted.

In doing our work, our primary perspective has come from our self-identification as Asian Americans, and among the core leadership, as "progressives." We had no explicit ideological party line. But the nexus of our struggles were clearly sited within Orange County, not Vietnam or China. As the core members worked on our own group "goals", we realized that we wanted to deal with oppression here, not "over there." While many if not most new immigrants feel a stronger tie to the homeland (and the struggles there), we took the position that our group would deal with local struggles, not those sited abroad.

I did not want the group to end up becoming, in practice, an anti-communist organization. At times this was difficult. I recall at one press conference, held to celebrate the release of an inmate we were helping, a core member yelled out that the "police are as bad as the communists"! A Vietnamese American, she was talking about police here, "communists" in Vietnam. And the same distrust and their hatred of "communists" would periodically appear in our internal discussions.

How then, as a Leftist, was I able to work with people who openly express such views? Given the history of red-baiting in the U.S., it is understandable that even non-communist leftists shudder when they hear such an outburst. Yet for the typical Vietnamese immigrant to our shores, it is likely that he or she lost everything in his or her bid for "freedom." For many, they are just victims of war; their side lost, and they are now suffering because of it. On a human level, it is easy to empathize with their plight; refugees are no more responsible for their situation than you or I are for what our President does in our name. But as a long-time community organizer, I've realized it is more productive to view the hatred of Vietnamese communism as an antipathy toward a one-party state. In fact, in the work of AWARE, this anti-state attitude comes in handy, for it is the state (and its law enforcement arm) that need to be challenged and made accountable to the people.

After all, we need to avoid falling into the trap of equating all "communisms." There are different historical conditions in each country that calls itself "socialist." And it makes no sense to make sweeping denunciations of "communism."

Communism was never monolithic.

But one issue that has emerged among AWARE members is whether one can be both "anti-communist" and progressive. To hard-line Leftists, that is an impossibility. In the American context, to be anti-communist has meant, traditionally, reactionary and rightwing. But it can also mean you are a "liberal." Anti-communists can be liberal social-democrats, concerned with alleviating the social conditions, while at the same time opposed to one-party systems.

The current campaign in Little Saigon to tie human rights conditions to trade ties with Vietnam illustrates the differing perspectives on this issue. To some, it's just another attempt to bash communism. And it, again, is hypocritical, since you can walk down Bolsa Avenue in the center of Little Saigon and buy almost anything from Vietnam. And local consumers keen for a taste of their homeland, do buy the products. Yet, those wanting to stop trade argue, especially, that it is just the "Chinese" merchants on Bolsa who are trying to make a buck.[14]

But one can take a progressive stance against global transnational capitalism by criticizing certain aspects of the trade. Does it really help the people there, or do the western corporations that are invading Third World countries like Vietnam just want to make money while exploiting the workers there (such as paying them cents to make Nikes that sell for over $100 here)? This type of a more progressive critique may win adherents on the Left, but merely bashing Vietnam for trading with the U.S. doesn't hack it. Not only will American Leftists be turned off, so will conservatives, for they are the ones behind the corporate invasion.

In this post-modern era, it is likely that one's politics is a mixture of Left and Right. Whether that is progressive depends, of course, on how one defines the term. But in community organizing, one needs to avoid labeling individuals as one or the other; it is perhaps sufficient to agree on common goals and strive towards that.

Many Vietnamese immigrants, for example, have grown up in the U.S., entered college and become idealistic about serving the people. Some have become ardent community activists, yet "torn between feeling an obligation to respect our parents' past yet not want to continue the legacy of war."[15] Activists like myself have to face the fact that many of their otherwise progressive comrades may not be able to agree with us on certain political issues, especially over what I (and their former compatriots in their homeland) would call the liberation of the Vietnamese in 1975. Can we still work together? For some, no, but AWARE does not claim to be a political party. Community work always necessitates working compromises, if you will, with a heavy dose of realism. We need to learn from the communities where we work, and not just be missionaries with a message, although it doesn't mean giving up on your principles or political ideology. It is, in fact, a two-way encounter. What is necessary, then, for cooperation to work and the struggle to advance, is to lay aside our differences and "agree to disagree." That, of course, is easier said than done. And to keep our eye on the "prize" as it were, as our overreaching goals.

That is not to say that there are no Leftwing, pro-Vietnam, Vietnamese in the U.S. Of course there are, and in the recent past, a few have surfaced. However, their mostly hidden story remains to be told. In the sixties, some students sent by the South Vietnamese government to study or do military training in the U.S. actually decided to stay, becoming anti-war activists in the process. One of those taking a strong public stance against the war was David Truong, whose father had run for president in Vietnam. The progressive, former Stanford student ended up serving time in prison, set up on a bogus "espionage" charge by a fellow Vietnamese working undercover for the U.S. Some also helped in arranging Jane Fonda's visit to Hanoi, at the height of the war. Many of them now studiously avoid being openly critical of, and live away from, Little Saigon. They have chosen to have a lower profile, especially during the years of intimidation by those seeking to "liberate" their homeland. One who recently emerged in the public eye again Hong Van Huynh, a one-time anti-war activist, who now heads the California chapter of the Vietnam-American Friendship Association. Hong was himself assaulted when he showed up protesting the 1999 anti-communist protests in Little Saigon.[16] And I know of one Vietnamese American college student who was successfully recruited by a sectarian, Leftwing party in Southern California. That student had had his mind opened up when he entered college. He started reading magazines such as *CovertAction Quarterly* and other progressive journals. Although his family background is typical of his fellow immigrants, he considers Ho Chi Minh the liberator of Vietnam against American imperialism. Another student I met is Hmong; he asked about material on Laos. I suggested he read William Blum's The CIA: A Forgotten History (Zed Books), which had a chapter on the CIA's nefarious activities in Laos. He did and his mind was forever changed; he no longer saw Vang Pao, as a respected community leader but as one who followed the dictates of the CIA.

That Vietnamese immigrant youth should question their elders' beliefs should come as no surprise to those of us who were anti-war activists in the 60s. Then, the establishment complained about the "generation gap." In fact, each new generation creates its own dreams, and seeks its own way of achieving those aspirations. And that is the fear that grips the elders of Little Saigon: that their children will forget the past, and the battles they waged. It is a reality that has already come to pass in Vietnam itself, where the American War is just history, with the inhabitants there more interested in the future and making a living or improving their lot than they are in reliving the past.

But in Little Saigon, such nonconformity with the "party line" here is regarded with suspicion still. One Vietnamese American student told me his mother called him a "communist" for supporting Tran's right to display the flag and the picture of modern Vietnam's founder. Another student, the son of a former economics minister in the Thieu regime, was also called "communist" for arguing for trade with Vietnam.[17] The party line, as it were, must, at any cost, be upheld. During the protests, when word spread that there were students from Vietnam studying in Orange County, protesters prepared to battle those "communist" infiltrators. They were never located. Instead, anyone who showed up supporting Tran was attacked, including whites. Yet it is not just youth who dare question their elders; Le Ly

Hayslip, whose biographies were made into the Oliver Stone movie, "Heaven and Earth," and whose nonprofit foundation works to help Vietnamese kids, criticized her fellow compatriots for not according Tran his civil rights.[18] For what she and I wrote in *The Los Angeles Times*, we were labeled in youth movement manifestos (reprinted in the *Viet Bao Kinh Te*) as writers worth counteracting.[19]

As an activist *cum* academic librarian, then, I remain hopeful about the youth of Little Saigon and the impact of the written word to inspire them. While it is true that students tend to read less these days, the anarchic openness of the Internet means that, despite corporate attempts to overwhelm us, alternative views, if they get indexed by the right search engines, have a way to reach inquiring minds. We need as activists to do more to share our activist work with others, and describing our efforts on a home page on the Internet is a wonderful way to spread the gospel.

Our perspective as Asian American activists has meant that we were interested in uniting the various Asian American ethnicities in a common struggle. In practice, again, that was a struggle. Recent immigrants tend not to identify as Asian Americans, their primary identification being their own ethnicity. While many parents remained "old country," their offspring were likely to be as Americanized as the next kid. One of the kids detained and photographed in Garden Grove, Minh Tran, then 14, was already quite vocal about her civil rights. Told by a Garden Grove police officer not to come back to "my city" on another occasion, she shot back: "This is America. I can go wherever I want!"[20] She became fervent about her eventual, successful, lawsuit, convincing her parents she should do it.

Because our core members were Chinese, Japanese and Vietnamese, groups in the community that didn't like us tried to attack the makeup of our group. At one public forum before a municipal body, a representative of a social service organization, we were told, attacked some of us for being, basically, the wrong ethnicity. We even had a Japanese in our group, he apparently told the body. While we saw our primary identification as Asian American activists, we discovered that others would use that to smear us. Given the history of Vietnam, it is clear that relations among the various ethnic groups there have not always been cordial. In particular, Chinese Vietnamese have been singled out, both in Vietnam and overseas. However, these ethnic-specific attacks often mask other agendas, with the "other" ethnicity an easy target for scapegoating.

In fact, Vietnamese and other Southeast Asian youth we helped never questioned why a Chinese or a Japanese and not just another Southeast Asian would be interested in helping them fight for their civil rights. I suspect that such a model— Asians helping other Asians—could be empowering, especially in a community where so-called "community leaders" were in bed with the police.

One community leader who did help us, albeit largely behind the scenes, was the first Vietnamese American elected to public office, Tony Lam.[21] A registered Republican, he had worked for Rand Corporation in Saigon interviewing defectors to the U.S.-supported puppet regime before settling in the States. Although he served on city council, he helped us in many ways, including inviting everyone from

AWARE at a press conference (for the newly released inmate), to his restaurant, Vien Dong, in Garden Grove, for a sumptuous, and free meal.

Lam also went out of his way to arrange a meeting with his city's police chief, but when we arrived at the police station, another police officer noticed our AWARE buttons, and the police chief refused to let us meet with him. We were left standing in the parking lot. Apparently, we were told, he feared we would end up suing him. For Lam, the city councilman, it was a slap in the face; he stood with us fuming and swearing at the police chief for treating a city official like this.

But Lam would also later run afoul of others in Little Saigon, including those who tried to unseat him and former CIA agents.[22] Because he favored trade ties with Vietnam, he was labeled "communist". Since he did not show up (on the advice of the Westminster city attorney) at the huge demonstrations in early 1999 in Little Saigon over a video store owner's display of Vietnam's flag and a portrait of Ho Chi Minh, he was roundly berated during what turned out to be the 53 days the anti-communists besieged the store.[23] After the store owner was arrested for video piracy and police raided the store, a small group of several dozen demonstrators decided that Lam's restaurant a few miles away deserved to be the next target, so for several more weeks, demonstrators stood outside his restaurant harassing patrons and pouring urine in view of the diners. They also attacked the establishment for serving Hanoi food. Eventually, the same demonstrators took their demonstration outside the Bowers Museum in Santa Ana, which was hosting an exhibition of art from Vietnam. There, I saw Lam hung in effigy, along with Ho Chi Minh; with the effigies dragged along the sidewalk and stomped upon. Lam, who later filed a civil suit against the protesters, was later to win in court.[24]

We also wanted to work in solidarity with other progressive organizations, including non-Asian ones. The group we ended up working most closely with was one created in the late 90's to fight police harassment and redevelopment in the Latino community, United Neighborhoods.[25] The group in many ways became the leading grassroots group in Orange County (it is now part of LULAC, League of United Latin American Citizens), helping many residents fight the system. We both (together with other community groups) testified before the May 1997 hearings on police gang databases held by the California Advisory Committee to the U.S. Civil Rights Commission in Costa Mesa.[26] Since then, United Neighborhoods has expanded from Anaheim (it now has a youth chapter in Santa Ana) and works closely with the Los Angeles regional office of the U.S. Civil Rights Commission on a number of cases. United Neighborhoods, under the leadership of the indefatigable Josie Montoya, has been generous in their outreach to AWARE in our common struggle against the state.

At a 1997 UCLA conference entitled, appropriately enough, "Serve the People," we met many other progressives who work in ethnic communities throughout the nation. The political diversity within communities can only increase. One example is the shift away from the Republican Party registration among Vietnamese Americans, with more joining not just the Democratic Party (whom I have no faith in) but also third parties. This will only continue. My continuing belief is that as more Asians get involved in community work, they will be radicalized and become effective warriors against the post-modern, transnational capitalist state.

ENDNOTES

1. Christian Collett, "One-way Dialogue: Republicans Blunder in Outreach to Vietnamese Voters," *Orange County Register*, September 29, 1999, Local News p.8.

2. Nick Shou, "Invisible Enemies," OC Weekly, March 5-11, 1999, 20-24, posted at http://www.ocweekly.com/ink/archives/99/26lede-schou.shtml; and Barbara Sher, Dan Tsang, et al, "More on the Face of Ho Chi Minh: Progressive Respond," *Change Links* (North Hollywood), 8/11 (March, 1999). p.2, posted at: http://www.labridge.com/change-links/FactSheet.htm.

3. Jason Cohen, "The War at Home," *LA Weekly*, February 26-March 4, 1999, posted at: http://www.laweekly.com/ink/99/14/news-cohn.shtml.

4. Listen to my interview with Talmo on KUCI's Subversity program, "Human Rights Hypocrisy," March 9, 1999. Posted as a RealAudio file at: http://kuci.org/~dtsang/subversity/Sv990309.ram.

5. Daniel C. Tsang, "Little Saigon Slowly Kicking the Redbaiting Habit," *The Los Angeles Times*, January 31, 1999, M6. Posted at: http://sun3.lib.uci.edu/~dtsang/redbait.htm.

6. Daniel C. Tsang, "Guerrilla in the Midst: The Man Behind the Human-Rights Rhetoric," *OC Weekly*, Posted at: http://www.ocweekly.com/ink/archives/99/27news5-tsang.shtml.

7. Carl Ingram, "Davis Vetoes Racial Data Legislation," *The Los Angeles Times*, September 29, 1999, p. 3.

8. Earl Ofari Hutchinson, "Take a Step Against Racial Profiling." *The Los Angeles Times*, September 28, 1999,

9. Daniel C. Tsang, "DWUS: Driving While a UCI Student," *OC Weekly*, April 23-29, 1999, p.11. Posted at: http://www.ocweekly.com/ink/archives/99/33news2-tsang.shtml.

10. Daniel C. Tsang, "Garden Grove's Asian Mug Book Settlement," *Policing by Consent* (April, 1996), pp. 8-9. Posted at: http://sun3.lib.uci.edu/~dtsang/ggamfs.htm.

11. Daniel C. Tsang, "Is 'Innocent Until Proven Guilty" A Lost Principle? Taking Photos of Teens and Linking Them to Gangs Because of What They're Wearing Reveals Lack of Sensitivity by Police," *The Los Angeles Times*, August 30, 1993, p. B5 (Home edition) and p.B9 (Orange County edition). Posted at: http://sun3.lib.uci.edu/~dtsang/lostprin.htm.

12. Daniel C. Tsang, "Moral Panic over Asian Gangs," *RicePaper* (University of California, Irvine), 4/1 (Autumn 1993), 18-21.

13. Ibid.

14. Nick Schou, "Ho Chi Minute Rice: Congress Debates Trade with Vietnam, Little Saigon Goes Shopping ," *OC Weekly*, June 25-July 1, 1999, p.13. Posted at: http://www.ocweekly.com/ink/99/42/news-schou.shtml.

15. Tram Quang Nguyen, "Black and White, Red All Over: A Vietnamese American Examines the Turmoil in Little Saigon," *Gidra* 1/1 (Spring, 1999), p.15.

16. Daniel C. Tsang, "Scars and Stripes: What's Behind Those Yellow Flags in Little Saigon," *OC Weekly*, March 5-11, 1999, p. 12. Posted at: http://www.ocweekly.com/ink/archives/99/26news1-tsang.shtml.

17. "A Dissenter Emerges," *OC Weekly*, February 25-March 4, 1999, p. 16. Posted at: http://www.ocweekly.com/ink/archives/99/25news5-staff.shtml.

18. Le Ly Hayslip, "Being Free in America Means Letting Other People Speak Out," *The Los Angeles Times*, February 24, 1999, p.7.

19. Daniel C. Tsang, "Hearts and Blinders: The Propaganda War Continues in Little Saigon," *OC Weekly*, April 30-May 6, 1999, p.13. Posted at: http://www.ocweekly.com/ink/archives/99/34news3-tsang.shtml.

20. "Racial Harassment Suit Filed," OCN (Cable TV), May 19, 1994.

21. Seth Mydans, "A Vietnamese-American Becomes a Political First," *The New York Times*, November 16, 1992, p. A11.

22. Daniel C. Tsang, "Redbaiting in Little Saigon: Despite His Cold War Credentials, Westminster City Council Member Tony Lam Faces Ostracism from the CIA's 'Lost Commandos'," *OC Weekly*, April 25-May 1, 1997, p. 10.

23. Jason Cohen, "Roasted Lam," *OC Weekly*, March 5-11, 1999, p. 22. Posted at: http://www.ocweekly.com/ink/archives/99/26news4-cohn.shtml.

24. Esther Schrader, "Grass-roots Organization is Making a Statement," *The Los Angeles Times*, October 12, 1997, p. 17.

25. H.G. Reza and Louise Roug, "Westminster Councilman Wins $8,500 from Political Foes," *The Los Angeles Times*, Orange County edition, September 21, p. B1.

26. Daniel C. Tsang, "GREAT No More: But a New Gang Database is Ready to Take Its Place," *OC Weekly*, July 11-17, 1997, p. 10. Posted at: http://sun3.lib.uci.edu/~dtsang/greatnm.htm.

PERSONAL IS STILL POLITICAL
Reflections on Student Power[1]

John Delloro

"*Only through personal participation in the practical struggle to change reality can you uncover the essence of that thing or class of things and comprehend them... If you want knowledge, you must take part in the practice of changing reality. If you want to know the taste of a pear, you must change the pear by eating it yourself.*"[2]

A few years after the garment workers' victory over manufacturer Jessica McClintock, Mao's thoughts on the dialectical relationship between theory and practice would help me to reflect on my experience in the Garment Workers Justice Campaign. In my attempt to "change reality," I uncovered my own weaknesses and broadened my understanding of the world. It was my first entry into the Asian American Movement. When I joined the seamstresses in taking on the garment industry, I was an undergraduate at UCLA. I didn't realize the depth it would begin my own personal liberation. It was as much a personal journey as a political one.

Dancing On the Picket Line

I had denied my racial identity for much of my life. Growing up in predominantly white middle class neighborhoods, I had ignored and dismissed much of the racism around me in order to survive. As I grew older and interacted with other people of color, I had begun to question myself and slowly recognized the self-hatred that buried all my memories of racism and shielded my eyes from reality. Denying myself for too long, I felt that I had a lot of catching up to do and needed to understand what it meant to be Asian American. Consequently, I read everything I could get my hands on about Asian American history. However, I knew that it wasn't enough to know the past struggles of Asian Americans but to be engaged in current ones. A young Asian American woman handed me a flyer and told me about the picket at the Jessica McClintock boutique protesting the exploitation of Asian immigrant women. I learned that twelve Chinese immigrant women, denied $15,000 in back wages, were demanding accountability from garment manufacturer Jessica McClintock. When she asked me to come to the picket, I knew that I would be there.

When I arrived at the site, I joined the long circle of people chanting "Jessie, Jessie, you're no good, pay the workers like you should!" With each line of protest verse I shouted, I remembered my long years of ignorance. With each step, I raised my voice higher. Next thing I knew, someone is handing me a megaphone. I continued shouting until it became a song and I was jumping up and down to the rhythmic pattern of the chants. I felt very emotional. I felt all the frustration and rage inside me getting out. I was exploding with anger at the system that mistreated these women and pulled the wool over my own eyes. I was shouting down the great betrayal of the promise given to my parents and my ancestors.

As I walked in more pickets, I could not ignore the large number of strong Asian American women in the campaign. A majority were UCLA undergraduates. When I was invited to a planning meeting and I got more involved, our working together brought about both a political awakening and personal revelation. In my previous pursuit of understanding Asia America and my relationship to a larger society, I did not make enough of an effort to understand the particular issues facing Asian American women. As an Asian American man, I began to realize our struggles are closely intertwined. I could not effectively confront institutional oppression, if I did not take responsibility for my own sexism.

I understood that to be Asian American is to be part of a collective identity that shares a common historical memory—an identity of resistance. Its collective nature demanded that you couldn't focus on a single gender (male). It also means that I cannot leave it to Asian American women to educate me but that I had to take the initiative to learn. Of course, it has been and still is a difficult process since the nature of oppression is to make itself invisible to those that are privileged for the oppression.

With that in mind, I delved into studying the issue through my own individual efforts and participating in different study groups. I saw the racism of the mainstream women's movement. I was disgusted by the several predominantly White middle class female organizations that had awarded McClintock, a White woman, for establishing a successful clothing industry empire. In 1993, Working Women had named her one of the top fifty Women Entrepreneurs of America and she was also among twenty of the America's top business leaders invited to a breakfast with Bill Clinton at the White House. The Asian immigrant women sewing her dresses received no such accolades for their work.

On further reflection, I realized that the oppression that Asian American women face is a complex interaction of racism and sexism and not an either/or experience in which racism and sexism can be separated. In other words, the experiences of Asian American women is distinct from Asian American men and White women. Asian American college women, mostly middle-class, outnumbered the Asian American men who were involved in the campaign. Several of my sisters in the campaign had repeatedly told me that they joined this struggle because the issue resonated with their experiences as Asian American women. The campaign made visible strong Asian women challenging a rich White woman. This image shattered the stereotype of the passive and docile "oriental geisha." I remember one woman explaining to me that she noticed that whenever she challenged men, including Asian American men, they would dismiss her as being too sensitive or a "bitch." In truth, she had only stepped outside the bounds of the accepted image of an Asian American woman as patient and agreeing listener. It would have been different if she were a man of any race. Even the disrespect to other women of color is different because Asian American women's lives are invisible in racial discourse. Asian American women are part of the "model minority." When my API sisters heard how McClintock treated the Asian seamstresses' demand with incredulous contempt, it resonated with their daily experiences.

Jessie needed to open her eyes to this force.

Asian women were rising up, and I needed to wake up, too.

Enter the Pyramid

Item: Under United States law, garment manufacturers are not legally liable to garment workers. Manufacturers use the subcontracting system to insulate themselves from the conditions of the garment shop. The structure can be likened to a pyramid with the manufacturers on top, contractors in the middle and the seamstresses at the bottom. The cutthroat competitive bidding system between contractors for manufacturer bids drives the wages of workers and working conditions down. Since contractors are considered independent businesses, manufacturers reap the lionshare of the profits without the responsibility to the workers who sew their dresses. [3]

Item: Asian and Latina women make up a majority of the U.S. workforce in the garment industry. Manufacturers have expanded their operations globally, pitting women of color in the U.S. against a mostly female workforce in the third world.

Item: Denied $15,000 in backwages, 12 Chinese immigrant women demand accountability from clothing manufacturer Jessica McClintock and call for a national boycott.

I was moved by the strength of these women to stand up to McClintock. They were standing up to not only Jessica McClintock but also the whole industry. With an issue of this size, we knew that we needed to build more public pressure on the company. We had to step outside the Asian American community. Identifying worker justice as a point of unity, we linked our struggle with other worker campaigns such as Justice for Janitors, which were predominantly Latino and Latina employees. In the process of assisting each other, I came to embrace a perspective that criticized capitalism as a system.

During a Justice for Janitors union contract battle, others and I joined the janitors in carrying out a civil disobedience at the intersection of Rodeo Drive and Wilshire Boulevard. in Beverly Hills. As we chanted "El pueblo unido, jamas sera vencido,"[4] I distinctly became aware of the larger struggle of working people. It wasn't just about Asian Americans. As we sat down in the middle of the intersection, we were together fighting for worker dignity. Even as the police carried us away, it was a powerful feeling chanting with my Latino brothers and Latina sisters.

I also became acutely aware of our own power. We had stopped the city of Beverly Hills from continuing business by blocking their busiest intersection. Similar to the Jessica McClintock boycott, we hit the businessmen in the pocketbooks. They had to pay attention. I understood that workers and consumers united wield tremendous economic power.

It also became clear to me that despite the potential power of workers and consumers, for-profit corporations controlled the economy. How can working families survive when decisions are based on profit margins? In order to fight back and control their lives, garment workers had to call a boycott and janitors had to take the streets.

I was convinced that capitalism could never be a just system. The pyramid needed to be turned upside down. Only a democratically controlled economic system would set conditions for a better society. The garment workers created the wealth that Jessica McClintock enjoys. I truly believe that those who create the wealth have a moral claim to a position of power in the system. No one can have true control of his or her life without power. The strength of socialism is its promise to place the human person at the center and not at the service of the economy. What would this system look like? I don't know but I do know that it is only in struggle that we can see what is possible.

Student Power: Building the L.A. Support Committee for Garment Workers Justice Campaign

I not only politically grew through this struggle but I learned how to begin to implement my ideas and beliefs. I learned to organize. Korean Immigrant Workers Advocates (KIWA), a community-based Korean immigrant worker center, guided and trained others and me in the art of organizing. Recognizing the important role of students in social change, members of KIWA conducted "Summer Activist Trainings" that taught many of us many of the basics of organizing. We learned many useful concepts, such as the difference between an issue and a problem, or discerning between strategy and tactics. We also learned many practical tools such as writing a good press release. SAT trainers taught us how to conduct a power analysis as part of the process in preparing a campaign plan. We learned to layout a campaign by identifying our goals and objectives, and then developing strategy and tactics. Most importantly, we learned the importance of one-on-one meetings with people in order to build an organization.

Although Asian Immigrant Womens Advocates (AIWA), an Asian immigrant womens center based in northern California, originally contacted KIWA about the Garment Workers Justice Campaign, KIWA provided us an open space to do the majority of the planning and forming of the Los Angeles support for the campaign, which was based in the Oakland. We were able to practice what we had learned and test our ideas. Since we were all from UCLA, we looked towards our campus resources to aid the workers. Through our student networks on and off campus, we educated about the issue and brought it to other campuses and student organizations. For example, we successfully gained the endorsement of UCLA's largest sorority, Alpha Phi, to boycott Jessica McClintock dresses. They even joined us in a picket-line and attempted to deliver into the store a human-sized card declaring their boycott of the dresses. We also initiated an independent study, which developed into a course that focused on the garment industry and the Asian American communities. Several group projects came out of the class that aided the campaign. For example, one group of students constructed a freestanding exhibit about the garment industry and the McClintock issue. We circulated it to different campuses in order to educate and gain support. Eventually, the issue was even taught in a couple undergraduate classes on different campuses. Of course, we continued to mobilize people to the bi-weekly picketlines at the Beverly Hills Rodeo Drive boutique.

It was very rewarding to see the campaign grow. As our leadership skills developed, we saw new student leaders emerge. I especially remember a group of Asian American women from University of California, Santa Barbara who attended one of the pickets at the Rodeo Drive McClintock boutique. They had recently learned about the issue from one of their undergraduate courses. I later found out that they were so inspired through their participation that they formed on their campus Asian Sisters for Ideas in Action Now! (ASIAN!), an anti-racist, anti-sexist and anti-capitalist student organization. When the campaign ended in victory for the workers, we felt that we all won. After a three and a half year struggle, we saw the fruits of our efforts.

I was convinced of the power of students to affect change. I'm reminded of a presentation at the Summer Activist Training in which Glenn Omatsu emphasized the importance of Asian American students in "joining the working poor to challenge oppression." He explained that with the rise in Asian Americans entering elite universities, Asian American students have more access to resources than previous generations and can greatly help the community. The LA Support Committee of the Garment Workers Justice campaign is living testament to his words.

However, in retrospect, I feel that student power has its limitations. In the case of the LA Support Committee for the Garment Workers Justice Campaign, the other students and I came from privileged backgrounds, which separated us from the everyday experiences of the seamstresses. Without any real accountability to the workers, we could easily miss the big picture. An incident recalled by Eric Watt illustrates this point:

> *..sometimes students are so caught up with the logistics of activism that they forget the movements are for real people who lead real lives. To broaden their concern with self-empowerment, one question we constantly have to ask the student is "Who is the movement for?" For example, in an action of the Garment Workers Justice Campaign, the students decided to send a targeted manufacturer, Jessica McClintock, a human-sized Valentine's card. On this card, students would write messages to demonstrate their support for the exploited garment workers. However, students wrote words like "bitch" and "white devil," which reflect more of their own frustrations than the actual struggle of the workers.* 5

I was one of those students and I remember writing " We will bury you Jesse!" It felt empowering to write how we felt about Jessica McClintock. But it was true:

we had confused our frustrations with the workers' struggle. The women weren't saying "I will bury you Jesse!" but " We want to be paid and given the respect and dignity of a human being." I realize now that in order to fight for a system that places the human person at the center, then we also need to do the same in our organizing approach, in our daily lives and interactions.

Beyond the Garment Workers Justice Campaign

About a year ago, I met with a healthcare worker who is a few years younger than me. We had been engaged in a campaign to organize a union in her hospital. I had intended to break the news to her that I may be leaving the campaign. Several of my co-workers had already quit and left. I wanted to explain to her that I couldn't in good conscience continue working for this union because I felt that the leadership disrespected my voice and several of my co-organizers.

She only shook her head unable to comprehend my words. She only repeated, "Why are you leaving us?"

She never attended an elite university. She never was part of any student group. She has a two-year old daughter with no husband or father in sight. She is standing up and fighting for a better life for her daughter. She is organizing a union.

My reasons made no sense to her. Only than did I realize she didn't have the luxury of leaving.

Today, as a professional organizer for the past 3 to 4 years, I see the same mistakes again. I have seen many of my peers recently graduate from college and directly enter professions as organizers in trade unions or non-profit community organizations. I have seen many of my cohorts leave with great frustration. Several state that they leave because they felt the workers were not being included in development of strategy and they themselves were being disrespected. It was never about bread and butter issues of feeding or spending more time with our families. We must be honest with ourselves. When we leave a campaign, we are leaving the workers. We must accept this consequence and realize the luxury that we have in choosing to leave. It is a privilege that will always separate privileged staff like us from most working people. As many of us young people become professional organizers, I cannot help but wonder if we are only creating a new class of privileged professionals.

Despite my concerns, students can play an integral role in the transformation of society. The Garment Workers Justice Campaign is proof of the power of a student and workers alliance. However, in order for college-educated young people like me to begin to work towards social change, I feel that we need to acknowledge and adequately address our own frustrations.

First, young, college-educated people like me need to be honest about what we seek to gain personally for our part in workers' struggles. It would be disingenuous and ultimately disempowering for us to discard our feelings and say that our feelings are not as important as the workers' struggle.

Second, we need to acknowledge and understand that our frustrations stem from a real place of disempowerment. We are beneficiaries of the Civil Rights and

Power Movements and had the fortune of a college education. We have all these ideas and tools to affect change but we are oftentimes denied the opportunity to take responsibility for them. No institution exists except the ones we create or change that allow us this freedom to exercise our power and potential.

Third, we need to create a safe space to express these frustrations. I have seen little trust between many of my peers. We are in the position where we see our disempowerment but we have no right to claim it. The current organizing culture doesn't allow us to own our feelings, but to disregard it for something higher. I have heard young organizer say that they left because of the treatment of the workers, rather than to their own feelings of helplessness.

Only when we confront our own helplessness can we grow. And ultimately, our personal growth must correspond with political struggle. We need to continue to organize around an agenda that places the issues of Asian immigrant women workers at the forefront of an Asian American Movement that joins in a multi-racial effort to challenge international capital, and that builds new institutions of power. I believe our work will be much more fulfilling and effective if guided by the larger vision of an anti-racist matriarchal socialist society.

ENDNOTES

1. I am greatly indebted to Susan Suh. Our discussions about this topic and related issues greatly helped shape the ideas in this paper.

2. Zedong, Mao. "On Practice." Selected Works of Mao Zedong V.1. Foreign Language Press. Peking (1967). p. 300

3. The following example illustrates this great contradiction. 12 garment workers collectively would only receive a sum total of $5 (about 41¢ a garment worker per dress) for one Jessica McClintock dress selling for $135. They would all have to sew thirty-five dresses collectively to buy one dress that sells for $135. In 1991, Jessica McClintock made about $145 million in profit.

4. Spanish translation: "The people united will never be defeated!"

5. Wat, Eric C. "Beyond the Missionary Position: Reflections on Teaching Student Activism from the Bottom Up." Teaching Asia America: Diversity and the Problem of Community. Ed. by Lane Ryo Hirabayashi. Rowman and Littlefield Pub. Inc. Lanham, New York, Boulder, Oxnard (1998). p.169.

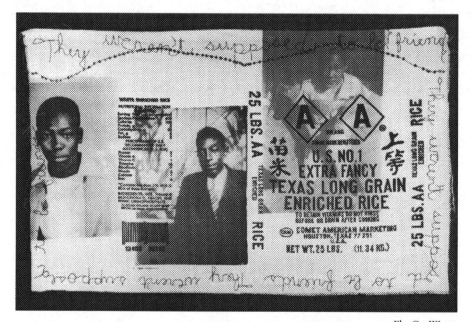

Flo Oy Wong
"They weren't supposed to be friends" 1993
mixed media - rice sack, silkscreened photos, sequins 20" x 32"

THE ART AND POLITICS OF ASIAN AMERICAN WOMEN

Nellie Wong

*Women who are fully aware of the present moment have to
know how to shed every rose-colored fantasy. Our joy is a
battle within a storm and not playing the harp under the moon
or reciting poetry in front of a flower.*[1]

Ever since I read this statement by Ding Ling, the late woman writer of China, I began to think more clearly about Asian American culture, art, literature and writing. Ding Ling's fiction was feminist in its portrayal of the conditions of Chinese women. The heroism of her women characters struck a chord within me. I began to view my own writing with brighter, clearer eyes. I opened them to the full spectrum of the courage and militancy of a tradition long hidden from me. As a socialist feminist, I had hungered for the words and songs of women. I had wanted to know the deeds of women who wrote as fighters for women's freedom. And, indeed, as fighters for the freedom of men and children, all the oppressed, not only in my own childhood community of Oakland Chinatown, but in the larger community of the entire world.

I wrote to shatter the silence of the past. I wrote to sing of my pains and sorrows against a backdrop of the external world, and to forge a link to my sisters and brothers of the Chinese American community. And I wrote to connect with those members of other communities who were a spirited part of the writing movement— women, other Asian Pacific Americans, Blacks, Chicanos and Latinos, American Indians, immigrants, workers, and lesbians and gays.

Especially I had to reach deep into the voices of the past of my ancestors, the women I saw as warriors: Li Ching Chao, Wu Tsao, Chiu Chin, and the unknown women of my parents' ancestral village in Toishan, in Guangzhou, China: the sweet, the bitter, the melancholy, the raucous, the humorous, the militant, the joyful, the celebratory, which pulled and pushed me to face oppression squarely in the face, to be brave and to act, and to join the movements toward radical, social change. For me, passion, politics and art formed an intricate whole—to fill the gaps, rips and tears of inactivity and passivity, to be with, and of, and for the people, both the dead and the living.

For many years now, my writing has been inextricably linked to my politics as a socialist feminist. Writing, in its fullest and myriad forms, must express the voices of the community, and it must provoke, challenge and move people to create, to change, to act. And when I speak of community, I speak not only of the Chinese American community, I also speak of the community of other people of color, Jews, women, sexual minorities, workers, immigrants, elders, youth, and people with disabilities. All of these people inform my creative writing eyes and ears, all of whom I embrace for we are the ones who are surviving against the grain.

As I searched for the voices that would speak to me as a Chinese American woman worker, I discovered a palette of hues and textures that formed the fabric of literature, worldwide, urban and rural, that made me cry, laugh, and sing. From the work of writers and poets like Yannis Ritsos, Rosario Castellanos, Roque Dalton, Sui Sin Far, Leonel Rugama, Ralph Ellison, Louis Chu, John Okada, Pat Parker, Hisaye Yamamoto, and others, I became convinced that literature must survive. It must move from shore to shore, from continent to continent. It must inform our reality, and our reality must find sustenance in our creative expressions.

The search for the literature of others was a necessity for me. I first wrote to fight back against the oppression as a female—criticizing the sexism in the Miss Chinatown U.S.A. contests. And I wrote to fight back against the censorship of the self because Chinese American cultural tradition dictated that my role as a woman was only toward marriage and motherhood. I also wrote to fight against the censorship of editors who disagreed with my socialist feminist politics, who said I could not write, such as what Hanging Loose Press did, who held my manuscript, The Death of Long Steam Lady, for a whole year and then refused to publish it. West End Press subsequently published this manuscript in 1986.

My writing became a catalyst for change, for personal and collective liberation. My passion, my politics and my art began to coalesce. The community I sought began to take shape, and I realized that I could no longer sit on the sidelines and watch the world go by. Indeed, I could not let myself remain a victim of racism, sexism and censorship, of invisibility. History's lessons became permanent images. Life sprung anew, and I began acting on my desire for full liberation, by joining the Women Writers Union which was born out of fighting racism and sexism in the Creative Writing Department at San Francisco State where the works of Tillie Olsen and Grace Paley were not considered major enough for a graduate student's oral examinations.

Five years of activism in the Women Writers Union led me to join Radical Women and the Freedom Socialist Party, two socialist feminist organizations which not only envision radical social change, but theoretically and programmatically carry it out in the feminist, left, people of color, anti-war, and labor movements. Crucial to my decision was the FSP and RW's perspective on the link between politics and art, that writing was not done in a vacuum, that writing and literature flowered from our daily lives as secretaries, gardeners, teachers, plumbers, electricians, typesetters, unionists and radicals.

I once thought that writing fell from the skies—that if somehow I was "blessed," the creativity would magically become mine. However, as a Marxist and Trotskyist,

I began to discover the link between work and art, between the internal and the external, and between the private and the political. I realized that art was inextricable from being a woman worker.

Leon Trotsky, a co-leader of Lenin in the 1917 Russian Revolution, wrote and spoke about the necessity of art and literature. Trotsky bravely stood and fought for a society that would be governed by workers, by people like ourselves. Trotsky wrote:

> *Art like science not only does not seek orders, but by its very essence, refuses them. Art is a function of the nerves and demands complete sincerity . . .*[2]

The Emergence of Unbound Feet

To my joy, in the late 1970s, I was a founder of Unbound Feet, a collective of six Chinese American women writers. The other co-founders were Nancy Hom, Genny Lim, Canyon Sam, Kitty Tsui and Merle Woo. An Asian American cultural renaissance bloomed in the late 1960s and 1970s. The Third World Strikes, particularly at the University of California Berkeley and San Francisco State University, among others, helped to catapult an explosion of art and literature that connected to the people of color and women's movements. We six women found each other because we were feminists who wrote and believed that performing our original works would make Asian American art and culture more accessible to the larger community. We wanted to dismantle the invisibility of Asian American women in particular and to express our lives through our art and social activism. Unbound Feet was the vehicle for our feminist voices. Unbound Feet's statement of purpose said,

> *As writers and cultural workers, we believe in the power of words as a tool for radical social change. We believe that our writing is a political act, and that politics and art cannot be divided . . . We have experienced oppression because of our race, sex, sexuality, and class; therefore, we speak out from a multi-issue base. We do not believe in isolating political struggles, such as separating ourselves from men or non-Asians as a method of social change, but believe that real equality can only come about by all oppressed groups working together. As feminists, our work examines, questions, and challenges traditional roles and relationships, breaks down stereotypes, and moves toward linking women's experiences together all over the world.*[3]

From October 1979 through February 1981, Unbound Feet wrote and performed almost a dozen works of poetry, prose and dramatic pieces. Our themes focused primarily on our identification as women of Chinese and Chinese Korean ancestry who were feminists. The Unbound Feet name symbolized our ongoing liberation from our Chinese foremothers whose feet were bound to the present day as U.S. women of color who were fighting racism, sexism, homophobia, invisibility and discrimination. While we were a women's collective, we were not separatist nor anti-male. Our composition was lesbian and heterosexual, our ages ranged from the 20s to the 40s.

As I look back, Unbound Feet was a tremendous, spirited expression of the politics and art of Asian American women. We performed at the Oakland Museum, the Chinese Culture Center, the Woman's Building in Los Angeles, La Pena Cultural Center in Berkeley, and for Chinese for Affirmative Action in San Francisco. Other venues included college campuses: San Jose State University, University of California, Los Angeles and Berkeley, and Mills College in Oakland. Our reputation spread because of our bold voices in both ensemble and individual works and as Asian American feminists. Our audiences were multicultural, feminist, Left, lesbian and gay, students, young and old, women and men. We received excellent reviews in community newspapers.

Unbound Feet also planned to publish a book. During our one and a half years of existence, we juggled work as secretaries, electricians, artists, teachers and mothers. Writing and practicing our performances became a part of our creativity with various time constraints and other responsibilities. However, the Unbound Feet experiment dissipated with our final performance of "Yellow Daughters" at the University of California, Berkeley.

Unbound Feet's Differences Emerge

While Unbound Feet built its reputation as Asian American feminist writers, our differences as feminists emerged from our planning of "Yellow Daughters," a performance sponsored by Asian American Studies (AAS) at the University of California, Berkeley. "Daughters" was set for February 6, 1981, with initial negotiations for a performance contract based on Asian American Studies paying for publicity and technical costs and a performance fee. Relying on this agreement, we issued publicity and spent time and money on silk-screened posters. Meanwhile we made several attempts to get Asian American Studies to put in writing our oral agreement. Finally, Asian American Studies told us we had "misconstrued" the agreement. They would not pay for publicity and technical costs and the only payment we could expect would be a performance fee. We also wanted free seats for low-income students.

All six of the Unbound Feet collective members met and discussed the dilemma: to go on with the show, to cancel, or to fight back. We were angered by the sexist condescension used by AAS throughout our discussions and we decided to confront this mistreatment by issuing a statement at the end of the performance.

During this same period, students in AAS had begun their own battle against a similar patronizing and unilateral treatment by the AAS administration. The students' objectives were to have a voice in the decision-making process, to help save AAS from several financial cutbacks, and to have the administrators of AAS accountable to the community by not allowing such crucial courses such as community languages to be cut. Merle Woo fully supported the students' demands, and her job was on the line as a lecturer in AAS. Because Unbound Feet connected the students' struggle with its own as an expression of its multi-issue feminism, we arranged to have a student representative speak out at the end of the performance. We felt that our statement and the students' statement together would demand that AAS be accountable to the community.

The Opposition Finally Speaks Out

Afterwards, we all met to evaluate the performance. At that meeting, Genny, Nancy and Canyon said they had not really wanted to make the statement, that those of us who were "stronger, more vocal," forced them into it, by "mind-twisting and head-bending" them. This was an attack on Kitty, Merle, and me. This was also red-baiting: radicals have historically been accused of brainwashing and forcing their opinions on others. The opposition had ample opportunity to voice their dissension; they actively participated in writing the statement and we unanimously agreed to issue it. They kept their disagreements quiet and resented us for their own silence. Exploited peoples have often dealt with their oppression by internalizing their anger and by keeping silent. Therefore, Kitty, Merle and I were dismayed that this tactic was used in our collective. This is why a true feminist perspective is necessary: to abandon self-contempt and to externalize the criticism and place it where it belongs.

Merle and I were open about our socialist feminist politics and our affiliation with Radical Women and the Freedom Socialist Party, but an Unbound Feet member red baited us by stating:

Unbound Feet did not form to engage in direct politicing (sic), organizing, or party building . . .[4]

Another said she wasn't going to buck the AAS faculty because they sat on grant boards and she didn't want to jeopardize her own funding.

All six Unbound Feet members were political women. We were activists in the Asian American, women, lesbian and gay, Left, art and writing movements. At no time, during the existence of Unbound Feet, did we "force our politics" on the collective. No one can force her politics on another person. We were strong and vocal; however, we wanted to build Unbound Feet as a truly feminist entity. We took risks stating what we thought, thereby refuting the stereotype of Asian American women being passive and quiet. As long as we wrote and performed our art, there was no problem except for the juggling of our responsibilities as workers and activists to those of Unbound Feet as a collective. Genny, Nancy and Canyon wanted to dissolve Unbound Feet because we openly criticized Asian American Studies for its mistreatment of us. To them, fighting sexism and racism in the Asian American establishment was divisive to a racial unity that was false. The community was already divided. We merely exposed those divisions and criticized them. How dare we, Asian American women, charge Asian American Studies with sexist treatment? How dare we "air our dirty laundry" in public when AAS was fought for in the turbulent 1960s to become a reality and a part of the curriculum? The women who wanted to dissolve Unbound Feet and all that we had fought for and done in one and a half years retreated from taking a political stand.

To criticize AAS was healthy. Criticism is a positive moving force. Being Asian American alone does not guarantee freedom from conflict. There were and are political divisions based on sexism, class bias, and ideological differences. Being Asian American women and feminists precisely means that we had no choice but to take a stand. Clearly, the survival of Unbound Feet was at stake, and Genny, Nancy and Canyon chose to resolve this conflict by first resigning, then dissolving the collective, and renouncing the name. They incorporated the Unbound Feet name without consultation with Kitty, Merle and me and withdrew money from our joint savings account. They also hired an attorney who said that our funds were being held "in trust" for all of us.

Kitty, Merle and I were aghast at their obstructionist tactics. We viewed our conflict not as personal, but one of principles and politics. The dispute involved not only the six in Unbound Feet, but the movements who had made our emergence and survival possible and the communities we represented. If three of us were wronged, the groups we represented were wronged. The opposition refused to act on the principles of democracy and feminism and believed they could silence the politics of our struggle by trying to settle it as a "personal" dispute among the six of us.

The issue of the name, Unbound Feet

The name, Unbound Feet, was central to our struggle. Kitty, Merle and I wanted to continue the collective as Unbound Feet Three. The name, Unbound Feet, symbolizes the active liberation of women; in particular, Asian women who suffer from sexism, racism, and class oppression. Genny, Canyon and Nancy tried to stop us from using the Unbound Feet name by their attempts to "dissolve" what we had built through our political and artistic work.

The six members of Unbound Feet finally settled the dispute; the money was divided equally among us, but only through a protracted struggle that affected all of the communities we represented. We had connected our right not to be mistreated by AAS to the students' fight against the growing conservatism of the department. For Kitty, Merle and I, and for our communities, we were expressing our vision that we had a responsibility to defend our democratic rights, multi-issue feminism, and the freedom to speak out as radicals. "To move towards freedom we must take stands as well as to write and perform our art" as stated in the Unbound Feet Three statement, is still true today.

Unbound Feet: Legacy to Liberation

Unbound Feet had to happen. It was necessary and an expression of the powerful, ongoing movement for the liberation of Asian American women. While all six former members of the collective are still artists and activists in their own right, the Unbound Feet collective writings and performances document a bright light of power and strength of the Asian American and feminist movements. We showed our communities that Asian American feminism was possible and that politics and art are indeed intertwined and that the collective, through struggle, can be a powerful force in improving our lives from exploitation and discrimination. Voicing our lives, however, is only a part of what we must do.

The 1970s, 1980s and 1990s have seen more art and writing by Asian Americans. Many of the novels, fiction, and poetry now available to us by such writers as Maxine Hong Kingston, Amy Tan, Gus Lee, Lois-Ann Yamanaka, Gish Jen, Fae Myenne Ng, Garrett Hongo, David Mura, Jessica Hagedorn, Meena Alexander, Marilyn Chin, and Chitra Banerjee Divakaruni, among others, represent a broad range of talent. And, I expect, as we head toward the millennium that more Asian American voices will be heard.

What I fear, however, is the mainstreaming of Asian American literature to the point of focusing only on being published. Where are our dissident voices for the still exploited, still discriminated against? Where, indeed, are the voices that challenge the status quo of an America that survives on the profits made from the super-exploitation and oppression of women, people of color, and queers? And how will the voices of Asian American radicals be heard?

The writings of the most oppressed have been censored by the racist, sexist, big-business mentality of publishing houses. And small, women's and people-of-color presses still struggle against the onslaught of profit-chasing publishers. Still, I am buoyed by poets such as Mila Aguilar whose poem, "To a Foreigner," challenges bourgeois assumptions:

You are a foreigner indeed,
Foreign to the rhythm of our struggle.
In the face of class murder,
How can we be lyrical? [5]

Poet and educator Merle Woo makes it very clear what she is fighting for in her poem presented at the 1981 Gay Freedom Day parade in San Francisco:

I march, stand, and fight with socialist feminists because
In its purest
Most fulfilled definition
In theory and action,
It is Revolutionary Feminism which is a
Fight for everyone who is oppressed
In one way or another
And which has as its goal
The certainty that
Those on the Front Line of Freedom will inherit the Earth [6]

Ding Ling's words, stated on International Women's Day in 1942, "Our joy is a battle within a storm and not playing the harp under the moon or reciting poetry in a front of a flower," still ring true. I am not saying that Asian American women must write only about factory or farm workers or can't enjoy a walk in the woods. But until we eradicate inequality of the sexes, racial and national oppression, anti-immigrant and anti-gay violence, violence against women and children, all engendered by our inhumane capitalist system, we Asian American women have a responsibility to challenge the status quo, speak out against censorship, and build a movement so that one day we will be free.

Our legacy to liberation means we must keep unbinding our feet, walking tall with broad shoulders, and working in concert with our sisters and brothers of all races so that our multicultural voices of love for social justice will be heard and that our literature and art will be a flowering of all the people.

ENDNOTES

1. Thoughts on the Eighth of March, 1942
2. Leon Tratsky on Literature and Art, "Art and Politics in Our Epoch," p. 106
3. Statement of Purpose, Unbound Feet, undated
4. "The Struggle of Unbound Feet," issued by Unbound Feet Three, July 12, 1981
5. A Comrade is as Precious as a Rice Seedling, Mila Aguilar. Kitchen Table: Women of Color Press, 1984.
6. "The Front Line of Freedom," *Freedom Socialist Newspaper*, 1981

"MAKE IT SNAPPY!" WHAT RHYMES WITH 'SOVIET SOCIAL-IMPERIALISM'?
The Line, The Music, and The Movement
Chris Kando Iijima interviewed by Fred Ho

Born December 19, 1948. Assistant Professor of Law at the University of Hawaii working primarily with native Hawaiian, Filipino and Southeast Asian students, communities underrepresented in the legal profession. Born and raised in New York City, Morningside Park and 121st St. Parents are Kazu and Takeru Iijima, formerly affiliated with the CPUSA who broke with the party because of its support for Japanese American internment during World War II. Now in their 80s, both parents continue to be activists and maintain a progressive world view. Kazu Iijima was an office worker, a typist and also worked as a domestic worker in her younger years. Takeru Iijima was a musician and aspiring conductor. He was discouraged from being a conductor because he was Japanese. He worked as a church organist and taught music in public schools before his retirement.

Fred Ho: What was the time you became radicalized and politically active?

Chris Iijima: I really don't remember, but I believe my first political venture was when I was young during a NYC teachers strike. My dad hated the teachers union (the UFT) and worked with an African American community organization in Brooklyn, the East New York Alliance, which organized their own schools during the teachers strike. He was volunteering with them and told me to come down. I was in high school at the time in 1960 or 61. The civil rights movement was taking off. But that was my first grassroots political activism working with these kids, in a storefront, in a community.

FH: Describe the rise of the Asian American Movement in NYC.

CI: There were two things simultaneously going on: the college students at Columbia University uptown and Asian Americans for Action downtown. Triple A was started by my mom and Minn Matsuda. At first it wasn't supposed to be anything majorly political and just Japanese American. It was anti-Vietnam War. My mom asked me to join, so I did. I was at that time active around the Vietnam War, trying to get out of the draft, occupying buildings at Columbia where I was attending college. I was already fairly conscious. My mom and dad were part of the parents organization that supported the Columbia students' takeover. They thought, and they were right, that I wasn't getting any real exposure to Asians and Asian Americans, and this was an Asian war, etc. They partly started, I think, Triple A, for me and my sister, Lynne, to get our heads together. When they started Triple A in 1969-70, there maybe were a half dozen people. Then we had the idea that there should be more than just Japanese in it. We first met in people's homes and then found a warehouse place down in Little Italy where we had to take a freight elevator. It was me, my mom and dad, Minn, my sister, and then Don Yee, Yuman and his brother Yohan (I don't remember their last names) and they were both students—they both were very political. There were other Nisei like Aiko Abe and eventually Yuri Kochiyama, a loose outcropping of Asians who didn't fit in doing community organizing since it was a mix of Japanese and Chinese, so it eventually evolved into this anti-imperialist, anti-Vietnam War, anti-racist group. It had a newsletter. We organized around anti-Vietnam War and anti-U.S./Japan Security Treaty issues as well as racial/identity issues.

Don, Yuman and Yohan were also being drawn to organizing in Chinatown and that's when people began to coalesce around I Wor Kuen. About 5 or 6 of us from AAA went into IWK. Triple A is where I met Nobuko. In 1970, we were going to the Japanese American Citizens League (JACL) national convention in Chicago to get them to come out against the War. We rode out there in a van, with a number of folks including Yuri, Nobuko and her brother Bob, Don Yee. That's where Nobuko and I started to perform. We needed something to present to the youth that wasn't going to be a speech. We were desperate. We thought of guerilla theater, but people said we needed a better kind of presentation. And so we said, OK, we'll sing. We wrote our own songs, a tune called "People's Beat" and "We are the Children"(laughs). I remember we first played some of these songs in New York at a function so that we could raise support to go to Chicago. Nobuko and I sang, and I also played guitar.

People liked our performance both in New York and Chicago. They never saw anything like it. At the JACL convention we met people from Los Angeles and had met people like Warren Furutani earlier. When we went to LA we met folks from Yellow Brotherhood, Asian American Hardcore like Mo Nishida. People would invite us to L.A. to sing. It was all somewhat haphazard, there was no gig in the traditional sense. We'd go out there and often made it up as we went along—arranging gigs while we were there. We met Charlie in New York later on. We all travelled a lot. If you notice, Charlie and Nobuko rarely sing together on the same song. The reason why was because we never officially practiced. We were constantly on the move and actually never had a name for the group. The name A Grain of Sand came from one of the songs we did on this album for Barbara Dane and Irwin Silber's record company, Paredon. Barbara Dane heard us and I guess she thought we were interesting—Asians singing this political stuff—she said this should be documented. At first we were reluctant to do it, but we agreed so long as we could write our manifesto in the liner notes. I'm sure you heard, the album is pretty rough, we did it in a day or two and we just put it out there. We were glad we did it just to document it.

Charlie played guitar professionally, he used to give lessons and he could read, which I couldn't do playing the guitar. I played french horn, and could read on that instrument, but my guitar reading skills weren't good. I knew music theory. Nobuko had a long background in jazz singing. At one point we had to write our songs for the Yellow Pearl Anthology project by Basement Workshop. I panicked, and to this day I don't even know what I wrote was accurate or not. We just did it.

I didn't and don't primarily see myself as a musician or cultural worker. That identification was a real pull, and we used to have a lot of talks about what we were doing. I was in Triple A and in this group, Asians in the Spirit of the IndoChinese. (I don't remember when I got out of IWK.) Nobuko and I spent a lot of time on the Upper Westside working with Latinos in the squatters' movement. I never saw myself as a musician, even to this day because I don't work at it like a craft. I appreciate people who take their cultural work seriously, working at a craft and a profession. I don't do that, and so I don't consider myself a musician or artist because I don't put in the time necessary.

[Our music group] A Grain of Sand was like the internet of its day. We connected people. People either knew us personally or knew our music. People in different cities who were getting into this Asian American consciousness and they'd find out about each other through us. We'd travel to Philly, San Francisco, LA, or wherever and tell people about what people in other cities were doing, give out their phone numbers, etc. In this way, people who felt isolated could see themselves as part of something larger. We articulated common political themes that were nationally arising in a way that different geographically separated groups could identify with and with each other. We also were able to join with other communities and contribute something as Asian Americans.

That, I think, was our main contribution. A lot of that had to do with the fact that we were ready to up and go. People would call and we'd just get out there.

FH: Who were your models? Some have described you as the Asian "Peter, Paul and Mary."

CI: We always hated the comparison to Peter, Paul and Mary. Nobuko always felt restricted musically. She had always been used to working with jazz groups and fairly sophisticated musicians. She also did some classical stuff. And she was a professional trained dancer and musician. She always felt more artistically constrained by what we were doing. And understandably. We never rehearsed. We never really sat down and worked out arrangements. It was, I got a phone call, they want us to come to Boston, let's go. We also had very disparate influences. I've always admired the Last Poets, they were it for me. If I had any political/artistic influences, it was them. My vocal influences and what I wished I could sound like (laughs)...Bill Withers, Kenny Rankin, Otis Redding, Sam Cooke...guys I wished I could've sounded like.

We would do student performances, but very few. Because at that time there were no official student organizations, so while we did student concerts at colleges, the vast majority of performances were community concerts: churches, in storefronts, small halls, a few clubs in LA, NY, and SF, or even someone's living room. We never did any really big venues except demonstrations. We also did Madison Square Garden for Puerto Rican Liberation Day. We had sung with a lot of the Puerto Rican Socialist Party people, we had recorded on their label, Coqui Records. The title of that recording was "Venceremos." Actually it was just me and Nobuko on that recording. It was a 45 lp, the A side was "Venceremos" and the backside was "Somos Asiaticos."

We had gone around with artists associated with nuevo cancion (the New Song Movement of Latin America) like Pepe y Flora. We'd sing with them in some venues and that's why the PSP asked us to do the record. It was in that whole period when a lot of Puerto Rican singers like Noel Hernandez or Roy Brown would come to New York to do concerts. We used to do gigs with Pedro Pietri, Pepe y Flora, it was great, I loved it. Rarely were we ever paid fees, it was just room board and pass the hat. We even sometimes paid our travel to L.A. Usually they'd figure out a way to get us out there. People inside the JACL, for instance, would figure out a way to fund us so we could go to California and then we'd go around California.

1972-3 was probably the most active period for us performing. We recorded in 1973. We were performing weekly at our height. When I say performing, I'm not talking only about shows. It was a very different concept. We were asked once by these squatters to sing on the window ledges of this building. Among the squatters on Friday nights, they'd have this thing called People's Cafe and we'd go and perform. That's what I loved about it: I really didn't get the sense that we were "performers," except when we were with people who really were, and that was a thrill. On the Coqui record they brought in these quatro players from Puerto Rico who were just mind-bogglingly great musicians. That was fun.

FH: Give me some background on political history, like the Asian Study Group and Workers Viewpoint Organization (WVO).

CI: There was a group called the Asian Center. The leadership was Bill Kochiyama and my dad. That was a place for essentially everybody not in Chinatown. It was located on 16th Street between 6th and 7th Avenues. It was a storefront we got and funded by donations. It was opened to all these groups around 1973. One of the groups was Asians in the Spirit of the IndoChinese (ASI). It had a lot of people from City College like Eddie Kochiyama, Jan and Brenda Sunoo. It was to make sure there was Asian presence in the anti-War movement. Folks at City College in that group, particularly Jan and Brenda, along with Michio Kaku, began to talk a lot about theory. That's where I first heard about Asian

Study Group. I never was a member of ASG although I joined one their study groups. Remember there was this whole thing about everybody getting into study groups? There was a real pull to get people from ASI to get into study groups. It was the very beginning of theoretical M-L, party-building, etc.

I don't really know how WVO began, my sense tho that it was an outgrowth of ASG with Jerry Tung. I had been in IWK, but not that long. To be honest, I've also had a problem with democratic-centralist organizations. I really tried. But maybe I'm too individualistic or not disciplined enough. I never was very good nor did I take discipline very well. I didn't last very long in IWK.

FH: When did you join WVO?

CI: I don't think one ever really "officially" joined WVO; I was officially in AAFEE. It was a different kind of period. When IWK started you had to identify yourself as IWK, that was the thing to do. When ASG-WVO came around, it became the whole "open-closed" membership thing. There were the "open" organizations and then the "closed" organizations. I don't remember ever being tapped on the shoulder and being told, you're a member of WVO. All I remember that was important was being identified with the line. The only open organizational affiliation I had was with AAFEE. I was a member of a closed WVO study group—that was the major thrust—being recruited into a WVO study group. This was the mid-1970s.

FH: How did you feel about and view the contention being IWK and WVO?

CI: It was very difficult because I had a lot of friends in both IWK and WVO. Much of my beginning political life was with people in IWK. Yuman was a chairperson of IWK...Don Yee. . . .personally it was very difficult. Part of the psychosis of the time was that we were so locked into defining, defending, and promoting the "correct line." Anybody that didn't follow the line was automatically a right-wing opportunist, counter-revolutionary, revisionist pig. People in WVO were always saying I was too liberal, too right-wing, too opportunist because I maintained friendships with people in L.A. In L.A. at the time, the East Wind Collective was going with IWK-LRS. Then the L.A. Storefront people were flirting with the Communist League. They were my friends. Even though I was wrapped up into the party-building thing, it was very hard not to feel these were still my good friends. I felt a lot of inner conflict, constantly flipping back and forth. That's why I was so terrible as a cadre: part of me was reading "What Is To Be Done?" and in my head, these friends were counter-revolutionaries, but in my heart, they couldn't be. I wasn't able to discuss my friends with party-building people...so when I saw them it became sort of like cheating on a wife. I'd go to LA and seek my friends out, to just hang with them behind the back of the organization and we'd try not to talk about politics. Luckily to this day they were as "liberal and individualistic" as I was. We've been able to come through that period, but it wasn't easy. That's why I consider people in L.A. as some of the closest people I know because they taught me how valuable friendships were. Thirty year friendships with people like Warren Furutani are so

247

important to me because they withstood terrible testing since many relationships were splintering all over the place. It was pretty bad.

FH: This is the first time I've heard any one describe it as psychosis, you may be very accurate in describing it as it was very vicious at times. I know having been in IWK, our view of you from what we were being told was that Chris Iijima is an opportunist and on the wrong side.

CI: Yeah, yeah. I mean everybody who wasn't in your group was an opportunist. That was the bizarre part of it: OL, RCP, everybody was a right-opportunist or a Trostkyite. Everybody was an opportunist—but us. Thank god my priority at this time was cultural work. I was told to get a music group together. Your job is to create a revolutionary culture. Hey, I read Lu Xun, I figured I could do that, I thought. The group was called May Day Singers. I remember sitting around—and it was kinda laughable—trying to figure out how to put the line into lyrics. The May Day Singers were considered "advanced workers"—although the reason they were considered "advanced" I think in retrospect was basically because they liked to sing and were willing to sing with the May Day Singers. I spent a large amount of time trying to figure out how to put the line into a particular song.

FH: The WVO line?

CI: Yes—basically it was "anti-revisionist, anti-right opportunism" songs—whatever that was. We had one song about fighting right-opportunism. We had the Chinese Communist Party approach to words, but "make it snappy." There was a directive to make songs that were anti-Soviet social-imperialism. And you really had to have those words in there somewhere. I admit that I bought into that. I've always felt it was important to have some political content in a song so that concept itself wasn't a problem for me. The stretch was how do you do it. When in fact it was probably impossible. I didn't fight the idea that "it should be political and reflect something." But I did fight that it had to be the line and half the time I didn't know what the line was. I thought I knew it. But half the time, I think nobody knew it. I know we in the May Day Singers often didn't know what it was. But, of course, you said you did and faked it. So as a result, of course, much of it was ludicrous. We'd sit there and ask, "what rhymes with Soviet social-imperialism?" Not a whole lot (laughs).

FH: I know your understanding of WVO is superficial, but why do you think so many Asians were attracted to it? And then later on, I'm told, that a number of African Americans came in. Tell me why?

CI: What made WVO attractive to Asian Americans is that WVO was into this theory thing. It was very attractive to me to get into a study group. I'd never heard of that before, and they were doing that in China, wow. This whole legitimacy about theory, about China, and that was attractive, I think, to a lot of Asians.

FH: Who promoted that? Jerry Tung, Michio Kaku...? Who were seen as the leading theoreticians with the light bulbs above their heads?

CI: Jerry was the Man, he was the Chairman. There were legends about how his father fought the Klan down south. You'd talk to the guy and he knew Lenin backward and forward. He was a smart guy. Also, AAFEE had a large reputation in the broader Asian American community. It was attracting a lot of community. That combined with the theory/China association was a very powerful lure. African Americans came in the merger between the Revolutionary Workers League and CWP. RWL had a lot of splits, but it also had a relationship with the former Palante [refers to the newspaper of the Young Lords Party] people, PRRWO (Puerto Rican Revolutionary Workers Organization—the antecedent to the Young Lords Party [editor]). So, there was this Asian-Black-Puerto Rican appeal. But it really was the emphasis on theory that drew a lot of people. I mean I was into it. I wanted to talk about "The National Question." I was in this heavy-duty study group that was reading stuff that I still couldn't read probably to this day.

FH: What do you think were the significant accomplishments of WVO during that era?

CI: Not just WVO, but for all those groupings, I think the one good thing was that it made people take the notion of what it took to make a revolution seriously. It meant organization, planning, strategy, thinking beyond throwing rocks in a demonstration or strumming a guitar. That was a contribution that all the groups made. The motivations for many of the people involved were very noble. Some of the best people were involved. That's the shame of it all. It was a shame that so many people got blown out, burned out. I was never good at democratic-centralism ("d.c.") anyway, and this was it to the max.

FH: Most people don't know what d.c. was like. Describe it some more.

CI: Here's an example from doing cultural work. Here's the line, write a song with the line. Period. You don't write anything else that's not the line. It's your job to write songs, perform songs, that illustrate the line. That was my understanding of d.c. when it came to cultural work.

FH: So it really wasn't democratic, but directives.

CI: It was a lot of centralism, but not a lot of democracy, which was true of most groups.

FH: How did they get you to do this?

CI: They didn't have to GET me to do it—I was willing and wanting to do it. Although I have to say that probably in retrospect, I didn't understand it very well, if at all. What I think people wanted me to do was what I had done with Nobuko and Charlie. To go out, spread the word. That's what they wanted us to do, how they envisioned us working. The problem was that the way it was set up, it couldn't be done that way. It was too controlled. So my understanding of d.c. was that you were given a task to do, a line to push and spread, and that was your job, your political work. To that extent, as a theoretical matter, I don't have a problem with that, because everybody does that in some manner.

FH: That's what most people do at their jobs, except they're getting a paycheck.

CI: Yeah. That in and of itself is not a big thing. But somewhere along the line, it got divorced from the mass base, from real people. That it sort of fed on itself, that it got further and further isolated from people. You don't realize it....and finally, there came a day, I turned around and realized, we're talking to a smaller and smaller group of people, literally talking to each other, talking to fewer and fewer people...because there was a time when everybody was splitting from one another. Splits here, splits there. More and more smaller groups of people hating everybody else. It was bizarre.

FH: What do you feel drove this thing, a tidal wave...

CI: I wish I knew. I think a lot of it was being alienated from and not listening to people with whom we were trying to organize. I accept my own responsibility for being a part of it. I believed that if only people would understand the line. If they didn't it was their problem. A lot of people got into this head because many of them weren't doing anything real—with real people and real problems.

FH: Were you still in touch with the CWP people after the Greensboro killings in 1979 [4 members of the CWP were murdered by the KKK in an anti-KKK rally organized by the CWP—editor]?

CI: At that time I wasn't really so much working with them, although I still was occasionally working with May Day Singers. I remember going down to Greensboro and performing at the funeral.

FH: So were you part of the process in which the CWP becomes the New Democratic Movement and rejects revolution?

CI: No. I have to say that there were a number of years when I didn't want to hear about any kind of politics. That was during that period.

FH: Describe what your lives were like during the 1970s, party-building time?

CI: I was different from others. A lot of people actually went to work in factories, and I didn't. My life was never radically altered in the same way as others who actually quit their jobs, became factory workers and began to organize. I never did that. My major thing was going out to Brooklyn and working with the May Day Singers. And that was pretty enjoyable. We'd be asked to go to an event and sing, and we would.

FH: I think you're very aware that in NYC there's a certain toxicity has been in the political soil for a very long time, which people refer to as the AAFEE-IWK war. Talk about that, your feelings, why it still continues in someways even though both entities don't even exist anymore.

CI: Because it was so bitter. I knew my political beginnings at least in Chinatown were with people in IWK. Like Don Yee, I used to consider him one of my closest friends, and I haven't seen him in years.

FH: Don Yee, who was married to Sasha Hohri, I remember, left IWK around the late 1970s, by 1978. Yuman was gone by them. Virgo was still around, but he was like a lessor figure. Obviously Gordon Chang and Carmen Chow (then-spouses) were still around and major leaders. Was that same kind of continuity replicated in WVO?

CI: No, my recollection is that there was a lot of turnover. It was hard to figure out how things worked. It was just sort of guilt by association: "Chris, that rotten opportunist with WVO. Don't talk to so-and-so, she's with October League, and that person's with Wei Min She/RCP...and so-and-so's with LRS"...you got bagged with an identity over time.

It was pretty bitter, there were a lot of fist fights. You couldn't leaflet in front of each other's event or there'd be a fistfight. Or you'd go on purpose to leaflet so there'd be a fistfight...I mean it was one of those deals.

I'm now talking again to people who used to be Wei Min She. I used to be very close to people in WMS. When Charlie, Nobuko and I used to sing, one of the places we used to always sing was the Everybody's Bookstore of WMS. We used to do International Hotel stuff. Steve Louie, Terry Dofu, Steve Wong...all those guys. But I always knew there was this big rift between WMS and IWK in San Francisco Chinatown, even before LRS and RCP. That's partly why it got so bad because it just carried over from the previous days.

I respected a lot of the folks involved in the Food Coop in New York Chinatown which had people like Bea Hsiao in it, but it wasn't led by WVO-AAFEE at that time. It was pre-AAFEE. They were beginning to organize people in Chinatown thru a food coop. They became a study group, maybe a WVO study group. That was a heavy influence on me, because I thought they were people doing good work. Sorry, that's a digression.

But as far as the toxicity, I think it was very, very bitter and only now just in the past few years or so have I talked with people who were in Wei Min like Steve Louie or Steve Wong. And before I used to be very close to people in Wei Min. Another good example is Rocky Chin, who I haven't really talked to in years because he was in IWK-LRS. We just started talking more recently because he's a lawyer and I worked with his daughter who went to Smith College. She was very active in ECASU (East Coast Asian Students Union). There also is Greg Morozumi who is doing great work in the Bay Area even now. I've worked with him recently with in connection with La Peña, and respect and like him a lot, but would have never worked with him before because of the whole LRS/WVO rivalry. I'm grateful to have been able to start clearing out of that kind of toxic atmosphere.

Back then, people got immediately tagged for who you were affiliated with. Then there were people who were independents like Yuri. Everybody was scrambling to get Yuri to come over to their organization because of her stature, and the Kochiyama family as a whole. I mean they were like turf. It was a very difficult time. I think there was a lot of promise and the promise just didn't get fulfilled. Just think about all the people who were the leadership of every major Asian American community organization who got drawn out of these groups, at some level, into party-building whether it be study groups, joining groups.... They all left their organizations to get involved in this. The major political leadership of the Asian American Movement, and this is probably true of the Puerto Rican Movement—the young leadership of both of these movements all went into party-building. I don't know about the Black Liberation Movement. But many well known African American political movement leaders got into party-building. Many of these people then got divorced from all the other stuff they had been doing. For a couple of years you had these very concentrated things going on. If you think about all these people associated with all these organizations, and this is especially true for the Puerto Rican Movement, it was a pretty impressive and dedicated group of people, many of whom I think never got back into activism. That's a tragedy, I think. That's why that legacy for young people isn't there. So many of the people who began a lot of the stuff just aren't around anymore.

FH: What do you think has been the positive legacy?

CI: There's a huge amount of potential goodwill among my generation for young people that hasn't really been tapped. In the past year and a half, Nobuko, Charlie and I have been called on to do all these performances for younger people. The first time we did it was (since the 1970s) for this award event honoring Yuri Kochiyama in San Francisco. It was a group working with African American and Asian American youth. They named an award after Yuri. They called Nobuko to ask if the three of us would sing in honor of this award named after Yuri. We said yes, and that was the first time we got back together again. We rehearsed a half hour before, did some of the old songs, and did it. UC Berkeley had heard we were going to do this and they financed our travel. We'd have to do a concert a Berkeley. They literally forced their Asian American Studies students to go to it. They required them to go, they took attendance. It was a captive audience (laughs)...We had a major concert there. There are a lot of students from Asian American Studies so it was a huge crowd. Surprisingly enough, the kids liked it. Their initial reaction was probably, oh god, let me outta here. But they liked it. The word spread among people that had never heard us before that we're not so terrible. So we started getting calls. We do one about every other month now. It sort of reminds me of like in our day we'd hear Delta Bluesmen, and you'd think of them as a link to history. I guess that's how some might perceive us—living history. We've been to Santa Cruz, Purdue, Michigan, Univ. of Mass. La Peña, Japan America Theater. Now Nobuko is listing us as part of the Great Leap Productions. We sing in Spanish in some songs and these kids are blown away that there are Asian Americans who actually used to sing for Spanish-speaking people. A new concept. It's been a lot of fun. The only pressure I feel is I want to be relevant to them, that this isn't just oldies or this is the way it was, but there's this history and tradition of Asian American activism that happened before you were born. I think that's what blows young people away. The idea that there is now a 30-40 year history of activism by American-born Asians. The ones most affected are political college students who've felt isolated that they're the only ones swimming against the tide, nobody really cares, everybody's into an "A Magazine" mentality [Asian American yuppie-ism—editor] but nobody wants to do anything political...they felt isolated and suddenly they feel more connected to a long Asian American activist tradition which says—this is your historical legacy. That's huge, and that's why they're fun to do.

Minn Matsuda and Kazu Iijima
Founding members of Asian Americans for Action (Triple A)
Photo credit: © Corky Lee

COMBATTING SEXISM AND SEXUAL HARASSMENT

Asian Pacific Islanders For Community Empowerment (API FORCE)

API FORCE recognizes that an organization dedicated to progressive vision and change must provide for its members a working and social environment free from sexual harassment, exploitation, and intimidation. Failing to do so would jeopardize its commitment to building a conscientious community based on mutual respect and consideration. API FORCE believes that sexual harassment is a violent act in which one person demeans and humiliates another. Although sexual harassment can occur to both men and women, it has historically been an expression of power by men over women. As an organization committed to a progressive vision which includes ending sexism, we adhere to a no-tolerance policy of sexual harassment in all its forms. Where sexual harassment is found to have occurred, API FORCE will act to stop the harassment, discipline those responsible, and prevent a recurrence according to the following policy:

What To Do About Sexual Harassment

The following are some key ways for dealing with sexual harassment, and they do not necessarily need to be followed in this order.

Direct Communication

An individual may act on her or his concerns about sexual harassment directly, by addressing the other party in person or in writing, describing the unwelcome behavior and its effect and stating that the behavior must stop. Copies of a sent letter should be kept by the writer.

Third Party Intervention

The creation of a Sexual Harassment Committee, whose constituents are not API FORCE members yet are familiar and allied with the organization, can provide arbitrary third party intervention to investigate harassment claims and decide upon issues of culpability. Persons with complaints should feel free to contact any member of the committee and request an investigation, soon after which the committee would convene to discuss appropriate procedures. Possible suitable measures include arranging a private meeting between the committee and each of the parties involved to try to clarify perceptions and insure that the parties are comfortable with their future interactions. Other actions, such as a mediated discussion among the parties or an open forum among API FORCE members, could also be explored in appropriate cases. Any act that is decided to constitute sexual harassment will result in prompt and certain expulsion from API FORCE.

Advice

The Sexual Harassment Committee can help the individual plan on how to confront the offending party in person or in writing. The committee can also provide further references and resources to the individual concerning sexual harassment.

Every Individual's Rights

Every person has the right at any time to raise the issue of sexual harassment without fear of reprisal. API FORCE will not permit reprisals against a person who in good faith reports or provides information about sexual harassment or behavior that might constitute sexual harassment. API FORCE will respect the confidentiality and privacy of individuals reporting or accused of sexual harassment to the extent reasonably possible.

People who feel that they have been harassed or know someone who is should know that it is usually best to act promptly. Correcting the situation immediately or at least talking with someone familiar about the issues and ways to respond would help safeguard an environment respectful of all. Ignoring the situation and hoping that it will correct itself is oftentimes just an implicit consent for the harassment to continue. Keeping records or a journal and saving any letters, e-mail, or notes received can all be very helpful as evidence, along with recording the dates, times, places, witnesses present, and the nature of the harassment.

Sexual harassment is not something one brings upon oneself. Oftentimes, one is not alone in feeling that she or he has been harassed by a certain party. Deciding to deal with the situation would help prevent others from being harmed and uphold basic principles of just treatment and respect for all. The structure and content of this policy are based much on the policies at various universities and a few organizations throughout amerika. The policy can go into effect immediately after general approval by API FORCE members.

The Sexual Harassment Committee should then be formed to begin addressing cases as soon as they arise. This policy should be subject to periodic review.

TO SERVE THE MOVEMENT

The Revolutionary Practice of Yuri Kochiyama

Diane C. Fujino

Yuri Kochiyama is arguably the most renowned Asian American woman activist. For close to four decades she has been an indefatigable worker for justice. She has struggled for countless political issues in numerous social movements, including the Black Liberation Movement, the Asian American Movement, the Puerto Rican independence movement, and the political prisoner movement. Yet, Yuri is more than a political being. She is a compassionate, well-rounded person. She loves community sports. She brought encouragement to Japanese American soldiers fighting in World War II when, from inside a concentration camp, her Sunday School class and supporters wrote to an astonishing 13,000 Nisei GIs. She is highly developed in her sense of ethics and in her duty to serve humanity. And she inspires others to enhance their humanity by helping those around them, by caring about injustices, and by participating in the collective movements to build a better world.[1]

People are not born revolutionaries; they develop their political ideology and practice. Yuri's development involved a slow twenty years of consciousness raising. Then, as a wife, mother of six children, and part-time waitress, she exploded into political activism in the early 1960s. Except for a couple of significant factors, Yuri's early life holds few keys to predicting her later participation in the revolutionary movement. Born on May 19, 1921, the child of Japanese immigrants, Yuri was raised in a well-to-do, middle-class family. During a period of rampant residential discrimination, her father built a custom-designed house in a White neighborhood in San Pedro, a port town in south Los Angeles. Perhaps in part because of their economic position, Yuri was able to shield herself from direct experiences with race, class, and gender discrimination. She was popular in school, serving as the first female student body vice-president and joining the high school tennis team. She dated White boys from her high school, which was unusual for Nisei of that period.[2] Yuri also managed to avoid doing much housework. The gender norm of 1930s America dictated that mothers train their daughters to become "good wives" and "good mothers." Japanese American families tended to follow this norm. But Yuri was so busy participating in extracurricular activities that she rarely helped her stay-at-home mother with chores, except to wash dishes. In fact, her twin brother remembered doing more housework than Yuri. But Yuri denies this, stating that neither she nor her two brothers did much housework.[3]

Yuri's ability to evade traditional gender roles did not stem from a feminist consciousness. She was simply too busy. This lack of consciousness reflected her overall apolitical stance. To Yuri, the world was colorblind and discrimination did not affect her. She maintained this rosy outlook even when she was denied sales clerk jobs in White establishments. However, she regularly received job offers, always unsolicited, as a domestic worker for middle-class White families. Still, her ability to break from prescribed gender and cultural norms, to a degree anyway, was a hint of her later rebelliousness.

In many ways, Yuri's apolitical stance, her provincialness, her readiness to defend US government actions—even as the government incarcerated her family and people—and her ability to minimize the existence of racism give no indication that she would later develop into a revolutionary.[4] But two factors in her early experience help to explain her political growth. First, Yuri was a whirlwind of community service. She was a Sunday School teacher and a counselor to multiple pre-teen girls groups, including the YWCA Girl Reserves, the Girl Scouts, and Blue Birds. She was so involved in these girls' lives and committed to her role as advisor that she invited the girls to weekend slumber parties at her home. Yuri was also a sports enthusiast. In addition to playing on the high school tennis team, she covered many sporting events as a journalist. At the young age of 16, she had the audacity to ask the local newspaper sports editor if she could write for them. The paper gave her a trial coverage, which she apparently passed, because she began reporting on local sporting events for the San Pedro News-Pilot. For her dedication to building community in San Pedro, her hometown friends organized hero's gatherings in her honor in 1958 and again in 1989.[5]

Yuri carried her devotion to community service into the concentration camps. Inside the Santa Anita "assembly center" in Los Angeles, Yuri's Sunday School class began sending postcards to Nisei soldiers who were not only facing down war, but also race discrimination inside the armed forces. Inside the Jerome, Arkansas concentration camp—where Yuri's family was later sent—the girls gained many supporters. Children brightened up the postcards with colorful crayola drawings, the young women wrote the letters, older adults helped with addressing and mailing, and some Nisei soldiers like Yuri's brother made regular monetary contributions to help pay for stamps and materials. Soon, the group in Jerome was writing to an incredible 13,000 Nisei soldiers. How does Yuri know this number? She painstakingly recorded the names and addresses of every soldier to whom they wrote. When she left Jerome, she asked her mother to continue the recordings. This type of detailed, even obsessive, record-keeping behavior has followed Yuri throughout life. Today she records every incoming phone call and incoming and outgoing letter—and Yuri receives numerous calls and correspondence daily—in an effort to remember people's news and kindness and to not forget to respond to their requests.

The second characteristic that foretold of Yuri's later revolutionary growth was her openness to new ideas, her flexibility in adapting to new situations. Moreover, the trauma of being forcibly removed and incarcerated as well as her father's false arrest, imprisonment, and premature death in January 1942 moved Yuri to gradually re-examine her views. When she was relocated from her predominantly White neighborhood to the all-Japanese concentration camps in April 1942, she grew in her racial identity. Yuri, then 21, reflected: "Going to camps is where, for the first time, I came to know my own people. And in doing so, I started, finally, to see myself as a Japanese American....In camp, under duress, the best and worst come out. I think it was mostly their strengths that came out. I was really proud to be Japanese." In addition, Yuri sought out opportunities to listen to the opinions of more political, mature internees. In this way, she learned about the discontent of the Japanese Americans inside the concentration camps and of the racial discrimination they faced.[6] Though her political consciousness would develop slowly over the next two decades, the incarceration experience represented the planting of seeds, which in the fertile soil of the Civil Rights Movement, would eventually blossom into political activism.

Yuri's adaptability is also seen in the ease with which she moved from a spacious, custom-built house in San Pedro to a tiny one-room sleeping unit in New York following her marriage in 1946 to Bill Kochiyama, a veteran who fought with the famed all-Nisei 442nd Regimental Combat Team. One would suspect that such an economic drop would have been difficult on someone who grew up in relative prosperity. But to Yuri, rather than being a hardship, this new life presented her with exciting opportunities to meet varied and interesting people.

Throughout the 1950s, Yuri and Bill continued their active community work, primarily providing services—housing, entertainment, friendship—to Japanese and Chinese soldiers passing through New York on their way to the Korean warfront. The group they founded to support the GIs, the Japanese Sino Service Organization, was unique in its pan-Asian focus.[7] While Yuri would say they were only filling a need, this multi-ethnic vision foreshadowed her later work in bridging multiple movements and communities. In the context of the emerging Civil Rights Movement, Yuri grew in her awareness of social injustice, primarily through first-hand experience with discrimination and by reading newspaper coverage of protests.

Yuri's dedication to community service, her flexibility and open-mindedness, her efforts to escape prescribed gender and cultural roles, and her boldness cannot be minimized. These were the key elements that became reworked and transformed into her political activism.[8] Yuri's commitment to the collective, to helping others, to building up community help explain why she became involved in the political happenings of her community when the Kochiyamas moved to Harlem in 1960. They had not moved to Harlem for any political reason. The location of Bill's job enabled their family, now with six children aged one to thirteen, to move into a larger apartment in a newly opened housing project. The Kochiyamas soon found themselves in the midst of a growing Black movement. They joined a community-based organization located a block from their home, the Harlem Parents Committee, and became involved in the civil rights struggle for culturally relevant education for Black children.[9] They had not sought out a political group per se; rather, they were simply getting involved in the fabric of their community. At the same time, Yuri was now open to political concerns as a result of experiencing discrimination in the concentration camps and among the poor in New York housing projects. Here we see how Yuri's openness to new ideas and flexibility enabled her to work within an explicitly political and all-Black group for the first time. Once exposed to political ways to fight oppression, Yuri plunged into political activism. She continued her whirlwind of community service activities, but now in ways that politically challenged the social institutions that created inequality.

Yuri's civil rights activism led to her introduction to a person who would inspire in her a revolutionary transformation. Yuri and her teenage son Billy were among the more than 600 activists arrested during a protest against the Downstate Medical Center's failure to hire Black and Puerto Rican construction workers. It was during their hearing in October 1963 at the Brooklyn Courthouse that Malcolm X appeared.[10] Yuri excitedly and hesitantly moved forward to meet this giant of the Black movement. At the time, Yuri's politics reflected that of the predominant Civil Rights Movement. She disagreed, for example, with Malcolm's stance against integration. Yet she was attracted to Malcolm's radical politics, despite being, at age 42, considerably older than the urban youth who championed Malcolm. But her open-mindedness allowed her to hear new perspectives. And she was drawn to the logic of Malcolm's ideas and to the sincerity of his practice. After Malcolm attended a program for Japanese anti-war activists held at the Kochiyama's in June 1964,[11] Yuri began attending Malcolm's weekly speeches at the Audubon Ballroom in Harlem and joined his Organization of Afro-American Unity. She quickly became immersed in revolutionary nationalist politics. At the time of Malcolm's death in 1965, the radical Black Liberation Movement was emerging. And it was in this climate that Yuri's activism developed.

In 1969, Yuri made the organizational commitment to revolutionary nationalist politics by joining the newly created Republic of New Africa (RNA), a formation seeking Black liberation through the establishment of a Black nation in five states in the US South (Alabama, Mississippi, Louisiana, South Carolina, and Georgia). At that time and today, Yuri believes that the road to liberation for Blacks is through the establishment of a sovereign nation in the US South—a controversial stance with which many radicals disagree. Yuri also agreed with the anti-capitalist and pro-socialist ideology of the RNA. While the RNA tended to use more Afrocentric terms such as "African communalism" or "ujamaa" more often than the term "socialism," their politics fall into the socialist rubric. Their Declaration of Independence, written in 1968, states that the nation seeks "to place the major means of production and trade in the trust of the State to assure the benefits of this earth and man's genius and labor to Society and all its members." And in a political statement, the RNA wrote: "Another aspect of New Afrikan Nationalism is that We are Black Scientific Socialists, that is, We are Black people that adhere to the principles of scientific socialism....Another name for the scientific socialist society We are struggling for is New Afrikan Ujamaa."[12] Robert Williams, then RNA president, stated it plainly, "I envision a Democratic socialist economy wherein the exploitation of man by man will be abolished."[13]   And Gaidi Obadele, first vice-president, declared, "We don't have any hang-ups on socialism, which we call 'ujamaa,' which is broader than socialism. It's an African conception of the organization of society. It means we have total responsibility for one another."[14]   Yuri too notes that socialism would be the economic system of the New Afrikan nation.

The US government's massive efforts to stop the swelling radical social movements of the late 1960s also shaped Yuri's politics.   When the FBI's counter intelligence programs (COINTELPROs) viciously attacked the Black Panther Party, the RNA, and other radical groups,[15] many of Yuri's comrade-friends ended up in prison as the targets of political repression.   Already a night owl, Yuri would stay up until the wee hours of the morning writing letters to the prisoners, creating eye-catching leaflets announcing political events and court dates, and writing press releases, articles for newsletters, and letters to newspaper editors.   Her weekdays were filled with political meetings and her weekends with visits to prisons.   No doubt, Yuri's own incarceration experiences as well as her father's false imprisonment and premature death during World War II inspired her passion for supporting political prisoners.

In the 1970s, Yuri also began supporting Puerto Rican prisoners of war, incarcerated for their efforts to liberate their homeland from US colonial rule.   At the time, five Puerto Rican nationalists, including Lolita Lebron and Rafael Cancel Miranda, were incarcerated since the 1950s for armed attacks on the US president's residence and US Congress.[16] While clearly controversial, Yuri defends their actions. After all, international law gives the right to colonized people to resist imperialist structures by any means necessary, including armed struggle.[17]   To this day, Yuri defends the right to armed struggle and armed self-defense.

In 1977, Yuri participated in what was one of the most exciting events of her colorful life.   She and 28 other activists, virtually all Puerto Rican, closed down the Statue of Liberty and hung the Puerto Rican flag across Ms. Liberty's forehead.   This media-catching event was part of the motion that won the unconditional release of the five nationalists in the late 1970s.[18] And twenty years later, in September 1999, the Movement won the release of eleven Puerto Rican prisoners of war incarcerated since the early 1980s for their efforts to liberate their patria.   In a life of intense political activity for numerous social issues, the struggle to free political prisoners is dearest to Yuri's heart.

Simultaneous with her work for political prisoners and the Black Liberation Movement, Yuri began working in the Asian American Movement, which emerged as a distinct social movement in the late 1960s.   Not surprisingly, Yuri worked in the radical wing of the Asian American Movement to oppose imperialism and to challenge the purpose and content of US education.   She worked with the first pan-Asian political group in New York City, Asian Americans for Action (AAA or Triple A), to oppose US military encroachment into Vietnam, Cambodia, Laos, and Okinawa.[19] She also supported the student struggles to gain ethnic studies at City College of New York, and taught one of the first Asian American Studies courses there.   Moreover, Yuri worked with Japanese American activists, often to ensure that no other groups had to enter concentration camps. During the early 1970s, she worked with AAA in a successful campaign to repeal Title II of the 1950 Internal Security Act, which created six concentration camps in which to place any persons who "might probably" engage in espionage or sabotage. AAA recognized that, "This is a 'legal' weapon designed to clamp shut and terrorize anyone who dares to question established policy."[20] In the late 1970s, she helped found Concerned Japanese Americans to oppose the potential lock-up of Iranian Americans during the Iran hostage crisis. And when New Yorkers began working to gain Japanese American redress and reparations in 1980, Yuri worked with East Coast Japanese Americans for Redress (ECJAR) to galvanize the community to testify at the New York hearing of the Commission on Wartime Relocation and Internment of Civilians (CWRIC), a location the New York Nikkei community demanded and won. Bill Kochiyama testified at that 1981 New York CWRIC hearing and Yuri testified before the national CWRIC in Washington DC. The efforts of ECJAR, which affiliated with the National Coalition for Redress/Reparations, and other organizations succeeded in winning monetary compensation for the unconstitutional incarceration of 120,000 Japanese Americans during World War II.[21]

In the 1990s, Yuri remains as committed as ever to revolutionary change. Yet as times have changed, so too have some aspects of her practice. These differences reflect her maturation as an activist as much as the transformation of the Movement itself. First, Yuri now has greater awareness of her role as a political leader. In the 1990s, for the first time, she speaks on the national college circuit, regularly gives activist advice to young people, founded organizations in which she provides key leadership, and permitted video and book projects to be produced about her life. Even still, Yuri has not played the role of traditional leader; she has not been a theoretician, a major decision-maker, a well-versed strategist, or until recently, a main organizer. Yuri defines her own role as that of a worker: "I'm just another activist and not a leader type...I'm just one of the thousands and thousands who participate in the Movement." But Yuri is a leader, though of a non-traditional variety. She has worked to bridge numerous communities and movements across racial, ideological, and interpersonal barriers. She has given unsparingly of her time, her resources, herself to the collective struggle for justice over the past four decades. And she has inspired thousands to become active by her concern for each individual, her moral courage, and her practice. For these reasons, Yuri is respected—by renowned Movement leaders and young activists alike—as a serious organizer and esteemed friend. It is the Asian American Movement that enabled Yuri to develop her full potential as a leader—as a role model, founder of organizations, and nationally recognized speaker. As far back as three decades ago when the Asian American Movement emerged, young Asian American activists turned to Yuri for leadership and inspiration. But it has only been in the 1990s that she is widely regarded as a Movement leader, and though she does not verbalize this, her actions demonstrate an understanding of this role.

A second way Yuri has changed over the years is that the pace of her political activities has slowed down, just as the frenzy of the Movement has declined from its height in the 1960s and 1970s. Plus, a stroke suffered in March 1997 has forced Yuri to acknowledge her physical limitations. Third, just as the Movement is less "hard-lined" than in the 1970s, so too is Yuri. The radicalness of her politics has not changed, but today, she interacts with people in more flexible ways. She adjusts her speeches depending on her perception of the audience. And in the case of Asian American college students, Yuri's talks are often less radical than talks she gives to African or explicitly Leftist audiences. For example, at the Brecht Forum and the Marxist School, her solution for social change was, "We must challenge the system of capitalism." But on the same topic, this time for the multiracial newsletter, *Shades of Power*, she wrote: "If we want to change society, we must begin by transforming ourselves; learning from one another about one another's history, culture, dreams, hopes, personal experiences;" nowhere does she mention the capitalist system.[22] Some criticize Yuri for being liberal—moving away from controversial positions to maintain superficial harmony.[23] And there are times when Asian American audiences want to hear more radical analyses. But Yuri does this strategically to raise political consciousness and motivate people to action based her perception of their awareness.

What can we learn from Yuri's practice? There are at least four themes for social change embodied in Yuri's life. First, Yuri is humanizing. To her, people expand their humanity by participating in the collective struggle for justice. This is the political philosophy that guides her actions in life and in the Movement. More than any words, her deeds have inspired people to grow as human beings. From writing to 13,000 Nisei soldiers to working in soup kitchens and shelters to bringing people together to struggle for revolutionary change, Yuri exemplifies a humanizing practice. By doing good works for someone other than oneself, by working for causes larger than oneself, and by working to eradicate structures that maintain oppression, people expand their own humanity by becoming part of the international human community. Moreover, Yuri advocates that self-transformation is necessary for societal change. At the same time, she believes that structural change is necessary for humans to truly be liberated from the corporate profit seeking, discrimination, consumerism, and individualism that fuels capitalist oppression.

This last point segues into the second theme of Yuri's political practice. Her activism reflects an ideological belief in radical, grassroots transformation within the context of worldwide liberation. Yuri is not simply about helping people in the short-run. While it is certainly commendable to serve the hungry and shelter the home-less—and Yuri has done this—she also recognizes the significance of opposing systemic oppression. This requires radical transformation to attack the root causes of oppression, namely imperialism, capitalism, racism, sexism, and heterosexism. And Yuri believes that the best way to bring about systemic changes is by struggling at the grassroots level. Unlike mainstream thinkers who rely heavily on institutional structures, on change coming from politicians, lawyers, or judges, she believes that genuine social change comes from the masses of people collectively working for justice.

She believes in people power. And her political practice for the past four decades has been a testament to the radical, grassroots struggle.

The third theme that emerges from Yuri's practice is an opposition to polarization. She is a master bridge builder. To counter the creation of artificial boundaries that separate groups, Yuri actively works to connect social issues, movements, and communities. At another level of bridge building, Yuri does not lose sight of the individuals involved in the Movement. She has a special ability to nurture the political inclinations of young people and to inspire them to work for social change. She does this not only by being a living example of what it means to struggle for justice and by sharing her stories about the Movement, which are phenomenal, but also by asking the youth about themselves, by making them feel that their ideas and activities are important. And at yet another level of bridge building, Yuri connects the individual with the larger issue of social justice. She values each person's contributions, recognizing that there are individuals involved at every level of the Movement who create the motion that collectively triggers change. What Yuri understands in a dialectical way is the Movement brings out the best in people, who in turn, enhance their own humanity by working in the movement for justice.

The fourth theme represented by Yuri's life and political practice is an unending dedication. Yuri has a passion for justice. She is courageous. She has stuck to her political beliefs despite criticism from loved ones and political comrades. She has risked losing jobs and getting arrested. And she has put her health in jeopardy in her fight for justice. She has stayed up until the wee hours of the night to write to political prisoners, to compose articles for newsletters or newspapers, to finish mailing leaflets for an event. She remains a committed worker in the fight for justice. Yuri's comrade Herman Ferguson, one of today's foremost Black revolutionary leaders, said: "Yuri is a revolutionary soldier....A revolutionary soldier is committed to the destruction of the enemy in word and deed, is...someone you can trust fully,...who is not afraid of the enemy, who has cleansed herself of the negativity of humanity. I can count all the revolutionary soldiers I know on one hand and still maybe have a thumb left. Malcolm X was in that vein, and so is Yuri."[24]

In the end, people will assess Yuri's contributions to the movement for justice, not by her breadth of knowledge or her ideas or her organizing abilities, all of which are commendable, but by her revolutionary practice.

ENDNOTES

1. Information for this chapter comes from the author's extensive interviews with Yuri Kochiyama from December 1995 through March 1998; from the author's interviews with Yuri Kochiyama's family and comrades from June 1996 through February 1999; primary sources such as Yuri Kochiyama's diary during World War II; secondary sources including books, newspaper articles, and Movement publications; and informal interactions and discussions with Yuri Kochiyama and a number of her friends and political associates.

2. Mei Nakano, Japanese American Women: Three Generations, 1890-1990 (Berkeley: Mina Press, 1990), 111; Jere Takahashi, Nisei, Sansei: Shifting Japanese American Identities and Politics (Philadelphia: Temple University Press, 1997), 42-44.

3. Yuri Kochiyama, interview with author; Peter Nakahara, interview with author, February 17, 1999.

4. Mary (Yuri) Nakahara diary, "The Bordered World," vol. 1, 1942, Japanese American National Museum.

5. Kochiyama family, Christmas Cheer, 1958; Steve Marconi, "San Pedro's Favorite Daughter Given a Hero's Return," *San Pedro News-Pilot*, August 7, 1989.

6. Kochiyama diary, vol. 1, 1942.

7. Kochiyama family, Christmas Cheer, 1956, 1960; Yuri Kochiyama, interview with author.

8. This building of old elements into something new is what Engels referred to as "the law of the negation of the negation." As explained by Dialego: "Negation involves the movement of something from an old stage to a new and higher stage so that the elements of the old are carried forward and reworked into the new....When we speak therefore of the 'negation of the negation' we do not merely mean that something has changed twice over. We mean that there has been a spiral development upwards, carrying the past into the future, remaking it in the process" [ital. in original] (Dialego, Philosophy and Class Struggle, Chicago: Imported Publications, 1978, 21).

9. Luther Whitfiel Seabrook, Parent Advocacy for Educational Reform: A Case Study of the Harlem Parents Committee (UMI Dissertation Services, University of Massachusetts, 1978).

10. Yuri Kochiyama's letter to Malcolm X, October 17, 1963.

11. Kochiyama family, Christmas Cheer, 1964; Rea Tajiri and Pat Saunders, Yuri Kochiyama: Passion for Justice (video, 1993); Yuri Kochiyama, speeches; Yuri Kochiyama, interview with author.

12. RNA, "Political Statement," n.d.

13. Robert Sherrill, "...We Also Want Four Hundred Billion Dollars Back Pay," *Esquire,* January 1969.

14. ibid.

15. Ward Churchill and Jim Vander Wall, Agents of Repression: The FBI's Secret Wars Against the Black Panther Party and the American Indian Movement (Boston: South End Press, 1988); Ward Churchill and Jim Vander Wall, The COINTELPRO Papers: Documents from the FBI's Secret Wars Against Dissent in the United States (Boston: South End Press, 1990); Lennox S. Hinds, Illusions of Justice: Human Rights Violations in the United States (Iowa City: School of Social Work, University of Iowa, 1978); Imari Obadele, Foundations of the Black Nation (Detroit: House of Songhay, 1975); Imari Obadele, Free the Land, (Washington, D.C.: House of Songhay, 1984).

16. Rafael Cancel Miranda, panel discussion at "The Double Life of Ernesto Gomez Gomez" video showing, Critical Resistance conference, Berkeley, CA, September 25, 1998; Ronald Fernandez, Prisoners of Colonialism: The Struggle for Justice in Puerto Rico (Monroe, ME: Common Courage Press, 1994); Rea Tajiri and Pat Sanders, "Yuri Kochiyama: Passion for Justice" (video, 1993).

17. "Basic Principles of the Legal Status of the Combatants Struggling Against Colonial and Alien Domination and Racist Regimes," UN General Assembly Resolution 3103 (XXVII), December 12, 1973; "Declaration of the Granting of Independence to Colonial Countries and Peoples," UN General Assembly Resolution 1514 (XV), December 12, 1960; and "Programme of Action for the Full Implementation of the Declaration on the Granting of Independence to Colonial Countries and Peoples," UN General Assembly Resolution 2621 (XXV), October 12, 1970. See Nozomi Ikuta, ed., *Proclaim Release!* (2nd ed., 1996, 6, 32-36).

18. Mary Breasted, "30 in Puerto Rican Group Held in Liberty I. Protest," *The New York Times*, October 26, 1977; "Puerto Rican Demonstration: Statue of Liberty Takeover," *San Francisco Chronicle,* October 26, 1977; Ronald Fernandez, Prisoners of Colonialism, 1994; Rea Tajiri and Pat Sanders, "Yuri Kochiyama: Passion for Justice" (video, 1993); Yuri Kochiyama, interview with author.

19. Asian Americans for Action newsletters: December 1969, October 1970, February-March 1972; Kazu Iijima, "Brief History of AAA and the NY Asian Movement," speech, n.d.; Glenn Omatsu, "Always a Rebel: An Interview with Kazu Iijima," *Amerasia Journal*, 13, (1986-87): 83-98; William Wei, The Asian American Movement (Philadelphia: Temple University Press, 1993).

20. "Infamous Concentration Camp Bill: Title II—Emergency Detention Act," Asian Americans for

Action newsletter, October 1970: 8. For information on Title II, see Raymond Okamura, "Background and History of the Repeal Campaign," *Amerasia Journal*, 2 (1974): 74-94.

21. Rockwell Chin, "The Long Road: Japanese Americans Move on Redress," *Bridge*, Winter 1981-82; Leslie T. Hatamiya, <u>Righting a Wrong: Japanese Americans and the Passage of the Civil Liberties Act of 1988</u> (Stanford, CA: Stanford University Press, 1993); William Minoru Hohri, <u>Repairing America: An Account of the Movement for Japanese-American Redress</u> (Pullman: Washington State University Press, 1988); Bill Kochiyama, testimony at CWRIC, November 23, 1981; Yuri Kochiyama, interview with author.

22. Yuri Kochiyama, "Black-Asian Interactions in History," speech, Brecht Forum, June 18, 1997; Yuri Kochiyama, "A History of Linkage: African and Asian, African-American and Asian-American," <u>Shades of Power: Newsletter of the Institute for Multiracial Justice</u>, Spring 1998.

23. To understand this meaning of liberalism, see Mao Zedong's essay, "Combat Liberalism."

24. Herman Ferguson, interview with author, June 19, 1996.

SECTION THREE

MOVEMENT BUILDERS

"Every generation, out of realative obscurity, must find its own mission; and either fulfill or betray it."

FRANTZ FANON

INTERNATIONAL HOTEL

Mobilization spilling to the other side of Kearney Street

SFPD Tac Squad charge line in front of the Asian Community Center and the International Hotel

Top Photo credit: Revolution Books
Bottom Photo credit: Workers Committee to Fight For the International Hotel and Victory Building

YURI KOCHIYAMA

With Justice in Her Heart

interviewed by *Revolutionary Worker*

Y uri Kochiyama has been a dedicated fighter against the injustices of the system for almost 40 years. During World War 2 her family was forcibly removed from their home to an internment (concentration) camp along with 120,000 other Japanese-Americans. While at a camp in Arkansas, Yuri came face-to-face with the segregation of the Jim Crow south. The parallels between the oppression of Black people and the treatment of Japanese-Americans were striking. In 1960, Yuri and her husband Bill Kochiyama moved to an apartment in a housing project in Harlem. Yuri became involved in the Civil Rights Movement and was part of the major struggles of the '60s and '70s, especially the national liberation struggle of Black people and other oppressed nationalities. She has supported political prisoners and the fight of oppressed people against imperialism around the world.

Yuri Kochiyama was in the Audubon Ballroom in Harlem the day Malcolm X was assassinated and held him in her arms as he lay dying. She supported the work of the Black Panther Party. She took part in the takeover of the Statue of Liberty in 1977 to demand freedom for Puerto Rican political prisoners. Yuri and Bill Kochiyama were part of the successful fight to gain reparations for people of Japanese descent who were incarcerated during World War 2.

Recently, the RW had the opportunity to interview Yuri Kochiyama in her Harlem apartment. We talked for hours over snacks and tea that Yuri had spread out in her living room. We sat amidst stacks of leaflets for upcoming political events and mementos of her life, including beautiful photos of Malcolm X and pictures of her husband Bill who died a few years ago. Though she's now 77 years old and recently suffered a stroke, Yuri continues to remain active. She still speaks publicly, attends political events and protests and is working on her autobiography. Yuri Kochiyama has given her heart and devoted her life to the struggle of the people. Her commitment to change the world remains strong and her passion for justice is contagious.

Revolutionary Worker: Why don't you start by talking about your experiences growing up. What was it like with the intense racism against Japanese-Americans during World War 2?

Yuri Kochiyama: Well, first I'd better tell you what my name is. I was using Mary

Originally published in *Revolutionary Worker* #986, December 13, 1988

Nakahara when I was young, my maiden name. And I was born and raised in San Pedro, California. San Pedro is a small working class town on the coast. It's about 20 miles out of Los Angeles and it's a shipping and fishing town. But I must say that when I was young I was totally apolitical. I was very small town-ish, you know, provincial and also quite religious-going to Sunday school and teaching Sunday school in fact. So I was totally different from what I became. But it took me a long time. I mean it's not something that I changed into, transformed to overnight. It was through years and years of just living and learning and having different people come into my life.

Of course the biggest thing that happened was World War 2, the bombing of Pearl Harbor, December 7, 1941, which changed not just my life or Japanese-Americans, but changed the life of everyone here in America. After all, never had war come so close to this country and then eventually, of course, as it became a world war it affected the whole world. Until that time, I was just living a comfortable life, actually a middle class life in San Pedro. I wasn't even aware of the terrible situation for Jews in Europe in the '30s that was moving into the '40s. By 1941 I had just finished junior college-two years. And as I said, I was not political and I was not socially aware. So it was like an abrupt kind of a change when the U.S. government or President Roosevelt declared that all Japanese would have to be evacuated. It certainly changed our life.

But before that happened, on December 7, 1941 while the bombs were still falling on Honolulu, the FBI came to our house and took my father. At first we didn't know where they were going to take him. I was the only one home. Everyone else was away. And then we found out that he was taken to the federal prison on Terminal Island. My mother was so worried because the very day before he was taken, which would be December 6, he had just come home from the hospital where he had surgery for stomach ulcers. So he was very weak. And yet the FBI came in and asked for Mr. Seiichi Nakahara and I said, "Well, he's sleeping right now." And they just said, "Where is he?" And I said, "Well, he's in the bedroom." And they just walked in and went right to the bedroom and shook him up and told him to put on his slippers and bathrobe and they took him out. I didn't even have a chance to ask where they were taking him.

Then in a few days we found out through our lawyer that he was taken to the federal prison. My mother kept getting in touch with anyone who had any power in that town to see if she could get him out of the prison into the hospital until he got better. And I don't know how long it took-maybe it took a couple of weeks-but they put him in the local hospital, San Pedro Hospital. But that was the hospital where all the merchant marines that were injured in the South Pacific were being taken to. And so my father was taken there, too. And my mother said she was so shocked the first time she went to the hospital-they opened up one huge room where all these people were being brought in, the merchant marines-and only around my father's bed they had a sheet around it and it said "prisoner of war." And my mother was afraid that all those guys in

270

there would be wanting to beat him up or she couldn't imagine what they were going to do to him. So she asked the hospital if he could have a room of his own. I don't know if it was a matter of days or weeks, but they did put him in a room by himself.

So he was taken away right on December 7, the day of the bombing. My mother had been seeing my father at the prison, but the whole family got to see him for the first time on January 7. My twin brother was attending U.C. Berkeley and he said, "You know, they don't want Japanese students on the campus. They would like to get us all off." And he said, "We're all trying to get off the campus, but we can't even buy tickets at the train station or bus station." We said, "Well, hitchhike if you can." But at the time we thought, too, maybe that wasn't the safest thing. We didn't know how he came home, but he came home. And as soon as he came home, he did the American thing. I mean he wanted to-he wanted to join the U.S. service. And so he went to the draft board. And it seemed strange-here my father was taken by the FBI and yet the draft board said oh, it's fine, he could join the U.S. army.

My older brother, three years older, he also immediately tried to get in to volunteer, but his health wasn't that good. He has asthma and other problems. So he was rejected. But my twin brother Pete got into the service. And I remember on January 13—he had just gone into the service and they were outfitting him and he was still at the local army station right in our town-I went with my brother to see my father. And Pete was so proud, wearing his American uniform. But when my father saw my brother walk in the room, he thought that he was a police or someone to interrogate him and he was just shaking. And we couldn't figure out why. By the time we saw my father, we could see that something was happening to his mind. He asked, well, who beat you up or something like that, because his mind was being affected with the interrogations. We said oh, nothing happened to us.

My mother kept asking the army authorities if they could let my father come home until he got better and then they could take him back again. The following week, on January 20, we got word that they were going to send him home and we were so happy. But they sent him home because they knew he was dying. And he came home in the evening and by the morning, the next day, 12 hours later, he was gone. And then, of course, the FBI called and said if anyone comes to the funeral, they would be under surveillance and there was already a five mile travel ban [for Japanese people]. But a lot of our Japanese friends came to the funeral. And of course, sure enough, the FBI was there looking everybody over.

RW: You were old enough to remember being evacuated to the concentration camps?

YK: Yeah, because I was 20, 21.

RW: What was that like?

YK: Well, at first we couldn't believe it. There was a lot of stuff in the paper that evacuation might take place. But we didn't believe it. We said no, no. Not this country. This country is supposed to be the symbol of democracy and humanitarian concern and we didn't think it could happen. But we saw how quickly things were moving to getting us out. On February 19, President Roosevelt declared 9066, which gave the military on the west coast the power to remove the Japanese or do whatever they thought best for the safety of the west coast. And so things moved along quite quickly and by April 1 all people of Japanese ancestry were being moved out of the area.

Our group, which was the Los Angeles area, Long Beach, San Pedro, Wilmington, Gardena, went by a car caravan. Others went by buses or trains or in different ways. And of course none of us knew where we were going. We were going to "assembly centers." No concentration camps were built yet.

We were sent to Santa Anita, which was the largest assembly center. There were maybe 30 assembly centers throughout California and the west coast.

We were only supposed to bring what we could carry. Anyway, we didn't know if we were going to stay long. We thought well, it could be only for a couple of weeks, a couple of months. We didn't know how long we were going to be sent to camps. We didn't even know that Santa Anita was going to be a temporary stop. We thought we might be in a camp in California for the rest of the time. We didn't know we were going to be sent inland.

But 120,000 people of Japanese ancestry—70 percent who were American citizens who were born here and 30 percent who were our parents, who were not allowed to receive citizenship so they were considered aliens-were sent out. We were all moved from California, Oregon, Washington. 120,000 Japanese were removed. And the army did it rather smoothly, I think, because the Japanese were so cooperative. This was one way that we could show we were true Americans, I guess. There may have been some Japanese who were against it, but I don't think they could have fought back. I mean, the hysteria against the Japanese was so strong.

RW: We know this is a famous story and you've been asked to tell it many times. But can you describe when you first met Malcolm X?

YK: It was at the Brooklyn courthouse and Malcolm walked into the foyer and all the Black young people ran down and circled him and were shaking his hands. But since I wasn't Black, I didn't think I should go down there because at that time, there was an article in Life magazine where a white student came into Harlem, the Shabazz Restaurant and saw Malcolm, went up to him and said, "What can I do for you?" and Malcolm just said, "Nothing." And she went out crying. Benjamin Karim's book says Malcolm regretted that. He didn't want to treat her like that but he had some Nation of Islam lieutenants with him and they were watching him carefully, so he responded the way he thought he should.

I kept edging closer to the group and I thought, now or never. I thought how could I attract his attention. And he looked up and I couldn't believe it. I said, "Can I shake your hand?" He looked at me strange, like, what is this Asian woman doing here? And he said, "What for?" And I said, "To congratulate you."

And he said, "For what?" And I said, "For what you're doing for your people." And then he said, "And what am I doing for my people?" And I didn't know what to say, but I said, "You're giving direction." And then all of a sudden, I don't know, he just changed his demeanor and he smiled and he came out of the group and he held out his hand. So I ran forward and I grabbed it. I couldn't believe I was shaking hands with the Malcolm X.

I didn't know hardly anything about the civil rights movement and I didn't even know there was such a thing as the Black liberation movement, but I said, "I admire the things you're doing and saying, but I don't agree with you about something-your strong stance against integration." Can you imagine having the nerve to say I don't agree with you? And he just said, "I don't have the time to give a two or three minute lecture on the pros and cons of integration." Then he said why don't you come to the office.

Well that never happened because on November 22 Kennedy was killed and Malcolm made the statement about "chickens coming home to roost," and he was silenced by Elijah Muhammed. I thought, I'll never see Malcolm again, because I think he was taken out of the 125th Street office. And so it just sort of ended there for a while. It wasn't until the Hiroshima-Nagasaki World Peace Study Mission toured the country. They were speaking out against nuclear proliferation. That group had three writers and they wanted to meet Malcolm more than any other person in America. It gave me a chance to hope to try to get in touch with him again. I left messages at the office, though no one let me know whether Malcolm would comply.

We couldn't believe it but on June 6 when we were having a reception, Malcolm showed up. When he came here, he first thanked the Japanese for coming to Harlem. That was the year that Harlem had "The World's Worst Fair"-when the World's Fair was happening in Flushing Meadows. So the Japanese went to "The World's Worst Fair." And it was a good thing because all the while coming across the country they had never seen anything like it. They were invited to all these nice luncheons and garden parties in churches and schools. And then they came to Harlem where they saw one of the worst blocks on 114th Street, the Jesse Grays section. They came to see "The World's Worst Fair"-the actual living conditions of the people-and they saw broken stairwells and toilets that wouldn't flush and bathtubs that were clogged and all the garbage on the streets because the sanitation department hadn't picked it up. The Japanese saw all that. Then when they came to our apartment, Malcolm said to them, "You have been bombed and you saw that we have been bombed, too...by racism."

And then we had a little program. Malcolm spoke of his respect for China. He admired Mao because Mao fought against foreign domination, against corruption in his own government and against feudalism. And then he mentioned Vietnam. Now this was 1964, and I don't know if America had started to send its troops over-they were sending advisers to Vietnam. But he said if America starts sending troops, I hope you will protest. And it was too bad he didn't live long enough to see how the anti-war movement mushroomed and became so big. But he was speaking out even then.

He was so open when he was here and he was so gracious to everyone. He shook hands with everyone. People said he probably wouldn't shake hands with whites. Not true. He shook hands with everyone and he was as warm to whites as to Blacks.

RW: You lived in Harlem during the 1960s. What was it like?

YK: It was like the movement was coming up north from the south. But one of the most exciting things that was happening, in '59 or so, Cuba won its revolution. So we were having a lot of meetings, everybody would be sitting around here on the floor and we would listen to people who had just come back from Cuba. People would bring over videos on Cuba. It was just exciting what was happening. And then at the same time, '59, '60, '61, there were people who were going on the Freedom Rides down south. And we would be inviting people like Jim Peck who came back out of the hospital with 57 stitches in his face. It was in Alabama that he was beaten. And then of course the biggest thing was probably the death of Patrice Lumumba [a revolutionary leader in the Congo] around '61 and Black people were going to the UN and were doing actions down there.

It was like something was happening continuously once it became the '60s. We just moved here in the '60s. A lot of children were being hit by cars because above 110th, there weren't traffic signals on every block. So Harlem Parents Committee organized all the parents to bring their toddlers and we put all the kids on the streets to stop traffic. This was on 131st and Fifth Avenue, because so many children had been hit there. At that corner is a school and a little park across the street. And yet cars were coming through there without stopping. But after we had the demonstrations, traffic signals were installed.

The Puerto Ricans did something similar in their section, throwing garbage in the street just to get the sanitation department to pick up the garbage. We even made it possible that trains coming into 125th Street had to slow down to lessen the noise.

Living in the '60s in Harlem was really exciting.

RW: There was a progression nationwide from the civil rights movement to the Black liberation movement to people trying to figure out revolution like the Panthers and the Young Lords. What impact did that have on the neighborhood?

YK: Well, at first we were in just the civil rights movement with the Harlem Parents Committee. 1961, '62, '63 was strictly civil rights kind of things. But by '64 and '65—Harlem started having demonstrations against the war before downtown was doing it, because the Yorubas (an African religious group) were marching then and I think it was because Malcolm was speaking out against the eventuality of a war in Southeast Asia. The people here were already alerted. And I think that the people here were ahead of the people in the mainstream anti-war movement.

The Africans were trying to free themselves from the colonization by Europeans and Malcolm would talk about that every week. I could not help but feel that between Martin Luther King and Malcolm X, Malcolm X was more "on target."

And so I think the atmosphere in Harlem was much, much more radical than what was happening downtown in the civil rights movement and I think we were lucky to be living up here to hear some very good speakers. So many people go to hear speakers because they're known by the media. But here in Harlem, people just get up and the kind of things they speak about are things that you may not read about in the newspapers. But I think that's what educated us. It was more Afrocentric.

I was in both the civil rights movement and the Black liberation movement and they were so different, just totally different. I think King was hoping that we would all want to go into the mainstream, while Malcolm was saying we've got to stay away from the mainstream and get away from the jurisdiction of the United States. And when Malcolm spoke about nationalism, he was speaking about independence and sovereignty and a nation of his own, a Black nation. So that in itself was different. But it was good that there were both of these movements-that you could see the differences and people could make a choice of which movement they wanted to follow.

And while this was going on-now we're talking from about '60 to '65 because Malcolm didn't live beyond '65—we were hearing a lot about what the Puerto Ricans were doing. The Puerto Ricans wanted independence and they were fighting against the colonization by the United States. So I think this is important because if we did not know about the Puerto Rican movement, we would not see how there were so many people all over the world who were trying to free themselves from imperialism. And I think the '60s really pointed out how important it was to know about the dangers of imperialism.

By 1960 my kids were from about 2 to 15 or 16 and all this impacted on them. I had two daughters who were in fifth and sixth grade to eighth and ninth grade and they had just started taking ballet. But once they started hearing about the movement, they didn't want to go to ballet class. They said they were going to go with me to demonstrations. So they gave up their ballet and then they started going with me everywhere to demonstrations.

When my older daughter Audee was 15, she went to Macomb, Mississippi with a high school SNCC (Student Non-Violent Coordinating Committee). The same year, my son, Billy, 17 going on 18, was finishing high school and he didn't even go to his high school graduation. His fellow members of a group called Students Against Social Injustice went out and raised the money so that he could go to Mississippi. And he went to Mississippi and stayed there the whole summer.

Audee and Billy lived with Black families. It was an experience that they would never forget. Almost 15 years later, my husband and I went down to

Mississippi and met the very family that my son stayed with. It was nostalgic.

I think coming up to Harlem in the '60s was the best time that we could have come because everything was happening and it also involved our children. The children were all engulfed by all of this action. And then we even had the younger ones involved that could hardly walk yet. But we'd put 'em in the stroller and take them here and there and other people would carry them to the marches too. It was a good experience for them. Later, I took my grandchildren, Zulu and Akemi.

Also, I'd like to say how lucky I was to have the kind of husband I had—someone who was so open, broad-minded, sensitive, who enjoyed people, who was an active father and homemaker and a thoughtful husband. Also I was lucky to have children who thought of family as a priority but had other interests, other than the struggle. Our family was very close, made more tightly knit because of the several tragedies in our family-losing two children. We are forever grateful to all the people who came into our lives at the time, supporting us, also opening doors and windows to a fuller life.

RW: You've been active in the movement to free political prisoners for many years, including the fight to free Mumia Abu-Jamal. And you have gone out to talk to different groups about Mumia. What response do you get?

YK: Once people learn about Mumia, they can't help but love Mumia because not only was he such a radical and such a courageous kind of guy and his support for the MOVE group has been contagious. He has supported everyone, all the underdogs and the marginalized. And when you think of it, there has been no political prisoner who has been able to galvanize so many people the way Mumia has-and not just here in this country, but all over the world. And I'm amazed that 26 members of the Diet [top government body] in Japan are supporting Mumia, too.

But people won't believe how Mumia and I got started corresponding. It had nothing to do with the movement. It had nothing to do with political prisoners. I couldn't believe it but one day I got a letter from him and he wrote in Japanese-Hiragana, which is one of the forms of writing Japanese. There's Katakana, the simplest. Then there's Hiragana and then there's the regular Chinese calligraphy. But he was using the Japanese Hiragana and I couldn't believe it. And I said how did you learn? And he said he was studying Japanese just by himself in prison.

But how this came about was that I had just read something by Velina Houston, the famous Black/Asian/Indian playwright. She wrote about a Black samurai in the sixth or eighth century. And so I wrote to Mumia about him and he said, "You won't believe it but I've just been reading about him myself." But just before that he wrote in Japanese, and that's how we got started to know each other.

The other day we had a four-way conversation with Assata Shakur, thanks to Susan Burnett. Assata expressed her admiration for Mumia. She said he is extraordinary, bringing people together. I think that's maybe his calling. But it's just that he has so much courage to come out with the kind of issues he has supported, especially his support for the MOVE people. I think the police department can't forget that. But his contribution to the struggle will be forever remembered. And he has already left a mark in the struggle.

There's a question of what makes Mumia different from other political prisoners. And I just say, well he has the same quality of leadership and courage and yet his humbleness gives him another dimension.

RW: You've taken a strong stand in support of the right of oppressed nations to wage armed struggle for liberation from imperialist domination. And you traveled to the Philippines and Japan to talk about your experience as a member of one of the international delegations that went to Peru to defend the life of Abimael Guzmán, the leader of the Communist Party of Peru, who is in prison. Could you talk some about this?

YK: About Peru—I felt privileged to be able to travel under the auspices of the IEC, the International Emergency Committee. There was such a difference between our experience in the Philippines as with the experience in Japan. The people in the Philippines understood so well what it was to be colonized because they have been colonized. They knew what Peru had gone through historically with what happened to them through Spain's colonization.

We were invited by Bayan, which has a membership of 1.5 million people and 21 different organizations. Gabriella, the women's group, comes under it and there are about five different college organizations. The press people, reporters come under it. Even the religious orders. I couldn't believe it, but we even met with the Catholic nuns and other sisters. We met with the street sweepers, the jeepney drivers, the fishermen, the farmers, the unemployed. They all came under Bayan and Bayan also has a couple of very revolutionary groups.

The news reporters were really interested because some of the news reporters that came to our sessions were people who themselves had been imprisoned under the Marcos government. They understood so well about what the indigenous and the poor people in Peru had been going through. You didn't even have to tell them that there's no way that Peru is going to change unless it's through revolutionary change. They understood.

But when we went to Japan, it was totally different. I think one of the reasons was sadly because Fujimori is Japanese. They seem to be so proud that a Japanese was head of another nation. In Tokyo, we met with many organizations. They were supposed to be progressives or liberals. Some were with the churches. But they were not for Sendero Luminoso. [The Communist Party of Peru is called "Sendero Luminoso"-Shining Path-in the mainstream press-RW note]. They did not think that it was necessary for them to wage that kind of struggle and probably they didn't like them because they were communists.

But when we went to Kyushu, an island south of the main island of Japan, it was different. We were meeting with mostly workers and they told us not to use the word leftist there, but I think the groups we met were leftist and we also met with Burakumin, the group that's considered outcasts in Japan. The only thing they told us was that they didn't think we should meet with Peruvians in Japan in Kyushu, even if they were there, because they were being watched carefully and we might endanger them.

But in Honshu, the main island, the one group that understood what the Peruvian outcasts-the indigenous and the poor-what they were going through, were the Koreans because they themselves were marginalized people in Japan. And we met with a group of Koreans and I thought that was just wonderful to be able to meet with them.

RW: The documentary film "Yuri Kochiyama: Passion for Justice" shows you lecturing and speaking to young people of different nationalities. A lot of our readers are young, involved in different struggles and trying to figure out where they fit in and how to carry the struggle forward. What would you say to them?

YK: I've spoken to kids as young as second and third graders. A school here in Harlem-the teachers were both Black and white, but the students were all Black-asked if I would come and speak to them about Malcolm X. And I couldn't believe how much these second and third grade students already knew about Malcolm. But it was because their parents knew about Malcolm. And I've spoken to junior high schools, one in Greenwich Village. I've spoken to about six high schools and to colleges all over the country, and the enthusiasm and interest of the students, regardless of what age, has amazed me. And it's been very, very heartening. They really are interested. They really want to change society. They want it to become a better society than they are living in now.

What I would say to students or young people today. I just want to give a quote by Frantz Fanon. And the quote is, "Each generation must, out of its relative obscurity, discover its mission, fulfill it or betray it."

And I think today part of the mission would be to fight against racism and polarization, learn from each other's struggle, but also understand national liberation struggles-that ethnic groups need their own space and they need their own leaders. They need their own privacy. But there are enough issues that we could all work together on. And certainly support for political prisoners is one of them. We could all fight together and we must not forget our battle cry is that "They fought for us. Now we must fight for them!"

ALEX HING

Former Minister of Information for the Red Guard Party and Founding member of I Wor Kuen

interviewed by Fred Ho and Steve Yip

Fred Ho: Alex, let's talk about some biographical information. What's your birthday.
Alex Hing: January 8, 1946.
FH: Where were you born?
AH: I was born in San Francisco Chinatown, born at the Chinese hospital on Jackson Street
FH: What were the names of your parents?
AH: My father's name was Ah Hing Senior and my mother's name is Bertha Lew Hing.
FH: What did they do?
AH: My father he's passed away. He was a magician, he was a performer and my mother basically was an assistant in his act but she also held clerical jobs and eventually she was a supervisor in the credit department in the TransAmerica Corporation.
FH: Were they primarily English speaking, Chinese speaking or bilingual?
AH: My mom was primarily English speaking and my dad was pretty much bilingual.
FH: And how do you classify yourself?
AH: English speaking.
FH: Let's talk about your experiences growing up particularly in a family of performing artists and what were your experiences like and how you got politicized, how you become aware of oppression, about racism, and how did you become a radical activist.
AH: Okay. I became aware of racism just growing up in Chinatown, that made me aware of racial discrimination and racism. Growing up, I had kind of a strange childhood. I think growing up in Chinatown is strange to begin with because it's a very closed community. At that time Chinatown was primarily American born and immigration was not open until 1965. So most of the time when I was growing up I hung out with the same group of, basically English speaking, American born youth. And everybody's parents knew everybody else's so it was very closed, very tight. And most of the people had pretty much working class jobs, like bus driver, postal worker, things like that or running a grocery store in the community or some kind of service. Lot of people working in restaurants

Interview transcribed by Celina Lee of Asian Revolutionary Circle and garment shops. Since my family were entertainers, I always felt a little different than everybody else because my father would be home when most other fathers would be working and he would be working when most other fathers were home. And because my mom worked during the day as well as worked with my father, he did household chores, like he did the shopping for instance, he cooked dinner and did the laundry. So I always felt kinda different because this wasn't everyone else's experience, and when you grow up you want to be the same as everyone else. We were different. Another thing that was different and I didn't find this out until I was 16, was that my father was half-White. But he actually, culturally, was more Chinese than my mother who was completely Chinese. So it was weird because I grew up and I felt different than everybody else and I thought it was because I didn't speak Chinese and a lot of my schoolmates spoke Chinese. There were only a few that didn't. But my mother who was 100 percent Chinese, she was an assimilationist. She would always correct our grammar and made sure we spoke perfect English. My older brother went through Chinese school and he didn't do that well. Since I was more rebellious and had a bigger temper, my mom made a wise decision not to send me to Chinese school because she knew I wouldn't do well in there at all. So I didn't speak Chinese with the people I grew up with, and then I was also one-quarter White, which I didn't know consciously, I felt that people would tease me.

FH: And how did you get politicized? What made you a radical as opposed to your other siblings?

AH: In my teen years, I got into trouble with the law. Some of my friends also got into trouble with the law and some got sent to California Youth Authority and those people, that went to the Youth Authority, that was like a real prison. Log Cabin was pretty much the last stage before you went to Youth Authority. So I went to Log Cabin Ranch, but before that I did sixty days at the Youth Guidance Center. And the Circumstances around my winding up there were political. I had sixty days to think about why I was there. What happened was, we used to hang around these pool halls on Kearny Street and one day we're in the pool hall, I think it was in the Manila, right where the Kearny Street Workshop used to be in the I-Hotel. This place called the Manila Pool Hall. We were hanging out there. And one kid comes in, a Chinese guy, he said that he just gotten jumped by these three white guys. And they were walking through Chinatown and let's go get them. So this guy's name was Byron Chow, who actually at that time his father owned a pretty big garment factory. And then there were these two white guys that hung out with us that we knew from high school. They liked our culture and they liked hanging out with us and they were in the pool hall, too. This one Italian-American named Franconie and this Russian guy named Bill Poppin. So there were two White guys and two Chinese guys and we went looking for these guys who beat up Byron. We found them. and we jumped them and we pretty much kicked the shit out of them and then, you know, we went back to the pool hall. and then later on that day, I get visited by the cops and apparently I had broken one guy's arm. So all of us went to court and the two white guys, they weren't even charged. They weren't even charged. The three guys that got jumped, they basically snitched on me and Byron and Byron was able to get a lawyer because his parents were rich. I was the only one there without any legal representation. I already had a criminal record and so out of all four of us I was the only one that did time. I asked, "Why me?" The only thing I could think of in my rudimentary consciousness was well, there's race, that was obvious, and then there also was class too, because why was Byron walking around?

FH: What year was this?

AH: I was sixteen so whenever that was.

FH: 1962?

AH: Yeah, 1962. So I had like sixty days to think about this and the courses that I was taking at the Guidance Center were unusual because I was the only one of my crowd that was on the college track. You know, during the sixties the state started a battery of tests, you either got academic courses that trained you to go to college. Or you were in the shop courses. So all the guys I was hanging out with took all these really neat courses like print shop, electric shop, wood shop and I was into this algebra, calculus, French, all this stuff. When I was in the juvenile hall, and the counselors found out what kind of curriculum I had they freaked out because they didn't have the books. Because most of the kids that went to juvenile hall were on the shop track and had to put in some amount of schooling. They were taught basic math and basic English. So they let me do self-study, and that's where I started to read history and that's where I became, I think, a conscious revolutionary. When I was 16, I started to read world history. I started to question, Why am I reading only a White history because I was Chinese, I knew that we went back before the Greeks. So how come we merited only a half a chapter?

FH: Were you reading revolutionary literature then or not?

AH: Not really. I was reading basically high school textbooks. The other thing that I noticed was not only was it White civilization, European civilization - the darkest they ever got was Egypt and from reading Egyptian history you would think it was White history, too, the way they taught it. But basically I started to notice a pattern that what seemed to mankind's history was going from one war to another war to another war. Just jumping from war to war and I thought that was a stupid way to organize society. So by the time I got out of that sixty days I pretty much had a basic outlook which I still haven't changed to this day which is that American society at least is pretty much racist and that, and that the resolution to most societal problems is dealt through warfare, which I feel is not the best way to handle things.

FH: And how did the Leway kids start because from my reading it started somewhere around '67? Can you talk about the beginning of Leway and how you got involved?

AH: Yeah. OKAY. To tell the truth, I wasn't directly involved in the formation of Leway. And I'll go a little bit more into my biography and dovetail it when we get back to Leway. So after I did that sixty days I tried to really go straight because I had this kinda theory in my head and I wanted to get my life back together but it wasn't to be, and circumstances put me back in, and I went to this Log Cabin Ranch. So during that whole period of time I was locked up pretty much for a whole year, which was a long time when you're very young. And when I came out of the Log Cabin, I decided that the only way I could break out of the cycle personally was to stay away from Chinatown. Chinatown was not good for me if I hung out in Chinatown with my old friends again. The first day I got out of Log Cabin my cousin comes up in a stolen Chevrolet and said, "Let's go for a cruise." I mean, I had to, I just had to get away from that. I went to City College, and basically what I did was I went to school and I went home and all I did was study and try to stay away from my old crowd, who at that time were getting busted again hanging out at the pools halls.

At San Francisco City College I fell into this group of people who were very close to SDS (Students for a Democratic Society) and at that point I was opposed to the war in Vietnam. And when I met these White radicals on campus who wanted to talk about the Vietnam War, I fell into that crowd and at that time, City College was very, very repressive. The only political student organizations they allowed on campus were the Young Republicans and the Young Democrats. And we wanted to bust that open because we felt that the Democrats were the ones waging the war at that time. Republicans were even worse. So we wanted to raise the question of US involvement in Vietnam and we started to hand out flyers. We started to sponsor these forums around the war. And the campus authorities pretty much tried to shut us down. So we had a mini-free speech movement at City College where we picketed and held demonstrations for free speech. We decided that we should form a slate and take on the student government. So we ran, I ran at the head of the slate. I ran for president of the student body at City College. It was my last year at City College. There were like two thousand votes cast and I lost like by fifty-four. It was a real close race. And the politics around that campaign, pretty much changed that campus. They pretty much granted all of our free speech demands and actually the guy on the opposite side who actually won the election, he basically started to move a little bit more towards the liberal position. I was by then pretty much a revolutionary. From then on, I was hooked into these student radicals. I wanted to go to UC Berkeley because I thought that was where the action was. I started to hang around with a group of leftists who lived Haight Ashbury. I moved to the Haight and was part of that movement. It was the alternative movement in the Haight but it was more political than the hippies, and the people I hung around with were political. I think some of the people, I didn't know at the time, were actually in the CPUSA or had parents that were in the CPUSA. Maybe they weren't in it themselves but they were very close to the

CPUSA and also people who were close to SDS. I got involved with the Peace and Freedom Party when the Peace and Freedom Party decided to petition to go on the ballot in California to run Eldridge Cleaver as President. This was around the whole time when the Panther thing was happening. In college, that's when I started to read revolutionary literature. I started to read <u>Red Star Over China</u>. I started to read <u>The Autobiography of Malcolm X</u>. Both those books, you know, really struck me as right on. I didn't get into theory per se then, but you know, I was a history buff. Read Malcolm's autobiography and <u>Red Star Over China</u>. I worked on the Peace and Freedom Party campaign and that's how I came to know some of the Panthers because the Panthers were also involved in the campaign. I went door to door, in the Filmore district registering voters, signing up petitions to the Peace and Freedom Party. It was actually quite successful. The Peace and Freedom Party got on the ballot and through that process, I came to know the Panthers and started to really follow the Black Panther Party and I actually wanted to join the party but at the time they weren't accepting non-Blacks. I felt that I had gone pretty much full circle. That I had experiences with these White radicals and that wasn't really my calling. I decided to go back to Chinatown and hang out with my old gang, my old crowd and to try to politicize them. That's when I went back down to Jackson St. after being away for all these years.

I was involved in Stop the Draft Week too. We all went to the Stop the Draft, all those anti-war things. So I went back to Chinatown and started to connect that with my old crowd. Leway had already formed. I'll give you the background to that now.

What happened during the time I was gone was that the rest of the people that I was hanging out with they also got tired of the same cycle of getting arrested and getting out. Since Chinatown was very closed, once you were arrested, you couldn't get a job in the community. You were blackballed. It was very difficult also to get a job outside the community because of racism. There was a cycle where people would go to jail, come out and not find anything to do and get busted again. People were tired of that. Around this time the Johnson administration had a lot of money for this War On Poverty and stuff. There was this agency called Youth For Service and one of the key players there was a Chinese American. His job was to try to work with the youth in Chinatown to help solve this crime problem. He was able to funnel money and help these youth basically by the pool halls they were hanging out in. The idea behind that was cooperative capitalism. From the beginning, if you thought about it, it wasn't gonna work but they decided to try it. They got some money from the Youth For Service. Basically it was federal money, city money and pretty much bought the pool hall. The idea was to run the pool hall for profit.

Pretty much Ron Kansaki was the business mastermind behind that. They bought the pool hall and the idea was the pool hall would bring income. The money would hire youth. They would save the money and started a soda foun-

tain next door. They also started to have a garment co-op. This was before the
Wei Min She garment coop..

Even though that program was running, people were still getting in trou-
ble with the law. And the money from Leway had to go a lot to legal aid. Like
bail, attorneys, etc, etc… The reason why that didn't work was now you have a
place that was funded by federal money and at that time the KMT, the Six
Companies, completely controlled Chinatown. Completely controlled
Chinatown. They saw Leway as a big threat. Here's where all the kai-doy hung
out. All the bad kids were all in this one place and they were working with the
federal government. They're a bunch of commies, you know. So repression was
focusing on Leway.

When I went back to hang out at Leway, I consciously tried to politicize
that crowd. People there were miles ahead of me already, I felt. There were peo-
ple who had already been making contact with the Panthers and in much deep-
er ways than I could. There were some sisters who actually had Panthers as
boyfriends.

FH: How many do you say?

AH: Oh, a good half dozen.

FH: These were Asians? Were they Chinese American or Japanese American?

AH: Pretty much Chinese American. They had boyfriends who were actual Panthers.
So they were up at the headquarters a lot. Some sisters were really politicized
and some of the brothers down at Leway were also pretty much aware that there
was a revolution happening. There was no doubt in our minds that it was hap-
pening and that the Panthers were in the forefront of that. And that if we real-
ly wanted to get out of our situation we had to hook into that process. From
within Leway a core group of us, I would say no more than a dozen, it was prob-
ably about eight or ten of us started to consciously talk about what was wrong
with Leway and perhaps we should model what we want to do after the Black
Panther Party. Like I said some of the sisters had already known some of the
Panthers and, invited some of the Panthers to come down to Leway. So what
happened was Bobby Seale and David Hilliard just dropped in one night on
Leway and they got their minds blown. They had no idea because they, the
Panthers, had the stereotype of Chinese youth, too, you know like, slide rule, go
to school, glasses.. When they went into Leway, it was like a Black thing that
they saw pretty much. The music that was played out of Leway was jazz, soul
music, that was the kind ambience it had. People wore dark clothes, field jack-
ets, sunglasses in the middle of the night, shooting pool, smoking cigarettes.

FH: But do you know approximately what year?

AH: It was probably early 1968 or late 1967.

Steve Yip: Let me interrupt with one question. Were you aware at the time that peo-
ple from the Chinese Marxist Left were actually observing you during the Leway
days? Did they actually try to offer any aid at that time?

AH: We weren't really aware of the previous Marxist-Leninist activity in the community. I think our thing was more like a spontaneous happening and we didn't understand that there was anything prior to us.

SY: You know my dad's crowd? I was a nerdy Chinese kid living in West Oakland but he was already bringing up the question of Leway to me and trying to get me to go into Leway. I was like seventeen but I never went to Leway. In my retrospection they were already paying attention, even before the Red Guards came out, they were already paying attention to what Leway was doing.

AH: Actually in retrospect, I felt that soon after we formed the Red Guards. There was a piece of Left history that was already there. Like I said, we weren't aware of that. We had our own situation and you have to understand what that was like. It was really, really repressive. It was like every time we left the pool hall we would get stopped if we were in a car. This was even before we became the Guards. The police would come in and pretty much shakedown Leway. The landlord would start to increase the rent. This is even before we became the Red Guards. There was a tremendous amount of repression and I think that's what forced people into a more revolutionary position.

FH: So when did Leway stop and how did the Red Guard Party start?

AH: Leway never really stopped. What happened was, David and Bobby came down and saw the situation and basically said that what we were doing was correct but we needed to form an underground revolutionary core which we already had. We had, like I said a group of eight or ten of us who were not satisfied with Leway who wanted to build an organization, a revolutionary organization similar to the Panthers. If the Panthers would've recruited us we would've joined on the spot. But they didn't. What they did instead was they invited us to go up to their headquarters on a weekly basis and start studying with them. So that's when we started to get introduced formally to revolutionary theory. We went up to...

SY: Filmore or Oakland?

AH: Both. We went to the national headquarters in Oakland and then we went up to the Filmore St. headquarters and then we eventually went up to Eldridge's house and had these weekly study sessions at Eldridge's house on Marxism and Leninism. It started with the Red Book, which we had already been reading and then we went from the Red Book to more longer tracts of Mao, like "On the State," "On Contradiction" and "On Practice" and we basically were studying the exact same things the Panthers were studying. We started to read Frantz Fanon, we started to read Che Guevara, Fidel Castro, all that literature at the time we systematically went through. The study group... the core went to the Panthers and then we went back down to the pool hall and started to replicate that study session with the people who didn't go to the Panthers. So we started to form cells. We took pretty much our directions from the Panthers. We started to put out this little newsletter and we came out in the open. What happened was on the surface of it was Leway and nobody knew this Red Guard being formed. It took several months for us to surface in public. We were hammering out our program our whole underground apparatus. We were serious because there was so much repression going on against the Panthers, that we realized that if we came out in the open without already some kind of underground apparatus that we could be very seriously damaged. I guess it's pretty much well known by now that there was, in the Bay Area at least, there was this underground where you could wind up in Cuba overnight if you wanted to. It was hooked into the Weather underground, Panther underground. That was all hooked up. We kinda hooked our piece into that. So we were part of that thing. We had to get that together. Weapons training, discipline, all that and plus the study and then to come out with a mass program. During that time there were couple of events when the Red Guards wasn't open yet that the Red Guards actually did political work. One of the things that we did was to support the students at San Francisco State College. So we made a decision that we would go out there and support the Third World Strike. We went to the picket lines, we raised money, we provided whatever support we could, we also leafletted the community to support their demands.

FH: When did the Red Guards actually came out?

AH: It was early '69.

FH: March '69?

AH: Yeah, early '69.

AH: These Chinese foreign students wanted to have us work with them on a celebration commemorating the 50th anniversary of the May 4th Movement. They came to the Red Guards to see whether we would support that and we said yeah, we would support it, but we think it's totally irrelevant to what's going on in the community. Who gives a shit about what happened 50 years ago in China. Right? We said there is more important stuff happening with the Chinese community now. We're being messed over now. We need jobs. We ran down our whole program. Of course we would support this thing but we felt that we wanted it to be more relevant. So we agreed on what we wanted to do was out of that commemoration of the 50th anniversary of the May 4th Movement, put forward a demand to rename Portsmouth Square to Sun Yat-sen Park.

FH: What year was that?

AH: This was probably '69. We said that we wanted to come out as the Red Guards. We would join them. We would support them. But we wanted our piece. We wanted to have a presence as the Red Guards. So there was a two line struggle. They were afraid of the Red Guards. They wanted to have their own thing. But they couldn't have their thing without our support because we could bring people there, we could provide security. They were afraid the KMT would move in and shut it down. So basically what we worked out was a two stage rally. We provided security for the whole thing and leafletted the whole thing, it was a tremendously successful event. The first part was run by the students and they talked about the May 4th Movement and then we came in. We came in blasting the "East is Red," marching in. We had these handmade Chinese flags and these handmade Red Guard armbands. We all wore field jackets. If we were armed, we didn't display them. I think we were armed with concealed weapons and then we had people posted on the perimeter of the park, on the roofs with rifles. We marched in and it looked like we took over the rally but it was actually agreed upon. That they would have their piece and we would have our piece. A couple of months after that, we invited the Black Panther Party to come and speak at Portsmouth Sq. in support of Free Huey. That again was another tremendously successful rally and that's when I first realized that there other people besides us. Some of these older people would come out and when we passed the bucket, we'd pass the hat around, there would be some money in that. There was real money there. I had the sense that there's something more here than meets the eye. That we were tapping into something we knew nothing about. What cinched that was we had a celebration of China's national day, October 1st, because one of our demands was that the U.S. recognize Beijing and not Taiwan. I actually was involved in this political theater for a while, so I was very close to the people who ran this. Remember the Committee?

SY: It was on Broadway.

AH: It was on Broadway. Actually we had our headquarters there after we got kicked out of Leway. The Red Guards had their headquarters there.

FH: So you were kicked out of Leway? Tell why you were kicked out.

AH: The whole thing got shut down 'cause we couldn't afford the rent. We were homeless for a while.

FH: When was it shut down?

AH: Oh, man. We opened in 1968. Yeah, it was probably shut down by '69.

FH: After the Red Guards came out?

AH: Almost immediately after the Red Guards came out. I doubt that we lasted more than six months in that storefront. The whole thing got shut down.

FH: How long were you guys underground before you came out as the Red Guards? About how long?

AH: It was a good six, seven months. Let me explain that. After we came out we did the showing of the film "The East Is Red." There was a theater there and so we showed the film. We had three showings. We only planned to show it once and we were having a celebration. We were going to show "The East Is Red" and serve a dinner. We ripped off food you know, they used to just deliver stuff and leave the stuff on the sidewalk and we would just help ourselves and we would use the kitchen in the Committee and cook up this roast duck and everything and rice. So we had this big celebration. We originally planned to have this one celebration. The place was packed and people demanded that we keep this going. So we showed it three nights in a row to a packed house. I don't know if people kept coming back or different people or what. Then I definitely knew that there were some people there before us. And actually some people came up to shake our hands to say to us, if we need help, they'll be around, great job… and again, there was money.

So after that, repression started to really come down on the Jackson St. headquarters, both the Red Guards and Leway. I don't think the cops, KMT made any distinction between Red Guards or Leway even though we did. Because there were some people who were in Leway who absolutely refused, they were anti-communist and refused to go along with the Red Guards thing. In the beginning of the Red Guards we pretty much recruited everybody because when the Panthers came down it was zing and you know, everybody was like, "Yeah, that's right, that's right." But when they found out that we were in it for the long haul, people started to get cold feet and dropped out. We had dug up the basement and we set up a shooting range. We were reloading ammo down there. We had target practice down there. This is in the sub-basement. Like cops would come in, they would like just start smashing everything, tearing posters off the wall. Leland Wong, he made that famous poster. It was the Year of the Pig so Leland Wong made up an Emory Douglas-like poster.

It was like, Year of the People Off the Pigs. It was the Chinese community rising up and slaughtering these pigs. And it was like an Emory poster so we had that up. The cops would come in and they would go furious, and would tear it down. They would start smashing things and they would start searching people. The landlord, the KMT owned the building, they would just triple the rent so basically we had to shut down. We had to leave that place because there was so much heat on it. People were starting to get arrested. Our funds started to be depleted, we had spent so much money on bail and legal defense. We actually had free legal defense at that time and we did run some programs out of the pool hall. We hooked up with the San Francisco Newsreel that became the Third World Newsreel and we had our weekly film showing on revolutionary films. We had different people come and lecture from the Panthers to different progressive organizations that was in the Bay Area. It was kind of like a networking thing. Eventually under the Panthers' direction we started a Breakfast for Children for Program which was a big flop because unlike the Black community, there's no Chinese parent who will allow their children to go to school without eating first. But we started it because the Panthers said we should do it and, "OKAY, if they say we should, let's do it." What happened was a lot of the African American kids from the projects started to come to our Breakfast Program. That's how we got closer to the African Americans that actually lived in Chinatown. We got to know their parents through their kids. We realized that this wasn't working. We shut that down and what we started to do was to serve lunches in the park to the elderly. That was more successful. They were already in the park and they really appreciated the lunch and we served it free. We got "donations." And we would put out these lunches.

So we had these programs and we also got involved in different coalitions with Alice Barkley to fight the gentrification of Chinatown. There was a plan to turn the Chinese playground into a parking lot. We protested that. We went on a petition drive to prevent the tuberculosis testing center from being shut down and then there was the Guangzhou temple and then there also was the infamous education struggle where, this is going on the heels or during the Third World Strike at State College, there was also community demands for improving the public education in the elementary, junior high schools, and high schools, particularly in the elementary schools. So, that was spearheaded by Alice Barkley.

FH: What do you think was the most significant thing about the Red Guard Party during its time?

AH: I feel the most significant thing about the Red Guard Party was that we opened up Chinatown to politics.. Before we hit the scene, people from Steve Yip dad's generation, they were repressed. They were just shut down. After the left was shut down in the fifties, the KMT and Six Companies dominated, just completely dominated Chinatown. Even when Johnson came in with this anti-poverty money, liberals like Alice Barkley were having a really hard time getting themselves established. They had what they called it, economic opportunities program, EEOC?

SY: Yeah, EEOC.

AH: They had a very small office. Planned Parenthood had a very small office and that was it. George Woo was doing something with the Wah Ching immigrant youth [a Chinatown gang] and then there was like Cameron House and some churches, social service organizations. They were not that effective because every time they really tried to do something, the KMT would say, "That's communist," and those guys would back off. They were so scared that they would back off. So when the Red Guard Party came, we said, "We're communists. We are really communists and we're gonna take you on because you're the enemy. These people aren't communists. We're communists." We created a left, the right was already there. We created a left and what that did was create a middle for all these other forces to exist. So I would say that before we came along there was no other political activity other than the KMT and we created that space for other politics to happen in Chinatown.

SY: How did the Red Guards choose your leadership?

AH: It was pretty much self-chosen. In the beginning we had this core that came out of Leway. This core was in fact the leadership. We basically sat down and, "OKAY. Here's the Panther's structure. Who wants to be this? Let's make Fook the chairman. Fook, you're the chairman, OKAY? Shut up. You're the chairman. We're gonna make you the chairman cause you look the baddest out of everybody. This is how we did it. Teddy, you're Minister of Defense and that's unquestionable because you're the baddest dude around. You know, we basically went like that. I was Minister of Information because I went to college, that's pretty much how it happened.

FH: Were there any women in the leadership of the Red Guards?

AH: Yeah

FH: How many?

AH: Not that many. A couple. I have to be honest, OKAY. No. In the beginning no.

SY: Wasn't Diane in leadership? Big hair?

AH: In the beginning not the central core leadership. There were a bunch of guys who were in the Central Committee. But the women were the backup and did most of the work.

FH: How big was the Red Guards at its height?

AH: Well, like I said when we first came out we recruited almost everybody. It would not be a stretch to say we had 200 people. That lasted a hot minute. We got down to around two dozen in the core, which I thought was a fairly sizeable amount.

FH: Out of that two dozen, what percentage were women?

AH: Half.

FH: Talk about how the Red Guards ended and the transition to I Wor Kuen.

AH: OKAY. I want to go a little bit into this. So we're doing all this stuff and what happened was when the cops shut down the Jackson St. office there were a lot of people in Leway who were pissed at us. I think Ron Kansaki hates my guts 'til today because of that; because they thought that Leway was happening and if it hadn't been for the Red Guards they could've still had Leway today. I don't think so. But any case history didn't work out that way. There were a lot of people who were in Leway who pretty much blamed us for messing up their stuff because the whole thing got shut down. From there what happened was we were homeless. We had that office on Broadway St. for a while, and we tried to go into the I-Hotel. We weren't allowed, pretty much, to open a Red Guard office in the I-Hotel. So, what happened was, we worked with other people who had organizations. Pretty much the Asian Legal Services was where we went, because we had this whole legal services apparatus already set-up. We were really developed in that sense, we could get people out of jail, we had legal contacts. We knew exactly what to do and we had attorneys working with us. So when the Asian Legal Services piece opened up pretty much the people in the Red Guard who were more into doing the mass work went into that. So within the Red Guard during that period of time we didn't have any headquarters. There were two kinds of views that were developing and this was similar to what was happening with the Panthers. Some people felt that it's time for us to go underground. Let's start waging the armed struggle. Let's start hooking it up. Let's start getting it on now. And there were other people who said, "Well, we still need to do mass work. We still need to do political work. The community is not ready to sustain that yet and we have to have some connection to doing aboveground political work. So we were kinda like in this limbo situation and this was like after I had come back from that trip to Asia.

FH: With the Panthers?

AH: Yeah. When I came back there was no headquarters. People were floating around and I felt we had to do mass work and other people there were kinda already going off. What happened was at that time, Carmen Chow and Gordon Chang had moved from New York to the Bay Area and we had always been in touch with people from IWK from almost the beginning.

FH: How did you learn of them?

AH: They gave us a phone call out of the blue. They called us up at our headquarters. They said that they heard of us and if we knew about them. I said, "No. I had no idea." They explained that they were doing the same things and that we should keep in touch. We were ecstatic that this was happening in New York. So from time to time we would communicate on the phone or, I don't think through the post office that much, but from time to time we would call. And then after I went to China when I came back I landed in New York City and I got to know people from Asian Americans for Action (AAA), you know, Yuri Kochiyama. I also met Jeannie Yonemura and Carmen and the people from IWK when I was in New York. So when Carmen and Gordon moved to the Bay Area, what happened was that…

FH: Do you know what year?

AH: I think it was 1971. I think the direction we were headed was that we were gonna go under, join the Black Liberation Army or whatever. Some of us started to have discussions with Carmen and Gordon about forming a national organization. It made sense to me at that time. What happened was that they were very critical of the Red Guards' ultra-military position. I think that we were also critical of them being too intellectual having no idea what the situation was all about. What happened was we had a meeting of the Red Guards and we said that, "Look we are at a crisis now. These people are offering us to, kinda like a second breath, but we would have to join their organization and form a San Francisco chapter and make it a nation-wide organization and we know that the rest of you can't afford to that." There were some people who couldn't do aboveground work. They were wanted. They couldn't, absolutely couldn't do that, even if they want to they couldn't do it. So we basically said, "Well we're still comrades. If you guys want to go under, do your thing, you have all our support. We're not gonna stop you. But we feel that the rest of us want to join this national organization. It wasn't a split or anything like that. It was more like a dissolution. The people that wanted to go under, they went under as far as I was concerned. Then the rest of us we started to have these meetings with Carmen and Gordon and we formed the San Francisco chapter of IWK. Immediately that started to grow. Basically a lot of students joined in.

FH: This is before my entrance to IWK, which was 1976-77. I understand that the merger took place in the summer of 1971 and that there were 2 two-line struggles going on. One of course around this question of the ultra-militarism versus mass work. The other part of it was around the question of male chauvinism and non-monogamy. Can you talk about the kind of politics that were being discussed between the members of the Red Guards and the I Wor Kuen? How that struggle took place since you were on different coasts?

AH: The New York chapter was the chapter that was dealing with the non-monogamy, male chauvinism issue. That wasn't an issue with us in San

Francisco. The issue for us in San Francisco was the purely military point of view and basically the struggle was to get us to see that we should primarily do mass work rather than primarily build an army. How that was resolved was that we said, "Well, people who wanted to do under, go under and the people that wanted to do mass work join IWK." Now those of us that joined IWK we still came into it with a very heavy militaristic background. That's our background. That was our upbringing. That's the whole way we viewed things. That was a continuing struggle within IWK for at least a few months, if not a year or two to get a handle on that.

FH: I Wor Kuen adopts Marxism-Leninism-Mao Zedong Thought around 1974. What was that process?

AH: Actually, 1972 was a very significant year. Because, unbeknownst to a lot of people, the democratic-centralism of IWK formally dissolved. So that means the organization actually shut down, for a period of about a year.

FH: Okay. Why?

AH: The reason why to this day I do not know, but I said right on, because I felt depressed under this democratic-centralism, I couldn't do this, I couldn't do that. I couldn't really say what I felt.

SY: In 1972?

AH: Yeah. And it was like a crisis. I think people were having a hard time understanding the relationship between mass work and a revolutionary core organization. So IWK had set up all these mass organizations like Chinese Progressive Association (CPA), there was also a childcare center, there was a women's health clinic, there were a bunch of programs that were basically run by IWK cadre. And what the relationship between that and IWK was, people had a hard time figuring out and so people just said let a hundred flowers bloom, let's dissolve this democratic centralism, let's all work together and see what we can come up with. And in my opinion, that was the best time, because that was when we formed this Bay Area Asian Coalition Against the War, there was a lot of mass activity going on and people weren't really, you know, people basically got to do what they want. At least that's the way I felt. And then what happened was, at the end of that experiment, people said that what we needed to do was form a Marxist-Leninist organization, and the main task would be party-building. So that's how that happened. It came out of a period where the democratic-centralism of the organization was dissolved and then it re-formed on the basis of Marxism-Leninism.

FH: How was that done? And who spearheaded that? Was there a summation that this period where DC was dissolved that things weren't working right? I mean, that's a big leap from kind of everybody doing their own thing to party-building.

AH: Yeah, because we were still all working together, we were all in the same group, we just had less meetings to go to. We didn't have this IWK meeting to go to because when we met as IWK, we couldn't figure out what to discuss. And then there was all this mass work happening. Right, so we just thought that we would do the mass work until we got enough experience that we would kind of come back to sum it up. And I guess what happened was a bunch of papers were circulated, around the importance of building a Marxist-Leninist organization, based on the working class and criticizing some of the lumpen-proletariat or non-Marxist way of looking at revolution. And setting party-building as a main task or if it wasn't set then, it was set almost immediately afterwards. But the thing was that we should form IWK based on Marxism-Leninism.

FH: Who introduced or was pushing ML in this new IWK?

AH: I think it was pretty much Gordon Chang, and Carmen. Now, I thought that it was redundant because I had already considered myself, since the time we formed the Red Guards, as a Marxist-Leninist because the Panthers were formed around an ideology that was Marxist-Leninist and I thought it was redundant. I said, I'm already a Marxist-Leninist, but I came to understand that maybe my understanding of it wasn't that deep. In other words, because I didn't uphold the primacy of the working class, because I always had this kind of Panther lumpen-proletariat point of view. And so when those papers came down about the importance of the working class and the working class being the vanguard and understanding class society within that, when those papers came down, there was also, implicit within it, a critique of the Panther Party's politics and ideology. So I would say that when those papers came down, it was a break with Huey's ideology. Huey was going off on the deep end then anyway, he was going off on this inner-communalism and all that stuff. So this was an attempt to reform the organization on a more traditional Marxist-Leninist ideology.

FH: Talk a little bit about how a national organization functioned, since you were on opposite coasts. How did you get things done, how did you coordinate?

AH: I guess there was a lot of travel and a lot of clandestine phone calls. A lot. And actually, it wasn't really running that tight as I later came to understand.

FH: Give me an example.

AH: Later as I came to understand that New York pretty much had a real strong leadership and was pretty much left to fend on its own because it had a strong leadership. But what happened was when the decision was made to center the organization in the Bay Area, that some of the leadership from New York was siphoned off and started to come to the Bay Area, right. So there was a drain on the New York leadership.

FH: Why was the decision made to center it in San Francisco?

AH: I guess because that was where the Asian movement was really more developed. New York is New York and then there's Boston right, in the East Coast. But in the Bay Area there were formations that were like Asian American, like there was in Japan Town, there was like San Jose, Sacramento, there were different spontaneous things happening all over the place.

FH: How big was the IWK Central Committee around 1974-75?

AH: I can't say, you know, half a dozen.

FH: Okay, so it's not that large, about six. And were you on it from the beginning?

AH: I was never on the IWK Central Committee. I was frozen out when that thing came back together. I had a too militant…

FH: But your wife of that time was on it.

AH: Yeah, right.

SY: That's the Central Committee, six people? That wasn't like the Politburo or Executive Committee, that was the Central Committee?

AH: We called it the Central Committee. I don't think it was more than eight.

FH: It's always been touted that the Central Committee was always majority women, was that the case?

AH: I believe so.

FH: About what percentage? Four out of six? Five out of six? Six out of six? Were there any men?

AH: There might have been, say if it was eight, there might have been a couple of men, but I even doubt that many.

FH: So quite a large majority.

AH: Right, ninety percent, eighty percent.

FH: Okay. Why?

AH: Good question.

FH: Try to explain it.

AH: You know what? Okay, you want me to go off on that, why?

FH: Yeah, yeah okay.

AH: I think this is my Chinese mother theory. You laugh, so now you know, end discussion, right?

FH: Go ahead. Just talk about it.

AH: But I think that, kind of like coming on with the rise of feminism and also I think traditionally, Asian men, deep inside no matter how macho and male chauvinistic we are, really always respect our mothers, in the family. And actually if you take a look at traditional Asian families, the woman's role is actually very strong, really strong. That's true in Japanese families, the guy's usually tough and stoic, but who does the finance, who takes care of the household and all that. You know, in Japanese societies, women's role is very strong. Even though for external purposes that's not the case. Also I think in my experience growing up, Chinese mothers anchor the family, play a very, very strong role in a different way. So I think that kind of like that cultural thing, dovetailing with feminism, kind of cemented that.

FH: You know, I'm just going to throw out my two cents. I have a different view on it. I think it has to do more with the higher percentage of educated Chinese American females than males that were involved with the organization.

AH: That could be, too.

FH: Quite a lot of them were very highly educated, from very educated families. They could do administrative work much better than the males, they could do the memos, they could do the correspondence, they could come out with position papers more easily, they were writers, you know.

AH: There was that too, and also the working class women were secretaries, so they could write. They could do the processing, and all that stuff. Yeah, I agree with that too, I think maybe both of those things were a factor because if you take a look at the Asian woman, traditionally, they're stronger than what most people percieve.

FH: Right, right. Are you comfortable about naming names about who were some of the prominent members?

AH: I can't do that.

FH: Okay, alright. Let's talk about the IWK relationship to other Left-wing organizations at that time that had Asian background, came out of the Asian movement like Wei Min She/RU, Asian study group, Workers Viewpoint for the CWP. What do you think, I mean, looking at it now, in late 1999, your own perception of what happened back then in terms of relations with those organizations, how much of it you think was really based on matters of principle disagreement, for example, on really fundamental different perspectives, politics, and how much of it had other aspects to it?

AH: I agonize over that today. Today I believe that we probably, the left probably, could have taken the whole thing if we had gotten together. I think the influence of the left was so tremendous and so huge that if we had figured out how to get together...

FH: How to make a party...

AH: ..we could have taken it. We could have taken it. Now, my viewpoint is this: Marxist-Leninists know how to take power. They have problems after they seize power what to do with it. I think it becomes a little abusive. So I think you need to have this kind of really tight discipline seizing power, then I think you have to kind of let it go after you get it. But I think if you take a look at the influence that the left had, in all aspects of society, in all the key areas where there was stuff happening, that was all led by leftists, conscious revolutionaries. And the problem was that we spent an inordinate amount of time fighting each other. An inordinate amount of time fighting each other—over phraseology. And I think that there were some actual differences, there were actual differences in perspective, but via what was attacking us or what came later with the Reagan revolution, it was not that important. You know, not that important, that we could've said later for this, here's the enemy, let's unite, let's fight the enemy. I think a lot of it on one hand is that the movement was led by intellectuals and then I also think that there was this history in Marxism-Leninism of ruthless two-line struggle, right. So that wherever there was a line there was an opposite then, there was a two-line struggle. No matter what position there was always at least two lines. People would stay up writing papers and struggling over these things when actually the right-wing really took us by surprise. I don't think that it was an illusion, we thought we could build a party and take it if we had figured out how to work together. Look at Chinatown, if we had gotten together in Chinatown, it would be a different Chinatown today I believe. The I-Hotel would still be standing for instance, but you know come the I Hotel eviction night, one wing was fighting the other, we couldn't get together, people were fighting each other. And they, the system, saw that and moved in. So I think that there were real differences, but how important they are in the whole light of history—not that important. Not that important.

FH: Let me ask you, who chose the name IWK? How the name come about?

AH: IWK was… I don't know. They did that in New York.

FH: And how about the Red Guard Party?

AH: The Red Guard Party, actually the Panthers chose that for us. We wanted to call ourselves like the Red Dragons or something like that. We wanted to be like a street gang. They said that the Red Guard was more political and see, people in the Red Guard knew that, "Good, you call yourself the Red Guard you'll really gonna freak fucking people out." I don't know if we should do this but they said, "Do it." So we did it.

FH: Was it Bobby Seale or Eldridge?

AH: I think it was Bobby. It might've come from Eldridge but I think it was Bobby that said, "No. No. You gotta call yourself the Red Guard Party."

MORITSUGU "MO" NISHIDA

interviewed by Fred Ho

"**M**o" Nishida is a revolutionary activist in Los Angeles. He works as a janitor in Little Tokyo, the Japanese American community of downtown Los Angeles. His commitment to both the struggle of Asian Americans and of "lower-tier" workers has remained staunch through many political and personal difficulties. Today, he continues his activism as a organizer and supporter of the Jericho Movement to free U.S. political prisoners. As evidenced in both the interview below and his article earlier in this anthology, he continues to creatively enrichen U.S. revolutionary theory. This interview was conducted in Little Tokyo, Los Angeles, California on April 19, 1999.

Fred Ho: Mo, I thought first we could get some background information on you, when you were born, what your family background has been and how you got politicized? Maybe bring that into the sixties and then jump into how you became a Marxist and then the history of your involvement with the East Wind Collective. Then give me some background on East Wind: how that started, what its work was and the struggles in which it was involved, and its relationship to other left forces. Then let's talk about the question of the East Wind merger with the League of Revolutionary Struggle and your views on that. Finally, we can go more into your overall views on what's going on today.

Moritsugu "Mo" Nishida: OK. I was born on August 11, 1936 in Boyle Heights in the Japanese hospital of Los Angeles. Before the war, my dad worked in the produce market and he was a crate salesman. He did different jobs like truck driving and stuff like that. He worked basically in the produce market. He was a young Issei who came over here in 1924. He was 14 when he came across. My mother was born of the Maruyama clan in Japan and was brought over here as an infant. She was the oldest of 10 kids. She's basically a Nisei although she was classified as an Issei enemy alien during the war. We grew up in the west side, in Seinan right around Foshay Junior High School in the southwest district of the pre-war Japanese community. There are a lot of Buddhaheads out there still today. My dad still lives there. I live out there right now, but gonna move into Chinatown.

Interview transcribed by Kye Leung of Asian Revolutionary Circle

FH: What were the names of the communities again?

MN: S-E-I-N-A-N, that's southwest in Japanese. We had the Hollywood district, that's J-flats, uptown, that's the Koreatown section right now. Boyle Heights, J-town, those were the inner city Japanese neighborhoods in LA. You go a little further to Gardena, Sawtelle- the remnants of the community are still there. My family was pretty small: my dad, I was born in 36, my next sister was born in 41 just prior to the war. My youngest sister was born in 48.

When the war broke out we were evacuated to Santa Anita Assembly Center.

My mom had a nervous breakdown in camp...But at the time, I was young and didn't have too many emotions about what was happening. That's one of the things I'm trying to dig up, to get to that emotional thing. I know there's a lid on it. I think lot of us Niseis have that kind of experience, that's why motherfuckers are dying all over the place, from suppression, you know that energy to push that shit down, getting all that stress remaining and stuff. Immune system going down. I know for my own survival it's important to get that sucker out. In Santa Anita we go to housing in Orange Mess. My grandparents were in White Mess, that's what they called the different blocks. The people from Seinan—our area—were shipped to Amachi, Colorado. Sent there in the dead of winter and southern California people don't have those kind of clothes to deal with those dustbowl conditions, that cold-assed weather in Colorado. I imagine there was a lot of suffering. I don't have a lot of memories of it, just the fun part. Seeing snow, living in snow, must've been cold like a motherfucker. I remember when they first turned the water taps on and shit like that, there were rumors, I don't know if I saw it, or was told stories that snakes and lizards were coming out the water tap and shit like that. That was our introduction to Amachi, Colorado...it seem like it was right after they started drafting [Japanese American men into the U.S. army] right out of camp that caskets start coming back. They sent a person from Washington to give us a pep talk on how brave these guys were, giving their life for freedom and democracy and all that shit.

FH: You talking about the 442nd [an all-Japanese American regimental combat team in World War Two that suffered high casualties and exemplified themselves in bravery at the front lines of battle—editor]?

MN: Yeah. I can remember distinctly at that age, talking about, "That White boy full of shit talking about fighting for freedom and democracy." No fucking kid in first or second grade can draw those conclusions. So I had to be reflecting the sentiment and the talk around most adults in camp, or at least around me.

FH: Tell me more about the sixties and the stuff that started to jump off with the Panthers and how did Asian American Hardcore start up and what was your involvement with that?

MN: I was in school when the Civil Rights thing started off at Cal State LA. I roomed with this English guy and some of our friends were demonstrating down at the federal building here in LA about the shit going on in Birmingham [then-Governor "Bull" Connor had police on horse back with cattle prods and dogs attacking civil rights marchers—editor]. Next thing we knew this guy disappears for about a week. After he came back, we asked, "What happened to you?" He said, "Well, I went down to the demonstration and what they had done was deputized all kinds of White people out there. What the White people did was go fuck all these young kids up that were demonstrating out there." Fuck this shit. That's when I started going to the demonstrations. That's the first step for me, just going down there. Brought back memories of camp and shit like that. Of course we were getting pressure from the bloods on campus. "What side are you on motherfucker?" they'd question us. Can't sit off by yourself with those Asians/ Buddhaheads sitting up there talking shit and playing cards acting like the world was cool. So there was a lot of that kind of pressure.

About that time I was thinking about going to graduate school. My grades were not good but I was thinking about going because I had a professor who would've sponsored me. Funny thing is, in academia, as long as it's far away, you got these goddamn liberals who'll support you, but as soon as integration hit Pasadena, all those fucking liberals started getting that peculiar color: the red neck and face all puffy. They call them yokels, rednecks, but I don't know what they call those professors but they look just like them. So I said fuck that shit. I left school and went back to the community and started doing social investigation, talking to people. I started talking to some of the younger people and then the Are You Yellow? conference came up. At the conference Penny Nakatsu and some people from AAPA (Asian American Political Alliance) came down. From there we went to organizing Oriental Concerns on all the campuses. We had every campus in Southern California or at least in the LA area organized, or being organized. That was a pretty good action.

FH: Oriental Concern was a student group? So it predated the Asian student unions?

MN: Right, right. All kinds of good feelings and identity kind of stuff. But you know the Civil Rights thing was cooking right along and the Vietnam War thing was starting to get hot. For me I was drinking a lot those days. I had one foot in the drinking circuit, my friends and I were drinking, were pretty much getting fucked up along with many others. We're trying to figure out how to get the others into the Movement when the Panther shit came out. That was electrifying. Bad motherfuckers. We needed to think of shit, need to get something going. Started talking to some old friends. We started drawing some of the old gangbangers into the movement and stuff. Yellow Brotherhood formed right around that time with Victor Shibata and those guys.

FH: Tell me how Yellow Brotherhood started.

MN: I don't know how much Panther influence had on them but the way they started reflected the Panther line. They had spontaneously formed, you probably have to talk to Victor about this, to talk about the drug problem they had emerged out of. They were dropping reds and doing all those things. Watching the younger guys get fucked up and most of these guys had tried to straighten

their lives out. They went back and started working with their own young peo-
ple in the West Side. They were trying to recruit people to do the people's work,
too, so they were coming around different political events and stuff like that
talking their stuff where everyone's talking "Serve the People". We had a meet-
ing where we had Penny come down to USC (University of Southern
California). She was talking about how at San Francisco State they were using
student body funds to fund community organizations and centers in the com-
munity. She was talking about this when one of the YB guys yells out,
"Motherfucker you want to talk all that shit. We got all kinds of drugs and shit
going on in the community." They laid down the whole rap; fucked everybody's
mind. "Wow, who are these young cats?" Some of us wanted to hook up with
some of these guys 'cause that was our experience, too. It turned out that they
were hard-liners.

FH: What do you mean by that?

MN: No drugs whatsoever. We were dabbling, right. We still smoking dope, drop-
ping acid and doing those kind of things. They said that was a no-no. They also
used different methods in dealing with youngsters. Every now and then they
whacked them when the kids got out of hand. Acting like a good old time
Buddhahead parent. What some of the Nisei parents didn't have the balls to do
with their own kids.

FH: Yellow Brotherhood started what year?

MN: About the time of the State strike, everything's about 1968. A lot of us tried to
join the Black Civil Rights Movement. But we ain't Black so we get this, espe-
cially from non-California bred Blacks who don't understand the Asian oppres-
sion and struggle, so to them, if you're not Black then you're White. So we get-
ting all kind of bullshit like that. Of course in California we all grew up togeth-
er and it's a different situation. We got this uncomfortable vibe so we started
thinking about, "What about us? Where do we fit in? We ain't White so what's
going on?" We started looking at our own community. We're an oppressed
community. That's when we started coming back into our own community.

FH: How many people were in Yellow Brotherhood? Was it Japanese American,
Chinese American, mixed?

MN: The non-white Asian population of Los Angeles at that time was predomi-
nantly Japanese. The Chinese population lived by the city produce market on
San Pedro Street and 9th Street. There was a corridor which basically was from
Jefferson Boulevard along San Pedro Street to Little Tokyo and up to Chinatown
(Spring and Macy—now Cesar Chavez). At that time, the whole area was heav-
ily Japanese and Chinese. Out here in the West Side we all grew up together,
we all hung together. Japanese, Chinese, Koreans, Filipinos, so we all kinda grew
up together. That was the kinda makeup of the group, the makeup of the young
people that they dealt with. Predominantly Japanese but not exclusively
Japanese.

FH: How big was Yellow Brotherhood?

MN: I say probably a dozen, fifteen, twenty people in the core, the senior guys. Then shit, about thirty to fifty youngsters.

FH: Were there women in there?

MN: Yeah.

FH: About what proportion female to male?

MN: The seniors, I don't think so.

FH: Mostly males?

MN: Yeah. Brothers growing up together, most of them were together as a gang (The Ministers). The youngsters, probably a fourth or fifth, twenty percent. The sisters had a real hard time relating to the group in terms of their negative self-image. Most of the Yellow Brotherhood were males; females suffered a very low self-esteem and wanted to runaway from the Japanese community. This is something particular to the psychological oppression of the Japanese community. That denial of and wanting to get away from something that's Asian.

FH: Did you join Yellow Brotherhood?

MN: Not really. I knew Victor and a lot of the guys. I stayed close to them. I knew their philosophy was a little bit different than mine so I didn't actually join them. I'm from the West Side, too.

FH: What kinds of things were they doing?

MN: They used to go out rounding up kids and stuff like that. If kids get too rambunctious they tied them up and shit like that, sit on them. If they got too rambunctous they ran toe-to-toe with them.

FH: Were they doing any political study?

MN: No. Although Victor was political, out of the whole bunch he was the only one open to that. Most of them were into this do-good thing. Most of Yellow Brotherhood was into helping the community by straightening out the youth, something the Nisei parents couldn't or weren't able to do. As a consequence we formed Hardcore. We knew that we needed to get the people coming back out of the joint and the people that were fucked up there we knew. Our main guy who started Hardcore was a dealer, a major dealer. He knew everybody. People would come by his house to get high. Even though Yellow Brotherhood made a big splash, it wasn't dealing with people coming out of jail or prison. Hardcore was started in 1968-9.

FH: Was Hardcore explicitly a political group?

MN: No, not in the sense that we formed a political line and such, but we openly identified ourselves with the Panthers. We had the Japanese American Community Services (JACS) office in Little Tokyo where we did serve the people work. At that time, there were direct needs people could see with their own eyes. Not like now where everything's fucking hidden. Fucking redevelopment destroyed all or most of the low-cost housing. So the Panther philosophy was redemption. For people that are fuck ups, you go out there and work with the people; serve the people and as you serve the people, the people look up to you and respect you; and your self- esteem goes up. You become more serious about who the fuck you are and what contributions you gonna make to the community. So we used the same philosophy. We openly identified with the Panthers and we openly identify with revolution. We worked in the community through the JACS office and propagated our line like that. People supported us. We didn't get any money from anybody. But people dropped food off and stuff like that. There were a few guys like Russell Valpariso, Ray Tasaki, real prominent members of our group who were once big-time fuck ups before they became activists. It was a remarkable achievement for them guys to come into the Movement and clean up and become activists, even though the overall recidivism—the fall-back rate—was high like in the Panthers. But there are enough guys that made it, that made the experience not only worthwhile, but tells us that we were on the right track.

FH: Was Hardcore mixed Chinese and Japanese or primarily Japanese American?

MN: Yeah, like I said, LA was predominantly Japanese, predominately American-born. The Chinese community was real small, centered around Chinatown and the produce market. Immigrants were starting to come in. So the nature of the community was a lot different. Some of the American-born kids went to work there, like my homeboy Gil. Made some real penetration with the Wah Ching (a Chinese immigrant youth gang-editor) and workers there. But the main group of people that who came into work in Chinatown mostly came out of UCLA. They ended up being WVO (Workers Viewpoint Organization) and LRS (League of Revolutionary Struggle) cadres. They were afraid of the youth. They came in with this elitist kind of thing. Pushed Gil and the homegrown brothers outta the way. Kinda took over a lot of the stuff that was going on.

FH: What percentage of Hardcore were women?

MN: Maybe ten percent.

FH: Roughly how big was Hardcore?

MN: The cadres were probably maybe half a dozen. The regular people up to twenty, twenty-five. Constantly changing.

FH: So you had actually a cadre organization?

MN: Not really. When I say cadre I mean the people who were relatively clean and who were dedicated to the development of the organization and working with people.

FH: Did you have any political identity? Did you see yourself as nationalist, Marxist?

MN: We saw ourselves as Maoist.

FH: Did you use that term?

MN: Yeah. Yeah. We were Chairman Mao soldiers. We identified clearly with the Panthers, the Panther line. For our people, we were willing to link up with anybody else that was willing to link up with us but our work was in our community.

FH: Tell me more about the history of Hardcore. When does it end and what happened to it?

MN: Hardcore like I said, develops out of people coming out of prison, develops out of people on drugs that wanted to get off drugs, people coming from court diversions or people that we just knew and who we just drew in. We had a place, two houses. Actually there were three. But when I was there, we had two. One was on 23rd St.. This was Doctor Noguchi's, the famous coroner.

FH: Really!?

MN: We had supported him in his fight [a highly publicized court case in which Noguchi, "coroner to the stars," challenged his dismissal by the Los Angeles Board of Supervisors for mismanagement as racist—editor]. He let us have the place rent free and we cleaned up the yard and stuff like that. It was small place and we filled it up with people. Then we took over the 32nd Street house. We had that place for $1 a year. That was a bigger place so we spent more time there. So we were around a couple of years as Hardcore. We were sending people to the Black Workers Congress and stuff like that, hooking up. We went to the JACL national convention in Chicago and hooked up with Shinya Ono. He was in jail after the Days of Rage [at the Democratic National Convention which led to the famous Chicago Seven trial—editor]. There's this humongous picture of this cop about to kill the motherfucker. Shinya got a hard head. Anyhow they hooked up with him there and went to visit him in Cook County jail. Talked about getting him paroled out to the West Coast. Then they went to New York to meet Yuri Kochiyama. So we developed our connections all the way across the country, nationally. Some of us went to Seattle. We were hooked up with Alex Hing and the Red Guards pretty early on. And the future J-Town Collective people. So our connections were pretty set from early on through Hardcore to JACS and JACS was a central focus for a lot of people coming in so we could redirect them to wherever they wanted to go. Our thing was the Asian involvement.

So they come back, Shinya gets paroled out to us and Shinya comes with all these credentials. He probably started in the Communist Party. He was one of the founding members of IWK and also a Weatherman. So Shinya comes in with a lot of prestige. He starts talking to us about we need to separate our serve the people lines from our political lines, that we can't mix all the stuff together. Most of us are new in the game so we didn't know if he's right or wrong. It sounds reasonable. Can't have these dope addicts hanging around all the time. Having to worry about getting your ass busted all the time kind of stuff. So we went for it. That's when we formed CWC. Community Workers' Collective.

FH: What year was that?

MN: 1970, 1971 something like that. The dates, I'm really fucked on dates.

FH: I'll keep asking, do your best.

MN: We got a house in Boyle Heights that this old rich guy let us rent. Then Community people got together and got donations and paid the rent for the first couple of years. That was real good. At least the people supported our serve the people work. The house was run collectively. We had two types of meetings in the house: one to discuss political work areas and two, around the running and functioning of the house. Backing up, when we form CWC, there's a split. There's a group that said we need to keep going and do this serve the people work as the primary focus of our lives and stuff. So they split off and form the New People's Hardcore. Another group wanted to be more explicitly political, those that form Community Workers Collective. It wasn't an antagonistic split, just a difference in focus and priority.

FH: And you went in which direction?

MN: I went with CWC. Community Workers' Collective. OK let me put it in focus. About this time, I guess it's around 1969, that's when the Panthers get attacked and the COINTELPRO (FBI Counterintelligence Program) slaughter takes place. A lot of us were ready and waiting for word from Huey to say, "Fuck them, let's go." Make some impression on revolutionary America. We weren't chickenshit! Word never did come down. We knew that Huey's line, the lumpen leadership line, was full of shit. We didn't have anywhere to go theoretically. Instead of going deeper into Mao, I think this has to do with Shinya and his background and the growing influence of the WVO (then-Asian Study Group—editor), but they start really pushing the study of Marx, Engels, Lenin and that kind of stuff. Talking about we got the solution, that the others didn't have it, we got it. We didn't have anywhere to go with the Panthers and none of us had enough sense to go deeper into Mao. That's when the CWC started a study group to study the classics. I didn't join right away. I had gotten some criticism earlier about being male chauvinist and elitist and all. I said, "Fuck it. I don't need to be a part of most of this stuff. I'll just go along and be a soldier." But I was getting a lot of pressure from different friends around the country saying, "How come you're not a part of the group? You're living in the same fucking house. Everybody else is in it." I eventually joined 6 months after it formed. It was always a small collective, never more than maybe 15–20 people. I thought we had the healthiest trend of all the groups.

MN: We tried to form coalitions involving radical groups out of the different communities around common issues as Asians. The political alignments in the different communities were similar. For example, in the Japanese community you had the conservative establishment types like the Japanese Chamber of Commerce, the American-oriented assimilationist types like JACL and then us on the left. In the Chinese community you had the Six Companies as part of the conservative community establishment, the CACA (Chinese American Citizens Alliance) who were mainstream liberal reformists, and IWK, WVO and us. Filipinos had similar political array of forces. The Somoans also with the traditional tribal chiefs, the Somoan Church Federation, and Omi Faatasi as the left. So we met with Samoans, Filipinos and with Chinatown people.

FH: So the CWC turned into the East Wind Collective? How did East Wind come about?

MN: The majority of the people that formed East Wind were from CWC and Shinya was the main driving force. He becomes the leading light for the group. Like I said, I personally feel we were probably the most open and the most Maoist of all the groups around. WVO never promoted Mao as a center of focus for their study and shit like that. IWK is a little better, not a hell of a lot. 'Cause the Red Guards were the ones that promoted Mao. When IWK takes over they did Alex in, the women there—Carmen [Chow, later Carmen Chang after marrying Gordon Chang—editor] and her sister (Wilma). There were three or four women in top leadership in IWK. They had developed a reputation of fucking up men. They purged Shinya from IWK and then when they merged with the Red Guards they did Alex's ass in. They demoted his ass to rank-and-file cadre.

FH: Right, right he was never on the Central Committee of IWK nor later the LRS.

MN: This motherfucker come off the street dedicated to revolution. I mean shit, he's supposed to be up there in the leadership, there's a lot of criticism of him, but still…

FH: So East Wind started about 1970? Do you know the year?

MN: That East Wind formed? I would have to say around 1970.

FH: Were you a member of East Wind from the beginning?

MN: No.

FH: When did you join East Wind?

MN: Not too long after it formed, maybe within six months to a year.

FH: Why did East Wind form? What was the reason for it?

MN: There was a need for a cadre organization, a political cadre organization in the community to give analysis and to give overall direction and then for us to be involved in the party-building process.

FH: How big was East Wind?

MN: At least a third were women. You can say that they played a fairly prominent role in the organization. Shinya's presence kinda overwhelms a lot things then. That's the personality cult. From hindsight, I know that's what it was. There was a period when we weren't even more than two dozen strong in membership and we still had a fucking bureaucracy! Can you imagine that? What the fuck, you know? Shinya had a lot of good ideas, like one of the things we always tried to do was to keep a balance between personal life and political life as part of the organization. We never separated the personal from the political. So that in cadre unit meetings we would talk about both. I think that was healthy. Our central committee wasn't just made up strictly by political awareness, but also included representation by work areas (we had labor, community, youth), gender and age balance as well. You know, a three-in-one combination. It was pretty healthy. We tried to do our own theoretical work. We drew our own positions. Early on we took a position on the Black national question. Kinda charted out what we saw as the development of the White nation in America.

FH: Your view was that there was a Black nation?

MN: Yeah, there is. I believe that heart and soul. There is an emerging Chicano nation here. The White Nation gets consolidated when the Atlantic northeast bourgeoisie wins the Civil War. The Confederacy was just that, a loose confederacy of states. After the Civil War, the imperialist white nation in the north-east expands and conquers the whole territory with the annexation of the south-west and feudalism develops in the U.S. based on the latifundia, land grants, etc. inherited from the Spanish colonization. Simultaneously, feudal development takes place in New Africa [what some who call the Black nation in the South—editor] during post-Civil War sharecropping; by the 20th century, it becomes all absorbed and consolidated into the U.S. imperialist-dominated multinational state. This is the principal contradiction: between the White oppressor nation and the oppressed nations and nationalities.

The woman question is also a fundamental contradiction. Then I didn't fight very hard for that. But now, fuck it. I believe that. The woman question is a fundamental contradiction. I believe it was good that we were trying to do our own theoretical work. We were getting shot down all the time. We put these position papers out there and these motherfuckers would be sniping away at us.

FH: Like who?

MN: Who? The fucking WVO people. They were supposed to be the theoreticians right? We put out our position statements and all of a sudden there would be a fucking avalanche of shit coming from all over talking about us as petty-bourgeois and nationalist and all this other kind of crap. A good example is the SLA.

FH: Simbionese Liberation Army?

MN: There was universal condemnation of these fuckers. No analysis, just universal condemnation. "These motherfuckers are ultra-leftist revolutionaries that just wanna go out there and they might even be provocateurs or stuff like that." Everybody said that shit. Our position was that we didn't think that the SLA's approach was a cool way of making revolution and promoting consciousness and stuff like that. But what they did in terms of the food program and shit like that raised a lot of consciousness, you know. We thought that was a very good thing. This whole thing about armed struggle we didn't think this was the time. People have to understand the background of the people involved—Cinque and people like that—and where he was coming from. So we tried to give an analysis and tried to split it between the pros and cons—what we thought helped promote revolutionary consciousness and what didn't. We put that out there and more people dumped shit on us. We just said, "Fuck you." We held our ground.

FH: What kind of mass work was East Wind doing?

MN: Most of our work was in the Japanese community. We basically had leadership over the JACS office. We had work going on in Boyle Heights working with youth, working with community people for a community center. We had a rice distribution program. We wanted to be able to supply good rice cheaply for the community and we came up with the idea of a large rice buy and distribution program. But none of the rice traders would do business with us. Then this company that sold rice to Vietnam agreed to sell us rice. The Vietnam War had ended, so they were looking for new business. The first bags of rice were good rice. But then we found the other bags to be what the Japanese call kuzu meshi or broken rice. These cocksuckers, man, you could see it was a deliberate attempt to bullshit us because the first rolls that we were able to access as samples was good rice. Everything fucking after that was kuzu meshi, birdseed. Motherfuckers said, "We're not giving you your money back. We're not gonna give an exchange." So we started a big struggle with this company. The JACL intervenes and stabs us in the back, kissing the White man's ass. But the community, two, three hundred strong ordinary community people with their kids and everything coming out to demonstrations. But our petty-bourgeois tendencies showed us outright. We were building up steam and then around Christmas-New Year, the leading cadres start saying, "Aw man, the people are getting tired. The people are getting tired." Some of us were like, "Hey, people ain't getting tired. You're getting tired. Fuck this shit." We got the momentum. People are interested. People coming to the meetings. People coming out to the demonstrations. We gotta keep this up. We let it slide for about a month and we could never build up again after that. Ultimately the resolution was that they did some exchange for us. I took a trip right after that, up north to Sacramento. I go up to the Delta and hang out at Walnut Grove in Back of the Yards, the Japanese section there. I thought that if ever we had a nation in America it was up there.

FH: For a brief time, some people put out an Asian cultural nation position.

MN: Yeah. We tripped out on that. We never took that seriously. We never found a basis for the nation. Autonomous villages, communities, some kind of autonomy like J-town, Chinatown was feasible. In fact it was like that. San Francisco Chinatown had its own telephone exchange at one time. You call into Chinatown you had to go through the Chinatown Exchange to get in.

FH: Tell me about GIDRA [a popular Los Angeles-based Asian American newspaper—editor]. What was going, and who was part of that, and what was the relationship with East Wind?

MN: GIDRA was four or five people who coughed up $50-$100 and bought a word processor. I think some of these people were Mike Murase, Evelyn Yoshimura, Colin Watanabe, and those guys that come out of UCLA. Came out of Oriental Concerns. I think the GIDRA organizers get radicalized around the U.S. invasion of Cambodia. Colin gets popped (arrested) and the community responds to his and others' defense. Also Asian Radical Movement (ARM) shows up— Steve Tatsukawa, Laura Ho, Suzie Wong—all pretty much egged on by their White leftist mentors, to show us how be revolutionaries. They decide that they wanted to develop a newspaper. So they put together fifty bucks and bought a word processor and they started a newspaper. It was pretty much a mixed bag. We had, maybe two people in East Wind that worked on the paper and we had access. We never thought we would control it or anything. I think if we did, shit we would've had different kind of politics, made it more political. There was a real strong hippie trend in Southern California. They came out of Long Beach State. That's the Hiroshima (a popular Japanese American band—editor) people and the GIDRA people. So there's all that…

FH: …counter-culture.

MN: That was ok. It was all part of the rebellion. I always felt that it was a positive thing because it did represent the rebellion and that we had an organ the left had access to anytime it wanted to. They were not afraid to print our shit. We had a hell of a time with *Rafu Shimpo* (the Japanese American daily in Los Angeles). I been fighting with them for thirty years as far as printing our political views. But we need something like GIDRA again that supports the cultural rebellion. They've resurrected GIDRA but I don't think it looks too healthy. Too middle-of-the-road.

FH: Talk to me about the polemics going on between East Wind, Workers Viewpoint Organization, IWK, the interaction that eventually leads to a merger process between East Wind and the League of Revolutionary Struggle after the IWK-ATM merger [c.f. Ho article on IWK—editor]. Talk to me about these relations. Those were the three main groups—WVO/CWP, IWK/LRS and East Wind in Los Angeles—in which you could see a lot of Asians in their ranks.

MN: Well, from what I recall, the major polemics were around the national question. It was crystal clear to us that WVO didn't recognize the national question as a fundamental contradiction in America. One of the things that disgusted me was, this was not too long after the Greensboro murder of 4 WVO/CWP cadres, and we've been studying the national question for a while. Reading what everything Stalin and Lenin had put out. Developing our own positions. We got a hold of the Black national question documents developed by the Comintern (Third Communist International—editor). Then we're told by WVO/CWP, "hey, we got this guy coming up now from our political department that could run it down to you." So OK. Turns out he was one of these nerds from Princeton or Harvard or some shit like that. So I asked, "How long this cat been in the organization?" "Oh, six months. He's smart. He's read all these books and he knows what's going on." So I took time to listen to him. What the fuck, anybody can quote something out of a book. That's what they were throwing at us and this guy was supposed to be the authority. Fuck you, you know. We just shined him on after that. We knew what Jerry Tung [general secretary of the WVO/CWP—editor] was like. Jerry stayed in Progressive Labor way too long around the Vietnam national question (PL condemned the Vietnamese National Liberation Front—editor). That motherfucker was sucking out of Whitey's ass all the way man, up until it got so ugly what the old White left was doing to the national question. The CPUSA took the same fucking line that all nationalism was reactionary and will lead to a Third World War. Fucking CPUSA was putting us down.

FH: When and why did you leave East Wind?

MN: I left just before the merger (between East Wind and the LRS—editor).

FH: About '78ish?

MN: Yeah. Anyhow, I find out that the Central Committee for almost a year was dysfunctional. We have four people on the Central Committee and possibly three of them are in depression and aren't even attending Central Committee meetings. But they were attending work unit meetings. We had different units: a Little Tokyo unit, Boyle Heights unit, workers unit. They were attending the work unit meetings and participating but hiding this shit. They didn't report anything from Central Committee. So after I leave the organization I found out that the fucking organization, leadership was dysfunctional. I ask one of the guys on the Central Committee and said, "What's going on? How come nobody said nothing? Why wasn't this brought up?" He said Shinya said that the contradictions between the leadership and the led in the organization is an antagonistic contradiction and it's OK to tell people lies. I wanted to punch the motherfucker out there. I asked him, Can you believe that? How come you didn't bring it up? Did you question it? He said no. So I knew we were in the cult of personality. Pretty obvious. I don't know what to say to something like that. You got fucking idiots participating in an organization who listen to crap like that, fuck you, what kind of organization can you have? That blows my mind.

FH: Why did you actually leave?

MN: I was gonna get to that. It comes down to the same bullshit. It was around defense of the Sun building.

FH: In Little Tokyo?

MN: Yeah. In Little Tokyo, the community was fighting redevelopment. We as an organization had said that we are gonna stand and fight and hold that motherfucker down. If the cops want us, they were gonna have to take it from us. We have to show the community that we have some balls and we're willing to defend our people. That was the majority position in East Wind, which I was a part of, that we should occupy the building and defy the cops. The minority trend was that we should just do a token thing and then give it up to them. We took it to a community meeting and about one hundred people showed up. Talked about the defenses and stuff like that. We put the majority position out there and it of course carried the day. IWK came up with this thing about the minority position.

FH: What do you mean?

MN: That you just put a token defense force in there and don't occupy the goddamn building. What we wanted to do was occupy it, run classes, do stuff, run programs out of the building 24 hours. Keep it going and if the cops come, let them come. Fuck them. They said no. IWK said we just put a couple of people there and put a token force there and if they come let them take it. At the East Wind meeting, the position was stand and fight. Occupy the building. Fill it up with our people, run programs and serve the community and politicize them. At the community meeting, the same thing. When the concrete practice comes out we assigned two people down there and we don't develop no programs no nothing to occupy the building. So the cops come 3 o'clock in the morning like they always do and bust our people and haul them off to jail. East Wind leadership capitulated against its own majority membership position and the community which had voted with the majority position. East Wind fought for the majority position but did nothing to implement it, nothing to organize the defense and occupation. I was in the process of leaving. I was living in J-town. This guy comes up and tells me, ,"Hey man, they took 'em." These community people were watching, looking out for us. Some of them said that if things went down, the people would be willing to fight and back us up. One of the brothers told me, "You people are full of shit." What can I say? I raise the issue in the organization and a reoccurring pattern had developed. We take a position at a plenum. These two positions would come up. It would seem kind of coincidental but much of the leadership would be with Shinya in particular. The leadership would end up in the minority position and be defeated at plenum. But when we implement the line it's always the minority position that would be implemented. I'd questioned what happened to the leadership person. He replied by saying maybe he should quit or step down. We said no, that ain't even the question. The question is whether you can fucking accept criticism and change. It ain't about throwing anybody out or purging anyone or doing any of that bullshit. So he agreed to stay. Now we came to the merger. His line is that we're too small and disconnected and we don't have a good perspective on stuff. We can't see the bigger picture. That's true. What about line? We got positions. We got positions developing on the women question. We got a hard position on the national question. We got tentative positions on the gay and lesbian thing, the White working class, the Asian American working class. We got all this kind of developing stuff. I had worked on that shit, we had positions that we can negotiate and talk about. Where are these fucking people coming from?

FH: Were you pro or anti inclusion of gays and lesbians?

MN: They should have all the rights and privileges that everybody else in this society should have so they should be apart of this revolutionary organization. They got revolutionary politics and they should be a part of it.

FH: That's very different from a lot of M-L groups that were anti-gay and lesbian.

MN: That's Stalin shit and promoting it throughout the whole international communist movement. Cubans are down on gays and lesbians and in Vietnam, they're killing them. We had that International meeting in Vancouver with those strong and beautiful Vietnamese women. Because the Vietnamese Party had such a fucked up position in my opinion on the gay/lesbian thing, those goddamn [White American] lesbians wanted the main thing the Vietnamese women to talk about was this and not the bombing and invasion by U.S. imperialism. So we had to throw them out. Fucked up White women, what do you expect? White liberal women, too. Well we had a lot of positions. Tentative positions all that. Fucking years of mass work. Shinya gonna say, "Throw all that out the window because we ain't big enough. We ain't got a national perspective." He was doing other shit that was fucked up. I knew about it 'cause he would confide in me periodically. I bullshit him. He was still talking to Weather people. He wouldn't report that to the organization. I didn't have enough sense to report it either. I think we have to have an underground wing, straight up, like the Black Liberation Army. We don't all have to be coming in the same way like most of the other groups. IWK have their positions. WVO have their positions. All those suckers. I figure if we were gonna form the Party, the Party should have the broadest experience of work that represents the American revolution. You can't be just one way. At least in the work. So I was so disgusted with the motherfucker and by the group because the group would not stand up. We had another problem concerning organizational line. There's two ways of approaching leadership and one is the laundry list approach. You get up there and write down all the shit you want to discuss., what the problems are and stuff like that. Then you say, ok, one leadership person takes top half and other person takes bottom half. They go off their ways and develop it. The other way, the leadership takes the whole list, sits down and discusses it and then divides it. You have this responsibility so that, the leadership the people who are going to be the presenters or whoever leads it have boundaries and understanding where everybody is coming from. So you have a central kind of approach to the goddamn thing whereas the other way people go off and do their own goddamn thing, come back and you might have something that clashes. In one of our work units, it constantly happened. The fucking meeting would dysfunction after a while. How come this is going on? So we went back and did some studying. Mao talks about that shit, talks about "dispersed methods of leadership" versus "democratic-centralist" leadership. They bring that up and try to fight it out in the cadre unit. Fucking rank and file and other people don't say shit, wouldn't take a position, didn't want to offend the leadership. Fuck that. All this stuff was coming to a head so I figure, "Well I'm leaving", and I was gonna start to raise some criticism right away and they asked me not to. So I said, "OK, I won't." What I said basically was that, "I think the merger process is full of shit, this mechanical merger and not on line." They wanted me to leave saying that I had left for personal reasons. After a year I could expect them to produce a position paper that states what lines they united with LRS around, what was the basis of the merger. I thought that was pretty reasonable. So I agreed and didn't raise criticism then. They never did produce that. Though you talk to them they still say, "Oh, we merged on the basis of a line." You ask what line then? They can't say. The crowning point was me and this brother had left together, maybe we left separately, but we teamed up afterwards and we went to the merger announcement meeting. They saw us there and sent fucking Mark Masaoka over to talk to us. He says to us: "We don't want you guys to ask any questions." What do you mean you don't want us to ask any questions? "We don't want you guys to ask any questions." Well, fuck you, you know. If anybody is allowed to ask questions, we will ask questions. I will anyhow. Bullshit, is what you call it. It was fucked up. All the people there shined us off and treated us cold as dogs, hoping like hell we would leave. Then they announce the merger, talk all their bullshit and said, "We will not take any questions from the floor." That blows the meeting. Is that cold, eh? Fucking me and Tats were cracking up, chicken shit motherfuckers. That was when I really got disgusted with them. Of course my life after that went through some rough times...got divorced by my ex-wife, went back to J-town, stepping into downtown Los Angeles, I got strung out pretty quick after that.

FH: Was that connected to depression and related to what was going on politically?

MN: Yeah, sure. It was all of that. Moving back to J-town, getting a divorce, leaving the organization. Really disappointed to see what was going on and have people turn against you so easily, that kind of unprincipled bullshit. And I liked drugs. I was working in the city wholesale produce market. That's a hotbed for drugs down there and get fucked up everyday until I got really strung out behind that fucking dust. Couldn't even work after awhile. But I was a "revolutionary drug addict." I was always trying, even then, being fucked up, trying to organize some bar girls who were pissed off at the one of the owners and something like that, trying to get them organized. Went through two tenant organizations while fucked up. Kept working. This is different from other who have "dropped out." Their perspective is dropping out and staying in the suburbs. I dropped out and but I stayed in J-town in the middle of the depression. Nowhere I could hide from anything. Shit, walk out and open the door to my fucking room and hell, it's in the middle of the hallways of the fucking hotel. It's hard to explain that to fucking middle class people. Anyhow I made it. Chairman Mao said that it takes ten years to make a stupid fucking intellectual into a worker. I was more stupider than most, it took me about twelve years. I'm still alive. I should've die two or three times.

FH: What did you think when you heard about the collapse of the League of Revolutionary Struggle?

MN: Well, I didn't understand it. I got a hold of their paper, their dissolution paper. I forgot how I got a hold of it. I think I got it through Warren Furutani. I thought to myself, this is a bunch of bullshit what they said. They made all kinds of statements that were outright lies—not even fabrications—just outright lies about how the LRS doesn't boast nor fight with other groups about who was most correct, most revolutionary, etc., etc., makes me wanna puke. Fuckers be fist-fighting the WV people in Chinatown over who would be selling their newspaper on what corner. Jerry's group folded up and I got a hold of some of the papers on that. I couldn't figure out what the hell was going on. So it was the late 80s and early 90s, right? My perspective living in Little Tokyo was that, shit, things hadn't changed. It was getting worse. How come all these suckers are caving in? I was confused about that for a long time and then I run across all these suckers and they be uptight. All these suckers who once were talking about HOW CORRECT THEY WERE, now look at them, they be running away. They got nothing to say. I'm still friends with some of them. So I was trying to get some of them to talk to me. Let's sum it up man. Fuck it, we got lessons to learn from all this bullshit. I've been doing this for ten, fifteen years now, asking people to sum it up. But most of the LRS Asians wanted to just close-up, cave in and all follow Carmen.

FH: A lot of the Asians went along with the capitulation. Not all of us, I didn't. But most of the Asians went with her. That was a clear cult of personality because even she had resigned as general secretary but she was promoted on a speaking tour to the whole organization nation-wide to argue for giving up Marxism, socialism and revolution.

MN: Wow. That far?

FH: Yeah. Oh yeah.

MN: Whoa. That's betrayal. Shit. I didn't know about that. I wish I would've known so I would've been there. Fuck her. I was living in a dump. So tell me about giving up socialism. Fuck them people. If that was the basis for the liquidation, shit, I don't think how anyone with any heart can go with that. Fuck. That's saying capitalism will last forever and that's ok. Fuck that. That's bullshit. Lousy ass motherfuckers.

FH: Well she's now a corporate lawyer.

MN: Yeah, right. I know her ex-husband is a big shot at Stanford. Suck shit out of a straw. Fuck 'em. She can't say shit about Shinya [at an earlier time Carmen Chow had accused Shinya Ono of being an agent-provocateur, according to Mo Nishida—editor].

FH: I got a letter from Shinya about a week ago. He's in Japan you know, became a Buddhist. He declined writing something for this anthology because he said, he doesn't think in that framework anymore. He's trying put it all in the past and doesn't want to recollect anything.

MN: Wait until it gets hot and then he'll be come back and then we're gonna have to bomb his ass.

FH: The liquation of the LRS went along both racial and generational lines, with many Chicanos not going along with it, but almost all the young people that were recruited in the 80s going along with the liquidation. But the class composition of the League in the 80s was changing a lot because the LRS was recruiting a lot from the more elite schools, Stanford, Berkeley, UCLA. What did you think of the LRS work in the redress and reparations movement for Japanese Americans during the 1980s?

MN: Redress—an apology, good. Reparations—monetary compensation, even better. But what they should've also done was raise the demand for return of the land taken from the Japanese. That would've made the struggle more of a revolutionary one—for return of the lands. We might not have gotten it, but still it should have been raised, especially by revolutionaries. The reformism of the LRS shows up in its dominant line in the reparations struggle. A revolutionary group would have raised the land demand, even if it was a conspicuously minority position, to do revolutionary educational work around.

FH: Very true, I hadn't thought of that, and to come to think about it, I agree. So what's your perspective today? Do you still believe in the need for a M-L party? What are your views of the movement today? What do you think of this Asian American Left Forum? I know that some of the younger generation are trying to talk to you about the history and stuff.

MN: Let me just make a comment about the one on people coming and talking to me. There have been a few, maybe one or two, other than yourselves, that are serious about revolution, but as far as the young people that are coming out, coming up the last ten years, there's only been one person and that's Ryan. [Yokota]. But other than that, like I said, I feel that people want to read the shit out of the books. These are the kids out of the universities, mainly around the UC system and UCLA in particular. A big disappointment. I see this Left Forum as being mainly those university and UCLA people and there's a big strong elitism. For me, my identity is as a worker. Maybe a working class intellectual. I went to school so I have the intellectual abilities and training at least. I'm a worker and that's what I identify as and I feel the chauvinism from the young people. Who the fuck is this guy? What's he got any business talking to us about stuff. They'd rather listen to a trade union bureaucrat or UCLA professor. I see that, I feel that. Not a direct put down, but I feel that.

So saying that, my perspective is that ain't nothing changed. Since the sixties and the 70s, fuck, the community's in worse shape now than it's ever been. because everything's hidden now, at least in the Japanese community. We still haven't developed a Japanese working class organization. That's my dream—to develop a revolutionary national motion in our community made up of working class people. My belief as a revolutionary nationalist is that either our communities are going to be a part of the reserves of imperialism like they always been or they could be a part of the forefront of the oppressed people, part of that united front against imperialism. We tried that in the 60s getting educated youth to help lead that struggle, the leading force of that struggle. Well, the 60s and 70s proved to us that was wrong. It's the working class that got to organize itself and take the leadership of the community. Move it so that we could influence the community and move it into part of the revolutionary united front. So my whole thing is working with, trying to penetrate the working class and raise consciousness and do that. That ten year process about leaving East Wind and coming back into the community and going into the whole drug scene became a part of my development as a worker. I survived so I am a worker. My politics haven't changed. I'm a still a revolutionary nationalist. I'm still a Maoist. I'm still a Malcolmite. But I'm a Maoist in the truer sense now. I believe that it's the working class that has to provide the main force and the leading force. I think that the working class in America, particularly most of our communities, are literate enough to understand Marxism, Leninism and Mao Zedong Thought without any intervention by intellectuals. I think there's now the cultural basis for the direct transmission of our teachers' teachings. Not like in 1930s China or Japan where people with third grade education were the main force in the working class or like it was here even in our community in the 1930s. That's the basis.

I'd like to emphasize the two-tiered nature of the U.S. working class and leading role/force of the lower tier because of imperialist domination of oppressed nations within its borders and the oppressed nationalities. The working class as a whole has to be seen strategically as the main force, but we, the lower working class, have to be organized in our communities as the leading political force. It's the poorest sections of the innercities where the lower working class lives. That's where we have to go, to organize and build our bases along the lines of George Jackson's "Black commune" idea. From this base, we need to seize the leadership of the trade union movement from the "bosses of labor" and their business union lackeys. That's my view.

We don't need the introduction of educated youth who can't join or take leadership from the lower working class. The educated youth who want to join the revolutionary movement must commit class suicide and make that supreme sacrifice of their ego, creature comforts, etc., and show that they are serious about coming to terms with the historical materialist flow of reality.

Yeah, we gotta have a Party. Shit, you gotta have leadership. If you gonna throw a dance, you gotta have somebody coordinating the fucking thing. The Party is still our central task. How do we approach that? Obviously self-proclamation ain't doing it. I think the encouragement is for everybody to experience as much as they can and do what you can you can to promote revolutionary consciousness among the people. Malcolm teaches us by any means necessary. Mao talks us about walking with two legs, defending yourself with two hands. From that basis of everybody doing whatever it takes to form their own cadre units, form their own political consciousness-raising processes that's going to come together to eventually to form a party and it ain't going to be through no self-proclamation. That's real clear. The other thing I'm really clear about now is the repudiation of Stalin. Fuck the motherfucker. There's a whole trend of leading revolutionary organizations going on right now that's promoting him, defending him, like Sendero Luminoso in Peru led by that professor, Abimael Guzman, or Jose Maria Sison, another professor, and the Philippines Communist Party. I think it's important that both Guzman and Sisson and their parties have promoted the armed struggle again. I think that's the high point. That's what it's really all about. Before that our people were trying ways with revolutionary struggle with their hands tied behind their backs. You got to go with both hands. That armed struggle is gotta be seen as viable alternative and those two promoted that and have shown that it can be done.

FH: But they also uphold Stalin?

MN: Yeah. That's the contradiction as I see it. Stalin put a hurt on us. The cocksucker is not a dialectician for one thing. How the fuck can he be a fucking Marxist or Leninist without being a dialection? In any reading of Lenin, Lenin takes account of the other side, especially inner-party struggles. Gotta have a right to speak up, you can't smash that shit down. He talks about those fuckers, the Mensheviks, like they're dogs but he don't say they shouldn't have a right to speak. Goes over and bends backward and argues for organs and stuff for them to put their views out. Mao's the same way, talks about the Hundred Flowers. People don't understand that shit. Then you gotta weed out the weeds and find the sprouts. Stalin betrayed the movement. White man calls it "realpolitik." As far as my politics is concerned, I'm against Stalin. The leading light as far as I'm concerned in this day and age—in theory and practice—is Chairman Mao and Amilcar Cabral. Cabral talks about class suicide . He made his own Party and the Party betrayed their people. That's a heartbreaker. Robert Mugabe (of Zimbabwe), I met him. I love that son of a bitch. At the time I met him I thought he was a living Buddha. He smashed imperialism over there, too. That's real clear: you can't live with imperialism. Fuck them, you gotta kick them out. Look at South Africa, Mandela betrayed his people. Shit. Both Mugabe and Mandela can be considered bourgeois nationalists. They broke the back of white supremacy but did not move to the second and more important step of liberation of all their people through the nationalization of all large land holdings and redistribution of that land, nationalization of all foreign holdings and all nationally important industries, for starters. They still got those Azanians over there though, who're still struggling: One bullet, one settler. Cold shot, but maybe that's what it has to come down to. Just to say that party-building is the central task and to start forming cadre units isn't enough. The thing is to develop mass practice and consciousness-raising and using mass line politics. Develop a presentation of dialectical materialism in a way that anyone can understand. That should be relatively easy. It doesn't have to be garbled or any of that crap from Marx, Engels, Lenin. Go to Mao and you go to nature, human experience, and you can break all that shit down. Dialectical materialism. People will see that's the most logical thing in the world because it represents real life. The thing about the mass line, mass line politics. How democratic centralism really works. All those things we gotta be ready to share with the people in a way that's logical to them and try it out. Like the run we just come back on. The Native Americans call it the circle, the talking circle. That's the basis of democracy where everybody speaks their piece and everybody listens. You gotta respect each other's opinions and views, and then you come to a decision, that's the centralism. We tried to practice that on our run. The central focus is to make sacrifice. We gotta be honest with people, like Cabral talks about, "Tell no lies, claim no easy victories." Making revolution we gonna have to make sacrifices. We gotta give up a lot of these creature comforts, things that we take for granted. We have to make sacrifice so that the next generation will see that people are serious. How can you look at this bunch from the sixties and take them serious now? They totally discredited the revolution and the revolutionary aspirations of young people. What the fuck? So they can go ego trip. "Oh yeah, a lot of my friends is the vice president of this university." So fucking what? All these schools do is take the best of our young people and fuck them up. And it takes years and years of hard work to take that away, to overcome that side. That's a part of it too., That's a part of building character. If you gonna build good, strong, loving people, people gotta suffer. Fuck. Japanese people have that saying, "*Kuro shi na kattara honto no ningen ni nara nai*"—If you don't suffer you can't become a real human being. Can't have it made all your whole life and think you have soul. It don't work like that.

Red Guard rally in Portsmouth Square
San Francisco
Photo credit: Franklin Fung Chow

RICHARD AOKI

interviewed by Dolly Veale

Richard Aoki is one of the pioneers of the Asian Pacific American revolutionary movement in the U.S. However, he is better known for his role in relation to the Black Panther Party (BPP). Richard's place in the BPP's history was portrayed in the 1997 film "Panthers" (as a Chinese man). In this interview, Richard recounts this part of his life's journey as a leader in the vortex of the 1960s Black liberation struggles, as well as the Asian Movement. Richard also played a unique role as a political "bridge" between the two revolutionary nationalist streams (Black Power movement and the Asian students/youth movement) in forging unity between these two oppressed and rebellious segments of Amerikkkan society.

Many political activists who have known and worked with Richard Aoki over the years have found one noteworthy quality about him: through all the ups and downs of his personal and political life, he has remained principled in how he deals with political differences. Richard has not been known to indulge in personal or political slanders, rumors, or gossip to deal with the multitude of (real or supposed, light or serious) political and ideological differences within the ranks of the revolutionary movement. Instead he is known for engaging in straight-forward and principled debate, discussions, and political relations. Such political integrity is important to uphold.

Many people know that the government worked overtime to exploit and manipulate differences within the BPP, and between the BPP and other organizations. Those were and are favorite tactics of the political police to destroy and demoralize radicals forces and organizations, including through the FBI's infamous COINTEL-PRO (counterintelligence project). There is a profound lesson here—that there were people like Richard who did not fall into those traps and avoided playing into the government's hands. In this respect, Richard sets a good example for the growing revolutionary and youth movement of today.

Richard has continued to participate in various struggles against the injustices and inequalities inherent in U.S. capitalist society. A recent example was his support for the students during the April 1999 ethnic studies struggle at U.C. Berkeley. He has spoken at many forums and protests, including in those to free his ex-BPP comrade from death row—Mumia Abu-Jamal.

Even as the powers-that-be work overtime to divide and conquer, Richard's story is testimony to the fact that what unites the people is greater than what divides us. His story helps to illustrate that the people have a common enemy against an exploitative and oppressive system, and a common struggle for liberation. Nonetheless it also took a conscious decision on his part to resolutely throw his lot with the Black liberation struggle, to boldly step up to the cutting edge of the most revolutionary (and controversial) element of that time. This interview highlights some of Richard Aoki's key contributions to the "legacy to liberation."

Dolly Veale: Can you describe your childhood experiences in the U.S. internment camps during World War II, then after the camps, growing up in West Oakland, California among Black youth in the 1940s and 1950s, being one of the few Asian families there?

Richard Aoki: In retrospect my early childhood experiences were instrumental in the development of my politics. First of all being born Japanese in America, then being jerked off to a concentration camp for 3 1/2 years solely because of my ancestry was a bit mind boggling. To experience the concentration camp environment is a mind blower. But being in an all Japanese environment for that period of time gave me an idea of my culture. I had to learn how to speak Japanese, especially with the older people.

I was 4 years old when the war started and we were interned, so I was the right age to attend the camp schools, to start kindergarten there. In kindergarten I was chosen to play George Washington in the school pageant honoring the "father of our country". I got real excited about it and ran home and told my father what the big deal was. Disasterville struck. Needless to say I was in no physical shape to participate in the school pageant. My father was incensed that I didn't have the good sense to realize that I was not the father of "our country", no way, shape or form. Nor would I ever be, never, NO, because the nature of this society. I got the message. There was no way I could forget the message: I should not think in terms of George Washington, this was not my country by a long shot. In fact "my country" put me in this camp. I was born here unfortunately. Yes, I'm Asian American, Asian from my heritage, American unfortunately for where I was born. Yes, that was the kind of a funny experience.

My father briefly taught Junior High School in the camp. He resigned after he got to the section on American democracy because he looked at the kids while speaking about democracy, freedom, justice; and all the kids had to do was look out the window and see the barbed wire fences, the watch towers with search lights, the half track with 50 caliber machine guns. It didn't compute. The kids weren't getting the message, and righteously so. They were old enough to realize this picture didn't focus right for them. He also told me that he was opposed to war and that he would not serve in the U.S. military. Towards the end of World War II, the U.S. government got a little desperate for manpower, and came into the camps to recruit. My father was among those that refused to go. He could be classified as a No-No boy.

DV: Can you explain what the No-No boys were?

RA: No-No boys were those Japanese American youth who were eligible for the draft, who in order to serve had to sign a document saying whether or not they supported Japan. If they said yes, of course, they would have the bad news. If they said no, that was OK. Once they passed that hurdle and that hoop they had to sign another document affirming their allegiance to the United States, yes or no. Anybody that put two no's on the questionnaire automatically was not involved with the military and called a No-No boy [see endnote—editor].

The way my father explained it was that his entire family was in the concentration camp, run by the Americans and now they are asking him to fight the Japanese. That doesn't compute with him. How could he go and fight a war knowing his whole family is incarcerated including being liquidated if things didn't go right?

There was a fear that was in the camps that was kind of underscored. What would happen if the war went badly and Japan had won? There were discussions during and after the war that I recall hearing about, what the Japanese would do to the Japanese Americans. One consensus was that the Japanese Americans would be assimilated into the Japanese imperial empire. Another thought was the Japanese militarists would execute all the Japanese-Americans for several reasons. Number one, security or unreliability. Number two, contamination of the culture through exposure in birth. And number three, the Japanese imperialists weren't much into being kind, when you consider the mass atrocities committed by the Japanese military such as the rape of Nanking. There was the decimation of the civilian population of China, and the rape of Manila in the Philippines.

Getting back to the No-No boys, my father fell in that category. It was also the title of a book by John Okada that was somewhat of a semi-experiential narrative on what drove the No-No boys on, or one No-No boy. The fact that my father's generation were split during the war regarding their loyalty to the United States, we could never have a dinner conversation after the war to discuss the war, and the role that everybody in the family played, because people were on both sides. In fact one uncle, he died before the information was released, but I knew that he had served in M.I.S.—Military Intelligence Service—a special group of Japanese-Americans who were sent to the battle fronts to be translators for the U.S.

My family was among the first to be relocated so we got to the camp as it was being constructed or parts of it were being constructed still. We were sent to Topaz, Utah - in the middle of the scenic Utah desert, one of about 10 camps that were established during World War II to hold 120,000 of us. When I first got to the camp with my family I didn't go out at night because of the sifting out process among those loyal to Japan and those loyal to the U.S., and it grew very violent. The weapons they used were construction equipment that was lying around. I saw a guy get his head split open, and a number of people were killed. To this day the figures have not been officially released but I saw for myself. It was not a happy camp. Things did stabilize as the administration went on and people settled in.

Anyway we were abruptly jerked from the concentration camp and relocated to a Black ghetto which was West Oakland. Don't forget this is the end of the war, housing is real bad in California, especially in the Bay Area where we were originally from. And being Japanese-American made the rental department a little confined. The only place that many Japanese could apply to live after the war were in ghettos and barrios where housing prices were not that high. West Oakland in the 1940s and 1950s was essentially a self- contained community economically, politically, and socially. It was and still is a segregated ghetto.

I was about 8 years old. West Oakland to me, was a nice place to grow up in, even though at first, I was considered an outsider. It took me about a year to establish roots in the community and maybe several dozen fights, but once I had proved myself to the brothers on the block I was pretty much left alone. 8 years old and I learned how to fight real fast, I swear to god. I mean like every day [knock knock], "Can Richard come out and play?" Well Richard didn't want to come out and play at all. Richard doesn't have the mathematical gene, but it's no contest out there, until my father said "you got to go out there and play. If you don't go out there and play I'm gonna beat your butt". I said "if I go out there and play they are gonna beat my butt". He said, "Well the chance of you getting your butt beat is 100% if you stay here. You got a better chance out there". Again not having that mathematical gene I could calculate that I got no chance in here but I got a chance out there so over a period of one year I was able to establish my place in that community.

And my immersion in the African American culture totally, was one of the best things that ever happened to me. I had a chance to really enjoy the richness of the culture. Also I had a chance to see the down side like the brutality out there on the streets perpetrated by the police. One incident I remember one night I was out. Two white cops stopped this wino on the street, and he threw up and some of it by chance landed on the pants of one of the cops, so they beat him half to death, even before they got to the notorious front steps of the City Hall. At that time, the Oakland City Hall contained the City Jail and it was rumored that the front steps of the City Hall was the most dangerous place in Oakland for any Black person. They had a tendency to fall down those steps when they were being dragged off to jail. At least that is what the report said, "Prisoner fell down the steps".

I didn't see it as injustice per se. I just saw it, like how quaint, it's kind of familiar, you know, people of color don't seem to get a break around here. Then speaking with a lot of the people who lived in the neighborhood I got an idea of segregation, racism, discrimination, which I was starting to become aware of—a view of American society that was not very positive. Be that as it may, I managed to survive in the ghetto, went to school, made friends, even ran in a street gang called The Saints that was made up of Black kids, several other Asians, two white kids that lived on the block, who were poor whites. Both of them have ended up in prison. Friendships I made there in West Oakland stood up over the last 40 to 50 years.

DV: I understand you joined the U.S. army after high school and then developed opposition to the Vietnam war. Can you describe that process?

RA: From 1956 to 1964 I was in the U.S. army. I didn't do anything exciting, it was just "3 hots and a cot", $72.50 in cash a month for a buck private. I picked up a lot of skills in that period of time. From 1956 to 1964 militarily it was a transition period—the U.S. was gearing down from Korea, but were gearing up for Vietnam. I could see that as early as 1960 because contrary to what people say about John F. Kennedy, he was one of the worst warmongers I have ever seen as President. I was in the military when he quietly activated the 5th and 10th Green Berets. We didn't know where they were going to go. Now here is where they make mistakes. To be in the Green Berets, as you know, was counter-insurgency. They have a policy that you have to speak another language in addition to English. And they were taking in a lot of Eastern Europeans in 1960, almost all the people they selected. I thought still we're gonna fight in Europe. But ironically that first group of Green Berets were sent to Vietnam, their second language is Eastern European language [laughs]. It was kind of weird, but that's the military.

Probably around 1960 or so, I began to have questions about U.S. involvement in Vietnam. I developed opposition to the war I think because of the disparity between what Washington/Wall Street was saying about the war and what I actually experienced. I'm a grunt. Who am I to question? When my enlistment ran out in 1964 I was up at the regimental headquarters with my duffle bag and my eagerness to leave. I signed out for my discharge paper. Then the regimental clerk said I have another set of papers—your reenlistment papers for another 8 years. However, the moment I signed the discharge papers I was a civilian. So the clerk called the colonel. The colonel came in his bathrobe to talk to me about reenlistment. I was offered the chance to go to officer candidate school and promotion to second lieutenant in 22 weeks. The second thing I was offered was to be assigned, or transferred, to the 101st Air Borne, the screaming eagles. I had applied twice but had been turned down. The third thing I was offered was a $3,500 "reenlistment bonus". In the barracks we used to called it blood money, but Washington called it reenlistment bonus. The grunts would call it blood money cause we knew that bordered on mercenaryism. I declined their bribes.

I came back to Berkeley, attended Merrit College in Oakland and got involved in the Vietnam Day Committee demonstrations in 1964. That's when

I began running into representatives from all the political tendencies in Berkeley—all twenty million of them. I decided that revolutionary socialism looked like the answer, joined a group that espoused it, but kept my roots in the West Oakland community and began to develop my own thoughts about the theoretical power struggle and what needed to be done. In 1966, I transferred to U.C. Berkeley. There was all kinds of movements resisting the status quo—resistance to the draft; resistance to segregation; resistance to union busting. All these movements were also part of the backdrop to the development of organizations like the Black Panthers. In fact, the third month after I transferred to U.C. Berkeley, in October 1966, the Black Panther Party was formed.

DV: How did you know Huey P. Newton and Bobby Seale?

RA: Well through the families, the Seale family, the Newton family, the kids had big families, and everybody knew everybody in that West Oakland area. I knew Huey's brother Melvin, he was my age. Once you know the family, you know what it's like, and I kept in touch with them while I was in the service. I knew Huey's reputation before. I was more familiar with Bobby because he was older and he had also gone into the military, so we had a sort of bond there. But in his case he signed up for the Air Force for 4 years and when his enlistment was up to about 3 1/2, some officer called him the "n" word and he had to defend himself. So he was kicked out. Once I was in the military, especially on leave coming back here, I was a homie, I'd run into Bobby and say "Hey how's it going, what you doing, what's happening". By 1966 I knew that most of the home boys on the block were not happy with events that were occurring.

By 1966 Malcolm X and Medgar Evers had both been killed. The only organization that seemed to be doing anything, seemed to be the more radical groups, among them surprisingly enough was the Nation of Islam. They were considered the most dangerous organization in the U.S. then. So looking at something like Nation of Islam which at first I really thought might be the answer, but since I had been studying at Berkeley I could see its limitation in their theoretical construct. The mythology of it - the myth about the evil scientist Yaku who created the white person and white people are mutations and all that. Other names would come up on the table, like "what about this group"? "No man, a little shaky", groups such as the traditional Communist Party, USA or the Progressive Labor Party, which we didn't feel were revolutionary. I also had a personal beef against the CPUSA, because I discovered in my research that at the beginning of World War II, they were the ones out there screaming and hollering for us to be put in the concentration camps. Recently I got an e-mail that a leading member of the CPUSA had passed away. He played a key role for the old CPUSA within the Japanese community. They almost lynched him in Tule Lake, the maximum security camp, when the CPUSA sent him there to pass the good word out—to tell internees to join the U.S. Army.

DV: Before deciding to become a revolutionary, there was period when you were doing this and that on the streets. What changes did you go through to decide to become a revolutionary?

RA: This is the decision I had to make. One time, Huey and I had the idea of emulating one of his friends who was the number one pimp in North Oakland. We didn't want to compete with him so we went to West Oakland and looked over the possibilities there and in the process got to talk to a lot of prostitutes. And he and I could just not become pimps. We talked to the women and they were in bad shape. I mean they were out there because they were mothers trying to make ends meet. Yes they made lots of money, relatively speaking, but it's a hard life. Huey and I couldn't see profiting over somebody's misery. We thought about other lines of work, but hey, in the ghetto you know there ain't too much going there. Pimping was lucrative, the most esteem/elevating for a male, not for the female, that was a different story, but for the men it was big time. I found out years later about our "role model", that a lot of people in the community wanted to blow that guy's head off. At the time, we didn't realize that came with the territory. We just saw the fancy clothes, the two .45s the guy carried around.

That was before the BPP was founded, maybe in 1964 or 65. We were checking things out. I think it was to Huey's credit. Lot of people bad mouth Huey, but I knew a Huey that was human, and he and I didn't jive about this. But Bobby didn't want to hear none of this stuff. He was married and his wife would have been all over him. But Huey and I were footloose and fancy free and so we prowled the streets a lot together. Got into a lot of trouble but the important thing is we were open—open to helping the community someway, somehow because we could see things weren't going right. We could also see that there were political movements and stuff. Thank god Berkeley was right there because any questions we had we could always run to Berkeley for the theoretical part. The conditions we knew because we lived in the community, so that part wasn't that hard.

DV: When you and Bobby and Huey were sitting around, how did you decide to form the Black Panther Party?

RA: When I decided to be associated with the Trotskyites, one thing they encouraged me to do was to read. So I not only read their stuff, but I read everything that was published. I hooked up with Bobby and Huey at Merrit College and we were hanging out. Huey wasn't a student then but Bobby and I were. Then Huey and I used to run the streets at night, like anybody, doing this and that.

I was going to Merrit for the first couple of years, but I was involved in Berkeley through the Vietnam Day Committee. And through the VDC I was able to scan the political spectrum because that was a broad based anti-war movement. And in the process of scanning the groups I formed certain political opinions, right or wrong, about their role in the cosmos. I could see a lot of them weren't gonna play a big role in the cosmos. Sectarian groups with three people in them. I'd say "Man your line is good, where are the others?" They'd say "It's just the three of us."

We were mainly trying to figure out what we were gonna do, what is to be done I think would be a better characterization. It's not like we sat down and said revolution is the answer. We sat down and said, look, we got our backs up against the wall and nothing's working. These regular groups, the civil rights groups, and I'm labeling that constrictivly, don't seem to be delivering the goods. In fact, the passive, non-violence whatever ain't working out, too many people are getting unnecessarily killed. And we recalled what Malcom had to say— yeah the KKK don't come marching down Harlem. I'll never forget that. Why don't they come marching down Harlem? Huey, Bobby and I looked at each other and said, why don't they? Because we there! They ain't going nowhere in Harlem, nowhere. So I started putting together what I was involved in with theoretical stuff that I was playing with. I could see that something revolution-ary was on the horizon. To make a long story short, the Black Panther Party was formed because the three of us, and others contributed in a way, came up with a 10 point program. There were two organizations that influenced the forma-tion of the BPP—one was the Lowndes County Freedom Organization of Alabama. They were for voting rights. Their logo was the Black Panther. That's where we lifted that from. The patrols were out of CAPS, the community action patrols in LA. They had tape recorders and they had movie cameras. But they didn't have self defense weapons. We just kind of added that.

DV: It was added because Huey studied law and found out there was a legal loop-hole, at that time, where you could carry unconcealed weapons in California legally?

RA: I'll give that to you. We got a program. Let's compare our program with the other groups and start recruiting because three do not make an organization, I mean we got to have other people you know. That's when we hit the pool halls and the bars to look for recruits. And that was the first wave including Bobby Hutton, the Forte brothers, the Harrison boys. We were recruiting people and I remember Huey and I were sitting at a table side by side. Applications forms were coming in and we were reviewing them. Stamping them and giving them their card with our signatures on it. This was at our first headquarters in North Oakland down there on Grove Street (now called Martin Luther King, Jr. Way). One young kid came and he asked the question, "am I gonna get hurt? I mean, my mamma tells me I shouldn't even be in here." We said, "Well your mamma's right on most things, but you come to the right place". He said "will I die?" Huey said "we ain't gonna bullshit you, this is dangerous". I complimented Huey on being honest. I was biting my tongue cause we wanted numbers but to lie to people, to tell them "no" wouldn't be right.

DV: You, Huey and Bobby sat down and wrote the 10 point program?

RA: I recall we did with a bottle of scotch, but there are different interpretations of it. We thought it was a lot of fun. Bobby was working for a poverty center. This was a weekend, I remember that. And the poverty center had a mimeo machine so we were able to print that out and the whole nine yards in the middle of the night. The 10 point program was the result that we got to have a program. We all knew that you can't get nowhere without a program.

The exact points just evolved - looking at the material conditions, such as housing, employment, etc. We had one on police brutality. Now we just kind of threw the 10 items out there to see how many of them would fly, you know, what were the real sore points. We discovered it was the police that most people in the community were concerned about. We lived in the community too and people said to us "Look, you jive asses, if you want to do something you get the police off our backs." That's the one most people could identify with. You know, housing, other groups were dealing with it. But no other group was really dealing with the police at the time. So that's when we came up with the shot gun patrol thing.

I became one of six field marshals in the history of the BPP. Like Geronimo Pratt, I had been in the military. Skill is a skill, you know, skill is like computers, a tool. So what tools do people need in order to take care of certain business. To me, a rational person does not stop police brutality by running up in front of them and getting your head beaten. That doesn't work. What's the next best thing? We were going to "police the Police" in Oakland. In order to deter them, and this is what we were more interested in, the basic philosophy was if we tail the cops with our cameras and our shotguns and our tape recorders, the chances of brutality occurring would be less because the police knew that the focus was on them, they may not be as apt to brutalize people. There were a number of incidents where we actually did prevent a lot of brutality.

Another thing we discovered, or I discovered years later, the crime rate in Oakland went down as the activity of the BPP grew. So what happened is we took a lot of young bloods that had been out there doing senseless things and we were giving them a purpose. Now that didn't come in the party program, but if they bought the party program they had a family. They had a party. Somebody told me recently that those years were probably the most intense, fastest years in American history. That people are still reeling from that particular period. I'm talking about the period from about 1965 to 1970. Those 5 years were a historical turning point in American history. Not that anything like a revolution occurred, but it was a revolutionary movement that was nationwide.

DV: How did the BPP handle this thing where people had to get out of the life on the streets to become a revolutionary?

RA: Definitely our reputation was in the 'hood. We were well established and respected where things come from and the fact that we were there. It was a difficult question, but that's the way we did things. I'll give you an example. One time Bobby, Huey, and myself had to go to a very private political meeting and we had to have two body guards to back us up. So, we scooted over to San

Francisco and the three of us took care of the business while the two body guards killed time waiting for us to get back. We found out when we got back to Oakland, that the two body guards had scored on some illegal substances and that they were in the car that we were driving back from San Francisco. They were summarily dismissed from the BPP rather quickly, because the premise was yes, life is hard, but if you are on duty you do not engage in illegal activities that would draw bad news to the organization. That was about it.

DV: Did you help introduce Huey and Bobby to Mao and his Little Red Book ("Quotations from Chairman Mao Zedong")?

Mao's Red Book would have been discovered sooner or later by the Panthers organization. There is no doubt in my mind. But being also involved in the Asian Movement, I suddenly found myself having information access that other individuals or organizations didn't have. When I was at Berkeley I started running into a lot of people, not just from Berkeley but who were actually from other places, including international linkages. I talked to them and let them know that we're freedom fighters in this country and we need help. At that time the distribution of Red Books was illegal in this country, unless you had a license which China Books in San Francisco did, I found out later. But we discovered that Canada had diplomatic relations with the People's Republic of China and that a trade vessel would dock in Vancouver that had tons of Red Books. This was late 1966, early 1967. So it was arranged to get a couple of cases from Canada across the border into the U.S. and distribute them here and to do two things with it. Number one, to use the Red Book for political education because that's excellent, it's a basic training book. And number two, to go up to UC Berkeley's Sproul Plaza and sell it to raise money. Hey, all movement organizations need money and this was a good tactic. I stuck with the political end. I said yeah, money, we can always get money, but politics is something else. It was really, to me, the first thing, the political consciousness. Now politically Huey probably bought the Red Book more than Bobby. Of course I was more than sold on it because it was the best pocket thing I could carry around. I didn't have to argue a lot. I could say look at this.

I hadn't read all of Mao, but I was starting to read Mao. I had already finished Marx, Engels, and brought it all the way up to Fidel, Che and Fanon. Then Mao sort of grabbed my attention because there were strong Maoist tendencies in the movement in the 1960s so you don't want to disregard something that's important. It wasn't, parenthetically, until the 3rd World Liberation Strike that I'd see Maoism really start moving.

DV: How did other political forces relate to or influence the BPP?

RA: We actually knew all the CPUSA people in the area that were Black. They stayed away from us. They didn't want to see us. They thought we were crazy because we weren't following their line which was loyalty to Moscow. The other thing is they were putting the brakes on the national liberation movement here.

We looked to people like Robert F. Williams who was one of our heros.

Today I think not too many people are aware of who he was and what he did. In the '60s Robert F. Williams was a NAACP chapter president from Monroe County, North Carolina, somebody you wouldn't think would be too radical. He did something different—he armed his branch of the NAACP against Klan activities. I'm sure he must have been in trouble with the national headquarters of the NAACP because this was not their line. In the process of his struggle against the Klan he wrote a book, Negroes with Guns. Now that's an interesting title. [Recently reprinted by Washington State University Press—ed.] You know I bought that book and I read it. And I read about the struggle, along with that book, People With Strength by Truman Nelson, a white civil rights activist. And between those two books and newscasts and newspaper accounts I began to develop a healthy respect for Rob Williams. I tried to contact him. Things didn't come through. Then he was framed on a kidnapping charge. He had to leave this country. He next appeared in Havana, Cuba as a guest of Fidel Castro. I maintained contact with Rob Williams. Surprisingly enough correspondences between Havana and Berkeley took place and I was asked to be one of the distributors of his newspaper called *Crusader*. The thing that surprised me was that our mail was uninterrupted, at least on the surface, but I think he understood, anything he and I wrote to each other would be neutral. His thing was "would you be a distributor"? And I'd reply "I would be happy to." I wouldn't talk about nothing else, OK.

So every month or so I'd get my little copies of the *Crusader* and would go out and pass them out to everybody I knew because Robert F. Williams had respect. What capped it off in a way was when the relationship between the Soviet Union and the People's Republic of China started deteriorating, Robert F. Williams left Cuba and relocated in China. That blew the minds of everybody in the movement. I mean it's one thing to be with Fidel, but to be an honored guest of Mao Zedong and in a way "anointed" by Mao. There were pictures that he sent showing him with Chairman Mao that led me to think, "Wow, the only African-American revolutionary", quote unquote, "he must be revolutionary!" You have to remember a lot of things in the '60s passed real fast, but, Robert F. Williams did not pass fast. You could see his reputation was solid amongst those who were serious about the African-American Liberation struggle. He had done something that was revolutionary. Number one, he armed a NAACP chapter, and it was important enough to get him railroaded out of this country. I mean we all knew it was a railroad job. When Fidel welcomed him you don't know how good that made a lot of people feel because had he stayed here, he would have been a casualty of the FBI, I'm convinced of that. Then to cap it with being a guest of the People's Republic of China!

DV: So when the split took place between China and the Soviet Union in 1963 or 1964, Robert F. Williams went with the China side?

RA: Otherwise Fidel wouldn't have asked him to leave Cuba. We wondered what the hell was happening! Because Fidel was getting his economic support from the

Soviet Union. He got it all. Well, Robert F. Williams was a revolutionary. So where could he go from Cuba? So when he pops up in Bejing, you know my head turned. Of course I turned ahead of others who hadn't seen that turn of events. Because by this time I was internationally in check, so I knew the Sino-Soviet split was significant. Plus I was in correspondence with the guy. Of course I'm not going to write to him and say look here brother, I know why you had to move. He understood. I understood why he had to move. Now our correspondences continued. I opened this letter, with a stamp with the Vietnamese doing their thing and stuff, I said wait a minute. A lot of his letters would have Vietnamese type stamps on them even though they were from the Peoples Republic of China, you know a stamp of Vietnamese shooting down a U.S. warplane. The fact that Robert F. Williams, a man with his stature, was over there, how do you think it made us feel, I'm excited, "Hey Huey, Bobby, look at this. My man Robert F. Williams is now in China." "Wow what's he doing there, Richard?" I said "poor Fidel, he had a bad decision to make. I'll tell you why he's in China brother, because the Soviet Union sold the people out and put the pressure on Fidel. Fidel's got to keep his country going, and they put the screws on him and so he put Bob Williams out."

DV: Did Robert F. Williams' book influence you guys a lot?

RA: The title did, I'll tell you that. <u>Negroes with Guns</u>, we laughed about that. I know Bobby and Huey read it because I thought that was the best seller of the year. I'm sure all of us read that one. I'm sure they all didn't read <u>People with Strength</u> which was more political, it was a leftist non-sectarian account of what happened in Monroe County, North Carolina. It made me feel good that Williams was not off base politically. I mean any crazy can arm their NAACP chapter. But what he did!

A friend of mine who is African American, who was in my BPP branch, I asked him a couple of years ago "what was it about me that you thought was different?" He said "you were crazy. Don't take offense." I said, "You said I was crazy, I mean how else could I take it?" He said "any non-Black who stepped up to help Blacks positively was crazy for the 60s, I just got to tell you a fact, Richard". In retrospect that person was right. Any person of color who did not step forward in the '60s to support the Black liberation movement was really doing themselves in because there's a saying from Nazi Germany. When they came for the Jews, I didn't do nothing. When they came for the communists, I didn't do nothing. When they came for the labor leaders, I didn't do nothing. When they came for the intellectuals, I didn't do nothing. When they came for me, I was alone. So common sense dictates to me that any group that's in the forefront of the struggle for liberation of ethnic minority people has got to be the group that's supported. Because once they kill that group off, they are coming after everybody else. So if you are a person of color there's no other way for you to go except to be part of the Black liberation struggle. It doesn't mean submerge your own political identity or your whatever, but the job that has to be done in front, you got to be there. And I was there. What can I say.

DV: Besides Mao's Red Book, what were some of the other tools that the BPP used for mass political education?

RA: Because I was the first Minister of Education and there ain't been one since that time. Malcolm X was the first grade reader, The Autobiography of Malcom X, because it was written in simple enough language that ghetto kids could understand it. Then the reading list got a little more complex as it went up. To me, I guess at that time the Red Book was the best thing around. It was small and accessible. Not only it was popular, it was accurate. I mean, I couldn't disagree with the various quotations there. I mean nobody could really, if they think about it, could disagree. We needed the books for the classes, in the beginning, political education classes. That was my job, that's why I was at U. C. Berkeley. My job since I was the highest ranking Panther at Berkeley, was to get that knowledge and come back to the community. I was also looking into the Asian Movement to see if we could develop an Asian version of the BPP.

Then the Third World Strike at UC Berkeley happened. Some of the Black students had already been conditioned by the BPP, in fact some of the members of them at UCB were Black Panthers members. The Latino movement was getting off the ground. Native Americans had already formed the Native American Movement. And Asians had formed Asian American Political Alliance in 1968, of which I was a spokesperson. So, in 1969 when the strike occurred we not only had theoretical agreement, we had organizations that we could move in and link up to go forward together. That was the whole thrust of the strike—the solidarity. Meanwhile I had already talked with Huey about alliances back in 1967, before things got really hot. He said "what is your feeling about the hippies?" For Huey to ask me a direct question, caught me off guard a little bit. I said, "What you mean?" He said "Are they revolutionary, or not? Man, we need help, you know, and you're the one who know these things." I said "Well that's an interesting question. Basically they're reformist, basically they are sons and daughters of those rich people, but they got some conscience, that's the reason why they are hippies." Huey bought uniting with the hippies. I couldn't believe it. The thing that surprised me on a couple of occasions, Huey was ahead of me in some areas. Huey gave the BPP a broader vision.

Well, everybody knew Huey was heavy. There's no question about that. I mean he was basically illiterate because of the school system, but when he needed to learn, when he needed to understand the penal code, he understood it. We used to laugh at him. He beat the charges many times, with himself as attorney. One time he revealed to me what he was going to do on his latest legal escapades. I said "oh man, I'll visit you," but he beat the charges! Another time they hit him with 44 counts of burglary. He went to a real attorney. The real attorney said I can cut a deal for you, and Huey said "I ain't come here to cut a deal." The lawyer said "you can plead to 8 of those 44 and you won't have to serve but county time." I said "what are you gonna do?" He said "I'm fighting this one. I'm cutting that lawyer loose. I'm gonna do it." He beat that too! I defend Huey. A lot of people don't think too much of him. I guess I'm narrow in a way because all I recall is the good stuff that he represented, that he and I went through. He went internationalist far faster than me. I mean, he understood that—things like Robert F. Williams, Mao, the Viet Cong. And one of the things I respected about Huey was he was a good street fighter.

DV: Isn't it true that both of you were good street fighters, but you had more grounding in some Marxist theory?

RA: Yeah. We understood enough, the comedy of errors, but we took care of business. That's the way it was. We didn't go out of our way, there were bullies in our 'hood, but we weren't the bullies. We were the more level headed types but we learned how to fight because we had to fight the bullies and the police and whoever else messed with us. Huey was heavy and he could back it up. There are a lot of people who are heavy but they can't think worth a shit, or they can think a lot but they can't do anything. Huey was a good combination of the two. I've been very proud and privileged to speak on his defense after his death. Give the brother credit where credit is due. Lord knows what he went through.

I had an advantage, I was schooled in the Marxist classics. That was the good thing about having the experience that I had all the way through. There was one jump I had because I was quick enough on the uptake to make some sort of analysis. Now whether my conclusions were right or wrong is a different story. There are some issues I messed up on but other things like proletarian internationalism, man, that's where I draw the line. We're talking about proletarian internationalism we talking about a big battle here. Even with AAPA at UC Berkeley, I'd try to neutralize the negative stuff that was coming down on the movement and try to put proletarian internationalism as the answer to it. I guess I was pretty articulate even in those days. I studied Hegel in its original German text when I couldn't understand the English translated version. And I was twice as confused. As somebody later said that's the way you should have been, now you read Karl Marx and you get a better picture. I had the luxury of a little time to study that stuff too. Since I studied it before things heated up, as they were heating up I had a frame-work.

I know I'm a little biased but the formation of the BPP was one of the greatest things that happened to 20th century America as far as the struggle for freedom, justice, and equality in concerned. It may not have been the perfect organization with the perfect program, but it made a difference. I'm amazed that even to this day how much of a difference it has made, not only in the world, but in my personal life, that I hooked up with something that has been reinforced time and time again that it was the correct thing to do at that time. And I wouldn't take anything away from the brothers and sisters because there was sisters in there too.

DV: Could you talk some more about the role of women in the Panthers?

RA: Yeah, one has to recall that the feminist movement is really an outgrowth of the civil rights struggle. If you look at American history the suffrage movement and the abolitionist movement were pretty tight prior to the civil war. After the civil war they were parting of their ways and each group went along its separate route. I have my own opinions on the gender issue, but when it comes to the BPP organization, the women, as in any revolutionary group, seem to come to the fore in leadership positions. Well, the first female that joined was Joan, also known as Tarika Lewis just fresh out of high school and rose to leadership position. Erika Huggins was another one (whose husband was killed in the early part of the movement) who played a tremendous role with the educational institute in East Oakland. I can't omit Kathleen Cleaver because she served as an inspiration to many of the women who joined afterwards. I can mention others I've known but at this point Tarika and Erika and Kathleen are the three that I point out who were female members of the BPP that did accomplish a lot.

At the 30th anniversary reunion of the BPP in 1996 in Oakland, I had a chance to have a long talk with Kathleen about events we were both involved in during those years. Over the years, I had wondered about my political participation in the BPP, some basic questions I had to answer. I had a chance to talk to a lot of people, and Kathleen and Bobby both reinforced that I had done the right thing. That reunion dispelled any doubts I may have had about my righteous participation in the BPP. And then the warm reception I received as a "veteran fighter." an "O.G.", at the 30th anniversary of the UCB Third World Strike in 1999, also made me feel it was all worth it.

DV: Going back to your earlier point about how people responded most to the 10 point program was on fighting police brutality, how do you see the application of collective resistance, of group self defense today?

RA: I've always thought of collective self defense, it's nice. I like it. I like it, yeah, but I'm afraid people will get too carried away by focusing on the instrument and not on the instrumentor. In other words, the police departments are merely the state being utilized to crush class aspirations, but they are not the total enemy. I pushed that as hard as I could way back then because you can spin your wheel on that issue. People would be fools if they don't fight back against police brutality, so resistance is natural but the one danger I always kept in the back of my mind was it would get too focused on just that one issue, and keep it there. I think today as 30 years ago, that is an area that is full of mine fields. And in the future, the way this society is going, it is going to be a flash point as it has been for numerous other things.

DV: What other lessons would you draw from your history for today?

RA: I have not given up on any of the basic principles that I stood for 30 years ago. I feel the task we started 30 years ago remain unfinished. National liberation was an important question in the 1960s and it remains important today. I consider myself a Marxist-Leninist—Marx for the philosophy and Lenin for how to do it. But I consider myself more Maoist than anything else. Based on my experience, I've seen where unity amongst the races has yielded positive results.

333

I don't see any other way for people to gain freedom, justice and equality here except by being internationalist.

ENDNOTE

The U.S. Government administered a loyalty questionnaire to every adult internee in the concentration camps in 1943. Two questions were particularly troubling to the internees. One question asked if they would swear allegiance to the U.S. And forswear allegiance to Japan, and the other question asked if they were willing to serve in combat duty wherever ordered. Those who answered "no" to both questions were called "No-no boys." The internees had different reasons for answering "no"—from not having had any previous allegiance to Japan and thus not being able to forswear that allegiance, to wanting to avoid separation from family members, to protesting the U.S. Government's unconstitutional incarceration of Japanese Americans. But all "no-no" respondents were deemed unloyal and segregated into the Tule Lake concentration camp.

SECTION FOUR

THE ARTS
THE STRUGGLE FOR IDENTITY AND REVOLUTION

"National Liberation begins as an act of culture."
AMILCAR CABRAL

One week after the assault and eviction, the Workers Committee to Fight For the International Hotel, lead by a veteran Chinese labor organizer, holds a march on Kearny Street to the I-Hotel

The workers Committee in front of the I-Hotel one week later. In spite of the police ring, a crew from the Workers Committee infiltrate the line, climbed to the roof and unravel a banner from the rooftop calling for a re-occupation of the I-Hotel.

DA MENTO HOSPITO

Richard Hamasaki

Eh, somebudi lik make one
big freeway tru my vallee
dey lik bill 'em reel beeg
and strong man
lik one battl ship
so dey can send all dem kars
an trucs an busses
t'rew da mowntans
an make moa
condos an macdonals and purlridges
so da turists, an da grunts, an da locos
can bang each a'da moa

not only dat, but the air fors guys
lik hapai dere missos
tru da mowntans from heekem to mokapu
an bak

one na'da hi'way aint gonna
keel dis iland brah
dis iland alredi dyin—
da hungri politishans
da govament
an da beesnees mens
tink dey can ku'aku'ai da aina
lik one prostitoot

eh, so wat if get one moa hi'way
tru da mowntans
who gives a fricken "A"
about da farmas
da fishamens
da fresh wata
da wind

337

da rain
an da makas
yeh, da eyes,
da makas dat luk da mowntans
an spak da new hi'way runnin
tru da vallee
da eyes dat see nottin'
but one beeg town

an pretti soon
we can drive dawreck—
from halawa prison oneway
to da hawaii state mento hospito
in kaneohe

ENDNOTES FOR "MENTO HOSPITO"

This poem is written in Hawai'i Creole English, or Pidgin. In Hawai'i, Pidgin is a widely spoken language, utilized mostly by native speakers of many ethnicities. Disparaged for decades, in recent years writers of Pidgin have been producing voluminous work, defiantly disregarding criticism and a plethora of negative stereotypes.

First published in the 1980s in a newsletter associated with the University of Hawai'i (UH), this poem has been informally reprinted and used in a number of UH classes. In the 1980s, Professor Charlene Sato, who recently passed away, rendered this poem into Pidgin orthography. Sato's essay "Linguistic Inequality in Hawaii: The Post-Creole Dilemma" provides a comprehensive and enlightening analysis of the politics of language, the marginalization of the Hawaiian language, the demonization of Pidgin, and the inequities created when teaching "standard" English only to elite groups of select students in Hawai'i (in <u>Language of Inequality</u>, Wolfson, N. and J. Manes, editors, Berlin: Mouton, 1985).

This poem was composed in the early 1980s, protesting the construction of the controversial, multi-billion dollar H-3 highway. Recently opened, the freeway destroyed lives, lifestyles, and countless ancient Hawaiian sites, altering forever O'ahu's landscape on both sides of the Ko'olau mountains. Although touted by many, this massive highway project promises even more change: more congestion and pollution, further devastation of indigenous flora and fauna, and significant population and construction project increases on a Pacific island already bursting at the seams.

BEHIND BARBED WIRE

for Grandpa Senri and Grandma Yoshino Nao

Injustice provokes poetry
ruptures imprisoned memories

prolongs the will despite deprivation
laughing in its sleep, sullen even in pain

alone, withdrawn from its own bones' rhythm
groaning this evening, the tide too low for flight

like shadows or a long and tender serpent's tongue
it reaches, picks rusted locks, opens gates

drifts through fences
beyond walls and barriers

tastes, then drinks
mutters and moans

finds humor even in poor company
humiliations lingering in its mind

gazing at mountain peaks
reverberating with urgency

escaping past censors through barbed wire,
iron bars, armed guards

This ancient electricity heats the brain
with thoughts incarnadine

resurging family stories
of cunning artistry

of grandparents hiking through desert
finding then carving stone

grinding black ink with water
wet brushes touching paper

ENDNOTES FOR "BEHIND BARBED WIRE":

This poem is dedicated to my maternal grandparents, Senri and Yoshino Nao, and for their children, who were born in San Francisco: Chiyo Wada, Makoto Nao, Kimi Matsumoto, Chiye Hiura, Setsu Hamasaki, Kazu Harano, Michi Hatano, and Isamu Nao. Shortly after World War II, my grandparents and six of their eight children were evicted and incarcerated, along with some 120,000 immigrants and American citizens of Japanese ancestry. My grandparents, along with several of their children, were first incarcerated at California's Tanforan Racerack, then at a "relocation camp" in Topaz, Utah. Many thousands more, of various ethnic backgrounds, suffered loss and humiliation at the hands of "fellow" Americans acting on behalf of Executive Order 9066. Despite economic ruin, personal defamation, and U.S. government-condoned segregationist policies, my grandparents, along with many others who were incarcerated at Topaz and elsewhere during the war, refused defeat and found solace in art, music, sports, dance, theater, photography, teaching and other endeavors, both creative and community-related. As a child, I remember being told about and seeing the handiwork of my grandparents—double palm-sized rock slabs gathered from their walks through the deserts and surrounding hillsides of Topaz, Utah— beautifully conceived, carved, and smoothed into stone sumi-ink recepticles utilized for grinding and mixing the trademark black ink employed by Japanese calligraphers, poets and artists. In 1982, my brother Mark Hamasaki and I were commissioned by the editors of Bamboo Ridge Press to design and print—on our old Multilith offset press which enabled us to print several publications from our own literary vehicle, 'Elepaio Press—the first edition of <u>Poets Behind Barbed Wire</u>, a special issue edited and translated by Jiro and Kay Nakano and published by Bamboo Ridge (1983). This collection, won a book award from Ishmael Reed's Before Colombus Foundation and featured the works of four poets and an artist, all of Japanese ancestry and residents of Hawai'i, who were incarcerated in American concentration camps during World War II. The featured Hawai'i artist was George Hoshida, and the four Hawai'i tanka poets were Keiho Yasutaro Soga, Taisanboku Motokazu Mori, Sojin Tokiji Takei, and Muin Otokichi Ozaki.

GUERILLA WRITERS

golden rules of english?
conspiracies of languages?

memories unwanted
works are left unknown

if what's to be spoken
needs to be written
sabotage the language

ignore the golden rules

guerrilla writer
barbarize the rules

conspire against
double talk

turn ivy towers
into a babbling school

if what's to be written
mustn't be forgotten

transcribe oral messages
record stories and songs

unleash a conspiracy
of languages

guerrilla writer
barbarize the rules

Recorded and performed in "Most Powerful Nation," Hawaii Amplified Poetry Ensemble, 1989.

SHAKUHACHI

for Grandma Kenzo and Grandma Asano Hamasaki

Look at the strong shoot
bowing below noon wind's mouth
hear smooth hollow sound
soon to be seasoned on earth
bamboo woodwind, five-holed flute

O shakuhachi
measure of eight, the wind song
blown by the bent man,
share with all your inner thoughts
let us hear the birds and wind

In the bamboo grove
near the rock's base where wind moves
hoof beat and bird cry
of two and two together

341

wood tapping and moaning notes
The ancient rhythm
the moving foot stirring air
Eat of the new shoot
sing with the stem of the root
warrior, home from the war

Railroad ties rotting
beneath moist undergrowth near
the old sugar mill
trees swaying at the cliff's edge,
"Plantation's gone," cries the flute

ENDNOTES FOR "SHAKUHACHI":

My paternal grandfather, Kenzo Hamasaki, a Japanese immigrant laborer, arrived at Pa'auilo Sugar Mill on the island of Hawai'i in 1898, the same year Hawai'i was annexed to the United States. He was 21 years old. Five years prior to annexation, haole businessmen, with the aide of the United States marines, illegally overthrew the sovereign nation of Hawai'i and deposed Queen Lili'uokalani. My grandmother, Asano, would later join Kenzo in Hawai'i and also worked for the plantation while raising five sons, all of whom were born in Pa'auilo.

The "warrior" in the fourth stanza is a reference to my father, Richard Noboru Hamasaki, who was born in 1919 in a plantation shack near the cliffside of Pa'auilo adjacent to the now abandoned sugar mill. My father was drafted into the U.S. Army shortly before the attack on Pearl Harbor. Subsequently, my father served in three wars in various capacities, the first two of which included fierce combat experiences, WWII, the Korean War and the Vietnam War.

This poem, structured in tanka-style, is arranged syllabically, 5-7-5-7-7, and each stanza should be capable of standing independently. Presently, but probably not for very much longer, the Pa'auilo Sugar Mill stands, empty and abandoned. Long ago, sugar and pineapple barons permanently reconfigured the Hawaiian landscape and imported thousands of immigrant workers. Recently, one by one, the plantations have been shut down and thousands of workers have been laid-off while the land lies fallow, awaiting for yet another phase of exploitation despite the fact that thousands of Native Hawaiians are on Hawaiian Homes' waiting lists, many of whom will die landless.

LE CAPITALISME NUCLÉAIRE AUX ÎLES PACIFIQUES

Hiroshima and Nagasaki, coastal cities of new-found commerce:
In time, soothing winds blow again even in embittered remembrance,
and a good rain can wash the blood
from the inventor's conscience.

A fine mist weaves new shrouds, in gratitude to
planners, strategists, consultants, specialists, entrepreneurs, politicians,
especially our own, in this high stakes game of "storing" nuclear waste,
worse than ravaging hurricane or tsunami, earth's bane.

Bikini, Enewetak, Moruroa, Fangataufa,
each an umbilicus, portals of our vast ocean body,
but the horror is real, human as lamenting hearts,
refugees of the stillborn, their atolls irradiated with abandon.

Seas emerge as negotiable dumpsites,
expansive churning chameleon fields,
for nuclear holocaust
invisibly toxic for the next twenty-five thousand years.

What conundrums lowered overboard,
secreted cunningly below our waters,
Pandora's gifts inevitably unpackaged by the salty sea
unleashing with each tide, a plague upon all our houses.

And for what? For how many millions of nuclear dollars a day?
billions exchanged for those who must slake their thirst upon island rains,
undermining hunger and the dwindling abundance of seafood
melting on the taste buds of our offspring yet unborn.

ENDNOTES FOR "LE CAPITALISME NUCLÉAIRE AUX ÎLES PACIFIQUES"

In the Pacific Ocean, the United States (between 1946 and 1958), Britain (from 1952 to 1957), and France (from 1966 until recently) have staged well over 200 separate nuclear "tests" in the air and seas surrounding the Marshall Islands, Kiribati, and in "French" Polynesia. The toll of suffering experienced by our fellow human beings in Oceania is manifested in the high rate of radiation-related illnesses such as birth defects, cancer, leukemia, miscarriages and thyroid disease which often plagues local populations located near these former nuclear "test" sites. The toxic consequences of these deadly nuclear "experiments" and the far-reaching presence of poisonous nuclear waste in our earth's food chain have yet to be fully realized.

Despite France's recent curtailment of detonating nuclear bombs in the Pacific, the U.S. continues to utilize some 700,000 square miles of land and water in the Marshall Islands in the North Pacific Ocean as impact zones for inter-continental ballistic missiles launched from Vandenburg Air Force Base in California. Many of Hawai'i's seemingly ubiquitous and restricted U.S. military bases, sitting on prime Hawaiian land, are repositories for nuclear weapons storage sites as well.

Recently, the media has announced multi-billion dollar proposals for nuclear storage waste in Micronesia, particularly in the Republic of the Marshall Islands. This poem obviously protests any attempts to further poison our wansalawata (one-salt-water) as the Pacific Ocean is called in Melanesian Tok Pisin (Pidgin), a language spoken (and written) by over a million people in Papua New Guinea.

WHATEVER HAPPENED TO KALĀHUIPUA'A

Visiting "Mauna Lani," translated heavenly mountain—
  renamed no doubt for its hotel, golf course, condominiums

Renamed "Mauna Lani," for reasons "unknown" to all
  except it's easier pronounced or recalled

Though many would point to the breathtaking view
  and try to impose symbolism or even royal metaphor

"Mauna Lani," foreign in the image it conveys
  among lava flows with springs and beaches and sand

Whatever happened to Kalāhuipua'a?
  by the sea with fishponds far from mountains and snow?

Today Kalāhuipua'a is stripped of its name—
  a place changed, a memory, a conspiracy

Couldn't this ocean resort easily be called "Family of Pigs,"
  or "Pig Gathering," for the wild country pua'a?

Since the power of words is life
  so the power of the name in death must prevail

Just keep calling this place Kalāhuipua'a—
  in memory of its people, their pua'a, and those who usurped the nation.

ENDNOTES FOR "KALĀHUIAPAʻA"

Kalāhuipuaʻa is translated literally in this poem and is a wahi pana, or sacred name-place of Native Hawaiians. Located on the island of Hawaiʻi, the ancient landscape of the former Kalāhuipuaʻa has been radically altered in order to construct an elite resort. A "new Hawaiian" name, Mauna Lani, has been imposed on this traditional wahi pana, whose landscape has now been permanently altered.

Nearly all of Hawaiʻi's luxury resorts are constructed with cathedral-high ceilings. These absurdly high ceilings are designed with gambling in mind. And while gambling is presently illegal in Hawaiʻi, every year new legislation is proposed only to be narrowly voted down. If and when these hotels offer gambling, drop-ceilings can easily be installed, concealing one-way mirrors for hidden video cameras and concealed security catwalks found in major casinos throughout the world. The man-made geographical change that transpired when Kalāhuipuaʻa was destroyed was devastating, to say the least, and examples abound throughout Hawaiʻi, of destroyed landscapes and the imposition of foreign names upon these once revered places. Each wahi pana has characteristics, stories, and memories unique to its place and to the aboriginal peoples who settled here from Oceania. In effect, not only is the land being altered, thanks to "development," but how many traditions which date back 40,000 ago, when humans first began voyaging into the Pacific, have been forever extinguished?

Many thanks to ʻIlima Piʻianaia for escorting and guiding me, in the early 1980s, to Kalāhuipuaʻa prior to its complete alteration. Inspiration for the first drafts of this poem arrived quickly, as soon as ʻIlima had shared the original name with me and as we walked through Kalāhuipuaʻa ancient and memorably exquisite natural landscape, wending our way through bulldozed tracts of lava fields where now stands one of the world's most exclusive resorts, yet another playground for the "rich and famous."

KAMAPUAʻA HAD BALLS

a set of balls
  perfectly hung

his mother sang names to his ears
  and the magic of names is power

Kamapuaʻaʻs the pig
  he created valleys and springs

    He came to a goddess with his balls
  and stopped her with pū hala and olomea

345

and ferns that brush away lava

He cut men down with his teeth
  and fucked their wives against mountains

    Kamapua'a
  your balls contain your power

              in the mountains the cleavage is narrow
        where the pig herd runs over your back

    where no woman has ever stopped you
      where the valleys are wet and steaming

ENDNOTES TO "KAMAPUA'A...":

Kamapua'a is a legendary Hawaiian kupua, or "demi-god," half-human and endowed with god-like powers and strength. In traditional Hawaiian literature, folklore and orature, Kamapua'a is a chiefly trickster and has the ability to "morph" himself into many forms including plants, fish, and other animals or shapes. Various legends also portray Pele, the goddess of the volcano, and Kamapua'a as having both adversarial as well as mutually co-dependent relationships. Metaphorically and geographically, one can interpret that Kamapua'a represents land areas where Pele's volcanic flows are contained or repulsed. In contrast, where Pele reigns supreme, Kamapua'a is vulnerable and often overwhelmed. Traditional Hawaiian and Polynesian poets and priests personified nature exquisitely, celebrating various attributes of natural phenomena metaphorically as well as portraying competitiveness and even collaboration between natural elements—such as the uniqueness and differences between fresh water that gives life to the dry land above and the salt water giving sustenance to the oceanic world below. Traditional Hawaiian literature also discerns and acknowledges differences, conflicts and uniqueness of the sexes rather than merely stereotyping simplistic ploys of male characters and heroes. Kamapua'a, in this poem, is celebrated ironically, his machismo ego and virtual powers had to be reckoned with. Kamapua'a also seems to live metaphorically in our present society in the form of powerful, intelligent, "charming," yet unsatiable, mischievous, and even rapacious males. Furthermore, Kamapua'a manifests himself geologically, where symbolic "male" images of the land can be seen in constant symbiosis and "competition" with the "female" images of the Hawaiian landscape. Pele, with her volcanic powers, provides a powerful contrast to Kamapua'a. She is, after all, still creating new lands, a most significant, pervasive and productive power, especially for we who are surrounded by the hungry "island-eating" yet life-sustaining sea.

PSEUDO-AUTOBIOGRAPHY

Thien-bao Thuc Phi

Why didn't I change my name?

Let me tell you so you can remember this

P-H-I a strange last name for a Vietnamese

T-H-I-E-N dash B-A-O a name more suited to a girl

this name I bore this name I wore growing up in phillips
no I didn't move there/ to be radical I grew up there

and back then growing up in a multicultural context meant
you were gonna get your ass kicked by all different colors of the rainbow

thought this shit was the same as Vietnam
where my birth was the calm before the fall
that tumbled us all
across the ocean

I thought the whole world was pushin me
thought the whole world was a pirate trying
to hold my head under the sea
so in America I lashed out I smashed mouths
I offered testimony with bloody knuckles and chipped teeth
that little asian guys could fight over useless nothing too

but growing up in phillips wasn't all blue
like the times me and my crew would buy red ice pops
in slender plastic sleeves and suck em down
on the way around to cockroach park
we'd sit on the swingsets
dangle our legs and watch the older kids play
basketball
until the sun sank like a golden ball
into a white net of clouds

but when I turned teen it seemed life
turned into a white teen prom date wet dream
and us melanin enhanced and financially challenged
boys faded into the backdrop
we pushed heavy steel carts across the blacktop
at Cub Foods / fellow fools
whose tongues kept rolling even after the carts stopped

I was still running from two languages
so I hopped
till I got hip to this one called rhyme
but was it a crime
I didnt know if I could call the rhyme mine
tongue twisting to signify
I just hip hopped
till I couldnt stop
and flipped flopped
traditional poetry scripts

I memorexed the texts
while my minds eye/
would rewind/ the celluloid
my mind memorized
the imprinted history of those racist times
those faceless crimes
when they said we were
off kilter like a koi's eyes
and wanted to hide
our murders and imprisonment
I put it together with my people's current predicament
and it all seemed
to cement
my non-future

I sought to suture my wounds
wounds I would later learn was ours
not just mine
but at the time
I mimed chaos by writing on streetsigns
to pass the empty times
I got delirious with eddie murphy
who said us asian guys had little dicks
and in reality we were invisible to all the chicks
so I picked up sticks

and smashed car hoods to prove manhood
my body swam in unrest cuz my mind undressed
and was sleeping with stress
I became what was villianized though I was
demaculinized
while more and more broken car antennas
showed up on lawns in my neighborhood
and back then I didn't know why

I thought I would get wise by pursuing
high education so I got a full ride

a scholarship to hop the scholar's ship
but by now I knew not to trust
any rides
the white man offers you on a boat see
a family of refugees/ stuck beneath the sea/
reminded me/ thusly/
they haunt me/
their salt still buying time in my eyes

but I went to the college
learned I wasn't fucked up
I just had "issues"
dis oriental became disoriented
so I stuck to other Asians
but there was some evasion
cuz a lot of those yolkless eggs
souled themselves out by the dozen
seemed my people loved every other color
while hating ourselves
caught up in America's mental cells
invisible death row
wishing we were white and pretending to be multicultural
by rolling up egg rolls
once a year for white folks

I met some who I hoped to call Asian brothers
but I found most talked shit about
who they called faggots
and kept their lip zipped on politics
cuz whites had a tight grip on their dicks
and besides
it might scare off the white chicks

I wasn't one of those cutoff dicks so I tried
to stick with the sisters

but I found most of them to be enamored with
white boys and black boys
demonizing me and my castrated brothers
while seeing all others as individual human beings
particularly making excuses for the not one
but two faces
of the so called raceless caucasians

I met white boys who thought their hand
on their Asian girlfriend's ass was a visitor's pass
into the Asian community
while looking at me like
a dirty thief tugging on their sleeve
for a hershey
these white boys talked revolution
with a raised fist
to get with my sis
acting like
they wouldn't be the first on my hit list

trying to get all marco polo on our yoko ono

I wouldn't let them call me brother
cuz I know my mother
and if she bore a boy like them
she would've raised them better

there seemed to be no hope
asian sisters got exoticized
from True Lies
to the cover of Picture Bride

while asian brothers got demasculinized and demonized
in pop culture genocide
dissed everywhere from textbooks to the classifieds
get half a look or half a paragraph in some book
and we're supposed to be pacified

so now I hide
in the open

balance my need to be better than the nothing
they gave me

and the need to be the beast that they made me

but I won't be
one of those tragic asians
selling yellow fever and dissing my fellows
while fleeing to white folks
who are supposedly faultless
fuck that grandstand handstand hop sing shit
i'm no door jamb i'd rather jamb doors
wide open

and while no one
and I mean no one
ever taught me that Asian men are beautiful
now I'm self-taught

let me remind all of you
of my name
because I won't go away

Thien-bao Thuc Phi
it's not going to change

ACT LIKE YOU KNOW

Her hair is very black and its getting in her eyes
cuts a dramatic outline against the sky
cloudy and big
as a father and a mother.

She is as Vietnamese as the Mekong
as American as powerbook colonialism
explosive like random terrorism
and colorful like creative vandalism

Her hair is very black but she doesn't let it get in the way
when she talks
and if you can't keep up
its the Doppler effect
for you   baby
speech   cryptic   elliptic
like light up neon numbers
on security key pads

you know I don't know what scares me more you know she says
you know she says
the gunshots
or the fact
that I keep brushing my teeth
after I hear them outside my window

you know?
I-I mean it doesn't scare my mom
doesn't stop my mom from rising out of sleep at 3AM
some nights to walk among the vegetables and flowers she planted
and declare her love for summertime
you know?

Her hair is black but it doesn't swing in the way of her walk
steps with carefully measured attitude and/
just the right amount of altitude-
walks like the Hai Ba Trung probably walked,
she walks like a Vietnamese pop song.
you know she says you know she says
for me standing on a street corner with no where to go
is the same as standing on the ledge of a cliff
and looking downwards you know she says you know

she watches as all the neon lights in the city
glow and slam together
like the curved spines of a school
of fish in twilight time

watches as crew cut white boys in sharp white luxury sedans
park in Phillips so they can "get a piece of the rock"
broken cruise ships inside tiny glass bottles
you know she says
I would take all the newspapers in town
and make a pair of wings if the paper wasn't so thin
she says you know she says

and you act like you know
cuz she isn't here to answer any of your questions
she is busy having hair that is black
among amber waves of grain
she is busy planting her colorful words
so that on every street

her mothers flowers will have room to grow
you know
she will not be answering any questions
cuz she is busy
looking into the bleached blond blue contact eye of the world
and struggling to stay awake.

CALLING

it was tough for all of us
those times it seemed
our arms braced between the American dream
and not being seen
raised on this street called 26th
and Bloomington
slipping through the seams in this country's
multi-culti quilt
we called it the same old shit

they called us gook, chink, blanket ass
spick nigger coon
and what was really sad is we called each other that too
went to school and they called us new names:
Native American Asian American
Latino Latina African American and Mixed
while treating us the same way
they called it progress

we called each other Beaulieu, Saice,
Mustafa, Nguyen,
we talked about hip hop and minimum wage jobs
and the girls who broke our hearts
in languages that they call ebonics, pidgen,
res accented, or improper broken english
we called it talkin shit
or I was just fuckin with you

we ran in the confused streets of Phillips
from the police
from the crazies
from our own mothers
we ran

till our chests burned and our hearts
hungered for any place to call home
we ran but we didn't call it running no
we called it hangin we called it doing something
we called it surviving

so remember those times
like when we were sitting around a table
and we heard over the radio
how that gangsta who once chased you with a knife
and once chased you with a steel bar and once
stuck a loaded gun in your gut
remember when we heard he got shot dead
and we didn't know how to feel about it
and we called it life

when the streetlights ran low lookin
like wingless angels with hazy lazy haloes
we sat in damp basements playing nintendo
listening to yo-yo and de la soul
eatin ho-hos drinking ice cold cokes
we called it the days

and sometimes we turned our stereos
up till they would blow stories from the trees
and we danced in those basements or in
the lunchroom or in that building remember
that building Guillermo painted a mural on the
outside wall about respect
we danced a modern day ghost dance we break danced
we salsa'd we cha cha'd we danced becuz we wanted
to impersonate the electricity running
beneath the city that no one is supposed to dig for
we danced becuz we had air in our lungs
that we didn't know what to do with
we danced becuz no one could stop us
we called it living

so when you get out of your fancy college
learning about postmodernist deconstructionist
while still not knowing how to fix your own ride
when you're sitting in Uptown in some cutthroat
coffeeshop with a Phillip Levine book

and a borrowed Powerbook acting like you're no joke

when you can no longer tell
if you're liberating yourself thru expression
or selling your oppression

when they pretend to listen to you
but still wish YOU
WOULD
GO
QUIETLY

remember there were those of us
living here
who called you friend

SURVIVING THE TRANSLATION

She doesn't know what language
this mirror translates her into

she started at age 14 taping her eyes open wide
at night to blind out the look she was giving herself
in the mirror
wishing her reflection yielded to blond not black
standing on her toes to gain
a couple inches.
She takes a sponge soaked in bleach and runs it
over her chinese japanese dirty knees
she gets dizzy
cuz the mirror seems to be turning and turning
and the bleach is burning and burning
this is her forever churning and never learning
yearning a desire for a boy whose whiter
cuz next to him she might look a little lighter
but what's inside of her don't get brighter
and something inside of her dies as she dyes
her hair
her cries the saline solution for eyes blinded
by blue contact cataracts

that burn to the touch
a torch in the form of a zippo
on a grasshut
her yellow skin painting her a Miss Saigon slut
although she's a virgin her outside is fuckin her insides
she doesn't seem to have any allies
white women demonize China for footbinding
while wearing wonderbras and killing themselves with exercize
white boys say they're colorblind
blinded to the fact that they treat her like an
exotic vacation to Sai Gon or a Mai Tai

and some of her Asian brothers tired of getting beat
instead of standing beside her/ pass right on by her
trying to prove manhood by chasing
any white girl that apple pies their eyes
so she tries to get by
trippin about a trip to hell
wishing she wasn't just a mere white slip of herself

she goes to work
a cocktail waitress
getting her ass slapped by salt and pepper haired powerbook VIP's
who've been to the Phillipines
plastic like the packets of saltines
she delivers to tables with pate and buffalo wings
she wishes she could fly out but these white angels
endanger her with their haloes and spangles
left featherless she floats down and stays
child of earth/dazed homeless and heavenless
feeling as authentic as the oriental food section at the supermarket
tugging at her apron lone and lost her mind targets
dreams of Hollywood
but would they let her be real
she could be an uptight sexpot dragonlady on Ally McBeal
maybe hook up with Spielberg
but it looks like he forgot her
cuz he's busy memorizing geishas
she could get television hung as yet another next Connie Chung
too late to begin or she could be a prodigy on Violin
her mind snaps back to the present
the tray of drinks she balances
all bounce back wavy reflections

of herself
her lightened hair feigned amber waves of grain
her blinking blue eyes imitation stars

she stops and puts her apron on the bar
steps away from the whites who
haunt, with hoarse voices, as ghosts
she puts her hands against the glass of the door
and pushes it open, not pausing to check the reflection
she takes out the blue contacts and turns
them into two identical prescription drops of rain
whose final destination is the storm drain
she walks off into the night wondering
if this is a real start
if she can say
this time black eyes and black hair I am
this night I dream how delicious it is to be me
not some white man's sex fantasy
or pieces of white people's pity
but the yellow and black that I learn myself
to love to see
she keeps walking and wonders
if she can make this last
she breathes in the air
and wonders if she can survive
the translation.

YOUNG ASIAN IN LOVE AND IN MOTION

there's barely enuf time to strap on those leather boots and swing
your arms in that dark peacoat,
leave the buttons undone and wrap the straps
around loose while we open the door to

city lights,

cars that cough one eyed like pirates locked on land

we need to move we need to move
before we get stiff like jello
in the icebox,

can't get cold, can't congeal,
we need the motion we need the motion
even this far from the ocean
and on the 21 someone leans over
whispers deep in my ear there's no sex
like
wander
lust.
we can't be far now, we only just started
to smoke,
the lighter flame can stand up to the wind and highlight our skin
young yellow and perilous
and float through the city like the glaciers did,
cut this mothafucka up,
carve these twin cities a new river
so we can flow like frozen

phantom
ships in the fog

under street lamps whose bulbs need replacing
SO WHAT if it snows in march, this is not my room
where the most consistant love is a space heater
and the peaches in heavy syrup demand romance
while we shy away from the sharp edges of the can
we just need to move,
you can't freeze and be in motion
at the same time
so we got to scissor kick through the streets
till we find a shore and keep from drowning so
fuck uptown fuck downtown and god knows
fuck st paul
leave those white scenesters behind who have adopted
someone else's revolution,
they're no better than Disney
dizzy with their own special effects and drunk off acuumba matata
skimmed and trimmed down like Pocahontas
and leaving bare bones the last place they swarmed

fuck
them.

Please.

Bilingual fellow yellow sister this may be just
one night when we're out and about skimming
the land of a thousand lakes with no ice skates,
one night where we avoid point: once upon a time to
point: happily ever after,
one night where we are not prey
to soda commercials soloflex or buns of steel,
maybe just maybe this is one poem that doesn't need to be written
cuz it's happening right now right here as we speak its throwing sparks
in the dark we don't have a spare minute to write down the details
this world this life is holding on to our shirttails
we can write it down next time, we got sequel.

I WAS BORN WITH TWO TONGUES
for the two tongues collective

I was born with two tongues:
one the mekong, red river the other
flowing fluid I pushed soil and carried my people
like suntanned angels on syllables
past the stone tablets of scholars
and premeditated foreign dollars
I dodged the friendly fire of soldiers
who called it love
their eagle wings clipped
and holstered
their red white and blue bolstered
by hershey bars and bayonets
one hand a grenade
the other a pomegranite

I was born with two tongues:
one of salt, the other silt
and I combined them to bridge the bering
born to the earth on a tide of blood
my mother bore me past pirates
and patriots and politicians
who all sounded the same
my father fell in fans of flame
then fastened them on me
so I could fly fearless
then I realized these tongues

of salt and silt
were father and mother

and with these two tongues
called father and mother
I learned the two halves could grow uneven
in this land where whites
only love me when I'm crying or dying
I loved my parents and hated them and
never knew them
then I became them and feared them
loved and forgave them
I rose and fell with voluptuous vietnamese cadences
and beat myself with the blunt edges of english

and now these two tongues I am born with
are yin and yang
prophecy and memory
armed and in harmony
with these two tongues
versus evil I disperse terse verses
that make racists reverse

I use these two tongues
to twist with the tongues
of the woman I love
& to write love
in the three languages between us
until she throws her head back
and sings insanely two songs
of losing and finding
of love and unwinding

and I will tell you this with two tongues
until we all realize
these two tongues
are one

MIRROR IMAGES

Faith Santilla

Kasama
Companeras
Sisters and Brothers
It is through our oppression, pain and suffering that we are
Mirror images of one another

A war is being waged on our bodies, our land and our nations
From supply and demand
From the rise of command of
Imperialist namebrands and
U.S. military stations

Sensationalism of insatiable visions of
Too many males
Impels and impales our struggle for
True equality

Barbie idolatry, leading us to
Barbie ideologies
Leaving us out to die from
Eating disorders or sweatshop occupations

So now,
Where are the warriors that we once were?

Where is Gabriela who fought alongside Diego?
Where is Malinxe?
All of whom drove out the Spanish
While Uncle Sam was on his way

To hand you NAFTA
And to me, APEC
'Cause Presidents Estrada and Zedillo got
American dog collars around their necks
Trained to sit, heel and stay

Well today
Let me tell you
She is in the
Subcomandante Ramona
She is in Ka Juliet
She is the peasant woman whose basic rights have gone unmet

She is
Engaged in tribal warfares
Against a fascist regime in the Cordilleras
She is down the street from here
Celebrating her quincenera

She rallies in Nickerson Gardens
Is picking asparagus up in Stockton
And not too far away
She organizes strawberry workers in
Watsonville

She works
In the factories
And in the sugar mills
Below minimum wage
She is sitting in the audience
She is performing up on stage

She is chanting,
"Imperyalismo! Ibagsak"
She is chanting ,
"E-Z-L-N"
And she is forwarding the revolution
Breastfeeding two babies
And still holding up half the sky

And that is why my kasama
Companeras
Sisters and Brothers
It is through our histories and
Eventual victories that we are
Mirror images of one another.

SUPPOSE REVOLUTION

Cheryl Deptowicz

We weren't supposed to grow up complete
in ourselves
in our dreams
in our trusts.

We weren't supposed to want
change
time for leisure
a better life.

We weren't supposed to know words like justice or call each other comrades.
We weren't supposed to feel when we saw
a homeless man on the streets
a hungry child too weak to cry
a wife recently beaten
a co-worker fired.

We're supposed to
say it's okay
turn our backs
roll up our car windows
look the other way
retch in nonchalance.

He's only a lazy bum.
It's only a dirty flea infested child.
She's only a weak woman who probably asked for it.
He's only a slacker.

We weren't supposed to grow up red.
Red like the silk robes of imprisoned prostitutes in Bangkok.
Like the eyes of a fiery bull or the flag of his Spanish matador.
Red like a dew-dropped Hawaiian hibiscus flower.

Like the flushed cheeks of a newly-sexed teenager.
Red like the swollen bulging tear ducts of an abandoned child.
Like the blood dripping from the bruised lip of my hip hop lover pulled over
    by cops.
Red like the fire of a ghetto rebellion.
Like the rage of a million workers laid-off.
Red like the molten lava beneath our feet ready to erupt.

We weren't supposed to know you.
Yet for millions, billions, trillions, gazillions, everywhere,
You are the ardor of desire
The fire in excitement
The infatuation of craving
The affection of fancy
The love in warmth
The emotion in tenderness
The intensity of anger
The passion in souls...

Revolution, worldwide.

YUGOSLAVIA, CALIFORNIA

Angry advocates count close to 60,000 homeless in the City of LA
The government slashes away
Over 600,000 displaced Kosovars in Yugoslavia by the 70th day.
The government slashes away
NATO powers aim indiscriminately
24 hour air raids sting me.
Bridges
Hospitals
Homes
All destroyed
Affirmative action
Welfare
Jobs
All destroyed

I wake up in Yugoslavia, California
Scarcely two hours into sleep and
the ghetto bird gawks chillingly
circling my roof.
It bellows commands of put your hands up and freeze.

The propellers ring in my ears.
The searchlight blinds my dozing eyes.
The homeless along the alley are jolted awake and try to hide.
The chosen suspect is apprehended.
I hear Eugene Debs:
"While there is a soul in prison, I am not free."

From my bed, I think of the suspect
From which camp, this time?
From the browns?
the blacks?
the yellows?
the reds?
or the working whites?

Was it over drugs as they say on the 11 o'clock news?
Or gang banging as the newspapers would ooze?

Grogginess spins my head
My mouth a cottonball
I think of Mumia in death row
I think of my mother in Stockton Correctional Facilities
Both are innocent but
Racist judges, handpicked juror,s and demonizing trials
try to convince me otherwise.

But the manipulation and the cover-up
 won't work because like the average jane,
I'm two paychecks away from being out on the streets.
My body and politics look like the targets on surveillance screens ready to
aim and fire.
I have no millions to protect myself from their slanderous lies.
No proper enough business suit to give me access to their boardrooms (not
that I'd oblige).
Handcuffs are made for wrists like mine.
Bullets and bombs are tested on people like me, neighborhoods and countries
like mine.
Because I refuse to wear my ball and chain in silence.

Free Mumia!
Free All political prisoners!
Mama, I'm coming to free you.
Your cellmate too!
Free us all.
Break down the wall.
I wake up in Yugoslavia, California.

Ilustration credit: © Todd Hyung-Rae Tarselli

Duck's FEET

Nellie Wong

Ma Ma was lucky
Never had her feet bound
She was the daughter of a peasant
And peasant girls were needed
To work in the fields
Their large, handsome feet
Walked miles for water
Stood for hours planting seed

Stories spilled forth
About Chinese women
Whose feet were bound
From age 6 or 7
Because some emperor
Didn't want his empress
To be running loose
Around the palace
She might be chasing
After an illicit affair
And only the emperor
Was blessed with that privilege

Ma Ma was lucky
She was born into poverty
No high-mindedness
For this peasant girl
With a loud voice
With duck's feet
Nor for her sisters and cousins
Who plowed, cooked and sewed
Unable to dream of
Four-inch feet

Pained from young girlhood
This ritual imposed
On her wealthy sisters
Ensconced in compounds

Taught to be ladies
Who needed to walk,
With the aid of servant girls
Their hands against the walls
Lest they trip and fall

Exotica, the bourgeois man's dream
Sexual fantasies of tasting
These lily feet
No bigger than a six-year-old girl's

Ma Ma was lucky
The village of the Yee clan
Was happy if there were
A few grains of rice
Some bock choy
And bits of pork

And yes sometimes
Some duck's feet
Braised slowly in soy sauce
With ginger and garlic
Duck's feet, a banquet
Over long grain rice
Some homemade wine
And cool grass jelly
To alleviate hot summers,
Flies hovering like invited guests

Ma Ma was lucky
She came to America
Only to see Bah Bah's cousin's wife
With bound feet
She was called Fourth Auntie
We children called her Ah Thlee Moo
She wore round, wire-rimmed glasses,
Her black hair a short bob
As a child I thought

Ah Thlee Moo was a lady
Only ladies had bound feet
Even in America

Those dead ladies
If they could talk
Would have loved
The duck's feet
Of their poor relatives
Planting rice in the blazing sun

Those dead ladies
If they could talk
Would have cut off
Their bound feet
Would have grown
If they could
New, beloved duck's feet

WHAT DOES IT MEAN?

What does it mean to me,
A Chinese American woman,
To have Mumia sitting on Death Row
For over 17 years?

What does it mean to me,
A retired worker, a poet,
To have "The Voice of the Voiceless"
Writing us from his prison cell?

What does it mean to you and me,
Working people, radicals, socialists, anarchists,
That this capitalist system
Killed Sacco and Vancetti,
Bombed MOVE in Philadelphia?

What does it mean to the sisters and brothers,
Puerto Rican revolutionaries,
That Clinton offers clemency
With restrictions attached?

What does it mean to people of the First Nations,
Cherokee, Mohawk, Menomonee, Lakota,
That the Indian Wars are still on,
Killed Jancita Eagle Deer, Anna Mae Pictou Aquash?

What does it mean to the imprisoned.
Our sisters and brothers in Dublin, Lompoc,
That freedom is beyond the padlocked bars,
That nothing is free is this land of the free?

What does it mean to Leonard Peltier, Marilyn Buck,
The women on welfare with children to feed,
That the lives of women and people of color
are disposable trash in the eyes of the oppressor?

Let's let brother Mumia know what we mean
Let's let brother Ruchell McGee know what we mean
Let's tell them we, the people, understand
That until there are no 60 richest families
Running havoc on our lives
That until there are no more IMFs, GATTs, WTOs
That until the workers control industry
That until the First Nations get their lands back
That until Affirmative Action is a natural process
That until there are no more sexual slaves in Russia, Korea, America
That until violence ceases against lesbians, gays, bi's, transgenders
That until there is no more HIV, brown lung disease, cancer
That until Mumia and all other political prisoners walk free
That until we have socialism which means
A planned economy and everyone gets their needs met

That we mean business, not waging war in Iraq, Yugoslavia, Indonesia
That we mean the guys in suits cannot buy us off
Put us in highrise buildings, giving us perks
Here's a nice office for you
Here's a bonus for you
Here's a chocolate bar for you
So we don't make noise
So we sleep in front of the TV
So we think we're free
Passive, compliant, obedient
So they think they've crushed us

When our resistance must threaten the powers
Of domination, incarceration, disintegration,
Abomination, militarization, gentrification

'Cause what it means is Revolution
revolution of our minds, our bodies and souls
revolution for the working class, by the working class,
the poor, disabled, youth, elders, the unprotected

'Cause what it means is Revolution
revolution for the homeless, the evicted
revolution for single moms, gay parents
revolution for runaway teens, locked out children

'Cause what it means is Revolution
revolution without borders
revolution for all the races and sexes
revolution for you and me

'Cause we're gonna take the power
our women power, our men power,
our children power, our workers' power

'Cause we run the factories, the minefields
the assembly lines, the strawberry fields
the railroad lines, airlines, and cyberspace

Let's tell Mumia
He's gonna be free
That the spirit of Malcolm is with us
That it doesn't matter that I'm Chinese,
She's Jewish and he's Nicaraguan
Our children are Cuban, Jamaican, Korean

'Cause we know what it means
to fight back and win
'Cause we know what it means
why Mumia's been on Death Row
these past 17 years

'Cause Mumia stands against police brutality
against racism and brutalization of women
against invasion of Third World countries
against violence against our youth

'Cause Mumia gives us hope
his words, his courage, his very life

That's what it means
It means Revolution
On our terms, in our time

R E V O L U T I O N
Spell it out, spell it!
Sing it out, sing it!
Carry it out, carry it!
REVOLUTION!

Especially written for MUMIA 911, an International Day of Art to Resist the Execution of Mumia Abu-Jamal and to DEMAND a new and fair Trial, ILWU Hall, 255 9th Street, San Francisco, California

DANCING OUTSIDE THE AMERICAN DREAM
History and Politics of Asian Dance in America[1]

Peggy Myo-Young Choy

The Legacy of Invisibility

"I am a thief and I am not ashamed. I steal from the best wherever it happens to me . . . . I am a thief and I glory in it. . . . "
Martha Graham, from The Notebooks of Martha Graham[2]

These are the words written by the late Martha Graham in her dance notebooks. Graham is considered one of the foremost pioneers of modern dance in America. On the day following her death in April, 1991, *The New York Times* eulogized Graham as " . . . . a prime revolutionary in the arts of this century and the American dancer and choreographer whose name became synonymous with modern dance. . . ."[3] Dance historian Deborah Jowitt emphasizes how Graham would "start from scratch, concentrating on the pulse of the body."[4]

But Graham herself openly admits that she did not start from scratch. Not only is she proud of her thievery, she does not acknowledge those people from whom she has plundered. It is difficult to ignore the incongruity in the photograph of Graham which appeared with obituaries in both *The New York Times* and *Dance Magazine.*[5] In this portrait, taken in 1984 by Hiro, she sits on a chair of Chinese design, with her hands shrouded in her sleeves. It seems that Graham wants to look more like a Chinese dowager empress rather than what she really is—an Anglo choreographer.

In a public radio feature I heard on Graham in 1990, she is quoted as saying, "I tried to teach people exotic ways to move." What are some of these "exotic ways" of moving? As someone who has studied Graham's technique, it seems evident to me that some of her movements—particularly those in which the dancer is seated on the floor—are borrowed from the South Asian yoga tradition. She also borrowed from Japanese and Chinese theater forms.[6] Her early choreography expressed Asian themes, including pieces such as "The Three Gopi Maidens," "Three Poems of the East," and "Flute of Krishna" (all choreographed in 1926), and "Chinese Poem" (choreographed in 1928).[7] Her choreography was often located in and about sets designed by Asian American sculptor, Isamu Noguchi (of Japanese-Caucasian ethnicity).

Other Asian—specifically Southeast Asian—influences are decipherable in her own dance notes. For her work, "Night Journey," she writes, "Rise into 2 Bali turns...Rise into Javanese foot movement... "[8] There is no evidence that Graham ever studied Southeast Asian (i.e. Javanese or Balinese) dance. We do know that she studied at the Denishawn School in Los Angeles, from 1916 to 1923, and subsequently joined the Denishawn Company.[9] In fact, it was Ruth St. Denis (founder of the Denishawn School along with Ted Shawn) who inspired Graham to be a dancer. Seeing St. Denis perform in 1911, Graham reminisces: "She was more than exotic— I realize now she was a goddess figure. I knew at that moment I was going to be a dancer."[10]

We also know that in 1922, she performed a "pseudo-Javanese dance" choreographed by her teacher, Ruth St. Denis. Those knowledgeable about Javanese dance can tell you that the hand position pictured does not exist in Central Javanese dance vocabulary. The head is angled skyward with chin held high and mouth open, and the toes curl under instead of up. These are all aberrations of the dance. St. Denis as choreographer and Graham as dancer felt little need for accurate, respectful representation.

Writing in 1988, Jowitt refers to St. Denis as, "perhaps the most famous of all Oriental dancers . . . . who found the East to be a storehouse of guises." According to Jowitt, "Asia was her better self."[11] While Jowitt is aware of the phenomenon of Orientalism and its impact on dance,[12] she writes this statement without questioning the term "Oriental" itself, and thus lends credence to attempts by Anglo choreographers like St. Denis to use what they thought to be Asian culture. Nevertheless, Jowitt refrains from any critical analysis which would view St. Denis as one who exploited Asian culture in her attempt to become the "exotic other." By doing so her career, ultimately affirmed Western hegemony.[13]

In a poem, St. Denis describes her own portrayal of a Chinese boddhisatva in her 1926 solo, "White Jade":

"I am Kuan Yin on the Altar of Heaven . . . . my body is the living temple of all Gods."[14]

She physically appropriated the Chinese boddhisatva image, and by so doing, arrogantly and erroneously asserted her ego in direct contradiction to the meaning of Kuan Yin—that is, of compassion and egolessness. She also attempted to portray an Indian beggar-prostitute in the "Nautch Dance"—a dance of the same title exists in India but bears no resemblance.[15] St. Denis created yet another imagined Asian image in her work, "O-mika," with her portrayal of a Japanese prostitute who entertains prospective customers with dances including a sword dance. St. Denis even sought to portray "Madame Butterfly"[16]—the premier example of the Orientalist female stereotype—the exotic, flower-like beauty who ultimately destroys herself because of her love for an Anglo male. Elaborate quasi-Asian stage settings augmented St. Denis' "transformations." According to Jowitt:

Dances came to her [St. Denis] in the form of pictures, of landscapes. . . . These luminous settings—a vine-draped temple in India, a Chinese shrine, a bazaar, a Japanese brothel. . . .—were keyed to a transformation of herself.[17]

By appropriating what she thought to be Asian images in Asian settings, St. Denis created imagery that crystallized stereotypes for the American public to digest into their psyche for years to come. St. Denis says of herself, ". . . . I had to be an Indian—a Japanese—a statue—a something or somebody else—before the public would give me what I craved."[18] Of course, St. Denis was not an Indian nor Japanese. Implicit in St. Denis' statement is the sense that Anglo Americans prefer to watch the exotic "other" on stage in the form of Anglos trying to be Asian rather than Asians being themselves.

In the 1990s, Anglos continue to frame themselves within Asian terrain. Dancer and choreographer Molissa Fenley situates herself in the middle of a Japanese-style rock garden setting designed by Richard Long, and calls her dance "contemporary" dance.[19] American dance history books almost without fail include Isadora Duncan, St. Denis, Graham, Cunningham, and usually end with Twyla Tharp.[20] What is absent from these books are dances by and about Asians. The history of Asians dancing in this country is invisible and unacknowledged. But we know we are more than "a something or a somebody else."

It is time to renegotiate terms such as "modern dance" and "contemporary dance," because these terms legitimize thievery and the invisibility of Asians (not to mention other people of color). These terms cut off the past and ignore the dance history and dance knowledge of Asians in this country. Such renegotiation is fraught with difficulty because these terms are part of the political, cultural and economic hegemony of the dominant white settler society. Nevertheless, as part of this renegotiation process, it is crucial to rewrite American dance history to include the dance works of Asians and other people of color.

Asian Americans Dancing: Talking Story to Pierce the Silence

Asians have been choreographing in America since at least the 1930s. For example, my grand-aunt, Ha Soo Whang, was choreographing and teaching Korean dance to the Hyung Jae Club women and girls in Honolulu in the 1930s. Halla Pai Huhm began her Korean dance school in Honolulu between 1949 and 1950.[21] In my attempt to begin to piece together this silenced history, I "talked story" with a number of Asian American women choreographers, a process in itself empowering. I present four stories here.

Martha Nishitani

At the time I spoke with Martha Nishitani in 1991, she was 71 years old. She was designated "Asian American Living Treasure" in 1984 by the Northwest Asian American Theater. She established her own school of creative dance in Seattle. She says she was influenced by Doris Humprey and Martha Graham, but went on to develop her own technique. In 1952, she performed her work about the fall season called, "Transit into Dormancy."

Her incarceration at Camp Minidoka during World War II left some intense memories—of barbed wire, of soldiers with guns. Yet, she does not think the internment limited her choreography. She did not grow up with knowledge about Japanese culture. However, she thinks her love of nature and her slow movements are reflections of her Japanese ethnicity.[22]

Janice Mirikitani

Known foremost as an Asian American poet, Janice Mirikitani minored in dance at UCLA's School of Fine Arts. There she learned Graham technique which held dramatic appeal for her. She has often used dance as an adjunct to her poetry.[23]

In 1983, she choreographed a piece for her poem, "Prisons of Silence," for the Asian American Dance Collective. Her preoccupation with the internment and redress was due to her family's incarceration. She herself was there as an infant. Her parents' silence about the experience created a lot of anger in her. The piece was her strategy of resistance and assertion of herself. In 1988, she worked with non-professional dancers—women recovering from crack and cocaine abuse. In 1990, she choreographed a piece for those afflicted with AIDS.

Sun Ock Lee

Sun Ock Lee studied dance in Korea from the age of nine. She learned Korean dance from Yi Mae Bang, and also studied ballet, modern and Indian dance. At 13, she enjoyed learning Graham technique. After coming to New York in 1969, she developed her own form of meditational dance, called Zen Dance/Son Mu, which was based on her own exploration process and Buddhist practice. Not satisfied with only dancing "traditional" Korean forms, she felt a need to "break away and take a leap to find my own voice."[24] She believes her Zen Dance/Son Mu could not have developed in Korea. "If you want to see your homeland, you have to leave your homeland. If want to win over the enemy, you have to know the enemy."[25] Living in New York gave Lee a clear sense of her identity as a Korean who crosses geographical and cultural borders.

Alleluia Panis

This is Alleluia Panis as she appears in the cast of Fred Ho's "A Song for Manong," as choreographer and dancer in 1988. She came with her family from the Philippines to live in San Francisco during the 1960s. At Galileo High School, she learned modern dance from Klarna Pinska, a protegé of Ruth St. Denis. Alleluia herself learned and performed St. Denis' "Nautch Dance"—the solo depicting an Indian beggar-prostitute. As a teenager, Alleluia did not feel uncomfortable performing the dance. From her perspective at the time, it was a theatrical exercise.[26] She was supported and encouraged by Klarna Pinska, who Panis felt was sensitive about race issues.

Sun Ock Lee
Photo credit: John Chang McCurdy

Martha Nishitani
Photo credit: Uyeno

Alleluia Panis
Courtesy of Fred Ho

Towards the Creation of Asian American Dance

Water-tight or "pure" experiences do not exist for any of us as Asian American dancers. Within the boundaries of our dance lives we have met with Anglo dance forms through the mainstream performance world and institutional curriculum. We have met with Asian dance forms and Anglo distortions of Asian forms. The racist ramifications of the famous Anglo "pioneers" like Graham need to be highlighted. For myself, I felt that with the Graham technique there was a place for me as a dancer of Asian ethnicity, whereas I felt at the margins with ballet. Did I feel more accepted in modern dance because I vaguely sensed the influence of Asian forms however grossly distorted, however appropriated? Or was it because the Asian members of Graham's company—such as Takako Asakawa—fulfilled our need for role models? Unaware of the Orientalist history out of which emerged "modern dance," I believed I had discovered some sense of my own Asian identity, but in fact, I was learning that Orientalist history through movement. Yet, for all of the Asian women spoken with, as well as myself, having studied and enjoyed Graham technique, we have since gone beyond. I now teach a class called "Asian American Movement," which integrates Asian American literature, improvization, meditational movement, Asian dance and martial arts—all of which form the basis for my choreography. Through my choreography, I connect with an "imagined lineage" of women—most of whom I have never met. For example, my work includes portraits of the Korean *sajin shinbu* (picture brides), *chongshindae* (comfort women, sex slaves to the Japanese military), and other fearless women, such as Black Panther Assata Shakur and Sarraounia, the queen of Burkina Faso.

Resistance and the assertion of our own dance comes through our process of searching for and claiming our heritage in America. It means navigating through stereotypes and what others assert as representations of our selves, and moving through our own processes of identity formation through creation of new work. As we learn more about our ancestor's performance knowledge and how they brought this knowledge here as settlers, we have the responsibility to learn about it deeply, respectfully and carefully. Our excavating the past includes looking at the history of our ancestors, as active people with bodies in perpetual movement. They brought with them from their home countries valuable strategies of health and indigenous knowledge of the body—herbs for tired and sick bodies, massage after a beating or a day's hard labor in the fields. We are left to our own renewable resources (such as ki energy) to create strategies of resistance to survive in a country that does not acknowledge the diversity of our identities, let alone our active participation in the creation of this country's cultures. It is a daily struggle to "move the center,"[27] to create pathways to visibility, to alter the hegemonic perception that there are only a few legitimate ways to move.

During the 1960s and 1970s, according to Alleluia Panis, many Asian American choreographers did not want to touch "ethnic" dance for fear of being labeled for life and kept out of the mainstream dance world.[28] When we as dancers can engage in both political and artistic change, when we can openly acknowledge our roots which extend as deeply into the past as they grow towards future transformation, we can imagine the beginnings of an Asian American history of movement.

Peggy Myo-Young Choy
Photo credit:
Steve Eliasen

Sources Cited

Clifford, James The Predicament of Culture: Twentiety-Century Ethnography, Literature, and Art (1988), Cambridge, Harvard University Press.

Foster, Susan Leigh Reading Dancing: Bodies and Subjects in Contemporary American Dance (1986), Berkeley, University of California Press.

Graham, Martha The Notebooks of Martha Graham (1973), New York, Harcourt Brace Jovanovich, Inc.

Gruen, John "Molissa Fenley: A Separate Voice," in *Dance Magazine* (1991), May, pp. 38-41.

Hardy, Camille "Martha Graham, American Pioneer, May 11, 1894-April 1, 1991," in *Dance Magazine* (1991), June, V. LXV, no. 6, pp. 18-19.

Jowitt, Deborah Time and the Dancing Image (1988), Berkeley, University of California Press.

Kisselgoff, Anna "Martha Graham Dies at 96; A Revolutionary in Dance," in "Obituaries," in *The New York Times*, April 2, 1991, V. CXL, no. 48,558, pp. A1, B7.

Said, Edward Orientalism (1979), New York, Vintage Books.

Sorell, Walter "Martha and the Myth," in *Dance Magazine* (1991), V. LXV, no. 7, pp. 53-57.

Wa Thiong'o, Ngugi Moving the Centre: The Struggle for Cultural Freedoms (1993), London, James Currey.

ENDNOTES

1. The first version of this article appeared in *Movement Research Performance Journal*, no. 4, winter/spring 1992. Other publications featuring this article include, *Forward Motion*, Vol. II, No. 3, July 1992; and *Inside Arts*, Sept. 1993.
2. Graham, p. xi.
3. Kisselgoff, p. A1.
4. Jowitt 1988:164
5. Kisselgoff, p. B7; Hardy, p. 19.
6. Jowitt, pp. 214-226.
7. Sorell, p. 56.
8. Graham, p. 158.
9. Hardy, pp. 18-19; Kisselgoff, p. B7.
10. Mason, p. 28.
11 Jowitt, pp. 125, 147.
12. Jowitt, pp. 49-65.
13. See Edward Said's ground-breaking discussion in Orientalism (1978) and James Clifford's discussion of "Orientalism" in his book, The Predicament of Culture (1988).
14. Jowitt, p. 128.
15. Purnima Shah, personal communication.
16. Jowitt, p. 129.
17. Jowitt, pp. 136-137.
18. Jowitt, p. 137.
19. The title of one of the three solos danced in the rock garden is called "Bardo," (a term from Tibetan Buddhism) and is danced to a "mantra" by Somei Satoh. (Gruen 1991:39) The Asian influence is unacknowleged. Typically, dance critic Anna Kisselgoff emphasizes Fenley's solitary individualism which relates to no tradition. She writes, "Molissa Fenley remains one of the experimental dance scene's most independent choreographers, admirably beholden to no faction or fashion." (Gruen 1991:39)
20. Examples include Susan Leigh Foster's Reading Dancing Bodies and Subjects in Contemporary American Dance and Deborah Jowitt's Time and the Dancing Image.
21. Mary Jo Freshley, personal communication, 5/91.
22. Martha Nishitani, interview, 5/91.
23. Don Mar, interview, 5/91.
24. Sun Ock Lee, interview, 5/91.
25. Ibid.
26. Alleluia Panis, inteview, 5/91.
27. See Ngugi wa Thiong'o's seminal book, Moving the Centre: The Struggle for Cultural Freedoms.
28. Ibid.

THE BROWN POWER POET
Serafin Malay Syquia (1943-1973)

Fred Houn

Serafin ("Serf") Malay Syquia was one of Pilipino America's most powerful poetic voices. At the time of his death at the early age of 30 from a brain tumor, Syquia had emerged as a leading and prolific Third World writer and deeply committed political activist. Moved by the upsurge of third world peoples' struggles abroad and in the U.S., Syquia, a product of the late 1960's, left a career as a stockbroker virtually overnight to consume his life activity and creative energy in the struggles of his Pilipino American community and the movement for social change. Indeed, his strength as a poet/artist stemmed from mirroring his own personal transformation as it increasingly connected with the collective life of the Pilipino American masses in both his art and social practice.

A quite and gentle man, his poems, however, expressed an unmitigating anger and determined opposition to the exploitation of the Pilipino people (both in the U.S. and in the Philippines). Serafin loved his people. His art and life were devoted to the self-respect, dignity, and empowerment of Pilipinos, Asians, and Third World peoples. His sacrifice, energy and spirit of revolutionary optimism represented the finest of that generation of Asian American cultural workers.

His first experience in political struggle was the movement to save the International Hotel in San Francisco's Chinatown/Manilatown, a historic battle to defend a Third World community from destruction. Through his involvement with the I-Hotel, he became very close to and was touched by the lives and struggles of the manongs, the elderly Pilipino male workers. Many of his poems capture the experiences and personalities of the manongs.

With other Pilipino American writers, such as Oscar Penaranda, Emilia Cachapero, Bayani Mariano, and Al Robles, Syquia worked daily in the Filipino American communities. The lives, the language and stories of the Filipino American masses became the inspiration for their poetry. Indeed, these young writers had also emerged at the forefront of a new Pilipino American cultural movement that expressed pride in Pilipino American identity ("Brown is Beautiful/We are an Oppressed People") — writers that sought to inspire the people to struggle. Syquia was probably the leading developer of a Pilipino American poetry of resistance: culture to expose the lies of racist stereotyping, to be a force for irresistible beauty and irrepressible truth.

Syquia was one of the coordinators of Ating Tao ("Our People"), formed at San Francisco State University as a Pilipino American performing arts/theater collective. Ating Tao combined traditional Pilipino and modern dance, music, and poetry and agitprop theater, and performed extensively to Pilipino American communities throughout the West Coast.

He was also part of the core of Black, Asian, Latino and Native American writers that formed Third World Communications in 1971, a cutting-edge alliance of a number of the major contemporary oppressed nationality writers of that period, including Janice Mirikatani, Roberto Vargas, Ntozake Shange, Jessica Hagedorn, Buriel Clay, among many others.

A serious writer, Syquia was constantly writing and perfecting his craft. He had studied creative writing at San Francisco State University where he earned both his bachelor and masters degrees. His literary influences were broad, though his major inspiration came from writers with a militant political vision. These included: Imamu Amiri Baraka, Pablo Neruda, Amado Hernandez, Janice Mirikitani, Kay Boyle (his professor at State), as well as William Carlos Williams and e.e. cummings.

Syquia was very aware of the Pilipino American tradition based on the lives and stories of the manongs. So many unpublished poems by Serafin Syquia were discovered after his death that they could comprise an important collection documenting his contributions to the continuum of Pilipino American literature. Along with such writers as Carlos Bulosan, Philip Vera Cruz, Joaquin Legaspi, Bienvenido Santos, Sam Tagatac, N.V.M Gonsales and the oral traditions of the Pinoy workers, Serafin Syquia remains an example to this and future generations of Pilipino and Asian American cultural workers.

Writings by Serafin Syquia are found in the following:

Selected Poems: Serafin Malay Syquia, published by friends, 1973;

Two Poems by Serafin Syquia, broadside, published by Anita Burrows, 1973;

Anthologies:

Time to Greez!, Mirikatani, et al., Glide and Third World Communications, 1975;

Perspectives, E.O.P. Third World Journal, San Francisco State University, 1973;

Liwanag, Liwanag Publications, 1976

Kapatid, San Francisco State University journal, 1971

AION, Asian American Publications,1971

Flips, An Anthology of Poems, Syquia, editor, 1971.

Special thanks to Luis Syquia, Mrs. Amelia Syquia, and Janice Mirikatani.

REVOLUTIONARY ASIAN AMERICAN ART
Tradition and Change, Inheritance and Innovation, Not Imitation!

Fred Houn

Several Scores of days detained in this wood house
All because of some inked rules which involve me.
Pity it is that a hero has no way of exercising his power.
He can only wait for the word to whip his horse on a homeward journey.

From this moment on, we say goodbye to this house,
My fellow countrymen here are rejoicing like me.
Say not that here everything is western styled.
Even if it were built with jade, it has turned into a cage.

Poem carved into barracks wall by an anonymous Chinese immigrant while detained at Angel Island Immigration Station.

Revolutionary Traditions in Asian American Culture and Art

At the time that the first Chinese contract laborers were brought to America, in China, Cantonese opera actor Li Wenmao was leading an armed uprising against the Chinese imperial government in 1854 during the Taiping Rebellion. All performances of Cantonese opera were subsequently banned and went underground. Thus, for more than a decade, Cantonese opera could only be openly performed abroad in overseas Chinese communities.

Cantonese opera was especially prevalent and popular in the Chinese community in America among the early Asian laborers and is one of the earliest forms of Chinese American culture, gradually evolving to incorporate the experiences of the Chinese in America. (An early example is a Cantonese opera about Angel Island presented in the early-20th century.) As an early Chinese American cultural form, Cantonese opera is also an example of the revolutionary roots of the Asian American cultural tradition.

The tradition of Asian American culture and art is essentially progressive and contains a strong revolutionary current. This should come as no surprise since culture reflects the objective condition and character of the people. Since Asian/Pacific peoples in America have been continually oppressed, the dialectic would suggest that there has been resistance.

Other early Asian American folk cultural forms include oral tradition of folk stories, ballads, chants and folk songs brought over by the early Asian laborers from their peasant oral traditions. Carried over from their homelands, these oral traditions were a common part of life in the Asian labor camps along the West coast and became increasingly shaped by the struggle to survive in America, i.e. the contradiction between the dreams of Gold Mountain and the painful and brutal realities of contract labor.

Other examples include: The *muk-yu-go* (wood-fish song), a form of narrative chant derived from the popular Cantonese oral narrative tradition. While chanting, a fish-shaped wood block was beaten for rhythm. An example of such a chant appeared in a publication in Canton in 1905 during the boycott of American goods to protest the extension of the Chinese exclusion laws in the U.S. This piece was entitled "Nights Cantos of the Gold Mountain Man", and conveyed feelings of banishment and indignation over the agony and injustices faced by the Chinese in America.

Another example is the 46-syllable Cantonese folk song form called the *seisapluk jigo* with its 8-line patterns and 5-5-7-7-3-5-7-7 syllables, each ending with a rhyming syllable. These were often written and sung in the colloquial language. The only remaining collection of these folk songs is an anthology of over 1,000 of such pieces published in two volumes in 1911 and 1915 entitled *Jian Shan Geji* (Songs From Gold Mountain), of which 246 of these songs have been translated into English by Professor Marlon Hom of UCLA.

Of course, there is an example of the poetry carved into the wooden barracks of Angel Island – hundreds of anonymous poems of the pain, loneliness, suffering and anger from being incarcerated in that hell-hole interrogation station.

One of the earliest examples of published Asian American literature is a collection of stories called *Ku Shehui* (The Bitter Society), published at the turn of the century and complied as a collective literary outcry against the extension of the Chinese exclusion laws.

This is the folklore of Asians in America. By definition, folk culture is a collective body of community-derived traditions and forms with no specific authors or creators, simply a part of the community's life. As such, folk forms and literature may not necessarily be well crafted works, serving more as a functional part of daily work, ceremonies, rituals and social life, as distinct from art which developed primarily for aesthetic expression. We can clearly see that this beginning Asian American cultural tradition has been closely rooted to the Asian communities and to the lives of Asian workers. The themes of these traditional works express common feelings and experiences of separation, loneliness, disappointment, bitterness, pain, anger and struggle.

Asian American culture and literature cannot be correctly defined as works solely in the English language. Rather, the great body of the Asian American cultural tradition emanates from the working class Asian communities and is in the Asian languages and dialects.

I am opposed to the mistaken idea that early Asian American literature is represented by Lin Yutang, Pardee Lowe, Etsu Sugimoto, Jade Snow Wong and other privileged writers of the merchant, high scholar, diplomatic and business class in America. These writers wrote in English for white publishers and to reach a white audience. As reflective of that small emerging petty bourgeois class of Asian Americans, their literature sought white acceptance, promoted the boot-strap path and projected their class interest: to be accepted by white society as model minorities, to be a credit to their race. They portrayed Chinatown as exotic, often apologizing for their community. Their literature was not the literature of the vast masses of Asians in America. It is my contention that even as literature, their writings are narrow and limited in their emotional breadth and experience, whereas the vast body of literature emanating from the working class communities evokes and conveys a broader range of feelings and expression.

During the 1930s and 1940s, there was an active literary movement in San Francisco's and New York's Chinatowns influenced by the strong presence of Left organizations in American labor and oppressed nationality struggles.

Chinese Americans Marxist writers were especially catalytic in generating many new community publications. Most of these were in Chinese. At first, the themes of these writings dealt mainly with China's national salvation from warlordism, feudalism, and foreign imperialism. But as the Asian workers' struggles in the U.S. intensified, these publications came to address the struggle and lives of Chinatown workers and small business.

One of the main writers in this Chinatown literary movement was Ben Fee (president of the Chinese Workers Mutual Aid Association – CWMAA – and Chinese section leader of the then—revolutionary Communist Party USA). Ben Fee was later "found" by Frank Chin as an example of an original "Chinatown Cowboy" type for Chin's own self-serving purposes, totally disregarding the fact that Ben Fee was a communist.

Along with Ben Fee in San Francisco was Happy Gin Fu Lim, then-secretary of the CWMAA. While Ben Fee wrote in the old-style of writing, Happy Lim was an exponent of the new literature and developed and organized the New China Alphabet Language Association.

One of the giants of Asian American literature who wrote in that era was H.T. Tsiang, all but totally unknown to today's generation of Asian American writers. Tsiang was a communist intellectual and writer who wrote for the most part in English.

Tsiang published four books, three of which he self-published because the white capitalist publishers would not do so. Tsiang boldly published their rejection letters to him in his books. Tsiang's novel about a New York City Chinatown laundryman, And China Has Hands, is extremely funny, satiric and witty, yet politically very advanced and profound. Tsiang was hip before hip was hip, even making cameo appearances himself in his own books. Tsiang claimed to have distributed 16,000 copies of his The Hanging On Union Square, boldly denouncing the censorship of him as a revolutionary Chinese American writer for his proletarian politics. The endings to his books are caught up in sweeping socialist romanticism, but that was typical of that era of Left-wing writers and researchers need to reclaim these great Asian American literary giants.

One of the most powerful of the critical realist writers of this era was Carlos Bulosan. His <u>America is in the Heart</u> is, as E. San Juan Jr. describes, "a veritable masterpiece in a genre of chronicling a young man's pilgrimage that in turn symbolizes the collective rite of passage of the Filipino working class in exile."

These writers represented diverse stylistic tendencies. They were also activists in the class struggle, which gave their work truthful beauty and vitality. This has been the revolutionary heritage of Asian American literature and culture.

Further examples in this progressive heritage include the profusion of art, sculpture, crafts and poetry from the Japanese Americans interned during the concentration camps – passionate, filled with vibrant realism.

Though not Leftist, artist and writers such as Miné Okubo, Toshio Mori, Hisaye Yamamoto, Sui Sin Far (Edith Eaton) created moving works about the lives of the community people – stories about their work, families, love and conflicts. Often of a personal nature, yet these writings are intimately connected to community life, filled with compassion, sensitivity and a depthful understanding.

And another example of a great work of Asian American literature connected to the community and to the lives of its people is Louis Chu's <u>Eat a Bowl of Tea</u>, a classic in Asian American writing. Chu, in my opinion, was an innovator, a Chinese American innovator whose own writing voice was able to realistically capture the feelings and meanings of everyday Chinatown communication. Simply, but in all of its complex profundities.

It is my contention that Asian American art is not the loose collection of voices of artists who happen to be Asian American. Rather, Asian American culture and art is a collective body of folk and art traditions, a continuum to which our works will be judged. And I have tried to argue that within this continuum, there are different class tendencies. The strongest and most powerful works have been closely connected and rooted in the community, to the lives of the Asian American working class, while those works representing the Asian American petty bourgeoisie are more water-down and white-assimilated and are weaker examples, peripheral to the thrust of this continuum. For Asian American cultural criticism, the point is not that each work represents a voice of a specific artist's experience, but what that voice is saying about Asian American life. Thus we can not evaluate an artistic work solely by the subjective intentions of the artist, but must deal with its impact in the real world.

What Makes Revolutionary Art Revolutionary?

In evaluating art, content is always primary—i.e., the ideas of the work. All art is propaganda—it propagates ideas and feelings—but certainly not all propaganda is art.

We must be clear that art is not above or separate from society. The artist is not dispassionate or neutral to the world. A revolutionary analysis of culture and art deals with the class interest which it serves: the question of art for whom? But this question must not be treated mechanically, i.e. by a simplistic numerical count of the audience whereby the majority must be workers. Art must reach broadly and include and reach different classes, but it must be clear whose interests it serves. And how are the revolutionary interests of the working class and oppressed peoples served?

Revolutionary art must intensify class antagonism; it is partisan, takes a stand with the masses; it attacks the enemy. It is art that accuses! Not to simply describe oppressive realities, but ultimately gets at why, and thereby makes us wise. Being "Wise to the whys" compels us to rise and to act, to change reality. Revolutionary art boldly exhibits contradictions, the weaknesses and failures among the people, yet reveals the causes, shows the motion of our struggles. Revolutionary art will also celebrate resistance. This is how revolutionary art serves the interests of the oppressed and exploited.

Another question: art about whom? Again, we can't be mechanical and one-sided. The subjects of revolutionary art must also be broad—revolutionary art must be meaningful and relevant to the working class masses, the very people whom ruling class art degrades and/or ignores.

There must be the broadest range of artistic forms. We must be clear that even aesthetics are class partisan, that society conditions our tastes, values and norms about what is beautiful and what we should love. Ruling class bourgeois aesthetics promote fear, alienation, submission, depravity: culture and values based on the supremacy of property ownership. The ruling class seeks to enforce its own image upon the world, its ideology and world view, as well as to keep the people in a state of confusion and impotence with a host of fads and trendy diversions, but never to offer clarity about exploitation and oppression.

Revolutionary art must be artistically powerful and political revolutionary. It must inspire a spirit of defiance, or class and national pride to resist domination and backward ideology. Revolutionary art must energize and humanize; not pacify, confuse and desensitize. this is the liberating function of art, freeing the imagination and spirit, yet focusing us to our revolutionary potential.

I am adamantly against one-dimensional, so-called "correct" proscriptive forms that petty bourgeois critics try to label as "political art." I'm also not in favor of the errors of socialist-realist art with its glorified "socialist heroes," but favor imaginative critical realism, a sensuous rendering of the colorful material world. Art can fill us with love, with hope and with revolutionary vision.

Ultimately society must be transformed through the organization of people for socialist revolution. Artists can contribute a critique of capitalist society. This is critical realism: to criticize appearances and obscured social relations, to show that social life is fundamentally class struggle and to expose and shatter the lies and false consciousness imposed on the people. To be an effective revolutionary artist, therefore, revolutionary ideology and talent are required. Artists play key roles in affecting consciousness and can help to transform the working class from a class-in-itself to a class-for-itself.

The artist takes a stand through the practice of creating art and in his/her role in real struggle. After all, art comes from life. Revolutionary and progressive artists must delve deeply into the lives of the people, to be integrated with them.

Revolutionary ideas and spirit demand revolutionary artistry, not mediocrity and sycophancy. Revolutionary art is about what is coming into being. Therefore, it is innovative, not imitative or mimicking fads. Asian American artistic innovation will come from embracing and incorporating the broad tradition of Asian American culture in a creative leap in response to the actual leap in the level of struggle of the people. Innovation will not come about by abandoning Asian American culture for the "individual" and "universal." We must realize that the universal is expressed by the particulars. A full and deep grasp of the specificity and particularity of our experience naturally evokes the universal and makes for a truly rich and profound universality.

We need to study and grasp the traditional forms, not to be academic experts, but to create a living contemporary art through taking what is useful, positive and rejecting the negative and backward. Tradition must serve liberation, to unite and focus us toward transforming the world.

Speech presented March 21, 1985 at Kearny Street Workshop, San Francisco.

APPENDIX

HISTORICAL DIAGRAMS OF THE REVOLUTIONARY ASIAN PACIFIC AMERICAN MOVEMENT

History can't be reduced to or accurately depicted as a linear diagram such as implied by historical trees. Nor can history "begin" at one singular, unitary point. Nor does history "end," as many apologists for capitalism would have us believe. We have tried to give some "visualization" of the revolutionary Asian Pacific American movement in the development of nationwide organizations such as I Wor Kuen (later the League of Revolutionary Struggle, Marxist-Leninist), Wei Min She (of which the majority of its membership joined the Revolutionary Union/Revolutionary Communist Party), the Workers Viewpoint Organization (later the Communist Workers Party) and the Union of Democratic Filipinos/Katipunan An Demokratikong Pilipinos (KDP), along with smaller, more regional-based groups, newspaper collectives, many of which were explicitly revolutionary or anti-imperialist with revolutionary activists working in or emerging from them.

Diagram I. U.S. OLD LEFT. Two main currents ran through much of the first half of the twentieth century in the U.S. Left. While both have their roots in 19th century American socialism, which overwhelmingly was (White) European American, a clear ideological and political demarcation occurred in the 1920s.

One current was a communist current, inspired, influenced and catalyzed by the establishment of the Soviet Union as the first socialist state. The Communist Party USA was formed out of the older White socialist movement with infusions from "non-White" radicals and revolutionaries, such as members from the African Blood Brotherhood. During the late 19th and early 20th century, a Japanese Marxist, Sen Katayama, played a leading role in founding both the communist parties of Japan and the U.S. Katayama has not been properly recognized for his contributions to American Marxism.

The Communist Party USA grew considerably during the struggles of the 1930s and was highly influential in many U.S. social movements and struggles of that era. Much has been historically documented of their role, though Chinese American historian Him Mark Lai is probably the only scholar who has examined and documented the activity of Chinese American Marxists during this time. The CPUSA, in its better political period with regard to minorities ("people of color," "Third World peoples," "oppressed nationalities," etc.), had over a dozen different language newspapers, led numerous mass organizations, and had widespread influence among militants, artists and organizers, including Filipino American writer Carlos Bulosan (cited as one of Asian Pacific America's literary greats), community and labor organizer Karl Yoneda (c.f., Ganbatte, Yoneda's autobiography), Ben Fee (a prominent organizer in both San Francisco and New York Chinese American communities), and many others whose stories and deeds need greater attention and recognition (a subject for another book). Yoneda and Bulosan are cited in the diagram because they are the most prominent. In addition, the CPUSA's adoption of the Black-belt Negro Nation thesis as expounded by the Comintern (the Communist International, a gathering of communist parties worldwide under the leadership of the Soviet party) is significant for giving special emphasis and political priority to "the national question" in the U.S. An outgrowth of this emphasis on the "national question" was the Chinese Workers Mutual Aid Association, a largely immigrant, working class Chinese American grassroots mass organization, and precursor to many of the mass organizations that emerged out of the Asian Pacific American Movement during the New Left period.

The other current, while socialist, opposed the Soviet Union's "Stalinism," and embraced Stalin's arch-opponent, Leon Trotsky, and "Trotskyism." For the most part, the Trotskyists continue to be overwhelmingly White and labor-focused in their base organizing. However, several major splits occurred in the Trotskyist socialist current, and one significant outgrowth for the Asian Pacific American Movement was the formation of the Freedom Socialist Party and Radical Women which recruited leading Asian Pacific American women activists and cultural workers/writers, specifically Merle Woo, Nancy Kato, Nellie Wong and Emily Woo Yamasaki (Woo, Wong, Woo-Yamasaki have respective articles in this anthology).

THE UNIVERSE THAT INCUBATES THE BIRTH OF THE ASIAN PACIFIC AMERICAN REVOLUTIONARY MOVEMENT. By the 1960s, with major events internationally such as the Soviet Union's invasion of Poland, Hungary and Czechoslovakia, the rise of Third World independence and national liberation struggles, the Sino-Soviet split in the international Marxist-Leninist camp, the start of the Cultural Revolution in China, as well as domestic developments such as the Black Power, the anti-Vietnam War movements, etc., the New Left emerges. The New Left had very little ties to the Old Left. The Communist Party USA by the 1950s had gone into retreat suffering from many setbacks as a result of McCarthyism and the Cold War, and from its own political reformism. The Trotskyist socialist camp had been rocked by splits and by its own increasing white chauvinism and irrelevance to youth and to the new forces and upsurges of the 1960s.

The New Left is really born from the international and domestic conditions and upsurges particular to its generation and historical period. Many analyses exist elsewhere of a fuller discussion of the causes, conditions and distinctions of the birth and rise of the American New Left. This anthology analyses one component of this New Left: the Asian Pacific American revolutionary movement. It must be noted from the interviews conducted by veteran militants in this anthology that very little direct connection initially existed between the older Chinese American (and some Filipino and Japanese American) Marxists with the young revolutionaries. However, as the New Left came to recognize and appreciate its precursors, as part of every generation's need and requirement to do historical study, to make summation, a process of "rediscovery" and "reclamation" unfolded. Hopefully, future generations of APA radicals and revolutionaries will find this anthology useful to maintaining continuity, drawing lessons and making summations.

THE REVOLUTIONARY ASIAN PACIFIC AMERICAN MOVEMENT (PART OF THE NEW LEFT)—Nationwide organizations are extracted in diagrams 2 to 6.

Diagram 2: I WOR KUEN/LEAGUE OF REVOLUTIONARY STRUGGLE. A history and summation is found in Section One by Fred Ho, with supplementary narrative by Ray Tasaki (the Japan Town Collective), the interviews of Alex Hing (Red Guard Party and I Wor Kuen/LRS) and "Mo" Nishida (East Wind Collective).
Diagram 3: WORKERS VIEWPOINT ORGANIZATION/COMMUNIST WORKERS PARTY. C.f. Chris Iijima interview.
Diagram 4: UNION OF DEMOCRATIC FILIPINOS (KDP). C.f. articles by Estella Habal, Helen Toribio and Ninotchka Rosca.
Diagram 5: WEI MIN SHE/REVOLUTIONARY UNION/ REVOLUTIONARY COMMUNIST PARTY. C.f. articles by Steve Yip and Dolly Veale.
Diagram 6: SMALLER REVOLUTIONARY AND ANTI-IMPERIALIST ASIAN PACIFIC AMERICAN MOVEMENT GROUPS. Some of these groups were revolutionary, others were explicitly anti-imperialist and/or included leading activists who were revolutionaries or became revolutionaries out of these projects. Note that 1989 marks the beginning of the "non-revolutionary" period, as three major nationwide organizations have dissolved (viz., KDP, WVO/CWP, IWK/LRS). APA revolutionaries from Wei Min She continue in the RCP as do APA veterans and newer activists in the Freedom Socialist Party/Radical Women. By the 1990s, new grassroots radical and militant activist organizations appear, though none truly nationwide. These include Youth for Filipino Action (a very promising youth group which self-destructs after a few short years), the Gabriela Network (founded by Ninotchka Rosca and which trains new radicals such as Carolyn Antonio), various prisoner support organizations which have overlapping memberships of new leading radicals (Wayne Lum, ManChui Leung) initiated and inspired by the tireless Yuri Kochiyama, and others. The only explicitly revolutionary (though not Marxist or socialist) group is the Asian Revolutionary Circle in Boston.

Note that while many activist groups have arisen during this time, they were not included because many of them are supported primarily by foundations and state monies, have hired staff as leadership and do not explicitly locate themselves as part of the U.S. Left or radical movement. The ones that are included do not rely upon external grants, aren't led by paid staff, and have principles of unity or mission statements that identify with the broader U.S. left. While study groups and other circles exist scattered throughout the U.S., and individual APA radicals and revolutionaries may be found in other socialist, Left and anarchist groupings, they are not cohered by a focus in the APA community and struggles or are too informally structured. Also not included are support groups for overseas/international struggles. While these groups have interacted with the APA movement, their primary focus has not been the struggle in the U.S.

RESOURCES

Much archival material exists in two special collections: The Steve Louie Collection at the University of California, Los Angeles, and the Fred Ho Collection at the Dodd Center, University of Connecticut-Storrs.

Two videos available from Peoples Video Network are recommended featuring a number of the authors from this anthology in two important forums held in New York City during August and November, 1998 organized by the Asian Pacific American Ad-Hoc Committee. The first forum was entitled "Asian Pacific Americans and Revolutionary Socialism" held at Hunter College, and the second was "Aziatic Uprising: An Intergenerational Dialogue" at Columbia University. For information or to order, contact: Sue Harris, 212.633.6646, People's Video Network, 39 West 14th Street, New York, NY 10011.

HISTORICAL DIAGRAM 1
UNITED STATES OLD LEFT

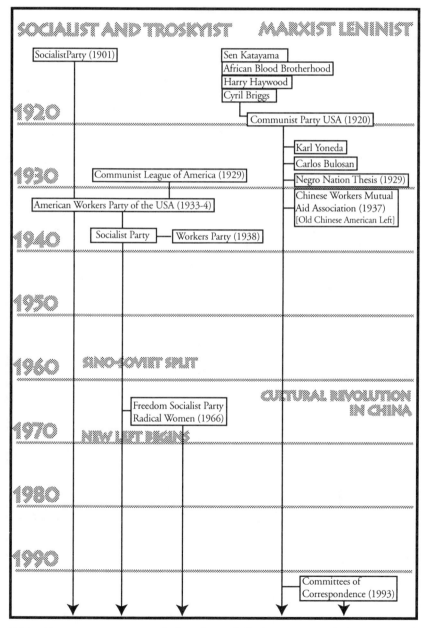

This diagram is not intended to be a full description of the U.S. Left history, but only a cursory description relevant to the topic of this book.

HISTORICAL DIAGRAM 2
ASIAN PACIFIC AMERICAN REVOLUTIONARY MOVEMENT

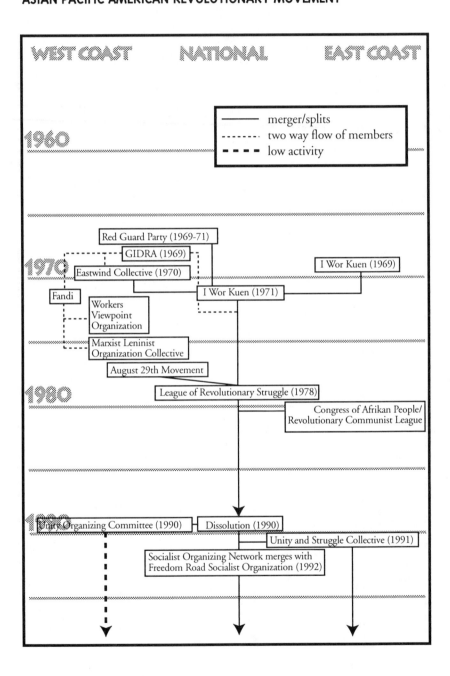

HISTORICAL DIAGRAM 3
ASIAN PACIFIC AMERICAN REVOLUTIONARY MOVEMENT

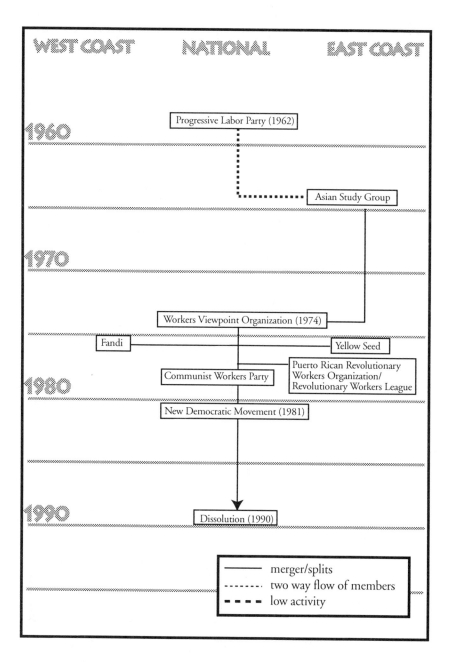

| WEST COAST | NATIONAL | EAST COAST |

1960 — Progressive Labor Party (1962)

Asian Study Group

1970

Workers Viewpoint Organization (1974)

Fandi — Yellow Seed

Communist Workers Party — Puerto Rican Revolutionary Workers Organization/ Revolutionary Workers League

1980

New Democratic Movement (1981)

1990 — Dissolution (1990)

—————— merger/splits
- - - - - - - two way flow of members
▬ ▬ ▬ low activity

HISTORICAL DIAGRAM 4
ASIAN PACIFIC AMERICAN REVOLUTIONARY MOVEMENT

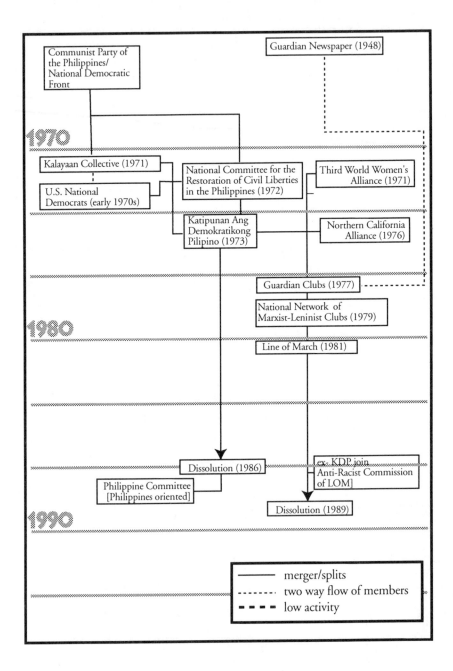

HISTORICAL DIAGRAM 5
ASIAN PACIFIC AMERICAN REVOLUTIONARY MOVEMENT

WEST COAST   **NATIONAL**

1960

Students for a Democratic Society

Revolutionary Youth Movement II

Yellow Caucus/
Peace and Freedom Party

UC-Berkely Asian American
Political Alliance and
Third World Liberation Front

Revolutionary League

Chinatown Coop
Garment Factory

October League

1970 Asian Community
Center (1969-70)

East Bay Asians
for Community Action

Revolutionary Union

Everybody's
Bookstore (1970)

Wei Min She (1971-5)

J-Town Workteam/
Taishu Newspaper

dissolves and most join RCP   Revolutionary Communist Party (1975)

Foreign Students from
Hong Kong and Taiwan

1980

1990

——— merger/splits
------- two way flow of members
- - - low activity

HISTORICAL DIAGRAM 6
ASIAN PACIFIC AMERICAN REVOLUTIONARY MOVEMENT

WEST COAST/ PACIFIC	NATIONAL	EAST COAST

1960

WEST COAST/ PACIFIC	NATIONAL	EAST COAST
Third World Liberation Front (1969)		Asian American Political Alliance (1968)
Japantown Collective (1971)		Asian Student Union,
Bay Area Asian Coalition Against the War		City College of NY
[includes IWK, WMS, Kalayaan, JTC] (1972)		Asian Americans for Action
Eastwind Collective		Asians in the Spirit of Indo-Chinese People
Yellow Brotherhood		Chickens Come Home to Roost
Asian American Hard Core		
New Peoples' Hard Core		
Community Workers Collective		
Asian Revolutionary Movement		
Fandi		
GIDRA Newspaper		
In Struggle		
Third Arm, HAWAI'I		
Rodan Newspaper		

1970

1980

1990

WEST COAST/ PACIFIC	NATIONAL	EAST COAST
	Gabriela Network	
		Youth for Filipino Action
API FORCE		David Wong Support Commitee
ASIAN!		Yu Kikumura Support Committee
League of Filipino Students		Asians for Mumia/ Jericho
ACTION		Ad-Hoc Committee
		South Asians Against Police
	Asian Left Forum	Brutality and Racism
		Asian Revolutionary Circle

400

RED GUARD PROGRAM AND RULES

1969

Red Guard

We the Red Guard want an end to the exploitation of the people in our community by the avaricious businessmen and politicians who are one of the same. We want an immediate end to the brutal harassment of our people by the racist pig structure. We dedicate ourselves in exposing the ruthless landlords and businessmen who oppress the Chinese people. Jobs and inadequate medical facilities do not meet the needs of our people and we will work with determined people to institute reforms. Relevant education and decent housing are among the other immediate goals which the poor Chinese people are striving for. Chinatown must not remain the same economically and culturally backward community it is. Now is the time for change! The people shall be freed from the wraths of the oppressors. We should rid our ranks of all impotent thinking. All views that over-estimate the strength of the enemy and underestimate the strength of the people are wrong. The oppressed peoples and nations must not pin their hopes for liberation on the sensibleness of imperialism and its lackeys. We will only triumph by strengthening our Unity and persevering in our struggle.

OUR POLITICAL PROGRAM

1. We want freedom. We want power to determine the destiny of our people, the Yellow Community.

We believe that Yellow people will not be free until we are able to determine our destiny.

2. We want decent housing, fit for shelter of human beings.

We believe that if the white landlord will not give decent housing to our Yellow community, then the housing and the land should be made into cooperatives so that our community, with government aid, can build and make decent housing for its people.

3. We want education for our people that exposes the true nature of this decadent American society. We want education that teaches us our true history and our role in the present-day society.

We believe in an educational system that will give to our people a knowledge of self. If a man does not have knowledge of himself and his position in society and the world, then he has little chance to relate to anything else.

4. We want all Yellow men to be exempt from military service.

We believe that Yellow people should not be forced to fight in the military service to defend a racist government that does not protect us. We will not fight and kill other people of color in the world who, like Yellow people, are being victimized by the white racist government of America. We will protect ourselves from the force and violence of the racist military, by whatever means necessary.

5. We want an immediate end to POLICE BRUTALITY AND MURDER of Yellow People.

We believe we can end police brutality in our Yellow community by organizing Yellow self-defense groups that are dedicated to defending our Yellow community from racist police oppression and brutality. The Second Amendment to the Constitution of the United States gives a right to bear arms. We, therefore, believe that all Yellow people should arm themselves for self defense.

6. We want freedom for all Yellow men held in federal, state, county and city prisons and jails.

We believe that all Yellow people should be released from the many jails and prisons because they have not received a fair and impartial trial.

7. We want all Yellow People when brought to trial to be tried in court by a jury of their peer group or people from their Yellow communities, as defined by the Constitution of the United States.

We believe that the courts should follow the United States Constitution so that Yellow people will receive fair trials. The 14th Amendment of the U.S. Constitution gives a man a right to be tried by his peer group. A peer is a person from a similar economic, social, religious, geographical, environmental, historical and racial background. To do this the court will be forced to select a jury from the Yellow community from which the Yellow defendant came. We have been, and are being tried by all-white juries that have no understanding of the "average reasoning man of the Yellow community."

8. We want adequate and free medical facilities available for the people in the Yellow community.

We know that Chinatown has the highest density area next to Manhattan. It also has the highest TB and sickness rate in the nation.

9. We want full employment for our people.

We believe that the federal government is responsible and obligated to give every man employment or a guaranteed income. We believe that if the white American businessmen will not give full employment, then, the means of production should be taken from the businessmen and placed in the community so that the people of the community can organize and employ all its people and give a high standard of living.

There are thousands of immigrants coming into Chinatown every year and it is almost impossible for them to find gainful employment.

10. We demand that the United States government recognize the People's Republic of China.

We believe that MAO TSE-TUNG is the true leader of the Chinese people; not CHIANG KAI SHEK. The government of the United States is now preparing for war against the Chinese People's Republic and against the Chinese people. The racist government of the United States has proven that it will put only peoples of color in concentration camps, Japanese were placed in concentration camps; therefore, it is logical that the next people that will be going are the Chinese people; because the United States is gearing it's war time industrial complex for war against China.

SUMMARY

It is stated in the Declaration of Independence that ..."all men are create equal; that they are endowed by their Creator with certain unalienable rights that among these are life, liberty, and the pursuit of happiness. That, to secure these rights, governments are instituted among men, deriving their just powers from the consent of the governed; that, whenever any form of government becomes destructive of these ends, it is the right of the people to alter or abolish it, and to institute a new government, laying its foundation on such principles, and organizing its powers in such forms, as to them shall seem most likely to effect their safety and happiness."

OUR LEADER MAO TSE-TUNG STATES:

"The Socialist system will eventually replace the Capitalist system; this is an objective law independent of Man's will. However much the reactionaries try to hold back the wheel of history, sooner or later revolution will take place and will inevitably triumph."

RULES OF THE RED GUARD

Every member of the RED GUARD throughout this country of racist America must abide by these rules as functional members of this party. CENTRAL COMMITTEE members, CENTRAL STAFFS, AND LOCAL STAFFS, including all Captains subordinate to either national, state, and local leadership of the RED GUARD will enforce these rules. Length of suspension or other disciplinary action necessary for violation of these rules will depend on national decisions by national, state, or state area, and local committees and staffs where said rule or rules of the RED GUARD WERE VIOLATED.

Every member of the party must know these verbatim by heart. And apply them daily. Each member must report any violation of these rules to their leadership or they are counter-revolutionary and are also subject to suspension by the RED GUARD.

THE RULES ARE:

1. For all meetings, everyone must attend and be on time. (Penalties will be enforced severely if there is no legitimate excuse.)

2. Those not employed, must report daily to receive assignments and to submit Daily Reports. Those who are employed, must submit a weekly report, and receive new assignments.

3. All special and emergency meetings must be called through the CENTRAL COMMITTEE members only.

4. Party members cannot be so HIGH to the point that they cannot function properly.

5. Party members cannot have narcotics or weed in his possession while doing party work.

6. Party members should not carry any form of weapon which can get you busted unless assigned.

7. Party members must not use, point, or fire a weapon of any kind at any one except the Enemy.

8. Anyone outside the party that wants information must be referred to the OFFICER OF THE DAY (It will be posted on who OD is.)

9. Party members must not commit any crimes against other party members or YELLOW people at all, and endanger or jeopardize themselves or the party.

10. When arrested give only name and address. Anything else said or signed will be used against you.

11. All members must attend POLITICAL EDUCATION CLASSES, MEETINGS and ACTIVITIES.

12. Any person that wants to join the RED GUARD will undergo a six-month BASIC TRAINING program. Acceptance to Party Membership will be decided by the REVIEW BOARD after basic training.

8 POINTS OF ATTENTION

1. Speak politely
2. Pay fairly for what you buy.
3. Return everything you borrow.
4. Pay for anything you damage.
5. Do not hit or swear at people.
6. Do not damage property or crops of the poor, oppressed masses.
7. Do not take liberties with women.
8. If we ever have to take captives do not ill-treat them.

3 MAIN RULES OF DISCIPLINE

1. Obey orders in all your actions.
2. Do not take a single needle or a piece of thread from the poor and oppressed masses.
3. Turn in everything captured from the attacking enemy.

12 POINT PLATFORM AND PROGRAM

I Wor Kuen

Asian people in Amerika have been continually oppressed by the greedy, traitorous gangsters of our own communities and by the wider racist exploitative Amerikan society. We have been bombarded by the media (newspapers, T.V., radio, and schools) with false ideas about how we should accept our position in this society. They have tried to brainwash us and have even coerced us into going overseas and fighting against our own people in S.E. Asia.

But, Asian Amerikans have been fighting back against the oppression of this country ever since we first tasted the bitterness of Amerika's racism and exploitation. The long and heroic history of the Asian Amerikan struggle inspired and strengthened us in our purpose. No longer can we endure these oppressive conditions. We cannot let our ancestors' struggles go down in vain. We know who are our real enemies and friends and we have found new strength for we are joining our sisters and brothers within this country and around the world to fight for freedom and justice against the rulers of this country.

We have tried the peaceful means of petition, courts, voting and even demonstrations. But our situation remained the same. We are not free.

We want to improve the living conditions of our people and are preparing to defend our communities against repression and for revolutionary armed war against the gangsters, businessmen, politicians, and police. When a government oppresses the people and no longer serves the needs of the people, we have the right to abolish it and create a new one.

We are working for a world of peace, where the needs of the people come first, which is without class distinctions and is based upon the love and unity of all peoples.

The following 12 points are what we are fighting for:

1. WE WANT SELF-DETERMINATION FOR ASIAN AMERICANS.
The masses of Asian people in Amerika live in ghettoes which are like small colonies. The Amerikan capitalists continually attempt to make profit off us by trying to alter our entire way of life for their own benefit. We want liberation from this enslavement so we can determine our own destinies.

405

2. WE WANT SELF-DETERMINATION FOR ALL ASIANS.

Western imperialists have been invading and colonizing countries in Asia for the past 500 years. Amerikan imperialism, concentrating in Asia is now engaged in the most sadistic and genocidal war of aggression the world has ever seen. We want an immediate end to Amerikan imperialism.

3. WE WANT LIBERATION OF ALL THIRD WORLD PEOPLES AND OTHER OPPRESSED PEOPLES.

People of color, Asian, Black, Brown, Red are all fighting for liberation from Amerika's racist oppression. Millions and millions of white people are also rising up to fight our common oppressor. We recognize that only when the oppression of all people is ended can we all really be free.

4. WE WANT AN END TO MALE CHAUVINISM AND SEXUAL EXPLOITATION.

The thousands of years of oppression under feudalism and capitalism have created institutions and myths of male supremacy over women. Man must fight along with sisters in the struggle for economic and social equality and must recognize that sisters make up over half of the revolutionary army. Sisters and brothers are equals fighting for our people.

5. WE WANT COMMUNITY CONTROL OF OUR INSTITUTIONS AND LAND.

Those institutions in our communities such as the police, schools, health, housing, transportation, sanitation, anti-pollution, and welfare must be controlled by and serve the needs of our people and not be geared to the making of money. We want an end to our community being used to make profit for outsiders, such as slumlords and tourist agencies.

6. WE WANT AN EDUCATION WHICH EXPOSES THE TRUE HISTORY OF WESTERN IMPERIALISM IN ASIA AND AROUND THE WORLD: WHICH TEACHES US THE HARDSHIPS AND STRUGGLES OF OUR ANCESTORS IN THIS LAND AND WHICH REVEALS THE TRULY DECADENT EXPLOITATIVE NATURE OF AMERIKAN SOCIETY.

The Amerikan imperialists have tried to justify their world empire by covering up the inhuman deeds they perpetrated in Asia and to the rest of the Third World. They also try to brainwash us in school with racist history which does not tell of the degradation, oppression and humiliation Asians and other Third World People have been forced to suffer in Amerika. We want to learn of the heroic and inspiring struggles Asian people have conducted throughout the world as well as in Amerika.

7. WE WANT DECENT HOUSING AND HEALTH AND CHILD CARE.

The institutions of housing, health, and child care are set up only to make money for landlords, doctors, hospitals and drug companies. We want housing, health, and child care that gives us life and not slow death.

8. WE WANT FREEDOM FOR ALL POLITICAL PRISONERS AND ALL ASIANS.

Our Asian brothers and sisters in Amerika's racist jails should be set free for they were not tried by their peers (other Asian brothers and sisters). Political prisoners are jailed because they fought for their freedom and basic rights as human beings. They all must be set free.

9. WE WANT AN END TO THE AMERIKAN MILITARY.

The Amerikan military machine is butchering people throughout the world, especially in Asia. The end of the Amerikan military will be one of the greatest events in the history of the liberation of mankind. We want all Asian Amerikans exempt from military servitude.

10. WE WANT AN END TO RACISM.

White racism has been oppressing Third World People for the past 500 years. Although we recognize and firmly support the progressive white people in the anti-imperialist struggle, we should continue to struggle against white racism on all levels. The racism among Third World People toward each other is being broken down and a new unity is being created in our struggle against our common enemy.

11. WE WANT AN END TO THE GEOGRAPHIC BOUNDARIES OF AMERIKA.

From its beginning, Amerika has been a robber country. It stole land by the use of armed force from native Americans, Chicanos and Latinos, and other peoples. Amerika can now only maintain its present boundaries both internally and externally by the threat and use of violence. We want free passage of all people to and from Amerika. The people of the world have built Amerika, and they must now determine its destiny. Amerika has also tried to blind those who live here as to the realities of socialism by restricting information from and travel to the People's Republic of China, Cuba, Albania, North Korea, and North Vietnam. We want open boundaries and an end to immigration and emigration harassment.

12. WE WANT A SOCIALIST SOCIETY.

What exists in Amerika today is a society where one man in order to survive must exploit his fellow man. We want a society that works for the fulfillment of human needs. We want decent housing, health, child care, employment, sanitation, and old age care. We want a society where *no man or woman* will die due to lack of food, medical care or housing, where each gives according to his ability and takes according to his need.

ASIAN STUDIES MANIFESTO

Asian Students Committee of City College, New York (CCNY), December 1973

Boreysa Tep, Richard K. Wong, Jean Yonemura

WE BELIEVE THAT THE DEPARTMENT OF ASIAN STUDIES SHOULD:

1. BE ONE VEHICLE TO SERVICE THE ASIAN STUDENTS AT CCNY

One of the main reasons that Asian students fought for the establishment and development of a Department of Asian Studies was to serve the needs of Asian students, who total more than 1000 since the 1969 Third World student struggle for Open Admission. Thus, Asian Studies was created to promote an awareness of our position as Asians in America and to provide the CCNY community with Asian history from an Asian perspective. Courses about Asia already offered by City College failed to serve this function, since they were taught from a Western perspective and Asians were systematically excluded from teaching these courses, while courses on Asians in America were non-existent.

Asian Studies should provide students with a perspective to analyze the problems that face Asians in America and in the world and provide them with the ability to determine their future roles in their communities and in society. Asian Studies should also encourage students to unite as Asians to actively deal with their common problems. The Asian Studies Department should promote values based on cooperation and mutual assistance rather than the widespread American social values of individualism and the quest for material wealth. In these ways, Asian Studies become one important vehicle to serve Asian students.

2. PROVIDE A PROPER WORLD PERSPECTIVE

The developing nations of the world are situated in Asia, Africa and Latin America. In the course of their development, the U.S. government has clearly interfered with the destinies of these developing nations through its military, C.I.A., International investments and other U.S. establishments. A few examples would suffice: China, Vietnam, Cambodia, Chile, Puerto Rico, Africa, Indonesia, and the Middle East. These examples cannot be viewed in isolation from one another, for they are all connected to the U.S. foreign policy of intervention, and they recur again and again.

Students pushed for an Asian Studies Department because they were dissatisfied with the perspective that was given by the academic establishment which failed to discuss the oppression of Asians by imperialist and colonialist powers of Europe and the United States, and the related problems of racism and discrimination against Asians in the U.S.

These problems are of great interest to students at CCNY, especially Asian students. These concerns must be incorporated into the Asian Studies curriculum at all levels and must be integrated with any analysis of the situation facing Asians in America and in the world.

3. HAVE STUDENTS PARTICIPATE IN POLICY-MAKING DECISIONS (PERSONNEL, BUDGET, EDUCATIONAL POLICIES).

Students historically have been denied a voice in departmental policies — i.e. curriculum, personnel, and budget — by the governing bodies of the universities (the administration and the faculty). But one change coming about from the nationwide movement of University reforms has been the granting of the right to students of participating in the decision-making processes of Higher Education.

The Asian Studies Department at City College was established largely by students playing the leading role in its conception and development. Without the active and organized push by Asian Students for an Asian Studies Department, it would not exist here today. Students continue to be in a unique position to provide input into the policy-making decision in the Department, since they are the ones directly affected by such decisions involving course offerings, teachers, programs and so forth. Without students, there can be no Asian Studies, no college or universities.

We therefore believe that students must be guaranteed an equal voice and vote in policy-making decisions as faculty.

4. PRESENT THE HISTORY OF THE ASIANS IN AMERICA

It has been said that, except for the Native Americans, the United States is a country of immigrant peoples. American history, as it is taught in our schools, primarily concentrates on tracing the history of the European immigrants and their descendants. The conception of American history is distorted, since it has neglected almost totally the major role that Blacks, Latinos, Asian and Native Americas have played in building this country.

Asian Studies, therefore, should present the background of Asian people in America — why our forefathers had to leave their homelands, what their lives in America were like, what kinds of struggles they engaged in to maintain their lives and jobs, what their vital contributions have been in building the American West, how we live today as Asians in America. An understanding of our Asian 'roots' will lead to a more complete understanding of the various peoples that make up America today.

5. APPLY ITS RESOURCES TO LEARN FROM THE HELP OF THE ASIAN AMERICAN COMMUNITIES

Asian American history teaches us that our people have been historically concentrated in such urban 'ghettos' as Chinatown because of common backgrounds as Asian immigrants and children of Asian immigrants, because of limited job opportunities, and because of discrimination against Asians by the larger American society. Many problems still face the people of our communities today, such as unemployment, bad working conditions, substandard housing, high cost of living, and inadequate educational and health care facilities.

We recognize that Asian Studies program and money alone cannot solve the problems of Asian communities—the community people themselves will be the main component in broad social change. Too often, though, society teaches students to seek upward mobility through higher education to help solve the communities' persistent problems—we might call this 'brain drain', and this is part of the overall problem. Asian Studies can play a role in bringing students back to the community by exposing them to the community's problems and needs, by learning from the community people themselves, by helping students to find ways to solve the community's problems.

We must use all of our people's resources from all walks of life to fight for the rights and better livelihood for Asians in America, and to develop alternatives for the future. We seek to unite the students and community in a common effort, and not to promote escape from community issues and problems.

6. PRESENT AN ASIAN PERSPECTIVE OF ASIAN HISTORY

The peoples of Asia built one of the earliest civilizations in the world which has contributed to the development of the arts, philosophy, religion, literature, and science in other parts of the world. Beginning in the 19th century, Asia's vast human and natural resources have been the target for profit-seeking Western imperialist nations. Asian people have since been waging struggles for their independence and have again brought Asia to the attention of the world.

Western writers have depicted Asians as immoral, wicked, untrustworthy "heathens" ruled by weak and backward governments, in an effort to justify Western subjugation of Asia through inflicting massive violence and bloodshed on her people. Here in the United States, traditional scholars have institutionalized this viewpoint in schools of Asian Studies which serve the U.S. government and business interests in Asia during times of war and peace.

The CCNY Asian Studies Department must teach Asian history from an Asian perspective, through its early period to the Asian struggle against Western subjugation to the current struggles of Asian peoples to set up independent modern states.

7. PROVIDE EMPLOYMENT FOR ASIANS WHO HAVE A PERSPECTIVE THAT IS CONSISTENT WITH OUR DEPARTMENT'S PRINCIPLES

Racial discrimination has barred Asian scholars and teachers from employment and/or promotion in the very field that relates to their own backgrounds and countries. Therefore, we wholeheartedly support hiring Asian faculty who can teach from an Asian perspective, according to the analysis and principles we put forward in

Ethnic and Area Studies.

At this point, it is important to stress that Asian American Studies is the backbone of Asian Studies at CCNY. At the same time, it is a brand new field, so that Asian American programs at colleges across the country do not yet offer programs beyond a B.A. degree; and because of its pioneering nature, we cannot expect to judge prospective faculty by traditional academic standards when the field has not had time to develop as a discipline. The Asian Studies Department must pay close attention to recruiting faculty with extensive experience working in Asian communities, developing Asian American curricula or developing viable methodology to research and study Asians in America.

With a common outlook on the Department, faculty and students will be able to continue to the founding tradition of working together to expand and improve the Department.

8. PROMOTE UNDERSTANDING OF THE COMMON STRUGGLES OF THIRD WORLD PEOPLES.

Asian Studies, Black Studies and Puerto Rican Studies were formed in 1971 as a result of the CCNY Third World student strike of 1969. At that time, Black, Latina and Asian students began to realize that Third World peoples must stand up for the educational right of our peoples to attend City institutions of higher education and to learn our true histories as non-white minorities in America. Only through uniting have we gained our Ethnic Studies Departments, and only through understanding that our unity extends beyond the college campus into our urban communities can we continue to build.

Asian Studies must at all times promote unity among Ethnic Studies Departments, and, in a broader sense, among the Third Word students and communities through its course offerings, programs, activities and public standpoint.

WE THEREFORE RESTATE OUR PRINCIPLES...WE BELIEVE THAT THE DEPARTMENT OF ASIAN STUDIES SHOULD:

1. BE ONE VEHICLE TO SERVE THE ASIAN STUDENTS AT CCNY.
2. PROVIDE A PROPER WORLD PERSPECTIVE.
3. HAVE STUDENTS PARTICIPATE IN POLICY-MAKING DECISIONS (PERSONNEL, BUDGET AND EDUCATIONAL POLICIES).
4. PRESENT THE HISTORY OF ASIANS IN AMERICA.
5. APPLY ITS RESOURCES TO LEARN FROM AND HELP THE ASIAN AMERICAN COMMUNITIES
6. PRESENT AN ASIAN PERSPECTIVE ON ASIAN HISTORY
7. PROVIDE EMPLOYMENT FOR ASIANS WHO HAVE A PERSPECTIVE THAT IS CONSISTENT WITH OUR DEPARTMENT'S PRINCIPLES.
8. PROMOTE UNDERSTANDING OF THE COMMON STRUGGLES OF THIRD WORLD PEOPLES

CONTRIBUTORS

Carolyn Cervantes Antonio was born in the Philippines but has spent most of her life in the northeastern United States. A coordinator of GABRIELA Network, a Philippine-U.S. women's solidarity organization, she has focused her energies on working for international women's rights and human rights. An aspiring poet, she previously worked for Kitchen Table: Women of Color Press.

Asian and Pacific Islanders for Community Empowerment is a Bay Area-based (San Francisco/Oakland/San Jose) political organization. Born out of the struggle to defeat California's racist Proposition 187, API ForCE has been an organizing vehicle for Asian Americans who want to make progressive change in the areas of immigrant rights, affirmative action, economic justice, international solidarity, and anti-Asian violence since January of 1995. API ForCE welcomes all persons of Asian and Pacific Islander ancestry, stands in solidarity with other people of color and supports the human rights and dignity of all people. API ForCE envisions a new society based on multiculturalism, democracy, mutual respect, and economic and social justice for all.

Franklin Fung Chow was born in San Francisco at Franklin Hospital on May 29, 1936. Number One Son of Margaret Eunice Leong and Chow Hing Cheun. Weighing in at 5 lbs. and 7 ozs. at 8:10 AM. Attending physician: Dr. Margaret Chung. Attended and graduated from Commodore Stockton (now known as Gordon Lau) Elementary School and formerly known as The Oriental School), Francisco Junior School, George Washington High School, San Francisco City College and San Francisco State College with a BA Degree in Sociology in 1965. Veteran of the Korean Conflict with service in Texas and Rabat, Morocco. Real Estate Salesperson with Frank Yip Realty. Director of Summer Youth Programs for the Chinatown and North Beach Economic Opportunity Council. Investigator for the U.S. Equal Employment Opportunity Commission (EEOC) Civil Rights Analyst for the U.S. Commission on Civil Rights (USCCR) Retired from Federal Service in 1996. Ordained Elder and Deacon of the Presbyterian Church (USA). Participant on the March on Washington for Jobs and Freedom of August 28, 1963.

Originally from Hawai'i, **Peggy Myo-Young Choy**—through her work as a choreographer and activist—re-envisions/re-embodies the politics, history, and cultural aesthetics of what it means to be an Asian American woman in America. Her fresh, irreverent work is inspired by traditional Asian movement and music. She has received many awards and commissions for choreography from the Atlantic Center for the Arts/NEA to collaborate with Fred Ho, Cornell University, Princeton University, and Danspace Project's Commissioning Initiative. In 1994, she received the Woman of Achievement award from the Wisconsin Minority Women's Network. Her articles on Asian American performance have appeared in *Forward Motion, Movement Research Performance Journal, Inside Arts,* and *The Encyclopedia of Asian Americans.* Featured as outstanding choreographer in *Ms. Magazine* (1995), she has choreographed two innovative suites, "Seung Hwa: Rape/Race/Rage/Revolution" which premiered at DTW in 1995, and "Ki-Ache:Stories from the Belly" which premiered at Danspace Project in 1997.

John Delloro is a Pilipino American living in Los Angeles. Currently, he works as a community/political organizer for SEIU Local 399, the healthcare workers union. He has been organizing clergy and community members to support a worker organizing drive in the Catholic Healthcare West hospital system and to expand access to healthcare. Prior to this current job, he briefly organized workers at the MGM Hotel for the Culinary Union (HERE Local 226) in Las Vegas and later worked as researcher assistant at the University of California Los Angeles Labor Center where he conducted a literature review tracing the ideological development of the United Auto Workers. As a college student, he was active in the Los Angeles Support Committee for the Garment Workers Justice Campaign.

Diane Fujino is a Japanese American Sansei from Los Angeles. She is a founding member of ASIAN! (Asian Sisters & Brothers for Ideas in Action Now!), a radical Asian group based in Santa Barbara that has organized around anti-imperialist issues, affirmative action, and garment workers. She also works with the Interfaith Prisoners of Conscience Project to support political prisoners. She has been particularly active supporting Puerto Rican Prisoners of War, visiting California political prisoners, and organizing to free Mumia Abu-Jamal. She teaches in the Asian American Studies Department at the University of California, Santa Barbara. Her classes focus on the Asian American Movement, Asian women in the global economy, race relations, and Japanese American history. She is currently writing a biography of Japanese American revolutionary Yuri Kochiyama.

Estella Habal is a mother of four and grandmother of three children. She was a political activist for most of her adult life and continues to be active in Filipino community politics. She is currently completing a doctorate in history, and teaching part-time at various colleges in the San Francisco Bay Area.

Richard Hamasaki's home is in Kāneohe on the island of Oahu, Hawai'i. Beginning his teaching career at the Hawai'i Poets in the Schools Program in 1975, he has taught language arts to elementary school students, and has worked with remedial reading students at Central Intermediate School—where he was also a lead language arts teacher for the Indo-Chinese Refugee Assistance Project. In 1980, he co-developed and founded—with the late Native Hawaiian poet Wayne Westlake (1947-1984)—a literature course at the Ethnic Studies Program at the University of Hawai'i, Mānoa, a course which identified and examined the imaginative literature produced by poets, chanters, musicians, playwrights and authors of Hawai'i, from traditional Native Hawaiian composers and authors to contemporary novelists. Richard is currently teaching secondary English at the Kamehameha Schools, a private school for children of Native Hawaiian ancestry. He produces, edits and creates a number of collaborative art projects including a self-published art and literary magazine, *Seaweeds and Constructions* (1976-1984).

Fred Ho is a professional Chinese American baritone saxophonist and composer. He leads the Afro Asian Music Ensemble and the Monkey Orchestra. He's a producer, writer, and has been a revolutionary activist for 25 years. His many recordings and publications can be obtained via his production company website: www.bigredmedia.com. In 2000-2001, he will be co-editing with Professor William Mullen a new anthology on the subject of African American and Asian American connections in culture and radical politics. Fred

Ho will also complete a new book of his own essays. He has received three Rockefeller Foundation awards, two National Endowment for the Arts fellowships (in Jazz Composition and Opera/Musical-Theater), two New York Foundation for the Arts Music Composition Fellowships. In 1988, he was the first Asian American to receive the Duke Ellington Distinguished Artist Lifetime Achievement Award from the 17th annual Black Musicians Conference at the age of 30. He has composed four operas, two martial arts ballets and numerous extended works.

Born and raised in Queens, **Corky Lee** has been documenting the vibrant and fast merging Asian and Pacific Islander American community for over 20 years. Self-appointed as the "undisputed, unofficial Asian American photographer laureate," Lee labored for years in obscurity, and followed his own mission doggedly wherever it might take him: a Chinatown bar at dawn; a press conference on rising anti-Asian violence; a photo call for Pan Asian Repertory Theater; a parade or public ceremony; a picket line. Lee's work has been described as "only a small attempt to rectify omissions in our history text books." Lee balances a full-time job at a printing operation with his lifetime mission of community activism through photography.

ManChui Leung was born in Hong Kong and raised in Vancouver, Canada. She is a member of the Third World Alliance, a Third World unity anti-capitalist organization. Currently she is organizing against pro-prison hysteria and is committed to prisoner and political prisoner support work with the David Wong Support Committee, the Yu Kikumura Support Commitee and Asians for Mumia/ Jericho. She is also a member of Persimmon Space, an organization for Asian and Pacific Islander Lesbian, Bisexual and Transgender Women. She is currently working as an HIV/AIDS educator in New York's Chinatown, *free*lancing as a graphic designer and searching for the questions yet to be asked about the Asian and Pacific Islander Left.

Wayne Lum's political work has focused on prisoners' support, especially of political prisoners in the United States. A member of the David Wong Support Committee since 1992/1993, he is also a founding member of the Yu Kikumura Support Committee and Asians for Mumia/Jericho. He served as a coordinator of the Outreach Committee, New York City for Jericho 1998.

Thien-bao Thuc Phi was born in Sai Gon and raised in Phillips, South Minneapolis. He frequently visits area schools/colleges as a workshop leader / teacher / lecturer / performer. He is Minnesota's Grand Slam Poetry Champion for the second year in a row, and has also won at the Nuyorican Poets Cafe in New York. He would like to dedicate his work to Jody Natsue Koizumi, whose encouragement and love have proven invaluable.

Revolutionary Worker is the Voice of the Revolutionary Communist Party USA. Published weekly in English and Spanish editions, the Revolutionary Worker creates revolutionary lines of communication. It links people from many different fronts of struggle—to share their stories and experiences. It connects its readers to the revolutionary movement—in the U.S. And worldwide. Contact: www.mcs.net/~rwor or at PO Box 3486, Merchandise Mart, Chicago, IL 60654.

Ninotchka Rosca, who grew up in the Philippines, is a writer and activist. In the late 1970s, she fled under threat from the Marcos Dictatorship and is currently a New Yorker. Two volumes of her short stories, one non-fiction book and her two novels have been published. She co-founded GABRIELA Network, a Philippine-US women's solidarity organization, and the Philippine Workers Support Committee. She has been involved in the Philippine national democratic movement in one way or the other since the '60s. Since 1989, she has worked on the issues of freedom of expression, women's rights and human rights, lending her skills and voice to a number of cause-oriented organizations. She considers these issues as crucial to the struggle against neo-colonialism and certainly crucial to the advancement of humanity. In 1992, she was given the American Book Award. She is finishing her third novel, "The Woman From The Other Side of the Ocean."

Faith Santilla is a Pilipino American performance poet based in the Los Angeles area.

Tinku Sengupta is a teacher and founding member of South Asians against Police Brutality (SAPBR). SAPBR was founded in New York City in 1998. Other members of the SAPBR convening committee participated in the drafting of the article included in this anthology as a collective attempt to document their work.

Marge Yamada Taniwaki spent her formative years behind barbed wires at Manzanar, one of the ten major U.S. concentration camps for persons of Japanese ancestry during World War II. Having lost everything in their forced evacuation from Los Angeles, her family struggled to re-establish itself after being released from prison and traveling to Denver, Colorado where she and her siblings grew up in the inner-city neighborhood of Five Points. Marge remains a community activist while working a survival job. Her three decades of activism include participation in local as well as national Asian/Pacific community organizations. Marge is a founder of Making Waves: Asians In Action, a local network of Asian activists which performs political theatre. Because coalition work helps to effect social change, Marge has served with the Moyo Nguvu African Cultural Arts Center, works to end the "relocation" of Dineh from their traditional homeland in Arizona, and to stop commercial logging of communal land in the San Luis Valley of Colorado.

Todd (Hyung-Rae) Tarselli is currently imprisoned in Pennsylvania's only Super-Max prison. Todd writes about himself: "I use art to express my beliefs and ideas as a contribution to the revolution. Despite the punishments given for my beliefs I have not and will not give up the fight or allow an oppressive system to break my spirit. The revolution is not just believing in something; it's doing something that you believe in."
To write to Todd: BY-8025, 175 Progress Drive, Waynesburg, PA 15370-8090.

Ray Tasaki presently lives in San Jose, California and teachers computer graphics in a vocational training center, working with a disenfranchised and disadvantaged population. He was a member of the Japan Town Collective, I Wor Kuen, and the League of Revolutionary Struggle until 1986.

Born in the Philippines and raised in Hawai'i, **Helen Toribio** received her Bachelor of Arts degree from the University of Hawai'i, Mānoa, 1975. She was a member of Katipunan ng Demokratikong Pilipino (KDP) from 1978 to 1986. She received her Masters degree from the University of San Francisco in 1995, and is currently instructor of Asian American Studies at City College of San Francisco and at San Francisco State University.

Dan Tsang is an Asian American Studies, Politics and Economics bibliographer at the University of California, Irvine. He founded *Gay Insurgent: A Gay Left Journal*, and was a plaintiff in Tsang v. CIA, an ACLU-supported lawsuit against the CIA for spying on him. He hosts "Subversity," a public affairs interview program on KUCI, webcast on the Net (kuci.org:8080).

Dolly Lumsdaine Veale was born in Shanghai, China in 1948, emigrated to Hong Kong in 1955 and then to the U.S. in 1960. She is a veteran of the struggle at University of California, Berkeley to establish Asian Studies in the early 1970's. From 1970 to 1977, she took part in the struggle for the I-Hotel in San Francisco's Chinatown/Manilatown as an activist with the Asian Community Center. In 1973, she joined the Asian anti-imperialist group Wei Min She. She became a founding member of the Revolutionary Communist Party (RCP) in 1975, and has been its Bay Area branch spokesperson since the early 1980s. Between 1979 and 1982, Dolly was arrested 16 times for political activities, including many arrests for selling the *Revolutionary Worker* newspaper in the streets.

Flo Oy Wong is a contemporary mixed media installation artist born and raised in Oakland, California's Chinatown. Wong began her fine arts career at the age of forty, having received a Bachelor of Arts degree in English from the University of California, Berkeley in 1960. Prior to her art career, Wong taught elementary school. As a narrative artist, Wong uses rice cloth sacks, Chinese funeral paper, suitcases and other found objects to tell stories; Wong focuses on the personal, family, cultural and collective to visually present the extraordinary voices of ordinary people. Co-founder of the San Francisco based Asian American Women Artist Association in 1989, Wong was instrumental in helping to increase the visibility of Asian American women artists in exhibitions locally and nationally.

Kent Wong is Director of the University of California Los Angeles Labor Center, serving the education and research needs of workers and unions throughout California. He teaches Labor Studies and Ethnic Studies at UCLA, and directs an undergraduate program in Labor Studies. He is Founding President of the Asian Pacific American Labor Alliance, the first nationwide Asian American labor organization within the AFL-CIO, and served as President from 1992-1997. A recipient of a Kellogg National Fellowship, Kent has written extensively on labor issues for various journals and newspapers.

Nellie Wong was born in Oakland, California, the first daughter of Chinese immigrants from Toishan, China. She has worked as a secretary and administrative assistant for most of her life. She is now retired after working as a Senior Affirmative Action Analyst at the University of California, San Francisco for fourteen years. Nellie is the Bay Area Organizer for the Freedom Socialist Party and is also active in Radical Women, a socialist feminist organization. She is the author of three collections of poetry: Dreams in Harrison Railroad Park (Kelsey Street Press, 1997); The Death of Long Steam Lady (West End Press, 1986); and Stolen Moments (Chicory Blue Press, 1997). Her work has appeared in numerous anthologies and journals including *This Bridge Called My Back: Writings By Radical Women of Color; Bridge, Asian American Perspectives; The Berkeley Fiction Review; The Iowa Review; Skin Deep; No More Masks*, among others. She was a cofounder with Merle Woo of the Asian American feminist writing and performing group, Unbound Feet.

Merle Woo has taught as a lecturer for 27 years in the Educational Opportunity Program and Women Studies Program at San Francisco State University and Ethnic/Asian American Studies and the Graduate School of Education at University of California, Berkeley. She fought and won two free speech and multi-discrimination cases at UC Berkeley. In 1997, Woo was fired from SFSU after teaching in Women's Studies for ten years, because she is a socialist feminist lesbian, a member of the Freedom Socialist Party and Radical Women, and fought for student democracy and community and lesbian-related courses. Today she is a political organizer and works as a receptionist. She is also a widely-published poet and essayist.

416

Emily Woo Yamasaki is the New York organizer for Radical Women (RW), a member of the New York City branch of the Freedom Socialist Part (FSP) and the local coordinator of the Comrades of Color Caucus of RW and FSP. Here in New York City, she was the organizer for the International Feminist Brigade to Cuba in 1997. Emily has written articles for the "Voices of Color Column" of the *Freedom Socialist* newspaper on issues including racial tensions between Blacks and Asians, Chinese immigrants, her visits to Cuba and the dangers of anti-Semitism, some of which are featured in the newly published anthology *Voices of Color.* Emily is a longtime lesbian activist and also a member of the New York chapters of GABRIELA Network and the Labor Party.

Steve Yip was born and raised in the San Francisco Bay Area. He was one of the founders of the Asian Community Center and Everybody's Bookstore in San Francisco Chinatown/Manilatown in 1969-70, and a co-founder of Wei Min She in 1971. Steve was a political prisoner at the Federal Correctional Institution at Danbury for most of 1981. His incarceration resulted from a political action on May 30, 1980 at the United Nations that called attention to the threat of inter-imperialist nuclear war. In 1985, Steve coordinated the "Draw the Line" campaign that published a national statement exposing and condemning the police bombing of the radical MOVE organization compound that murdered 11 Black people, five of them children. He currently is an activist in New York City, a supporter of the Revolutionary Communist Party, and active in Asians for Mumia/Jericho network, New York organizer in the October 22nd Coalition to Stop Police Brutality, Repression and Criminalization of a Generation. Steve is also East Coast assistant to Carl Dix, National Spokesperson for the RCP. Contact: PO Box 400381, Brooklyn, NY 11240-0381.

BIG RED MEDIA INC.

NIGHT VISION A New Millennium Vampyre Opera
Libetto by Ruth Margraff   Double CD @ $25 ea. qty:_____

LEGACY TO LIBERATION: Politics & Culture of Revolutionary Asian Pacific America Book @ $20 ea. qty:_____
Anthology by Fred Ho with Carolyn Antonio, Diane Fujino, ManChui Leung and Steve Yip (AK Press)

ALL POWER TO THE PEOPLE!: The Black Panther Ballet Suite
featuring Fred Ho and the Afro Asian Music Ensemble   CD @ $25 ea. qty:_____

WARRIOR SISTERS: The New Adventures of African and Asian Womyn Warriors   Double CD @ $25 ea. qty:_____

YES MEANS YES, NO MEANS NO, WHATEVER SHE WEARS,
WHEREVER SHE GOES!
Fred Ho and the Afro Asian Music Ensemble   CD @ 15 ea. qty:_____

MONKEY: PART TWO
Fred Ho and the Monkey Orchestra   CD @ $15 ea. qty:_____

MONKEY: PART ONE
Fred Ho and the Monkey Orchestra   CD @ $15 ea. qty:_____

TURN PAIN INTO POWER!
Fred Ho and the Afro Asian Music Ensemble   CD @ $15 ea. qty:_____

THE UNDERGROUND RAILROAD TO MY HEART!
Fred Ho and the Afro Asian Music Ensemble   CD @ $15 ea. qty:_____

2000 WOMYN WARRIORS/SHEROES CALENDAR   Calendar @ $10 ea. qty:_____

SOUNDING OFF! Music as Subversion/ Resistance/ Revolution
edited by Ron Sakolsky and Fred Ho.   Book with CD @ $20 ea. qty:_____

ASIAN PACIFIC AMERICANS AND REVOLUTIONARY SOCIALISM FORUM   Video @ $20 ea. qty:___.____
4 hour video sponsored by the Ad-Hoc Committee, Hunter College, New York City, August, 1998
Produced by Big Red Media Inc., Peoples Video Network with Wayne Lum,

AZIATIC UPRISING! INTERGENERATIONAL DIALOGUE FORUM   Video @ $20 ea. qty:_____
4 hour video sponsored by the Ad-Hoc Committee, Columbia University, New York City, November, 1998
Produced by Big Red Media Inc. and Peoples Video Network

Mail this entire form with check or money order to: SUB-TOTAL   _____

BIG RED MEDIA   (ADD 8.25 SALES TAX FOR NY STATE)
443 12TH STREET, #1H
BROOKLYN, NY 11215-0177. usa   _____
www.bigredmedia.com
                                                   SHIPPING AND HANDLING
                                                                    $4.00

THANK YOU! bigredmedia@hotmail.com   TOTAL: _____